Cost–Benefit Analysis for Investment Decisions

First edition.
Cambridge Resources International Inc.
Suite #617, 1770 Mass. Ave., Cambridge,
MA 02140, USA
+1 613 770 2080

About the Authors

Dr. Glenn P. Jenkins
Professor of Economics,
Queen's University, Canada
& Eastern Mediterranean University, and
Institute Fellow Emeritus,
Harvard University

He founded the Program on Investment Appraisal and Management at Harvard University and was its director from 1985 to 2000. Since 2000, he has been the director of the Program of Investment Appraisal and Risk Analysis at Queen's University, Canada. He has conducted numerous seminars and courses on this subject for governments, private organizations, and professional staff of major international organizations. His research and advisory work has been primarily in the area of public finance. He has been Assistant Deputy Minister of Finance, Government of Canada (1981–84); and President of the Society for Benefit Cost Analysis (2011).

Dr. Chun-Yan Kuo
Senior Fellow,
John Deutsch International, and
Adjunct Professor of Cost–Benefit Analysis,
Queen's University, Canada

He is a leading author and practitioner in the field of the project appraisal. He has served as an adviser to a wide range of developed and developing countries. He has held senior positions with the Department of Finance, Government of Canada, and The International Tax Program, Harvard University; and he was a Visiting Professor at National Chiao Tung University, Taiwan, (2004–05). In 2007, he was one of the experts who prepared the *Canadian Cost–Benefit Analysis Guide: Regulatory Proposals* for the Treasury Board of the Federal Government of Canada.

Dr. Arnold C. Harberger
Professor of Economics,
University of California,
Los Angeles, and
Gustavus F. and Ann M. Swift Distinguished Service
Professor Emeritus,
University of Chicago

He is one of the pioneering academicians and professionals in this field. His writings have formed the analytical principles found in the state-of-the-art methodology for applied investment appraisal. He has acted as an economic consultant to many governments and international agencies, including serving as the Chief Economic Advisor to USAID for the period 2005–10. He is a Member: National Academy of Sciences of the U.S., Fellow: American Academy of Arts and Sciences, Fellow: Econometric Society, President: Western Economic Association (1989–90), Vice President: American Economic Association (elected for 1992), President: American Economic Association, 1997, and Distinguished Fellow: American Economic Association, 1999.

Foreword

Few published works have histories as long or as convoluted as this book. It all began with the awakening of my interest in cost–benefit analysis and applied welfare economics during my own graduate studies (1946–49) at the University of Chicago. This interest was nurtured by work in Latin America (starting in 1955) sponsored by USAID and its predecessor ICA, and in India starting in 1961–62 under the sponsorship of MIT's Center for International Studies in collaboration with India's Cabinet-level Planning Commission. Out of these experiences came a series of professional papers that formed the background of a graduate course in Project Evaluation at the University of Chicago starting in 1965. Many of these papers were collected in my book, *Project Evaluation*, first published in 1972 and currently available as a Midway Reprint from the University of Chicago Press.

Glenn P. Jenkins took that course as a graduate student and almost immediately began to put it to practical use. Even while still a graduate student, he consulted on these matters with branches of the government in his native Canada. He continued these Canadian exercises during his appointment as Assistant Professor of Economics at Harvard University, culminating in a year of leave from Harvard, working with the Canadian government's Ministry of Industry, Trade and Commerce and its Department of Regional Economic Expansion. Chun-Yan Kuo was a member of the team that evaluated a number of important Canadian government projects at that time. I, too, was involved with these Canadian entities at that time and subsequently, but in the meantime was also accumulating cost–benefit experience in Colombia, Panama, the Philippines, Spain and Uruguay, as well as at the World Bank, where I served steadily with its teaching arm, the Economic Development Institute, from 1962 through the 1960s and most of the 1970s.

Professor Jenkins's Harvard appointment evolved into a senior position with the Harvard Institute for International Development. His first foreign assignment in this role was to Malaysia, where his first task was to give a full-length course in economic project appraisal, under the sponsorship of the National Institute for Public Administration and the Economic Planning Unit of the prime minister's office. This course was very well received, so much so that Jenkins was asked to develop a manual on the subject, following the main lines of that course. It was in the resulting monograph that my name first appeared, placed there by Jenkins in an act of pure kindness, recognizing the role of my Chicago graduate course in the development of his own subsequent thinking. In the mid-1980s, the resulting manuscript began to be used as the main text of an intensive summer course (for participants from developing countries) that HIID offered, under Professor Jenkins's direction.

Our separate collaborations with the Canadian government continued, nearly always dealing with project evaluation and often overlapping (i.e., with the two of us working jointly on a given problem). This phase of our work reached something of a climax when Jenkins was appointed Assistant Deputy Minister (ADM) of Finance in Canada's government, a post he held from 1981 to 1984. During this period, I consulted regularly with the Department of Finance as well as with other branches of the Canadian government. In some of these activities, Kuo, then a senior Department of Finance official, also collaborated. It was in this period that I first learned that I had been (since 1977) the co-author of this manual. And it was here that I first began to actually participate in successive revisions of and additions to the book's text. On completing his service as ADM, Professor Jenkins returned to Harvard and soon started the HIID course referred to above. I ended up making brief appearances in this course every single year. More important, perhaps, was a tradition that developed of my staying on for a week or so after each of these visits in order to work jointly with Professor Jenkins, continuously editing and updating one part or another of the book. Out of these sessions, and of other work that each of us was doing in other contexts and/or under other auspices, many new ideas were incorporated as time went by. Among them were the analyses connected with distributional weights, the concept of basic needs externalities, the formalization of stakeholder analysis, and the introduction of the notion of a shadow price of government funds.

Perhaps the story of one such new idea is worth telling in detail. Around 1998, Professor Jenkins, Kuo, and I were contracted by the World Bank and the binational commission in charge of the project to undertake a certain component of the research needed for the evaluation of a major bridge project, a planned linkage of Argentina and Uruguay, across the Rio de la Plata, going between the cities of Buenos Aires and Colonia. Our job was to advise concerning the so-called "national parameters" of the two countries. What were the relevant opportunity costs of capital in Argentina and Uruguay? What about the corresponding opportunity costs of foreign exchange? And, finally, of labour? It was in pursuing the economic opportunity cost of foreign exchange that we ran into a snag. The almost standard way of handling this question seemed straightforward enough. The project authority was assumed to go into the foreign exchange market and buy the necessary divisas (say, dollars) using local currency (say, pesos). As we pursued this standard model in one of our post-course sessions in Cambridge, we found that it was not consistent with a full general equilibrium of the economy. The new demand for foreign exchange was assumed to arise because of an increased demand for tradable goods. As a result, the real price of the dollar would rise, and with it the price level of tradables.

Hence, the supply of tradables would increase. But the rise in the price level of tradables would stimulate the demand for non-tradables, the output of which would then also increase. Increases in the output of both tradables and non-tradables did not jibe with economic theory (except under conditions of recession or depression), so something was wrong.

As we tried to resolve this paradox, we found that the "standard" analysis suffered from a missing link. It did not incorporate the way in which the pesos were raised, which were then to be spent on tradables. The raising of these pesos (presumably in the capital market) would displace both consumption and investment, and hence reduce the demand for both tradables and non-tradables. Starting from this reduced demand for both, one could then contemplate the demand for both of these aggregates increasing, thus resolving our paradox. No paradox was present in both tradables and non-tradables increasing if we measured these moves from a position where both had been reduced from their starting position. This end result laid bare the fact that the whole idea of an economic opportunity cost of foreign exchange was not a stand-alone concept. This concept had a natural and unavoidable twin, which we called the *shadow price of non-tradables outlays* and which we from that point on built into our book's analysis.[1] This concept captured the economic costs involved when money was raised in the capital market and spent on non-tradable goods or services. It performed exactly the same function as the economic opportunity cost of foreign exchange, differing only in that it traced a scenario where the spending was on non-tradables rather than tradables.

The evolution of the book continued, but it was occurring too slowly, even for our own satisfaction. This led to our inviting Chun-Yan (George) Kuo to join us as a third co-author. Professor Kuo had been associated with the Harvard Program from its inception and had continued his affiliation with it when it was moved to Queen's University after HIID's untimely demise. With his addition to the team, the preparation of the manuscript for publication advanced more rapidly, bringing us to the present moment.

I close this preface on a personal note. Beyond Jenkins's generosity in making me a co-author some five years before I knew about it, I ended up being the beneficiary of coming first, as our names appeared in alphabetical order. I always felt this left readers with an inadequate appreciation of the extent of Professor Jenkins's role. He was the sole writer of the initial version of the book and the sole director of the course whenever it was given, whether at Harvard, or at Queen's, or in any of the numerous other venues in which versions of varying lengths were presented over the years. These other versions include

---

[1]There had been earlier writings that sensed the underlying problem, but none in which its solution was fully developed. See Blitzer et al. (1981) and Jenkins and Kuo (1985). The joint work outlined above is described in detail in Harberger and Jenkins (eds.), *Cost-Benefit Analysis* ("Introduction", pp. 1–72). See also Harberger, Jenkins, Kuo, and Mphahelele, "The Economic Cost of Foreign Exchange in South Africa", *South Africa Journal of Economics*, 2004; and Harberger "Some Recent Advances in Economic Project Evaluation", *Cuadernos de Economia*, 2003 (v. 40, no. 120), pp. 579–588.

numerous presentations at the World Bank; the African, Asian, and Inter-American development banks; plus multiple presentations in Argentina, Azerbaijan, Bolivia, Chile, Indonesia, Malaysia, Nicaragua, Philippines, South Africa, Sri Lanka, Thailand, and Uruguay.

For the final published version of the book, I therefore insisted that Professor Jenkins's name come first. I promised to write this foreword in order that readers would have a reasonably clear understanding of our respective roles.

Arnold C. Harberger

Table of Contents

Chapter Eighteen: The ABCs of Electricity Project Analysis

Chapter Nineteen: An Integrated Appraisal of Combined-Cycle Versus Single-Cycle Electricity-Generation Technologies

Preface

This book, *Cost–Benefit Analysis for Investment Decisions,* represents a culmination of work in this field by its authors over a period of more than 40 years. Many of our colleagues and students have played important roles as the intellectual contents of this text were developed. Those who have made specific contributions during the long gestation of this manuscript include Ernesto Fontaine, Alejandra Cox-Edwards, Donald Tate, Savvakis Savvides, Graham Glenday, M. Baher El-Hifnawi, G.P. Shukla, Vijdan Korman, Andrey Klevchuk, Pradip Ghimire, and Aygul Ozbafli.

The editing of this volume has benefited from the assistance of a number of people. Initial drafts were expertly prepared by Dorothy Lee and Pradip Ghimire. A special thanks to Sharon Sullivan, who led the editing effort and who, with the expert assistance of Stephanie Stone as copy editor and Gabriel Taiwo as graphics designer, successfully moulded this publication into its present form.

The preparation of this book has been guided by two main objectives. First, the approach must be firmly rooted in the disciplines of finance and economics, and structured to reflect the principles of these disciplines. Second, it must address the practical needs of analysts faced with evaluating a broad gamut of real-world public and private sector projects.

This book has evolved over time through its use as the core reading material in the Program on Investment Appraisal and Management, which was initiated at Harvard University in 1984 and which since 2000 has been offered at Queen's University in Canada. Through that programme and many shorter courses taught to groups around the world, thousands of professionals have been trained in this discipline using various earlier drafts of this book as their primary teaching materials. Alumni of this programme have used these same earlier drafts to train thousands more in universities and government institutions around the globe. As a result of these experiences, we have gained many insights and have introduced many improvements dealing with real-world applications of the principles outlined in the text. Hence, this book is designed so that it can be used both in the classroom as a reference manual and to help professionals apply the principles of investment appraisal in a wide array of settings and sectors.

This book has evolved over time through its use as the core reading material in the Program on Investment Appraisal and Management, which was initiated at Harvard University in 1984 and which since 2000 has been offered at Queen's University in Canada. Through that programme and many shorter courses taught to groups around the world, thousands of professionals have been trained in this discipline using various earlier drafts of this book as their primary teaching materials. Alumni of this programme have used these same earlier drafts to train thousands more in universities and government institutions around the globe. As a result of these experiences, we have gained many insights and have introduced many improvements dealing with real-world applications of the principles outlined in the text. Hence, this book is designed so that it can be used both in the classroom as a reference manual and to help professionals apply the principles of investment appraisal in a wide array of settings and sectors.

Earlier versions of this text have been used in several dozen programmes taught to enhance the professional development of the staff of multilateral financial institutions, including the World Bank, the African Development Bank, the Asian Development Bank, the Inter-American Development Bank, and the Caribbean Development Bank. Recently, the World Bank has provided generous funding to modify the basic training materials so as to make them more applicable for the analysis of infrastructure projects with private sector participation. This interaction has contributed to our thinking and in particular to reinforcing the importance of making this text directly relevant for the development professionals who need to apply the principles of cost–benefit analysis to real-world decision-making.

It is not easy to summarize the many ways in which this book differs from other texts and/or manuals on cost–benefit analysis. In part, it still bears some marks of its origin in an economic graduate course. Even though this aspect has been toned down over the years, this book delves more deeply into issues of concept and methodology than do most cost–benefit texts. Moreover, it quite consciously builds on the long tradition of applied welfare economics, as it was developed by a series of great economists going from Adam Smith to David Ricardo to Jules Dupuit, John Stuart Mill, Alfred Marshall, Vilfredo Pareto, Harold Hotelling, and James Meade, down to the present time. It is from this great tradition that economists learned how to quantify the gains from trade and the costs of monopoly and to evaluate policies such as price controls, export subsidies, agricultural support programmes, and the like. These results, plus many others developed in the 200-odd-year evolution of applied welfare economics, emerged from a rigorous, disciplined application of economic principles. There is nothing casual or ad hoc about this great tradition.

We have consciously and constantly strived, in developing the materials in this book, to remain faithful to this tradition. In seeking answers to new questions, we have tried always to base our work on economic fundamentals. Any measure of benefits and costs over time *must* be expressed in real terms, but cannot plausibly be carried out "at constant prices of a given base year". It is a basic economic truth that there is great economic benefit in the act of taking copper bars from the ongoing economy when their price is one real dollar per pound and returning them to the economy when it values them at three real dollars per pound (so long as the real opportunity cost of capital is covered). But then we must find a way of defining the real dollar that is capable of capturing such movements in relative prices. That role is played in economic theory by choosing one price or price index to be what we call the *numeraire*, our basic unit of measurement. We face this choice and conclude that the only two reasonable candidates for a numeraire are a country's consumer price index and its gross domestic product (GDP) deflator. With the first of these, we measure all benefits and costs in "consumer baskets"; with the second, our measurement is done in "producer baskets".

The mere fact that we have to have a numeraire has important implications for the discount rate to be used in project analysis. The project starts with our extracting purchasing power from the rest of the economy; the pay-back comes later as the project yields its benefits over time. The question is, of course, are these benefits worth the costs that were entailed as purchasing power was extracted in order to do the initial investment? Economic logic and rigour require that both the extraction of resources and the subsequent benefit flows be evaluated in the same units — in our case, either in consumer baskets or in producer baskets. So what about the discount rate? In the process of extracting resources, we displace either investment or consumption that would otherwise have taken place and possibly also draw some new capital funds from abroad. On the displaced investment, the economy loses the future flow of earnings that it would have yielded; on the displaced consumption (which means increased saving), the economy suffers a loss unless the savers earn a rate of return covering the "supply price" of these savings. Thus, fundamental principles of applied welfare economics tell us that the economy has suffered a loss unless a project yields benefits sufficient to cover the lost productivity (from displaced investment) plus the genuine economic supply price of any newly stimulated savings plus the marginal cost (to the economy) of the funds drawn in from abroad. The project, in order to be worthwhile, has to generate benefits (translated into numeraire units) sufficient to cover the costs (also expressed in numeraire units) that were entailed in raising the investment resources in the first place.

Then comes the question, what is the mechanism by which these resources are raised? Investment and consumption can be displaced by new taxes, but which taxes? Each new tax law is different from the last, and this makes the choice of a standard or typical tax package arbitrary. Moreover, we would hardly ever be able to link the funds from a particular project to a particular tax package.

Once again, economic fundamentals come to the rescue. The capital market (which in some developing countries is simply the banking system) is in fact the "sponge" that absorbs any net new funds the government might have in any day, week, or month. The capital market can also be relied on to generate the purchasing power to cover any current cash deficit or shortfall. The capital market is thus truly the government's marginal source and use of funds. Typically, when expenditures end up bigger than expected, the government borrows more. When receipts turn out to be unexpectedly high, it borrows less (and sometimes pays down its outstanding debt). There is a big added dividend to the use of the capital market as the standard source of funds, since it is typically the source of private sector funds as well. Hence, the economic opportunity cost of capital is derived from an essentially similar scenario, regardless of whether the investment is being done by the private or the public sector.

The methodology of cost–benefit analysis applies quite easily and naturally to commercial-type ventures (whether private sector, public sector, or joint projects between the two) whose costs and benefits consist overwhelmingly of cash outlays and cash receipts. But what do we do with benefits and costs that are not in this form? The answer here is a little complicated. Some non-cash benefits and costs can be quantified by direct application of economic analysis. Thus, we have economic studies that estimate the value that commuters place on the time they spend going to and from work, and the costs involved in ships waiting in line to enter a port or canal, and the value that recreational users place on their visits to parks, museums, etc. Then we have other benefits that can be set by the analysts themselves (in the absence of other instructions) or by public sector authorities attempting to put values on particular non-market goals. In this vein, we have values denoting "society's" willingness to pay for added fulfilment of the basic needs of the poor, or for added economic activities in a given region or industry. Finally, we have a range of areas in which neither of the previous answers can plausibly apply. National defence benefits and those linked to a nation's culture, history, and traditions come to mind here. For these, the standard answer of professional economists is that we have little or no claim of professional expertise in setting values on such elements. Instead, we try to quantify those items that we are professionally equipped to estimate, and derive measures of costs and benefits for just those items. We then confront our audiences with statements like, "In this project, the direct economic costs exceed its direct economic benefits by $200 million. We leave it to the authorities to decide whether its national defence or other non-quantifiable benefits are worth this cost."

In addition to its heavy reliance on economic fundamentals, this volume emphasizes what we call an *integrated* analysis of projects. In this aspect, we incorporate financial and stakeholder analyses in addition to a strictly economic one. The clearest motivation for our doing so is the fact that many projects that have the potential to be highly beneficial in strictly economic terms run into trouble because they face difficulties on the financial or the stakeholder side. The financial analysis is central in the sense that it tries to capture *all* the relevant financial flows connected with a project. Far too often, evaluators will neglect such items as routine maintenance and repair, or recurrent expenditures for insurance, record-keeping, or supplies. Financial analysis can also call attention to situations in which particular outlays are dependent on fragile and unreliable sources of funds — sometimes on state budgetary items that are subject to capricious fluctuations from year to year or from administration to administration. Finally, the financial analysis, by setting down all of a project's outlays and receipts (usually in a spreadsheet format), establishes a solid basis for the subsequent economic analysis, helping to ensure that it provides comprehensive coverage.

The stakeholder analysis is also related to the financial one, but in a different way. Many projects require collaboration, or at least tacit acceptance, from a number of stakeholder groups if the projects are to succeed, or perhaps even if they are to get started. Agricultural projects depend on the contributions of farmers, truckers, middlemen, and perhaps exporter interests. Regional development projects require willing help from experts from outside the region. Projects to enhance medical services in rural areas often founder because of the reluctance of experienced physicians to relocate there. The function of the stakeholder analysis is to see to it that provision is made, within the framework of the project, to ensure that each critical group of stakeholders has an adequate incentive to carry out its required role.

In addition to presenting the methodologies that apply to the general financial, stakeholder, and economic analyses, this volume deals with a number of particular types of projects that are commonly encountered in developing countries — e.g., those dealing with transportation, electricity, potable water, and irrigation. The relevant chapters are mainly devoted to exploring the specific aspects that set these classes of project apart from others. Of particular importance here is the quantification of benefits in cases where they are not captured by a market price or in which the relevant prices are not good measures of the corresponding benefits. These chapters can serve as roadmaps guiding analysts through the landscape that is special for each class of project. These general roadmaps are supplemented in most cases by examples drawn from real-world project evaluations in the area in question. These are presented in summary form with the intention of focusing on the particular activities that give each type (e.g., roads, dams, electricity systems) its special characteristics.

Chapter One

The Integrated Analysis

1.1 Introduction

The goal of a proper project evaluation is to prevent bad projects from going ahead and good projects from being rejected. This book aims to help public officials and private analysts to develop and evaluate investment projects in order to promote the economic and social well-being of the country in question. The book progresses from the formulation and definition of a project to the data requirements for the evaluation, and then to the criteria used for accepting a good or rejecting a bad project from both the financial and the economic viewpoints, before finally dealing with the analysis and management of the many types of uncertainty faced by various stakeholders. These components are integrated into the analysis in a consistent manner.

Government investment expenditures should ideally be in the public interest. Such expenditures can be in the form of government investment, public–private partnership arrangements, or other forms of government intervention. This implies that resources should not be reallocated from the private to the public sector unless such a move is likely to benefit residents. In situations where private investments are being undertaken with financial support from either governments or development finance institutions, it is important to know the financial viability of such activities. Financial failure often leads to a contingent liability coming due at the expense of a public body. For an activity with contingent liabilities to be undertaken in the first place, it should be clear that its economic benefit exceeds its economic cost. Regulations impose both investment and operating costs largely on the private sector, in the hope of either creating or preserving benefits for the people. Many developed-country governments now require that cost–benefit analyses be undertaken to evaluate regulatory interventions. In each of these situations, account must also be taken of how the benefits and costs of these actions are distributed among the relevant stakeholder groups. These themes will be addressed under the headings of the financial, economic, and stakeholder analyses of what is referred to here as simply a "project".

By their very nature, investment projects offer uncertain benefits and costs over the life of a project. Even a project's investment costs are often subject to overruns as a result of technical difficulties and delays in implementation. These uncertainties must be taken into account in the course of a project's evaluation. Risk analysis and ways of reducing risk through the use of contracts are thus basic elements of the integrated project evaluation framework developed in this book.

Some public sector projects or programmes such as health care and education may not be properly assessed using the standard framework of cost–benefit analysis because of difficulties in quantifying their benefits in monetary terms. This book will show how the evaluation of such projects or programmes can be handled using the techniques of cost–effectiveness analysis.

1.2 Targeted Users of the Book

This book is intended for a variety of users. First, it serves as a guide to those in finance and planning ministries, national government treasuries, budget bureaus, and even line ministries who are responsible for making public sector investment decisions. In short, it addresses the needs of any group involved in the formulation, evaluation, and implementation of projects. Second, the book is intended to educate the private investment community on the economic and social aspects of investment appraisal. Third, it provides a methodology that can help taxpayers as well as international development and lending institutions to be confident that the money allocated for public investments will be spent in a responsible and productive way. Fourth, the book contains theoretical developments and practical applications to real-world cases that will be of interest to the academic community.

With such a wide audience, the book needs to be comprehensive yet not become mired in abstract theory or complicated calculations and technical refinements. Thus, we have tried to present the theory underlying our analyses in a clear and accessible fashion, yet without bypassing important details. Similarly, we have tried to choose our real-world cases in such a way that they illustrate how basic principles should be applied and at the same time guide practitioners through the steps that must be taken in carrying out real-world applications.

1.3 Project Definition

Public investments are key policy instruments used by governments in pursuing their overall development goals and strategies. The chosen projects should fit into the overall development strategy, within the limited resources that are available. In principle, governments should maintain a running list of potential projects, out of which priorities for further evaluation and eventual construction should be continuously selected.

1.3.1 Definition of a Project and Building Blocks for Evaluation

In capital budgeting, a project is the smallest separable investment unit that can be planned, financed, and implemented independently. This helps to distinguish a project from an overall objective, which may consist of several interrelated investments. Often, projects form a clear and distinct portion of a larger and less precisely identified objective or programme. While it is possible to treat an entire programme as a project for the purposes of analysis, it is far better to work with individual projects. Broad programmes are very likely to contain both good and bad components. It is precisely the task of project evaluation to identify and select those with the greatest positive impact.

The principles and methodology set out in this book can be applied to the full range of projects, from single-purpose activities such as small infrastructure projects to more complex multi-component systems such as integrated rural development and area development schemes. The basic definition considers a project to be "any activity that involves the use of scarce resources during a specific time period for the purpose of generating a socio-economic return in the form of goods and services".

After a project's objectives and scope are defined, a number of key modules should be identified. This will include the project's market and competitors, the technology and inputs required for the project, and how the project is likely to be financed.

a) *Demand Module:* This identifies the likely users of the project's output as well as the likely valuation of its products. Are the products destined for domestic use or for sales abroad? Are there alternative sources capable of meeting the likely demand? The analysis should initially be based on secondary research, but may also involve consultations with potential users and beneficiaries. The expected volumes and unit values over the life of the project should be examined and forecasted. The information identified provides the basic data for a profile of the project's costs and benefits, while the breakdown between tradable and non-tradable purchases and sales is needed in order to separately apply the relevant exchange rate to the foreign part. Analysts must make serious efforts to incorporate into their work the likely future trends of relative prices — real exchange rates, relative product prices, real wage rates, etc.

b) *Technical Module:* This examines the technical feasibility of the project's investment and operating plans, alternative project scales, location, and the timing of the project's implementation. Technical parameters should be determined separately and clearly laid out for each of the investment and operating phases. In the process, engineering data in terms of inputs by type (machinery, equipment, and material), quantity, cost, and time of use should all be specified. In the case of labour, the types of skill and number of workers required and the expected real wage rate should also be determined.

Project analysts should also identify potential bottlenecks for key project inputs, especially workers with particular skills. This information will provide the basic construction and operation cost year by year over the life of the project, i.e., the project's profile.

For certain projects it is important to identify any technological uncertainties. In such cases, some guarantees from the suppliers should be sought and incorporated into the evaluation. In addition, a number of project sizes and associated inputs or costs should be estimated by technical or engineering experts. This information will help analysts to identify the project that has the optimal scale and timing.

c) *Project Financing:* The possible sources of debt and equity financing for the project should be examined, since the terms of financing can have a significant impact on the financial viability of a project. Where borrowed funds are involved, the amount of debt, interest rates, and repayment schedules should all be spelt out and closely examined. Alternative schemes of financing, such as build–operate–transfer, may be contemplated in certain cases.

1.3.2 A Project as an Incremental Activity

An important element in the investment appraisal is to examine the incremental impact of the project: that is, how net receipts, net cash flows, or net economic benefits in the presence of the project can be expected to differ from those that would prevail in its absence. The with/without distinction should be clearly and carefully maintained in order to avoid the inclusion in the "with-project" scenario any benefits or costs that would exist "without" the project being undertaken. The "without-project" situation does not imply that nothing is done to the current situation if the project is not undertaken. In principle, it is a sort of moving picture of how the relevant items and markets would naturally evolve if the project did not go ahead, but with "good" decisions being taken on all other (non-project) matters at each step.

In this context, it is important to conceptualize two states of nature: one with the project and the other without the project. The former identifies the revenues and expenditures associated with the case in which the project is undertaken, while the latter refers to all relevant benefits and costs that are likely to prevail if the project were not undertaken. Comparing the two, a project usually involves incremental net expenditures in the construction phase, followed by incremental net benefits in the operating phase. The incremental net cash flow (or net economic benefits) refers to the net of benefits minus outlays that occurs with a project, minus the corresponding figure that would have occurred in the absence of the project. In this way it is possible to properly identify the additional net benefit flow that is expected to arise as a result of a project. From this, the corresponding change in economic well-being that is attributed to it can be measured.

1.4 An Integrated Approach

Traditional approaches to investment appraisal have tended to carry out a financial analysis of a project completely separately from its economic evaluation. The integrated project analysis developed in this book measures benefits and costs in terms of domestic prices for both financial and economic appraisal. The stakeholder impacts are then identified and allocated to the different parties. Since project costs and revenues are spread over time, uncertainty becomes an issue and is first dealt with in the financial analysis. Its consequential effects are then assessed in the economic analysis. There follows an overview of how an investment project is evaluated through an integrated financial, economic, risk, and stakeholder analysis.

1.4.1 Financial Appraisal

The financial analysis of a project investigates whether the project is financially viable. It is a cornerstone of many capital investment projects. The requirements for data and the assessment of the commercial viability are briefly outlined below.

a) Data Requirements

The module starts with the projection of the volumes of outputs, inputs, and deliveries that constitute the principal financial flows of a project. It then proceeds to generate the financial cash flow statement of the project by taking into consideration, where relevant, such items as accounts receivable, accounts payable, and changes in cash balances. The final result will yield the expected flows of financial receipts, financial outlays, and hence the net cash flow of the project, period by period over its life.

In forecasting benefits and costs over the life of the project, a key decision concerns whether to work exclusively with real (i.e., inflation-corrected) magnitudes or whether to carry out some of the analysis in nominal terms, before converting them to real terms. In this book the economic analysis is always carried out in real terms, and the financial analysis usually (though not necessarily) in nominal terms. The guide as to whether this exercise should be performed is whether key elements exist (such as nominal debt, nominal tax components, or nominal rental contracts) that are fixed in advance in nominal terms and whose conversion to real terms thus varies under different assumed future inflation rates.

The data on benefits should identify whether they accrue domestically or abroad. Correspondingly, expenditures on each item (including machinery, equipment, and material inputs) should also be separated according to whether or not the item is internationally traded. The breakdown is important for analysing foreign exchange implications in the economic appraisal. In the case of workforce requirements, it is essential to classify labour by occupation and skill type in order for a proper estimate of the economic opportunity cost of labour to be obtained.

Project financing may also be a key variable for the commercial viability of a project. Its debt/equity structure and the terms of interest rates can have an impact on tax liability and on the cash available to cover its costs. Thus, it is necessary to make some reasonable assumptions about these parameters. In the case of projects with private equity participation, the required market rate of return on such capital will influence the viability of the project from the investor's point of view.

b) Development of the Financial Cash Flow Statement

A project's viability is very much determined by the timing of the cash receipts and disbursement. Thus, the projection of these items needs to be carried out carefully so as to alert the analyst in advance to possible periods of illiquidity (or even liquidity crisis) in the future. Items such as accounts receivable, accounts payable, changes in cash balances, prepaid expenses, and inventories should all be accounted for in constructing the financial cash flow statement. Yearly tax liabilities (where relevant) should be estimated following the accounting and tax rules of the country in which the project is located. Expected future changes in tax and tariff rates should be built into the project profile.

Very often, the project will still have assets at its projected closing date. In such a case, the likely future (real) market value of such assets should be incorporated as part of the final year's net benefit. Normally, such residual values will be estimated by applying standard real economic depreciation rates for the different asset types.

Once the financial cash flow statement of the project is completed, its potential viability can be assessed. Since the project has different stakeholders who are mainly concerned with their own interests, financial cash flow statements can be generated for each such group. For government-sponsored and government-related projects, a minimum of three financial cash flow statements are usually developed from different viewpoints — banker's point of view, owner's point of view, and government budget point of view.

- The banker's (or total investment) point of view examines the expected possible receipts and expenditures of a project, considering the investment base to be the sum of equity and debt capital, and the annual cash flow to be the amount available for distribution to both equity holders and creditors.

- The owner's point of view considers capital outlays to consist only of the owners' (equity) funds. Loans are treated as inflows when they arrive, and amortization payments are treated as outflows.
- From the government budget viewpoint, the government will ensure that the relevant government departments have enough resources to finance its obligations to the project.
- Where a government project is expected to stand on its own, the financial flows accruing to the relevant entity – including receipts from sales, fees charged, and cash inflows from earmarked taxes or budgetary allocations – all count as benefits, but tax revenue changes unconnected with the entity do not appear in the financial analysis (though they are, of course, part of the economic analysis of the project).

The financial cash flow statements vary between these different points of view. For example, the financial profile from the banker's perspective may start with cash flows expressed in current prices. These may then be deflated by the relevant price index to arrive at real values for this profile. Because the banker would like to know whether the net cash flow is sufficient to repay the loans from different financing arrangements, the starting point for a credit analysis is the net cash flow from the total investment. Since the banker's viewpoint looks at the project as a whole, such a project profile serves as a natural base for the development of the project's economic profile, which also looks at the project as a whole, but includes a wider range of benefits and costs.

The nominal financial cash flow statement from the total investment point of view can be augmented by the proceeds of debt financing, but reduced by the interest payments and principal repayments of the loans, to obtain the net nominal cash flow from the owner's point of view. These values are then deflated by the inflation price index to determine the cash flow in real prices (in a given year) from the owner's point of view. An owner or investor of the project will be expecting to receive a rate of return on the project no less than his or her real private opportunity cost (net of inflation) of equity financing. Using this opportunity cost as the discount rate, a private equity owner would expect the discounted net financial cash flow over the life of the project to be greater than zero. This private discount rate would normally cover the risk associated with the operating and financial leverage of the project as well as the risk that is due to uncertainty.

c) Evaluation Criteria

There are alternative criteria for determining the financial attractiveness of a project. However, the net present value (NPV) of the project is widely accepted as the most satisfactory criterion for the evaluation of project profiles. As such, when a project is being appraised from the viewpoint of equity holders or owners, the relevant cost of funds or discount rate is the return to equity that is being earned on its alternative use. The project will be commercially viable if the NPV of the discounted cash flows is greater than zero. If the NPV is less than zero, the investors cannot expect to earn a rate of return equal to its alternative use of funds, and thus the project should be rejected.

Other criteria that are also used in the business community include internal rate of return, benefit–cost ratio, pay-back period, and debt service coverage ratio. Each of these measures has its own shortcomings. However, the debt service coverage ratio is often regarded as a key factor in determining the ability of a project to pay its operating expenses and to meet its debt servicing obligations. This measure is particularly relevant when considering a project from the banker's point of view.

The government usually provides key social sector projects or a wide range of services, such as health care and education. The issues involved in this undertaking tend to generate low or no revenues at all from the project. However, the financial analysis can still be relevant as a framework for presenting the yearly requirement of funds for continuing with the project.

1.4.2 Risk Analysis and Management

The financial analysis and results have so far been based on the deterministic values of project variables. It is, however, highly unlikely that the values of all a project's key variables, such as the rate of inflation, the market exchange rate, and the prices and quantities of inputs and outputs, will be projected with certainty throughout the life of the project. Hence, a project's NPV and other summary measures are subject to uncertainty and risk. Adapting the analysis to cover uncertainty is thus an important part of an integrated project evaluation.

The first step in conducting a risk analysis of a project is to identify the key risk variables using sensitivity and scenario analysis. The variables chosen should not only represent a large share of relevant benefits and costs but also experience a significant amount of variation in terms of the final outcome. It is usually necessary to focus only on the uncertain variables that contribute to the riskiness of the project in a significant way.

Once the risk variables are identified, the second step is to select an appropriate probability distribution and the likely range of values for each risk variable, based on the past movements of values of the variable and on expert opinion. The relationships between variables are also important and need to be specified. Monte Carlo simulation is a well-established device for generating a probability distribution of project outcomes. Such an exercise would produce an expected probability distribution of a project's NPV, based on the underlying uncertainty surrounding each of the key risk variables specified. From this cumulative probability distribution it is possible to discern the probability that the project's estimated NPV will exceed $1 million, $10 million, or any other given value. The expected mean, median, mode, deciles, and quartiles of the NPV distribution can also be derived. With so much uncertainty in a project, a proper project evaluation should provide some assessment of the expected variability of a project's net return, the probability of obtaining a negative NPV, and how this uncertainty affects the net benefit flows to the key stakeholders.

There are different kinds of uncertainty and risk associated with a project. Uncertainty can be related to suppliers, customers, or project financing. People may view uncertainty and risk differently in terms of their tolerance of risk. Contractual arrangements for managing risk are both a common and an essential component of certain projects. Thus, consideration must be given to redesigning or reorganizing a project to reallocate risk more efficiently. For example, there may be alternative financing arrangements that would help to redistribute some of the risk to a stakeholder who is willing to accept the risk at a low cost to the project, and hence make a project more attractive. There may be contracts that project managers can enter into with their customers/end-users or their suppliers. These different arrangements could create incentives or disincentives that would encourage a project's participants to alter their behaviour so as to improve the project's overall performance. The effects of such contractual arrangements are an integral part of the appraisal of a project. Monte Carlo simulations can be used to help in gaining an understanding of the nature and magnitude of the variability of the project. They can also be used to measure the impact of different contracts on the variability of the project's outcome.

1.4.3 Economic Appraisal

The economic appraisal of a project deals with the effect of the project on the entire society and inquires whether the project is likely to increase the total net economic benefit of the society, taken as a whole.

a) Rationale and Underlying Assumptions

Economic cost–benefit analysis is an important component of applied welfare economics, a branch of economic science that has steadily evolved over more than 200 years. A great deal of that which applied welfare economics has to contribute is based on the following three simple postulates.

1. The competitive demand price for an incremental unit of a good measures its economic value to the demander and hence its economic benefit.
2. The competitive supply price for an incremental unit of a good measures its economic resource cost.
3. Costs and benefits are added up with no regard to who the gainers and losers are.

When no distortions are present, the demand price and supply price of a good will coincide, making its economic value clear. But distortions (of which taxes are paramount) complicate the analysis.

In reality, many distortions prevail in the economy of any country, including, among others, personal income tax, corporate income taxes, value-added tax, excise duties, import duties, and production subsidies. These distortions would have a considerable impact on the economic valuation of capital, foreign exchange, and goods or services produced or used in the project in question. They should be properly assessed and incorporated into the economic appraisal.

For example, the benefits of a project's output should be measured by the demand price inclusive of a value-added tax or a general sales tax, rather than the market price received by the project in the financial analysis. On the other hand, if there is a production subsidy in the project, the resource cost of inputs used in the production should include the subsidy as part of the cost in the economic analysis. Non-tax distortions such as air pollution and water pollution also generate external costs, which should be assessed and accounted for in an economic analysis.

Many public projects (e.g., roads and schools) have outputs that are not sold in an open market. Nonetheless, an economic analysis must somehow try to capture and evaluate the total economic benefits of the output of the goods and services generated by these projects.

b) Development of the Economic Resource Statement

Like the financial cash flow profile in the financial appraisal, the economic appraisal needs to reflect all benefits and costs (whether or not these are financial in nature) and identify whether they accrue to direct project participants or to other members or entities in the society (including the government).

Goods and services in the economy can generally be classified as internationally tradable or non-tradable, and they are evaluated differently in the economic appraisal. A good or service is considered internationally tradable if a project's requirement for an input is ultimately met through an expansion of imports or a reduction of exports. Conversely, the output produced by a project is a tradable good if its production brings about a reduction in imports or an expansion of exports. Land, buildings, local transport, public utilities, and many services are almost intrinsically non-tradable. In addition, there are potential tradable goods whose prices are "unhooked" from the world price structure. These include goods that would normally be considered to be internationally tradable but are rendered non-tradable by particularly high or prohibitive tariffs, and also goods that are potentially tradable but whose internal price lies above the free on board (FOB) export price or below the cost, insurance, and freight (CIF) import price.

For non-tradable goods and services, the economic price of a project input or output is based on the impact that an additional demand for the input or supply of an output has on both the demand and the supply of the good in the market. For example, suppose a project increases the production of a good. The additional supply by the project results in a decrease in the market price, which will cause consumers to increase their consumption but cause some of the existing producers to cut back their production. The economic benefits produced by the project's output should be measured by the weighted average of the value of additional consumption enjoyed by consumers, which is the amount consumers are willing to pay (the demand price, which is the price inclusive of taxes, if any) and the value of resources released by the existing producers (the supply price or the value inclusive of subsidy but net of taxes). The demand and supply weights are determined by the response of additional demand and the cutback in supply with respect to the reduction in the market price.

By the same token, when a project demands an input, its additional demand will result in an increase in price, which in turn will stimulate existing consumers to cut back their consumption and induce producers to increase their production. The economic cost of the inputs demanded by the project should be measured by the weighted average of the forgone consumption (valued by the price inclusive of taxes) and the value of the cost to society of the resources (measured by the price excluding taxes but including subsidy, if any). Again, the weights are determined by the response of consumers and suppliers to the change in market price.

Labour is generally considered a non-tradable good. However, the economic cost of labour varies by occupation, skill level, working conditions, and location, depending upon the project in question.

Once the economic benefits or economic costs have been calculated, they replace the values used in the financial analysis for value of receipts or expenditures in the financial cash flow statement. The simple calculations or a conversion factor can be created by taking the ratio of the economic benefits or costs to its corresponding financial prices of outputs or inputs and then simply multiplying the financial receipts or costs by the corresponding conversion factors to arrive at the economic benefits or costs for construction of the economic resource statement.

In the case of tradable goods, distortions may include customs duties on imported inputs of a project or those imported items that the project output will replace. An export tax or export subsidy on the output of the project is also a distortion and should be accounted for in the economic evaluation. In general, the economic prices of these tradable goods are all equal to their border price, converted at an exchange rate reflecting the economic opportunity cost of foreign exchange.

There are certain projects in which consumers are willing to pay more than the value of the prevailing market price. In such cases, their gain in consumer surplus should be incorporated as an additional economic benefit and reflected in the economic profile of the project. This takes place most often in public sector projects, such as enhancement of water supply schemes or road improvement projects. Conversely, there are also projects that generate pollution or other negative environmental externalities. In these cases, items such as pollution or congestion costs should be evaluated and accounted for in the economic analysis of the project.

c) Evaluation Criteria

Once the economic profile has been constructed, the economic discount rate is used to estimate the project's NPV. The relevant discount rate is the economic opportunity cost of capital in the country in question. This hurdle rate applies not only to investments financed solely with public funds but also to the economic evaluation of investments undertaken by the private sector. An economic NPV greater than zero implies that the project is potentially worthwhile. That is, it would generate greater net economic benefits than the normal use of equivalent resources elsewhere in the economy. However, if the NPV is less than zero, the project should be rejected on the grounds that the resources invested could be put to better use if they were simply left in the capital market.

As with the financial appraisal, Monte Carlo simulations can be used to generate a probability distribution of the NPV of the project.

1.4.4 Stakeholder Impacts

It is important for the sustainability of the project over time to identify the winners and losers and how much they would gain and lose as a result of the project's implementation. The financial and economic analyses of the integrated project analysis will provide the basic data for estimating the specific stakeholder impacts. In the financial analysis, there are several groups or parties affected by a project. Each such group's benefits and costs can be analysed to determine who gains and who loses as a result of a project. The purpose of this distributional analysis is to see whether the benefits of the project will actually go to the targeted groups, as well as to ensure that no specific group is subjected to an undue burden as a result of a project. The magnitude of any burden can be measured by the present value of the incremental net benefit flows that are expected to be realized by that group. Among the main stakeholders affected by a project are generally the project's suppliers, consumers, the project's competitors, labour, and the government. The impact on government is mainly derived from the externalities generated by taxes and subsidies.

1.5 Cost–Effectiveness Analysis

The capital investment project has so far been evaluated in the context of a cost–benefit analysis. However, there are certain projects in which benefits of the project are difficult to quantify in monetary terms. These projects include health, nutrition, education, water supply, and electricity generation. In this case, an alternative approach, cost–effectiveness analysis, is commonly employed.

Cost–effectiveness analysis compares the costs of achieving a given outcome by alternative routes. By simply choosing the lowest cost of achieving a given benefit, it avoids the necessity of placing a monetary value on the benefit. Where the output in question has several dimensions, an index can be developed that places plausible weights on these different aspects (e.g., speed, convenience, accessibility, etc.) and that option chosen that yields the lowest cost per index unit. This variant is sometimes called cost–utility analysis.

Once a project is approved, managing and monitoring the progress of the project is important for organizations in terms of time, cost, and performance. It requires the establishment of an implementation schedule for the project, and progress is assessed against this schedule. The ex-post evaluation focuses on the outcome of the project to determine whether the economic and social goals of the project have been achieved and what the impacts on stakeholders of the project are after its implementation.

1.6 Organization of the Book

This book consists of 20 chapters. Chapter 2 describes the evolution of project cycle and the links among the various components of a project's development. It starts with the project definition, moves on to discuss building blocks and data requirements for appraising projects, and finally integrates the various components into the evaluation framework.

Chapter 3 examines the first major component of the overall evaluation framework: how to perform the financial analysis of a project. The purpose of a financial analysis is to estimate whether a project is financially sustainable, i.e., how it will cover its financial cost expenditures. For projects that have direct participation from the private sector, the question is whether the investors will find the project to be in their interests. The accuracy of the financial analysis depends heavily on the accuracy of the technical, marketing, and commercial analyses used to construct a project's investment, financing, and operating plans. Accurate estimation of the NPV of the project's net cash flows requires consideration of potential vulnerability to inflation as well as an estimate of the appropriate cost of capital that can serve as the private discount rate.

Project criteria are presented in Chapter 4, including debt service coverage ratios as a measure of a project's sustainability. The dominant criterion used in project evaluation, namely the NPV, is described in detail. This is conducted against a backdrop of one of the key attributes of any investment project, namely its time dimension. Net economic benefits must also be discounted or accumulated to a given point in time before they can be added up or otherwise compared. Chapter 5 discusses how a project's NPV helps to answer important questions, such as the appropriate initiation date, scale, duration, and termination date of a project.

The financial analysis is based on the deterministic value of each of the input and output variables of a project over the life of the project. The actual outcomes, however, are unlikely to be exactly as projected because of the uncertainty in the future over the life of the project. This uncertainty needs to be factored into a project's financial analysis. Chapter 6 introduces uncertainty and risk analysis into the financial appraisal by examining the respective merits of sensitivity, scenario, and Monte Carlo analyses, with emphasis on the last of these. Measures necessary for dealing with uncertainty, such as different types of contracts and instruments of project financing, are presented. The risk analysis also extends to the associated economic and distributional impacts of the project.

Chapter 7 presents the three basic postulates for applied welfare economics. These include the concepts of consumers' and producers' surplus and a definition of the different kinds of economic distortions and externalities. The chapter outlines how the three postulates can be used to estimate the economic prices of goods and services, first in the absence, and then in the presence, of distortions. The extension of the financial analysis to incorporate the additional costs and benefits linked to externalities shifts us to an economic framework, focusing on costs and benefits as they affect society as a whole.

Since the economic analysis, like the financial analysis, relies on the NPV criterion as the basis for decision-making, an economic discount rate is needed to calculate the present values of the net economic benefit streams. Chapter 8 provides the methodology for calculating the economic discount rate. Similarly, an estimation of a shadow price for foreign exchange is needed to reflect the distortions that exist in the tradable goods sector. These distortions are the source of a foreign exchange externality that causes the economic opportunity cost of foreign exchange to differ from the market exchange rate. In addition, a corresponding premium should also be estimated and accounted for in the case of expenditures on non-tradable goods and services, which are influenced by the same externalities that apply to the tradable goods sector, as described in Chapter 9.

The processes for determining the domestic price of tradable and non-tradable goods are fundamentally different. Chapter 10 deals with the measurement of the economic price of tradable goods at project sites under various situations. Chapter 11 develops an analytical framework to measure the economic price of non-tradable goods or services when all repercussions of a project output or purchase of project inputs are taken into account.

Chapter 12 examines the economic opportunity cost of the labour involved in a project. The project wage is the financial cost of labour. However, its economic cost, or shadow wage rate, can differ from the financial cost because of various distortions prevailing in labour markets.

The distributional analysis, also known as stakeholder analysis, can be important for the sustainability of a project. It is possible to identify major groups or parties affected by a project when one moves from the financial analysis to the economic analysis. They can be assessed in order to determine who will benefit and who will lose from the project, and by how much. This helps to identify and quantify the impacts of a project on various interest groups. This analysis is presented in Chapter 13, and its purpose is to ensure that no specific group is subjected to an undue burden nor presented with an unwarranted benefit as a result of a project.

Chapter 14 deals with two additional issues frequently raised in cost–benefit analysis. One is the shadow price of government funds and how it should be treated in our framework. The other is how distributed weights should be dealt with in the analysis of a project. In its ultimate analysis, poverty is the inability of households or residents to meet their basic needs, including health, nutrition, water and sanitation, education, and housing. A project that addresses these issues is more valuable to society and should be given preference over another project that has the same financial and economic values but does not cater to these special areas. The concept of a basic needs externality and how a project can be given credit for helping the neediest groups in society is addressed in this chapter.

In certain projects, it is rather difficult to quantify benefits in monetary terms. A cost–effectiveness analysis becomes a useful and effective criterion for making choices among projects or programmes. The description of this concept and application is outlined in Chapter 15.

Applications of the integrated appraisal developed above to specific sectors are illustrated in the remaining chapters of the book. Chapter 16 deals with various conceptual issues relating to transportation projects. The focus is on highway projects, including road improvements and newly constructed roads. Externalities connected with road projects, as well as those involving rail transport, are also discussed in this chapter.

Chapter 17 illustrates how a proposed investment in upgrading a gravel road to a tarred surface in South Africa should be evaluated. This is a project with no toll levied on road users, and thus no financial evaluation is carried out. However, from the economic perspective, the evaluation covers not only the assessment of savings in road maintenance costs by the Road Agency, but also the reduction in vehicle operating costs for road users as a result of the improvement of road surface, time savings for road users because of the increased speed of vehicles, and other fiscal externalities.

Chapter 18 describes the unique features and the problems of electricity investment projects. The principles of the marginal cost pricing of electricity applied to peak and off-peak hours, as well as resource cost savings by adopting least-cost alternative generation technologies, are particularly relevant to the investment in this sector. The conceptual discussion covers investments in both hydro and thermal electricity generation.

Chapter 19 demonstrates how the principle of least alternative cost is applied to the appraisal of a project aimed at expanding the capacity of the electricity-generation system in Adukki. It was originally proposed that a single-cycle thermal plant would be built and operated by an independent power producer (IPP), while the state utility is the only off-taker of the electricity generated by this plant. The price paid to the IPP is negotiated through a long-term power purchase agreement. This chapter illustrates how the financial and economic outcomes of the plant can be compared with those of a combined-cycle plant.

The final chapter, Chapter 20, applies the integrated investment approach to an assessment of whether an investment programme to upgrade the water and sewer utility in Panama is financially and economically feasible and sustainable. Estimates of the gross economic benefits or costs of the additional or reduced consumption of water are all based on the well-established welfare economics principles outlined in previous chapters. Nevertheless, the stakeholder analysis of this chapter causes concerns regarding the potential excess profits that could be received by a foreign concessionaire under the terms of the proposed concession.

The economic and social development of any country depends on the selection of sound investment projects. This book provides a theoretical and practical framework for project development and evaluation. It facilitates the preparation and assessment of projects to ensure that good projects are implemented while bad projects are not. Both decisions promote the economic and social well-being of the residents of the country in question.

References

Belli, P., J.R. Anderson, H.N. Barnum, J.A. Dixon, and J.P. Tan. 2001. *Economic Analysis of Investment Operations: Analytical Tools and Practical Applications.* Washington, DC: The World Bank.

Boardman, A.E., D.H. Greenberg, A.R. Vining, and D.L. Weimer. 2001. *Cost-Benefit Analysis: Concepts and Practice*, 2nd edition. Englewood Cliffs, NJ: Prentice Hall.

Brent, R.J. 2006. *Applied Cost-Benefit Analysis.* Cheltenham: Edward Elgar Publishing Limited.

Campbell, H.F. and R.P.C. Brown. 2003. *Benefit-Cost Analysis: Financial and Economic Appraisal using Spreadsheets.* Cambridge: Cambridge University Press.

Curry, S. and J. Weiss. 1993. *Project Analysis in Developing Countries.* New York: St. Martin's Press.

Dinwiddy, C. and F. Teal. 1996. *Principles of Cost-Benefit Analysis for Developing Countries.* Cambridge: Cambridge University Press.

Gramlich, E.M. 1997. *A Guide to Cost-Benefit Analysis.* Englewood Cliffs, NJ: Prentice Hall.

Harberger, A.C. 1987. "Reflections on Social Project Evaluation", in G.M. Meier (ed.), *Pioneers in Development*, Vol. 2. Washington: The World Bank and Oxford: Oxford University Press.

Harberger, A.C. and G.P. Jenkins. 2002. *Cost-Benefit Analysis.* Cheltenham: Edward Elgar Publishing Limited.

Little, I.M.D. and J.A. Mirrlees. 1974. *Project Appraisal and Planning for Developing Countries.* London: Heinemann Educational Books.

— 1991. "Project Appraisal and Planning Twenty Years on", in *Proceedings of the World Bank Annual Conference on Development Economics, 1990.* Washington, DC: World Bank.

Mishan, E.J. and E. Quah. 2007. *Cost-Benefit Analysis,* 5th edition. London and New York: Routledge.

Squire, L. 1989. "Project Evaluation in Theory and Practice", in H. Chenery and T.N. Srinivasan (eds.), *Handbook of Development Economics*, Vol. 2. Amsterdam: North Holland.

United Nations Industrial Development Organization. 1972. *Guidelines for Project Evaluation.* New York: United Nations.

Chapter Two

A Strategy for the Appraisal
of Investment Projects

2.1 Introduction

Every project has certain phases in its development and implementation. The appraisal stage of the project cycle should provide information and analysis on a range of issues associated with the decision-making on the project. First, the administrative feasibility of project implementation must be fairly assessed, and the marketing and technical appraisals of the project must be provided in order to evaluate its feasibility. Second, the financial capability of the project to survive the planned duration of its life must be appraised. Third, the expected economic contribution to the growth of the economy must be measured based on the principles of applied welfare economics, and a series of assumptions used to undertake this appraisal. Finally, an assessment must be made to determine whether, and how, the project would assist in attaining the socio-economic objectives set out for the country, along with an analysis to determine whether the project is cost-effective in meeting these objectives.

To carry out this task while offsetting some of the biases inherent in project appraisal requires a level of professionalism on the part of the analyst that is difficult or impossible to attain if project appraisal is carried out on ad hoc basis. For the appraisal of projects in the public sector, a corps of project evaluators must be established within the government with a view to developing a level of expertise in project appraisal that will significantly improve overall project planning and selection. These evaluators should not only be aware of a country's political environment but also have a general sense that their mission is to provide an accurate assessment of a project's viability based on professionally determined criteria.

There is often a tendency to examine the financial (or budgetary), economic, and distributional (or stakeholder) impacts of a project or programme as three independent outcomes. However, these three aspects of the overall performance of a project are generally closely interrelated and should be viewed as three parts of an integrated evaluation. For example, the distributional impact of a project cannot even be estimated without information on the financial and economic appraisal. Similarly, its economic efficiency can be impaired if it cannot rely on the project's revenues or the planned budgetary allocations needed for it to operate effectively.

The economic, financial, and stakeholder analyses of a project should also be closely linked because the information obtained at one stage of the appraisal may be essential for the completion of another aspect of the evaluation. For example, if we wish to know how much unskilled labour is benefiting from a project, we first need to know their wage rates and the numbers employed by the project. Such information is generally reported in the worksheets required to prepare the financial analysis of the project. If we wish to measure the impact of the project's pricing policy on the welfare of a particular group of people, the basic information on the project's customers and their relative consumption of the project's output will be found in the marketing module, which is required for the financial appraisal of the project.

A preliminary analysis of a public sector project that looks at financial variables alone is not very meaningful, no matter how accurately it has been carried out. The appraisal will be of more value to the public sector decision-makers if the analytical effort is spread out over all the important aspects of the project to derive its impact on the net economic well-being of society as a whole.

The identification, appraisal, and design phase of a project's development is composed of a series of appraisals and decision points leading to either the inception or rejection of the project. This process can logically be divided into four stages of appraisal and four decision nodes before the project receives final approval. These stages can be shown diagrammatically as in Figure 2.1.

Figure 2.1: Stages in Project Appraisal and Approval

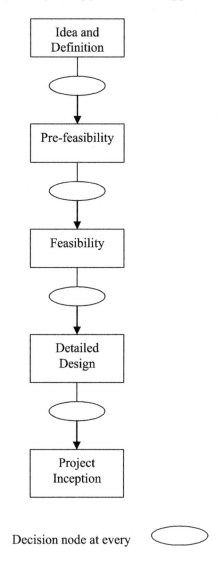

Decision node at every

2.2 Idea and Project Definition

The first and most important task of every procedure for project evaluation is to ensure that the prospective benefits of a project exceed its prospective costs. This is by no means a simple or straightforward task. In practice, it typically takes place in a sequence of stages (see Figure 2.1), each involving more time and resources than its predecessor, and as a consequence (one hopes), developing a more accurate picture of the project's likely costs and benefits. To be approved, a project should surmount each of the successive hurdles. A rejection, on the other hand, can take place at any stage. Some projects are so flawed that their gross inadequacies are shown up by even the very roughest initial screening. Other, less obviously flawed projects tend to be screened out in the pre-feasibility phases. The later stages of feasibility and detailed design may give rise to the rejection of some projects, but are more likely to be concentrated on such elements as the precise tuning and scale of the project, and the specific design and determination of its components.

Issues of design as well as other aspects of project strategy often involve much more than the simple quantification of a project's likely total costs and benefits. The way in which these costs and benefits are distributed can also weigh heavily in determining its feasibility. Many projects involve numerous different groups of stakeholders. For example, for an irrigation project, there are farmers, regional and local governments, the highway authority and highway users, the owners and residents of land to be flooded, the downstream users of the river's water, etc. While it may be that the project could be brought to fruition over the opposition of one or more of such groups, it is clearly more sensible for the sharing of benefits and costs to be arranged in such a way as to leave most of them contented. Indeed, no project will get under way unless it is designed (including the way in which costs and benefits will be shared) so that every stakeholder group that has some sort of "veto power" is precluded from exercising that power.

Financial issues can also come into play in many different forms. Stories are rife concerning beautiful, modern hospitals whose facilities are largely wasted because of inadequate budgets for equipment, medicines, and doctors' and nurses' salaries. Electricity systems that started in fine shape have fallen into disrepair and failed to bring the expected benefits because lagging adjustments of tariffs to inflation have impeded proper maintenance and have rendered it impossible to borrow to keep capacity in line with the growing demand. Road projects entailing large capital investments financed by borrowing have similarly failed to deliver their expected benefits owing to financial shortfalls that precluded adequate maintenance and repair. In almost of these cases there was no intrinsic deficiency in the project itself; instead, some sort of institutional rigidity was at fault. Experience tells us that it is the job of an effective project appraisal process to try first to foresee and then to forestall such financial difficulties.

It should be clear from the above that in cases where stakeholder interests play a significant role, and/or where the viability or success of a project is vulnerable to avoidable financial contingencies, these elements should be taken into account at each successive stage of the appraisal process. It is not prudent to leave them to be dealt with, almost as an afterthought, only at or near the final stage. This is why, in this book, we have tried to present an appraisal that permits the analyst to focus on economic, financial, and stakeholder considerations within a substantially integrated framework.

2.3 Pre-feasibility Study

The pre-feasibility study is the first attempt to examine the overall potential of a project. In undertaking this appraisal, it is important to realize that its purpose is to obtain estimates that reflect the correct order of magnitude of the variables in order to roughly indicate whether the project is sufficiently attractive to warrant more detailed design work.

Throughout the appraisal phase and, in particular, at the pre-feasibility stage, estimates that are clearly biased in one direction are often more valuable than mean estimates of the variables, especially when these latter are only known with significant uncertainty. In order to avoid acceptance of projects based on overly optimistic estimates of benefits and costs, the pre-feasibility analysis should use estimates with a downward bias for benefits and an upward bias for costs. If the project still looks attractive even in the presence of these biases, it stands a good chance of passing a more accurate evaluation.

The pre-feasibility study of any project will normally cover six different areas. These can be summarized as follows:

a) *Demand module*, in which the demand for the goods and services, and prices, or the relative needs for social services, are estimated, quantified, and justified.

b) *Technical or engineering module*, in which the input parameters of the projects are specified in detail and cost estimates developed.

c) *Labour and administrative support module*, in which labour requirements are specified for the implementation of the project, as well as for its operation, and sources of labour identified and quantified.

d) *Financial/budget module*, in which the financial expenditures and revenues are evaluated, along with an assessment of the alternative methods of financing.

e) *Economic module*, in which the project's economic costs and benefits as a whole are appraised from the viewpoint of the economy.

f) *Environmental impact assessment module*, in which the various environmental impacts of the project are identified and evaluated and proposals developed for their mitigation.

g) *Stakeholder module*, in which the project is appraised from the point of view of who receives the benefits and who pays the costs of a project. Where possible, quantification should be made in order to determine by how much each of these groups benefits or pays.

Whenever possible, the pre-feasibility study should use secondary research. Such research examines previous studies on the issues in question and reviews the specialized trade and technical journals for any important data that may be relevant to the appraisal of the project. Use of the research on commodities and technical aspects of projects from institutions or associations disseminating pertinent information is essential. Most technical and marketing problems have already been faced and solved by others. Therefore, a great deal of information can be obtained quickly and cheaply if the existing sources are used efficiently.

a) Demand Module

The demand module should be thought of as a first attempt at serious quantification of the benefits of the project. If the output of the project is directly marketed (such as telephone services), the module may consist of projecting the likely time path of its economic price (in real terms) and estimating the quantity demanded along that price path at each point in time. If the project provides a service (such as highway services), which might, though need not, be subject to a user charge, the appropriate procedure is to go directly to an economic evaluation of benefits and costs in real terms and then consider whether user charges are appropriate, how high they should be, and how they should be administered. In such cases, the willingness of the beneficiaries to pay is a key element in the estimation of benefits, even though total benefits may differ significantly from estimated toll collections. At the other extreme, there are projects in which the estimated user demand plays little or no role. In these cases, the value of the product of the project is typically established in other ways. Sometimes the value of the output of the project is seen by all to substantially exceed its cost. In these cases, resort is made to a fundamental economic principle: one should not attribute to any project a benefit that is greater than the cost of the least-cost alternative way of achieving the same result. Often in such cases, a "standard" alternative exists (for example, thermal electricity generation in the case of electricity), the costs of which are easily determined. The benefit of the project would then be considered to be the saving of costs that it provides, as against the costs of the "standard" alternative.

For the demand analysis of tradable goods, the key variables are the prospective levels and likely trends of their prices relative to the domestic price level (and to that of tradable goods generally). Here one can often find market analyses by the relevant producer associations and professional experts, including projections of prices and world output.

For the demand analysis of a product to be sold in the domestic market, it will be more important to begin primary research at the pre-feasibility stage of the project appraisal. The analysis will need to assess the overall marketing plan of the organization undertaking the project. The potential users of the product will often have to be surveyed before an accurate picture of its potential demand can be determined. If the product is to be sold in a competitive environment, a judgment should be made as to how the competitors in the market are likely to react. Such a judgment can be based on reviews of past actions as well as the institutional strengths and weaknesses of the competitors. Ultimately, the demand for the project's output will depend on the nature of the product, the competitive advantages of the project in supplying the product, and the resources spent to market the output.

In the case of public monopolies such as public utilities, government policies themselves may be important in determining the demand for the output. Extension of electricity supply to new rural areas and the development of new industrial complexes can have an important bearing on the future demand. The growth in the demand for the output of a public utility can often be projected accurately by studying the relationship over time of demand with respect to variables such as disposable income, industrial output, household formation, and relative prices. The study of growth in demand experienced by utilities in other countries with similar circumstances can also help to provide a good basis for projecting future trends.

The output of this module, if it is to be a commercial project, should be a set of forecasts of the following variables for the duration of the project:
- Quantities of expected output of the project, as well as the time path of associated real benefits.
- Quantities of expected sales and prices for goods to be sold domestically and not in competition with internationally traded goods.
- Sales taxes and export taxes that are expected to be paid on the project's output of the traded goods.
- Sales taxes to be paid on goods not traded internationally.
- Subsidies to be received on the basis of production, sales, exports, etc.
- Government regulations (such as price ceilings and floors, or quotas) affecting the sales or price of the output.
- Product trends in terms of technological developments and the expected product cycle.
- Trade restrictions that are not created by government regulation, and their impact.

b) Technical or Engineering Module

In this module, secondary research can be used very effectively. Engineering firms and technical experts in a particular field usually have considerable experience in other projects that have used either identical technology or similar techniques. Often there are many consulting firms or government agencies that have technical expertise in a specific area. The most important rule when using outside expertise to assist with feasibility studies is that the consulting group being employed to provide this information must be informed that it will not be considered for the design or management of the facility in the design and implementation phase. It is critical that the consultants used in the appraisal of a project are not placed in a position where they have a conflict of interest. Consultants should be hired at the appraisal stage to provide truthful information based on their experience in the past. The authorities may also wish to indicate to them that if their estimates for the current project prove to be accurate, they will receive favourable attention when the contracts are being awarded on future design activities for other projects. The consultants used to assist in the preparation of the appraisal should also be retained to check and approve the design and cost estimates developed by the group that has been given the task of preparing the final detailed plans.

If this procedure is not followed, there may well be a conscious effort on the part of the engineering or technical consultants to underestimate costs in order to have the project approved. Once the project is approved, they have an opportunity to obtain the more profitable task of preparing the detailed design of the project. Of course, the worst possible approach is to ask for free advice at the appraisal stage on the basis that the outside experts will be given a chance to do further work for payment if the project is attractive. It is a sad commentary on the performance of many governments in this area to note that these last two procedures are the ones often followed.

The output from the technical module of a pre-feasibility study should obtain the following information:

- The quantities of inputs, by type, that will be required for the construction of the project.
- The likely time paths of the real prices of these inputs and their probable sources of supply.
- The time paths of the labour requirements of the project, for each occupation and each category.
- The physical input requirements for the operation of the project, by year and by volume of output.
- The likely sources of supply for these inputs and the assumptions on which the time paths of their future real prices are based.
- Information on the technological life of the project.
- The nature and extent of the impacts that the project is expected to have on the environment.

c) Labour and Administrative Support Module

Project appraisal, to be effective, must not confine itself to examining the financial and economic costs and benefits on the assumption that the project can be built and delivered operationally and on time. This assumes a degree of management capacity that simply does not exist in many situations. Many projects have failed because they were undertaken without making sure the management and administrative expertise was available to be able to deliver the project as specified.

This module must reconcile the technical and management requirements of the project with the supply constraints on labour available to this project. If they cannot be reconciled, then the project should not be undertaken. A careful study of the labour markets should be made in order to ensure that the estimates of expected real wage rates to be paid are soundly based and that the planned sources of personnel are reasonable in the light of labour market conditions.

In general, labour requirements should be broken down by occupational and skill category, and these needs should be evaluated in terms of the possible sources from which they might be met. Where difficulties are foreseen, this information should be passed to the technical module so that possible revisions of the timing of the project can be considered.

d) Financial/Budget Module

The financial/budget module provides the first integration of the financial and technical variables that have been estimated by the previous modules. A cash flow profile of the project will be constructed, identifying all the receipts and expenditures that are expected to occur during the life of a project. Even in the pre-feasibility stage, an attempt should be made to provide a description of the financial flows of the project, identifying the key variables to be used as input data in the economic and stakeholder appraisal.

Initially, the financial cash flows will be expressed in terms of nominal prices over time because certain key variables, such as taxes and debt repayments, are calculated in terms of their nominal values. These nominal values are then converted into their real value equivalents by dividing by a numeraire price index. It is usually necessary to examine a project's performance in finance over time in terms of the real values of the financial variables in order to determine its financial robustness over time and, hence, its financial sustainability.

Because of the need for estimates of particular variables (e.g., foreign exchange requirements) for the purpose of making economic and stakeholder project appraisals, the level of financial detail required is considerably greater than that which is usually found in the financial appraisal of a private sector project. The financial module should answer a series of basic questions concerning the financial prospects and viability of the project. Four of the most important of these questions are outlined here.

- What relative degrees of certainty can be placed on each of the revenue and cost items in the financial analysis? What factors are expected to affect these variables directly, and in what way?
- What sources of financing will be used to cover the cost of the project? Does this financing have special features, such as subsidized interest rates, grants, foreign equity, or loans?
- What is the minimum net cash flow required by this investment to enable it to continue operations without unplanned requests being made to the government treasury for supplementary financing?
- Does the project have a large enough net cash flow or financial rate of return to be financially viable? If not, what sources of additional funds are available

and can be committed to assist the project if it is economically and socially justified?

If any one of these questions points to future difficulties, adjustments should be made in either the design or the financing of the project so as to avoid failure.

e) Economic Module

This module attempts to cover the full benefits and costs of a project in society or the economy. As the benefits and costs flow through time, they are expressed in real terms.

The distinction is made between the benefits and costs of the project as seen by the project owner and those perceived by the economy as a whole. Here the concern is with such items as taxes, subsidies, and other distortions flowing between the government and the project, with benefits that accrue to the project's users (in the form, say, of consumer surplus), and with externalities such as pollution and congestion, where costs are borne by people other than their specific perpetrators. A financial analysis will typically incorporate only the financial flows accruing to or paid by the project. Thus, the following key questions arise.

- What are the differences between the financial and economic values for each of the important variables? What causes these differences?
- With what degrees of certainty do we know the values of these differences?
- What is the expected value of economic net benefits?
- What are the probabilities of the different levels of net economic value being realized?

f) Environmental Impact Assessment Module

The environmental impact assessment module brings together the information from both the demand module and the technical module to assess the likely environmental impact of the project and to determine the most cost-effective ways of mitigating the negative impacts. The analysis undertaken in this module should, in many instances, quantify the physical impacts of the project on the environment and attempt to measure the economic costs and benefits of these impacts. In the assessment of the negative impacts, there is a need to consider the trade-offs that might exist between the benefits arising from the project and the environmental damage that is likely to occur. The alternatives and their economic cost for controlling the environmental damage should be compared to the economic cost of the damage that will be incurred. When the environmental costs are uncertain but have the potential to inflict significant damage, other ways of supplying the good or service that do not have the same potential for inflicting the environmental costs must be evaluated as alternatives to the project under consideration.

In a case in which the benefits or costs (and damages) cannot be quantified but the impacts are considered significant, the benefits and costs should be listed, substantiated, and properly documented in the analysis. Such intangible or qualitative items may have significant impacts on decision-making.

g) Stakeholder Module

The stakeholder analysis is concerned with the identification and, wherever possible, the quantification of the impacts of the project on the various stakeholders. These include the impact of the project on the well-being of particular groups in society, since a project seldom benefits everyone in a country proportionally. There is a need to identify political factors and long-term impacts of the project on the community that are not reflected by the changes in income. While this aspect of the appraisal may be less precise than the financial or economic analysis of a project, the stakeholder evaluation should be tied to the same project factors that are expected to reduce poverty or address the basic needs of poorer members of the community.

The following is an illustrative set of questions to be asked by the analyst when undertaking a stakeholder appraisal of a project.

- Who are the beneficiaries of this project, and who is expected to bear the costs?
- In what ways do those who benefit from the project receive those benefits, and how do those who bear the costs pay?
- What other political or social impact is this project expected to generate? How?
- What are the basic needs of the society that are relevant in the country? What impact will the project have on these basic needs?
- By what alternative ways (and at what costs) could the government obtain social results similar to those expected from this project (or programme)?
- What are the net economic costs of undertaking these alternative projects or programmes? How do their costs compare with those incurred by the project in order to achieve the same political or social objectives?

Two important principles should be remembered when evaluating the social impact of a project. First, the reasoning should be clear regarding how the project is going to produce the social impacts attributed to it. Second, as the government is usually undertaking many projects and programmes to reach its social objectives, the cost-effectiveness of this particular project must be compared with, at least, a benchmark of the costs that are incurred by the other policy instruments available. Only if this project is as cost-effective as other projects and programmes in achieving the social objectives should an additional benefit be attributed to it.

The set of questions outlined for a financial–economic–social appraisal of a project makes it clear that the aim is to categorize costs and benefits from the point of view of society as a whole. However, it should be recognized that some costs and benefits will be financial and directly generated within the project, and others will be financial but external to the project. It should also be emphasized that some costs and benefits will be measurable and valued at an imputed price, and others will be identifiable but measured and/or valued with some degree of uncertainty. The variety of types of costs and benefits should be borne in mind in interpreting the results of a social project appraisal. In particular, it is important not to be misled by the apparent simplicity of the net economic or social present values expressed as real numbers.

2.4 Feasibility Study

Once all the modules of the pre-feasibility study have been completed, the project must be examined to see whether it shows promise of meeting the financial, economic, and social criteria that the government has set for investment expenditures. A sensitivity analysis of the project must be made to identify the key variables that determine its outcome.

The function of the feasibility stage of an appraisal is to improve the accuracy of the measures of key variables if the particular project indicates it has a potential for success. In order to improve the accuracy, more primary research will have to be undertaken and perhaps a second opinion sought on other variables.

The important risk variables that affect the project's performance need to be identified. The methods of risk reduction, allocation, and management need to be developed and applied to the identified risk variables as part of the feasibility study.

At the end of this stage the most important decision must be made, namely whether the project is financially attractive to all interested parties in the activity and whether it should be approved. It is much more difficult to stop a flawed project after the detailed (and expensive) design work has been carried out at the next stage of appraisal. Once sizable resources have been committed to preparing the detailed technical and financial design of a project, it takes very courageous public servants and politicians to admit that it was a bad idea.

2.5 Detailed Design

Following the feasibility study, if the decision-makers give their approval for the project, the next task is to develop a detailed project design and make detailed arrangements for financing the project. Preliminary design criteria must be established when the project is identified and appraised, though expenditures on detailed technical specifications are not usually warranted at this time. Once it has been determined that the project will continue, the design task should be completed in more detail. This involves setting down the basic programmes, allocating tasks, determining resources, and setting down in operational form the functions to be carried out and their priorities. Technical requirements, such as labour needs by skill type, should be determined at this stage. On completion of the blueprints and specifications for construction of the facilities and equipment, the operating plans and schedules, along with contingency plans, must be prepared and brought together in the development of a formal implementation plan.

In summary, the detailed design stage of a project appraisal is when the accuracy of the data for all the previous modules is improved to the point at which an operational plan of action can be developed. Not only is the physical design of the project completed at this stage, but so is the programme for administration, operating, and marketing.

When this process is completed, the project is again reviewed to ascertain whether it still meets the criteria for approval and implementation. If it does not, then this result must be passed on to the appropriate authorities for rejection.

2.6 Project Implementation

If the appraisal and design have been properly executed, the selection of the project for implementation should entail only the completion of negotiations to finalize the conditions for financing and the formal approval of the project. The formal approval will require the acceptance of funding proposals and agreement on contract documents, including tenders and other contracts requiring the commitment of resources.

The implementation of a project involves the coordination and allocation of resources to make the project operational. The project manager will have to bring together a project team including professionals and technicians. This team will in turn have to coordinate the various consultants, contractors, suppliers, and other interested agencies involved in putting the project in place. Responsibility and authority for executing the project must be assigned. This will include the granting of authority to make decisions in areas related to personnel, legal and financial matters, organization, and administration. Proper planning at this stage is essential to ensure that undue delays do not occur and that proper administrative procedures are designed for the smooth coordination of the activities required for the implementation of the project.

The appointment of a project manager means that responsibility for implementation will fall within his or her jurisdiction. This will involve decisions regarding the allocation of tasks to groups within the organization and decisions regarding the procurement of equipment, resources, and labour. Schedules and time frames need to be established. Control and reporting procedures must be activated to provide feedback to policy-makers and the project manager.

When the project nears completion, preparation must be made for the phasing out of the construction activities and handover to the new operational management. The project completion will necessitate a scaling down and dismantling of the project organization. A transfer of project personnel and equipment to other areas of the operation will be required. These activities may occur over a considerable period of time. However, as the project becomes operational, it is essential that the skills, plans, and controlling organization be available to carry on with the function of the project in order to avoid excessive start-up costs, which can easily undermine the overall success or failure of the project.

2.7 Ex-post Evaluation

In the short history of formal cost–benefit analysis or project appraisal, considerably more effort has gone into the pre-evaluation of projects than into the review of projects actually implemented. For the development of operational techniques of project appraisal, it is essential to compare the predicted with the actual performance of projects. In order for this review of the strengths and weaknesses of implemented projects to be of maximum value to both policy-makers and project analysts, it is important that some degree of continuity of personnel be maintained within the organization's project evaluation teams through time.

In carrying out this evaluation, a review of the administrative aspects of the project development should be made immediately after the project becomes operational. The managers of the operational phase of the project must be made aware of the fact that an in-depth evaluation of the project's performance is to be carried out through time. In this way, the necessary data can be developed through the normal financial and control activities of the operation to enable an evaluation to be carried out at minimum cost.

The ex-post evaluation helps not only to assess the performance of a project and to give an ultimate verdict on its contribution to the country's development, but also to identify the critical variables in the design and implementation of a project that have contributed to its success or failure. The ex-post evaluation helps an organization to repeat successful experiences and to eliminate failures.

References

Baum, W.C. 1978. "The World Bank Project Cycle", *Finance and Development* 15(4), 10–17.
Cleland, D.I. and W.R. King. 1975. *Systems Analysis and Project Management.* New York: McGraw-Hill.
Food and Agriculture Organization of the United Nations. 2001. *Project Cycle Management Technical Guide*, prepared by Clare Bishop in collaboration with the Socio-economic and Gender Analysis Programme.

Gittinger, J.P. 1994. *Economic Analysis of Agricultural Projects.* Baltimore and London: Johns Hopkins University Press.

Goodman, L.J. and R.N. Love. 1977. "The Integrated Project Planning and Management Cycle", paper presented at United Nations Asian Centre for Development Administration, policy-level workshop on Administrative Support Planning for Development Projects, Kuala Lumpur, Malaysia (November).

Kaufmann, D. and Y. Wang. 1995. "Macroeconomic Policies and Project Performance in the Social Sectors: A Model of Human Capital Production and Evidence from LDCs", *World Development* 23(5), 751–765.

Little, I.M.D. and J.A. Mirrlees. 1974. *Project Appraisal and Planning for Developing Countries.* London: Heinemann Educational Books.

Noorbaksh, F. 1993. *Project Planning versus Project Appraisal.* Centre for Development Studies, University of Glasgow.

Thamhain, H.J. and D.L. Wilemon. 1975. "Conflict Management in Project Life Cycles", *Sloan Management Reviews* (Summer).

Ward, W.A. and B.J. Derren. 1991. *The Economics of Project Analysis: A Practitioner's Guide.* Economic Development Institute, World Bank.

Chapter Three

The Financial Appraisal of Projects

3.1 Introduction

The financial analysis of a project helps to determine its financial viability and sustainability. Since an integrated project analysis begins with a financial analysis, followed by an economic analysis, the concepts and data ought to be organized in a consequential and consistent manner. The comparison of either financial or economic benefits with their corresponding costs requires that all relevant data should be organized into a project profile covering the duration of the project's life. While a project profile is given by cash flows in the financial appraisal, in the economic appraisal the project's profile provides a flow of net economic benefits generated by the investment. This chapter explains how cash flow profiles of a project are developed and constructed in a consistent fashion. It also discusses how investment projects can be evaluated from different points of view.

3.2 Why a Financial Appraisal for a Public Sector Project?

It may appear that the financial appraisal of a project is of interest only to a private investor who wishes to determine the net financial gain (or loss) resulting from the project. Because public sector projects use public funds, the analysis from the public perspective is primarily concerned with the project's impact on the country's economic welfare. From a country's prospective, a project should be undertaken if it generates a positive net economic benefit. A project that yields negative net economic benefits should not be undertaken as it will lower the economic welfare of society as a whole. To determine the net economic benefits produced by a project, the appraisal needs to incorporate an economic analysis.

There are several reasons for conducting a financial appraisal for a public sector project. The most important one is to ensure the availability of funds to finance the project through its investment and operating phases. While an expected positive economic return is a necessary condition for recommending that a project be undertaken, it is by no means a sufficient reason for a successful outcome. A project with a high expected economic return may fail if there are not enough funds to finance the operations of the project. Many examples of development projects with expected high economic returns have failed as a result of financial difficulties. Water supply projects are typical examples of projects that generate substantial economic benefits because of the high economic value attached to water, but that receive little financial revenue because of low water tariffs. If the project is undertaken solely on the basis of a favourable economic analysis, with no consideration of financial sustainability, the project may fail owing to a lack of funds to maintain the system and service its debt. Other examples include projects such as public transport and irrigation, where services are usually provided at concessional prices.

A financial analysis enables project analysts to establish the financial sustainability of a project by identifying financing shortfalls that are likely to occur over the project's life, and thereby devise the necessary means for meeting these shortfalls. A key objective of a financial appraisal for a government project is to determine whether the project can continue to pay its bills throughout its entire life, and if not, how the shortfalls can be met.

In certain instances, the government approaches a project in the same way as a private sector investor would do in order to determine its financial profitability. This is necessary if private participation in the project is being contemplated. In this case, it is important to determine the profitability of a project and to estimate the value that a private investor would be willing to pay for the opportunity to participate. Ascertaining the financial profitability is also necessary when government policies are designed to encourage small investors or certain groups in society to undertake projects by providing them with grants or loans. Although the government's decision to provide grants or loans for these activities should be based on whether or not all small investors undertaking the project yield positive economic returns, the government will also need to determine whether the projects are financially sustainable.

Another reason for conducting a financial appraisal of public sector projects is directly related to understanding the distributional impacts of the project. For example, the difference between the financial price paid by individuals for a litre of water (found in the financial cash flow statement) and the gross economic benefit they derive from consuming the water (found in the economic resource flow statement) reflects a net gain to consumers. Similarly, the difference between the financial price (inclusive of tax) that a project faces and the economic cost of an input required by the project measures the tax gain to the government. Gains and losses of this nature will be difficult to establish on the basis of economic analysis alone.

3.3 Construction of Financial Cash Flows: Concepts and Principles

The financial cash flow of an investment project is a central piece of the financial appraisal. The cash flow statement of a project is a listing of all anticipated sources and uses of cash by the business over the life of the project. It can be illustrated as in Figure 3.1, in which the difference between receipts and expenditures is plotted against the sequence of years that make up the project's life. The net cash flow profile (measured by the difference between receipts and expenditures) is usually negative at the beginning of a project's life, when the investment is being made. In later years, when revenues from sales of output become larger than expenditures, the net cash flow becomes positive. Some projects that require significant investments to be made at intervals throughout the life of a project, such as the retooling of a factory, may occasionally also experience negative cash flows after the initial investment has been made. Other projects may have negative cash flows in their operating stage if they are producing a good or service that experiences wide swings in price or demand. Some other projects will even have negative cash flows in the final years of the project's life as costs are incurred to rehabilitate the project site or to compensate workers for their displacement.

3.3.1 Investment Phase

The first step in the construction of a financial cash flow statement is the formulation of an investment plan for the project based on the information developed in the technical, demand, manpower, and financing modules. The investment plan consists of two sections: the first deals with the expenditure on new acquisitions and the opportunity cost of existing assets, and the second deals with the financing aspects of the proposed investment. If there are different scales and/or locations under consideration, corresponding investment plans for each scale and/or location should be formulated. It is important that the investment plan should conform to a realistic time schedule, given the demand for the project's output, manpower, financial, and supply constraints in the economy, as well as the technical attributes of the project.

Figure 3.1: Financial Cash Flow Profile of a Project

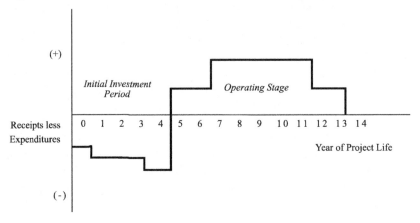

The investment plan will contain a listing of all the expenditures to be undertaken up to the point when the facility is ready to begin its normal operations. Each of these expenditures should be identified according to the year in which it is expected to occur. In addition, every expenditure should be broken down into two parts: first, the amount spent on goods and services traded internationally; and second, the amount spent on goods and services traded domestically. These categories of expenditure are in turn divided into the payments received by the suppliers of these goods, payments to the government (such as tariffs, value-added tax (VAT), etc.), subsidies received from the government, and subsidies for the purchase of the investment items. Expenditures on labour for the construction of the project should be identified by year and by skill level to provide a clear understanding of the project's cost structure and to determine whether there is a likely shortage of skilled workers. These breakdowns are also necessary for estimating the respective shadow price of labour in the economic analysis of the project.

a) Treatment of Assets

Depreciation expense, or capital cost allowances, is an accounting device used to spread the cost of capital assets over the life of these investments so that net income in any given year will reflect all the costs required to produce the output. However, depreciation expense is not a cash outflow, and thus should not be included in the financial cash flow profile of the project. The full capital costs of an investment are accounted for in the financial cash flow profile, since the amount of the investment expenditures is deducted in the year in which they occur. If any further capital charge, such as depreciation expense, was to be deducted from the cash flow profile, it would result in a double-counting of the investment opportunity cost of existing assets.

If the project under consideration is an ongoing concern or a rehabilitation project, whereby some of the project's old assets are integrated into the proposed facilities, the opportunity cost of these assets should be included in the cash flow statement, together with the expenditure on new acquisitions.

It is necessary to distinguish the "opportunity cost" of an asset from the "sunk cost" of an asset. The opportunity cost of using an asset in a specific project is the benefit forgone by not putting the asset to its best alternative use. In order to measure the opportunity cost of an asset it is necessary to assign a monetary value to it in such way that makes it equal to that which has been sacrificed by using it in the project rather than in its next-best use. Conversely, the value of an asset is treated as a sunk cost if the asset has no alternative use.[2]

The opportunity cost of the existing assets is generally included in the first year of the project's cash flow profile because the assets can be sold at that time if the project is not feasible. The financial opportunity cost of an existing asset is the highest financial price for which it can be sold. The highest financial price is typically the higher of the in-use value of the asset and its liquidation value. The in-use value of the asset is what it would sell for if it were to be used as an ongoing concern. The liquidation value is what the asset would sell for if broken into its different components and sold in parts. The costs of installing machinery and equipment, as well as their liquidation cost, are further deducted in order to derive the net liquidation value of the assets. When considering the opportunity cost of any production plant, account should be taken of the in-use value of the plant if it continues to be operated as it is.

The most appropriate way to determine in-use and liquidation values is through reliable market assessors. When estimating in-use values using assessors, the assessors' and sales agency's fees should be subtracted from the quoted value to obtain the net in-use value. Furthermore, when assessors give a liquidation value for a project's assets, the assessors' and sales agency's fees, as well as the expenditures incurred in dismantling the assets, should be netted from the quoted price to obtain a net liquidation value.

One approach to preparing an estimate of the in-use value of a set of assets is to consider their net replacement costs. The net replacement cost is the amount of expenditures that would have to be made today to build a facility that would provide the same amount of services in the future as would the assets that are now being evaluated. To estimate the net replacement value of an asset, two adjustments must be made to the historical purchase cost of assets. The first adjustment is for the change in the nominal prices of new assets, or the same type of asset, that can perform the same function as the asset being evaluated. This change in price is measured as the ratio of the current price or price index

---

[2]Sunk cost involves neither current nor future opportunity cost and therefore should have no influence in deciding what the most profitable thing to do will be. However, it should be noted that while the sunk cost of an asset should not be counted as a cost to a new project in examining its feasibility, any outstanding liabilities that are due to that asset may become the liability of the new project if the ownership is the same.

for this asset to the price or price index of the evaluated asset in the year it is purchased.

The second parameter that is needed in order to estimate an asset's net replacement cost is the amount of economic depreciation that the asset has experienced since it was purchased. The economic depreciation rate for an asset reflects the loss in the market value of the asset, which is generally different from the depreciation rate used for tax purposes. The purchase price of an asset adjusted for inflation and net of the cumulative amount of economic depreciation over the years since it was purchased represents the opportunity cost of the asset if it is used over its remaining lifetime in a project.[3]

Suppose the historical cost of a machine fully installed is A_0 and the machine's cumulated economic depreciation over years, expressed as a fraction, is d_t, the price index for this type of asset today is I_t, and the price index for this type of asset in the period it was initially purchased is I_h. Hence, net replacement value (in-use value) of the machine in year t can be estimated as follows:

(Net replacement value)$_t = A_0 \times (1 - \text{Proportion of asset depreciated } d_t) \times (I_t / I_h)$

The same calculation is carried out for the other types of existing asset. The sum of the above net replacement values for all existing assets needs further adjustments to account for the opportunity cost of land, inventory, and the excess of accounts receivable over accounts payable in year t in order to derive the total amount of the net replacement value. This value will be considered as the opportunity cost of the historical investments or all existing assets for the "without" and "with" project cases.

b) Treatment of Land

Land has an opportunity cost like every other asset when it is used by a project. Even if the land is donated to the project by the government, it should be included as part of the investment cost, at a value that reflects the market value of land in the project area.

Land is a very special asset because it does not depreciate in most situations. However, owing to improvements in infrastructure, the value of land being used by a project may increase much faster than inflation during the life of the project. In such cases, it is important not to include the increase in land value that is above inflation as part of the liquidation value of the project. In most cases, the increase in the liquidation value of land (particularly in urban areas) has nothing to do with the project under evaluation. Real increases in land value usually come about as a result of investment being made in public sector infrastructure. It is important not to attribute the increase in the real value of land to any

---

[3]Economic depreciation rates for plant and equipment may be obtained from the plant manufacturer, technical journals, or insurance companies that insure a plant's assets.

particular project in order to avoid introducing a bias toward land-intensive projects. The only exception to this rule occurs when the project either improves or damages the land. In such cases, the amount of the land improvement or deterioration should be added to or subtracted from the real value of the land measured at the beginning of the project to determine the liquidation value of the land at the end of the project.

Alternatively, the opportunity cost of land can be reflected in the cash flow profile of the project by an annual rental charge. This charge can be estimated by using the rental rate per dollar value of the land multiplied by the real value of the land for each period of the project's life. If the annual rental charge approach is used, then neither the initial cost of the land nor its final market value should enter into the cash flow profile of the project.

c) Investment Financing

The investment plan also deals with the means of and schedule for financing the investment expenditures. The financing may consist of equity, grants, domestic short-term and long-term loans, foreign loans, concessional loans, and other forms of foreign aid. They should be identified, and the disbursement schedules should be formulated. Which of these financings will be included in the cash flow statement depends on the point of view considered. While appraising the project from the owner's point of view, for example, the loan disbursement is a cash inflow, and the repayment of loan and interest payments are a cash outflow, as the owner is looking to the net receipts after paying all debts and obligations. The analysis from a banker's point of view, however, is not concerned with the financing, but instead is looking to determine the financial viability of the project to all investors, irrespective of whether they are debtors or shareholders.

In the case of public sector projects, it is the financial performance of the entire invested capital and not just the equity portion that is relevant for investors. Often, both debt and equity financing come from the same source, and the loans have been either explicitly or implicitly guaranteed by the government. The development of the financial cash flows of this project will therefore begin with no distinction being made between the return received by the lenders of debt and that received by the equity holders. In this case, the cash made available through borrowing is not considered as a cash inflow, nor are the interest or amortization payments on this debt considered as cash outflows.

The analysis of the financial cash flow from alternative points of view will be discussed in more detail later. Table 3.1 provides an example of an investment phase for a medium-scale mining project.

Table 3.1: Investment Phase for a Mining Project (million dollars)

Item	Year		
	0	*1*	*2....7*
A. Investment expenditures			
a) Site preparation, exploration, and development			
Materials:			
- Traded (CIF)	500.00	500.00	
Tariffs @ 12%	60.00	60.00	
VAT @ 10%	56.00	56.00	
- Non-traded	400.00	300.00	
VAT @ 5%	20.00	15.00	
Labour:			
- Skilled	150.00	100.00	
- Unskilled	200.00	250.00	
b) Equipment			
Traded (CIF)	600.00	2,000.00	
Tariffs @ 10%	60.00	200.00	
VAT @ 10%	66.00	220.00	
Total expenditures	**2,112.00**	**3,701.00**	
B. Financing			
Equity	2,012.00	1,201.00	
Domestic loan (short-term)	100.00	500.00	
Foreign loan (guaranteed by government)	0.00	2,000.00	
Total financing	**2,112.00**	**3,701.00**	

Interest during construction is an item that is often included as an accounting cost in the construction phase. It is included as a cost to reflect the interest forgone because funds have been tied up in the construction of the project. It is not a measure of interest that has actually been paid, but an accounting device to measure the opportunity cost of the funds employed in the project. If no interest has been paid by the project, then interest during construction is not cash expenditure and should not be included as expenditure in the cash flow statement of the project. On the other hand, if interest payments have been made during the period of construction, there is a cash outflow when the project is being examined from the viewpoint of the owner.

3.3.2 Operating Phase

The operating phase of the financial cash flow statement includes all cash receipts generated from the operation of the project, and all operating expenditures. Expenditures and receipts should be projected by year of operation. Like investment expenditures, operating expenditures should be broken down into internationally traded and non-traded items; and wherever possible, each expenditure item should be broken down into its components. For example, maintenance expenditures should be broken down into materials and labour. Expenditures on different types of labour (engineers, electricians, managers, etc.) should be identified and recorded separately. Any taxes or subsidies associated with the operating expenditures should also be identified and recorded separately wherever possible. These breakdowns are necessary for the economic analysis of the project and for providing a better understanding of the cost structure of the operating expenditures.

a) Adjustment for Sales to Find Cash Receipts

A project's viability is determined not only by the sales it generates but also by the timing of the cash receipts from the sales. A cash flow statement records sales transactions only when the cash from the transaction is received. Typically, projects forecast their sales as a single line item that comprises both credit and cash transactions.

A distinction must be made between sales and cash receipts. When a project makes a sale, the good or service may be delivered to the customer, but no money is transferred from the customer to the project. At this point, the project's accountants will record that the project has an asset called accounts receivable equal to the amount of the sale and the proportion of it that is not in cash. In other words, the buyer owes the project for the goods or services that he or she has purchased and not yet paid for. Until the buyer has paid for the goods or services received, the transaction will have no impact on the cash flow statement. When the buyer pays for the items previously bought from the project, the project's accountants will record a decrease in accounts receivable by the amount that the buyer has paid, and an increase in cash receipts. Thus, the cash receipts for any period can be calculated as follows:

Cash receipts for period (inflow) = Sales for period
+ Accounts receivable at beginning of period
− Accounts receivable at end of period

Suppose the accounts receivable recorded on the balance sheet at the beginning of the period is $2,000 and is then $2,600 at the end of the period. Sales for this period as recorded on the income statement are assumed to be $4,000. Total receipts or cash inflow for this period is calculated as follows:

Cash inflow = $4,000 + $2,000 − $2,600
= $3,400

Accounts receivable are typically measured as a percentage of sales. It is important to ensure that the accounts receivable selected for the project are consistent with the current performance of industry standards. It is also important to assess the likelihood of bad debts and to make allowances for them. Bad debts occur when a project's customers default on their payments. They simultaneously reduce the amount of cash inflows to the project and reduce the amount of accounts receivable at the end of the period.

Suppose, in the previous example, bad debts of $200 had been written off during the period. In this case, cash receipts for the period are determined as follows:

Cash receipts for period (inflow) = Sales for period
+ Accounts receivable at beginning of period
− (Accounts receivable at end of period + Bad debts written off during the period)

Cash inflow   = $4,000 + $2,000 − ($2,600 + $200)
= $3,200

It should be noted that the increase in cash receipts and the decrease in accounts receivable will be augmented by the VAT or other sales taxes associated with the sale of the items. These taxes are collected by the firm on behalf of governments and will be paid to the government later. Such sales taxes will now be included in the cash flow statement of the seller as part of the cash inflow when these payments are received, but the amount of sales tax will be subtracted from the net cash flow when the taxes are paid to final cash expenditures.

b) Adjustment for Purchases

A similar distinction to that between sales and receipts needs to be drawn between the purchases made by the project and its cash expenditures. The value of the transaction will be recorded in the cash flow statement only when and to the degree that cash is paid. When the project makes a purchase, the good or service may be delivered to the project, but it is possible that no money is transferred from the project to its vendor. At this point, the project's accountants will record that the project has a liability called accounts payable equal to a portion of the amount of the purchase that is not paid in cash. Until the project has paid for what it has received, the transaction will have no impact on the cash flow statement. When the project pays the vendors for the items it has bought from them, the project's accountants will record a decrease in accounts payable by the amount that the project has paid and an increase in cash expenditures. Hence, cash expenditures can be calculated from the value of purchases for the period, along with the value of accounts payable both at the beginning and ending of the period, as follows:

Cash expenditures for period (outflow) = Purchases for period
+ Accounts payable at beginning of period
− Accounts payable at end of period

Assume that total accounts payable at the beginning of a period is $3,500 and at the end of the period is $2,800, with the value of purchases from the income statement being $3,800. Total expenditure or cash outflow is calculated as follows:

Cash outflow   = $3,800 + $3,500 − $2,800
                       = $4,500

Accounts payable are typically measured as a percentage of total purchases or of a major input. It is important to ensure that the accounts payable on which the cash flow will be based are consistent with industry standards.

c) Adjustment for Changes in Cash Balance

Increases or decreases in cash balances can take place even when no changes occur in sales, purchases, accounts receivable, or accounts payable. When cash is set aside for the transaction of the business, the financial institutions that make loans to a project may require that a debt service reserve account be set up and funded. The accumulation of cash for this or other purposes represents an outflow in the cash flow statement and must be financed. Similarly, a decrease in cash held for transaction purposes is a source of cash for other uses by the project and thus is a cash inflow. Thus, if the required stock of cash balances to be held to carry out transactions increases within a period, this increase is recorded as a cash outflow. On the other hand, if cash balances decrease, this decrease is a cash inflow. At the end of the project, any cash set aside will ultimately be released back to the project as a cash inflow. The amount of cash to be held for facilitating the transactions of the business is typically a percentage of the project's expenditures, sales, or pattern of debt service obligations.

d) Adjustment for Other Working Capital Items

In order to carry out an economic activity, a certain amount of investment has to be made in items that facilitate the conduct of transactions. These items are working capital, including cash, accounts receivable, accounts payable, prepaid expenses, and inventories. The first three of these have already been dealt with above. Prepaid expenses such as insurance premia are recorded in the cash flow statement as other expenditures are made.

Changes in inventories are not recorded separately in the cash flow statement. When a project purchases a certain amount of raw materials, inventories of raw materials will increase. These inventories are financed through a cash outflow and/or an increase in accounts payable. If the inventories have been paid for in cash, a cash outlay will have been recorded in the cash flow statement. If they have been acquired on credit terms, no cash outflow will occur, and they will be recorded in the cash flow statement as an increase in accounts payable. The situation is similar when dealing with changes in the inventories of the final product. In this case, other inputs such as labour and energy are needed to transform raw materials into finished goods. To do this, additional cash expenditures will be required. A decrease in final good inventories implies that a sale has occurred. This in turn implies an increase in cash receipts or accounts receivable.

Since the components of working capital are developed independently in different ways, it is necessary to check for the overall consistency of working capital, to ensure that adequate provision has been made for working capital in order that the business transactions of the project can be carried out. This can be done by comparing the amount of working capital, estimated as a proportion of total assets of the project, to the industry average or to similar businesses that are operating successfully.

e) Income Tax Liability

Income taxes paid by the project should be included as an outflow in the cash flow statement. The income tax liability is estimated on the basis of the project's income statement following the accounting and tax rules of the country concerned. Year-by-year estimates of the cost of goods sold, interest expense, tax depreciation expenses, and overheads are all subtracted from the project's revenues to estimate the project's earnings before taxes. While estimating the income tax liability, provisions for loss carry-backward and -forward, if applicable, should be taken into account.

f) Value-Added Tax Liability

In most countries, VAT is levied on the goods and services sold domestically, while sales made to customers living outside the country are zero-rated. For a taxable firm, the value of sales will include the VAT collected by the project on behalf of the government. The cost of inputs that are taxed will include the VAT paid on these purchases. The payment made to the government, if the firm is taxable, is the difference between the VAT collected on the sales and the VAT paid on the purchase of inputs. These payments of VAT to the government are reported in the cash flow statement as an outflow. The net effect of this tax treatment is to largely eliminate the VAT from being a financial burden on the project.

When a project produces an output that is exempt from VAT, it will not be charging VAT when it sells its output. On the other hand, in most circumstances it will continue to pay VAT on its purchases of inputs. In this case, there will not be an additional line item reporting the VAT payment to the government. The net effect of the VAT is to increase the cost of the inputs and hence the financial cash outflow of the project.

The third possible situation occurs when the output of the project is expected to have a rate of zero imposed on the export sales. In this case, no tax is included in the sales revenues or cash inflows. The VAT will be levied and included in the inputs purchased by the project. The difference between the taxes collected on sales, i.e. zero, and the taxes paid as part of the input purchases now becomes a negative tax payment or a refund of taxes paid. This should be reported as a negative cost or a cash inflow to the project.

3.3.3 Cessation of Project Operations

When a new project acquires an asset, the entire expenditure on the asset is accounted for in the cash flow statement at the time that the expenditure actually occurs. It is quite possible, however, that the life of the project will not coincide with the life of all its assets, or that the span of the analysis will not extend as far into the future as the project may be expected to operate (e.g., railway projects). In such cases the residual value of the asset should be included in the cash flow statement as an inflow in the year following the cessation of operations.

When determining the residual value of the assets at the end of the project, it is preferable that all the assets be broken down into different categories: land, building, equipment, vehicles, etc. The residual value is taken as the in-use value unless it is clear that the facility will be shut down at the end of the project period. If it is to be shut down, the liquidation value should be used as the residual value. The in-use value is the value of the plant assuming that it will continue to operate as an ongoing concern. The liquidation value is the value of the assets if all components of the project are sold separately, and perhaps even the plant is taken apart and sold.

While dealing with the in-use and liquidation values in the future, the general guidelines are to use the cumulative economic depreciation over years. It is possible to use the depreciation rates from plant manufacturers or technical journals, or the depreciation rates used by insurance companies.

Land is a special asset that does not generally depreciate. The residual value of land recorded in the cash flow statement should be equal to the real market value of the land recorded at the beginning of the project, unless the project results in some improvement or deterioration of the land. For example, if a project involves an investment to improve the property, such as drainage of a swamp, the residual value of the project should include the increase in land value resulting directly from the investment made by the project. The opposite is the case if the project damages the land and its value. The residual value of the land must be reduced by the amount of damage caused by the project. Nevertheless, in many cases expectations may indicate that land values are likely to rise faster than inflation, although the increase is totally unrelated to the project.[4]

---

[4] Expected increases in land values are generally speculative; this implies that such increases might not be built into the residual value of land. Moreover, the purpose of the analysis is to appraise the project and determine its impact on its sponsors. Significant increases in land value may be sufficiently large as to lead to the implementation of the project and a misallocation of resources. Thus, the residual value of land should generally be the same as its real price at the start of the project.

3.3.4 Format for the Pro Forma Cash Flow Statement

While there is no specific format for presentation of the pro forma cash flow statement for an investment project, it is important that the data should be set out in sufficient detail so that the adjustments required by the economic and distributive appraisal can be easily applied to the financial cash flows. Entries for receipts and payments must be classified as outlined in the above discussion of investment and operating phases of the project. Receipts must be identified according to whether they arise from sales of tradable or non-tradable goods with all taxes. Payments should also be presented in a similar fashion, with all taxes, tariffs, and subsidies itemized separately. Labour costs must be identified according to the type of labour used.

The example of the mine will be used to illustrate the construction of the financial cash flow statement. The investment phase of the project was outlined in Table 3.1. It is now assumed that the mining project has an operating life of five years, and that the machinery and equipment will be liquidated as scrap at the closure of the mine. This is carried out in the year following the mine closure, at which time the scrap is expected to yield $1 billion. The land is assumed to have zero value after being mined. Table 3.2 contains the basic operating information required to develop the pro forma cash flow statements for this project. For example, accounts receivable and accounts payable are assumed at 20 percent of annual sales and purchases, inclusive of VAT, respectively. Desired cash balances are assumed to be equal to 10 percent of purchases of inputs. As the output of the mine is assumed to be exported, the export sales will be zero-rated for VAT.

A 10 percent royalty is charged on the value of export sales. This is paid directly to the government. No income tax is levied on this mining activity.

Using the data presented in Tables 3.1 and 3.2, the pro forma cash flow statement can be constructed in detail, broken down by commodity and labour type as shown in Table 3.3. This pro forma cash flow statement provides the basis for the financial and economic analysis of the project that will follow. It is the net cash flow from this statement that is used for the project profile shown in Figure 3.1.

Table 3.2: Operating Information for the Case of a Mining Project (million dollars)

Item	Year							
	0	1	2	3	4	5	6	7
Sales								
Traded			2,000.00	3,000.00	3,500.00	3,000.00	2,000.00	
VAT @ 0%			0.00	0.00	0.00	0.00	0.00	
Purchases of inputs								
Traded (CIF)			600.00	750.00	800.00	700.00	600.00	
Tariffs @ 10%			60.00	75.00	80.00	70.00	60.00	
VAT @ 10%			66.00	82.50	88.00	77.00	66.00	
Non-traded			200.00	250.00	320.00	200.00	200.00	
VAT @ 5%			10.00	12.50	16.00	10.00	10.00	
Operating labour								
Skilled			100.00	150.00	200.00	150.00	125.00	
Unskilled			50.00	70.00	90.00	80.00	60.00	
Working capital (end of period values)								
Accounts receivable		0	400.00	600.00	700.00	600.00	400.00	0
Accounts payable		0	187.20	234.00	260.80	211.40	187.20	0
Cash held as working capital		0	93.60	117.00	130.40	105.70	93.60	0

It should be noted that no VAT is collected on the sales on behalf of the tax authority, while VAT paid on purchases can be claimed back as input tax credits under most consumption-type VAT systems. Thus, a line for a VAT input tax credit is created in Table 3.3 in order to derive the impact of the net VAT payments, or refund of VAT paid, on inputs on the net cash flow for the project.

Table 3.3: Pro Forma Financial Cash Flow Statement for an Investment in a Mine (million dollars)

Item	Year							
	0	1	2	3	4	5	6	7
A. Receipts								
Foreign sales (traded goods)			2,000.00	3,000.00	3,500.00	3,000.00	2,000.00	0
VAT @ 0%			0	0	0	0	0	0
Change in accounts receivable			-400.00	-200.00	-100.00	+100.00	+200.00	+400.00
Liquidation value (scrapped assets)								1,000.00
Cash inflow			**1,600.00**	**2,800.00**	**3,400.00**	**3,100.00**	**2,200.00**	**1,400.00**
B. Expenditures								
a) Site preparation, exploration, and development								
Materials:								
- Traded goods (CIF)	500.00	500.00						
Tariffs @ 12%	60.00	60.00						
VAT @ 10%	56.00	56.00						
- Non-traded goods	400.00	300.00						
VAT @ 5%	20.00	15.00						
Equipment:								
- Traded (CIF)	600.00	2,000.00						
Tariffs @ 10%	60.00	200.00						
VAT @ 10%	66.00	220.00						
b) Input purchases								
- Traded goods (CIF)			600.00	750.00	800.00	700.00	600.00	
Tariffs @ 10%			60.00	75.00	80.00	70.00	60.00	
VAT @ 10%			66.00	82.50	88.00	77.00	66.00	
Change in accounts payable			-145.20	-36.30	-12.10	24.20	24.20	145.20
- Non-traded goods			200.00	250.00	320.00	200.00	200.00	
VAT @ 5%			10.00	12.50	16.00	10.00	10.00	
Change in accounts payable			-42.00	-10.50	-14.70	25.20	0	42.00
c) Construction labour								
- Skilled	150.00	100.00						
- Unskilled	200.00	250.00						
d) Operating labour								
- Skilled			100.00	150.00	200.00	150.00	125.00	
- Unskilled			50.00	70.00	90.00	80.00	60.00	
e) Change in cash held as working capital			93.60	23.40	13.40	-24.70	-12.10	-93.60
Cash "outflow	**2,112.00**	**3,701.00**	**992.40**	**1,366.60**	**1,580.60**	**1,311.70**	**1,133.10**	**93.60**
C. Tax payments								
a) VAT (payment, (refund))	**-142.00**	**-291.00**	**-76.00**	**-95.00**	**-104.00**	**-87.00**	**-76.00**	**0**
b) Royalty	**0**	**0**	**200.00**	**300.00**	**350.00**	**300.00**	**200.00**	**0**
D. Net cash flow	**-1,970.00**	**-3,410.00**	**483.60**	**1,228.40**	**1,573.40**	**1,575.30**	**942.90**	**1,306.40**

3.4 Use of Consistent Prices in the Cash Flow Forecast

When conducting a financial appraisal of a project, it is necessary to make a projection of prices for the inputs and outputs over the project's life. These prices are influenced by movements in the real price of the good in question and the effect of inflation. The factors affecting the real price are different from those affecting inflation. Real prices are determined by changes in the market demand and/or supply for the specific items, while inflation is usually determined by the growth of the country's money supply relative to its production of goods and services. Forecasts of inflation are generally beyond the capability or responsibility of the project analyst. The rate of inflation is basically a risk variable, and the analysis of a project should be subjected to a range of possible inflation rates. The critical task for the analyst is to construct a projection of nominal prices that are consistent with an assumed pattern of inflation rates through time and the projection of changes in real prices.

The projection of the future path of real prices is of particular importance if the price of one or more input or output is significantly above or below its normal level or trend. To understand the impact of real price changes and inflation on the financial viability of a project and how they are incorporated in the analysis, we first consider the definition or derivation of various price variables employed in the analysis.

3.4.1 Definition of Prices and Price Indices

a) Nominal Prices

The nominal prices of goods and services are those found in the marketplace, and they are often referred to as current prices. Historical data for nominal prices are relatively easy to obtain, but forecasting nominal prices in a consistent manner is a notoriously difficult task. The nominal price of an item is the outcome of two sets of economic forces: macroeconomic forces, which determine the general price level, or inflation, and the forces of demand and supply for the item, which cause its price to move relative to other goods and services in the marketplace. In order to construct a cash flow forecast in nominal prices it is necessary to take into consideration the movement of both real prices and the general price level.

b) Price Level and Index

The price level for an economy (P_L^t) is calculated as a weighted average of a selected set of nominal prices:

$$P_1^t P_2^t P_3^t, \ldots \ldots \ldots, P_n^t$$

The price level P_L^t can be calculated for any period (t) as follows:

$$P_L^t = \sum_{i=1}^{n} P_i^t W_i \qquad\qquad (3.1)$$

where: i denotes the individual good or service included in the market basket;
P_i^t denotes the price of the good or service at a point in time;
W_i denotes the weight given to the price of a particular good or service (i);
and
$\sum W_i = 1$.

The weights used for calculating a price level are defined as of a certain date. This date is referred to as the base period for the calculation of the price level. The weights established at that time will rarely change because the intention is to compare the level of prices of a given basket of goods between various points in time. Hence, it is only the nominal prices that change through time in equation (3.1), while the weights (W_1, W_2, ...,W_n) are fixed.

Instead of calculating the price level for the entire economy, a price level may be created for a certain subset of prices, such as construction materials or consumer goods. It is generally useful to express the price level of a basket of goods and services at different points in time as a price index (P_I^t). The price index simply normalizes the price level so that in the base period, the index is equal to 1. In order to calculate a price index that compares the price levels in two distinct periods, the following equation can be used:

$$P_I^t = P_L^t / P_L^B \qquad\qquad (3.2)$$

where P_L^t denotes the price level in Period (t) and P_L^B denotes the price level for the base period (B). For example, the consumer price index (CPI) is a weighted average of the prices for a selected market basket of consumer goods. The investment price index is created as a weighted set of goods and services that are of an investment nature. The change in the CPI for a broad set of goods and services is used to measure the rate of inflation in the economy.[5]

Suppose there are three commodities in a basket of consumer goods and their prices in Year 1 are $30, $100, and $50, as shown in Example 1. The corresponding weights of these goods are 0.2, 0.5, and 0.3. The price level in Year 1 is $71 using equation (3.1). If the prices of these three goods in Year 2 become $40, $110, and $40, respectively, the weighted average of the price level will be $75. Similarly, the price level in Year 3 as shown in the example is $79.

---

[5]In some countries, the best instrument for the measurement of inflation is the CPI; in others, it is the implicit GDP deflator.

Example 1: Nominal Prices and Changes in Price

	Assume Year 1 is base year		
Goods	**1**	**2**	**3**
Weights	0.2	0.5	0.3

Nominal prices Year 1: $P_1^1=30$ $\qquad P_2^1=100$ $\qquad P_3^1=50$

$$P_L^1 = 0.2\,(30) + 0.5\,(100) + 0.3\,(50) = 71$$

$$P_L^B = 71$$

Price Index $P_I^1 = 1.00$

Nominal prices Year 2: $P_1^2 = 40$ $\qquad P_2^2 = 110$ $\qquad P_3^2 = 40$

$$P_L^2 = 0.2\,(40) + 0.5\,(110) + 0.3\,(40) = 75$$

Price Index $P_I^2 = 1.056$

Nominal prices Year 3: $P_1^3 = 35$ $\qquad P_2^3 = 108$ $\qquad P_3^3 = 60$

$$P_L^3 = 0.2\,(35) + 0.5\,(108) + 0.3\,(60) = 79$$

Price Index $P_I^3 = 1.113$

Inflation rate: changes in general price level (measured in terms of a price index)

$$g\,P_I^2 = [(P_I^2 - P_I^1)/(P_I^1)] * 100 = [(1.056 - 1.00)/(1.00)] * 100 = 5.63\%$$

$$g\,P_I^3 = [(P_I^3 - P_I^2)/(P_I^2)] * 100 = [(1.113 - 1.056)/(1.056)] * 100 = 5.33\%$$

Using the price level in Year 1 as the base period, the price indices can be calculated as 1.00, 1.056, and 1.113 for Year 1, Year 2, and Year 3, respectively, using equation (3.2).

c) Changes in General Price Level (Inflation)

Inflation is measured by the change in the price level divided by the price level at the beginning of the period. The price level at the beginning of the period becomes a reference for determining the rate of inflation throughout that particular period. Hence, inflation for any particular period can be expressed as in equation (3.3).

$$gP_I^e = [(P_I^t - P_I^{t-1})/P_I^{t-1}] \times 100 \qquad (3.3)$$

Inflation is much more difficult to forecast than the changes in real prices because inflation is primarily determined by the supply of money relative to the availability in an economy of goods and services to purchase. In turn, the supply of money is often determined by the size of the public sector deficit and how it is financed. If governments finance their deficit by borrowing heavily from the central bank, inflation is the inevitable end result.

In the evaluation of an investment, it is not necessary to make an accurate forecast of the rate of inflation. However, it is essential to make all the other assumptions concerning the financing and operation of the project consistent with the assumed pattern of future inflation. In most countries, the rate of inflation is a risk variable that should be accommodated through the financial design of the project. For example, even though the historical rates of inflation in the economy may only be 5 or 6 percent, it may be useful to see whether the project could survive if the rate of inflation is much higher and much lower. If the analysis demonstrates that it will be severely weakened, it may be advisable to look at whether the project can be redesigned in order to better withstand such unanticipated rates of inflation.

d) Real Prices

Real prices (P_{iR}) are an important subset of relative prices, and are obtained by dividing the nominal price of an item by the index of the price level at the same point in time. They express prices of goods and services relative to the general price level, as shown by equation (3.4).

$$P_{iR}^t = P_i^t / P_I^t \qquad (3.4)$$

where P_i denotes the nominal price of a good or service at time (t) and P_I denotes the price level index at time (t).

Dividing by a price level index removes the inflationary component (change in the general price level) from the nominal price of the item. This allows identification of the impact of the forces of demand and supply on the price of the good relative to other goods and services in the economy.

Example 2 illustrates how real prices are calculated using equation (3.4). For instance, the real price of Good 1 in Year 2 is $37.87, which is obtained by dividing the nominal price $40 by the price index 1.056.

Example 2: Real Prices and Changes in Real Price

Goods	1	2	3
Weights	0.2	0.5	0.3
Nominal prices Year 1:	$P_1^1 = 30$	$P_2^1 = 100$	$P_3^1 = 50$
	Price Index $P_I^1 = 1.00$		
Real prices Year 1:	$P_{1R}^1 = 30/1$	$P_{2R}^1 = 100/1$	$P_{3R}^1 = 50/1$
	$= 30$	$= 100$	$= 50$
Nominal prices Year 2:	$P_1^2 = 40$	$P_2^2 = 110$	$P_3^2 = 40$
	Price Index $P_I^2 = 1.056$		
Real prices Year 2:	$P_{1R}^2 = 40/1.056$	$P_{2R}^2 = 110/1.056$	$P_{3R}^2 = 40/1.056$
	$= 37.87$	$= 104.16$	$= 37.87$
Nominal prices Year 3:	$P_1^3 = 35$	$P_2^3 = 108$	$P_3^3 = 60$
	Price Index $P_I^3 = 1.113$		
Real prices Year 3:	$P_{1R}^3 = 35/1.113$	$P_{2R}^3 = 108/1.113$	$P_{3R}^3 = 60/1.113$
	$= 31.45$	$= 97.04$	$= 53.91$
• Changes in real prices Year 2:			
Change in P_{1R}^2 $[(P_{1R}^2 - P_{1R}^1)/(P_{1R}^1)] =$			
	$(37.87 - 30)/30$	$(104.16 - 100)/100$	$(37.87 - 50)/50$
	$= 0.2623$	$= 0.0416$	$= -0.2426$
• Changes in real prices Year 3:			
Change in P_{1R}^3 $[(P_{1R}^3 - P_{1R}^2)/(P_{1R}^2)] =$			
	$(31.45 -$	$(97.04 -$	$(53.91 -$
	$37.87)/37.87$	$104.16)/104.16$	$37.87)/37.87$
	$= -0.1695$	$= -0.0683$	$= 0.4235$

e)   *Changes in Real Prices*

The change in the real price of a good or service can be expressed as:

$$\Delta p^t_{iR} = \frac{p^t_{iR} - p^{t-1}_{iR}}{p^{t-1}_{iR}} \tag{3.5}$$

where p^t_{iR} denotes the real price of good (i) as of a specific period.

Using Example 2 and equation (3.5), we can compute that the change in real price of Good 1 in Year 3 is -16.95%.

For each of the inputs and outputs, a set of projections must be prepared in the path of its real price over the life of the project. For items undergoing rapid technological change, such as computers or telecommunication equipment, the real price of those goods would be expected to fall.

There is one important input, however, whose relative price is almost certain to rise if there is economic development in the country, namely the real wage rate. If economic development takes place, the value of labour relative to other goods and services will have to rise. Hence, in the forecasting of real prices for a project, the potential for real wages to rise should be taken into consideration and built into the cost of inputs for a project over its life.

f) Inflation-adjusted Values

Inflation-adjusted values for prices of inputs and outputs are based on the best forecast of how real prices for particular goods and services are going to move in the future, adjusted by an assumed path of the general price level over future periods. In other words, they are a set of nominal prices that are built up from their basic components of a real price and a general price level. These inflation-adjusted values are generated in a consistent fashion. A common mistake made by project evaluators is to assume that many of the prices of inputs and outputs for a project are rising relative to the rate of inflation. This is highly unlikely. The price level itself is a weighted average of the prices of individual goods and services. Hence, in the forecast of the real price of the goods and services used or produced by the project, we would expect that approximately the same number of real prices will be falling as are rising.

To forecast the movement of the real price of a good or service, it is necessary to consider such items as the anticipated change in the demand for the item over time, the likely supply response, and the forces that are going to affect its cost of production. This analysis is very different from that which goes into the forecast of the general price level. This forecast is not so much a prediction, but a set of consistent assumptions. It is the inflation-adjusted values that are used in the estimation of the nominal cash flows of a project. They can be estimated using equation (3.6):

$$\hat{P}^{t+1}_i = P'_i(1 + gP^{t+1}_{iR})(1 + gP^{t+1}_I) \qquad (3.6)$$

where: $\hat{P}^{t+1}_i$ denotes the estimated nominal price of good (i) in year $t+1$; P'_i
denotes the nominal price of good (i) in year t;
gP^{t+1}_{iR} denotes the estimated growth in real price of good (i) between year
t and $t+1$; and
gP^{t+1}_I denotes the assumed growth in price level index from year t to
year $t+1$.

g) Constant Prices

It should be noted that real prices are sometimes referred to as constant prices, which, as the name implies, do not change over time. They are simply a set of nominal price observations as of a point in time that is used for each of the subsequent periods in a project appraisal. While nominal prices are affected by changes in real prices as well as changes in the price level, constant prices reflect neither of these economic forces. If constant prices are used throughout the life of the project, this ignores both the changes in real prices, which may have a profound impact on the overall financial position of the project, and the impact that inflation can have on the performance of an investment. The use of constant prices simplifies the construction of a cash flow profile for a project, but it also eliminates from the analysis a large part of the financial and economic information that can affect the future performance of the project.

Two specific prices, namely interest rate and the price of foreign exchange, play an important role in the financial analysis of projects, and are discussed below.

3.4.2 Nominal Interest Rate

One of the most important aspects of integrating expectations about the future rate of inflation (gP^e) into the evaluation of a project is ensuring that such expectations are consistent with the projections of the nominal rate of interest. Lenders increase the nominal interest rate on the loans they give to compensate for the anticipated loss in the real value of the loan caused by inflation. As the inflation rate increases, the nominal interest rate will be increased to ensure that the present value (PV) of the interest and principal payments will not fall below the initial value of the loan.

The nominal interest rate, as determined by the financial markets, is made up of three major components:

a) the real interest rate (r), which reflects the real-time value of money that lenders require in order to be willing to forgo consumption or other investment opportunities;

b) a risk factor (R), which measures the compensation that lenders demand in order to cover the possibility of the borrower defaulting on the loan; and

c) a factor $(1+r+R)$ gP^e, which represents the compensation for the expected loss in purchasing power attributable to inflation.

The expected real interest rate will be relatively constant over time because it is primarily determined by the productivity of investment and the desire for consumption and saving in the economy. The risk premium is typically associated with the sector and investor, and is known. Inflation reduces the future value of both the loan repayments and real interest rate payments. Combining these factors, the nominal (market) rate of interest (i) can be expressed as:

$$i = r + R + (1 + r + R)\, gP^e \qquad\qquad (3.7)$$

In order to explain this concept more fully, it is useful to consider the following financial scenarios. When both risk and inflation are zero, a lender would want to recover at least the real-time value of the money. If the real interest rate r is 5 percent, the lender would charge at least a 5 percent nominal interest rate. If the lender anticipates that the future rate of inflation will be 10 percent, he or she would want to increase the nominal interest rate charged to the borrower in order to compensate for the loss in purchasing power of the future loan and interest rate payments. Maintaining the assumption that there is no risk to this loan, equation (3.7) can be applied in order to determine what nominal interest rate the lender would need to charge in order to achieve the same level of return as when there was no inflation:

$$
\begin{aligned}
i \quad &= r + R + (1 + r + R)\, gP^e \\
&= (0.05) + (0) + (1 + 0.05 + 0) \times 0.1 \\
&= 15.5\%
\end{aligned}
$$

Thus, the lender will need to charge a nominal interest rate of at least 15.5 percent to achieve the same level of return as in the zero-inflation scenarios.

Now, suppose the risk premium (R) is 3 percent. In this case, the nominal interest rate that is consistent with a 5 percent expected real interest rate and an expected rate of inflation of 10 percent is calculated as follows:

$$i = (0.05) + (0.03) + (1 + 0.05 + 0.03) \times 0.1 = 18.8\%$$

If the rate of inflation is expected to change through time and if refinancing of the project's debt is required, the nominal interest rate paid must be adjusted to be consistent with this new expected rate of inflation. This should have little or no direct effect on the overall economic viability of the project as measured by its net present value (NPV); however, it may impose very severe constraints on the liquidity position of the project because of its impact on interest and principal payments if not properly planned for.

3.4.3 Expected Nominal Exchange Rate

A key financial variable in any project that uses or produces tradable goods is the market rate of foreign exchange (E^M) between the domestic and the foreign currencies. This market exchange rate is expressed as the number of units of domestic currency ($\# D$) required to purchase one unit of foreign exchange (F). The market exchange rate refers to the current nominal price of foreign exchange. It needs to be projected over the life of the project. The market rate between the domestic and the foreign currency can be expressed at any point in time (t) as:

$$E_t^M = (\# D/F)_t \tag{3.8}$$

The real exchange rate, $E_{t_n}^R$, can be defined as follows:

$$E_{t_n}^R = \frac{\#D/I_{t_n}^D}{F/I_{t_n}^F} = \frac{\#D}{F}\frac{I_{t_n}^F}{I_{t_n}^D}$$

or:

$$E_{t_n}^R = E_{t_n}^M \frac{I_{t_n}^F}{I_{t_n}^D} \tag{3.9}$$

where $E_{t_n}^M$ denotes the market rate of exchange in year t_n; and $I_{t_n}^D$ and $I_{t_n}^F$ represent the price indices in year t_n for the domestic currency country and the foreign currency country, respectively.

The difference between the real and the nominal exchange rate at a given point in time, t_n, lies in the relative movement of the price index of the foreign country relative to that of the domestic country, as measured from an arbitrary chosen point in time, t_b (base year), to the time of interest, t_n. The cumulative inflation for the domestic country over a period of time is given by the domestic price index, $I_{t_n}^D$. The domestic price index at any point in time t_n can be expressed as the price index in any initial year t_0, $I_{t_0}^D$, multiplied by the cumulative change in the price level from time t_0 to t_n. This is given as follows:

The Financial Appraisal of Projects

$$I_{t_n}^D = I_{t_0}^D \prod_{i=1}^{n}\left(1 + gp_{t_0+i}^{de}\right) \qquad (3.10)$$

where gp_i^{de} is the rate of inflation in the domestic economy.

Similarly, the foreign price index at any point in time t_n, using the same reference year t_0 as the base year, can be expressed as the price index in any initial year t_0, $I_{t_0}^F$, multiplied by the cumulative change in the price level from time t_0 to t_n. This is given as follows:

$$I_{t_n}^F = I_{t_0}^F \prod_{i=1}^{n}\left(1 + gp_{t_0+i}^{fe}\right) \qquad (3.11)$$

where gp_i^{fe} is the rate of inflation in the foreign economy.

Substituting (3.10) and (3.11) into equation (3.9) allows the calculation of the nominal exchange rate in a future time period n as:

$$E_{t_n}^M = E_{t_n}^R \times \frac{I_{t_0}^D \prod_{i=1}^{n}(1+gp_{t_0+i}^{de})}{I_{t_0}^F \prod_{i=1}^{n}(1+gp_{t_0+i}^{fe})} \qquad (3.12)$$

For convenience when conducting a financial appraisal of a project, we can select the first year of the project, t_0, as the arbitrary reference point or base year for the calculation of the relative price indices. Using t_0 as the base year, the values for both $I_{t_0}^D$ and $I_{t_0}^F$ will be equal to 1 in that year. Hence, there will be no difference between the real and nominal exchange rates in that base period.

In the case where the initial price levels for the domestic and the foreign country are set to 1 in time period t_0, equation (3.12) for the market exchange rate can be simplified to:

$$E_{t_n}^M = E_{t_n}^R \times \frac{\prod_{i=1}^{n}\left(1 + gp_{t_0+i}^{de}\right)}{\prod_{i=1}^{n}\left(1 + gp_{t_0+i}^{fe}\right)} \qquad (3.13)$$

The real exchange rate will move through time because of shifts in the country's demand and supply for foreign exchange. It is very difficult to predict the movement of the real exchange rate unless it is being artificially maintained at a given level through tariffs or quantitative restrictions on either the supply or the demand of foreign exchange. In some situations, when the real exchange rate is believed to be currently either above or below its longer-term equilibrium level, a trend in the real exchange rate for a limited number of years may be projected. The ratio of the two price indices is known as the relative price index. If, through time, the domestic economy faces a rate of inflation different from that of a foreign trading partner, the relative price index will vary over time. If the real exchange rate remains constant in the presence of inflation, the change in the relative price index must result in a corresponding change in the market exchange rate.

Since the future real exchange rate is only likely to be known with some uncertainty, and the market exchange rate might not adjust instantaneously to changes in the rate of inflation, it is more realistic to allow some flexibility in the estimation of the market exchange rate. This is carried out by assuming a range for the distribution of possible real exchange rates around an expected mean real exchange rate. To incorporate this aspect, the above equation can be written as follows:

$$E_{t_n}^M = E^R \times (1 + k) \times \left(\frac{\prod_{i=1}^{n}\left(1 + gp_{t_0+i}^{de}\right)}{\prod_{i=1}^{n}\left(1 + gp_{t_0+i}^{fe}\right)} \right) \tag{3.14}$$

where k is a random variable with a mean value of 0.

3.4.4 Incorporating Inflation in the Financial Analysis

Much of the published literature on project evaluation recommends the exclusion of inflation from the appraisal process (Squire and van der Tak, 1975, 38). These methods account only for projected changes in relative prices of inputs and outputs over the life of the investment.[6] However, experience with projects suffering from financial liquidity and solvency problems has demonstrated that inflation can be a critical factor in the success or failure of projects. Correctly designing a project to accommodate both changes in relative prices and changes in the rate of inflation may be crucial for its ultimate survival.

Improper accounting for the impacts of inflation when conducting the financial analysis could have detrimental effects not only on the financial sustainability of a project but also on its economic viability. Assumptions regarding inflation will have a direct impact on the financial analysis of the project and may require adjustments in the operating or investment policies. Since an inadequate treatment of inflation may adversely affect the financial

---

[6]All of the following authors recommend that expectations of inflation be ignored in the evaluation of projects: Little and Mirrlees (1974); United Nations Industrial Development Organization (1972); and Curry and Weiss (1993). A more satisfactory treatment of this issue is provided by Roemer and Stern (1975, 73–74).

The Financial Appraisal of Projects

sustainability of the project, the economic viability of the project may ultimately be compromised if inflation is not properly accounted for.

It is important to realize that the ultimate analysis of the financial cash flows should be carried out on a statement prepared in real domestic currency. It is difficult to correctly analyse nominal net cash flow statements as it involves attempting to understand figures that reflect two changes: changes in the real price and changes in inflation. Moreover, when preparing the cash flow statement, certain variables such as tax liabilities, cash requirements, interest, and debt repayments need to be estimated in the current prices of the years in which they incur. The correct treatment of inflation requires that preparatory tables be prepared using nominal prices, and then the nominal cash flow statements deflated, to obtain the cash flow statements in real prices. Constructing the financial analysis in this manner ensures that all the effects of changes in both real prices and inflation are consistently reflected in the projected variables.

The steps required for incorporating inflation into the financial cash flow of a project in a consistent manner are as follows:

1. Estimate the future changes in the real prices for each input and output variable. This will involve the examination of the present and future demand and supply forces that are expected to prevail in the market for the item. For example, an examination of the real prices of many electronic goods and services will indicate that they have been falling by a few percentage points a year over the past decade. Real wages, on the other hand, tend to increase over time as the economy grows.
2. Develop a set of assumptions concerning the expected annual changes in price level over the life of the project and calculate the expected inflation rate.
3. Determine what the nominal rate of interest is likely to be over the life of the project given the expected changes in the price level estimated above.
4. Combine the expected change in real prices for each input and output with the expected change in the rate of inflation in order to obtain the expected change in the nominal price of the item.
5. Multiply the nominal prices for each item by the projections of quantities of inputs and outputs through time to express these variables in the current year's prices of the period in which they are expected to occur.
6. Begin the construction of a cash flow statement using the nominal values for the inputs and outputs.
7. Determine the financing requirements along with the interest payments and principal repayments, and include these items in the income tax statement and also in the cash flow statement.
8. Construct an income tax statement for each year of the project's life to determine income tax liabilities, with all variables expressed in their nominal values. Depreciation expenses, cost of goods sold, and interest expenses and income tax liabilities are estimated according to taxation laws of the country

in question. The estimated income tax liabilities are included in the cash flow statement.

9. Estimate accounts receivable, accounts payable, and any changes in the stock of cash that are reflected in the cash flow statement. This completes the construction of the projected variables in terms of their current values.

10. Construct the nominal cash flow statement from the total investment point of view by assembling all projected annual cash receipts, annual cash expenditures in current prices, and changes in cash balance over the life of the project.

11. Add loans received from bankers as cash inflow and subtract interest payments as cash outflow to construct the cash flow statement in current prices from the owner's point of view. Deflate all items in the owner's cash flow statement by the price index to arrive at real values for the cash flow statement. Note that loans, interest payments, and loan payments are also deflated and included in the cash flow statement in real prices.

12. Discount the net financial cash flow to the owners of the enterprise. The appropriate discount rate will be the real private opportunity cost of equity financing if the owner of the enterprise is a private owner. However, in the case of a public sector enterprise, the appropriate discount rate will be the target financial rate of return (net of inflation) set by the government.

13. Calculate the net financial cash flows accruing to any other points of view that are relevant for the project.

The development of pro forma financial cash flow statements in this way ensures that the impact of inflation on the financial performance of the project is correctly accounted for. At the same time, the final financial analysis is completed with the variables expressed in terms of the price level of a given year. In this way, the movement of such variables as receipts, labour costs, and material costs can be compared over time without being distorted by changes in the general price level.

When the financial analysis is carried out in terms of real prices, it is essential that the private opportunity costs of capital or the target financial rates of return used as discount rates be expressed net of any compensation for the expected rate of inflation. In other words, these discount rates must be real, not nominal, variables. If a nominal private cost of capital or target rate of return is used, the result will be a double correction for the expected changes in the general price level. Such practices will greatly distort the conclusions of the analysis concerning the financial viability of the project.

It should be noted that the real financial prices for the input and output variables developed above are used as the base on which to estimate the economic values for the benefits and costs of the project. Once these economic costs and benefits are estimated, an economic resource flow statement can be constructed. The structure of the statement should be similar to that of the financial cash flow statement. The difference between the two statements is analysed to determine the impacts of the project on various stakeholders.

3.5 Analyses of Investment Decisions from Alternative Viewpoints

Most investment projects can be evaluated from the perspective of the different actors or institutions directly affected by them. These actors or institutions in a commercial project are in fact stakeholders, including the owner or equity holder, the supplier of raw materials, the workers employed in the project, the bank or financing institution, the government's budget office, and the country as a whole. In the case of projects involving government intervention in the form of grants, subsidies, loans, or a joint venture, the stakeholders may be different from those listed here, depending upon the specific type of project. Nevertheless, it is necessary to conduct the analyses from the viewpoints of the various important stakeholders to ensure the project's sustainability and success. This minimizes the risk of a situation arising in which one powerful stakeholder who is adversely affected by the project is able to derail the entire scheme.

The most commonly undertaken financial analyses for commercial and government-related projects are from the points of view of owner, banker, government, and country. These are discussed below, focusing on differences in the variables included in the analyses from the different perspectives.

3.5.1 Banker's Point of View

A banker's first and foremost interest is to evaluate the overall strength of the project, i.e. to determine whether the potential loans the project may require are secured. Bankers see a project as an activity that generates tangible financial benefits and absorbs tangible financial resources. They disregard any distinctions in the sources of finance but ask whether the financial receipts generated from the operations of the project are sufficient to cover the investment and operating expenditures and whether they provide a sufficient return.

In what is also known as the total investment point of view, bankers take into account all financial benefits and costs of the project in order to determine the financial feasibility of the project, the need for loans, and the likelihood of repayment on loan and interest. Included in the total investment of a project are the financial opportunity costs of any existing facilities that are integrated into the new project. From this point of view, the historical costs of existing assets are irrelevant. Bankers typically have first claim on the project's assets and net cash flows, so a banker's net cash flow is the project's gross receipts, net of operating and investment expenditures.[7]

3.5.2 Owner's Point of View

The owner of a project examines the incremental net cash flow from the investment relative to what could have been earned in the absence of the project. Unlike the banker, the owner adds the loan to the net cash flows from the total investment point of view as cash receipts and subtracts payments of interest and loan repayment as cash outlays. If the project receives any grants or subsidies from the government, these should be included as receipts in the cash flow statement. Therefore, the only difference between the analysis from the owner's point of view and that from the banker's point of view is financing.

3.5.3 Government's Point of View

A project may require outlays from the government budget in the form of cheap credit, subsidies, grants, or other transfer payments, and it may also generate revenues from direct or indirect taxes and fees. The analysis from the government's point of view ensures that the relevant government ministry has enough resources to finance its obligations to the project. If the ministry is the project owner, the distinction between the cash flow statements from the owner's and the government's point of view is the difference in their opportunity costs of funds. If, on the other hand, the government's involvement is in the form of receiving taxes and/or providing some cheap credit, subsidies, or grants, the cash flow statement from the government's point of view will reflect these transactions.

Although the three views outlined above are the most typical points of view considered when conducting the financial analysis, it is important to analyse the impacts of the project on all the parties involved. For example, if the project under consideration is likely to have a negative impact on competitors, their reactions should be anticipated and proper adjustments made. It is thus necessary to estimate and signify the magnitude of the negative impacts on any affected group. These affected groups could include, for example, competitors, suppliers of inputs, and downstream processors as some of the stakeholders of the project.

---

[7]In a few cases there may be a subtle difference between the total investment point of view and that of the banker. Consider, for example, a government department that is encouraging the construction of low-income housing projects by repaying the interest on the housing loan. An analysis from the total investment point of view will not be concerned with the loan at all, whether subsidized or not. A banker, however, will definitely be more in favour of lending to a project that receives a government loan subsidy than to a similar project that does not receive the subsidy.

3.5.4 Country's Point of View

Evaluation from the country's point of view is especially appropriate when a project is undertaken by the government or involves some form of government intervention. When undertaking the evaluation from the point of view of the entire country, economic prices must be used to value inputs and outputs in order to reflect their true resource cost or economic benefit to society. The economic prices take into account taxes, subsidies, and other distortions in the marketplace. From the country's point of view, the activities that had to be forgone in undertaking the project should also be charged at real resource cost. Thus, the economic appraisal of a project adjusts the financial cash flow from the total investment viewpoint for taxes and subsidies, and ignores loan and interest payments because these represent flow of funds, not real resources.

3.5.5 Relationships between Different Points of View

A project can be thought of as a bundle of transactions that cause different individuals or institutions to incur different costs and receive different benefits. The evaluation of a project from several perspectives is critical because it allows the analyst to determine whether the parties involved will find it worthwhile to finance, join, or execute the project. If the outcome of a project is attractive to the owner but not to the financing institution or to the government's budget office, the project could face problems securing official approval and funding. Alternatively, if a project is attractive from the viewpoint of a banker or the budget office but unattractive to the owner, the project could face problems during implementation. In short, in order to ensure its approval and successful implementation, a project must be attractive to all the investors and operators associated with it.

To illustrate the different analyses available for evaluating a project, we provide an example of a project with the following stylized facts:

1. The project will last for two years, labelled Years 0 and 1. The project will be built during Year 0, start operating at the beginning of Year 1, and terminate at the end of Year 1.
2. During Year 0, $1,000 is spent in the purchase of machinery.
3. To finance the project, the owner will require a loan from a private bank equivalent to 50 percent of the initial investment cost. The repayment on the interest and the principal of the loan is due in Year 1. The loan carries a 10 percent interest rate.
4. The project generates $300 in sales in Year 1 and receives a subsidy equivalent to 50 percent of the sales value. Operating costs are $140 in Year 1. Taxes amount to $100.
5. The project sells its equipment at the end of Year 1 for $950.

6. The project creates pollution. The cost of cleaning up the area contaminated by the project has been estimated at $50 per year of operation. The government will not require the investor to clean up after the completion of the project.
7. The land required, which is currently owned by the developer of the project, has an opportunity cost, as it could have been rented to others for $30 per year.

The cash and/or resource flows of the project can be rearranged as viewed by the different actors — the owner, banker, government budget office, and country as a whole — following different accounting conventions. This is presented in Table 3.4.

Table 3.4: Net Resource Flow from Different Viewpoints (dollars)

		Financial Analysis					Economic Analysis	
Viewpoint	Owner		Banker		Government		Country	
Year	0	1	0	1	0	1	0	1
Sales		300		300				300
Operation cost		−140		−140				−140
Equipment	−1,000	950	−1,000	950			−1,000	950
Subsidy		150		150		−150		
Taxes		−100		−100		100		
Loan	500	−500						
Interest		−50						
Environmental externality								−50
Opportunity cost of land	−30	−30	−30	−30			−30	−30
Net resource flow	−530	580	−1,030	1,130		−50	−1,030	1,030

The returns of the project from the alternative viewpoints differ. Moreover, the analysis of the project from a financial and an economic perspective and from the viewpoints of the owner and the country can lead to four possible results, as shown in Figure 3.2.

Figure 3.2: Profitability Calculations from the Point of View of the Owner and the Economy

		Economic (Country)	
		+	(−)
Financial (Owner)	+	(A)	(B)
	(−)	(C)	(D)

In cell (A), the project ought to be undertaken because it generates net benefits to the owner and to the country. In cell (D), the project generates net losses to both parties and, consequently, should not be undertaken. In between are cases where the owners are motivated to take actions that are not consistent with the action that is best for the economy. In cell (B), the project is profitable to the owner, but generates a loss to society. This may occur for a project such as cultivation of a crop with extensive pesticides, which may harm people living in the project area. If the government increases its taxation of this activity, owners may find it unprofitable to invest in the project. If the government imposes taxes, the activity will shift from cell (B) to cell (D). In this case, the project should not be undertaken if it is unprofitable to society.

In cell (C), the project generates net economic benefits to society but net losses to the owners. Consequently, equity holders will not endorse or undertake the project on their own. Such an activity may include the cultivation of trees, which enhance watershed protection, biodiversity, and erosion control. Although these services benefit society, they do not generate enough income to the private owner. If the government provides subsidies in order to persuade investors to participate in the activity, the project will shift from cell (C) to cell (A). In such a situation it is socially profitable, and the owners will have an incentive to undertake the project.

This analysis demonstrates the importance of having projects that are attractive from both the financial perspective and society's point of view. In order for socially profitable projects to be implemented, they must be designed to be financially viable. On the other hand, projects that are financially attractive but have negative economic returns will cause damage to the economy, and are worse than doing nothing.

3.6 Conclusion

This chapter began with the presentation of the main concepts, principles, and conventions involved in the development of pro forma financial statements for an investment project. As projects usually last for many years, forecasts of capital investment, quantities, and prices of inputs and outputs over the life of the project are uncertain, but such projections are necessary for the financial analysis of its commercial viability.

We have described the process for making projections consistently over the life of the project. These include the movement of the real and nominal prices of inputs and outputs of the project, the nominal interest rates, and the nominal exchange rate, which are projected in a way that is consistent with expectations about the future rate of inflation.

Finally, an investment project often involves different stakeholders. Each will be concerned with the impact the project will have on them. To ensure the project's sustainability, the assessment of projects from different points of view is needed in order to minimize the adverse effect perceived by any of the stakeholders.

Appendix 3A: Steps in Constructing the Pro Forma Cash Flow Statements

The data requirements for conducting a project appraisal have been outlined in the current chapter. This appendix will provide a practical approach to constructing the financial cash flow statement starting from the very beginning. The construction of a cash flow statement requires that the data be organized in a number of preparatory spreadsheets that culminate in the cash flow statement.

1. All project parameters are extracted from the project documents and placed in a Table of Parameters. The Table of Parameters includes all the raw data required for construction of the cash flow statements. This will include prices, costs, production coefficients, financing terms, inflation and exchange rates, depreciation rates, working capital, and all other data that will be used in the analysis. It is imperative that all data entry in the spreadsheet be completed in the Table of Parameters. The construction of all other tables should be based on formulas and equations that are linked to the data in the Table of Parameters. This is crucial for maintaining the integrity of the spreadsheets for sensitivity and risk analyses.

2. After all the required data have been recorded in the Table of Parameters, a table of inflation and exchange rates is constructed. This enables domestic inflation and foreign inflation indices for the life of the project to be developed. These indices are based on the expected rates of domestic and foreign inflation. The table also contains a relative inflation index that measures the change in the general price level of the domestic currency relative to the foreign currency. It is used to determine the nominal exchange rate over the life of the project. There is no need to include exchange rates if none of the project's inputs are imported and none of its outputs are exported. The reference year for estimating inflation is usually taken as the first year of the project's life, for convenience. As a result, the relative inflation index for the first year of the project will be 1. Typically, the project analyst takes the real exchange rate as constant; the nominal exchange rate is affected only by the relative change in the inflation rates of the domestic and foreign currencies.

3. The next table(s) will contain all the data on sales and purchases, and will be used to estimate the unit cost of production. On the sales side, quantities produced and quantities sold are introduced. The expected sales prices over the life of the project should be determined. Quantities sold should be multiplied by nominal prices to generate revenues. To determine the nominal price of an item, changes in real prices are included, if any are expected, and the inflation index applied. If the sales are for the domestic market, the prices expressed in domestic currency and the domestic inflation index should be applied. If the project involves exports and the prices are expressed in

foreign currency, the foreign inflation index should first be applied to the real prices, and the result then multiplied by the projected market exchange rate. Prices of all inputs are determined in exactly the same manner. This includes labour of all types, and overheads. Total costs are aggregated and divided by the total quantity produced to determine the unit cost of production.

4. The next step is to estimate the cost of goods sold; this is used in the income tax statement to determine the project's income tax liability. Based on the inventory policy followed by the project and whether first-in-first-out (FIFO), last-in-first-out (LIFO), or another accounting method is used, physical units sold are identified in terms of when they were produced, and the respective cost of production is applied to each unit. For example, if all of a year's sales were produced in the same year, the unit cost of production of the year would be the relevant one. However, if only 70 percent of the sales of a year were produced in that year, with the balance produced in the previous year, the costs of goods sold would be determined by multiplying 70 percent of the sales by the unit cost of production of that year and the remaining 30 percent by the unit cost of production of the previous year.

5. The working capital table typically includes two sections. The first includes the impacts of working capital on the cash flow statements of the project. This includes changes in accounts receivable, changes in accounts payable, and changes in cash balances. Accounts receivable, accounts payable, and cash balances are typically based on the amount of sales or purchases and should be linked to nominal sales and/or purchases. In the second section, the project analyst will estimate the initial working capital requirements for the project. These will be financed either through equity or through debt.

6. The investment and depreciation schedule is prepared next. This table includes all investment data. The prices should be expressed in nominal terms. This table serves two purposes. The first is to determine the depreciation expense that will be included in the income tax statement used to determine the income tax liability. In this case, the rate of depreciation used is specified by the tax and accounting rules. The second purpose is to develop residual values for the project's assets. These are typically based on economic rates of depreciation for the depreciable assets. The economic rate of depreciation will be applied to the value of the asset in the year it was acquired. In this study, the residual values obtained will be in the purchasing power of the year of acquisition. Since the cash flow statement is constructed in nominal prices before being deflated to real prices, the residual values expressed in the purchasing power of the year of acquisition are adjusted to reflect the increase in price level over the life of the project.

Land is typically a non-depreciable asset. It will be adjusted for inflation only in order to arrive at the value of the land in nominal prices in the final year of the project.

7. The financing schedule typically includes all the loans by date of disbursement. Repayments of financing cost are estimated using nominal interest rates and are broken down by interest and principal. Interest expense is used in the income statement to help determine the tax liability of the project. If the loan is denominated in foreign currency and will be paid back in foreign currency, the entire repayment schedule should be worked out in foreign currency. The loan and repayment flows are then converted into domestic currency using the nominal exchange rates.

8. If the project is to pay taxes, an income statement should be constructed. The income tax statement is constructed in nominal terms. The cost of goods sold, depreciation and amortization expenses, overheads, and interest expense that have been prepared earlier are all subtracted from nominal sales. Net taxable income is then derived and the tax liability determined. The income tax liability is used in the cash flow statement, which is constructed in the next step.

9. All the elements of the cash flow statement have been prepared. The only step remaining is to assemble these components to construct the cash flow statement. We start with the cash flow statement from the total investment point of view.

   - Nominal cash receipts are typically made up of sales and changes in accounts receivable to adjust for credit sales, and the residual values of the project's assets. All receipts inclusive of VAT and other sales taxes are added up for each year to determine annual cash inflows.
   - Nominal expenditures are broken down into investment expenditures and operating expenditures, and included in the cash flow statement. If the project is using any existing assets, the opportunity cost of these assets should be included with the investment expenditures. Nominal operating expenditures inclusive of VAT and other sales taxes are included in the cash flows. Changes in the cash balance and accounts payable should also be included. Finally, the income tax liability is also part of the cash outflows. All expenditures are added up for each year to determine annual cash outflows.
   - VAT on sales is collected on behalf of the tax authority, and VAT paid on purchases can be claimed as input tax credit. Thus, the amount of VAT collected in excess of an input tax credit should be deducted as a cash outflow from the project.

- Nominal net cash flows are derived by subtracting the nominal cash outflows from the nominal cash inflows and adjusting for net VAT collected.

10. The cash flow statement in nominal prices from the owner's point of view is constructed by adding the debt as inflows, and interest and principal repayment as outflows to the cash flow statement estimated from the viewpoint of total invested capital.

11. The cash flow statement in real prices from the owner's point of view is estimated by deflating each item in the nominal cash flow statement by the corresponding inflation index for the year.

Appendix 3B: Impacts of Inflation on Financial Cash Flows

The effects of inflation on a project's financial condition include:
a) direct impacts from changes in investment financing, cash balances, accounts receivable, accounts payable, and nominal interest rates;
b) tax impacts, including interest expenses, depreciation, and inventories; and
c) the impact on the market exchange rate.

Inflation alters the amount and timing of the financial gains and losses of the various parties involved in a project, including the owner, the lender, and the government. Correctly accounting for these changes is necessary in order to determine how the overall project, and each of the interested parties, is affected by different levels of inflation.

3B.1 Direct Effects

a) Investment Financing

When estimating the amount of financing a project requires, it is important to distinguish between two types of cost increase. First, there are cost overruns, which are caused by incorrect estimates of the quantities of materials required or changes in the real prices of those materials. Second, there is cost escalation, which is attributable to general price level inflation. The "escalation" of costs that stems from pure price inflation should be recognized as normal and, if possible, should be anticipated and included in the project appraisal. If the project requires a loan or equity financing for future outlays, it should be recognized that the amount of financing needed will be affected by the amount of price inflation that takes place during the time of construction. Cost increases attributable to inflation are not overruns of real costs; therefore, additional borrowing that simply reflects the rise in the general level of prices should be planned for. If this condition is not adequately planned for at the appraisal stage, the project may experience a liquidity crisis or insolvency as a result of inadequate financing.

Table 3B.1 demonstrates the effects of inflation on investment financing. The project will be built during the first two years, operate for the following four, and then be liquidated in the final year. The total cost of construction will be capitalized at the end of the second year to determine the amount to be depreciated. Loans are obtained for 50 percent of the investment in fixed assets. Loan financing will have a nominal interest rate of 5 percent per year if there is no inflation, and interest will begin accruing during the construction period. The loan principal will be repaid at the end of the final operating year of the project (Year 5). The remainder of the financing requirements is covered by the owners' equity.

Table 3B.1: Project XYZ Financing (dollars)

Year	0	1	2	3	4	5	6
Inflation = 0%							
1. Price index	1.00	1.00	1.00	1.00	1.00	1.00	1.00
2. Investment outlays	5,000	5,000	0	0	0	0	0
Inflation = 25%							
3. Price index	1.00	1.25	1.56	1.95	2.44	3.05	3.81
4. Investment outlays	5,000	6,250	0	0	0	0	0
5. Impact on financing requirements	0	1,250	0	0	0	0	0

In this project, an investment of $5,000 is made in fixed assets in Year 0, and if there is no inflation, a further $5,000 is made in Year 1. If there is 25 percent inflation a year, the initial year's investment does not change; however, the nominal investment undertaken in Year 1 increases to $6,250.

The presence of inflation increases the nominal amount of the investment financing required by $1,250 even when there is no increase in its costs. For a 25 percent inflation rate, total nominal project costs increase from $10,000 to $11,250, or by 12.5 percent. The increased investment expense has three effects. First, it increases the interest costs to the project. Second, it increases the nominal amount of loan principal, which must be repaid by the project. Finally, it results in a larger nominal depreciable expense that will be deductible from future taxes. These effects have both positive and negative cash flow impacts, which are discussed below.

b) Desired Cash Balances

Cash balances are held by a project to facilitate transactions. A commercial enterprise will need to maintain an amount of cash on hand that is related to the value of sales and purchases it carries out. In addition, lenders may require that a substantial amount of cash balances or very liquid assets be held in a debt reserve account. If the demand for cash balances is a function only of the level of sales, and if sales remain constant with no inflation, then after initially setting aside the desired amount of operating cash, no further investments in the cash balances would be required. However, when there is inflation, the sales, receipts, and the cost of the goods purchased will rise even if the quantities of goods bought and sold remain the same. The resulting loss in the purchasing power of cash balances is referred to as an "inflation tax" on cash holdings (Jenkins, 1979). Its primary effect is to transfer financial resources from the project to the banking sector. In such a situation, the project will have to either increase its cash balances in order to conduct operations or substitute more physical resources to carry out these transactions.

The effects of an inflation tax on cash balances can be demonstrated using a simple comparison of two cases. The first case shows the cash situation for a project operating in an environment where there is no inflation. Sales will be $2,000 for each period from Year 2 to Year 5, and the desired cash balance is equal to 10 percent of the nominal value of sales. Hence, given the absence of inflation, after the initial $200 is placed in the cash account, there is no need to increase that balance. The PV of the cost of holding cash by the project is −$41 (Table 3B.2, line 6).

Table 3B.2: Project XYZ Cash Balance (dollars)

Year	0	1	2	3	4	5	6
Inflation = 0%; desired cash balance = 10%							
1. Price index	1.00	1.00	1.00	1.00	1.00	1.00	1.00
2. Sales	0	0	2,000	2,000	2,000	2,000	0
3. Desired cash balance	0	0	200	200	200	200	0
4. Change in cash balance	0	0	(200)	0	0	0	200
5. Real cash flow impact [4/1]	0	0	(200)	0	0	0	200
6. PV of holding cash @ 7% = (41)							

However, if the inflation rate increases to 25 percent per year, the cash balances must be increased to keep abreast of the increasing nominal value of sales. For the purpose of this example it is assumed that the number of units sold remains the same but their nominal value increases by 25 percent a year as a result of inflation. As a result, the desired stock of cash balances will increase, requiring an additional investment of cash in the project during each year if the desired level is to be maintained (Table 3B.3, row 4). After deflating these costs for inflation and discounting them, the PV of the cost of the cash needed to run the business is found to have increased substantially.

Table 3B.3: Cash Balance with 25 Percent Inflation (dollars)

Year	0	1	2	3	4	5	6
Inflation = 25%; desired cash balance = 10% of sales							
1. Price index	1.00	1.25	1.56	1.95	2.44	3.05	3.81
2. Sales	0	0	3,125	3,906	4,883	6,104	0
3. Desired cash balance	0	0	313	391	488	610	0
4. Change in cash balance	0	0	(313)	(78)	(98)	(122)	610
5. Real cash flow impact [4/1]	0	0	(200)	(40)	(40)	(40)	160
6. PV of holding cash @ 7% = (159)							

With zero inflation in Table 3B.2, the PV of the cost of holding real cash balances is −$41. However, when the inflation rate is 25 percent, the PV of the cost of maintaining the same level of real cash balances will be −$159, as shown

The Financial Appraisal of Projects

in Table 3B.3, line 6. This 288 percent increase in the cost of holding cash demonstrates clearly that in an inflationary environment, the need to continuously add to the stock of cash balances will add to the real costs of the project. Hence, project evaluators should incorporate a number of inflation projections in order to determine the sensitivity of total costs to the impact of inflation on the cost of holding the desired level of real cash balances.

c) Accounts Receivable

Accounts receivable arise from making credit sales. When goods are sold and delivered but the enterprise is still awaiting payment, the value of this sale is added to accounts receivable. Such credit sales are part of the normal process of conducting business. However, in the presence of inflation, the real value of the amounts that are owed to the seller decrease the longer they are left unpaid. This creates an additional financial problem for the management of the enterprise because they must be concerned not only with the normal risk of default but also with the fact that the receivables are falling in real value the longer they are left unpaid.

Table 3B.4 demonstrates the interaction between inflation and accounts receivable and the impact that this interaction has on cash receipts. As the inflation rate rises, the value of sales increases as a result of the higher prices of the goods, even when the number of units sold remains unchanged. This generally leads to an increase in the amount of accounts receivable. In this case, it is assumed that receivables will be equal to 20 percent of sales.

Table 3B.4: Accounts Receivable (dollars)

Year	0	1	2	3	4	5	6
Inflation = 0%							
1. Sales	0	0	2,000	2,000	2,000	2,000	0
2. Accounts receivable	0	0	400	400	400	400	0
3. Change in A/R	0	0	(400)	0	0	0	400
4. Real receipts [1+3]	0	0	1,600	2,000	2,000	2,000	400
Inflation = 25%							
5. Price index	1.00	1.25	1.56	1.95	2.44	3.05	3.81
6. Sales	0	0	3,125	3,906	4,883	6,104	0
7. Accounts receivable	0	0	625	781	977	1,221	0
8. Change in A/R	0	0	(625)	(156)	(195)	(244)	1,221
9. Nominal receipts [6+8]	0	0	2,500	3,750	4,688	5,859	1,221
10. Real receipts [9/5]	0	0	1,600	1,921	1,921	1,921	321
11. Change in real receipts [10–4]			0	0	(79)	(79)	(79)	(79)
12. PV of the change in real receipts @ 7% = (233)							

In spite of the fact that the nominal value of sales increases in each year that there is 25 percent inflation, Table 3B.4 demonstrates that the PV of the real receipts for this project decreases by $233 as a result of the higher rate of inflation. This is because inflation causes the real value of outstanding trade credit to fall. When this situation arises, businesses selling goods or services will attempt to reduce the length of the terms they give for trade credit, while businesses purchasing the product will have an additional incentive to delay payment. If sellers are not successful at reducing the terms they give for trade credit, they will have to increase the price of the goods they sell above what would be justified by the rate of inflation. Thus, it is important to include in a project evaluation the interaction of inflation and accounts receivable to determine how the real receipts of the business are affected by inflation.

d) Accounts Payable

Accounts payable represent the amount of money owed by a business to others for goods or services already purchased and delivered. When there is inflation, the buyer with the accounts payable benefits from having an outstanding balance because the real value of the obligation is falling during the period of time prior to the payment. This is simply the other side of the impact of inflation on accounts receivable, because one enterprise's accounts receivable is another's accounts payable.

Table 3B.5 shows how inflation affects a project's financial situation when accounts payable are 25 percent of annual purchases. Once again, it can be seen that inflation increases the nominal value of purchases; this also leads to higher accounts payable. The increased rate of inflation results in a net decrease of $155 in the PV of real expenditures. As shown in line 6, inflation increases the nominal value of purchases and creates a corresponding increase in nominal accounts payable in line 7. When converted to real expenditures, the buyer (the project in this case) benefits from the effects of inflation on accounts payable and will have a lower overall level of expenditure, as shown in line 11. This gives the buyer an incentive to extend the terms of the accounts payable to benefit from their falling real value. Hence, in the presence of inflation, the longer the outstanding accounts payable are held before being paid, the greater the benefit accruing to the buyer.

Table 3B.5: Accounts Payable (dollars)

Year	0	1	2	3	4	5	6
Inflation = 0%							
1. Purchases of inputs	0	1,000	1,000	1,000	1,000	0	0
2. Accounts payable	0	250	250	250	250	0	0
3. Change in A/P	0	(250)	0	0	0	250	0
4. Real expenditures [1+3]	0	750	1,000	1,000	1,000	250	0
Inflation = 25%							
5. Price index	1.00	1.25	1.56	1.95	2.44	3.05	3.81
6. Purchases	0	1,250	1,563	1,953	2,441	0	0
7. Accounts payable	0	313	391	488	610	0	0
8. Change in A/P	0	(313)	(78)	(98)	(122)	610	0
9. Nominal expenditures [6+8]	0	937	1,485	1,855	2,319	610	0
10. Real expenditures [9/5]	0	750	951	951	951	201	0
11. Change in real expenditures [10-4]		0	(49)	(49)	(49)	(49)	0
12. PV of the change in real expenditures @ 7% = (155)							

e) Nominal Interest Rates

Another way in which inflation alters the real net financial condition of a project is through its impact on nominal interest rates. Lenders increase the nominal interest rate on the loans they give in order to compensate for the anticipated loss of the real value of the loan caused by inflation. As the inflation rate increases, the nominal interest rate will be increased to ensure that the PV of the interest and principal payments will not fall below the initial value of the loan. This results in increased interest payments (in real terms) in the short term that compensate for the decreasing real value of the loan principal repayments over time.

The nominal interest rate i as determined by the financial markets is made up of three major components:
a) a factor r, which reflects the real-time value of money that lenders require in order to be willing to forgo consumption or other investment opportunities;
b) a risk factor R, which measures the compensation the lenders demand to cover the possibility of the borrower defaulting on the loan; and
c) a factor $(1+r+R)\ gP^e$, which is compensation for the expected loss in purchasing power attributable to inflation.

Inflation reduces the future value of both the loan repayments and real interest rate payments. The expected rate of inflation for each year of the loan is expressed as gP^e. Combining these factors, the nominal (market) rate of interest i can be expressed as:

$$i = r + R + (1 + r + R)\ gP^e \qquad\qquad (3B.1)$$

For example, if the real interest rate r is 5 percent and the risk premium and inflation are zero, the lender would charge at least 5 percent nominal interest. However, if the lender anticipates that the future rate of inflation (gP^e) will be 25 percent, he or she would want to increase the nominal interest rate charged to the borrower in order to compensate for the loss in purchasing power of the future loan and interest rate payments. Maintaining the assumption that there is no risk to this loan, the lender will need to charge a nominal interest rate of at least 31.25 percent by applying equation (3B.1) to achieve the same level of return as in the zero-inflation scenarios.[8]

For the project being analysed here, fixed assets investments are financed 50 percent by debt and 50 percent by equity. All other investments, such as initial supplies, are financed 100 percent by equity. In Tables 3B.6 and 3B.7, the loan schedule for the debt portion of the financing is calculated under the 0 percent and the 25 percent inflation rate scenarios.

Table 3B.6: Nominal Interest Rate of 5 Percent (dollars)

Year	0	1	2	3	4	5	6
Inflation = 0%							
1. Loan principal	2,500	2,500	0	0	0	0	0
2. Interest	0	(125)	(250)	(250)	(250)	(250)	0
3. Loan repayment	0	0	0	0	0	(5,000)	0
4. Real cash flow [1+2+3]	2,500	2,375	(250)	(250)	(250)	(5,250)	0
5. PV @ 5% = 0							

Table 3B.7: Nominal Interest Rate of 31.25 Percent (dollars)

Year	0	1	2	3	4	5	6
Inflation = 25%							
1. Price index	1.00	1.25	1.56	1.95	2.44	3.05	3.81
2. Loan principal	2,500	3,125	0	0	0	0	0
3. Interest	0	(781.30)	(1,757.80)	(1,757.80)	(1,757.80)	(1,757.80)	0
4. Loan repayment	0	0	0	0	0	(5,625.00)	0
5. Nominal cash flow [2+3+4]	2,500	2,343.70	(1,757.80)	(1,757.80)	(1,757.80)	(7,382.80)	0
6. Real cash flow [5/1]	2,500	1,875.00	(1,126.80)	(901.40)	(720.40)	(2,420.60)	0
7. PV @ 5% = 0							

As discussed above, the higher rate of inflation will increase both the nominal investment required and the nominal interest rate. The higher initial capital requirement must be repaid at the higher nominal interest rate, as shown in Table 3B.7.

---

[8]At this point, the subsequent adjustment of interest rates brought about by the impact of the taxation of interest payments is ignored, as is the impact of changes in net-of-tax interest rates on the demand and supply of loanable funds. For an excellent discussion of these issues, see Feldstein (1976).

The Financial Appraisal of Projects

A comparison of Tables 3B.6 and 3B.7 shows that the PVs of both loans are the same. This demonstrates that a loan with a 31.25 percent interest rate when inflation is 25 percent has the same PV as a loan with an interest rate of 5 percent when inflation is zero. The crucial differences are in the timing and amount of repayment. The higher nominal interest rate of 31.25 percent and higher inflation forces the project to repay its loans faster than if the inflation rate and nominal interest rates were lower. Table 3B.8 shows the difference between the project's cash flow in the two scenarios.

In real terms, the higher nominal interest rate increases the cash outflows (or reduces the net cash inflows) of the project during Years 1–4 but decreases the value of the principal that is due at the end of the project by $2,829.40. This is important in the evaluation of the sustainability of a project because the higher outflows during the early years of the repayment period could cause liquidity problems for the project if it is not generating sufficient cash inflows.

Table 3B.8: Comparison of Real Cash Flows (dollars)

Year	0	1	2	3	4	5	6
1. 31.25% interest with 25% inflation	2,500	1,875	(1,126.80)	(901.40)	(720.40)	(2,420.60)	0
2. 5% interest with 0% inflation	2,500	2,375	(250)	(250)	(250)	(5,250)	0
3. Difference in real cash flow [1–2]	0	(500)	(876.80)	(651.40)	(470.40)	2,829.40	0

3B.2 Effect on Tax-related Factors

Inflation has three impacts on the tax liabilities of a project. First, the higher interest payments shown in the previous section increase the amount of tax deduction. Second, inflation reduces the value of the depreciation allowances taken for earlier investments in the project. Finally, the method used to account for inventory has an effect on the nominal earnings that are used to determine the taxable income. These three effects to some extent offset one another.

a) Interest Deduction

Inflation can alter the financial feasibility of a project through the impact of increased nominal interest payments on the income tax liabilities of the enterprise. In most countries, interest payments are deductible from income for the calculation of taxes, while principal repayments are not deductible. When the expected rate of inflation increases, nominal interest rates rise in order to compensate the lender for the loss in the purchasing power of the principal outstanding and future interest payments. Table 3B.9 shows how inflation, through the way it converts some of the real value of the principal repayments into interest payments, causes tax payments to fall. The higher nominal interest payments are deductible from taxable income; hence, they serve to reduce the amount of taxes that the project would otherwise be required to pay.

Table 3B.9: Interest Expense (dollars)
Income tax rate = 30%

Year	0	1	2	3	4	5	6
Inflation = 0%; nominal interest = 5%							
1. Interest expense	0	(125)	(250)	(250)	(250)	(250)	0
2. Real tax savings [line 1×0.3]	0	37.50	75	75	75	75	0
Inflation = 25%; nominal interest = 31.25%							
3. Interest expense	0	(781.30)	(1,758)	(1,758)	(1,758)	(1,758)	0
4. Tax savings [line 3×0.3]	0	234	527	527	527	527	0
5. Price index	1.00	1.25	1.56	1.95	2.44	3.05	3.81
6. Real tax savings [4/5]	0	187.20	337.80	270.30	215.90	172.80	0
7. Change in tax savings [6−2]	0	149.70	262.80	195.30	140.90	97.80	0
8. PV of increased tax savings @ 7% = 706							

b) Depreciation Allowance

Another factor affected by inflation is the real value of the depreciation allowances for capital goods that are deductible for income tax purposes. Most countries base the deductions for depreciation expense (capital cost allowances) on the original nominal cost of the depreciable assets. If inflation increases, the relative value of this deduction will fall, causing the real amount of income tax liabilities to increase. As shown in Table 3B.10, a 25 percent rate of inflation causes the tax savings from depreciation expense deductions to fall by $1,090. This is equal to approximately 10 percent of the real value of the fixed assets being depreciated.

Table 3B.10: Project XYZ: Depreciation Allowance (dollars)
Straight line depreciation over four years; income tax rate = 30%

Year	0	1	2	3	4	5	6
Inflation = 0%; depreciable investment = 10,000							
1. Depreciation	0	0	2,500	2,500	2,500	2,500	0
2. Real tax savings [line 1×0.3]	0	0	750	750	750	750	0
Inflation = 25%; nominal depreciable investment = 11,250							
3. Depreciation	0	0	2,812.50	2,812.50	2,812.50	2,812.50	0
4. Tax savings [line 3×0.3]	0	0	844	844	844	844	0
5. Price index	1.00	1.25	1.56	1.95	2.44	3.05	3.81
6. Real tax savings [4/5]	0	0	541	433	346	276	0
7. Change in tax savings [6−2]	0	0	(209)	(317)	(404)	(474)	0
8. PV of change in real tax savings @ 7% = (1,090)							

c) Inventory Accounting

(i) First-In-First-Out (FIFO)

Further tax implications of inflation are experienced by commercial enterprises, which must account for inventories of inputs and outputs. In many countries, in order to determine the amount of taxable profit, companies are required to value inventories in their accounts on the basis of FIFO. This means that the price of the oldest inventories (first in) is the value that is used to determine the cost of the goods sold (COGS). The difference between the COGS and the sale price is the taxable revenue from the project.

The real value of taxable income generally increases by the rate of inflation because sale prices are affected immediately by the rate of inflation, while the COGS from inventories are valued using prices of a previous period, when the nominal prices were presumably lower. For example, if the project has a one-year inventory of final goods at the beginning of the year and the inflation rate for that year is 25 percent, nominal cost prices of the goods sold will be 25 percent lower than their selling prices one year later. The result is that the measured profits are artificially inflated, and this increases the tax burden in both nominal and real terms.[9] As shown in line 12 and line 5 of Table 3B.11, if the rate of inflation increases from 0 to 25 percent, the PV of real tax payments increases by $193.

---

[9]In 1974, this effect of inflation alone caused corporate taxable income in Canada to be overestimated by more than 30 percent. See Jenkins (1979), Chapter 2.

Table 3B.11: Inventory and Cost of Goods Sold — FIFO (dollars)

Income tax rate = 30%

Year	0	1	2	3	4	5	6
Inflation = 0%							
1. Sales	0	0	2,000	2,000	2,000	2,000	0
2. Purchase of inputs	0	1,000	1,000	1,000	1,000	0	0
3. COGS	0	0	1,000	1,000	1,000	1,000	0
4. Measured profits [1–3]	0	0	1,000	1,000	1,000	1,000	0
5. Real tax liability [4×0.3]	0	0	300	300	300	300	0
Inflation = 25%; nominal depreciable investment = 11,250							
6. Sales	0	0	3,125	3,906	4,883	6,104	0
7. Purchase of inputs	0	1,250	1,563	1,953	2,441	0	0
8. COGS	0	0	1,250	1,563	1,953	2,441	0
9. Measured profits [6–8]	0	0	1,875	2,343	2,930	3,663	0
10. Nominal tax liability [9×0.3]	0	0	563	703	879	1,099	0
11. Price index	1.00	1.25	1.56	1.95	2.44	3.05	3.81
12. Real tax liability [10/11]	0	0	361	361	361	361	0
13. Change in tax liability [12–5]	0	0	61	61	61	61	0
14. PV of change in tax liability @ 7% = 193							

(ii) Last-In-First-Out (LIFO)

Another system for accounting for the COGS is LIFO. As the name implies, the most recent goods purchased (last in) are used to measure the COGS (first out), and the prices of the project inputs are generally increasing at the same rate of inflation as the outputs sold. During the production cycle of a project, this is a benefit because the profits are not increased artificially by the presence of inflation. It also means that taxes will be lower as a result. However, LIFO also has a negative aspect because as the activity winds down, the level of inventories is reduced. The lower prices of the goods that were purchased in earlier years are now used to calculate the COGS, resulting in inflated profits and increased taxes, as shown in Table 3B.12, line 13. In real terms, the tax burden increased by $177 in Year 5 over the no-inflation scenario.

Comparing the effects of inflation on the tax liability in the FIFO and LIFO accounting systems, it can be seen that in both cases, inflation increases the taxes. With FIFO and 25 percent inflation, the PV of the tax liability increases by $193 (Table 3B.11), and with LIFO, the PV increases by $126 (Table 3B.12).

In addition to the cost difference, the timing of the tax burden is substantially different. Using FIFO, inflation increases the taxes in each period, whereas using LIFO results in no increase in taxes in the production period but in a larger tax liability in the final sales period.

The Financial Appraisal of Projects

Table 3B.12: Inventory and Cost of Goods Sold — LIFO (dollars)
Income tax rate = 30%

Year	0	1	2	3	4	5	6
Inflation = 0%							
1. Sales	0	0	2,000	2,000	2,000	2,000	0
2. Purchase of inputs	0	1,000	1,000	1,000	1,000	0	0
3. COGS	0	0	1,000	1,000	1,000	1,000	0
4. Measured profits [1–3]	0	0	1,000	1,000	1,000	1,000	0
5. Real tax liability [4×0.3]	0	0	300	300	300	300	0
Inflation = 25%							
6. Sales	0	0	3,125	3,906	4,883	6,104	0
7. Purchase of inputs	0	1,250	1,563	1,953	2,441	0	0
8. COGS	0	0	1,563	1,953	2,441	1,250	0
9. Measured profits [6–8]	0	0	1,562	1,953	2,441	4,854	0
10. Nominal tax liability	0	0	469	586	732	1,456	0
11. Price index	1.00	1.25	1.56	1.95	2.44	3.05	3.81
12. Real tax liability [10/11]	0	0	300	300	300	477	0
13. Change in tax liability [12–5]	0	0	0	0	0	177	0
14. PV of change in tax liability @ 7% = 126							

LIFO defers the increased tax burden attributable to inflation until a period when there is a need to lower the level of inventories. As the lower-priced inventories are drawn into the COGS, the difference between inflated sales values and older prices generates larger profits and increases the tax liability. Using LIFO could increase the overall risk associated with the project in a high-inflation environment if the reason for the enterprise wanting to lower the level of inventories was financial stress or business slowdown. In such a situation, the increased tax liability is concentrated in a few periods when the project is already facing problems, while with FIFO, the increased tax liability is spread out over each operating period. Hence, when conducting the appraisal, it is important to consider the type of accounting rules used for determining the COGS to assess how inflation might affect both the timing and the quantity of the tax liabilities to be paid by the project.

References

Aaron, H.J., ed. 1976. *Inflation and the Income Tax*. Washington, DC: The Brookings Institution.
Curry, S. and J. Weiss. 1993. *Project Analysis in Developing Countries*. New York: St. Martin's Press.

Feldstein, M. 1976. "Inflation, Income Taxes and the Rate of Interest: A Theoretical Analysis", *American Economic Review* 66(5), 809–820.

Finnerty, J.D. 1996. *Project Financing: Asset-Based Financial Engineering.* New York: John Wiley & Sons.

Francis, J. and R. Ibbotson. 2002. *Investments: A Global Perspective.* Upper Saddle River, NJ: Pearson Education, Inc.

Gittinger, J.P. 1982. *Economic Analysis of Agricultural Projects*, 2nd edition, Part Two. Baltimore, MD: Johns Hopkins University Press.

Harberger, A. 1965. "Survey of Literature on Cost-Benefit Analysis for Industrial Project Evaluation", paper prepared for United Nations Inter-Regional Symposium in Industrial Project Evaluation (October).

Henderson, J.W. and T.S. Maness. 1989. *The Financial Analyst's Deskbook: A Cash Flow Approach to Liquidity.* New York: Van Nostrand Reinhold.

Higgins, R.C. 2001. *Analysis for Financial Management.* New York: Irwin McGraw-Hill.

Jenkins, G.P. 1979. *Inflation: Its Financial Impact on Business in Canada.* Ottawa: Economic Council of Canada, Special Study Series.

Little, I.M.D. and J.A. Mirrlees. 1974. *Project Appraisal and Planning for Development Countries.* London: Heinemann Educational Books.

Merrett, A.J. and A. Sykes. 1973. *The Finance and Analysis of Capital Projects,* 2nd edition, Chapters 1 and 15. London: Longman.

Roemer, M. and J.J. Stern. 1975. *The Appraisal of Development Projects, A Practical Guide to Project Analysis with Case Studies and Solutions.* New York: Praeger Publishers.

Sandilands Committee. 1975. *Inflation Accounting: Report of the Inflation Accounting Committee*, Command Document 6225. London: Her Majesty's Stationery Office.

Savvides, S.C. 1999. "Market Analysis in Project Evaluation", Harvard Institute for International Development, Development Discussion Paper.

Squire, L. and H.G. van der Tak. 1975. *Economic Analysis of Projects.* Baltimore, MD: The Johns Hopkins University Press.

United Nations Industrial Development Organization. 1972. *Guidelines for Project Evaluation.* New York: United Nations.

Walker, C. and A.J. Smith. 1996. *Privatized Infrastructure: The Build, Operate, Transfer Approach.* London: Thomas Telford Publications.

Chapter Four

Discounting and Alternative Investment Criteria

4.1 Introduction

This chapter discusses the alternative investment criteria commonly used in the appraisal of investment projects. The net present value (NPV) of a project criterion is widely accepted by accountants, financial analysts, and economists as the one that yields the correct project choices in all circumstances. However, some decision-makers have frequently relied upon other criteria, such as the internal rate of return (IRR), the benefit–cost ratio (BCR), the pay-back period, and the debt service coverage ratio. The strengths and weaknesses of these criteria are examined in this chapter in order to demonstrate why the NPV criterion is the most reliable.

Section 4.2 explains the concept of discounting and discusses the choice of discount rate. Section 4.3 elaborates on and compares alternative investment criteria for the appraisal investment projects. Conclusions are made in the final section.

4.2 Time Dimension of a Project

Investment decisions are fundamentally different from consumption decisions. For example, fixed assets such as land and capital equipment are purchased at one point in time, and are expected to generate net cash flows, or net economic benefits, over a number of subsequent years. To determine whether the investment is worthwhile, it is necessary to compare its benefits and costs with those of alternative projects, which may occur at different time periods. A dollar spent or received today is worth more than a dollar spent or received in a later time period. It is not possible simply to add up the benefits and the costs of a project to see which are greater without taking account of the fact that amounts spent on investment today are worth more today than the same amount received as a benefit in the future.

The time dimension of a project's net cash flows and net economic benefits can be captured by expressing the values in terms of either future or present values. When moving forward in time to compute future values, analysts must allow for the compounding of interest rates. In contrast, when bringing future values back to the present for comparison purposes, it is necessary to discount them. Discounting is simply the inverse of compounding.

4.2.1 Time Value of Money

Time enhances the value of a dollar today and erodes the value of a dollar spent or received in the future. It is necessary to compensate individuals for forgoing their consumption today or lending their funds to a bank. In turn, banks and other financial institutions have to offer lenders interest in order to induce them to part temporarily with their funds. If the annual market interest rate is 5 percent, then 1 dollar today would be worth 1.05 dollars one year in the future. This means that in equilibrium, lenders value 1.05 dollars in one year's time the same as 1 dollar today.

4.2.2 Compounding

There are two main ways in which interest can be included in future values, namely simple interest and compound interest. Simple interest is paid only on the principal amount that is invested, while compound interest is paid on both the principal and the interest as it accumulates. Compound interest, which is the most commonly used way of charging interest, can cause the future value of 1 dollar invested today to increase by substantially more than simple interest over time. The difference is caused by the interest on the cumulative interest. The formula for compound interest payment is $V_t = (1+r)^t$, where V_t stands for the value in Year t of 1 dollar received in Year 0, and r denotes the rate of interest.

Interest may be compounded annually. However, it is common for interest to be compounded more frequently, for example, semi-annually, quarterly, monthly, or even daily. The number of compounding intervals will also affect the future value of an amount of cash invested today. Thus, the two factors affecting the future value of a dollar invested today are the time period of the investment and the interest rate.

Furthermore, when comparing two debt contracts, it is essential that they be judged on the basis of equivalent rates, for example, annual rates in the case of loan agreements, and semi-annual rates in the case of bonds. The magnitude of the interest rate is certainly a major determinant of the future value of a series of cash flow items.

4.2.3 Discounting

The discount factor allows the present value of a dollar received or paid in the future to be calculated. Since this involves moving backward rather than forward in time, the discount factor is the inverse of the compound interest factor. For example, an amount of 1 dollar now will, if invested, grow to $(1+r)$ a year later. It follows that an amount B to be received in n years in the future will have a present value of $B / (1+r)^n$. The greater the rate of discount used, the smaller its present value.

The nature of investment projects is such that their benefits and costs usually occur in different periods over time. The NPV of a future stream of net benefits, $(B_0 - C_0)$, $(B_1 - C_1)$, $(B_2 - C_2)$, ..., $(B_n - C_n)$, can be expressed algebraically as follows:

$$NPV^0 = \frac{B_0 - C_0}{(1+r)^0} + \frac{B_1 - C_1}{(1+r)^1} \cdots\cdots + \frac{B_n - C_n}{(1+r)^n}$$

$$= \sum_{t=0}^{n} \frac{(B_t - C_t)}{(1+r)^t} \qquad (4.1)$$

where n denotes the length of life of the project. The expression $1 / (1+r)^t$ is commonly referred to as the discount factor for Year t.

For the purposes of illustration, the present value of the stream of net benefits over the life of an investment is calculated in Table 4.1 by multiplying the discount factors, which are given in line 4, by the values of the net benefits for the corresponding periods, shown in line 3. The NPV of $1,000 is the simple sum of the present values of net benefits arising each period throughout the life of the project.

Table 4.1: Calculating the Present Value of Net Benefits from an Investment Project (dollars)

Items	0	1	2	3	4	5
1. Benefits			3,247	4,571	3,525	2,339
2. Costs	5,000	2,121	1,000	1,000	1,000	1,000
3. Net benefits (= 1−2)	−5,000	−2,121	+2,247	+3,571	+2,525	+1,339
4. Discount factor at 6% (= 1 / (1+r)^t)	1.000	0.943	0.890	0.840	0.792	0.747
5. Present values (= 4×3)	−5,000	−2,000	+2,000	+3,000	+2,000	+1,000
6. NPV	1,000					

Equation (4.1) shows that the net benefits arising during the project's life are discounted to Year 0. Instead of discounting all the net benefit flows to the initial year of a project, we could evaluate the project's stream of net benefits as of a Year k, which does not even need to fall within the project's expected life. In this case, all the net benefits arising from Year 0 to Year k must be cumulated forward at a rate of r to Year k. Likewise, all net benefits associated with Years $k+1$ to n are discounted back to Year k at the same rate r. The expression for the NPV as of Year k becomes:

$$NPV^k \quad = \sum_{t=0}^{n} [(B_t - C_t) \times (1+r)^{k-t}]$$

$$= \sum_{t=0}^{n} [(B_t - C_t) / (1+r)^t] \times (1+r)^k \qquad (4.2)$$

The term $(1+r)^k$ is a constant value as it is a function of the discount rate and the date to which the present values are calculated. The rankings of alternative projects will not be altered if the project's net benefits are discounted to Year k instead of Year 0. The present values of their respective net benefits discounted at Year 0 are all multiplied by the same constant term. Hence, the ranking of the NPVs of the net benefits of the alternative projects will not be affected.

4.2.4 Variable Discount Rates

Up to this point it has been assumed that the discount rate remains constant throughout the life of a project. This need not be the case. Suppose that funds are presently very scarce relative to the historical experience of the country. In such circumstances, the cost of funds would be expected to be currently abnormally high, and the discount rate is likely fall over time as the supply and demand for funds return to normal. On the other hand, if funds are abundant at present, the cost of funds and the discount rate would be expected to be below their long-term average. In this case, the discount rate would be expected to rise as the demand and supply of funds return to their long-term trend over time. This process is illustrated in Figure 4.1.

Figure 4.1: Adjustment of Cost of Funds through Time

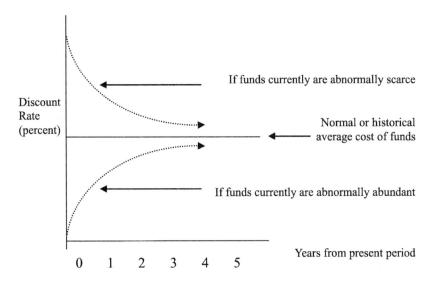

Suppose that the discount rates will vary from year to year over the life of a four-year project. The discount rate r_1 is the cost of capital, or the rate of discount extending from Year 0 to Year 1. The NPV of the project should be calculated as:

$$NPV^0 = (B_0 - C_0) + \frac{B_1 - C_1}{(1+r_0)} + \frac{B_2 - C_2}{(1+r_0)(1+r_1)} + \frac{B_3 - C_3}{(1+r_0)(1+r_1)(1+r_2)}$$

where r_1, r_2, and r_3 are the discount rates for Year 1, Year 2, and Year 3, respectively. Each discount factor after Year 2 will be made up of more than one discount rate. For example, the discount factor for Year 3's net benefits is $1/[(1+r_1)(1+r_2)(1+r_3)]$. The general expression for the NPV of the project with a life of n years, evaluated as of Year 0, becomes:

$$NPV^0 = (B_0 - C_0) + \sum_{i=1}^{n} \frac{B_i - C_i}{\prod_i (1+r_i)} \tag{4.3}$$

As in the case of the constant rate of discount, when comparing two or more projects, the period to which the net benefits of the projects are discounted does not matter, provided that the present values of the net benefits of each of the projects being compared are discounted to the same date.

4.2.5 Choice of Discount Rate

The discount rate is a key variable in the application of investment criteria for project selection. Choosing the discount rate correctly is critical given the fact that a small variation in its value may significantly alter the results of the analysis and affect the final choice of a project.

The discount rate, stated in simple terms, is the opportunity cost of funds that are invested in the project. In financial analysis, the discount rate depends upon the viewpoints of analysis. For instance, when a project is being appraised from the point of view of the equity holders, the relevant cost of funds is the return to equity that is being earned in its alternative use. Thus, if the equity holders are earning a return of 15 percent on their current investments and decide to invest in a new project, the cost of funds, or the discount rate, from their perspective for the new project is 15 percent.

When an economic analysis of a project is being conducted, the relevant discount rate is the economic opportunity cost of capital for the country. Estimating this cost starts with the capital market as the marginal source of funds, and involves determining the ultimate sources of funds obtained via the capital market and estimating the respective cost of each source. The funds are generally drawn from three sources. First, funds that would have been invested in other investment activities have now been displaced by the project. The cost of these funds is the gross-of-tax return that would have been earned by the alternative investments, which have now been forgone. Second, funds come from different categories of savers in the economy, who postpone some of their consumption in the expectation of obtaining a return on their savings. The cost of this part of the funds is the cost of postponing this consumption. Third, some funds may be coming from abroad, that is, from foreign savers. The cost of these funds is the marginal cost of foreign borrowing. Thus, the economic opportunity cost of capital will simply be a weighted average of the costs of funds from three alternative sources. The detailed methodology for measuring the economic opportunity cost of capital will be discussed later.

4.3 Alternative Investment Criteria

Various criteria have been used in the past to evaluate whether an investment project is financially and economically viable. In this section, six of these criteria will be reviewed, namely the NPV, the IRR, the BCR, the pay-out or pay-back period, the debt service coverage ratio, and cost-effectiveness.

4.3.1 Net Present Value Criterion

The NPV is the algebraic sum of the present values of the expected incremental net cash flows for a project over the project's anticipated lifetime. It measures the change in wealth created by the project.

a) When to Accept and Reject Projects

If the NPV of the project is 0, investors can expect to recover their incremental investment and also earn a rate of return on their capital that would have been earned elsewhere and is equal to the private discount rate used to compute the present values. This implies that investors would be neither worse nor better off than they would have been if they had left the funds in the capital market. A positive NPV for a project means that investors can expect not only to recover their capital investment but also to receive a rate of return on capital higher than the discount rate. However, if the NPV is less than 0, investors cannot expect to earn a rate of return equal to the discount rate, nor can they expect to recover their invested capital, and, hence, their real net worth is expected to decrease. Only projects with a positive NPV are attractive to private investors. Such investors are unlikely to pursue a project with a negative NPV unless there are strategic reasons for doing so. Many of these strategic reasons can also be evaluated in terms of their NPVs through the valuation of the real options made possible by the strategic project. This leads to Decision Rule 1 of the NPV criterion, which holds under all circumstances.

Rule 1: Do not accept any project unless it generates a positive NPV when discounted by the opportunity cost of funds.

b) Budget Constraints

Often, investors cannot obtain sufficient funds to undertake all the available projects that have a positive NPV. This is also the case for governments. When such a situation arises, a choice must be made between the projects to determine the subset that will maximize the NPV produced by the investment package while fitting within the budget constraint. Thus, Decision Rule 2 is:

Rule 2: Within the limit of a fixed budget, choose the subset of the available projects that maximizes the NPV.

Since a budget constraint does not require that all the money be spent, the rule will prevent any project that has a negative NPV from being undertaken. Even if not all the funds in the budget are spent, the NPV generated by the funds in the budget will be increased if a project with a negative NPV is dropped from consideration. It should be kept in mind that the funds assigned by the budget allocation but not spent will simply remain in the capital market and continue to generate a rate of return equal to the economic opportunity cost of capital.

Suppose the following set of projects describes the investment opportunities faced by an investor with a fixed budget for capital expenditures of $4.0 million:

	Project A	Project B	Project C	Project D
PV investment costs	$1.0 million	$3.0 million	$2.0 million	$2.0 million
NPV of net benefits	+$60,000	+$400,000	+$150,000	+$225,000

Given a budget constraint of $4 million, all possible combinations that fit within this constraint would be explored. Combinations BC and BD are not feasible as they cost too much. AC and AD are within the budget, but are overshadowed by the combination AB, which has a total NPV of $460,000. The only other feasible combination is CD, but its NPV of $375,000 is not as high as that of AB. If the budget constraint was expanded to $5 million, Project A should be dropped and Project D undertaken in conjunction with Project B. In this case, the NPV from this package of projects (BD) is expected to be $625,000, which is greater than the NPV of the next-best alternative (BC), $550,000.

Suppose that Project A, instead of having an NPV of +$60,000, has an NPV of −$60,000. If the budget constraint was still $4.0 million, the best strategy would be to undertake only Project B, which would yield an NPV of $400,000. In this case, $1 million of the budget would remain in the capital market, even though it is the budget constraint that is preventing the undertaking of potentially favourable Projects C and D.

c) No Budget Constraints

In evaluating investment projects, situations are often encountered in which there is a choice between mutually exclusive projects. It may not be possible for all projects to be undertaken, for technical reasons. For example, in building a road between two towns, there are several different qualities of road that can be built, given that only one road will be built. The problem facing the investment analyst is to choose from among the mutually exclusive alternatives such that the project will yield the maximum NPV. This can be expressed as Decision Rule 3:

Rule 3: When there is no budget constraint but a project must be chosen from mutually exclusive alternatives, investors should always choose the alternative that generates the largest NPV.

Consider three projects — E, F, and G — that are mutually exclusive for technical reasons and have the following characteristics:

	Project E	Project F	Project G
PV investment costs	$1.0 million	$4.0 million	$1.5 million
NPV of net benefits	+$300,000	+$700,000	+$600,000

In this situation, all three are good potential projects that would yield a positive NPV. However, only one can be undertaken.

Project F involves the highest expenditure; it also has the largest NPV, $700,000. Thus, Project F should be chosen. Although Project G has the highest NPV per dollar of investment, this is not relevant if the discount rate reflects the economic opportunity cost of the funds. If Project F is undertaken rather than Project G, there is an incremental gain in NPV of $100,000 over and above the opportunity cost of the additional investment of $2.5 million. Therefore, Project F is preferred. It is worth pointing out that the NPV of a project measures the value or surplus generated by a project over and above what would be gained or generated by these funds if they were not used in the project in question.

d) Projects with Different Lifetimes

In some situations, an investment in a facility such as a road can be carried out in a number of mutually exclusive ways. For example, the road services could be provided by a series of projects with short lives, such as installing a gravel surface, or by ones with longer lives, such as installing a paved surface. If the return on the expansion of the facility over its lifetime is such as to be an investment opportunity that would yield a significantly positive NPV, it would not be meaningful to compare the NPV of a project that produced road services for the full duration with the NPV of a project that produced road services for only part of the period. The same issue arises when alternative investment strategies are evaluated for power generation. It is not correct to compare the NPV of a gas turbine plant with a life of ten years to a coal-generation station having a life of 30 years. In such a case, the comparison must be between investment strategies that have approximately the same length of life. This may involve comparing a series of gas turbine projects followed by other types of generation that in total have the same length of life as the coal plant.

When projects of short duration lead to further projects that yield supra-marginal returns, the comparison of alternative projects of different lengths that will provide the same services at a point in time will require adjustments to be made to investment strategies so that they span approximately the same period of time. One such form of adjustment is to consider the same project being repeated through time until the alternative investment strategies have the same duration. Consider the following three types of road surface.

Alternative Investment Projects	Duration of Road
A: Gravel-surfaced road	3 years
B: Gravel–tar-surfaced road	5 years
C: Asphalt-surfaced road	15 years

Comparing the NPVs of these three alternatives lasting three, five, and fifteen years could produce misleading results. However, it is possible to make a correct comparison of these projects by constructing an investment strategy consisting of five gravel road projects, each undertaken at a date in the future when the previous one is worn out. A comparison could then be made of five gravel road projects, extending 15 years into the future, with three tar-surface roads and one asphalt road of 15-year duration. This comparison can be written as follows:

Alternative Strategies	Duration of Road
(i) (A + A + A + A + A)	15 years (i.e., 1–3, 4–6, 7–9, 10–12, 13–15)
(ii) (B + B + B)	15 years (i.e., 1–5, 6–10, 11–15)
(iii) (C)	15 years (i.e., 1–15)

Alternatively, it might be preferable to consider investment strategies made up of a mix of different types of road surfaces through time, such as:

Alternative Strategies	Duration of Road
(iv) (A + A + A + B + C)	29 years (i.e., 1–3, 4–6, 7–9, 10–14, 15–29)
(v) (A + B + B + C)	28 years (i.e., 1–3, 4–8, 9–13, 14–28)

In this situation, a further adjustment should be made to the 29-year strategy (iv) to make it comparable to strategy (v), which is expected to last for only 28 years. This can be done by calculating the NPV of the project after dropping the benefits accruing in Year 29 from the NPV calculation, while at the same time multiplying the present value of its costs by the fraction $(PVB_{1-28})/PVB$, where PVB denotes the present value of the benefits of the entire strategy, including Year 29, and PVB_{1-28} is the present value of the benefits that arise in the first 28 years of the project's life. In this way, the present value of the costs of the project are reduced by the same fraction as the present value of its benefits so that it will be comparable in terms of both costs and benefits to the strategy with the shorter life.

Although the NPV criterion is widely used in making investment decisions, alternative criteria are also frequently employed. Some of these alternatives have serious drawbacks compared with the NPV criterion and are therefore judged to be not only less reliable but also potentially misleading. When two or more criteria are used to appraise a project, there is a chance that they will point to different conclusions, and a wrong decision could be made (see, e.g., Ley, 2007). This creates unnecessary confusion and, potentially, mistakes.

4.3.2 Internal Rate of Return Criterion

The IRR for a project is the discount rate (ρ) that is obtained by the solution of the following equation:

$$\sum_{j=0}^{n} [(B_j - C_j) / (1+\rho)^j] = 0 \qquad (4.4)$$

where B_j and C_j are the respective cash inflow and outflow in Year j to capital. This definition is consistent with the meaning of an NPV of 0: that investors recover their invested capital and earn a rate of return equal to the IRR. Thus, the IRR and the NPV criteria are related in terms of the way they are derived. To calculate the NPV, the discount rate is given and used to find the present value of benefits and costs. In contrast, when finding the IRR of a project, the procedure is reversed by setting the NPV of the net benefit stream to 0.

The IRR criterion has seen considerable use by both private and public sector investors as a way of describing the attractiveness of a particular project. However, it is not a reliable investment criterion, as there are several problems associated with it.

Problem 1: The IRR may not be unique

The IRR is, strictly speaking, the root of a mathematical equation. The equation is based on the time profile of the incremental net cash flows, like those in Figure 4.2. If the time profile crosses the horizontal axis from negative to positive only once, as in Figure 4.2 a), the root, or IRR, will exist. However, if the time profile crosses the axis more than once, as in Figure 4.2 b) and Figure 4.2 c), it may not be possible to determine a unique IRR. Projects whose major items of equipment must be replaced from time to time will give rise to periodic negative net cash flows in the years of reinvestment. Road projects have this characteristic, as major expenditures on resurfacing must be undertaken periodically for them to remain serviceable.

Figure 4.2: Time Profiles of the Incremental Net Cash Flows for Various Types of Projects

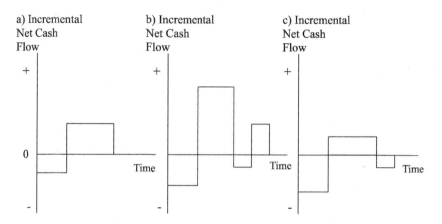

a) Incremental Net Cash Flow

b) Incremental Net Cash Flow

c) Incremental Net Cash Flow

There are also cases in which the termination of a project entails substantial costs. Examples of such situations are the land reclamation costs required to meet environmental standards at the closing down of a mine, or the agreement to restore rented facilities to their former state. These cases are illustrated by Figure 4.2 c). These project files may yield multiple solutions for the IRR; these multiple solutions, when present, represent a problem of proper choice of the rate of return.

Consider the simple case of an investment of $100 in Year 0, a net benefit of $300 in Year 1, and a net cost of $200 in Year 2. The solutions for the IRR are 0 and 100 percent.

Even when the IRR can be unambiguously calculated for each project under consideration, its use as an investment criterion poses difficulties when some of the projects in question are strict alternatives. This can arise in three ways: projects require different sizes of investment, projects are of different durations, and projects represent different timings for a project. In each of these three cases, the IRR can lead to the incorrect choice of project.

Problem 2: Projects of different scale

The problem of having to choose between two or more mutually exclusive projects arises quite frequently. Examples include two alternative buildings being considered for the same site and a new highway that could run down two alternative rights of way. Whereas the NPV takes explicit account of the scale of the project by means of the investment that is required, the IRR ignores the differences in scale.

Consider a case in which Project A has an investment cost of $1,000 and is expected to generate net cash flows of $300 each year in perpetuity. Project B is a strict alternative and has an investment cost of $5,000. It is expected to generate net cash flows of $1,000 each year in perpetuity. The IRR for Project A is 30 percent ($p_A = 300/1,000$), while the IRR for Project B is 20 percent ($p_B = 1,000/5,000$). However, the NPV of Project A using a 10 percent discount rate is $2,000, while the NPV of Project B is $5,000.

In this example, if a choice is made between Projects A and B, the IRR criterion would lead to Project A being chosen because it has an IRR of 30 percent, which is higher than the 20 percent for Project B. However, the fact that Project B is larger enables it to produce a greater NPV even if its IRR is smaller. Thus, the NPV criterion indicates that Project B should be chosen. This illustration demonstrates that when a choice has to be made among mutually exclusive projects with different sizes of investment, the use of the IRR criterion can lead to the incorrect choice of projects.

Problem 3: Projects with different lengths of life

In this case there are two projects, C and D. Project C calls for the planting of a species of tree that can be harvested in five years, while Project D calls for the planting of a type of tree that can be harvested in ten years. The investment costs are the same for both projects at $1,000. It is also assumed that neither of the projects can be repeated. The two projects can be analysed as follows:

	Project C	Project D
Investment costs:	$1,000 in Year 0	$1,000 in Year 0
Net benefits:	$3,200 in Year 5	$5,200 in Year 10
NPV criterion @ 8%:	$NPV_C^0 = \$1,178$	$NPV_D^0 = \$1,409$

$$NPV_C^0 < NPV_D^0$$

IRR criterion:	$p_C = 26.2\%$	$p_D = 17.9\%$

$$p_C > p_D$$

According to the NPV criterion, Project D is preferred. However, the IRR of Project D is smaller than that of Project C. Thus, the IRR criterion is unreliable for project selection when alternative projects have different lengths of life.

Problem 4: Projects with different timing

Suppose two projects, E and F, are started at different times and both last for one year. Project F is started five years after Project E. Both projects have investment costs of $1,000. They are summarized as follows:

	Project E	Project F
Investment costs:	$1,000 in Year 0	$1,000 in Year 5
Net benefits:	$1,500 in Year 1	$1,600 in Year 6
NPV criterion @ 8%:	$NPV_E^0 = \$389$	$NPV_F^0 = \$328$

$$NPV_E^0 > NPV_F^0$$

IRR criterion: $\rho_E = 50\%$ $\rho_F = 60\%$

$$\rho_E < \rho_F$$

Evaluating these two projects according to the NPV criterion would indicate that Project E should be chosen over Project F because $NPV_E^0 > NPV_F^0$. However, the fact that $\rho_E < \rho_F$ suggests that Project F should be chosen if the IRR criterion is used. Again, because Projects E and F are strict alternatives, use of the IRR criterion can result in the incorrect choice of project being made.

Problem 5: Irregularity of cash flows

In many situations the cash flows of a project may be negative in a single (investment) period, though this does not occur at the beginning of the project. An example of such a situation would be a build–operate–transfer (BOT) arrangement from the point of view of the government. During the operating stage of this project, the government is likely to receive tax benefits from the private operator. At the point when the project is turned over to the public sector, the government has agreed to pay a transfer price. Such a cash flow from the government's point of view can be illustrated as Project A in Table 4.2, where the transfer price at the end of the contract is $8,000.

Table 4.2: IRR for Irregular Cash Flows

Year	0	1	2	3	4	IRR
Project A	1,000	1,200	800	3,600	−8,000	10%
Project B	1,000	1,200	800	3,600	−6,400	−2%
Project C	1,000	1,200	800	3,600	−4,800	−16%
Project D	−1,000	1,200	800	3,600	−4,800	4%
Project E	−1,325	1,200	800	3,600	−4,800	20%
Results:						
Project B is obviously better than Project A, yet IRR$_A$ > IRR$_B$.						
Project C is obviously better than Project B, yet IRR$_B$ > IRR$_C$.						
Project D is worse than Project C, yet IRR$_D$ > IRR$_C$.						
Project E is worse than Project D, yet IRR$_E$ > IRR$_D$.						

This four-year project has an IRR of 10 percent. However, suppose the negotiators for the government were successful in obtaining a lower transfer price at the end of the private sector's contract period. The situation where the contract price is reduced to $6,400 is shown as Project B. Everything else is the same as Project A except for the lower transfer payment at the end of that period. In this case, the IRR falls from 10 to –2 percent. It is obvious that the arrangement under Project B is better for the government than Project A, yet it has a lower IRR. If the transfer price were reduced further to $4,800, the IRR falls to −16 percent, yet it is obvious that it is a better project than either Project A or Project B.

Now consider the situation if the government were required to pay an amount of $1,000 at the start of the project in addition to a final transfer price of $4,800 at the end. It is obvious that this is an inferior arrangement (Project D) for the government over the previous one (Project C), in which no upfront payment is required. However, according to the IRR criterion, it is a much improved project, with an IRR of 4 percent.

In the final case, Project E, the situation for the government is made worse by requiring an upfront fee of $1,325 in Year 0, in addition to the transfer price of $4,800 in Year 4. Yet according to the IRR criterion, the arrangement is more attractive with an IRR of 20 percent.

None of these situations are unusual. Such patterns in the case flow are common in project finance arrangements. However, the IRR is found to be a highly unreliable measure of the financial attractiveness of such arrangements when irregular cash flows are likely to exist.

4.3.3 Benefit–Cost Ratio Criterion

The BCR, sometimes referred to as the profitability index, is the ratio of the present value of the cash inflows (or benefits) to the present value of the cash outflows (or costs) using the opportunity cost of funds as the discount rate:

$$BCR = \frac{PV \ of \ Cash \ Inflows \ (or \ Benefits)}{PV \ of \ Cash \ Outflows \ (or \ Costs)}$$

Using this criterion, in order for a project to be acceptable, the BCR must have a value greater than 1. Moreover, for choices between mutually exclusive projects, the rule would be to choose the alternative with the highest BCR.

However, this criterion may produce an incorrect ranking of projects if the projects differ in size. Consider the following cases of mutually exclusive projects A, B, and C:

	Project A	Project B	Project C
PV investment costs	$1.0 million	$8.0 million	$1.5 million
PV benefits	$1.3 million	$9.4 million	$2.1 million
NPV of net benefits	$0.3 million	$1.4 million	$0.6 million
BCR	1.3	1.175	1.4

In this example, if the projects were ranked according to their BCRs, Project C would be chosen. However, since the NPV of Project C is less than the NPV of Project B, the ranking of the projects should result in Project B being selected; thus, the BCR criterion would lead to an incorrect investment decision.

The second problem associated with the use of the BCR, and perhaps its most serious drawback, is that the BCR of a project is sensitive to the way in which costs are defined in setting out the cash flows. For example, if a good being sold is taxed at the manufacturer's level, the cash flow item for receipts could be recorded either net or gross of sales taxes.

In addition, costs can also be recorded in more than one way. Suppose that a project has the recurrent costs. In this case, the BCR will be altered by the way these costs are accounted for. All the costs and benefits are discounted by the cost of capital at 10 percent and expressed in dollars.

	Project D	Project E
PV investment costs	$1,200	$100
PV gross benefits	$2,000	$2,000
PV recurrent costs	$500	$1,800

If the recurrent costs are netted out from cash inflows, Project E would be preferred to Project D according to the BCR because:

$BCR_D = (2,000 - 500)/1,200 = 1.25$

$BCR_E = (2,000 - 1,800)/100 = 2.00$

However, if the recurrent costs are instead added to the present value of cash outflows, Project D appears to be more attractive than Project E:

$BCR_D = 2,000/(500 + 1,200) = 1.18$

$BCR_E = 2,000/(1,800 + 100) = 1.05$

Hence, the ranking of the two projects can be reversed depending on the treatment of recurrent costs in the calculation of the BCR. On the other hand, the NPV of a project is not sensitive to the way the costs are treated, and therefore, it is far more reliable than the BCR as a criterion for project selection.

4.3.4 Pay-out or Pay-back Period

The pay-out or pay-back period measures the number of years it will take for the net cash flows to repay the capital investment. Projects with the shortest payback period are preferred. This method is easy to use when making investment decisions. The criterion puts a large premium on projects that have a quick payback, and thus, it has been a popular criterion in making business investment choices.[10] Unfortunately, it may provide the wrong results, especially in the case of investments with a long life, where future net benefits are known with a considerable degree of certainty.

In its simplest form, the pay-out period measures the number of years it will take for the undiscounted net cash flows to repay the investment. A more sophisticated version of this rule compares the discounted benefits over a

---

[10]This criterion has similar characteristics to the loan life cover ratio (LLCR) used by bankers. This might explain its continued use in business decision-making.

number of years from the beginning of the project with the discounted investment costs. An arbitrary limit may be set on the maximum number of years allowed, and only those investments that have enough benefits to offset all investment costs within this period will be acceptable.

The use of the pay-back period as an investment criterion by the private sector is often a reflection of a high level of risk, especially political risk. Suppose a private venture is expected to receive a subsidy or be allowed to operate only as long as the current government is in power. In such circumstances, in order for a private investor to go ahead with this project, it is critical that the pay-back period of the project is shorter than the expected tenure of the government.

The implicit assumption of the pay-out period criterion is that benefits accruing beyond the time set as the pay-out period are so uncertain that they should be disregarded. It also ignores any investment costs that might occur beyond that date, such as the landscaping and replanting costs arising from the closure of a strip mine. While the future is undoubtedly more uncertain than the present, it is unrealistic to assume that beyond a certain date, the net benefits are 0. This is particularly true for long-term investments such as bridges, roads, and dams. There is no reason to expect that all quick-yielding projects are superior to long-term investments.

As an example, two projects are illustrated in Figure 4.3. Both are assumed to have identical capital costs (i.e., $C^a = C^b$). However, the benefit profiles of the two projects are such that Project A has greater benefits than Project B in each period until Period t^*. From Period t^* to t_b, Project A yields zero net benefits, but Project B yields positive benefits, as shown in the shaded area.

With a pay-out period of t^* years, Project A will be preferred to Project B because for the same costs, it yields greater benefits earlier. However, in terms of the NPV of the overall project, it is very likely that Project B, with its greater benefits in later years, will be significantly superior. In such a situation, the pay-back period criterion would give the wrong recommendation for the choice between investments.

Figure 4.3: Comparison of Two Projects with Differing Lives using Pay-out Period

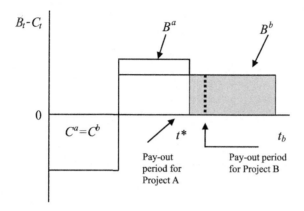

4.3.5 Debt Service Coverage Ratios

The debt service coverage ratio is a key factor in determining the ability of a project to pay its operating expenses and to meet its debt servicing obligations. It is used by bankers who want to know the annual debt service capacity ratio (ADSCR) of a project on a year-to-year basis, and to obtain a summary ratio of the loan life cover ratio (LLCR) (Yescombe, 2002).

The ADSCR is the ratio of the annual net cash flow of the project over the amount of debt repayment due. It is calculated on a year-to-year basis as follows:

$$ADSCR_t = [ANCF_t / (Annual\ Debt\ Repayment_t)]$$

where $ANCF_t$ is annual net cash flow of the project before financing for Period t and $Annual\ Debt\ Repayment_t$ is annual interest expenses and principal repayment due in the specific period t of the loan-repayment period.

The overall project's LLCR is calculated as the present value of net cash flows divided by present value of loan repayments from the current period t to the end period of loan repayment:

$$LLCR_t = PV(ANCF_{t\ to\ end\ year\ of\ debt}) /$$
$$PV(Annual\ Debt\ Repayment_{t\ to\ end\ year\ of\ debt})$$

where $PV(ANCF_{t\ to\ end\ year\ of\ debt})$ and $PV(Annual\ Debt\ Repayment_{t\ to\ end\ year\ of\ debt})$ are the sum of the present values of annual net cash flows and annual debt repayments, respectively, over the current period t to the end of loan repayment. The discount rates used are the same as the interest rate being paid on the loan financing. The LLCR tells the banker whether there is enough cash from the project to make bridge financing in one or more specific periods when there is inadequate cash flow to service the debt.

Table 4.3 illustrates the example of an investment of $2 million being undertaken with a proposal for financing that includes a loan of $1 million bearing a nominal interest rate of 15 percent, with a repayment period of five years (with an equal repayment) beginning one year after the loan is given. The required rate of return on equity is assumed at 20 percent.

Table 4.3 shows the annual cash flows net of operating expenses, along with the annual debt service obligations. The project is not attractive to the banker since the ADSCRs are low, at only 1.07 in Years 1 and 2, with no single years giving a debt service ratio of more than 1.47. This means that there could be a cash shortfall and an inability to pay the lenders the principal repayment and interest that is due.

Table 4.3: Calculation of ADSCR (dollars)

Year	0	1	2	3	4	5
Net cash flow	−2,000,000	320,000	320,000	360,000	440,000	380,000
Debt repayment	0	298,316	298,316	298,316	298,316	298,316
ADSCR		1.07	1.07	1.21	1.47	1.27
Year	6	7	8	9	10	
Net cash flow	100,000	200,000	480,000	540,000	640,000	
Debt repayment						
ADSCR						

The question now is how the ADSCRs can be improved. There are fundamentally only three alternatives:

- decrease the interest rate on the loan;
- decrease the amount of debt financing; or
- increase the duration of the loan repayment.

a) Decrease the Interest Rate on the Loan

If the terms of the loan can be restructured so that the ADSCRs look better, it may be attractive to the banker to provide financing. Table 4.4 shows the effect of obtaining a concessional interest rate or interest rate subsidy for the loan. In this case it is assumed that a 1 percent interest rate can be obtained for the full five-year period that the loan is outstanding. The ADSCRs are much larger now, never becoming less than 1.55; however, such a financing subsidy might be very difficult to obtain.

Table 4.4: Decrease the Interest Rate on the Loan (dollars)

Year	0	1	2	3	4	5
Net cash flow	-2,000,000	320,000	320,000	360,000	440,000	380,000
Debt repayment	0	206,040	206,040	206,040	206,040	206,040
ADSCR		1.55	1.55	1.75	2.14	1.84
Year	6	7	8	9	10	
Net cash flow	100,000	200,000	480,000	540,000	640,000	
Debt repayment						
ADSCR						

b) Decrease the Amount of Debt Financing

Table 4.5 shows a case in which the amount of the loan is reduced from $1 million to $600,000. Here, the ADSCRs are found to increase greatly, so that they now never fall below a value of 1.79. Since the amount of the annual repayment of that loan becomes smaller (equity financing is increased), the ability of the project to service the debt becomes much more certain.

Table 4.5: Decrease the Amount of Borrowing by Increasing Equity to $1.4 Million (dollars)

Year	0	1	2	3	4	5
Net cash flow	-2,000,000	320,000	320,000	360,000	440,000	380,000
Debt repayment	0	178,989	178,989	178,989	178,989	178,989
ADSCR		1.79	1.79	2.01	2.46	2.12
Year	6	7	8	9	10	
Net cash flow	100,000	200,000	480,000	540,000	640,000	
Debt repayment						
ADSCR						

c) Increase the Duration of the Loan Repayment

Table 4.6 shows the case in which the duration of the loan is increased from five to ten years. If a financial institution is able to extend a loan for such a long period, the annual debt service obligations will fall greatly. The result is that except for Years 6 and 7, the annual debt service obligation never falls below 1.61. In Years 6 and 7, the ADSCRs are projected to be only 0.50 and 1.00, respectively. This is due to a projected fall in the net cash flows that might arise because of the need to make reinvestments or heavy maintenance expenditures in those years.

Table 4.6: Increase the Duration of Loan Repayment (dollars)

Year	0	1	2	3	4	5
Net cash flow	−2,000,000	320,000	320,000	360,000	440,000	380,000
Debt repayment	0	199,252	199,252	199,252	199,252	199,252
ADSCR		1.61	1.61	1.81	2.21	1.91

Year	6	7	8	9	10	
Net cash flow	100,000	200,000	480,000	540,000	640,000	
Debt repayment	199,252	199,252	199,252	199,252	199,252	
ADSCR	**0.50**	**1.00**	2.41	2.71	3.21	

The question now is whether the project has sufficiently strong net cash flows in the years following Years 6 and 7 to warrant the financial institution providing the project bridge financing for these two years. This additional new loan would be repaid from the surplus net cash flows in later years. In addressing this question, the LLCR is the appropriate criterion to determine whether the project should qualify for bridge financing. The present value of the net cash flows remaining until the end of the debt-repayment period, discounted at the loan interest rate, is divided by the present value of the debt repayments for the remaining duration of the loan. It is also discounted at the loan interest rate. These estimations are presented in Table 4.7.

The LLCRs for Years 6 and 7 are 1.77 and 2.21, respectively. This indicates that there are likely to be more than adequate net cash flows from the project to safely repay the bridge financing that is needed to cover the likely shortfalls in cash during Years 6 and 7.

If for some reason the banks were not comfortable providing the bridge financing needed to cover the cash flow shortfalls during Years 6 and 7, they might instead require the firm to build up a debt service reserve account during the first five years of the loan's life from the cash that is over and above the requirements for servicing the debt. Alternatively, the banker may require the debt service reserve account to be immediately financed out of the proceeds of the loan and equity financing. This debt service reserve account would be invested in short-term liquid assets that could be drawn down to meet the financing requirements during Years 6 and 7.

Table 4.7: Is Bridge Financing an Option? (dollars)

Year	0	1	2	3	4	5
Net cash flow	−2,000,000	320,000	320,000	360,000	440,000	380,000
Debt repayment	0	199,252	199,252	199,252	199,252	199,252
ADSCR		1.61	1.61	1.81	2.21	1.91
NPV of NCF		2,052,134	1,991,954	1,922,747	1,797,159	1,560,733
PV of debt repayments		1,150,000	1,093,360	1,028,224	953,318	867,176
LLCR		1.78	1.82	1.87	1.89	1.80

Year	6	7	8	9	10	
Net cash flow	100,000	200,000	480,000	540,000	640,000	
Debt repayment	199,252	199,252	199,252	199,252	199,252	
ADSCR	**0.50**	**1.00**	2.41	2.71	3.21	
NPV of NCF	1,357,843	1,446,519	1,433,497	1,096,522	640,000	
PV of debt repayments	768,112	654,189	523,178	372,515	199,252	
LLCR	**1.77**	**2.21**	2.74	2.94	3.21	

It is sometimes the case that the financial institutions servicing the loan will stipulate that if the ADSCR ever falls below a certain benchmark, say 1.8, it must stop paying dividends to the owners of the equity until a sinking fund of a specified size is created or a certain amount of the loan is repaid. In this way, the lenders are protected from what might become an even more precarious situation in the future.

The actual benchmark requirements for the ADSCRs and the overall project's LLCRs will depend on the business and financial risk associated with a particular sector and the specific enterprise. The sensitivity of the net cash flows from the project to movements in the economy's business cycle will be an important determinant of what the adequate ratios for any specific project are. The existence of creditable government guarantees for the repayment of interest and principal will also serve to lower the benchmark values of the debt service coverage ratios for a project.

4.3.6 Cost–Effectiveness Analysis[11]

This is an appraisal technique primarily used in social projects and programmes, and sometimes in infrastructure projects, where it is difficult to quantify benefits in monetary terms. For instance, when there are two or more alternative approaches to improving the nutrition levels among children in a community, the selection criterion could simply be to select the alternative that has the least cost. A similar case occurs when there are two alternatives for providing

---

[11]See Curry and Weiss (1993) and Gittinger (1994) for discussion of cost–effectiveness analysis.

irrigation facilities to farmers in a certain region, for example, a canal system and a tube well network, and they cover the same area and provide the same volume of water in a year. The benefits in such cases are treated as identical, and, therefore, it is not necessary to quantify them or to place a monetary value on them if the problem is to select the project that will produce these benefits at the lowest possible cost.

This approach is also useful for choosing between different technologies for providing the same services, for example, when there are two alternative technologies related to the supply of drinking water or the generation of electricity. When the same quantity and quality of water per annum can be delivered using pipes of different diameters, and the smaller pipe involves greater pumping costs but has lower capital costs, a cost–effectiveness analysis may be used for making a choice. A similar situation occurs when there are two alternative ways of generating electricity, one with a lower investment cost but higher operating expenses (single-cycle versus combined-cycle technologies). Again, if the decision has been made to provide this service, there is no need to calculate the benefit in monetary terms. The cost–effectiveness analysis may be used in all such cases for selecting the best project or the best technology.

If the amount of benefits of the alternative projects differ, and if the benefits cannot be measured in monetary terms but can be physically quantified, the pure cost–effectiveness of a project can be calculated by dividing the present value of total costs of the project by the present value of a non-monetary quantitative measure of the benefits it generates. The ratio is an estimate of the amount of costs incurred to achieve a unit of the benefit from a programme. For example, in a health project, what are the costs, expressed in dollars, incurred in saving a person's life? Presumably, there are alternative ways to save a life; what are their costs? The analysis does not evaluate benefits in monetized terms, but is an attempt to find the least-cost option to achieve a desired quantitative outcome.

In applying the cost–effectiveness approach, the present values of costs need to be computed. While using the cost–effectiveness analysis, it is important to include all external costs – such as waiting time, coping costs, enforcement costs, regulatory costs, and compliance costs in the case of health care, offset by the salvage values at the end of the projects – and to choose the discount rate carefully. The preferred outcome will often change with a change in the discount rate.

Pure cost–effectiveness analysis can be extended to more sophisticated and meaningful ways of measuring benefits. A quantitative measure can be made by constructing a composite index of two or more benefit categories, including quantity and quality. For example, the cost–utility analysis in health care uses quality-adjusted life-years (QALYs) as a measure of benefits. The QALY measure integrates two dimensions of health improvement, namely the additional years of life (reduction in mortality) and the quality of life (morbidity) during these years. On the basis of the costs incurred, expressed in dollars, the decision-maker would still choose the option with the least cost per QALY achieved by the project or the programme (see, e.g., Garber and Phelps, 1997).

Cost–utility analysis attempts to include some of the benefits excluded from a pure cost–effective analysis, hence moving it a step closer to a full cost–benefit analysis.

One should be aware of some of the shortcomings inherent in the cost–effectiveness approach. It is a poor measure of consumers' willingness to pay in principle because there is no monetary value placed on the benefits. Furthermore, in the calculation of the cost–effectiveness ratio, the numerator does not take into account the scale of alternative options. Nevertheless, this ratio is still a very useful criterion for selection of alternative options when the benefits cannot be monetized.

4.4 Conclusion

This chapter first described the concept of time value of money and the proper use of the discount rate in project appraisal. It reviewed six important criteria used by various analysts for judging the expected performance of investment projects. While each one may have its own merit in specific circumstances, the NPV criterion is the most reliable and satisfactory one for both the financial and the economic evaluation.

For bankers and other financial lending institutions, measurements of the ADSCR and LLCR are the key factors that enable them to determine whether a project can generate enough cash to meet the debt service obligations before financing of the project should be approved.

The chapter has also discussed the situation in which the benefits of a project or a programme cannot be expressed in monetary values in a meaningful way; in such a case, a cost–effectiveness analysis should be carried out to assist in making welfare-improving investment decisions.

References

Boardman, A.E., D.H. Greenberg, A.R. Vining, and D.L. Weimer. 2001. *Cost-Benefit Analysis: Concepts and Practice*, 2nd edition. Englewood Cliffs, NJ: Prentice Hall.

Curry, S. and J. Weiss. 1993. *Project Analysis in Developing Countries*. New York: St. Martin's Press.

Garber, A.M. and C.E. Phelps. 1997. "Economic Foundations of Cost-Effectiveness Analysis", *Journal of Health Economics* 16(1), 1–31.

Gitman, L.J. 2009. *Principles of Managerial Finance*, 12th edition. Boston: Pearson Prentice Hall.

Gittinger J.P. 1994. *Economic Analysis of Agricultural Projects*. Baltimore, MD: Johns Hopkins University Press.

Gramlich, E.M. 1997. *A Guide to Cost-Benefit Analysis*. Englewood Cliffs, NJ: Prentice Hall.

Ley, E. 2007. "Cost-Benefit Analysis: Evaluation Criteria (Or: 'Stay away from the IRR')", paper prepared for the World Bank (November).

Pohl, G. and M. Dubravko. 1992. "Project Evaluation and Uncertainty in Practice: A Statistical Analysis of Rate-of-Return Divergences of 1,015 World Bank Projects", *The World Bank Economic Review* 6(2), 255–277.

Walker, C. and A.J. Smith. 1996. *Privatized Infrastructure: The Build Operate Transfer Approach.* London: Thomas Telford Publications.

Yescombe, E.R. 2002. *Principles of Project Finance.* London: Academic Press.

Chapter Five

Scale, Timing, Length, and Interdependencies in Project Selection

5.1 Introduction

In the previous chapter, it was concluded that a project's net present value (NPV) is the most important criterion for financial and economic evaluation. The NPV criterion requires that only projects with a positive NPV are approved. The next step is to endeavour to maximize the NPV in order to extract as much value from the project as possible. The aim should be to maximize the NPV of incremental net cash flows or net economic benefits. Of course, such optimization should not be pursued blindly, as it may have repercussions for other stakeholders that need to be considered in the final decision-making.

Project analysts often encounter a range of other important considerations. These include changes in project parameters, such as the scale of investment, the date of initiation of a project, the length of project life, or interdependencies of project components. Each of these is addressed in this chapter using the criterion of a project's NPV.

5.2 Determination of Scale in Project Selection

Projects are rarely, if ever, constrained by technological factors to a unique capacity or scale. Thus, one of the most important decisions to be made in the design of a project is the selection of the scale to which a facility should be built. In too many cases, scale selection has been treated as if it were a purely technical decision, neglecting its financial or economic aspects. When financial or economic considerations have been neglected at the design stage, the scale to which the project is built is not likely to be the one that would maximize the NPV. Thus, in addition to technological factors, the size of the market, the availability of project inputs, and the quality of manpower, etc. will also have a role to play.

The most important principle for selecting the best scale of a project (e.g., height of an irrigation dam or size of a factory) is to treat each incremental change in its size as a project in itself. An increase in the scale of a project will require additional expenditures and is likely to generate additional expected benefits over and above those that would have been produced by the project at its previous size. Using the present value of the incremental benefits and the present value of the incremental costs, the change in NPV stemming from changing scales of the project can be derived. In Figure 5.1, the cash flow profiles of a project are shown for three alternative scales. C_1 and B_1 denote the expected costs and benefits if the project is built at the smallest scale relevant for this evaluation. If the project is built at one size larger, it will require additional expenditure of C_2. Therefore, the total investment cost of the project at its expanded scale is $(C_1 + C_2)$. It is also anticipated that the benefits of the project will be increased by an amount of B_2, implying that the total benefits from this scale of investment will now be $(B_1 + B_2)$. A similar relationship holds for the largest scale of the project. In this case, additional expenditures of C_3 are required, and extra benefits of B_3 are expected. The total investment costs for this scale are $(C_1 + C_2 + C_3)$, and the total benefits $(B_1 + B_2 + B_3)$.

Figure 5.1: Net Benefit Profiles for Alternative Scales of a Facility

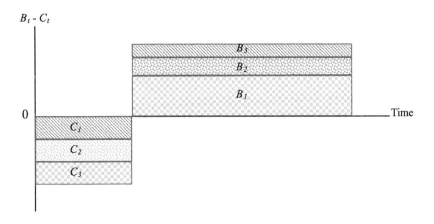

The goal is to choose the scale that has the highest NPV. If the present value of $(B_1 - C_1)$ is positive, it is a viable project. The next step is to determine whether the present value of $(B_2 - C_2)$ is positive. If the incremental NPV is positive, then this project at scale 2 is preferable to scale 1. This procedure is repeated until a scale is reached where the NPV of the incremental benefits and costs associated with a change in scale is negative. This incremental NPV approach helps in the choice of a scale that has maximum NPV for the entire investment. The NPV is the maximum because the incremental NPV for any addition to the scale of the project would be negative. If the initial scale of the project had a negative NPV but all the subsequent incremental NPVs for changes of scale were positive, it would still be possible for the overall project to have a negative NPV. Therefore, in order to select the optimum scale for a project, it is necessary to first ensure that the NPV of the overall project is positive, and that the NPV of the last addition to the investment to increase the project's scale is non-negative. This is illustrated in Figure 5.2, in which all project sizes between scale *C* and scale *M* yield a positive NPV. However, the NPV of the entire investment is maximized at scale *H*. After scale *H*, the incremental NPV of any expansion of the facility becomes negative. Therefore, the optimum scale for the project is *H*, even though the NPV for the entire project is still positive until scale *M*.

Figure 5.2: Relationship between NPV and Scale

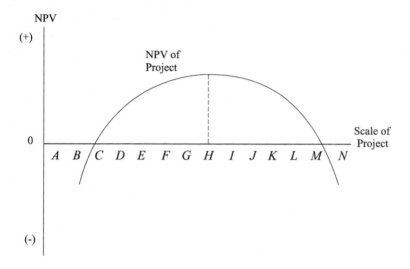

The optimal scale of a project can also be determined by the use of the internal rate of return (IRR), assuming that each successive increment of investment has a unique IRR. If this condition is met, the optimal scale of the facility will be the one at which the IRR for the incremental benefits and costs equals the discount rate used to calculate the NPV of the project. This IRR for the incremental investment required to change the scale of the project will be the marginal internal rate of return (MIRR) for a given scale of facility. The relationships between the IRR, the MIRR, and the NPV of a project are shown in Figure 5.3.

Scale, Timing, Length and Interdependencies

Figure 5.3: Relationships between the MIRR, IRR, and NPV

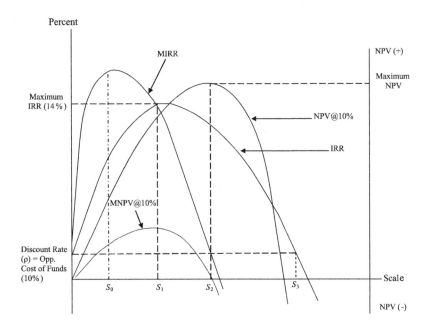

From Figure 5.3, it can be observed that in a typical project, the MIRR from incremental investments will initially rise as the scale is increased, but will soon begin to fall with further expansions. This path of the MIRR will also cause the IRR to rise for the initial ranges of scale and then to fall. At some point, the IRR and the MIRR must be equal and then change their relationship to each other. Prior to the point S_1 in Figure 5.3, the MIRR of the project is greater than the IRR: here, expansions of scale will cause the overall IRR of the project to rise. At scales beyond S_1, the MIRR is less than the IRR: in this range, expansions of scale will cause the overall IRR to fall.

The point at which the IRR equals the MIRR always corresponds to the scale at which the IRR is maximized. However, it is important to note that this is not the scale at which the NPV of the project is likely to be maximized. The NPV of a project obviously depends on the discount rate. Only when the relevant discount rate is precisely equal to the maximum IRR will S_1 be the optimal scale. If the relevant discount rate is lower, it pays to expand the project's scale up to the point where the MIRR is equal to the discount rate. As shown for the case in which the discount rate is 10 percent, this scale yields the maximum NPV at a scale of S_2 in Figure 5.3.

To illustrate this procedure for determining the optimal scale of a project, consider the construction of an irrigation dam that could be built at different heights. Because of the availability of water, the expectation would be that expansions of the scale of the dam would reduce the overall level of utilization of the facilities when measured as a proportion of its total potential capacity. The information is provided in Table 5.1.

Table 5.1: Determination of Optimal Scale of Irrigation Dam (dollars)

Time	0	1	2	3	4	5	...		
Scales	Costs	Benefits						NPV	IRR
S_0	−3,000	250	250	250	250	250	...	−500	0.083
S_1	−4,000	390	390	390	390	390	...	−100	0.098
S_2	−5,000	540	540	540	540	540	...	400	0.108
S_3	−6,000	670	670	670	670	670	...	700	0.112
S_4	−7,000	775	775	775	775	775	...	750	0.111
S_5	−8,000	865	865	865	865	865	...	650	0.108

Time	0	1	2	3	4	5	...		
Changes in scales	Incremental							Change in NPV	MIRR
	Costs	Benefits							
S_0	−3,000	250	250	250	250	250	...	−500	0.083
S_1-S_0	−1,000	140	140	140	140	140	...	400	0.140
S_2-S_1	−1,000	150	150	150	150	150	...	500	0.150
S_3-S_2	−1,000	130	130	130	130	130	...	300	0.130
S_4-S_3	−1,000	105	105	105	105	105	...	50	0.105
S_5-S_4	−1,000	90	90	90	90	90	...	−100	0.090

Notes: Discount rate (opportunity cost of funds) = 10 percent.
The depreciation rate of the dam is assumed to be zero.

In this example, the ΔNPV can be calculated for each scale of the dam from S_0 to S_5. Thus, the ΔNPV for S_0 is −500; for S_1-S_0, it is 400; for S_2-S_1, 500; for S_3-S_2, 300; for S_4-S_3, 50; and for S_5-S_4, −100.[12] Applying the above rule for determining the optimal scale would lead to scale S_4 being chosen because beyond this point, additions to scale contribute negatively to the overall NPV of the project. At scale S_4, the NPV of the project is +750; at scale S_3, it is +700; and at S_5, it is +650. Therefore, the NPV is maximized at S_4. If the project is expanded beyond scale 4, the NPV begins to fall, even though at scale S_5 the IRR of the entire project is still 0.108 (which is greater than the discount rate of 0.10). However, the MIRR is only 0.09, placing the marginal return from the last addition to scale below the discount rate.

---

[12]For perpetuity, the IRR can be calculated as the ratio of annual income to initial investment.

5.3 Timing of Investments

One of the most important steps in the process of project preparation and implementation is to decide on the appropriate time at which the project should start. This decision becomes particularly difficult for large indivisible projects, such as infrastructure investments in roads, water systems, and electricity-generation facilities. If these projects are built too soon, a large amount of idle capacity will exist. In such cases, the forgone return (that would have been realized if these funds had been invested elsewhere) might be higher in value than the benefits gained in the first few years of the project's life. Conversely, if a project is delayed for too long, shortages of goods or services will persist and the output forgone will be greater than the alternative yield of the funds involved.

Whenever a project is undertaken too early or too late, its NPV will be lower than the level it could have been if it had been developed at the right time. The NPV of a project may still be positive, but it will not be at its maximum.

The determination of the correct timing of investment projects will be a function of how it is anticipated that future benefits and costs will move in relation to their present values. Situations in which the timing of investment projects becomes an important issue can be classified into four different cases.

Case A — The benefits of the project are a continuously rising function of calendar time, but investment costs are independent of calendar time.

Case B — The benefits and investment costs of the project are rising with calendar time.

Case C — The benefits are rising and then falling with calendar time, while the investment costs are a function of calendar time.

Case D — The benefits and investment costs do not change systematically with calendar time.

Case A: Potential Benefits Are a Rising Function of Calendar Time

This is the case in which the benefits net of operating costs are continuously rising through time, and costs do not depend on calendar time. For example, the benefits of a road improvement project rise because of the growth in demand for transportation between two or more places. It can thus be expected that as population and income grow, the demand for the road will also increase through time.

If the project's investment period ends in Period t, it can be assumed that its net benefit stream will start the year after construction and will rise continuously thereafter. This potential benefit stream is illustrated by the curve $B(t)$ in Figure 5.4. If construction were postponed from t_1 to t_2, lost benefits amount to B_1, but the same capital in alternative uses yields rK, where K denotes the initial capital expenditure and r denotes the opportunity cost of capital for one period. Postponing construction from t_1 to t_2 thus yields a net gain of $AIDC$. Similarly, postponing construction from t_2 to t_3 yields a net benefit of CDE.

In this situation, the criterion for ensuring that investments are undertaken at the correct time is quite straightforward. If the present value of the benefits that are lost by postponing the start of the project from Period t to Period $t+1$ is less than the opportunity cost of capital multiplied by the present value of capital costs as of Period t, the project should be postponed because the funds would earn more in the capital market than if they were used to start the project. On the other hand, if the forgone benefits are greater than the opportunity cost of the investment, the project should proceed. In short, if $rK_t > B_{t+1}$, the decision should be to postpone the project; and if $rK_t < B_{t+1}$, the project should go ahead. Here t is the period in which the project is to begin, K_t is the present value of the investment costs of the project as of Period t, and B_{t+1} is the present value of the benefits lost by postponing the project for one period from t to t_1.

Figure 5.4: Timing of Projects: Benefits Are Rising, but Investment Costs Are Independent of Calendar Time

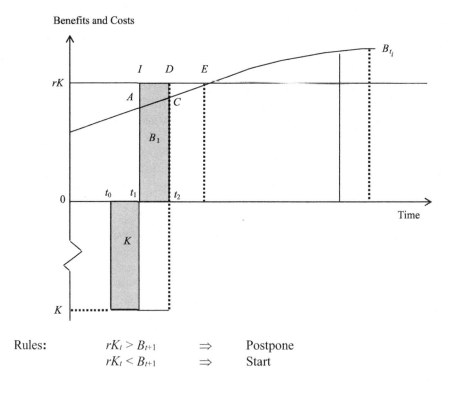

Rules: $rK_t > B_{t+1}$ $\Rightarrow$ Postpone

$rK_t < B_{t+1}$ $\Rightarrow$ Start

Scale, Timing, Length and Interdependencies

Case B: Both Investment Costs and Benefits Are a Function of Calendar Time

In this case, as illustrated in Figure 5.5, the investment costs and benefits of a project will grow continuously with calendar time. Suppose the capital cost is K_0 when the project is started in Period t_0 and the costs will become K_1 if it is started in Period t_1. The change in investment costs must be included in the calculations of optimum timing. When the costs of constructing a project are greater in Period 1 than in Period 0, there is an additional loss caused by postponement of $(K_1 - K_0)$, as shown by the area $FGHI$ in Figure 5.5.

Figure 5.5: Timing of Projects: Both Benefits and Investment Costs Are a Function of Calendar Time

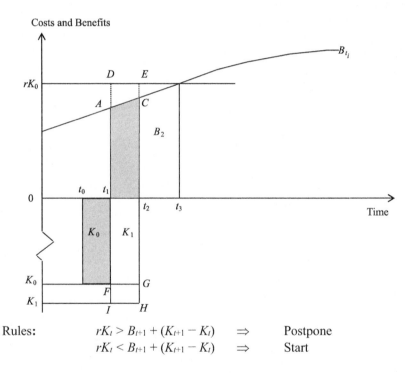

Rules: $rK_t > B_{t+1} + (K_{t+1} - K_t)$ $\Rightarrow$ Postpone
              $rK_t < B_{t+1} + (K_{t+1} - K_t)$ $\Rightarrow$ Start

In Case A, when benefits are a positive function of calendar time, the decision rule for the timing of investments is to postpone if $rK_0 > B_1$ and to proceed as soon as $B_{t+1} > rK_t$. Now, when the present value of the investment costs changes with the timing of the starting date, the rule is slightly modified: if $rK_0 > [B_1 + (K_1 - K_0)]$, postpone the project; otherwise, undertake the project. The term $(K_1 - K_0)$ represents the savings of the increase in capital costs by commencing the project in Period t_0 instead of t_1. The rule shows a comparison of the area t_1DEt_2 with $(t_1ACt_2 + FGHI)$. Hence, if investment costs are expected to rise in the future, the optimal option would be for the project to be undertaken earlier than if investment costs remained constant over time.

Case C: Potential Benefits Rise and Fall According to Calendar Time

In the case in which the potential benefits of the project are also a function of calendar time, but are not expected to grow continuously through time, at some date in the future they are expected to decline. For example, the growth in demand for a given type of electricity-generation plant in a country is expected to continue until it can be replaced by a cheaper technology. As the alternative form of technology becomes cheaper and more easily available, it is expected that the demand faced by the initial plant will decline through time. If the net benefits from an electricity-generation plant are directly related to the volume of production it generates, it would be expected that the pattern of benefits would appear similar to $B(t)$ in Figure 5.6.

Figure 5.6: Timing of Projects: Potential Benefits Rise and Decline with Calendar Time

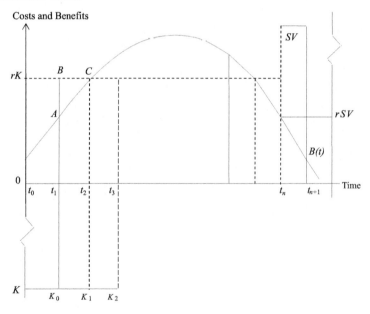

Rules: Start if $rK_{t_i} < B_{t_{i+1}}$

            Stop if $rSV_{t_n} - B_{t_{n+1}} - \Delta SV_{t_{n+1}} > 0$

            Do project if:

$$NPV^{t_i} = \sum_{i=t_{i+1}}^{t_n} \frac{B_i}{(1+r)^{i-t_i}} - K_{t_i} + \frac{SV_{t_n}}{(1+r)^{t_n-t_i}} > 0$$

Do not do project if:
$$NPV^{t_i} = \sum_{i=t_{i+1}}^{t_n} \frac{B_i}{(1+r)^{i-t_i}} - K_{t_i} + \frac{SV_{t_n}}{(1+r)^{t_n-t_i}} < 0$$

If the project with present value of costs of K_0 is undertaken in Period t_0, its first-year benefits will fall short of the opportunity cost of the funds shown by the area ABC. The correct point to start the project is t_1, when $rK_{t_1} < B_{t_2}$, and if the following project's NPV (measured by the present value of the area under the $B(t)$ curve minus K_1) is positive:

$$NPV = -K/(1+r) + \sum_{t=2}^{n}[B_t/(1+r)^t]$$

It is obviously essential that this NPV be positive in order for the project to be worthwhile.

The above formula assumes that the life of the project is infinite, or that after some time, its annual benefit flows fall to zero. Instead of lasting for its anticipated lifetime, the project could be abandoned at some point in time, with the result that a one-time benefit is generated, equal to its scrap value, SV. In this case, it pays to keep the project in operation only so long as $B_{t_{n+1}} > rSV_{t_n} - \Delta SV_{t_{n+1}}$, so it would make sense to stay in business during t_{n+1}. If $B_{t_{n+1}} < rSV_{t_n} - \Delta SV_{t_{n+1}}$, it would make more sense to shut down operations at the end of t_n.

In practice, there are five special cases in relation to scrap value and change in scrap value of a project:

- $SV > 0$ and $\Delta SV < 0$, e.g., machinery
- $SV > 0$ but $\Delta SV > 0$, e.g., land
- $SV < 0$ but $\Delta SV = 0$, e.g., a nuclear power plant
- $SV < 0$ but $\Delta SV > 0$, e.g., severance pay for workers
- $SV < 0$ and $\Delta SV < 0$, e.g., clean-up costs

In general, a project should be undertaken if the following condition is met:
$$NPV^{t_i} = \sum_{i=t_{i+1}}^{t_n} \frac{B_i}{(1+r)^{i-t_i}} - K_{t_i} + \frac{SV_{t_n}}{(1+r)^{t_n-t_i}} > 0 \tag{5.1}$$

If this condition cannot be met, and if
$$NPV^{t_i} = \sum_{i=t_{i+1}}^{t_n} \frac{B_i}{(1+r)^{i-t_i}} - K_{t_i} + \frac{SV_{t_n}}{(1+r)^{t_n-t_i}} < 0$$

the project should not be undertaken.

Case D: The Costs and Benefits Do Not Change Systematically with Calendar Time

This is perhaps the most common situation, in which there is no systematic movement in either costs or benefits with respect to calendar time. As illustrated in Figure 5.7, if a project is undertaken in Period t_0, its profile begins with investment costs of K_0, followed by a stream of benefits shown as the area t_1ABt_n. Alternatively, if it is postponed for one period, investment costs will be K_1, and benefits will be t_2CDt_{n+1}. In this case, the optimal date to start the project is determined by estimating the NPV of the project in each instance and choosing the time to start the project that yields the highest NPV.

It is important to note that in determining the timing of the project, the date to which the NPVs are calculated must be the same for all cases, even though the period in which the projects are to be initiated varies.

Figure 5.7: Timing of Projects: Benefits and Costs Do Not Change Systematically with Calendar Time

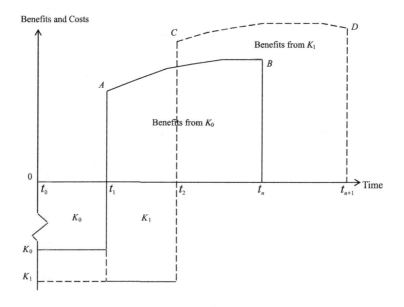

5.4 Adjusting for Different Lengths of Life

If there is no budget constraint, and if a choice must be made between two or more mutually exclusive projects, investors seeking to maximize net worth should select the project with the highest NPV. If the mutually exclusive projects are expected to have continuously high returns over time, it is necessary to consider the lengths of life of the two or more projects. The reason for wanting to ensure that mutually exclusive projects are compared over the same span of time is to give them the same opportunity to accumulate value over time. One way to think about the NPV is as an economic rent that is earned by a fixed factor of production. In the case of two mutually exclusive projects, for example, the fixed factor could be the building site, a right-of-way, or a licence. That fixed factor should have the same amount of time to generate economic rents, regardless of which project is chosen. What is required is a reasonable method of equalizing lengths of life that can be applied. This is elaborated with the help of the following two examples.

Example 1

Consider two mutually exclusive projects, Project A (three years) and Project B (four years), with the same scale of investment, and the net cash flows as shown in Table 5.2. All the net cash flows are expressed in thousands of dollars, and the cost of capital is 10 percent.

Table 5.2: Net Cash Flows for Projects with Different Lengths of Life (thousand dollars)

Time Period	t_0	t_1	t_2	t_3	NPV@10%
Net cash flows of Project A	−10,000	6,000	6,000		410
Net cash flows of Project B	−10,000	4,000	4,000	4,750	500

If the differences in the lengths of life were overlooked, Project B would be selected because it has the higher NPV. However, this would run the risk of rejecting the potentially better Project A with the shorter life.

One approach to addressing this problem is to determine whether the projects could be repeated a number of times (not necessarily the same number of times for each project) in order to equalize their lives. To qualify for this approach, both projects must be supra-marginal (i.e., have positive NPVs) and should be repeatable at least a finite number of times.

Assume that Projects A and B above meet these requirements. If Project A was repeated three times and Project B twice, both projects would have a total operating life of six years, as shown in Table 5.3.

In Year t_6, both projects can start up again, but there is no need to repeat this procedure. The construction of the repeated projects is initiated so as to maintain a level of service. For example, construction for the second Project B begins in Year t_3 so that it is ready to begin operations when the first Project B stops providing a service. Given the equal lengths of life for the repeated projects, they can now be compared on the basis of their NPV:

$$NPV \text{ of Project } A\text{'s repeats} = 410 + \frac{410}{(1.1)^2} + \frac{410}{(1.1)^4} = 1,029$$

$$NPV \text{ of Project } B\text{'s repeats} = 500 + \frac{500}{(1.1)^3} = 876$$

Given an equal opportunity to earn economic rents, Project A has a higher overall NPV and should be considered the more attractive project.

Table 5.3: Net Present Value for Repeating Projects

Time	t_0	t_1	t_2	t_3	t_4	t_5	t_6
Project A's NPV for each repeat	410	-	410	-	410	-	410
Project B's NPV for each repeat	500	-	-	500	-	-	500

Example 2

This example refers to the case in which a choice is to be made between mutually exclusive projects representing different types of technology with different lengths of life.

Project I (Technology 1)

$B_t\text{-}C_t$

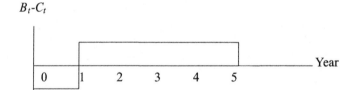

Project II (Technology 2)

$B_t\text{-}C_t$
C_t

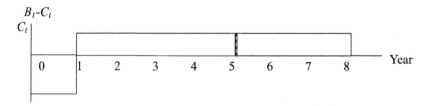

How can a decision be made between the two technologies using the NPV criterion? Suppose that the present value of the costs of Project I $[PV_0(C_0^I)]$ is

$100 and the present value of its benefits $[PV_0(B^I_{1-5})]$ is \$122. Similarly, the present value of the costs of Project II $[PV_0(C^{II}_0)]$ is \$200 and that of its benefits $[PV_0(B^{II}_{1-8})]$ \$225. A comparison of the NPVs of the two projects suggests that Project II is preferred to Project I because the NPV of Project II is \$25, whereas that of Project I is only \$22.

However, since these two projects represent two different types of technology with different lengths of life, the NPV of Project II is biased upward.

In order to make a correct judgment, it is necessary to make the projects comparable by either adjusting the lengths of life or calculating the annualization of net benefits. One option is to adjust Project II to make it comparable to Project I. The benefits for only the first five years of Project II should be included, and its costs should be reduced by the ratio of the present value of benefits from Years 1–5 to Years 1–8. This is expressed as follows:

$$NPV^I_0 = PV_0(B^I_{1-5}) - PV_0(C^I_0)$$

$$NPV^{II \, Adj}_0 = PV_0(B^{II}_{1-5}) - PV_0(C^{II}_0)\left(\frac{PV_0(B^{II}_{1-5})}{PV_0(B^{II}_{1-8})}\right)$$

Substituting in the values of costs and benefits of the two projects in the example gives:

$$PV_0(B^{II}_{1-8}) = \$225, PV_0(C^{II}_0) = \$200, PV_0(B^{II}_{1-5}) = \$180$$

Hence,

$$NPV^I_0 = \$122 - \$100 = \$22$$
$$NPV^{II \, Adj}_0 = \$180 - \$200(180/225) = \$180 - \$160 = \$20$$

After the adjustment, the NPV of Project I is greater than that of Project II; this means that Project I is better.

The second way of making the two projects comparable is to adjust the length of Project I. It is necessary to calculate the NPVs of Project I (adjusted) and Project II. The NPV of Project I can be adjusted by doubling its length of life. The benefits of Years 6–8 are then added to the benefits of Years 1–5. The costs are increased by the value of the costs to lengthen the project to Year 8, which is the present value of the costs in Year 5, reduced by the ratio of the benefits of Years 6–8 to the benefits of Years 6–10.

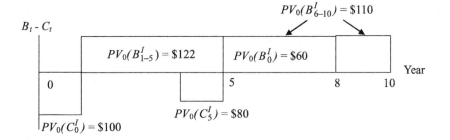

This adjustment can be expressed as follows:

$$NPV_0^{I\,Adj} = PV_0\left(B_{1-5}^I\right) - PV_0(C_0^I) + PV_0(B_{6-8}^I) - PV_0(C_5^I)\left(\frac{PV_0(B_{6-8}^I)}{PV_0(B_{6-10}^I)}\right)$$

Substituting in the present values of costs and benefits of the two projects in our example gives:

$$NPV_0^{I\,Adj} = \$122 - \$100 + \$60 - \$80(60/110) = \$38.36$$
$$NPV_0^{II} = \$225 - \$200 = \$25$$

Using this method, the NPV of Project I is still greater than that of Project II. Therefore, Project I is preferred to Project II.

The third way is to compare the annualization of the net benefits of the two projects. For Project I, the NPV is \$22 over a five-year period. The annualized value of the benefits can be calculated as follows (European Commission, 2005):

Annualized value^I = [\$22 × 0.10] / [1 − (1 + 0.10)$^{-5}$] = \$5.80

For Project II, the NPV is \$25 over an eight-year period. The annualized value of the benefits is:

Annualized value^{II} = [\$25 × 0.10] / [1 − (1 + 0.10)$^{-8}$] = \$4.69

Again, the higher NPV of Project II than those of Project I is due to a longer time horizon. When they are normalized for time period, it is shown that Project I is in fact preferred.

5.5 Projects with Interdependent and Separable Components

An investment programme will often contain several interrelated investments within a single project. It has sometimes been suggested that in such integrated projects, it is correct to evaluate the project as a whole and to bypass the examination of each of the sub-components. This argument is generally not correct. The analyst should attempt to break the project down into its various components and examine the incremental costs and benefits associated with each of the components in order to determine whether they increase or decrease the NPV of the project.

Suppose the task is to appraise a project to build a large storage dam, planned to provide hydroelectric power, irrigation water, and recreational benefits. Upon first examination of this project, it might appear that these three functions of the dam are complementary, so that it would be best to evaluate the entire project as a package. However, this is not necessarily the case. The irrigation water might be needed at a different time of the year than the peak demand for electricity. The reservoir might be empty during the tourist season if the water is used to maximize its value in generating electricity and providing irrigation. Therefore, maximizing the NPV of the whole package may mean that the efficiency of some of the individual components will be reduced. In this case, the overall project might be improved if one or more of the components were dropped from the investment package.

In appraising such an integrated investment package, the first step is to evaluate each of the components as an independent project. Thus, the hydroelectric power project would be evaluated separately. The technology used in this case would be the most appropriate for this size of electricity dam without considering its potential as a facility for either irrigation or recreational use. Similarly, the uses of this water supply in an independent irrigation project and in an independent recreational development should each be appraised on their own merits.

Next, the projects should be evaluated as combined facilities, such as an electricity-cum-irrigation project, an electricity-cum-recreational project, and an irrigation-cum-recreational project. In each of these combinations, the technology and operating programme should be designed to maximize the net benefits from the combined facilities. Finally, the combined electricity, irrigation, and recreational projects are evaluated. Again, the technology and operating plans will have to be designed to maximize the net benefits from the combined facilities. These alternatives must then be compared to find the one that yields the maximum NPV. It is frequently the case that the project that ends up with the highest NPV is the one containing fewer components than was initially proposed by its sponsor.

A common investment problem of the type that involves separable component projects arises when a decision is being made as to whether or not existing equipment should be replaced. When faced with this decision, there are three possible courses of action:

(a) Keep the old asset and do not buy the new asset now.
(b) Sell the old asset and purchase the new one.
(c) Keep the old asset and, in addition, buy the new one.

The present value of all future benefits that could be generated by the old asset (evaluated net of operating cost) will be denoted by B_o and the liquidation or scrap value of the old asset, if sold, SV_o. The present value of future benefits (net of operating costs) from the new asset will be expressed as B_n and the present value of the investment costs for the new asset as C_n. The combined benefits from the use of the old and new assets together will be denoted as B_{n+o}.

The first step is to appraise each of the three alternatives to determine which of them are feasible, i.e., which of the three generate positive NPVs. These comparisons are as follows:

- In order that alternative (a) be feasible, the present value of the future benefits from the old asset must exceed its liquidation value, i.e., $B_o - SV_o > 0$.
- In order for alternative (b) to be feasible, the present value of the future benefits from the new asset must be higher than the present value of its investment costs, i.e., $B_n - C_n > 0$.
- In order for alternative (c) to be feasible, the total benefits produced by both assets combined must be greater than the costs of the new investment plus the liquidation value of the old asset. In this case, the old asset is retained, to be used along with the new asset. This is expressed as $B_{n+o} - (C_n + SV_o) > 0$.

If each of the alternatives is feasible, a comparison must be carried out to determine which component or combination yields the greatest NPV. To determine whether or not to replace the old asset with the new one, it is necessary to calculate whether $(B_n - B_o) - (C_n - SV_o)$ is more or less than 0. If it is less than 0, the assets should not be exchanged. However, retaining the old asset while purchasing the new one would still be a viable option if $(B_{n+o} - B_n) - SV_o > 0$. This condition for retaining the two assets amounts to each one justifying itself as the marginal asset. Alternatively, if $(B_n - B_o) - (C_n - SV_o) < 0$ and $(B_{n+o} - B_o) - C_n < 0$, the old facilities should continue to be used without any new investment. Finally, if the conditions are $(B_n - B_o) - (C_n - SV_o) > 0$ and $(B_{n+o} - B_n) - SV_o < 0$, the old asset should be replaced with the new one.

One way to describe these comparisons is to define $(B_{n+o} - B_o)$ as $B_{n/o}$ and $(B_{n+o} - B_n)$ as $B_{o/n}$. In this notation, $B_{n/o}$ is the incremental benefit of the new asset in the presence of the old, and $B_{o/n}$ is the incremental benefit of the old asset in the presence of the new. The condition that is required for both assets to be present in the final package is that both $B_{n/o} > C_n$ and $B_{o/n} > SV_o$. This means that each component must justify itself as the marginal item in the picture.

This same principle governs in all cases where one has to deal with separable components of a project. Each separable component must justify itself as a marginal or incremental part of the overall project.

The careful examination of the alternative components of a potentially integrated project is thus an important task in the preparation and appraisal phase of a project. Failure to do this may mean that potentially valuable projects are not implemented because they were evaluated as part of a larger, unattractive package. On the other hand, wasteful projects might be implemented because they have been included in a larger integrated project that as a whole is worthwhile, but could be improved if the wasteful components were eliminated.

Complementarity and Substitutability among Projects

Once project analysts start to consider the interrelations between projects, a substantial number of possibilities emerge. It is instructive to examine these possibilities in detail. Denoting *PVB* as present value of benefits and *PVC* as present value of costs, we have the following cases:

$PVB_I + PVB_{II} = PVB_{I+II}$ Projects I and II are independents on the benefit side

$PVB_I + PVB_{II} > PVB_{I+II}$ Projects I and II are substitutes on the benefit side

$PVB_I + PVB_{II} < PVB_{I+II}$ Projects I and II are complements on the benefit side

$PVC_I + PVC_{II} = PVC_{I+II}$ Projects I and II are independents on the cost side

$PVC_I + PVC_{II} > PVC_{I+II}$ Projects I and II are complements on the cost side

$PVC_I + PVC_{II} < PVC_{I+II}$ Projects I and II are substitutes on the cost side

Independent projects will not be dealt with here. Examples of such projects would be a spaghetti factory in San Francisco and a highway improvement on Long Island. One project essentially has nothing to do with the other. A case in which projects are substitutes on the benefit side has already been examined. It is impossible for a multi-purpose dam to generate, as a multi-purpose project, the sum total that could be achieved if the benefits of the same project (e.g., a dam), independently maximized for each separate purpose, were added together. Thus, multi-purpose dams invariably entail substitution among the separate purposes.

Complementarity on the benefit side is relatively easy to deal with. An automobile will not function on three wheels, or without a carburettor. Hence, the marginal benefit of adding the fourth wheel, or the carburettor, is enormous. A more subtle case of complementarity on the benefit side, well known in the literature of economics, is that of an apiary project together with an orchard. The presence of the orchard enhances the benefits of the apiary; the presence of the bees also enhances the value of the orchard.

Whereas the separate purposes of multi-purpose dams are invariable substitutes on the benefit side, they are practically always complements on the cost side. To build one dam to serve several purposes will almost always cost less than the sum total of the two or more costs of building (at least hypothetically) separate dams to serve each of the separate purposes.

Cases of substitutability on the cost side are harder to find, but they clearly exist. A dam project that will produce a larger lake will clearly be competitive with a highway whose natural route would cross the area to be flooded. The total costs of the two projects together will exceed the sum of the costs of the two, considered above. Similarly, a project to urbanize an area is likely to compound the costs of a highway project going through that area.

Altogether, one must be alert to the possibilities of substitution and complementarity between and among projects. The underlying principle is always the same: maximize NPV. Its corollary is precisely the principle of separable components, as previously stated. Each separable component must justify itself as the marginal one. This becomes a problem where issues of substitutability are involved, though rarely so in cases of complementarity on both sides (benefits and costs). Perhaps the most interesting cases are those (like multi-purpose dams) in which complementarity on one side (in this case, the cost side) has to fight with substitutability on the other.

5.6 Conclusion

The timing and scale of projects are often important considerations in project evaluation. This chapter has discussed the issues and presented some decision rules for projects according to the NPV criterion. In addition, project analysts often face an issue of choosing between highly profitable, mutually exclusive projects with different lengths of life. Alternative approaches have been presented: either adjust the costs or benefits, or annualize the benefits in making a choice among mutually exclusive projects.

In reality, an investment often contains several interrelated investments, either substitute or complementary. The concept of the NPV of the project's benefits and costs can provide a powerful tool for selecting a project with single component or combination of components.

References

European Commission. 2005. *Impact Assessment Guidelines* (June 15) and *Annexes to Impact Assessment Guidelines* (June 15).
Harberger, A.C. 1972. "Cost-Benefit Analysis of Transportation Projects", *Project Evaluation – Collected Papers.* London: The Macmillan Press.
Pacheco-de-Almeida, G. and P. Zemsky. 2003. "The Effect of Time-to-Build on Strategic Investment under Uncertainty", *RAND Journal of Economics* 34(1), 166–182.
Szymanski, S. 1991. "The Optimal Timing of Infrastructure Investment", *Journal of Transport Economics and Policy* 25(3), 247–258.

Chapter Six

Dealing with Uncertainty and Risk in Investment Appraisal

6.1 Introduction

In the financial cash flow analysis, project variables such as input and output prices and their quantities have so far been based on their deterministic values, by which analysts make the best projection over the life of the investment project. The values of these variables used in the analysis and the resulting outcomes from a predictive model turn out to be single values with 100 percent certainty of occurring. In reality, uncertainty, which refers to variability in the value of some item such as a future commodity price, is always present, surrounding each of the future values of a project's key variables throughout the project life. In some cases, especially environmental and health projects, it is even more difficult to make projections because of a lack of scientific knowledge and the presence of technological innovation. The uncertainty is further compounded as the effects of the project are spread over a long period of time into the future.

This chapter describes how to move from the deterministic world developed previously to a dynamic and probabilistic world, in which uncertainty and risk in outcomes prevail, in order that the analysis can present more objective and realistic results for decision-makers. It also discusses how uncertainty and risk can be addressed and mitigated while managing the project. Section 6.2 explains why the risk analysis of an investment project should be considered as an integral part of the appraisal exercise. Section 6.3 defines risk for the purposes of investment appraisal, while Section 6.4 discusses how a project's risk variables can be identified and how the risk analysis of the project is conducted. Section 6.5 provides a conceptual framework for the potential use of contractual arrangements for shifting and mitigating project risks. Contracts provide a vehicle for redistributing risk among project participants. While contracts can create incentives to alter the behaviour of participants, they will also affect the overall return of a project. Section 6.6 describes a series of risks that are often encountered when arranging for project financing, and outlines a few of the contractual arrangements for mitigating and shifting these risks. Conclusions are made in the final section.

6.2 Importance of Risk Analysis in Investment Appraisal

A traditional financial cash flow analysis, similar to the analyses presented in Chapter 3, is based on single (deterministic) values for all of the project's variables. As a result, the outcome of the financial analysis is a point estimate of a project's net present value (NPV), internal rate of return, loan life cover ratio, and some other financial performance measures. The outputs of the economic and distributional analyses are also point estimates of the economic return and the gains and losses to the project's different stakeholders. The decision of whether to accept a project should not be made only on the basis of such information because the values for most of the project's variables are likely to change. While historical values of a particular variable are known with certainty, predicting future values is an entirely different matter. There is no guarantee that the projected values, irrespective of how they were arrived at, will actually materialize. This indicates that uncertainty or variability of key project variables will generate a largely unpredictable, single-value or "certainty equivalent" outcome of the project. As such, a project that may have appeared acceptable on the basis of the deterministic analysis may be much less desirable once the variability of the results is taken into account.

The financial cash flow analysis essentially deals with the values of cost and revenue items projected over the distant future. These values are rarely known with any degree of certainty. Each of the project variables affecting the NPV of a project is subject to a high degree of uncertainty. For example, the costs of building plants, the prices of machinery, oil, and other intermediate inputs, and the sales of the project outputs are all subject to changes in demand and supply in their respective markets that are difficult to project even for the next year or two, let alone for the next ten or more years. Similarly, macroeconomic variables such as the rate of inflation, the market exchange rate, and the interest rate are subject to changes in the economic conditions and government policies that go beyond the foreseeable future for the project analyst. However, these variables have an impact on both the financial profitability of the project and its economic viability.

It can be dangerous to make any judgments based only on the deterministic future values of project variables and the consequential NPV and debt service ratios because it is almost certain that they will never occur in reality. For example, estimates of time and vehicle operating cost savings resulting from improving a road can be uncertain owing to the unpredictability of the levels of passenger and cargo traffic in the future, these being key factors affecting the investment decision. These phenomena in effect make the pinpoint, single-value outcome of the project unpredictable. It is therefore unrealistic to rely on the deterministic values of the variables influencing a project decision. Rather, it is better to build the analysis based on probabilistic values of the project's input variables, which, in turn, will yield expected mean values as well as probabilities; these in their totality will represent the certainty equivalent estimate for achieving the project's output variables, such as the NPV.

Moreover, because such an analysis will reveal the pattern of possible outcomes (in the shape of a probability distribution), decisions can then also be made on the basis of individual tolerance of risk.

Uncertainty and risk analysis are important for a number of reasons. First, there is a need to reduce the likelihood of undertaking a "bad" project and of failing to accept a "good" project. It may be easy to avoid bad projects simply by making very conservative assumptions about the values of the key variables and then accepting only those projects that still have a positive NPV. For example, the estimates of the net cash flows from operations could be lowered by increasing the capital expenditures by 100 percent. If a project still had a positive NPV, this would support a belief that it may still be viable.

Second, once uncertainty is analysed and risk is understood, contractual arrangements may be put in place in order to lower the riskiness of a project's returns and to help save potentially good projects. For example, suppose the economic NPV of a project is positive on the basis of the deterministic analysis, but there is a large degree of variability in the returns, rendering the project unacceptable. It may be possible to mitigate the overall risk of the project through contractual arrangements among stakeholders, thereby saving a potentially good project from being rejected.

Third, one of the ways in which uncertainty can be reduced is to gather more data and information, to the extent feasible, about the key project variables in order to narrow their likely range and to determine more precisely the appropriate input probability distribution. To do this, the first step is to identify those variables that are key determinants of a project's NPV through sensitivity analysis. Otherwise, there is a risk that scarce resources will be wasted on research into many variables rather than focusing on the most critical ones. Moreover, attempting to estimate probability distributions for all or many input variables rather than just those that carry most of the risk will increase the level of complexity and exaggerate the problem of correlations among risk variables when applying a Monte Carlo simulation.

6.3 Definition and Measurement of Uncertainty and Risk

Risk analysis encompasses the identification of a project's risk variables and the uncertainty they represent, the analysis of the impacts of these risk variables on the project, and the interpretation of the results. A risk variable must be uncertain in terms of the difficulty in predicting its future values, as well as being significant in terms of its impact on the project outcome (see, e.g., Savvides, 1994). A good example would be the price of a major product of the project. Quite often, the price of a project's output is uncertain in the future, and it has direct consequences on financial viability for the investors as well as on the economic well-being of the nation as a whole.

Risk may result from the nature of uncertainty encompassing a particular variable and the availability of historical data on which to base an estimate of both the range of possible outcomes and their respective probabilities. For the purposes of illustration, consider the case of a tradable commodity such as sugar. Historical world prices are available, so it is possible to venture a schedule of prices and associated probabilities. However, despite having this information, there is still uncertainty as to what prices the project will face as there is no guarantee that the future will follow the same pattern as the past. A second level of uncertainty arises when the range of expected possible prices can be reasonably estimated, but probabilities cannot be attached to each value with any degree of confidence. A third level of uncertainty occurs when it is difficult to find any historical data or expert judgment on which to base a forecast for either the range of possible values or their respective probabilities. Based on the above definitions, it can be seen that project risk variables will involve different levels of uncertainty and variability.

It is important to realize that the uncertainty of a variable or group of variables does not necessarily result in a risky outcome. For example, a road project connecting two towns may be expected to generate a net economic NPV of $20 million under low estimates of road use, value of time, and operating cost savings. At the other extreme, under high estimates of road use, value of time, and operating cost savings, the project may be expected to generate an economic NPV of $100 million. In this case, the uncertainty in the input variables results in variability in the outcome, but not necessarily in any risk, as the project is expected to yield positive economic benefits under all expected states of nature. It is, however, more common to have a situation in which the project with certain probability may yield negative returns or values below an acceptable threshold.

There are several measures for assessing a project's risk. Two measures are used here: the probability of the project having a negative return or not meeting a certain threshold value for a particular outcome, and the expected loss from the project. While these two measures are typically used irrespective of the point of view of the stakeholder, the actual outcome assessed may vary from one stakeholder to another. For example, the main concern of a project's owner is the increase in net wealth as reflected by the financial NPV, while a banker's concern would be the project's ability to pay its debt services, thereby focusing on the probabilities of meeting targeted debt service coverage ratios (DSCRs). The government is primarily concerned about the probability of an overall economic benefit or a return to certain groups in society.

6.4 Steps in Conducting Risk Analysis

Risk variables are not only uncertain in nature but also significant in terms of their impact on the project outcome. The latter characteristic can be identified from sensitivity analysis. The analysis and management of the risk impacts can be carried out using the Monte Carlo simulation technique. The steps in conducting risk analysis are described below.

6.4.1 Sensitivity Analysis

The first step in conducting risk analysis of a project is to identify the risk variables. Sensitivity analysis is typically utilized in the identification of these variables. This analysis is a means of testing how sensitive a project's outcomes (e.g., financial NPV, economic NPV, DSCRs, gains and loss to different stakeholders) are to changes in the value of one parameter at a time. It is often referred to as "what if" analysis because it allows a financial analyst to answer questions such as, "*What* would happen to the NPV *if* variable *x* were to change by a certain amount or percentage?"[13] It should be noted that some of the input variables that have a significant impact on the financial outcome of a project may have a much smaller impact on the economic appraisal, and vice versa.

The following steps are used for conducting the sensitivity analysis on the financial results of a project:

1. Develop the deterministic financial cash flow model of a project and estimate its NPV and DSCRs, as explained in Chapters 3 and 4. This is called the base case analysis.
2. Conduct sensitivity analysis by altering either the values of the project input variables or the assumptions that underpin the values that were estimated. The variables can be specific to the project (such as prices, costs, and quantities sold) or macroeconomic variables, such as the performance of the economy (e.g., the growth rate of real gross domestic product, or GDP).
3. While holding the values of other variables constant, let the base case value of an input variable (price, for example) change by, say, 10 percent and calculate the percentage change in the financial NPV and DSCRs for certain years. The resulting numbers measure the degree of sensitivity of each of the project outcomes (e.g., financial NPV and DSCRs) to change in an input variable, while holding other variables constant.

This process is repeated for each of the input variables that are expected to have some impact on the financial outcomes of the project. For those variables that cause the greatest change in the financial outcomes, one can calculate what happens to the financial NPV as values for one variable are changed over their likely range. If the NPV turns negative after only a small change in a variable, it may signal that the project is financially risky to the investors and would need to be either rejected by them or restructured in a way that can mitigate the risks before the project is initiated.

---

[13]Most spreadsheet software programs allow for changes in either one or two input variables at a time. It is essential to carrying out sensitivity analysis before conducting Monte Carlo simulation. One of the uses of sensitivity analysis is also to check whether the financial cash flow model has been correctly developed, since it provides a good means of auditing the model and correcting mistakes.

The risk variables must satisfy two criteria. First, they must account for a large share of cash receipts (benefits) or cash disbursements (costs). Second, their impact on the projected results must remain significant within the range of probable values. Where it is possible to narrow down the margins of uncertainty by gathering additional information or by entering into an appropriate contractual arrangement, a highly sensitive variable will not qualify to be a risk variable. For example, if appropriate remedies in the form of undertakings and guarantees are provided by a contractor to build the project, then escalations in "capital investment costs" may cease to be an active risk variable. Moreover, in some cases, a variable could have a wide range of values, but its variation may not have much impact on the NPV unless it represents a considerable share of the revenues or costs. If an input accounts for 1 percent of the project cost, having a large fluctuation is unlikely to create much uncertainty in the financial results of the project. Similarly, a variable could constitute a large proportion of revenues or costs, but it will not be a major source of risk unless it is expected to vary considerably. For example, if the tariff for the electricity received by a power producer is fixed, the price of electricity is not going to be a source of risk even though the price is a major determinant of the project's revenues.

That being said, sensitivity analysis has a number of limitations. First, although it accounts for the likely range of values for a variable, there are no probabilities attached to the values in a range. As a result, sensitivity analysis does not recognize that certain values are more likely to occur than others. Second, input variables are altered one at a time without taking into account any relationship between variables. When the selling price of a product varies, for example, it is likely to affect the quantities sold, but also the revenue projections. This shortcoming can be rectified by conducting the scenario analysis on revenues rather than selling prices, or by specifying a formula link or some correlation between variables in the deterministic base case model. Third, how the results of a sensitivity analysis are viewed may depend on the risk preferences of investors or other stakeholders. That is to say, what one individual may consider unduly risky, another one who is less risk-averse may consider acceptable.[14] For these reasons, it is difficult to derive a general decision rule about whether to accept or reject a project based on sensitivity analysis alone.

6.4.2 Scenario Analysis

A scenario analysis simultaneously changes two or more variables to determine the joint, or combined, effect. It recognizes these interrelationships to be altered in a consistent manner at the same time. Scenarios can be based on macroeconomic factors such as the performance of the economy (e.g.,

---

[14]It should be noted that investor risk preference affects all aspects of capital investment decisions; thus, it has an impact not only on sensitivity analysis but also on scenario analysis and Monte Carlo simulation risk analysis.

expansion, normal, recession), industry-specific factors such as the behaviour of competing firms, or project-specific factors such as the possibility of a technological breakthrough.

The general steps for conducting a scenario analysis of a project are as follows:

1. Identify the key sets of circumstances, usually based on the major sources of uncertainty, that are likely to determine the success or failure of a project. For example, scenarios are sometimes defined as worst (pessimistic) case, expected (best-guess) case, and best (optimistic) case.
2. Adjust the values of each of the variables in the financial or economic analysis to be consistent with each scenario.
3. Calculate the values of the different project outcomes required (such as financial NPV and economic NPV) for each scenario.

In some cases, the interpretation of the results is easy. For example, if the NPV is positive even in the worst case, the project can be accepted; if the NPV is negative even in the best case, the project should be rejected. However, if the NPV is positive in the best case and negative in the worst case, the results are more difficult to interpret, but a decision can still be made with the knowledge of the "downside" and "upside" risk potential. If the downside risk is too great, further measures may be necessary to mitigate the risk if the project is to be undertaken.

The main shortcoming of scenario analysis is its failure to take into account the probabilities associated with each scenario, even though it allows for interrelationships among variables. Second, the scenarios themselves are likely to be discrete rather than continuous. This presents no problem in some cases, where an event either happens or does not happen, but in others, the scenarios that are defined may not fully reflect all of the possible situations that could arise. Third, it is rather difficult to determine the various scenarios that are relevant for decision-making before the range of possible outcomes for the project has first been determined.

6.4.3 Monte Carlo Analysis

Monte Carlo analysis is a natural extension of sensitivity and scenario analysis. It uses a random-sampling process to approximate the expected values and the variability inherent in the assumptions, which are expressed as probability distributions for the most sensitive and uncertain parameters (risk variables). It is a computer-aided methodology through which many possible project scenarios are generated using a random selection of input values from the specified probability distributions. Monte Carlo is a scientific technique (originally devised and used in the physical sciences) through which it is possible to simulate how the project may develop in the future. It creates multiple versions of the future, based on what are considered to be possible, by studying and defining the expected variability of the input parameters used in the projected financial and economic model. This is made possible by expressing the uncertainty of input variables as probability distributions. Using customized software, the computer then selects values randomly, but in accordance with their specified probabilities; these are inserted into the parameter table of the financial cash flow model to generate a series of possible project outcomes. This process is repeated numerous times (1,000 to 10,000) to produce a number of probability distributions (and statistics) of project results; the distributions also include the variability of the project and represent the wider picture of the expected risk and return to the investors, financiers, and other stakeholders in the project. Thus, the technique can also be employed to assess the potential benefit or costs of financial contracts used to mitigate some of the project's risk. Risk analysis using Monte Carlo methodology is therefore a useful tool in developing contracts to mitigate and manage project risk.

Monte Carlo analysis addresses the main concerns regarding sensitivity and scenario analyses. By identifying probability distributions for the uncertain variables, a defined distribution can be obtained for each of the specified variables according to historical data or subjective judgments by professional experts in the field. The distribution tells us the expected value of the outcome as well as the probabilities of higher and lower values for the outcome. The analysis allows for the modelling of a large number of scenarios that generate a random, and therefore methodologically objective, probability distribution of the outcome resulting from the combined effect of all the specified input probability distributions.[15]

The following steps are required to undertake a Monte Carlo risk analysis of a project:[16]

1. Identify risk variables that not only constitute a large share of the revenues or costs of the project but are also uncertain in nature.
2. Link each risk variable in the financial cash flow model of the deterministic case.
3. Assess how likely the risk is to occur and determine whether any truncation limits are needed. Truncation allows an analyst to put a ceiling on the value of a variable.
4. Select the probability distribution (uniform, triangular, normal, step, or discrete) and the range of values for each risk variable.[17] The appropriate

---

[15]A crucial part of any Monte Carlo exercise is the setting and handling of correlated risk variables during the simulation phase. For more on the treatment of correlated variables in Monte Carlo simulation, please refer to Pouliquen (1970) and Savvides (1994).

[16]At least three software programs are available for this purpose: RiskEase, Crystal Ball and @risk.

[17]For the symmetrical distributions (uniform, triangular, and normal), the range is completed by indicating the minimum and maximum values. For the normal distribution, the range can also

Dealing with Uncertainty and Risk in Investment Appraisal

probability distribution is selected based on a historical series of values or the opinions of experts in the field.[18]

5. Identify and manage the relationship among correlated variables to avoid inconsistent simulation results.

6. Select the model results that the computer program is supposed to monitor and report during the simulation.

7. Specify the desired number of simulation runs (usually 1,000 to 10,000) and then run the simulations.[19] Each run represents a scenario where a particular value for each identified risk variable is selected according to the specified probability distribution, correlations among variables, etc.

8. Present a series of statistical measures, such as the expected financial NPV, economic NPV, and variability of the outcomes.

Statistical measures of the project outcomes generated from Monte Carlo simulations are important. They are briefly described below.

1. *Expected Value*: The expected value is a probability-weighted average of the outcomes of the simulation runs. Since the probability of each run is equal to the inverse of the number of simulation runs, the expected value is the same as the arithmetic mean of the results (e.g., the mean NPV).

2. *Variability and Risk*: The variability of the outcomes can be measured by their range (maximum value minus minimum value), their variance, or the coefficient of variation, which is the standard deviation divided by the mean.

   The riskiness of a project can also be measured by the probability of achieving a negative outcome, which is displayed as the expected loss from the project. The expected loss and expected gain provide a measure of the cost associated with making the wrong decision when approving or rejecting a project. The expected loss is a probability-weighted average of all the negative outcomes. It is the expected value of the loss that might be incurred following a decision to accept a project. It is important because it gives an indication of what is really at stake (or at risk) from taking a decision to invest in the project. On the other hand, the expected gain is a probability-weighted average of all the positive outcomes. It is the expected value of the gains forgone following a decision to reject the project.

---

be set by specifying the mean and standard deviation. For the step and discrete distributions, it is necessary to define a series of intervals or discrete values, along with their probability weights. These probabilities must add up to 1.

[18]For example, when dealing with the projected traffic on a new road, the projected number of visitors to a clinic, or the projected number of students in a classroom, the opinions of experts should be used in identifying the probability distributions and ranges.

[19]It should be noted that the larger the number of input risk variables, the harder it is to determine the minimum number of runs required to obtain plausible results. However, given the speed of computers, this does not represent an obstacle as it is feasible to run a large number of simulations.

The expected loss ratio (el) defines risk as being dependent on both the shape and the position of the cumulative probability distribution of returns (e.g., NPVs) relative to the zero "cut-off" mark. The ratio is calculated as the ratio of the absolute value of the expected loss divided by the sum of the expected gain and the absolute value of the expected loss, as follows: [20]

$$el = \frac{|Expected\,Loss|}{Expected\,Gain + |Expected\,Loss|}$$

The expected loss ratio can vary from 0, when there is no expected loss, to 1, when there is no expected gain.

Instead of a single point estimate of a project's NPV, Monte Carlo simulation generates a probability distribution of the NPVs based on the underlying uncertainty surrounding each of the key risk variables. The main question is how this additional information alters the decision criteria for accepting or rejecting projects.

The distribution of NPVs can be presented either as a frequency distribution or as a cumulative probability distribution. Figure 6.1 illustrates the latter for NPVs from three points of view: the owner, the banker, and the economy. Any point on the cumulative probability distribution indicates the probability that the NPV will be equal to or less than the corresponding value on the horizontal axis. By the same token, 1 minus any point on the cumulative probability distribution indicates the probability that the NPV will be greater than the corresponding value on the horizontal axis. The farther to the right the distribution is, the more attractive the project. Several decision rules can be drawn.

---

[20]These measures of risk and the decision rules relating to Monte Carlo simulation are taken from Savvides (1994).

Figure 6.1: Net Present Value Distribution: Cumulative Probability

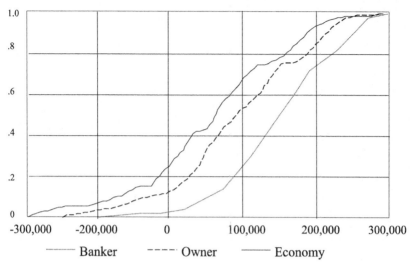

Decision Rule 1: If all of the cumulative probability distribution lies to the right of the zero cut-off mark, the NPV has zero probability of being negative. The project should therefore be accepted.

Decision Rule 2: If all of the cumulative probability distribution lies to the left of the zero cut-off mark, the NPV has no chance of being positive. The project should therefore be rejected.

Decision Rule 3: If the cumulative probability distribution crosses the zero cut-off mark, there is a risk of having a negative NPV that must be weighed against the probability of obtaining a positive return. The investment decision is indeterminate through purely objective criteria. It really rests on the risk profile of the investor. The cost of making a mistake about whether to approve a project, as measured by the expected gain and the expected loss, and the magnitude of the probability of a negative NPV, are factors that should be taken into account in making this decision.

Decision Rule 4: If the cumulative probability distributions of the returns of two mutually exclusive projects do not intersect at any point, the project whose probability distribution curve is farthest to the right should always be chosen (Figure 6.2). This is because given the same probability, the return of Project B is always higher than the return of Project A.

Figure 6.2: Mutually Exclusive Projects: One with a Higher Return

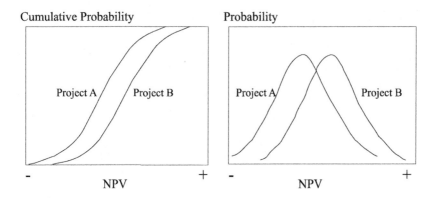

Figure 6.3: Mutually Exclusive Projects: High Return versus Low Loss

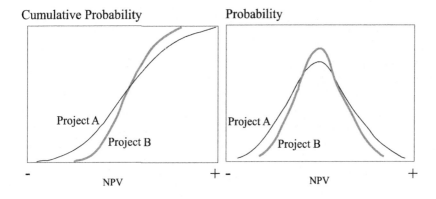

Decision Rule 5: If the cumulative probability distributions of the returns of two mutually exclusive projects intersect at any point, the decision rests on investors' risk predisposition. In Figure 6.3, Project B is less risky than Project A. However, the expected value of Project A's NPV could be higher than that of Project B. Whether the added return of Project A is worth the added risk depends in part on the degree of investors' risk aversion. The rules, given the risk predisposition of the investor, are shown below:

a) If risk-neutral, it is uncertain which project is best.
b) If risk-averse, Project B may be preferred to Project A.
c) If risk-lover, Project A may be preferred to Project B.

6.5 Risk Management with Contracts

Any step that can be taken to reduce the variability of the returns of a project will generally help to reduce its risk. One way to reduce a project's risk exposure is to enter into contractual arrangements. In the case of certain commodities, forward and futures contracts can be bought or sold to hedge risks. Gold or platinum producers, for example, can sell futures contracts to lock in a price today for delivery at some time in the future. While these futures markets are very useful for an operating company, the duration of the contracts is usually short, and they can be costly to obtain. Consequently, they often do not provide the kind of sufficiently long-term contracts that would allow a new mining company to be established. That is why companies seek to secure long-term contracts that will permit them to arrange their financing, to invest in the necessary physical capital, to hire workers, and to begin operations in a stable environment. The key to a stable environment is managing risks in such a way that the parties to a contract have incentives to abide by the terms of a contract and to avoid actions that would undermine it.

6.5.1 Risk Reallocation

When managing risk, a way must be found to redesign or reorganize a project in order to reallocate risk efficiently. The aim is not to reduce risk to one party by shifting it to others — a zero-sum game — but rather to gain an efficiency perspective, where, with the right contract, one party can gain substantially without corresponding cost to the other parties. The objective is to reallocate risk to those who can best bear it. This section explores how contracts (i.e., contracts with purchasers, suppliers, and workers that govern the operation of a project) can be used and implemented to share risk efficiently.

Contract efficiency has a number of attributes. One of these is the degree of risk aversion. Customers or suppliers who are perhaps more optimistic or who are simply less averse to taking chances are more willing to accept risk; they will assign a lower cost of risk to an uncertain situation than others who are less willing to "go out on a limb". Another attribute of efficiency is the comparative advantage for different project participants to diversified risks. For example, large international mineral contractors are able to diversify geologic risks by undertaking exploration activity in many sites around the world.[21] They are better able to reduce that risk than the government or an organization that owns one potential reserve.

---

[21]Blitzer et al. (1984) provide a comparison of alternative contracts for offshore oil exploration in Ecuador.

a) Risk-Sharing Contracts that Limit the Range of Values

If a project's risk is deemed to be unacceptably high, the key sources of risk should first be identified and isolated. For example, suppose that a project to build a water pipeline has been proposed. The water is going to be used for mining activities. A pipeline requires a major capital expenditure, and at the very least, it is likely that lenders will require assurances that the debt service for the pipeline will be met. To be economic, the pipeline must be used at a high rate of capacity utilization to justify its costs.

i)   A common type of contract for this type of project is a take-or-pay contract, which would bind potential water users (the mineral companies) to take a certain volume of water when the product is available or to make at least minimal payments sufficient to cover debt service on the pipeline. The mineral companies that will use the water are offering assurances to water suppliers and indirectly guaranteeing the debt service for lenders. The mineral companies might be willing to enter into such a contract in order to have the pipeline project proceed.[22]

ii) Suppose that instead of a water pipeline, the project is a pipeline to transport natural gas to be used for industrial purposes. One possible contractual arrangement to ensure the uninterrupted sales revenue of natural gas at the required level could be a specific price-escalator clause, which would index the price of natural gas to the prices of close substitutes, e.g., coal or oil. This provision would cause gas suppliers and customers to share any oil price risk, and would help protect the pipeline from a drastic decrease in throughput.

iii) Another approach that could be used to attract and retain customers would be to offer customers a limited product-price range. In this scenario, gas suppliers would offer their customers a ceiling on gas prices. Suppliers would thereby assume the risk of natural gas prices above the ceiling. Typically, such a contract will have to be approved by the lenders to ensure that there is no undue strain on the project's ability to repay its debt.

Another source of risk might be the availability of natural gas for the pipeline. Suppliers may have to be induced to give this pipeline project through such measures as minimum quantity guarantees. If a minimum gas price for natural gas is used to induce supply, purchasers would be signalling their willingness to assume more of the price risk. Bonuses could be offered for maintaining consistency of supply, and penalties could be imposed for supply interruptions. Where the quality of the goods supplied is an issue, supply

---

[22]In some situations, the much stricter all-events-full-cost-of-service-tariff arrangement can be used. Under such a contractual arrangement, customers are obligated to pay under all circumstances, i.e., whether the product is available or not. This type of contract is sometimes referred to as a hell-or-high-water contract because purchasers must pay "come hell or high water" (i.e. no matter what happens).

contracts would also have to include terms that would clearly state the minimum acceptable quality.[23]

These types of arrangements can be analysed by incorporating the contract terms into a spreadsheet model. For example, take-or-pay contracts can be modelled using the IF function in Excel. Price-escalator clauses can be introduced as equations linking gas prices to oil or coal prices; the oil and/or coal prices may themselves be risk variables for simulation purposes. Contract limitations that establish floor or ceiling prices or deliver minimum quantities can be captured while modelling the risk analysis.

The effect of these contract provisions is to change the expected value and/or the variance of the distribution of project outcomes. An increase in the expected value or a decrease in the variability of project outcomes would make a project more attractive to investors. For example, the introduction of a ceiling price on natural gas could be 141odeled by truncating the distribution of gas prices at that ceiling. The truncation has the effect of taking the probabilities of a price above the ceiling and assigning them to that value.[24] The results are twofold: the expected price of natural gas would be lower, and the variance of the gas revenue would be lower because the range of possible values is reduced. This contract provision would make the project more attractive to customers and less attractive to gas suppliers. Provided that gas suppliers would continue to fulfil their contracts, investors might find the pipeline project to be more attractive because gas customers have a greater incentive not to switch fuels. While the project may have given up some of its returns through such a contract, this arrangement also reduces the variability and riskiness of the returns.

b) Risk-Sharing Contracts that Establish a Correlation between Revenues and Costs

A reduction in risk can be achieved by establishing a correlation between sales revenues and costs. This result is based on the same principle as portfolio diversification, in which the variance of the sum of two random variables that are combined in certain proportions is equal to the weighted sum of their individual variances plus a covariance term:

$$V(ax+by) = a^2V(x) + b^2V(y) + 2abCov(x,y) \qquad (6.1)$$

---

[23]It should be noted that when reallocating risk through risk-sharing agreements, it is important to maintain viability across the chain of intermediaries that are crucial in taking the product through to the final consumer. A risk-sharing contract that puts a vital intermediary in a precariously non-viable position will risk the success and the viability for all the stakeholders in the project.

[24]If in the simulation process the price of natural gas was above the ceiling, the model would insert the ceiling price; if the price of natural gas was below the ceiling price, the model would use the market price (Glenday, 1989 and 1997).

where x and y are two random variables, and a and b are two constants that could be scale factors or proportions.

In the context of risky net cash flows, let x be sales revenues (R), y be costs (C), $a = 1$ and $b = -1$. Equation (6.1) then becomes:

$$V(R-C) = V(R) + V(C) - 2Cov(R,C) \qquad (6.2)$$

The variance in the net cash flows, $R - C$, is equal to the variance in cash receipts plus the variance in costs *minus* two times the covariance between receipts and costs. If a contract can be drawn up that will create a positive correlation, and hence a positive covariance between cash receipts and some of the cost items, and if in the process the variance of the costs does not increase by more than twice the covariance, the variance of the net cash flows will be less than the sum of the variances of receipts and costs. Simply put, when the revenues and costs move in tandem, there will be less variability in the project's returns.[25]

Examples of such contracts include indexed bonds[26] and profit-sharing agreements with workers. In a profit-sharing agreement, let g stand for a proportion of the total costs (C) that is still paid to workers as a wage and h be the labour's share of profit after wages have been paid. Thus, the total cost will become:

$$C = gC + h(R - gC)$$

where R stands for gross revenue. The net profit will be:

$$R - C = R - gC - h(R - gC)$$

The variance of net profit will be:

$$v(net\ profit) = (1 - h)^2 v(R) + g^2(1 - h)^2 v(C) - 2g(1 - h)^2 cov(R,C) \qquad (6.3)$$

If $0 < g < 1$ and $0 < h < 1$, the variance of net profit will be lower than it was without the agreement. Thus, any contract that creates a positive correlation between revenues and supply costs is likely to have a similar effect.

---

[25]The reduced variability also puts a ceiling on the risk-upside, which is the possibility of excessive returns.

[26]A number of years ago, Pemex, Mexico's state-owned oil company, issued bonds whose interest rate was indexed to the price of oil. When the price of oil rose, interest rates would be higher, but Pemex would be better able to afford the higher rates; when the price of oil fell and the company was squeezed for cash, interest rates would be lower, which would help to keep the net cash flow to equity positive.

c) Other Risk-Reallocation Techniques

Contingent claims analysis can be used to value options that are available to either project managers or investors to manage risks. This is clearly advantageous if a firm is able to switch product lines, production techniques, or input suppliers; to expand capacity if sales are growing rapidly (where failure to expand could mean the loss of sales to larger firms); or to suspend production if revenues do not cover variable costs. The problem of quantitatively assessing overall project flexibility is beyond the scope of this manual, but the underlying principles should be kept in mind.

6.5.2 Contracting Risk

Contracting risk refers to potential unilateral departures from the contract terms by one party that may jeopardize the other party's position (Blitzer et al., 1984). If a contract is one-sided, or if circumstances arise that would cause one party to take action under the terms of a contract, that party is likely either to take defensive or evasive action or to simply walk away from the project.

For example, if a supplier has agreed to a price ceiling on materials that are used as inputs to a project, but as a result of shortages the market price for the materials has risen substantially above the ceiling, the supplier has an incentive to take action that would weaken the impact of the price ceiling. Such action might include the substitution of lower-quality materials or delayed deliveries. The effect of such action would be to reduce overall product quality or to disrupt regular production runs to such an extent that project managers would be willing to renegotiate the price-ceiling clause in the materials contract. These negotiations may take time and could disrupt a project's normal operations. This is why an efficient contract does not load too much risk, given the compensation, on one party. An efficient contract is a stable contract that is able to withstand unanticipated shocks without costly gaming behaviour or frequent renegotiation.

6.5.3 Incentive Effects

Efficient contracts can sometimes offer not only an improved allocation of risk, but also an incentive structure that will encourage project participants to change their behaviour in such a way as to improve project outcomes. Whereas risk sharing takes the distributions of the risk variables as given and tries to reallocate risk to those who can best bear it, risk management provides incentives for participants to alter their behaviour so as to change the probabilities of the outcomes. The challenge is to design a contract with incentives that are compatible with the project's objectives.

Many of the incentive problems that arise with a project are due to imperfect and/or asymmetric information. This gives rise to the so-called principal–agent problem, where the principal (owner) of the assets would like the agent (manager, employee) to manage the assets in the best interests of the owner. The problem is that the agent may understand the operations of the project better than the owner, and the agent probably has better data and information about how the project is progressing. It is very difficult for the owner to monitor the manager's activities and performance thoroughly, and, hence, the manager has some leeway to pursue his/her own objectives rather than those of the owner. The result is a less than fully efficient operation.

For example, workers who enter into a profit-sharing agreement and who possibly have membership on the company's board of directors will have more information about the company's financial situation and will experience a different set of incentives than salaried workers. On the one hand, profit-sharing workers will not only share in the risks, but will also be more willing to engage in activities that will help to boost profits. On the other, salaried or hourly paid employees would be more inclined to pursue their own interests (e.g., longer lunch breaks, more vacation time, etc.), which are unlikely to be the same as those of the owner.

Managerial incentives can also be affected by contracting risks, as mentioned in the previous section. If managers are suspicious of the owner's (government's) intentions, they will act in such a way as to benefit themselves at the expense of the owners. This could mean running the equipment for more than the optimal number of hours, failing to observe maintenance schedules, or failing to maintain good customer relations.

6.6 Risks and Mitigating Measures in Project Financing

6.6.1 Introduction

Governments' use of project finance as a source of capital for medium- and large-scale development projects has increased considerably over the past two decades. Project finance has also evolved over time, and continues to do so, into different structural forms with respect to ownership, operating, and financing. A common feature in project finance is that the project is structured as an independent legal entity. The ownership of the project can take one of many forms. For example, the project can be owned by a private sector company, a government enterprise, a multinational corporation, a joint venture between private companies, or a partnership between the private sector and the government. The increasingly popular public–private partnerships that use project finance include build–operate–transfer (BOT) and build–operate–own (BOO).

Project financing typically refers to limited-recourse financing, where the project's lenders have recourse to the owners in certain situations only. In other words, some of the project's risks are borne by the lenders, while others are borne by the sponsors or other creditworthy third parties. For example, lenders could have full recourse to the owners until the project is complete, after which their only recourse is to the project's assets and cash flows. Limited-recourse financing falls between two extremes: full-recourse financing, which is similar to corporate (collateral-based) lending, and non-recourse financing, where the lenders' only recourse is to the project's assets and cash flows (see Beale, 1984; Niehuss, 1982).

Project financing started in the oil and gas industry, where sponsors wanted to reduce their risk exposure and preserve their borrowing capacity, and lenders were protected by the large profit margins in the industry. Since then, the scope and use of project finance has expanded, and continues to do so. At present, it finds wide applicability in the financing of infrastructure as international and regional banks encourage the undertaking of these investments by private sector companies or through public–private partnerships. Project finance is no longer limited to large-scale capital projects, as medium-scale projects with capital costs as low as $5 million have begun to use project finance to raise capital. Many industrial projects are financed in this manner.

A typical project finance set-up is displayed in Figure 6.4. The project entity — the special-purpose vehicles (SPVs) — makes appropriate contractual agreements with service providers, commercial partners, and financiers. The latter make sure that the agreements are in place so that the project represents a bankable risk. A project finance structure becomes a public–private partnership when a public authority is directly involved and makes available to the project public sector assets and other resources through a concession agreement for the purpose of undertaking and executing an economic development project (such as an airport, a motorway, or a port and marina development).

Figure 6.4: Public–Private Partnership (PPP) Set-up

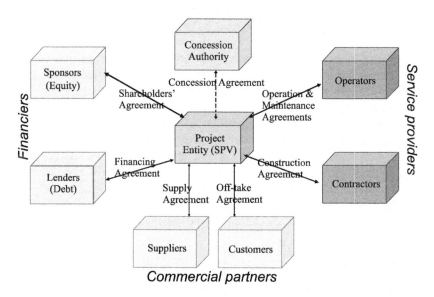

Governments in developing countries are increasing their use of project finance as a major source for raising capital for large projects. In particular, the use of project finance through BOT arrangements has become quite popular for large infrastructure projects in the power, water, and transportation sectors. The use of BOT enables governments to tap sources of capital that would not otherwise be available, attract the required expertise, or perhaps enhance the technology transfer process.

Project finance is not without its disadvantages and can be a more expensive means of finance than corporate (collateral-based) borrowing. The higher cost of project finance loans is attributed to higher interest rates and other charges and fees that are only applied to project lending. The higher interest rates are, in part, attributable to the additional risk to which the lenders are being exposed; they are also compensation for some of the expenses incurred in carrying out the different studies and in putting the deal together. These expenses and fees also include commitment fees, management fees paid to the lead underwriter, participation fees paid to other banks if the loan is syndicated, selling fees, and legal fees. In addition, closing project finance agreements is a lengthy and time-consuming process that often takes a few years, and projects' sponsors end up incurring some additional costs in putting the deal together.[27] Nevertheless, the main risks associated with project finance are better understood by both the project's lenders and owners and, as a result, contracts and other mechanisms are used appropriately to mitigate, spread out, and manage the risks.

6.6.2 Contractual Arrangements and Other Mechanisms for Mitigating Project Risks

Project risks and mitigating mechanisms are commonly approached from the point of view of the lenders. While the risks belong to the project, the mitigation mechanisms and contracts considered typically seek to eliminate or reduce the risk to a project's lenders. It is imperative that project sponsors 146nalyzes the risks and propose contracts to ensure that risks are being shifted in the most efficient way so that they are being undertaken by those project participants best equipped to bear them.

One of the misconceptions associated with risk in project finance is that lenders take a lot more risk when involved in project finance than they do in conventional corporate lending. This is not necessarily true. Banks have enhanced their abilities to 146nalyzes projects by hiring the necessary expertise. Consequently, their understanding of the nature of a project's risks and their magnitudes has improved significantly. This enables lenders to accept some low risks that they might not have accepted in the past had they not carried out

---

[27]For example, undertaking independent studies for the evaluation of reserves and certain risks, negotiating and preparing the different contracts, setting up certain funds, etc. all contribute to raising the cost of project financing to a project's sponsors.

detailed project studies. Since these detailed analyses are not commonly undertaken for projects using corporate lending, it may appear that lenders are bearing substantially more risk with project finance.

The critical period for most projects is the completion of the project and its preparation for operation. Lenders generally divide risks into two broad categories, pre-completion risks and post-completion risks. These risks and ways to manage them are briefly discussed below.[28]

a) Pre-completion Risks

Pre-completion risks include completion risk and participant risk. Completion risk is the risk that a project may not be completed. Completion is defined in physical, mechanical, and financial terms. Physical completion risk is the risk that the construction will not be completed within the specified time and budget, or will not be completed at all. Time delays also generally translate into cost overruns as a result of, among other things, accrued interest during construction and increases in the general price level. Mechanical or technical completion risk is the risk that the project cannot sustain production at a specified capacity for a specified period of time. Financial completion risk is the risk that the project cannot produce under a certain unit cost or that it cannot meet certain financial ratios for a specified period of time.

Lenders rarely accept completion risks and seek some sort of completion guarantee from the sponsors. These guarantees may take one of several forms. If the project is not completed on time or if there are cost overruns, project owners may be required to pay back the debt. Alternatively, project owners may be asked to absorb the project debt as a liability of the parent company and pay it according to a specified schedule out of the company's cash flows. A third alternative is for the project sponsors to guarantee completion by financing any overruns using new equity. It is clear that any of the above guarantees imply that prior to completion, project debt is treated as full-recourse debt or basically as the sponsors' debt. In the case of large development projects that are beyond the financial ability of the sponsors, the government may be called upon to provide a completion guarantee.

All of the above guarantees largely reduce the risk that the project will not be completed. In other words, by virtue of any of these guarantees, bankers have shifted the entire completion risk to the project sponsors or a creditworthy third party. The project's owners, on the other hand, should not be indifferent to guarantees.[29]

---

[28]More extensive discussions of the different risks can be found in various references such as Nevitt and Fabozzi (1995) and Finnerty (1996).

[29]For example, assuming the project debt as parent company debt may implicitly entail the first guarantee, which is to pay off the debt, hence providing more flexibility. When guaranteeing to complete the project from equity funds, will the sponsor commit unlimited funds, or does a cap exist? Perhaps a guarantee that has some elements from each of the three guarantees mentioned

The project's sponsors should also attempt to shield themselves from the completion risk or part of it, if possible, by passing it on or sharing it with other stakeholders. One way to accomplish this is through a turnkey arrangement or a fixed-price contract, with the contractor undertaking the construction of the project.[30] The project's analysts should assess whether or not the additional cost incurred in commissioning a turnkey project is necessary. In other words, has the contractor completed similar projects in the past on time and within budget? Have there been delays? Do they warrant a fixed-cost contract? Will the lenders be willing to accept the turnkey contract as their completion guarantee?

In certain situations, the project's lenders may agree to share construction cost overruns with the project's sponsors, up to a limit. Owners can pre-arrange other sources of cost-overrun funding, such as standby lines of credit. This will depend on the strength of the project's cash flows and whether or not they can cover additional debt repayments.

Lenders may be willing to share financial completion risks if these appear to be relatively low. Various conditions must be satisfied before lenders are willing to fully or partially accept completion risks. For instance, the project must be using a proven technology: lenders will seldom take the completion risk in the case of a new technology. Lenders will also require that the contractor has sufficient experience in undertaking similar projects and in completing them on time; that the expected cash flows are strong enough to withstand substantial cost overruns; that the project management and staff are competent; that procurement has been secured early; and that the political climate is stable. In a few cases and when all these conditions hold, some projects have succeeded in obtaining non-recourse financing from the lenders. Such non-recourse financing is more common for oil and gas production projects than for projects in other sectors.

One or more of the project sponsors may be financially weak, and may not be able to meet their financial obligations. Under certain legal structures for ownership, each individual sponsor is responsible for their share of the project's financial obligations and debt. If lenders are concerned that there are weak participants among the sponsors, they may require cross-default clauses on non-defaulting borrowers for the default of another borrower. Alternatively, lenders may seek third-party credit support for the weak sponsor(s). The most common form of this support is a letter of credit. If the lenders are concerned about the commitment of one of the sponsors, they may require pre-committed and/or additional equity, which will reduce their overall exposure to the project by lowering the debt/equity ratio.

From the sponsors' perspective, the cross-default may add to the financial burden of the non-defaulting borrowers and so may not be desirable to all sponsors. However, it may be possible in certain cases for the non-defaulting

---

above will work best for the sponsors without compromising the lenders. Another question that should be addressed is how force majeure would be handled during the completion phase.

[30]The most common of such contracts are known as EPC contracts. EPC refers to a contract covering engineering, procurement, and construction obligations.

sponsors to assume the debt of the defaulting sponsor(s) and buy their share in the project. If cross-default is not acceptable to the sponsors, third-party credit support or pre-committed equity may be preferable solutions.[31]

b) Post-completion Risks

Post-completion risks include raw material risk, resource risk, operating risk, market risk, political risk, force majeure risk, and abandonment risk.

i) Raw Material Risk

Raw material risk is the risk that the project will not be able to secure the sufficient supply of any of its raw materials to ensure the timely production of the project's output. This disruption may in turn jeopardize the sponsor's ability to service the project's debt. Raw material risk includes the risk of unavailability and the cost risk. If the project's sponsors do not own the sources of the project's main raw materials, lenders often require that the project has firm contracts with the suppliers of these raw materials.

Such contracts are beneficial not only to the lenders but also to the project's sponsors. First, obtaining this contract helps to secure the financing for the project. Equally importantly, it provides a great incentive to the supplier to adhere to the specified delivery schedule. These contracts can take the form of supply-or-pay arrangements. Under such a contract, a creditworthy supplier is committed to deliver the required amount of raw material to the project or to pay the project so that it can service its debt. How the suppliers can recoup such payments, if at all, is something that can be specified in the contract.

These contracts need not be zero-sum contracts, where one stakeholder has to lose in order for the other to gain. Long-term contracts with the project's suppliers can be beneficial to both the project's owners and the suppliers of the raw materials. For example, the supply price specified in the contract can be based on the long-run price of the raw material and can be indexed to reflect changes in the general price level or linked to the price of a close substitute. Alternatively, the input price can be linked to the price of the output itself.

Project owners will gain by securing the supply of the raw material at a price to be determined according to an already specified formula. The supplier of the raw material can also gain by securing a stable income stream. Both the owners and the suppliers are likely to gain owing to a lower variability over time in their cash flows as a result of the contract. In some instances it may be beneficial to the project's owners to pay a premium to secure a long-term supply-or-pay contract with its raw material suppliers. The availability of a spot market for the

---

[31] The legal structure of the project entity and issues of default need to be considered carefully to avoid any unexpected disruption to the project and distress to any of its sponsors before completion.

raw material can generally reduce the need for a contract to secure the long-run supply.

ii) Resource Risk

The resource risk is limited to mining projects. It is the risk that the mine will not have sufficient recoverable reserves. To deal with this risk, lenders often carry out their own geological surveys and analyses, or require the sponsors to carry out independent studies, to ascertain the quantity and quality of mineable reserves. Typically, lenders will consider providing project finance to a mining project if the amount of reserves to be mined is at least twice as much as the planned production. In other words, the loan-repayment period should not exceed half the mine's life. Whether the lenders have the technical staff to conduct their own analysis or the project's owners commission an independent investigation, this imposes an additional cost on the project's sponsors. This additional cost manifests itself in either higher interest rates charged by the lenders or increased expenditures to pay for the study. For projects that prove to have satisfactory reserves, lenders may be willing to assume the completion risk, or at least share it with the sponsors of the project.

iii) Operating Risk

This is the risk that the project may run into some operating difficulty that impedes its ability to generate sufficient cash flows to service the project's debt. In the case of proven technology and experienced operators and managers, lenders are usually willing to assume the operating risk. If the technology is relatively new, lenders will require performance guarantees from the equipment suppliers. With unproven technology, it is safe to say that project financing, if made available, will approach full-recourse financing, as the lenders will require at least completion guarantees and operating guarantees from the equipment supplier or the technology provider. The guarantees will be accepted only if the supplier or technology provider is creditworthy.

iv) Market Risk

The market risk is the risk that the project will not be able to generate enough revenues and cash flows to service its debt owing to low market prices of the output, an inability to sell the expected volume, or a combination of both. The risk of a low market price is known as price risk, and the risk of not selling sufficient volumes is known as volume risk. However, it should be noted that this standard way of describing market risk is an oversimplification of what is usually the main cause of failure of major projects (Flyvbjerg et al., 2003). Market risk is in fact both the most critical and the most difficult part to assess and evaluate in cost–benefit analysis. This is because it revolves around the wider and deeper subject of what constitutes project competitiveness.[32]

Lenders will be looking for guarantees that the output of the project will be sold. This requires long-term sales contracts for the project's output. Several types of sales contracts exist. Under a take-and-pay contract, the project's customers commit to buying a certain amount of the project's output if it is made available by the project. In other words, the project's customers will have to take and pay the amounts agreed upon even if they do not need them. This is perhaps the most often used of the long-term sales contracts, although not the one preferred by lenders. Such contracts should in principle be avoided because they are too one-sided, but may be necessary in some situations in order to make the project financeable. For example, an independent power producer will require such a contract from the utility to ensure continuous and sufficient sales.

The take-or-pay contract is a variation of the take-and-pay contract. Under the provisions of this contract, the project's customers will pay for a fixed amount of the product, whether or not it is available. A more radical form of the take-and-pay is the hell-or-high-water contract, under which customers pay even if the plant breaks down or if there is a stoppage relating to force majeure.

Throughput and cash-deficiency agreements are generally associated with pipeline projects. A throughput agreement stipulates that a specified amount of gas or oil will have to be shipped through the pipeline in a certain period of time. The specified amount is enough to generate sufficient revenues so that the project can pay all expenses and service the debt. A cash-deficiency agreement complements the throughput agreement by requiring the shipping companies to make cash payments to the project if for any reason the project does not have enough cash to service the debt. This payment by the shipper can be treated as an advance to the project and settled in the future in a manner that does not hinder the project's viability or its ability to service its debt.

All of the contracts mentioned above primarily secure specified sales (volume) levels, but can also be used to set prices. For example, the project's sponsors can agree with its customers on an initial selling price and a formula for indexing this price over time. The formula can include changes in general price levels, input prices, costs of substitutes, etc. Although including a large number of variables may sound conceptually appealing, it is likely to complicate the price estimation. In some cases, minimum prices can be specified in the contract.

When designing and analysing these contracts, all contracting parties should be creditworthy, and contracts should be reasonable and fair from all perspectives. Otherwise, contracts can, and will, be breached. Building some flexibility into the contracts is also advisable to avoid unintended hair-trigger breaches, which are the outcome of rigid clauses in the contracts.

---

[32]For an introduction to the subject of market analysis and the assessment of competitiveness of a project's market risk, see Savvides (2000).

The design of contracts can become more involved and complicated when multiple issues are being dealt with. Suppose, for example, that there are two projects, an oil-production project and an oil refinery. The refinery may wish to pursue throughput and cash-deficiency agreements with the oil-production project to ensure a continuous supply. At the same time, the oil-production project may wish to pursue a take-and-pay contract with the refinery to ensure the sale of its output. While the first set of agreements protects the lenders to the refinery against some risks, the second contract would increase the refinery's risk and hence have a negative impact on the refinery's ability to service its debt.

Another consideration when designing contracts is whether or not the entire output of the project should be under contract. The objective is for the cash flows guaranteed by contract to cover the debt servicing. If this is accomplished by having only a proportion of the project's output under contract, the lenders may readily agree to accept long-term sales contracts that cover only a portion of the project's output.

v) Force Majeure Risk

Force majeure risk is the risk that something outside the control of the lenders and sponsors would hinder the operations of the project. This includes natural disasters, such as earthquakes and floods, and other situations, such as strikes. Lenders may require the sponsors to seek insurance against force majeure risks or, alternatively, establish a debt service reserve fund that would be used to service the debt in such an eventuality. The financing provisions can also be structured in a way that allows for some restructuring in the event of a force majeure.

vi) Political Risk

Political risk covers a range of issues including nationalization, expropriation, currency inconvertibility and other controls on capital, and changes in tax laws. Some of these risks may be motivated by environmental concerns, the importance of which continues to increase worldwide and in developing countries in particular. Political risk is a concern for joint ventures and multinationals undertaking projects in developing countries.

There are several ways to protect the project's lenders against these risks. Governments can provide guarantees that the project will not be subjected to any of these political risks. Alternatively, governments can provide a guarantee that they will assume the project debt if the project is adversely impacted by any of these political actions. Project sponsors can also insure the project against political risks. Insurance can be sought from official sources such as the Multilateral Investment Guarantee Agency (MIGA) from the World Bank group and the Overseas Private Investment Corporation (OPIC) in the USA. Project sponsors can also seek private insurance from insurance organizations, such as Lloyds, that undertake such risks.

Political risk can be also mitigated if large international and regional financial agencies (such as the World Bank, the African Development Bank, the Asian Development Bank, and the International Finance Corporation) that have various other dealings with the country are involved. In fact, it may be to the benefit of the project in the host country to involve one or more of these financial agencies to signal the country's seriousness and commitment to the project.

Certain political risks can be avoided by establishing offshore escrow accounts, to be held in sound financial institutions. In such cases, a trust fund is typically created outside the project's country. The purchaser of the project's output will agree to deposit the proceeds of the sales directly into the fund. The trustees of the fund are obliged to service the debt, maintain some reserves, and then release the remainder to the project's sponsors. This mechanism is more readily applicable if the project's output is exported and the receipts are generated overseas. This scheme may be difficult to implement if the project's output is non-tradable and not generating foreign exchange. In other words, it may be difficult to use an offshore escrow account for infrastructure projects such as power, water and wastewater, and road projects.

vii) Abandonment Risk

The abandonment risk is the risk that the project owners will abandon the project before all project debt has been serviced. Project lenders are concerned that the project's sponsors may abandon the project during its operation stage if it is no longer profitable to them but still capable of generating the funds (at least partially) to service the debt. To protect themselves against abandonment, lenders formulate an "abandonment test" based on historical and projected costs and receipts. If the conditions in the test are fulfilled, sponsors may be allowed to abandon the project; otherwise, they have to continue to operate it to service the debt. If abandonment is only under severe conditions, the sponsors may have no recourse but to pay off the debt. For example, if the test provides that the project should be operated at the sponsors' cost while the revenues are used to service the debt, the owners may have no recourse but to pay off the debt. In other words, stringent abandonment tests can end up converting the loan from what appears to be limited-recourse financing to full-recourse financing.

viii) Interest Rate Risk

Floating interest rates can be risky. An increase in the interest rates can impair the project's ability to service its debt. This risk can be reduced by entering into interest rate swaps: a project borrowing at a floating interest rate can enter into an agreement under which it agrees to pay a fixed rate of interest and receive a floating rate of interest. Alternatively, the project owners can select an interest rate cap, which is a contract that protects the borrower (the project) against increases in interest rates by obligating another party, for a fee, to pay the difference between the market interest rate and the cap rate whenever the market interest rate is higher than the cap rate. To reduce the costs of the derivative, the borrower may choose a "collar" agreement, which provides for a ceiling as well as a floor condition. In such an arrangement, the cost of limiting the risk of high interest rates is offset against the possibility of gain in the event that the base rate falls below a certain point.

ix) Foreign Exchange Risk

There may be a currency risk if the project's receipts are in one currency and its costs are in another. Changes in the exchange rate can have detrimental impacts on the project's ability to service its debt. These risks can be reduced or partially hedged by taking out a loan in the currency in which the project will receive its receipts. Alternatively, the sponsors can use the forward or futures markets, or arrange currency swaps.

x) Rigid Debt Service and Hair-trigger Defaults

The terms of the loan-repayment period should take into account the economic life of the project and not put unnecessary pressure on the cash flows of the project in the early years. Rigid debt service may result in a project defaulting during a downturn even though it is still viable. To avoid these unnecessary defaults, debt servicing should be structured in a flexible manner and should avoid hair-trigger defaults. For example, debt servicing can be positively tied to a pre-agreed index (such the sales price) or the sales revenues, whereby the servicing increases when the sales revenues are above an agreed budget, and vice versa. In such cases, it is common for the financing bank to also demand to have some leverage over the management's decision to sell within a certain price range.

xi) Syndication Risk

It is quite common for the sponsors of large-scale projects to arrange their financing through a lead underwriter from a group of banks. This group is known as the syndicate. There is always the risk that the lead underwriter will not be able to secure the financing after negotiating the basic terms and conditions with the project's sponsors. This can delay the projects for long periods of time. To avoid such delays, the sponsors can try to secure a firm underwritten commitment from the lead underwriter(s). If this approach does not succeed, the sponsor can approach a group of underwriters to finance the project without creating a syndicate (each bank will co-finance the project based on separately negotiated loan agreements). This is commonly known as a club financing or project co-financing agreement, where the common factor is usually the fact that the co-financing banks make a separate agreement between them to share the available project collaterals and security available.

6.7 Conclusion

A project usually lasts for many years and faces a great deal of uncertainty, including the future values of project inputs and project outputs, the project financing arrangements, and the macroeconomic and political environment. A project analysis would be far from complete if it ended at the stage of deterministic evaluation. This chapter has shown how it is possible – and necessary – to move from the analysis of a deterministic world to a probabilistic world.

Project analysts have to first identify the key risk variables of the project in question using traditional sensitivity and scenario analyses, and then estimate correlation among risk variables with historical data to the extent available or with the help from experts in the area. This process takes into account the different ranges of possible values and different probability distributions for the risk variables employed in a Monte Carlo simulation of the project. The analysis presented in this chapter is indeed part of the integral project analysis approach, as it integrates key risk variables into the financial, economic, and stakeholder analysis of the project. Key project evaluation criteria for the financial and economic appraisal can all be summarized and presented based on the frequency or cumulative distributions for the items of interest, such as the financial NPV, the economic NPV, debt service coverage, and the expected loss ratio.

With the understanding of this technique, this chapter has presented a conceptual framework using numerous contracts to manage project risks in the most efficient manner. As project financing is also a key element for a successful project implementation, the possible pre-completion risks and post-completion risks have been identified, and some of the mitigation mechanisms and contracts presented that can eliminate or reduce the risks to the project's lenders, sponsors, and other participants in the project.

References

Arrow, K.J. and R.C. Lind. 1970. "Uncertainty and the Evaluation of Public Investment Decisions", *American Economic Review* 60(3), 364–378.

Balcombe, K.G. and L.E.D. Smith. 1999. "Refining the Use of Monte Carlo Techniques for Risk Analysis in Project Planning", *The Journal of Development Studies* 36(2), 113–135.

Beale, C.S. 1984. "Trends in Limited and Non-Recourse Financing", speech delivered to a project financing conference, @1984 The First Boston Corporation.

Blitzer, C.R., D.R. Lessard, and J.L. Paddock. 1984. "Risk-Bearing and the Choice of Contract Forms for Oil Exploration and Development", *The Energy Journal* 5(1), 1–28.

Finnerty, J.D. 1996. *Project Financing: Asset-Based Financial Engineering*, Chapter 3. New York: John Wiley and Sons.

Flyvbjerg, B., N. Bruzelius, and W. Rothengatter. 2003. *Mega Projects and Risk: An Anatomy of Ambition.* Cambridge: Cambridge University Press.

Flyvbjerg, B., M. Skamris Holm, and S.L. Buhl. 2002. "Underestimating Costs in Public Works Projects: Error or Lie", *Journal of the American Planning Association* 68(3), 279–295.

— 2005. "How (In)accurate are Demand Forecasts in Public Works Projects?", *Journal of the American Planning Association* 71(2), 131–146.

Glenday, G. 1989. "Monte Carlo Simulation Techniques in the Valuation of Truncated Distributions in the Context of Project Appraisal", paper presented at the 64th Annual Conference of the Western Economic Association (June).

— 1997. "Risk Sharing Contracts in Project Appraisal", *Canadian Journal of Program Evaluation*, 99-119.

Mun, J. 2004. *Applied Risk Analysis: Moving Beyond Uncertainty.* New York: John Wiley & Sons.

Nevitt, P.K. and F. Fabozzi. 1995. *Project Financing*, Chapters 10 and 11. Rochester: Euromoney Publications.

Niehuss, J.M. 1982. "An Introduction to International Project Financing", in R. Hellawell and D. Wallace Jr. (eds.), *Negotiating Foreign Investments: A Manual for the Third World.* International Law Institute.

Pouliquen, L.Y. 1970. *Risk Analysis in Project Appraisal.* World Bank Staff Occasional Papers No. 11. Baltimore, MD: The Johns Hopkins University Press.

Savvides, S.C. 1994. "Risk Analysis in Investment Appraisal", *Project Appraisal* 9(1), 3-18.

— 2000. "Market Analysis and Competitiveness in Project Appraisal", Harvard Institute for International Development, Development Discussion Paper No. 755 (February).

Schuyler, J. 2001. *Risk and Decision Analysis in Projects,* 2nd edition. Newtown Square, PA: Project Management Institute.

Vega, A.O. 1997. "Risk Allocation in Infrastructure Financing", *The Journal of Project Finance* 3(2), 38-42.

Chapter Seven

Principles Underlying the Economic Analysis of Projects

7.1 Objectives for Economic Investment Appraisal

Whereas a financial analysis of a project focuses on matters of interest to investors, bankers, public sector budgets, etc., an economic analysis deals with the impact of the project on society as a whole. The primary difference between an economic and a financial evaluation is that the former aggregates benefits and costs over all the country's residents to determine whether the project improves the level of economic welfare of the country as a whole, while the latter considers the project from the point of view of the finances of a particular institution or subgroup of the population.

A broad consensus exists among accountants on the principles to be used in undertaking a financial appraisal of a potential investment. There is also considerable agreement among financial analysts on the cash flow and balance sheet requirements for a public sector project to pay for itself on a cash basis. However, these accounting and financial principles are not a sufficient guide for undertaking an economic appraisal of a project.

The measurement of economic benefits and costs is based on the information developed in the financial appraisal, but in addition, it makes important use of the economic principles developed in the field of applied welfare economics. For a person to be a proficient economic analyst of capital expenditures, it is as imperative that he or she be conversant with the principles of applied welfare economics as it is that the financial analyst be knowledgeable about the basic principles of accounting. In the measurement of economic values, we begin by looking to the market for a specific good or service. The initial information for measuring its economic costs and benefits is obtained from the observation of the actual choices of consumers and producers in that market.

To better understand the nature of an economic analysis and how it relates to financial analysis, let us consider the case of a cement plant constructed on the outskirts of a town. In the financial analysis, the owners of the plant determine the profitability and financial attractiveness of the project. If the project has a positive financial net present value (FNPV) and relatively low risk, the owners will undertake the project because it will increase their net wealth.

If no one else in the country gains or loses as a result of the project, there would be almost no difference between the financial and economic analyses.

Consequently, when conducting an economic analysis, it may help from a conceptual standpoint to determine what groups, in addition to the project sponsors, gain or lose as a result of the project. For example, if the cement project pays wages higher than the prevailing market wages, the excess constitutes a benefit to workers. Thus, an adjustment to reflect their benefit would have to be included in the economic analysis. If the project pays income tax, this represents a financial cost to the project owners but a benefit to the government, and it would have to be estimated and included in the economic analysis. Furthermore, if one of the town's neighbourhoods is affected by pollution owing to emissions from the plant, the associated costs in terms of health and other lost amenities should also be taken into account in the economic analysis.

If the project's workers, town residents, consumers of cement (project and non-project), and the government represent all the parties impacted by the project, the net economic benefit or cost would be determined by adding all the gains and losses of these stakeholders to the gains or losses of the plant owners. If the final result is a net gain, then the cement plant increases the net welfare of the economy and should be undertaken; otherwise, it should not be undertaken. Note that economic viability does not require that every stakeholder perceives a net benefit from a project. Most projects will have both losers and gainers. However, if the gains outweigh the losses, the project is economically viable and should be undertaken. The underlying rationale is that a net gain implies that any losers from the project could be compensated.

This simple example explains the economic analysis of a project in its basic form. There are generally further adjustments that need to be carried out owing to differences between the market price and the economic price of tradable and non-tradable goods as well as differences between the financial cost of capital and its economic cost. These adjustments are discussed below.

This chapter is organized as follows. Section 7.2 presents the three postulates underlying the methodology of economic valuation. Section 7.3 shows how these postulates are applied to the economic valuation of non-tradable goods and services when there are no distortions in their markets. Section 7.4 introduces the concept of distortions and their applications to the economic valuation of non-tradable goods and services. Section 7.5 briefly discusses several other issues involving the three postulates. Concluding remarks are made in the final section.

7.2 Postulates Underlying the Economic Evaluation Methodology

The methodology adopted in this book for evaluating the economic benefits and costs of projects is built on the three postulates of applied welfare economics as summarized by Arnold Harberger (1971 and 1987). These postulates in turn are based on a number of fundamental concepts of welfare economics.

i) The competitive demand price for an incremental unit of a good or service measures its economic value to the demander, and hence its economic benefit.
ii) The competitive supply price for an incremental unit of a good or service measures its economic resource cost.
iii) Costs and benefits are added up without regard to who the gainers and losers are. In other words, a dollar is valued at a dollar regardless of whether the benefit of the dollar accrues to a demander or a supplier, or to a high-income or a low-income individual.[33]

What is the implication of these postulates for the economic analysis of a project? When a project produces a good or a service (output), the economic benefit or the economic price of each incremental unit is measured by the demand price or the consumer's willingness to pay for that unit. These postulates are firmly based on standard economic theory, but they also involve certain subtleties and conditions. The demand curve represents the maximum willingness to pay for each successive unit of a good as induced by changes in its market price. As such, the demand curve reflects indifference on the part of the consumer between having a particular unit of a good at that price and spending the money on other goods and services. As adjustments take place as a result of a project or other underlying event, the base assumption is that these are full adjustments over the whole economy. Individual prices and quantities may change in this and other markets, wages and incomes of different groups may rise or fall, but the economy is thought of as being always in equilibrium, with all markets being cleared. The reason for this is that we are comparing two future projections of the economy – one for the next 20 or 30 years without the project, the other for the same time span with the project.

The economic cost of a resource (input) that goes into the production of the project's output is measured by the supply price of each incremental unit of that resource. In other words, the economic cost of each incremental unit of an input is the price at which the supplier would only just be willing to supply that unit. The supply curve reflects the marginal cost of each unit to the seller under competitive conditions. In non-competitive cases the relevant economic cost of a unit is simply its marginal resource cost. Competitive suppliers will be indifferent as to whether to produce and then sell these particular units of the good at prices equal to their marginal costs. They are, of course, delighted if they receive more than its supply price for any unit. Again, adjustments along a supply curve take place in the context of the economy staying within its resource constraint, with equilibrium in all markets.

Finally, the third postulate concerns the distributional aspects of a project and how they should be incorporated into the economic analysis of projects. By

---

[33]This methodology can, however, be easily extended to allow for the benefits received by certain groups (e.g., the poor) to be given greater weight. The particular method by which this is accomplished is known by the term *basic needs externalities* and assigns special additional benefit values to projects that enhance the fulfilment of the basic needs of the poor.

accepting each individual supplier's and demander's valuations and then taking the difference between total benefits and total costs, the basic methodology of applied welfare economics focuses on economic efficiency.[34] The methodology in this book measures the net economic benefit of the project by subtracting the total resource costs used to produce the project's output from the total benefits of the output. In measuring the economic efficiency of projects, it adds up the dollar values of the net economic benefits, regardless of who the beneficiaries of the project are.

The first step in moving beyond pure efficiency considerations consists of what is called stakeholder analysis, which simply breaks down the overall benefits and costs of a project into component parts, delineating the benefits and costs for particular institutions (business firms, banks, etc.) or groups (consumers, farmers, labourers, the poor, etc.). This is clearly an important part of an economic appraisal. To help us deal with these issues, Chapter 13 contains a framework for identifying and measuring these distributive effects and offers some suggestions as to how this information may be included in the economic appraisal of a project.

7.3 Applying the Postulates to Determine Economic Evaluation of Non-tradable Goods and Services in an Undistorted Market

In this section, we work through a number of simple examples to illustrate how economic costs and benefits of non-tradable goods and services in a project are estimated using these three postulates in undistorted markets.[35] Distortions are defined in the context of this book as including taxes, subsidies, trade taxes, licences and quotas, monopoly markups, environmental externalities, congestion costs, and any other type of price or quantity restriction that causes the demand price of the item to diverge from its supply price (or more precisely, its marginal cost).

Although one might be hard pressed to find a market without distortions, we nevertheless start the analysis in the context of non-distorted markets in order to present the methodology in its simplest form. This simple case demonstrates that a difference may exist between financial and economic prices even in the absence of distortions.

To understand the impact of a project's demand for an input on the market for that input, we start by analysing that market. Similarly, to understand the

---

[34]The approach with basic needs externalities can be used as an alternative to distributional weights. Details of the analysis can be found in Chapter 14.

[35]A fuller explanation of the definition of a non-tradable is found in Chapter 11. At this point, it is sufficient to consider a non-tradable as a good or service where there is no incentive for domestic suppliers to export the item or for consumers to import the item. In such cases, the price of the item will be determined by the demand of local consumers interacting with the supply response of local suppliers.

impact of a project's output on the market for an output, we start by analysing the market for that output. Consequently, we start by developing a framework to show how the three postulates can be used to estimate economic costs and benefits in an existing market for a good or service (in the absence of a new project). We then proceed to show how the economic benefit of an output produced by a project can be estimated, and finally how the economic cost of an input used by a project is estimated.

7.3.1 Analysing Economic Costs and Benefits in an Existing Market (in the Absence of a New Project)

Figure 7.1(a) presents the demand curve for a good in an undistorted market. The demand price of the last unit is equal to the value consumers place on it. If the price were higher they would not buy that unit.

   If the market-determined price of the good is P^m and the quantity consumed at that price is Q^m, the economic benefit of the last (marginal) unit consumed is P^m, but the benefits of earlier (inframarginal) units will be greater than P^m. The maximum benefit derived from the first unit consumed is P^{max}, as shown in Figure 7.1(a). Applying the first postulate, the benefits of the successive units consumed are determined by the corresponding prices on the demand curve. Consequently, the economic benefit of the output of this industry (the quantity Q^m) is given by the area $OP^{max}CQ^m$.

   Figure 7.1(b) presents the other side of the market, namely, the supply side. The supply curve or marginal cost curve reflects the resource cost of producing successive units of the good. At the market-determined price P^m, the quantity Q^m is produced. While the resource cost of the marginal unit produced is P^m, that of each of the inframarginal units is less than P^m. Following the second postulate, the economic resource cost of producing Q^m is $OECQ^m$.

   Figure 7.1(c) combines the demand and supply curves for this market. Following the third postulate, we add up the economic costs and benefits to determine the net gain or loss in this industry. Since the benefits are represented by the area $OP^{max}CQ^m$ in Figure 7.1(a) and the costs are given by the area $OECQ^m$ in Figure 7.1(b), we have a net economic benefit given by the triangle $EP^{max}C$ in Figure 7.1(c).

   Although from this analysis it is clear that the industry is adding to the net wealth of the economy, we have not yet determined which group receives this net benefit of $EP^{max}C$. To answer this question, let us return to Figure 7.1(c). The only price observable in the market is P^m, and all Q^m units are bought and sold at this price. Consumers value each unit they consume at its corresponding price, as given by the demand curve, but they pay less than that price for all units consumed except the last one. This difference between how consumers value the output and what they actually pay for it is a net gain to consumers and is known as consumer surplus. Consumers pay an amount equal to OP^mCQ^m but enjoy a gross benefit of $OP^{max}CQ^m$. The net benefit perceived by consumers because they are able to purchase all units at a price P^m is equal to the triangle $P^m P^{max} C$ in Figure 7.1(c). This triangle is the consumer surplus.

Figure 7.1: Economic Costs and Benefits in an Existing Market

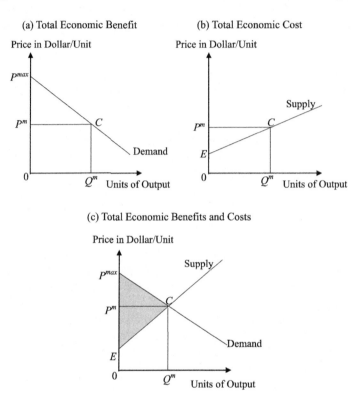

The fact that all units are sold at a price P^m implies that industry revenues, $OP^m CQ^m$, are larger than the economic costs, $OECQ^m$. The excess of revenues over resource cost, the triangle in Figure 7.1(c), $EP^m C$, represents a net profit (over and above their normal or "required" rates of return or other supply prices) to the owners of the factors of production. This difference is known as economic rent or producer surplus. It now becomes evident that the net economic benefit in this industry, as determined using the three postulates, is shared between the owners of the production factors used in the industry and the consumers of its output.

This analysis indicates that the gross economic benefits of the total output from this industry are greater than the financial revenues received by the suppliers within the industry, the difference being the consumer surplus enjoyed by the consumers of the output. It also indicates that the economic cost of producing the output is less than the financial revenues received by the suppliers, the difference here being the producer surplus enjoyed by the suppliers. The implication of these two facts is that the financial prices of inframarginal units are typically different from their economic prices (i.e., the price of the last or marginal unit), even in the absence of distortions. This point is further addressed below.

7.3.2 Analysing the Economic Benefits of an Output Produced by a Project

The previous analysis focused on an industry. In this section we consider the more common case of a new project. Suppose our project produces a non-tradable good such as cement. Figure 7.2 shows the supply and demand for this non-tradable good. The industry demand and supply curves prior to the introduction of the new project are denoted by D_0 and S_0, respectively. The new project produces a quantity, Q_p, and results in a shift in the industry supply curve from S_0 to S_{0+P}. The additional supply by the project results in a drop in the market price from P_0^m to P_1^m. As a result of the decrease in price, consumers demand more, and total consumption increases from Q_0 to Q_1^d. Also owing to the decline in price, existing suppliers will cut back their production from Q_0 to Q_1^s, as some of them can no longer profitably supply the same amount of the good at the new (lower) price, P_1^m. Q_p, the quantity produced by the project, equals the sum of the two quantities $Q_1^d - Q_0$ and $Q_0 - Q_1^s$.

Since the project sells its output at the new prevailing market price, P_1^m, the gross financial receipts to the project are given by $(Q_p \times P_1^m)$, which is area Q_1^s $AC Q_1^d$. To estimate the gross economic benefits of the project, we need to determine the economic value of the new consumption to the demanders and the value of the resources released by existing suppliers. These values are estimated using the first two postulates, as follows:

1. The additional consumption is valued, according to the first postulate, by the demand price for each successive unit or by the area under the demand curve $(Q_0 BC Q_1^d)$.

2. The resources released by other producers are valued, according to the second postulate, by the supply price (resource cost), along the "old" supply curve, not counting project output, of each successive unit or by the area under the supply curve $(Q_0 BA Q_1^s)$.

Figure 7.2: Economic Benefits of a New Project in an Undistorted Market

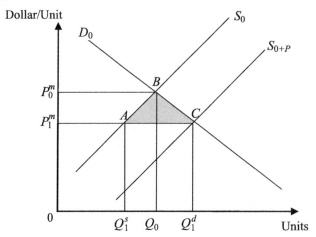

The gross economic benefits are given by the sum of the two areas above ($Q_1^s ABC Q_1^d$). It is important to emphasize that these benefits are gross. In other words, we have not yet netted from them the economic costs of producing the project's output. Saying that a project has positive gross economic benefits is the economic counterpart of saying that a project has positive gross financial receipts. The positive gross benefits alone do not indicate whether or not the project is economically viable, in the same way that positive gross financial receipts do not indicate whether or not the project is financially profitable.

The gross benefits are equal to the sum of the financial receipts to the project's owners ($Q_1^s AC Q_1^d$), plus the gain in consumer surplus ($P_0^m BC P_1^m$), less the loss in producer surplus ($P_0^m BA P_1^m$). In addition to the gross receipts to the project owners, consumers gain as a result of the reduction in price, and producers lose economic rents because of the reduction in price. It is worth noting that the gross economic benefits exceed the financial receipts to the project's owners owing to the net gain to consumers, as the consumers' gain more than fully offsets the loss in economic rents to the existing producers.

It is often the case that when the quantity produced by the project is relatively small compared to the size of the market, there will only be a small, most often imperceptible, induced change in the market price. In such a situation, and given that we are operating in an undistorted market, the gross financial receipts will be virtually equal to the gross economic benefits. In other words, there is little difference between the financial revenues generated by a project and its economic benefits to society. That difference will become significant only when the quantity produced by the project is sufficiently large to have a meaningful impact on the prevailing market price in the industry.

7.3.3 Analysing the Economic Cost of an Input Demanded by a Project

The following example demonstrates how the economic cost of a non-tradable input demanded by a project can be estimated using the three postulates. The industry demand and supply curves without the additional demand by the new project are denoted by D_0 and S_0, respectively (Figure 7.3). The new project demands a quantity, Q_p, and results in a shift in the industry demand curve from D_0 to D_{0+P}. The additional demand by the project results in a rise in the market price from P_0^m to P_1^m. As a result of the increase in price, existing consumers will cut back their consumption from Q_0 to Q_1^d, and producers will increase their production from Q_0 to Q_1^s at the new (higher) price, P_1^m. Q_p, the quantity demanded by the project, equals the sum of the two quantities $Q_0 - Q_1^d$ and $Q_1^s - Q_0$.

Figure 7.3: Economic Cost of an Input Demanded by a Project in an Undistorted Market

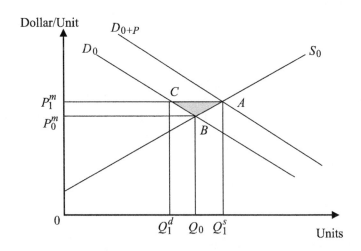

The project buys its requirement at the new prevailing market price, P_1^m, and incurs a gross financial expenditure of $(Q_p \times P_1^m)$, which is the area $Q_1^d CA Q_1^s$. To estimate the gross economic costs of the input demanded by the project, we need to determine the economic value of the consumption that is forgone by the existing consumers and the value of the additional resources used to accommodate the project's demand. These values are estimated using the first two postulates, as follows:

1. The cutback in consumption is valued, according to the first postulate, by the demand price for each successive unit given up by other consumers, the area under the demand curve ($Q_0 B C Q_1^d$).

2. The additional resources used to accommodate the expansion in output are valued, according to the second postulate, by the supply price (resource cost) of each successive unit, the area under the supply curve ($Q_0 B A Q_1^s$).

The gross economic cost of this input is given by the sum of the two areas above ($Q_1^d C B A Q_1^s$), which is equal to the financial cost to the project ($Q_1^d C A Q_1^s$), plus the loss in consumer surplus ($P_1^m C B P_0^m$), less the gain in producer surplus ($P_1^m A B P_0^m$). Owing to the increase in price brought about by the project's demand, existing consumers lose consumer surplus, while producers gain economic rents. The economic cost per unit with the implementation of the project can be measured by ($P_0^m + P_1^m$)/2, with linear demand and supply curves of any slope. However, it is worth noting that in this case, the gross economic cost is less than the financial cost paid by the project because net gain to producers in economic rent exceeds the loss in consumer surplus to the existing consumers. The changes in consumer and producer surplus are a direct result of the price increase.

If the quantity demanded by the project is relatively small compared to the size of the market, there will be a very small change, most likely imperceptitble, in the market price. In such a situation, and given that we are operating in an undistorted market, the gross financial cost to the project will be virtually equal to the gross economic cost. In other words, the triangle difference between the financial cost paid by a project for an input and its economic cost to the society will be negligible. The difference will become important only when the quantity demanded by the project is sufficiently large to have a substantial impact on the prevailing market price in the industry.

By determining the economic cost of each input used by the project and the economic benefit of its output, both of which are presented above, we will be in a position to determine the economic viability of the project by subtracting all economic costs from the gross economic benefits.

7.4 Applying the Postulates to Determine Economic Evaluation of Non-tradable Goods and Services in Distorted Markets

This section describes the impact of distortions on markets for goods and services whose domestic production satisfies all the domestic market demand for these items and whose domestic prices are not determined by their world prices. These are referred to as non-tradable goods. In general, the markets for a project's outputs and inputs are distorted, where distortions are defined as market imperfections. The most common types of such distortions are in the form of government taxes and subsidies. Others include quantitative restrictions, price controls, and monopoly markups (the excess of price over marginal cost). In project appraisal, we take the type and level of distortions as given when estimating the economic costs and benefits of projects. The task of the project analyst or economist is to select the projects that increase the country's net wealth, given the current and expected future patterns of distortions in the country.

While the presence of distortions in the markets for internationally non-tradable goods and services will render the estimation of economic costs and benefits, as well as the distributional impacts, slightly more complex, the methodological framework is still based entirely on the three postulates of applied welfare economics. When dealing with undistorted markets in the examples given above, the only difference between the financial receipts to the owners and the economic benefits is the gain in consumer surplus minus the loss in producer surplus. Similarly, the difference between the economic cost of the inputs used by the project and the financial expenditures borne by the project owners is the gain in producer surplus minus the loss in consumer surplus. In the absence of distortions, with the project causing only a minor change in financial prices, the financial receipts from the sale of the output will be for all practical purposes equal to the gross economic benefits, and the financial expenditures on the inputs will be similarly equal to their economic cost.

When a project produces an output in a distorted market, the market price will, as before, fall as a result of the increase in supply. Demanders will increase their demand, while non-project suppliers will reduce their supply. This outcome is identical to the case of an undistorted market. The economic benefit of the project's output will be measured as the sum of the value of the additional demand, measured by the demand price, and the value of the additional resources, measured by the supply price. In these respects also, the estimation process is similar to that of an output in an undistorted market.

7.4.1 Sales Taxes Levied on Output of Project

Taxes are imposed by governments primarily in order to raise revenues to pay for public sector expenditures.[36] When a value-added tax or a general sales tax (t_s) is imposed on an internationally non-tradable item, a divergence is created between the marginal value to consumers (P^d), which includes the sales tax and the marginal cost of the resources used in production (P^s), which does not include

---

[36]Some theorists of public economics assert that the purpose of raising revenues is to enable the government to perform functions that cannot be undertaken by the private sector owing to "market failures". These theorists sometimes add that the government is also required to adopt appropriate fiscal and monetary policies for the stabilization of the economy. Finally, they and others often justify expenditures in social sectors (health care, education) as being necessary for reducing income disparities and promoting equity.

the sales tax. In a situation when there is no other distortion in the supply of the item, the market price, P^m, will be equal to the marginal cost of production, which is defined here as the supply price, P^s. As a consequence, in this situation $P^d = P^s (1 + t_s)$ or $P^d = P^m (1 + t_s)$.

Let D_g denote the demand curve for an item, as shown in Figure 7.4. This curve shows the value of each unit of the commodity to the demanders, as measured by their willingness to pay. After deducting the part taken up by the tax, the amount available to suppliers is given by D_n, as shown in Figure 7.4. This is what suppliers will receive in order to cover their costs of production. The net-of-tax marginal cost of production is shown as the supply curve, S_0.

Suppose a new project demands a quantity, Q_p, causing the net-of-tax industry demand curve to shift from D_n to D_{n+P}. The additional demand by the project results in a rise in the net-of-tax market price from P_0^m to P_1^m. As a result of the increase in price, existing consumers, who must now pay $p_1^d = P_1^m (1 + t_s)$ per unit, will cut back their consumption from Q_0 to Q_1^d, while producers will increase their production from Q_0 to Q_1^s, the quantity demanded by the project (Q_p), which equals the sum of the two quantities, $Q_0 - Q_1^d$ and $Q_1^s - Q_0$.

When the project buys its requirement, the effect is to shift the net-of-tax demand curve to the right by the amount $[(Q_1^s - Q_1^d) = Q_p]$ of project purchases, i.e., D_{n+p}. The gross-of-tax demand curve will also shift to D_{g+p}. The project will make a gross-of-tax financial expenditure of $Q_p \times p_1^d$ $(= Q_1^d C'E Q_1^s)$, but the suppliers of this input will receive an amount equal to net-of-tax price multiplied by the quantity sold, $Q_p \times P^m$, or $Q_1^d CA Q_1^s$, to cover their costs. However, we see that the producers of this item do not increase their production by the full amount of the additional demand. To estimate the gross economic costs of the input demanded by the project, we need to determine the economic value of the incremental consumption that is forgone by the existing consumers and the value of the additional resources used to accommodate the project's demand. These values are estimated using the first two postulates, as follows.

Figure 7.4: Economic Cost of an Input Demanded by a Project (when a Tax Is Imposed on Sales)

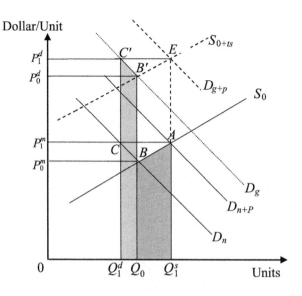

1. The cutback in consumption is valued, according to the first postulate, by the demand price for each successive unit given up by other consumers, the area under the demand curve inclusive of tax $(Q_1^d C'B'Q_0)$. This is reflected by the gross-of-tax demand price P^d.
2. The additional resources used to accommodate the expansion in output are valued, according to the second postulate, by the supply price (resource cost) of each successive unit, the area under the supply curve $(Q_0 BA Q_1^s)$. This is reflected by the net-of-tax supply price P^s or, in this case, the market price.

Thus, the economic cost of a project input can be measured by the sum of the supply price (P^s) multiplied by the change in quantity supplied (ΔQ^s) and the demand price (P^d) times the change in quantity demanded (ΔQ^d). That is:

$$P^e Q_p = P^s \Delta Q^s + P^d \Delta Q^d \qquad (7.1)$$

where $Q_p = \Delta Q^s + \Delta Q^d$. The ratios of ΔQ^s and ΔQ^d to Q_p become the respective weights of supply and demand, w^s and w^d, as a consequence of the project demand for the good. One can also rewrite equation (7.1) and calculate the economic cost as the quantity demanded by the project input multiplied by the following expected economic price of the good (P^e):

$$P^e = w^s P^s + w^d P^d \qquad (7.2)$$

The weights become an important factor in determining the economic price and, consequently, the economic cost of the good. These weights are generally determined by the own-price elasticities of supply (ε) and demand (η) of the good, which reflect the responsiveness of the quantity supplied to and demanded from a change in price of the good. They can be calculated as follows:

$$w^s = \varepsilon / (\varepsilon - \eta), \text{ and } w^d = - \eta / (\varepsilon - \eta) \qquad (7.3)$$

Readers should note that ε (the supply elasticity) is positive, while η (the demand elasticity) is negative.

These elasticities refer to an average elasticity representing the adjustments made by the market; as such, they are long-run elasticities of supply and demand. The relative shares of demand and supply vary from one good or service to another. However, the long time frame given by the economic life of a project typically implies a higher elasticity of supply than of demand, reflecting the relative ease of expanding production both within firms and by the addition of new ones.

For example, suppose there is a greater response in the existing supply than there is demand in the economy to the project demand. Let us assume $w^s = 2/3$ and $w^d = 1/3$ with the market price and sales tax rate, in which $P_0^m = \$120$ and $t_s = 0.15$. The economic price will then be calculated as:

$$
\begin{aligned}
P^e &= w^s P^s + w^d P^d \\
&= 2/3 \times 120 + 1/3 \times [120 \times (1+0.15)] \\
&= \$126
\end{aligned}
$$

Suppose that instead of a project demanding this good as an input into its production, we have a project that will increase the production of the good. The increase in project supply will shift the supply curve to the right, from S_n to S_{n+P}, as shown in Figure 7.5. The additional supply by the project results in a decrease in the net-of-tax market price from P_0^m to P_1^m. The fall in the market price will cause consumers to increase their demand from Q_0 to Q_1^d as the gross-of-tax demand price they pay falls from P_0^d to P_1^d. The decline in price received (net of tax) by producers of P_1^m will cause some of the existing producers to cut back their production from Q_0 to Q_q^s.

Figure 7.5: Economic Benefit of an Output Supplied by a Project (when a Tax Is Imposed on Sales)

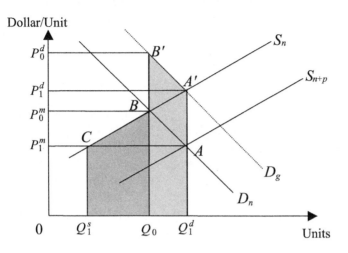

Since the project sells its output gross of tax at P_1^d but receives net of tax P_1^m, the gross financial receipts including taxes collected by the project are given by $(Q_p \times P_1^d)$, but the amount the project can keep net of taxes is shown by the area $Q_1^s CA Q_1^d$. However, the economic benefits produced by the project are measured by the following:

1. For the incremental increase in consumption of $Q_1^d - Q_0$, the consumers' willingness to pay, according to the first postulate, is the gross-of-tax demand price. This is shown as the sum of the amount consumers are willing to pay the suppliers plus the increase in the amount of taxes they are willing to pay the government (the area $BAA'B'$) for the additional consumption.
2. The value of resources released, according to the second postulate, is measured by the supply price $P^s = P^m$ multiplied by the reduction in quantity supplied of $Q_0 - Q_1^s$. This is shown in Figure 7.5 as the area under the supply curve $Q_0 BC Q_1^s$.

Using the same weights and prices as before, i.e., $w^s = 2/3$, $w^d = 1/3$, $P_0^m = \$120$, and $t_s = 0.15$, then the economic price of the good is:

$$P^e = w^s P^s + w^d P^d$$
$$= 2/3 \times 120 + 1/3 \times [120 \times (1+0.15)]$$
$$= \$126$$

In this case, when the change in the market price is small, the net economic benefits are greater than the financial benefits by the amount of additional tax revenue collected by the government. The additional tax accruing to the government will depend on the size of the tax rate and the incremental increase in the total supply of the good sold in the market as a consequence of the project.

7.4.2 Subsidies on Production

When a government wants to encourage the production of a non-tradable good, it may subsidize private producers to increase their output of the good or service. Figure 7.6 shows that the industry demand and supply curves in the absence of distortions prior to the introduction of the new project are denoted by D_0 and S_0, respectively. With a unit subsidy, where the government gives the producer a fixed amount per unit sold, the market supply curve will shift downward to the curve denoted by S_s ($= S_{0+subsidy}$). Now suppose a new project produces a quantity Q_p, equal to ($Q_1^d - Q_1^s$), which causes the industry supply to shift from S_s to S_{s+P}. The additional supply by the project results in a movement of the market price from P_0^m to P_1^m. As a result of the decrease in price, consumers increase the quantity demanded, and total consumption increases from Q_0 to Q_1^d. Also owing to the decline in price, existing suppliers will cut back their production from Q_0 to Q_1^s as they will no longer supply the same amount of the good at the lower price P_1^m. The quantity produced by the project, Q_p, equals the sum of the two quantities $Q_1^d - Q_0$ and $Q_0 - Q_1^s$.

Figure 7.6: Economic Benefits of a Project (when a Production Subsidy Is Present)

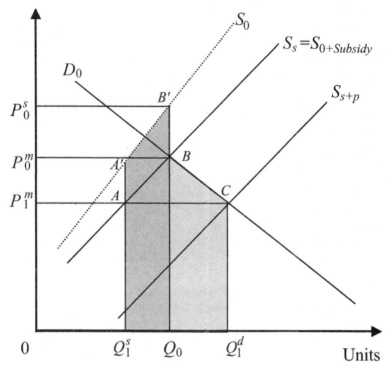

Since the project sells its output at the new prevailing market price, P_1^m,[37] the gross financial receipts to the project are given by $(Q_p \times P_1^m)$, which is area $Q_1^s A C Q_1^d$. To estimate the gross economic benefits of the project, we need to determine the economic value of the additional new consumption to the demanders and the value of the resources released by existing suppliers. These values are estimated using the first two postulates, as follows:

1. The additional consumption is valued, according to the first postulate, by the demand price for each successive unit, the area under the demand curve $(Q_0 B C Q_1^d)$.

2. The resources released by other producers are valued, according to the second postulate, by the supply price (resource cost) of each successive unit, the area under the supply curve without subsidy $(Q_1^s A'B'Q_0)$. This area includes the amount of production cost that was being paid by

---

[37]Here we assume that the project does not receive the subsidy. However, the economic value of the project output is the same whether or not the project output receives the subsidy.

consumers through the item's sales price and the amount of reduction in government subsidy shown by the area ($AA'B'B$).

Subsidy may be expressed as either a percentage of the market price or a proportion of total production cost. In this example, suppose subsidy is given at 40 percent of resources (k) spent on production of the good, and we also assume the responsiveness of the existing supply and demand to the change in price as a result of the project output as follows: $w^s = 1/3$, $w^d = 2/3$, $P_0^m = \$90$, and $k = 0.40$. The economic price of the good can then be calculated as:

$$P^e = w^s P^s + w^d P^d$$
$$= 1/3 \times [90/(1-0.40)] + 2/3 \times 90$$
$$= \$110$$

With the introduction of distortions in the form of taxes and subsidies, another stakeholder (the government) enters the picture. When there are other externalities created by pollution, monopoly markups, and price controls, the project will affect other groups in society. Consequently, when estimating the economic costs and benefits of goods and services in these distorted markets, we may expect additional benefits or costs and new players added to the list of beneficiaries or losers affected by the project.

The three basic postulates can also be used to determine the economic values for tradable goods and foreign exchange. These situations are treated in detail in later chapters.

7.4.3 Environmental Externalities

Suppose pollution is being created by an industry that is producing an input for our project. For example, some firms create waste products or effluents that are deposited in the atmosphere, in the waterways, and on the ground. This has a damaging effect on people and properties that are not directly involved in the production or consumption of the output. It is assumed that resources will have to be used now or at some future date to deal with this environmental damage. These resource costs are not recognized by the consumers of the industry's output nor are they reflected in the financial price of the item. Yet they must be included in its economic cost.

Let D_0 and S_0 denote the industry demand and supply curve of the good. If the impact on the environment is not completely internalized in the private production costs, the damage caused by the external impact of the pollution should be estimated and added to the input cost to the project, as shown in Figure 7.7.

Principles Underlying the Economic Analysis of Projects

Figure 7.7: A Project Buys an Input with a Pollution Externality

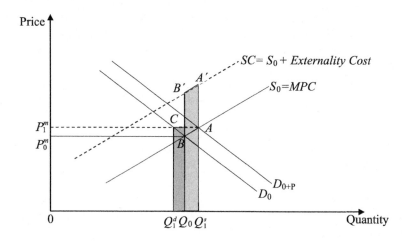

Suppose the project demands the good as a project input and causes the demand curve to shift from D_0 to D_{0+P}. As a result, the market price rises from P_0^m to P_1^m. The total consumption will decrease from Q_0 to Q_1^d, and other existing suppliers will expand their production from Q_0 to Q_1^s. Q_p, the quantity demanded by the project, equals the sum of the two quantities $Q_0 - Q_1^d$ and $Q_1^s - Q_0$.

In this case, the gross financial costs to the project are given by ($Q_p \times P_1^m$), which is shown by the area $Q_1^s A C Q_1^d$. The gross economic costs of the project are determined by the economic value of the forgone consumption by some demanders and the value of the resources increased by other existing suppliers plus the additional pollution cost. These values are estimated using the first two postulates, as follows.

1. The reduced consumption is valued, according to the first postulate, by the demand price for each successive unit, the area under the demand curve ($Q_0 B C Q_1^d$).

2. The additional resources demanded by producers alone are valued by the area under the supply curve as $Q_0 B A Q_1^s$. However, the total economic cost of production must also include the pollution externality of $BB'A'A$, yielding a total economic cost for $Q_0 Q_1^s$ of $Q_1^s A'B'Q_0$.

In this case, the economic cost of the project's input is greater than its financial cost to the project.

On the other hand, there are projects that may reduce the level of production of other producers who pollute the air or water. In this case, the project will create a positive externality owing to a reduction in the adverse impact on the environment as a result of these other producers cutting back their level of output.

In any event, the evaluation of environmental impacts may not always be straightforward and will often require a special environmental impact study. It may be noted that natural resource extraction and energy projects often produce environmental externalities, contaminating air or water. These environmental externalities are real and genuinely impose costs on the well-being of people within a country. Hence, these economic costs should be included as part of the economic costs of a project.

7.5 Other Distortions

There are other distortions in an economy to which the principles of the three basic postulates also apply. Two important areas in which other distortions play a significant role in causing divergences between economic and financial prices are the economic opportunity cost of capital and the economic opportunity cost of labour. These are briefly discussed in this section.

7.5.1 Economic Opportunity Cost of Capital

Different approaches have been used to determine the economic cost of capital. However, economic analysis suggests that the most plausible and widely applicable approach is to postulate that new expenditures are "sourced" in the capital market and that the normal destination of "free" funds is that they are returned to the capital market. In a small and open economy, this "sourcing" comes from three places: a) displaced investment (i.e., resources that would have been invested in other investment activities but are either displaced or postponed by our project's extraction of funds from the capital market); b) newly stimulated saving (as economic agents respond to increased interest rates); and c) additional foreign capital inflows (as foreign suppliers of funds also respond to the same stimulus).

Based on these three alternative sources of funds, the economic cost of capital can be estimated as a weighted average of the rate of return on displaced or postponed investments, the rate of time preference applicable to those who make additional savings, and the marginal cost of additional foreign capital inflows. In general, various distortions are associated with each of the three alternative sources of funds. The methodology will be described in detail in Chapter 8.

7.5.2 Economic Opportunity Cost of Labour

There are a variety of factors in the labour market that may create a divergence between the market wage and the economic cost of a worker at the project. We can start with the genuine supply price of labour, i.e., the wage rate (including fringe benefits) that a given employer (or project) has to pay in order to acquire labour services of any type and quality. The supply price of labour reflects the whole panoply of market and non-market incentives facing workers as they consider the options of being in the workforce or not, and once they are there, as they consider all the monetary and non-monetary factors that govern the desirability of working on the project vis-à-vis the many alternative options they face. This supply price is a key starting point for estimating the economic opportunity cost of labour, but to reach that target other distortions (especially taxes) must be added.

Sometimes the project is expected to pay net wages that are higher than the supply price of labour in the market. This is mainly the case when there are minimum wage laws or unionized labour. One can also find other reasons why some employers offer wages that exceed the prevailing market rates. In all such cases, a wedge is created between the wage actually paid to workers in a project and the cost incurred by the economy when such workers are employed on a project.

Whereas in calculating the economic cost of capital or foreign exchange we are dealing with a fairly homogeneous item, virtually the opposite is true in the case of labour. Wages differ by occupation, skill, experience, location, type of job, etc. We will be fully conscious of this extreme heterogeneity when we estimate the economic prices of different categories of labour in Chapter 12.

7.6 Conclusion

This chapter has presented the three postulates underlying the methodology of economic evaluation. We have first shown how the three postulates are applied to the economic valuation of non-tradable goods and services in an undistorted market and later how they apply when distortions are present.

In general, there are likely to be many distortions prevailing in an economy under evaluation. These distortions include, among others, value-added taxes, excise duties, import duties, and production subsidies.

Later chapters will give detailed explanations of the way in which distortions of various kinds enter into the estimation of the economic opportunity costs of foreign exchange, of capital, and of labour of different types, as well as of specific inputs and outputs, both tradable and non-tradable. We hope that the present chapter has given readers a useful overview, a point of departure for the more detailed analyses to come.

References

Boardman, A.E., D.H. Greenberg, A.R. Vining, and D.L. Weimer. 2001. *Cost-Benefit Analysis: Concepts and Practice*, 2nd edition. Englewood Cliffs, NJ: Prentice Hall.

Curry, S. and J. Weiss. 1993. *Project Analysis in Developing Countries*. New York: St. Martin's Press.

Harberger, A.C. 1971. "Three Basic Postulates for Applied Welfare Economics", *Journal of Economic Literature* 9(3), 758–797.

— 1978. "On the Use of Distributional Weights in Social Cost-Benefit Analysis", *Journal of Political Economy* 86(2), Part 2: Research in Taxation, S87–S120.

— 1984. "Basic Needs Versus Distributional Weights in Cost-Benefit Analysis", *Economic Development and Cultural Change* 32(3), 455–474.

— 1987. "Reflections on Social Project Evaluation", in G.M. Meier (ed.), *Pioneers in Development*, Vol. II. Washington, DC: The World Bank and Oxford: Oxford University Press.

Harberger, A.C. and G.P. Jenkins. 2002. Introduction to A.C. Harberger and G.P. Jenkins (eds.), *Cost-Benefit Analysis*. Cheltenham: Edward Elgar Publishing Limited.

Harberger, A.C., G.P. Jenkins, C.Y. Kuo, and M.B. Mphahlele. 2003. "The Economic Cost of Foreign Exchange for South Africa", *South African Journal of Economics* 71:2 (June), 298–324.

Hartwick, J.M. and N.D. Olewiler. 1986. *The Economics of Natural Resource Use*. New York: Harper and Row Publishers.

Hirshleifer, J., J.C. DeHaven, and J.W. Milliman. 1960. *Water Supply: Economics, Technology, and Policy*. Chicago, IL: University of Chicago Press.

Jenkins, G.P. 1999. "Evaluation of Stakeholder Impacts in Cost-Benefit Analysis", *Impact Assessment and Project Appraisal* 17(2), 87-96.

Jenkins, G.P. and C.Y. Kuo. 1998. "Estimation of the National Parameters for Economic Cost-Benefit Analysis for the Philippines", Development Discussion Paper, Harvard Institute for International Development, Harvard University (May).

Jenkins, G.P. and H.B.F. Lim. 1998. "An Integrated Analysis of a Power Purchase Agreement", Development Discussion Paper, Harvard Institute for International Development, Harvard University.

Little, I.M.D. and J.A. Mirrlees. 1974. *Project Appraisal and Planning for Developing Countries*. London: Heinemann Educational Books.

Mason, S., C. Baldwin, and D. Lessard. 1983. "Budgetary Time Bombs: Controlling Government Loan Guarantees", *Canadian Journal of Public Policy* 9(3).

Mishan, E.J. and E. Quah. 2007. *Cost-Benefit Analysis,* 5th edition. London and New York: Routledge.

Roemer M. and J.J. Stern. 1975. *The Appraisal of Development Projects*. New York: Praeger Publishers.

Squire, L. and H. van der Tak. 1975. *Economic Analysis of Projects*. Baltimore and London: Johns Hopkins.

United Nations Industrial Development Organization. 1972. *Guidelines for Project Evaluation*. New York: United Nations.

Vega, A.O. 1997. "Risk Allocation in Infrastructure Financing", *The Journal of Project Finance* 3(2), 38-42.

Wells, L.T. and E.C. Gleason. 1995. "Is Foreign Infrastructure Investment Still Risky?" *Harvard Business Review* (September-October) , 44-54.

Zerbe, R.O. Jr. and D.D. Dively. 1994. *Benefit-Cost Analysis in Theory and Practice.* New York: Harper Collins College Publishers.

Chapter Eight

Economic Opportunity Cost of Capital

8.1 Why Is the Economic Cost of Capital Important?

An investment project usually lasts for many years; hence, its appraisal requires a comparison of the costs and benefits over its entire lifetime. In order for it to be accepted, the present value (PV) of the project's expected benefits should exceed the PV of its expected costs. Among a set of mutually exclusive projects, the one with the highest net present value (NPV) should be chosen.[38] This criterion requires the use of a discount rate so that the benefits and costs that are distributed over the life of the investment can be compared.

The discount rate recommended here for the calculation of the economic NPV of projects is the economic opportunity cost of capital for the country. If on the one hand the economic NPV of a project is greater than zero, it is potentially worthwhile to implement the project. This implies that the project would generate more net economic benefits than the same resources would have generated if used elsewhere in the economy. On the other hand, if the NPV is less than zero, the project should be rejected on the grounds that the resources invested would have yielded a higher economic return if they had been left for the capital market to allocate to other uses.

In the process of project design, the economic cost of capital also plays an important role in the maximization of the potential economic NPV of a project. It is a critical parameter for decision-making on the optimum size of the project and the appropriate timing for the implementation of an investment. Both are key factors affecting the project's net benefits and its ultimate feasibility. In addition, the choice of technology for a project is influenced by the opportunity cost of capital. For example, a low cost of capital will encourage the use of capital-intensive technologies as opposed to labour- or fuel-intensive technologies.

---

[38]The benefit–cost ratio is often used as a decision criterion in an economic evaluation. However, the NPV criterion is known to be more reliable than other criteria for both the financial and the economic evaluation. For the financial appraisal, other criteria include the payback period, the debt service ratio, and the internal rate of return. Each of these criteria has its own shortcomings. Detailed discussions are presented in Chapter 4.

8.1.1 Choosing the Scale of a Project

An important decision in project appraisal concerns the size or scale of the facility to be built. It is seldom the case that the scale of a project is constrained by technological factors; hence, economic considerations should be paramount in selecting the appropriate scale. Even if the project is not built to its correct size, it may be a viable project because its NPV may still be positive, albeit less than its potential. The NPV is maximized only when the optimum scale is chosen.

As was discussed in Chapter 5, the appropriate principle for determining the scale of a project is to treat (hypothetically, and on the drawing board, as it were) each incremental change in size as a project in itself. An increase in the scale of a project will require additional expenditures and will generate additional benefits. The PV of the costs and benefits of each incremental change should be calculated using the economic discount rate.

The NPV of each incremental project indicates by how much it increases or decreases the overall NPV of the project. This procedure is repeated (at the planning, drawing-board stage) until a scale is reached at which the NPV of incremental benefits and costs associated with an increment of scale changes from positive to negative. When this occurs, the previous scale (with the last upward step of NPV) is the optimum size of the project. The effect that the economic opportunity cost of capital or economic discount rate has on determining the size of the NPV gives it a central role in determining the optimum scale of a project.

8.1.2 Timing of Investment

Another important decision to be made in project analysis relates to the appropriate time at which a project should start. A project that is built too soon could result in a large amount of idle capacity. In this case, the forgone return from the use of resources elsewhere might be greater than the benefits gained in the first few years of the project's life. In contrast, if a project is delayed too long, shortages may occur, and the forgone benefits of the project will be greater than the alternative yields of the resources.

Whenever a project is undertaken too soon or too late, its NPV will be lower than if it had been developed at the optimum time. The NPV may still be positive, but it will not be at the project's potential maximum.

The key to making a decision on this issue is whether the costs of postponement of the project are greater or smaller than the benefits of postponement. In the most straightforward case, where investment costs K remain the same whether the project is started in either Period t or Period $t+1$, the costs of postponement from Year t to Year $t+1$ are simply the economic benefits B_{t+1} forgone by delaying the project. On the other hand, the benefit of postponement is the economic return, r_e, that can be earned from the capital invested in the general economy. Thus, the benefit from postponement is equal to the economic opportunity cost of capital multiplied by the capital costs (i.e., $r_e \times K_t$).[39] One can see again that the value of the economic opportunity cost of funds is an essential component in deciding the correct time for starting a project.[40]

8.1.3 Choice of Technology

In order to be a worthwhile undertaking, any investment project must earn enough to cover the economic opportunity cost of capital. If this is not the case, the capital would be better allocated to other uses through the normal workings of the capital market.

Sometimes public sector projects face a financial cost of capital that is artificially low. This is the case not only when they can raise funds at an artificially low rate of interest because of government subsidies or guarantees, but also (typically) when they raise funds at the market-determined rate of yield on government bonds. In either case, the cost of capital perceived by the project may be far below its economic opportunity cost.

The use of a lower financial cost of capital instead of its economic opportunity cost would create an incentive for project managers to use production techniques that are too capital-intensive. The choice of an excessively capital-intensive technology would lead to economic inefficiency because the value of the marginal product of capital in this activity is below the economic cost of capital to the country. For example, in electricity generation, using a financial cost of capital that is lower than its economic cost will make capital-intensive options such as distant hydroelectric dams or nuclear power plants more attractive than oil- or coal-fired generation plants (Jenkins, 1985). Hence, it is necessary to have a correct measure of the economic opportunity cost of capital in order to make the right choice of technology.

8.2 Alternative Methods of Choosing Discount Rates for Public Sector Project Evaluation

The choice of the discount rate to be used in economic cost–benefit analysis has been one of the most contentious and controversial issues in this area of economics. The term "discount rate" refers to the time value of the costs and benefits from the viewpoint of society. It is similar to the concept of the private

---

[39]There are a number of cases in which the benefits and capital costs are also a function of calendar time. These are discussed in Chapter 5.

[40]This exercise applies when the benefits of the project in period t are the same, regardless of whether the investment was made in t, $t+1$, $t+2$, etc., and also when the stream of project benefits over time is increasing with time, i.e., $B_{t+2} > B_{t+1} > B_t$.

opportunity cost of capital used to discount a stream of net cash flows of an investment project, but the implications can be more complex. However, after much debate, a consensus, or at least a reasonably good understanding of the issues, has emerged.

In essence, four alternative approaches have been put forward on this issue. First, some authors have suggested that all investment projects, both public and private, should be discounted by a rate equal to the marginal productivity of capital in the private sector (Hirshleifer et al., 1960). The rationale for this choice is that if the government wants to maximize the country's output, it should always invest in the projects that have the highest return. If private sector projects have a higher expected economic return than the available public sector projects, the government should ensure that funds are invested in the private rather than the public projects.

Second, authors such as Little and Mirrlees (1974) and Squire and van der Tak (1975) have recommended the use of an accounting rate of interest. Their accounting rate of interest is the estimated marginal return from public sector projects given the fixed amount of investment funds available to the government. The accounting rate of interest is essentially a rationing device. If there are more projects that look acceptable than the available investible funds, the accounting rate of interest should be adjusted upwards; and if too few projects look promising, the adjustment should be made in the other direction. Therefore, the accounting rate of interest does not serve to ensure that funds are optimally allocated between the public and the private sectors, but acts only to ensure that the best public sector projects are recommended within the constraint of the amount of funds available to the public sector. This approach does not recognize the fact that if the funds are not spent by the public sector, they can always be used to reduce the public sector's debt. They will then be allocated by the capital market for use by the private sector.

Third, it has been recommended that the benefits and costs of projects should be discounted by the social rate of time preference for consumption, but only after costs have been adjusted by the shadow price of investment to reflect the fact that forgone private investment has a higher social return than present consumption. This method has been proposed by such authors as Dasgupta et al. (1972), Marglin (1963), and Feldstein (1964).

Fourth, Harberger and other authors have suggested that the discount rate for capital investments should be the economic opportunity cost of funds obtained from the capital market. This rate is a weighted average of the marginal productivity of capital in the private sector and the rate of time preference for consumption (Harberger, 1968; 1987). This proposal has been reinforced by the theoretical work of Sandmo and Dreze (1971) and Dreze (1974), and reconciled to a degree through the alternative approach of using a social rate of time preference in conjunction with a shadow price of investment, a method advocated by Sjaastad and Wisecarver (1977).

Many professionals have chosen to follow this weighted average opportunity cost of funds concept. Furthermore, Burgess (2008) has shown that under a wide range of circumstances, the use of the economic opportunity cost of funds as the discount rate leads to the correct investment choice, while other approaches lead to the selection of inferior projects.

In its simplest form, the economic opportunity cost of public funds, i_e, is a weighted average of the rate of time preference for consumption r and the rate of return on private investment ρ. It can be written as follows:

$$i_e = W_c r + (1 - W_c) \times \rho \tag{8.1}$$

where W_c is the proportion of the incremental public sector funds obtained at the expense of current consumption and $(1 - W_c)$ is the proportion obtained at the expense of postponed investment.[41]

8.3 Derivation of the Economic Opportunity Cost of Capital

The rates of interest observed in the capital markets are fundamentally determined by the willingness of people to save and the opportunities that are available for investment. In an economy characterized by perfect competition with full employment and no distortions, the real market interest rate would reflect the marginal valuation of capital over time and could be used as the economic discount rate. However, in reality there are distortions in the capital markets, such as business and personal taxes, and inflation; hence, market interest rates will reflect neither the saver's time preferences for consumption nor the gross economic returns generated by private sector investment. Both savers and investors must take into consideration taxes and other distortions when entering the capital market to lend or borrow.

The determination of the market interest rate is illustrated by Figure 8.1 for the case in which savers are required to pay personal income taxes on interest income and borrowers pay both business income taxes and property taxes on their investment. For the moment, the effects of inflation will be set aside so that all the rates of return are expressed in real terms. The curve $GS(r)$ shows the relationship between the supply of savings and the rate of return r received from savings net of personal income taxes. This function indicates the minimum net return that savers must receive before they are willing to postpone current consumption and save for future consumption. If there is a personal income tax, savers will require a return that is sufficiently larger than r to allow them to pay income taxes on the interest income and still have a return of r left. The savings function, which includes the taxes on interest income, is shown as $FS(i)$.

---

[41]For a more complete discussion of this derivation, see Harberger (1968; 1972).

Economic Opportunity Cost of Capital

Figure 8.1: Determination of Market Interest Rates

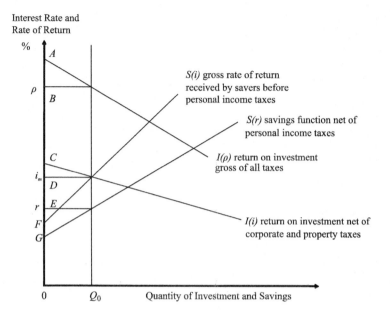

Interest Rate and
Rate of Return

%

S(i) gross rate of return
received by savers before
personal income taxes

S(r) savings function net of
personal income taxes

I(ρ) return on investment
gross of all taxes

I(i) return on investment net of
corporate and property taxes

0   Q_0 Quantity of Investment and Savings

At the same time, investors have a ranking of investment projects according to their expected gross-of-tax rates of return, which is shown as the curve $AI(\rho)$. If the owners of the capital have to pay property taxes and business income taxes, they will be willing to pay less for their investment funds than in a no-tax situation. $CI(i)$ reflects the rate of return that investors can expect to receive net of all business and property taxes. In this market situation, the interest rate i_m will be determined by the gross-of-personal-income-tax savings function $FS(i)$ and the net-of-tax demand for investment curve $CI(i)$.

The basic principle that must be followed to ensure that a project's investment expenditures do not ultimately retard the level of economic output of the country is that such investments must produce a rate of return that is at least equal to the economic return of other investment and consumption that is postponed, plus the true marginal cost of any additional funds borrowed from abroad as a direct or indirect consequence of the project. In order to form a general criterion for the economic opportunity cost of capital for a country, we must assess the sources from which that capital is obtained and attach an appropriate economic cost to each source.

For most countries, it is realistic to assume that there exists a functioning capital market. That is not to say that it is free of distortions, for it is the existence of distortions, such as taxes and subsidies, that prevents us from using the real interest rate in the market as a measure of the economic opportunity cost of funds. In addition, most governments and private investors obtain marginal funds to finance their budgets from the capital market and, during periods of budgetary surplus, typically reduce their debts.

Chapter Eight   *185*

It is true that the financing for a government's budget comes from many sources other than borrowing, such as sales and income taxes, tariffs, fees, and perhaps sales of goods and services. The average economic opportunity cost of all these sources of finance combined may well be lower than the economic opportunity cost of borrowing. However, this fact is irrelevant for the purpose of estimating the marginal opportunity cost of the government's expenditures. As with the estimation of the supply price of any other good or service, the marginal economic opportunity cost must reflect the ways in which an incremental demand will normally be met. Even in the very short run, most governments are either borrowing or, when enjoying a budgetary surplus, paying off some of their debt.[42] Therefore, if fewer public sector projects are undertaken in a given year, more funds will be available in the capital markets for private sector use.

This is not to imply that each year every government uses the capital market as its source or repository of marginal funds. However, the overwhelming evidence from observing developing and developed countries indicates that this is a fair characterization of the behaviour of most governments. As the economic discount rate is a parameter that should be generally applicable across projects and estimated consistently over time, it is prudent for a country to base its estimate of the economic opportunity cost on the cost of extracting the necessary funds from the capital market. The approach has a further advantage in that the capital market is clearly the marginal source of funds for most of the private sector. Hence, it follows that the economic opportunity cost of funds for both the public and the private sectors is based on the costs derived from similar capital market operations.

To estimate the economic opportunity cost of funds obtained through the capital market, we will first assume that the country's capital market is closed to foreign borrowing or lending. It is also assumed that taxes such as property taxes and business income taxes are levied on the income generated by capital in at least some of the sectors. In addition, we will assume that a personal income tax is applied to the investment income of savers.

In Figure 8.2, we begin with a situation in which the market rate of return is i and the quantity of funds demanded and supplied in the capital market is Q_0. At this point, the marginal economic rate of return on additional investment in the economy is ρ and the rate of time preference, which measures the marginal value of current consumption, is equal to r. Funds of the amount of B are then borrowed from the capital market to finance the project by the amount $(Q_s - Q_t)$. This causes the total demand in the economy for loanable funds to shift from $CI(i)$ to $C'I(i)+B$. However, the value of funds for investment elsewhere in the economy, and the net-of-tax returns to them, is measured by the curve $CI(i)$. The gross-of-tax return on the investments is measured by the curve $AI(\rho)$.

---

[42]Some of this debt may reflect foreign as well as domestic borrowings.

Figure 8.2: The Economic Opportunity Cost of Capital

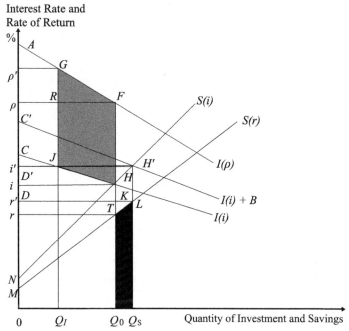

Interest Rate and
Rate of Return

Quantity of Investment and Savings

The increase in the demand for funds by the project will cause the market cost of funds to increase from i to i', thus inducing people to save more (postpone consumption) by an amount $(Q_s - Q_0)$. At the same time, the higher cost of funds will cause people to postpone investments by an amount $(Q_0 - Q_I)$.

The economic cost of postponing consumption is equal to the area Q_0TLQ_s, which is the net-of-tax return that savers receive from their increased savings. This is measured by the area under the $MS(r)$ curve between Q_0 and Q_s. With a linear supply function, this area is estimated by the average economic cost per unit, $[(r + r')/2]$, multiplied by the number of units, $(Q_s - Q_0)$. Postponed investment has a gross-of-tax economic opportunity cost, which is measured by the $AI(\rho)$ curve. This includes both the net return given up by the private owners of the investment measured by the curve $CI(i)$ and the property and business taxes lost. This opportunity cost is shown by the shaded area Q_IGFQ_0, of which Q_IJHQ_0 is the net return forgone by the would-be owners of the investment, and $JGFH$ represents the amount of taxes lost by the government. Again, this can be calculated by the economic opportunity cost per unit $[(\rho + \rho')/2]$ multiplied by the number of units, $(Q_0 - Q_I)$. For marginal changes in government borrowing, we can safely disregard the triangles RGF and KLT, which arise from the change in interest rates.

The economic opportunity cost of capital i_e can then be defined as:

$$i_e = \frac{r \times (\partial S / \partial i) - \rho \times (\partial I / \partial i)}{(\partial S / \partial i) - (\partial I / \partial i)} \tag{8.2}$$

where $(\partial S / \partial i)$ and $(\partial I / \partial i)$ denote the reaction of savers and other investors, respectively, to a change in market interest rates brought about by the increase in government borrowing.

Expressed in elasticity form, equation (8.2) becomes:

$$i_e = \frac{r \times \varepsilon_s - \rho \times \eta_I \times (I_T / S_T)}{\varepsilon_s - \eta_I \times (I_T / S_T)} \tag{8.3}$$

where ε_s is the elasticity of supply of private sector savings, η_I is the elasticity of demand for private sector investment with respect to changes in the rate of interest, and I_T/S_T is the ratio of total private sector investment to total savings.

Let us suppose that $\rho = 0.16$ and $r = 0.05$. Let us also assume that $\varepsilon_s = 0.3$, $\eta_I = -1.0$, and $I_T/S_T = 0.9$. In this case, the economic opportunity cost of capital can be calculated as:

$$
\begin{aligned}
i_e &= [0.05\,(0.3) - 0.16\,(-1.0)\,(0.9)] \, / \, [0.3 - (-1.0)(0.9)] \\
&= (0.015 + 0.144) \, / \, (1.20) \\
&= 0.133
\end{aligned}
$$

The economic opportunity cost of capital is 13.3 percent. Typically, it will be closer to the gross return from investment than the rate of time preference on consumption because the elasticity of private savings is generally much smaller than the absolute value of the elasticity of demand for private sector investment.

In equation (8.3), all the different groups of savers have been aggregated into one category, and all groups of investors have also been grouped into one sector. The aggregate elasticity of supply of savings and the aggregate elasticity of demand for investment can be disaggregated into their components as follows:

$$\varepsilon^s = \sum_{i=1}^{m} \varepsilon_i^s \, (S_i / S_T) \tag{8.4}$$

$$\eta^I = \sum_{j=1}^{n} \eta_j^I (I_j / I_T) \tag{8.5}$$

where ε_i^s refers to the elasticity of supply of the ith group of savers and (S_i / S_T) is the proportion of total savings supplied by this group; η_j^I refers to the elasticity of demand for the jth group of investors, and (I_j/I_T) is the proportion of the total investment demanded by this group.

Substituting equations (8.4) and (8.5) into equation (8.3), we obtain an expression for the economic opportunity cost of capital that allows for consideration of different distortions within the classes of savers and investors:

$$
i_e = \frac{\sum_{i=1}^{m} \varepsilon_i^s (S_i / S_T) r_i - \sum_{j=1}^{n} \eta_j^I (I_j / S_T) \rho_j}{\sum_{i=1}^{m} \varepsilon_i^s (S_i / S_T) - \sum_{j=1}^{n} \eta_j^I (I_j / S_T)}
\tag{8.6}
$$

The classes of savers will usually be differentiated by income groups that face different marginal income tax rates. There will also be savings by domestic businesses. However, it is not clear whether higher interest rates would affect the amount of business savings because the decisions that businesspeople make about whether or not to pay dividends are based more on business investment opportunities. Thus, the amount of business savings is assumed in this study to be independent of interest rates. We can also include in the broad class of savers the foreign savers who supply the funds to a country when it obtains funds from abroad. As the international capital markets become more accessible to domestic investors, we would expect the elasticity of supply of this sector to increase in relation to the other sources of savings. In some circumstances, the cost of foreign borrowing and the elasticity of supply of foreign savings might dominate the entire equation (8.6). It is therefore important to properly assess the economic cost of foreign borrowing; this will be discussed in Section 8.5.

On the demand side, investors are typically divided into the corporate sector, the non-corporate sector, housing, and agriculture, according to the different tax treatment provided to these sectors.

8.4 Determining the Economic Cost of Alternative Sources of Funds

Measuring the real rate of return to reproducible capital in a country is not an easy task. In most cases, the most consistent approach is based on the country's national income accounts. At the very least, the accounts presume to cover the full range of economic activities in the country (including such items as the implicit income from owner-occupied houses and the value added of many informal sector activities).

Employing this method of calculation, one starts from a past base period and the real amount of investment made during each period from the base year until the present. For these purposes, the amounts of real investment should be obtained by deflating nominal investment by the general gross domestic product (GDP) deflator (not the official investment deflator). The purpose of this is to express the capital stock of the country in the same units of account as those used to express the earnings of capital. Our methodology employs the GDP deflator as the general numeraire; it is used to convert all nominal values into real values.

If investment is available by component, it is desirable to carry out the estimates component by component (buildings, machinery, vehicles, inventories) in order to allow for different depreciation rates on these categories. Once an initial capital stock K_{j0} is estimated for each component, and its appropriate depreciation rate δ_j established, the time path of the capital stock is generated by the formula

$$K_{j,t+1} = K_{jt}(1 - \delta_j) + I_{jt}$$

where I_{jt} denotes the amount of new gross investment in each component.

Obviously, it is not possible to speak of a separate rate of return to different pieces of the capital stock of the same entity, so we express the rate of return as Y_{kt}/K_t, where $K_t = \Sigma K_{jt}$ and Y_{kt} is the income from capital at time t. It consists of the sum of interest, rent, and profit income, as recorded in the national accounts. If these items do not appear explicitly, it is usually possible at least to find a breakdown that includes wages and salaries as one category, corporate profits as a second, and the surplus of non-corporate enterprises as a third. Here the challenge is to separate the surplus of non-corporate enterprises into two components, one representing the value added due to time value of the owners and their family members, the other representing the gross return to capital in these enterprises.

However, this is not the end of the task. Since we are building up a stock of K_t of reproducible capital, its value should necessarily exclude that of land (although improvement to land, such as fences, canals, and even levelling, should be treated as reproducible). So from the income stream accruing to capital, we definitely want to exclude the portion that we estimate as accruing to land. In addition, we should exclude most elements of government capital from the capital base used to calculate its rate of return. Likewise, we should exclude from the relevant "return to capital" any income from these items. In some countries this would give us a rate of return straightforwardly based on the real earnings of reproducible private sector capital (in the numerator) and the real value of this private sector capital stock (in the denominator). However, in most countries these also exist in public sector productive entities such as electricity companies, railways, airlines, ports, and even manufacturing facilities, which behave sufficiently like other business enterprises to warrant being counted in the same calculation, alongside private business enterprises.

In order to see clearly the rationale for this treatment, readers should focus on the purpose for which we want to calculate the economic opportunity cost of capital in the first place. That purpose is best seen by visualizing the exercise of any organization or person — a private company, one or more individuals, a non-profit institution, the government itself — going into the country's capital market to raise money. This puts added pressure on that market and squeezes out other demanders for funds, while giving some additional stimulus to suppliers of funds in that market. We take the position that the actions of business firms and private savers are governed by natural economic motives, in the sense that we can take seriously the idea that they have reasonably well-defined supply and/or demand functions for funds as a function of interest rates and other variables in that country's capital market. We suggest that government (apart from those public enterprises that in fact behave like business firms) operates mainly with a different type of machinery — legislative acts and authorizations, budgetary decisions, administrative edicts, and the like. In short, we do not see previously authorized public investments being "naturally" squeezed out by a tightening capital market in the same way as we see this same phenomenon for regular business investments.

Our vision of the economic opportunity cost of capital is that as new demands for funds in a country's capital market squeeze out alternative investments, the country loses (or perhaps forgoes) the returns that would have been generated by these investments; at the same time, the country incurs the costs involved in covering the supply prices of the new amounts of saving that are stimulated by the new demand, in addition to whatever incremental costs are entailed in newly generated capital inflows from abroad.

We thus start with a weighted average of the marginal productivity, ρ, of displaced investments, the marginal supply price, r, of newly stimulated savings, and the marginal cost, MC_f, associated with newly stimulated inflows from abroad. This simple vision can be represented as:

$$EOCK = f_1\rho + f_2\,r + f_3\,(MC_f) \tag{8.7}$$

where f_1, f_2, and f_3 are the sourcing fractions linked, respectively, to sourcing from displaced investment, newly stimulated domestic savings, and newly stimulated capital inflows from abroad. Obviously, $f_1 + f_2 + f_3$ should equal 1.

A key element in this story is ρ, since f_1 is typically the largest of the three sourcing fractions. As previously mentioned, we conceive of ρ as representing the typical marginal productivity of the class of investments it is intended to cover. We recommend its estimation, as indicated above, on the basis of the ratio of returns to reproducible capital (net of depreciation but gross of taxes) in the productive sector of the economy to the value of reproducible capital in the productive sector of the economy. If the reproducible capital stock can be conveniently estimated only for the total economy, it would be advisable to reduce this stock by a fraction that is estimated to account for the bulk of public sector capital items, such as government buildings, schools, roads, etc., which are not basically business oriented.

In order to achieve the rate of return that represents the supply price r of newly stimulated domestic savings, we must certainly exclude the taxes on income from capital that are paid directly by business entities plus the property taxes paid by these entities, as well as by homeowners. In addition, we would want to exclude the personal income taxes that are paid on the basis of the income from reproducible capital.

If aggregate national accounts data are being used, we recommend subtracting from the gross-of-tax return to reproducible capital the full amount of corporation income taxes paid and the full amount of property taxes paid, adjusted downward to exclude an estimated portion falling on land. In addition, there is a need to subtract the full amount of personal income taxes paid on the income from capital, also adjusted downward to exclude the income taxes that are paid on the income derived from land.

When this is done, the remaining value covers not only the net-of-tax income received by individual owners of capital but also the costs of intermediation, which is most easily understood (in the case of bank loans) as the difference between the average rate of interest that banks receive on their loans and the average rate they pay to their depositors.

It is also possible to approach the estimation of the economic opportunity cost of capital in a more disaggregated way, distinguishing separate categories of displaced investment (e.g., corporate, non-corporate, and housing) owing to the different tax treatments they receive and distinguishing different categories of savings on a similar basis (e.g., savers with marginal tax rates of 30, 20, 10, and zero percent). For example, in the latter case, the higher an individual's rate of personal income tax, the lower their equilibrium rate of time preference for consumption will be. In a situation in which the market interest rate is equal to 0.08 and the marginal rate of personal income tax is assumed to be 0.1, the value of r is 0.072. Now consider a high-income individual who is faced with a marginal personal income tax rate of 0.4. This individual will have low rates of time preference at 0.048 guiding their decisions on how to spend their consumption over time. Thus, high rates of time preference and high discount rates correspond more closely to the decisions of the poor concerning the distribution of their consumption over time.

Furthermore, consumers who are borrowing in order to finance current consumption will typically have higher rates of time preference than those who only save. If the margin required by finance companies and money lenders over the normal market interest rate is M percentage points, the rate of time preference for borrowers on consumer loans is the sum of the market interest rate and M percentage points. Supposing M is 0.11, the rate of time preference for borrowers on consumer loans becomes 0.19, a rate that is often charged on credit cards, even in advanced countries. From these examples, we can see that as we move from the poor borrowers to the rich groups in society, which are net savers, the time preference rate can quite realistically fall from 0.19 to 0.048.

However, we believe that this approach, which we ourselves have often used in the past,[43] suffers from its de-linking from the aggregate national accounts framework. For example, our preferred framework deducts taxes actually paid, and thus incorporates all the effects of avoidance, evasion, and corruption as they occur in the country in question, while the disaggregated framework tends, perhaps naively, to make the assumption that the statutory marginal rates are rigorously applied.

8.5 Marginal Economic Cost of Foreign Financing

In this section we deal with the estimation of marginal economic cost of newly stimulated capital inflows from abroad as a result of project funds raised in capital markets. Foreign capital inflows reflect an inflow of savings from foreigners, which augment the resources available for investment. When the demand for investible funds is increased, this will not only induce domestic residents to consume less and save more, but will also attract foreign savings. When the market interest rate is increased to attract funds, an additional cost is created in the case of foreign borrowing. Not only is this higher interest rate paid on the incremental borrowing, it will also be charged on all the variable interest rate debt, both current and prior, that is made on a variable interest rate basis. Thus, it is the marginal cost of borrowing by the project that is material in this case (Harberger, 1980; Edwards, 1986).

If the interest rate on foreign borrowing by the project is i'_f, it reflects only the average cost of this financing. The marginal cost that is relevant is given by the sum of the cost of foreign financing of the additional unit and the extra financial burden on all other borrowings that are responsive to the market interest rate. This is shown in Figure 8.3.

---

[43]Jenkins (1973) and Barreix (2003). In the study by Barreix, the analysis was carried out using both aggregate and sector-disaggregated approaches, and demonstrated that both estimates were completely reconcilable.

Figure 8.3: Marginal Economic Cost of Foreign Borrowing

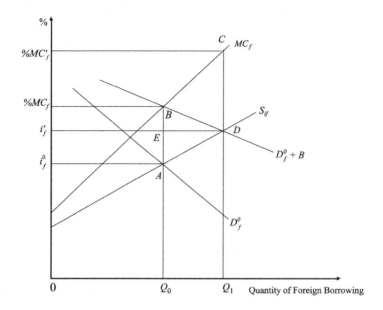

If a country faces an upward-sloping supply curve for foreign financing, the interest rate that borrowers have to pay will increase as the quantity of debt rises relative to the country's capacity to service this foreign debt. With a demand curve for foreign borrowing shown as D_f^0, the interest rate charged on such loans is shown at i_f^0 and the quantity of foreign borrowings Q_0. Now suppose that the demand for loanable funds B increases such that its demand for foreign loans shifts to $D_f^0 + B$. As a result of the additional funds $(Q_1 - Q_0)$ demanded in the capital market, there will be a slightly higher market interest rate, i'_f, paid to foreign savers. This higher interest rate i'_f will be paid not only on the foreign borrowing of this year but on any variable interest rate loans in its stock of foreign financing that are affected by the increased market interest rate for foreign financing. The latter also includes the country risk for the respective country. With the greater stock of foreign financing that must be serviced using foreign exchange, the lender faces a greater exposure to the risk of default from macroeconomic instability. As a consequence, the marginal economic cost of foreign borrowing, MC_f, is not given by the supply curve of foreign savings available to the country but by the marginal economic cost curve, which lies above the supply curve.

Algebraically, the marginal economic cost of foreign borrowing is shown as:

$$MC_f = i_f \times (1-t_w) + (\partial i_f / \partial L) \times (1-t_w) \times \phi \times L \qquad (8.8)$$

where t_w is the rate of withholding taxes charged on interest payments made abroad; L is the total value of the stock of foreign financing; ϕ is the ratio of the total foreign debt whose interest rate is flexible and will respond to additional foreign financing to the total stock of foreign financing for the country; and $(\partial i_f / \partial L)$ is the rate of change in the cost of foreign financing as the current foreign financing increases. Alternatively:

$$MC_f = i_f \times (1-t_w) \times \{1 + \phi \times (1/\varepsilon_s^f)\} \qquad (8.9)$$

where ε_s^f is the supply elasticity of foreign funds to a country with respect to the cost of funds the country pays on its new foreign financing.

Let us consider the case where $i_f = 0.10$, $t_w = 0.20$, $\varepsilon_s^f = 1.5$, and $\phi = 0.60$. Using equation (8.9), MC_f is equal to 0.112. In this case, with a market interest rate of 10 percent for foreign loans, the marginal cost of foreign borrowing would be 11.2 percent.

A final factor that needs to be considered when estimating the marginal economic cost of foreign borrowing is the effect of the expected rate of inflation. If gp_f denotes the expected rate of foreign inflation, then the marginal economic cost of foreign borrowing, MC'_f, after adjustment for inflation, can be derived as follows:

$$MC'_f = \frac{[i_f \times (1-t_w) - gp_f] \times [1 + \phi \times \dfrac{1}{\varepsilon_s^f}]}{(1 + gp_f)} \qquad (8.10)$$

To estimate the economic opportunity cost of capital in an open economy, we need to combine equation (8.7) with equation (8.10) and the estimate of gross-of-tax return from domestic investment ρ and the cost of newly stimulated domestic savings r. It is these rates of opportunity cost, along with their respective weights, that generate the weighted average rate that should be used as the rate of discount for all government expenditures.

8.6 Intergenerational and Risk-adjusted Economic Discounting

Questions have been raised as to whether a lower rate should be used for intergenerational discounting because many of the people affected by a particular project or policy may no longer be alive in the distant future (United States Environmental Protection Agency, 2000). However, there is little consensus in the economic literature on economic discounting for intergenerational projects or policies. There are several reasons for not favouring the use of different discount rates over the project impact period unless the opportunity cost of funds is abnormally high or low from one period to another.

Moreover, for projects in which capital expenditures are incurred at the beginning of the project while benefits are spread over the life of the project, applying one discount rate for the streams of costs and another for the streams of benefits can be problematic and empirically difficult for each project. The informational requirements are very demanding for converting all the streams of costs into consumption equivalents in a consistent manner. The problem becomes more complicated when the streams of costs and benefits occur simultaneously and are spread over all years. Using a weighted average of the economic rate of return on alternative sources of funds, the discount rate based on the opportunity cost of forgone investment and consumption can avoid the complicated adjustments.

The use of a risk-adjusted economic discount rate has also been suggested elsewhere to account for the systematic risk of future uncertainty (Brean et al., 2005). However, the discount rates derived above are associated with the average risk in the economy. Since the streams of uncertain future costs and benefits are mainly related to the input variables themselves, they are best dealt with using the Monte Carlo risk analysis, as described in Chapter 6, rather than the adjusted economic discount rates.

8.7 Country Study: Economic Cost of Capital for South Africa

This section illustrates how the economic opportunity cost of capital for South Africa is estimated following the methodology outlined in the previous sections. South Africa is considered a small, open, developing economy. When funds are raised in the capital market to finance any investment projects, those funds are likely to come from three different sources, as described in Section 8.4, namely funds released from displaced or postponed investment, newly stimulated domestic savings, and newly stimulated foreign capital inflows. Following equation (8.7), the economic opportunity cost of capital can be estimated using the sum of the values obtained by multiplying the opportunity cost of each of the three alternative sources of funds by the shares of the funds diverted from each of these sources.

8.7.1 Estimation of the Economic Cost of the Three Diverted Funds

a) Gross-of-Tax Return to Domestic Investment

Using the approach based on the national income and expenditure accounts, the return to domestic investment can be estimated from the GDP net of depreciation and the contributions made by labour, land, resource rents, and the associated sales and excise taxes. The total contribution of labour to the economy is the sum of wages and salaries paid by corporations and by unincorporated businesses. Since owners of unincorporated businesses are also workers, but are often not paid wages, the operating surplus of this sector thus includes the returns to both capital and labour. The labour content of this mixed income was estimated at 35 percent for South Africa during the period between 1995 and 1999.[44] The 35 percent figure is used and assumed throughout the period from 1985 to 2004.

Land is a fixed factor of production that makes a contribution to value added, especially in the agriculture and housing sectors. The contribution of land to the agricultural sector is assumed to be one-third of the total value added in that sector.[45] Regarding the housing sector, information is not available on the amount of value added produced by this sector, nor is it available for the value added of the land component for the sector. Hence, this component is not incorporated into the calculation.

In South Africa, resource rents arise owing to the fact that in the past, the mining of non-renewable resources such as gold, coal, platinum, and diamonds has made a substantial contribution to GDP. These specific resources are non-renewable; when exploited with the help of reproducible capital, they can yield substantial economic resource rents.[46] These resource rents should be subtracted from the income to capital in order to derive the income to reproducible capital.

Moreover, it should be noted that the value-added tax (VAT) implemented in South Africa is a consumption-type tax and allows a full credit for the purchase of capital goods. Hence, the VAT is effectively borne by the value added of labour and not capital; hence, it should be subtracted from GDP in order to derive the return to capital alone.

To arrive at a rate of return, the value of the income attributed to the stock of reproducible capital is divided by the total estimated value of the reproducible capital stock reduced by the value of the reproducible capital stock attributed to

---

[44]This figure was obtained from officials of the South African Reserve Bank in Pretoria.

[45]Data are not available for the agricultural sector alone, but are available on a combined basis for agriculture, forestry, and fishing. Because of the importance of agriculture in South Africa, it is assumed that the value added in the agricultural sector accounts for 95 percent of the total value added in the agricultural, forestry, and fishing sectors combined. Further, the assumption that the contribution of land is equal to one-third of the total value added of the agricultural sector is consistent with what has been estimated in countries of a similar level of development.

[46]Resource rents were estimated by Blignaut and Hassan (2001). However, the resource rents shown here are calculated based on the assumption that the real rate of return to the reproducible capital in mining is 10 percent for the period from 1985 to 1993. From 1994, resource rents are assumed to increase with the inflation rate owing to the absence of data for these years.

production of general government services. Over the past 15 years, the average real rate of return on investment in South Africa is estimated to be approximately 12.73 percent, as shown in Table 8.1.[47] The value of ρ is thus taken to be 13.0 percent for this exercise.

b) Cost of Newly Stimulated Domestic Savings

When project funds are raised in the capital markets, domestic savings in banks or other financial institutions are stimulated. The net-of-tax return to the newly stimulated domestic savings can be measured by the gross-of-tax return to reproducible capital minus the amount of income and property taxes paid by corporations and the personal income taxes paid by individuals on their income from investments. It is further reduced by the cost of the financial intermediation services provided by banks and other financial institutions. These costs of financial intermediation are an economic resource cost that increases the spread between the time preference rate for consumption and the interest rate charged to borrowers. Owing to a lack of detailed data in this sector, it is estimated by assuming that the value added produced by financial institutions accounts for one-half of the value added created by the total of all financial institutions and real estate. Furthermore, the intermediation services are estimated to be a further half of the value added in the financial institutions.[48] Hence, the amount of return divided by reproducible capital stock represents the net rate of return to households on newly stimulated savings. It also reflects the rate of time preference for forgone consumption.

Using national accounts data over the past 20 years, the cost of newly stimulated domestic savings, r, for South Africa is estimated at about 4.50 percent, as shown in Table 8.2.

c) Marginal Economic Cost of Foreign Financing

The real marginal cost of foreign financing, MC_f, can be estimated using equation (8.10). In South Africa, long-term debts currently account for more than 70 percent of total foreign debt. These long-term debts are mostly denominated in US dollars. The coupon rate charged by the US institutions ranges from 8.375 percent to 9.125 percent for US dollar bonds (South African Reserve Bank,

---

[47]This estimate is lower than the one shown in Kuo et al. (2003) for the following reasons. First, the amount of return to capital in the Kuo–Jenkins–Mphahlele study was measured gross of depreciation, and the reproducible capital stock was assumed to be the total stock in the economy, including that of general government services. Second, the national accounts data appear to have been revised substantially in some areas, especially since 1995.

[48]See Statistics South Africa, Final Supply and Use Tables, 1998. The fraction of value added in the financial institutions was about 48 percent of those in the financial institutions, real estate, and business activities combined. The share of operating surplus in the total value added in financial institutions was 53 percent.

2006). For this exercise, it is assumed that the average borrowing rate from abroad is about 8.5 percent per annum, with the GDP deflator of 2.5 percent in the United States.

The fraction of long-term loans outstanding with variable interest rates, ϕ, is about one-third.[49] If we include both long- and short-term debts with variable interest rates, they would amount to 53 percent of the total stock of South Africa's foreign debt. For the purpose of this exercise, we assume the amount to be about 50 percent. Thus, the following information is given: $i_f = 8.5$ percent, $t_w = 0$, $gp_f = 2.50$ percent, and $\phi = 0.50$. Assuming that ε_s^f is 1.5, one can obtain the value of MC'_f, which is approximately 7.80 percent.

8.7.2 Weights of the Three Diverted Funds

The weights of the three diverted funds depend upon the initial shares of the sources of these funds and their price responsiveness to changes in the market interest rates. We estimate that the average ratio of the total private sector investment to savings (I_T/S_T) for the past 20 years is about 73 percent. The average shares of total private sector savings are assumed to be approximately 20 percent for households, 65 percent for businesses, and 15 percent for foreigners.[50] Assuming the supply elasticity of household savings to be 0.5, the supply elasticity of business saving to be zero,[51] the supply elasticity of foreign funds to be 1.5, and the demand elasticity for private sector capital in response to changes in the cost of funds to be -1.0, one can estimate the proportions of each of the diverted funds. They are 9.48 percent from newly stimulated domestic savings, 21.33 percent from newly stimulated foreign capital, and 69.19 percent from displaced or postponed domestic investment.

8.7.3 Estimates of the Economic Cost of Capital

The economic opportunity cost of capital can be estimated as a weighted average of the rate of return on displaced private sector investment and the rate of return to domestic and foreign savings. Substituting the above data in equation (8.7), one can obtain an estimate of the economic cost of capital for South Africa of 11.08 percent.

The empirical results depend on the values of several key parameters, such as the supply elasticity of foreign capital, the initial share of each sector in total

---

[49]The percentage of long-term debts with variable interest rate declined from 69.9 percent in 1994 to 33.8 percent in 1999 (World Bank, 2001).

[50]These shares fluctuate from year to year in South Africa. This is also a parameter for sensitivity analysis.

[51]It is not clear whether higher interest rates would affect the amount of business savings. This is because businesses are more concerned with investment opportunities.

private sector savings, the average rate of return on domestic investment, resource rents, the labour content of mixed capital and labour income for unincorporated businesses, foreign inflation rate, etc. A sensitivity analysis is performed to determine how robust the estimate of the economic cost of capital is. The results indicate that the value would range from 10.74 percent to 11.49 percent.[52] Thus, a conservative estimate of the economic cost of capital in South Africa would be a real rate of 11 percent.

8.8 Conclusion

The discount rate used in the economic analysis of investments is a key variable in applying the NPV or benefit–cost criteria for investment decision-making. Such a discount rate is equally applicable to the economic evaluation, as distinct from a financial analysis, of both private and public investments. If the NPV of either type of project is negative when discounted by the economic cost of capital, the country would be better off if the project were not implemented. Estimates of the value of this variable for a country should be derived from the empirical realities of the country in question. Of course, the results of such a discounting effort are only as good as the underlying data and projection made of the benefits and costs for the project.

This chapter began with the presentation of alternative approaches to choosing discount rates for investment projects and a review of their strengths and weaknesses. An approach that captures the essential economic features uses a weighted average of the economic rate of return on private investment and the cost of newly stimulated domestic and foreign savings. Most practitioners have chosen to use a discount rate that follows this weighted average opportunity cost of funds concept. This chapter has described a practical framework for estimating the economic opportunity cost of capital in a small, open economy. The model considers the economic cost of raising funds from the capital market. It takes into account not only the opportunity cost of funds diverted from private domestic investment and private consumption, but also the marginal cost of foreign borrowing. For illustrative purposes, this methodology is applied to the case of South Africa.

---

[52]For example, if the supply elasticity of foreign capital is 1.0 instead of 1.5, the share of financing from foreign funds becomes smaller, but the marginal cost of foreign funds is increased. As a consequence, the economic opportunity cost of capital increases to 11.49 percent. On the other hand, if the supply elasticity of foreign capital is increased to 2.0, the economic cost of capital would be 10.74 percent. Perhaps the most important element in determining the economic cost of capital is the gross-of-tax return on domestic investment. If the average rate of return is 1.0 percentage point higher than 13.0 percent of the base case, the economic opportunity cost of capital would become 11.77 percent.

Table 8.1: Return to Domestic Investment in South Africa, 1985–2004 (million rand)

Year	GDP	Total Labour Income	Taxes on Products	Value-Added Tax	Subsidies	GVA in Agriculture	Resource Rents	Depreciation	Return to Capital	GDP Deflator Index	Expressed in 2000 Prices		Percentage Rate of Return
											Real Return to Capital	Capital Stock (Mid-Year)	
	(1)	(2)	(3)	(4)	(5)	(6)	(7)	(8)	(9)	(10)	(11)	(12)	(13)
1985	127,598	69,115	11,791	-	1,536	6,091	6,323	21,003	22,283	18.00	123,801	1,358,877	9.11
1986	149,395	80,969	13,946	-	1,814	6,831	8,994	26,348	22,725	21.07	107,850	1,377,945	7.83
1987	174,647	95,102	16,141	-	2,146	8,994	11,605	29,823	25,713	24.13	106,583	1,383,741	7.70
1988	209,613	111,556	20,936	-	2,241	11,149	12,269	34,521	35,504	27.79	127,766	1,391,734	9.18
1989	251,676	134,204	26,505	-	2,375	12,332	12,933	40,978	44,023	32.58	135,107	1,407,786	9.60
1990	289,816	158,557	29,153	-	2,488	12,184	13,596	45,990	50,249	37.64	133,494	1,425,970	9.36
1991	331,980	182,514	31,096	18,792	2,523	13,825	12,411	50,251	56,232	43.56	129,088	1,440,425	8.96
1992	372,227	209,129	33,190	17,506	4,519	13,056	11,227	54,227	66,457	49.91	133,156	1,448,246	9.19
1993	426,133	234,347	41,611	25,449	6,320	16,284	10,042	58,575	82,87	56.44	146,833	1,452,144	10.11
1994	482,120	260,776	48,373	29,288	6,400	20,252	11,005	64,500	98,830	61.86	159,775	1,458,980	10.95
1995	548,100	295,467	53,644	32,768	5,898	19,317	12,134	71,827	117,460	68.20	172,239	1,472,298	11.70
1996	617,954	332,191	58,119	35,903	5,635	23,720	13,115	78,817	137,366	73.71	186,353	1,492,361	12.49
1997	685,730	366,463	63,419	40,096	4,856	25,140	14,178	87,188	156,216	79.69	196,034	1,517,125	12.92
1998	742,424	401,632	74,473	43,677	6,923	25,434	15,271	96,615	158,848	85.83	185,067	1,544,460	11.98
1999	813,683	436,124	80,528	48,330	5,718	26,179	16,350	107,966	177,618	91.89	193,288	1,565,853	12.34
2000	922,148	478,812	87,816	48,377	3,886	27,451	17,792	119,237	226,708	100.00	226,708	1,580,321	14.35
2001	1,020,007	514,603	96,363	54,455	4,571	32,588	19,156	130,848	267,391	107.67	248,350	1,595,909	15.56
2002	1,164,945	564,357	109,820	61,057	4,664	44,179	21,126	149,329	329,119	118.74	277,180	1,612,489	17.19
2003	1,251,468	618,498	120,219	70,150	3,336	42,007	22,075	161,635	338,513	124.07	272,833	1,630,963	16.73
2004	1,374,476	676,231	146,738	80,682	2,671	41,323	23,377	172,394	372,402	131.39	283,428	1,656,231	17.11

Source: For the period 1985–2004, South African Reserve Bank, *South Africa's National Income Accounts 1946–2005* (June 2005).

Notes: GDP: gross domestic product; GVA: gross value added.

Column (2) is obtained from the sum of wages and salaries paid by corporations and 35 percent of net operating surplus generated by incorporated businesses.

Column (9) = (1) − (2) − (4) − 0.95*(⅓)*(6) − {(2)/[(1) − (3) + (5)]}*[(3) − (4)] − (7) − (8).

Column (12) is obtained from the total capital stock net of general government services.

Table 8.2: Cost of Newly Stimulated Domestic Savings in South Africa, 1985–2004 (million rand)

Year	GDP	Total Labour Income	Taxes on Products	GVA in Agriculture	Resource Rents	Depreciation	Income and Wealth Taxes Paid by Corporations	Income and Wealth Taxes Paid by Households	Wages and Salaries Received by Households	Property Income Received by Households	Value Added in FIs, Real Estates	Return to Domestic Savings	Real Return to Domestic Savings (Expressed in 2000 Prices)	Rate of Return to Domestic Savings (Percentage)
	(1)	(2)	(3)	(4)	(5)	(6)	(7)	(8)	(9)	(10)	(11)	(12)	(13)	(14)
1985	127,598	69,115	11,791	6,091	6,332	21,003	7,434	9,038	65,078	16,861	15,849	4,181	23,230	1.71
1986	149,395	80,969	13,946	6,831	8,994	26,348	8,486	10,512	75,444	18,772	17,312	2,096	9,949	0.72
1987	174,647	95,102	16,141	8,994	11,605	29,823	8,736	12,354	88,577	25,107	20,688	2,491	10,326	0.75
1988	209,613	111,556	20,936	11,149	12,269	34,521	10,194	14,468	103,565	34,228	25,069	6,746	24,276	1.74
1989	251,676	134,204	26,505	12,332	12,933	40,978	11,249	19,723	124,050	42,485	30,265	9,304	28,553	2.03
1990	289,816	158,557	29,153	12,184	13,596	45,990	15,284	23,831	146,240	49,541	36,039	8,338	22,151	1.55
1991	331,980	182,514	31,096	13,825	12,411	50,251	13,547	28,961	169,516	59,380	44,945	19,033	43,694	3.03
1992	372,227	209,129	33,190	13,056	11,227	54,227	10,963	35,650	193,250	73,942	53,265	26,341	52,778	3.64
1993	426,133	234,347	41,611	16,284	10,042	58,575	12,579	37,739	216,368	82,383	62,861	37,739	66,866	4.60
1994	482,120	260,776	48,373	20,252	11,005	64,500	14,565	45,280	240,416	94,052	76,491	46,132	74,580	5.11
1995	548,100	295,467	53,644	19,317	12,134	71,827	14,115	51,623	272,916	110,378	82,162	59,390	87,087	5.92
1996	617,954	332,191	58,119	23,720	13,115	78,817	21,408	59,496	306,225	121,807	94,122	66,332	89,987	6.03
1997	685,730	366,463	63,419	25,140	14,178	87,188	24,134	68,048	338,204	142,844	110,488	74,558	93,562	6.17
1998	742,424	401,632	74,473	25,434	15,721	96,615	29,935	75,422	370,589	155,866	122,227	63,557	74,048	4.79
1999	813,683	436,124	80,528	26,179	16,350	107,966	30,220	84,335	402,375	176,116	140,673	73,362	79,834	5.10
2000	922,148	478,812	87,816	27,451	17,792	119,237	33,248	87,848	440,299	206,496	156,252	109,440	109,440	6.93
2001	1,020,007	514,603	96,363	32,588	19,156	130,848	58,701	89,700	471,816	231,010	177,531	116,150	107,879	6.76
2002	1,164,945	564,357	109,820	44,179	21,126	149,329	68,807	95,801	515,053	271,925	204,590	153,266	129,079	8.00
2003	1,251,468	618,498	120,219	42,007	22,075	161,635	70,356	99,451	567,024	280,899	228,075	155,418	125,263	7.68
2004	1,374,476	676,231	146,738	41,323	23,377	172,394	75,343	108,628	618,215	305,088	247,514	169,534	129,029	7.79

Source: For the period 1985–2004, South African Reserve Bank, *South Africa's National Income Accounts 1946–2005* (June 2005). Statistics South Africa. *Final Supply and Use Tables 1998*.

Notes: GDP: gross domestic product; GVA: gross value added; FIs: financial institutions.

Column (12) = (1) – (2) – (3) – 0.95*(⅓)*(4) – (5) – (6) – (7) – (8)*{(10)/[(9) + (10)]} – (11)*0.5*0.5.

Column (14) is obtained by dividing Column (13) of this table by Column (12) of Table 8.1.

References

Barreix, A. 2003. "Rates of Return, Taxation, and the Economic Cost of Capital in Uruguay", PhD Dissertation, Harvard University (August).

Blignaut, J.N. and R.M. Hassan. 2001. "A Natural Resource Accounting Analysis of the Contribution of Mineral Resources to Sustainable Development in South Africa", *South African Journal of Economic and Management Sciences*, SS No. 3 (April).

Brean, D.J.S., D.F. Burgess, R. Hirshhorn, and J. Schulman. 2005. "Treatment of Private and Public Charges for Capital in a Full-Cost Accounting of Transportation", Report Prepared for Transportation Canada, Government of Canada (March).

Burgess, D.F. 1981. "The Social Discount Rate for Canada: Theory and Evidence", *Canadian Public Policy* 7(3), 383–394.

— 2008. "Removing Some Dissonance from the Social Discount Rate Debate", University of Western Ontario, London, Ontario (June).

— 2009. "Toward a Reconciliation of Alternative Views on the Social Discount Rate", paper presented at the Conference on "Discount Rates for the Evaluation of Public Private Partnerships", held at Queen's University, Kingston, Ontario, October 3, 2008.

Dasgupta, P., A. Sen, and S. Marglin. 1972. *Guidelines for Project Evaluation.* Vienna: United Nations Industrial Development Organization.

Dreze, J.H. 1974. "Discount Rates and Public Investment: A Post-Scriptum", *Economics* 41(161), 52–61.

Edwards, S. 1986. "Country Risk, Foreign Borrowing, and the Social Discount Rate in an Open Economy", *Journal of International Money and Finance* 5, Sup. 1 (March), S79–S96.

Feldstein, M. 1964. "The Social Time Preference Discount Rate in Cost-Benefit Analysis", *Economic Journal* 74(294), 360–379.

Harberger, A.C. 1968. "On Measuring the Social Opportunity Cost of Public Funds", in The Discount Rate in Public Investment Evaluation, Report No. 17, Conference Proceedings from the Committee on the Economics of Water Resources Development of the Western Agricultural Economics Research Council, Denver, Colorado (December), 1–24.

— 1972. "Professor Arrow on the Social Discount Rate", *Project Evaluation: Collected Papers.* Chicago: The University of Chicago Press.

— 1980. "Vignettes on the World Capital Market", *American Economic Review* 70(2), 331–337.

— 1987. "Reflections on Social Project Evaluation", in G.M. Meier (ed.), *Pioneers in Development*, Vol. 2. Washington: The World Bank and Oxford: Oxford University Press.

— 1997. "New Frontiers in Project Evaluation: A Comment on Devarajan, Squire, and Suthiwart-Narueput", *The World Bank Research Observer* 12(1).

Harberger, A.C. and D.L. Wisecarver. 1977. "Private and Social Rates of Return to Capital in Uruguay", *Economic Development and Cultural Change* 25(3), 411–445.

Hirshleifer, J., J.C. DeHaven, and J.W. Milliman. 1960. *Water Supply: Economics, Technology, and Policy.* Chicago: University of Chicago Press.

Jenkins, G.P. 1973. "The Measurement of Rates of Return and Taxation from Private Capital in Canada", in W.A. Niskanen et al. (eds.), *Benefit-Cost and Policy Analysis.* Chicago: Aldine.

— 1981. "The Public-Sector Discount Rate for Canada: Some Further Observations", *Canadian Public Policy* 17(3), 399–407.

— 1985. "Public Utility Finance and Economic Waste", *Canadian Journal of Economics* 18(3), 484–498.

Kuo, C.Y., G.P. Jenkins, and M.B. Mphahlele. 2003. "The Economic Opportunity Cost of Capital in South Africa", *South African Journal of Economics* 71(3), 525–543.

Lind, R.C., et al. 1982. *Discounting for Time and Risk in Energy Policy.* Washington, DC: Resources for the Future, Inc.

Little, I.M.D. and J.A. Mirrlees. 1974. *Project Appraisal and Planning for Developing Countries.* London: Heinemann Educational Books.

Marglin, S. 1963. "The Social Rate of Discount and the Optimal Rate of Investment", *Quarterly Journal of Economics* 77(1), 95–111.

Poterba, J.M. 1997. "The Rate of Return to Corporate Capital and Factor Shares: New Estimates Using Revised National Income Accounts and Capital Stock Data", Working Paper 6263. Cambridge, MA: National Bureau of Economic Research (November).

Sandmo, A. and J.H. Dreze. 1971. "Discount Rates for Public Investment in Closed and Open Economies", *Economica* 38 (November), 395–412.

Sjaastad, L.A. and D.L. Wisecarver. 1977. "The Social Cost of Public Finance", *Journal of Political Economy* 85(3), 513–547.

South African Reserve Bank. 2006. *Quarterly Bulletin* (June).

Squire, L. and H.G. van der Tak. 1975. *Economic Analysis of Projects.* Baltimore: The Johns Hopkins University Press.

United States Environmental Protection Agency. 2000. *Guidelines for Preparing Economic Analyses* (September).

World Bank. 2001. *Global Development Finance: Building Coalitions for Effective Development Finance.* Washington, DC: The International Bank for Reconstruction and Development/The World Bank.

— 2006. *Global Development Finance: The Development Potential of Surging Capital Flows.* Washington, DC: The International Bank for Reconstruction and Development/The World Bank.

Chapter Nine

Shadow Price of Foreign Exchange and Non-tradable Outlays

9.1 Introduction

The economic cost of capital, as measured in Chapter 8, deals with inter-temporal comparisons.[53] It links the annual flows of benefits and costs over a project's lifetime to its initial capital investment. In this chapter, we deal with another facet of the act of raising project funds from the country's capital market. This concerns the distortions that are affected not inter-temporally but at the point in time that the funds are raised. Investment and consumption expenditures by others in the market are displaced by the very act of raising the project's funds in the capital market. As a consequence, the government loses tariff revenue plus value-added and other indirect taxes. These losses must be counted in the economic evaluation of any project, in addition to those linked to the spending of project funds on tradable or non-tradable goods and services, and in addition to the inter-temporal distortions captured by the economic opportunity cost of capital.

The starting point of this exercise is the calculation of the economic opportunity cost, or shadow price, of foreign exchange (EOCFX) and the shadow price of non-tradable outlays (SPNTO). Before starting, it should be made clear that at that point, we are accounting for the distortions involved in sourcing the money for the expenditures, and in causing equilibrium to be

---

[53]The issue of how project funds are raised has been a source of constant discussion and debate. Our position – which we believe reflects a fairly close consensus among experienced practitioners – is that it is advisable to choose a standard type of sourcing for project funds, and that capital market sourcing is clearly the best candidate to serve as this standard. The next alternative would be sourcing from tax revenues, though here there are a large number of alternative ways of raising extra tax money, each involving a different weighted average of distortions. By contrast, capital market sourcing works on the basis of additional pressure in the capital market. We expect that an added demand for funds will have much the same effects regardless of whether the government is raising money to build a dam, or a private firm is borrowing to renew its stock of trucks, or a group of consumers is borrowing to finance a joint vacation trip. The capital market does not "see" the purpose for which the funds will be used; it simply "feels" the added pressure. It is thus the forces of the market that ultimately determine what expenditures will be displaced. Hence, we proceed on the assumption that a standard pattern of distortions that are involved in the actual act of displacing consumption and investment (dealt with in the present chapter), plus a standard pattern of inter-temporal distortions, impact the economic opportunity cost of capital – the rate of return – dealt with in the preceding chapter.

maintained in the market for foreign exchange, but we are explicitly not counting the distortions that are entailed (or engendered) as that money is spent, either on tradables (for which EOCFX captures the sourcing distortions) or on non-tradables (for which the sourcing distortions are captured by SPNTO). The procedure leading to EOCFX captures those distortion costs that are triggered each time money is sourced in the capital market and spent on tradables. Similarly, the calculation of SPNTO captures the distortion costs that are engendered each time money is sourced in the capital market and spent on non-tradables.

However, once that stage is reached, the repetitive aspect vanishes. One project might buy an import good with an 80 percent tariff plus a 20 percent value-added tax (VAT); another might import everything free of tariff and VAT; yet another might buy locally a taxed export product, leading to a loss of tax revenue for the government. It is similar for non-tradable goods: money may be spent on items that are heavily taxed, lightly taxed, heavily subsidized, lightly subsidized, or not subsidized or taxed at all. In all such cases, the analysis of each project must cover the specific distortions involved in the spending of project money, but this must be done separately, as part of the study of each project's costs and benefits — it cannot be incorporated into a standardized measure such as EOCFX or SPNTO.

Our cost–benefit analytical framework has been developed to convert the financial receipts and expenditures of a project into values that reflect their economic worth. The financial analysis uses the market exchange rate to convert the foreign currency values of traded goods into units of domestic currency. However, the market exchange rate does not usually reflect the economic value to the country of foreign exchange. In any such case, the conversion from foreign to domestic currency units should be carried out using EOCFX. EOCFX is also needed for the valuation of the tradable inputs that are used, directly or indirectly, in the production of the non-tradable goods and services.

The most common source of difference between the economic value and the market rate of foreign exchange stems from tariffs and non-tariff barriers. In a similar vein, we must incorporate export taxes and subsidies. These trade and other indirect tax distortions give rise to economic externalities each time that foreign currency is either extracted from or injected into the foreign exchange market.

To demonstrate how the economic value of foreign exchange may differ from its market value, we begin by considering a case in which it is the market exchange rate that moves to bring about an equilibrium of demand and supply. It is also assumed that the country cannot significantly influence the world prices of its exports or imports. Under these conditions, it is possible to measure the quantities of different traded goods in units of "dollar's worth" simply by counting copper in units of half a pound when its world price is $2.00 per pound, wheat in units of one-quarter bushel when its world price is $4.00 per bushel, and so on. In this way, the demand and supply curves for importables and exportables can be aggregates spanning many different commodities.

9.2 Determination of the Market Exchange Rate

Defining the exchange rate as the number of units of domestic currency per unit of foreign currency, the domestic prices of tradable goods will be linked positively to the market exchange rate. As the demand for foreign exchange is linked to the demand for imports, the quantity of foreign exchange demanded will fall as the market exchange rate rises, and vice versa. This is illustrated in Figure 9.1 (A and B). In Panel A, the demand for importable goods (AD_0) is juxtaposed on the domestic supply of importables (BS_0). The definition and implication of importable (and exportable) goods will be elaborated on in the next chapter.

For any given set of world prices for importable goods (assumed to be fixed at P_0^W), the domestic price will fall from P_0^I to P_2^I as the market exchange rate falls from E_0 to E_2. At each level of the exchange rate, the demand for foreign exchange is equal to the difference between the demand for importable goods and the domestic supply of these goods.[54] When the exchange rate is at E_0, there will be no net demand for foreign exchange because domestic production will be equal to the demand for these goods. As the exchange rate falls, the demand for importables will increase from Q_0 to Q_2^d, while their domestic supply will fall from Q_0 to Q_2^s. Hence, imports will flow into the country to fill this gap. When the quantity of imports is measured in units of foreign exchange, the demand for foreign exchange will increase with the fall in the exchange rate, as shown by the curve CD_0^I in Figure 9.1B.

---

[54]Since the demand for imports is an excess demand function, the elasticity of demand for foreign exchange will be greater than the elasticity of demand for importable goods, even when the domestic supply of these items is completely inelastic.

Figure 9.1: Importable Goods and the Demand for Foreign Exchange

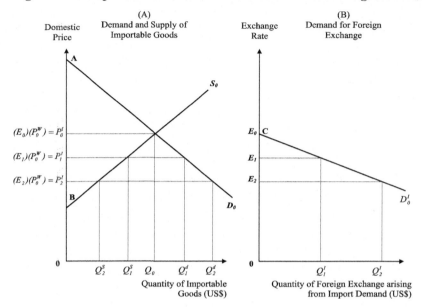

In a similar fashion, the supply of foreign exchange is derived from the domestic supply and demand for exportable goods. Because the world prices of these goods are fixed, their domestic prices will be tied to the country's exchange rate. An increase in the exchange rate will lead to an increase in the domestic price of each item, which will in turn cause the supply of exportable goods to increase. The relationship between the demand and supply of exportable goods and the supply of foreign exchange is illustrated in Figure 9.2.

Shadow Price of Foreign Exchange and Non-tradable Outlays

Figure 9.2: Exportable Goods and the Supply of Foreign Exchange

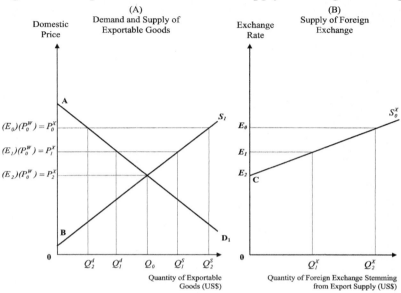

When the exchange rate is above E_2, the supply of exportable goods (denoted by the curve BS_1) will be greater than the domestic demand for these goods (curve AD_1). Hence, exports will amount to $Q_1^s - Q_1^d$ when the exchange rate is E_1. These sales of exports abroad can also be expressed as the country's export supply curve, which is a function of the market exchange rate, as shown in Figure 9.2B.

Determination of the equilibrium exchange rate requires that the quantity of foreign exchange demanded be equal to the quantity supplied. Combining Figures 9.1B and 9.2B into Figure 9.3 gives an equilibrium market exchange rate of E_1^m. At an exchange rate of E_0^m, there will be an excess supply of foreign exchange equal to $Q_1^x - Q_1^I$, while at an exchange rate of E_2^m there will be an excess demand of $Q_2^I - Q_2^x$. These situations can represent equilibria so long as capital movements or other transfers are present to finance the difference. Otherwise, market forces will lead to equilibrium at E_1^m.

Figure 9.3: Determination of the Market Exchange Rate

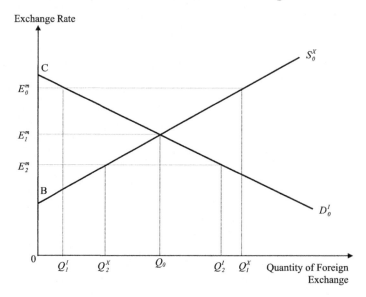

9.3 Derivation of the Economic Price of Foreign Exchange

For an economy that has no taxes, subsidies, or other distortions in the demand or supply of its tradable goods, the equilibrium market exchange rate (E_1^m) will be equal to the economic cost of supplying an additional unit of foreign exchange. E_1^m will also reflect the economic benefits of a marginal increase in the consumption of whatever goods or services might be purchased with an extra unit of foreign exchange. However, with the introduction of tariffs or subsidies on one or more tradable goods, a divergence will arise between the market price of foreign exchange and its economic value, expressed in units of the domestic currency of the country.

The study of the economic price of foreign exchange has traditionally been carried out using a partial equilibrium analysis. Such studies have looked only at the demand for imports and the supply of exports, giving no consideration to any externalities that might occur as the funds to buy imports are acquired or the funds generated by exports are deployed (Harberger, 1965; Bacha and Taylor, 1971; UNIDO, 1972; Fane, 1991). In this chapter, the traditional, partial equilibrium derivation of the EOCFX is first presented. The analysis is then extended using a framework that takes into account how funds for buying imports are sourced and how funds generated by exports are disposed of (Blitzer et al., 1981; Jenkins and Kuo, 1985; Harberger and Jenkins, 2002; Harberger et al., 2003).

9.3.1 A Partial Equilibrium Analysis

Nearly all countries levy tariffs on at least some imports, and subsidies or taxes are also sometimes levied on exports. Here, we will first examine the relationship between the market exchange rate and its economic value for the case where there is a uniform tariff on imports and a uniform subsidy on exports.

The tariff will bring about a divergence between the domestic valuation of imports (willingness to pay), given by the demand curve CD_0^I in Figure 9.4, and the demand for foreign exchange, shown by the curve TD_1^I. Consumers' evaluation of these imports does not change when the tariff is imposed. Nevertheless, the amount of foreign exchange they are willing to pay the foreign supplier will fall because they must pay the tariff to their own government in addition to the cost of cost, insurance, and freight (CIF) of the item to the importer. Thus, tariffs cause the economic value of foreign exchange to be greater than the market exchange rate.

A subsidy on the sales of exports will lower the financial cost of producing an item, as seen from the point of view of the domestic supplier. However, the economic resource cost of production is still measured by the before-subsidy supply curve BS_0^x, while the price at which producers are willing to export their goods is given by the curve SS_1^x, which includes the effect of the subsidy. Hence, subsidies will increase the supply of foreign exchange and cause the market exchange rate to be less than the EOCFX.

Figure 9.4: Determination of the EOCFX with Tariffs and Subsidies

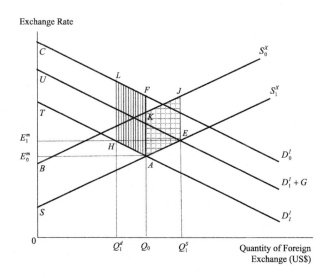

In such circumstances, the market exchange rate (E_0^m) will be determined by the interaction of the demand for foreign exchange (given by the net-of-tariff demand for imports TD_1^l) and the subsidized supply of foreign exchange SS_1^x (arising from the supply of exports). The intersection of these two curves at point A in Figure 9.4 will determine the initial market exchange rate (E_0^m). At this exchange rate, the amount of foreign exchange bought or sold in the market is Q_0 units. The value consumers place on the goods that can be purchased with a unit of foreign exchange includes the tariffs they pay. This value is shown as the distance Q_0F. At the same time, the resources required to produce an additional unit of foreign exchange is reflected either by the height of the supply curve that would have existed if there were no subsidy, BS_0^x, or the distance Q_0K. The existence of the subsidy means that producers will be induced to use a greater value of resources to produce an additional unit of exports than E_0^m, which is the market value of the foreign exchange that the country receives from its sale.

Now let us consider what economic costs are incurred when a project requires G units of additional foreign exchange. We do not inquire how the funds that are used to purchase this foreign exchange were raised (the traditional partial equilibrium assumption). On this assumption, all the foreign exchange bought by the project is generated through a rise in its domestic price. This is shown in Figure 9.4 by the shift in the demand curve for foreign exchange from D_1^l to $D_1^l + G$. However, the demand curve D_1^l still measures what people, other than the project, are willing to pay net of the tariff for each successive unit of foreign exchange. The project's action will cause the exchange rate to be bid up from E_0^m to E_1^m. This creates an incentive for exports to expand and for consumers to decrease their demand for imports.

Producers of exportable items will supply additional foreign exchange of $Q_1^s - Q_0$ as the market exchange rate increases from E_0 to E_1. The producers receive additional subsidy payments of $AKJE$ in Figure 9.4, which will be spent on factors of production and intermediate inputs. The total value of resources required to produce this incremental output is given by the area $Q_0KJQ_1^s$. At the same time, consumers reduce their demand for imports (foreign exchange) by $Q_0 - Q_1^d$. As they reduce their purchases of imports they will also reduce their expenditures on import duties, shown by $HLFA$ in Figure 9.4. These import duties reflect part of what consumers are willing to pay for the imports they are giving up. Hence, the total economic value of the reduction in consumption is $Q_1^d LFQ_0$.

Combining the resource cost of the additional supply of exports with the reduction in consumer benefits from the cutback in consumption, the total economic cost of the foreign exchange used by the project is found to be equal to the sum of the two areas $Q_0KJQ_1^s$ and $Q_1^d LFQ_0$. Algebraically, the value of these two areas can be expressed as:

$$EOCFX = E^m(1+k)(Q_1^s - Q_0) + E^m(1+t)(Q_0 - Q_1^d) \qquad (9.1)$$

where E^m is the market exchange rate, k is the amount of subsidy expressed as a fraction of the initial equilibrium exchange rate, and t is the tariff also expressed as a fraction of this exchange rate.

Expressing equation (9.1) in elasticity form, the EOCFX on a per unit basis (E^e) can be calculated as follows:

$$E^e = \frac{e^x E^m Q^x (1+k) - \eta^I (Q^I) E^m (1+t)}{e^x Q - \eta^I (Q^I)}$$

$$= E^m \times [1 + \frac{e^x k - \eta^I (Q^I / Q^x)t}{e^x - \eta^I (Q^I / Q^x)}]$$

$$(9.2)$$

where e^x is the supply elasticity of exports, η^I is the demand elasticity for imports, Q^I is the quantity of foreign exchange required to pay for imports, and Q^x is the quantity of foreign exchange earned from exports.

Equation (9.2) shows that the traditional measure of the economic cost of a unit of foreign exchange is equal to the market exchange rate plus (less) the net revenue loss (gain) experienced by the government in tax revenue from the adjustment of the demands and supplies of tradable goods, which accommodate the increase in demand for foreign exchange by the project. This EOCFX is often expressed in project evaluation as a ratio to the market exchange rate (E^e / E^m) . The percentage by which E^e exceeds E^m is typically referred to as the foreign exchange premium. To find the economic price of any given importable good, its CIF value (measured at the market exchange rate) is simply augmented by the foreign exchange premium, i.e., multiplied by E^e / E^m. For an exportable good, it is the free on board (FOB) price (measured at the market exchange rate) that is augmented by the exchange premium to arrive at the good's economic value.

Suppose an importable good has a financial cost of $150, inclusive of a 20 percent tariff that has been levied on its CIF price. As the tariff payment is not a resource cost to the economy, the value of this item net of tariff, $125, is the cost that must be paid in foreign exchange. Assume that the value of E^e / E^m is 1.10. In this case, to arrive at the economic value of the item ($137.50), its net-of-tax cost of $125 is adjusted by 1.1. The adjustment in this case lowers the economic cost to the project of this item below its financial cost, hence increasing the net benefits of the project.

This process of adjustment eliminates $25 of financial cost, while at the same time imposing $12.50 of additional cost to reflect the additional economic value of the foreign exchange, over and above its financial cost.

The object of this type of adjustment is to ensure that a project's use or generation of foreign exchange is priced to reflect its economic opportunity cost. For tradable goods the total conversion factor for a good is made up of two parts: (i) an adjustment factor, specific to the good, which eliminates from the financial costs any taxes that are directly levied on the item; and (ii) the premium reflecting the degree to which the EOCFX exceeds its market value $(E^e / E^m - 1)$.

9.3.2 EOCFX and SPNTO Using Funds in the Capital Market

Up to this point, the estimation of the EOCFX has explicitly not taken into account how the funds are sourced by the project to purchase the foreign exchange. This issue was raised and examined by Blitzer et al. (1981) when alternative fiscal instruments such as income or commodity taxes were used as ways to finance a project. Jenkins and Kuo (1985) also estimated the foreign exchange premium for Canada by developing a multi-sector general equilibrium model and assuming the funds were raised through a personal income tax. These assumptions are nevertheless not consistent with the economic opportunity cost of capital, where the capital market is postulated to be the source of funding for the project.

The act of raising funds in the capital market will reduce the demand for goods and services in distorted as well as undistorted markets, in both the tradable and non-tradable sectors. Hence, externalities are generated by the act of raising funds in the capital market. We here explore how the traditional measure of the EOCFX needs to be modified in order to take these additional externalities into account.

Once the focus is broadened to include externalities generated by the act of raising the funds involved (by whatever means), it becomes clear that the purchase of non-tradable goods must be treated in a similar fashion to tradables as there will typically be a difference between the financial cost and economic cost of outlays on non-tradables. The percentage difference between these financial and economic costs will be referred to here as the premium on non-tradable outlays.

The estimation of EOCFX and SPNTO is carried out here using a three-sector general equilibrium framework in which the funds used to finance the purchase of tradable and non-tradable goods are obtained through the capital market (Harberger and Jenkins, 2002). The three sectors are importable, exportable, and non-tradable goods and services. Distortions such as tariffs, value-added taxes, and subsidies are also present in the model. As before, the capital market is taken as the standard source of project funds, and the external effects involved in sourcing will be the same regardless of whether these funds are spent on tradables or non-tradables.

When a project is financed by extractions from the capital market, there are three alternative sources for these funds. First, other investment activities may be abandoned or postponed. Second, private consumption may be displaced as domestic savings are stimulated. Third, increased foreign savings (capital inflows) may be generated in response to additional demand pressure in the capital market. Different sets of external effects will be involved, depending on the particular sources (e.g., domestic vs. foreign) from which the funds were drawn and the types of expenditures made (e.g., tradable vs. non-tradable).

In order to cover all aspects of the problem, four source–use combinations are here considered. The alternative sources are the domestic and foreign capital markets. The alternative uses represent project spending on tradables and non-tradables. We begin by considering the case of sourcing the funds in the local capital market.

a) Domestically Sourced Funds Used to Purchase Inputs

When funds are extracted from the domestic capital market to finance the purchase of project inputs, there will be a displacement of investment or private consumption expenditures. These investment and consumption expenditures would otherwise have been made on importable goods, exportable goods, and non-tradable goods. The ultimate quantitative impacts on the demand in the market for these three broad classes of goods will also depend on whether the project uses the funds to purchase tradable or non-tradable goods.

Funds Used to Purchase Only Tradable Goods. When funds from the capital market are used to purchase importable goods, the natural result would be a net excess demand for tradables, together with a net excess supply of non-tradables. To eliminate this disequilibrium, the exchange rate has to rise, causing the price of tradables to increase relative to non-tradables. As a consequence, the domestic demand for importables and exportables will decline, and that for non-tradables will rise. At the same time, the producers of importables and exportables will find it profitable to produce more, and producers of non-tradables will produce less. The process will continue until a new equilibrium is reached in which there will be no excess demand or excess supply in the system.[55] In other words, the exchange rate will adjust so as to ensure that there is no excess supply of tradable goods in the final equilibrium.

In the market for non-tradables, the reduction in demand caused by the initial capital extraction is somewhat offset by an increase in the quantity demanded (substitution effect) owing to the decrease in their relative price. Similarly, the supply of non-tradable goods responds to the depressed market by contracting. Resources that are released from the non-tradables sector will be used to help accommodate the increased demand for tradables. Readers should recall that this entire analysis is carried out on the assumption of full economic equilibrium in the presence of existing distortions. Under this assumption, the total resources released from the non-tradable goods sector must equal the resources required for the additional production of importable and exportable goods.

In the case where funds are raised in the domestic capital market and spent on domestically produced exportable goods, the impact on the exchange rate turns out to be exactly the same as the case where the funds are spent on the purchase of importable goods.

Funds Used to Purchase Only Non-tradables. In this case, the capital extraction plus the spending of all the funds on non-tradable items results in an excess demand for non-tradables. At the same time, there is a reduction of spending on tradables owing to the extraction of funds from the capital market. To reach a new equilibrium, the relative price of non-tradables will have to increase, inducing resources to move from the tradables to the non-tradables sector. This adjustment process is the reverse of that described in the case of funds spent on tradable goods.

b) Foreign Funds Used to Purchase Inputs

When foreign funds are used to finance the project's inputs, the results are quite different from the case described above. Now there is no initial displacement of

---

[55]This follows from properties of demand functions that the weighted sum of all the compensated price elasticities of demand (and supply) across all of the goods will always be equal to zero. That is, the real exchange rate will adjust until there is no excess demand (supply) for tradable and non-tradable goods in the system. This can be expressed as follows:

$$(\partial Q_{d,i}/\partial E)\, dE + (\partial Q_{d,e}/\partial E)\, dE + (\partial Q_{d,nt}/\partial E)\, dE = 0;$$
$$(\partial Q_{s,i}/\partial E)\, dE + (\partial Q_{s,e}/\partial E)\, dE + (\partial Q_{s,nt}/\partial E)\, dE = 0$$

where E denotes the foreign exchange rate; $Q_{d,i}$, $Q_{d,e}$, and $Q_{d,nt}$ stand for the demand for importable, exportable, and non-tradable goods, respectively; and $Q_{s,i}$, $Q_{s,e}$, and $Q_{s,nt}$ stand for the supply of importable, exportable, and non-tradable goods, respectively. In addition, the extraction of funds through the capital market results in a reduction in demand in both the tradable and non-tradable goods sectors. The reduction in demand for non-tradable goods will discourage their production until their supply equals their demand. This ensures that the following equation in the non-tradable goods sector is satisfied:

$$(\partial Q_{d,nt}/\partial B)\, dB + (\partial Q_{d,nt}/\partial E)\, dE - (\partial Q_{s,nt}/\partial E)\, dE = 0$$

where dB stands for the amount of funds raised in the domestic capital market.

investment and consumption of tradable and non-tradable goods owing to the capital extraction.

Moreover, when funds come from abroad to purchase tradable goods, no excess demand is generated for either foreign or domestic currency. However, when foreign-sourced funds are spent on non-tradables, this will generate an increase in their relative price. At the new equilibrium, the supply of non-tradables will have increased and that of tradables will have decreased.

9.4 General Equilibrium Analysis: A Diagrammatic and Numerical Illustration

In this section we present concrete exercises in order to illustrate how the general analysis can be put into practice. The exercises will examine the two alternative sources of funds.

9.4.1 Sourcing of Funds in the Domestic Capital Market

Figure 9.5A shows the total supply and demand for tradable goods in an economy as a function of the real exchange rate E. For the moment, we assume that there are no distortions in either the tradable or the non-tradable sector.

a) Impacts of Project Demand with No Distortions

If the project demand for tradable goods is 600, it cannot be assumed that there is movement upward on the price axis to point E_u, as shown in Figure 9.5A, where there is a gap of 600 between T_0^s and T_0^d, the quantities of tradables demanded and supplied.[56] Instead, we must take into account the fact that in raising 600 of funds in the capital market, the demand for tradables has been displaced by some fraction (say two-thirds) of this amount and the demand for non-tradables by the rest (the other one-third).

---

[56]This is analogous to what was done in the partial equilibrium scenario, in which the sourcing of the funds was not considered.

Figure 9.5: Impact of Domestically Sourced Funds Used to Purchase Tradable Goods

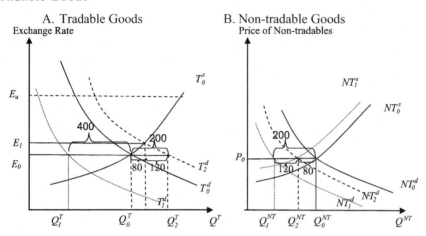

Hence, the scenario is that the demand curve for tradables is shifted to the left by 400 and simultaneously a wedge of 600 inserted, representing the purchase of tradable goods to be used in the project, between the new demand T_1^d and the supply curve of tradables T_0^s. As the entire 600 is spent on tradable goods, the demand for tradables shifts from T_1^d to T_2^d. At the exchange rate of E_0, there is now an excess demand for tradables of $Q_2^T - Q_0^T$, or 200. Simultaneously, in the non-tradable goods market (Figure 9.5B), there is an excess supply, also of 200 ($(Q_0^{NT} - Q_1^{NT}) = 200$). As a result, the real exchange rate rises from E_0 to E_1. The 600 of tradables resources used by the project comes from three different sources — a backward shift of tradables demand of 400, a movement backward along the "old" demand for tradables of 120, and a movement forward of 80 along the supply curve of tradables.[57] In the non-tradable goods market, as a result of the decline in its prices relative to tradable goods, demand will increase by 120, as shown in Figure 9.5B. The net reduction in the demand for non-tradable goods becomes 80. In the final equilibrium, the supply of non-tradable goods will be reduced by 80, and the resources released from this sector will be absorbed in the expansion of the tradables sector.

Figure 9.5 can be used for a whole series of exercises, each involving a different set of distortions. To this end, the demand and supply curves must be interpreted as being net of any distortions that are present in the system — in

---

[57]This assumes that $|\eta_T^d| = 1.5 \, \varepsilon_T^s$; here, η_T^d denotes the demand elasticity for tradable goods, while ε_T^s denotes the supply elasticity of tradable goods.

Shadow Price of Foreign Exchange and Non-tradable Outlays

particular, the demand for imports and the supply of exports are those that describe the market for foreign exchange. Thus, the import demand curve will be defined as being net of import tariff distortions and the export supply curve as being net of any export subsidy. Likewise, the demands for tradable and non-tradable goods will be defined to be net of the VAT distortion. (In making this assumption, we are in no way constraining people's tastes or technologies. However, it should be clear that using this artifice does not allow us to trace the economy's reaction to the imposition of new tariffs or value-added or other taxes or distortions). Figure 9.5 can be seen as representing the net position of different economies that have different tax setups, but that happen to have the same set of "market" demand and supply curves for foreign currency, for tradables, and for non-tradables.

Figure 9.6 tells the same story as Figure 9.5, but with important additional details. The connection between the two is the famous national accounting identity $(X^s - M^d) = (T^s - T^d)$, where X^s is the supply function of exports and M^d the demand function for imports. The shift of 400 in the demand for tradables now needs to be broken down into a portion (here -300) striking the demand for importables and its complement (here -100) striking the demand for exportables, as shown in panels A and B. These components cause corresponding shifts in the import demand curve (shifting to the left by 300) and the export supply curve (shifting to the right by 100), as shown in Panel C. With the purchase of 600 of importable goods, there is an excess demand for foreign exchange of $Q_d^{fx} - Q_s^{fx}$, or 200. The exchange rate will rise to E_1. This will cause the supply of exports to increase by 100 and the demand for imports to decrease by 100.[58]

---

[58]Assume that $|\eta_m^d| = \varepsilon_x^s$, where η_m^d denotes the demand elasticity for imports, while ε_x^s denotes the supply elasticity of exports.

Figure 9.6: Foreign Exchange Markets

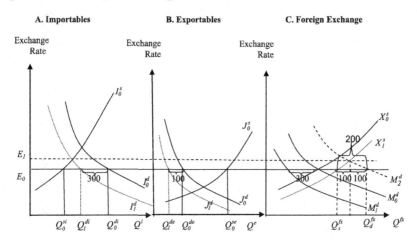

Note, however, that the movement along the supply curve of exports (+100) is different from the movement along the total supply curve of tradables (+80) and, similarly, that the movement along the demand function for imports (−100) is different from that along the demand for total tradables (−120). This simply reflects the fact that the demand for imports is an excess demand function $I^d - I^s$, where I stands for importables, and that the export supply is an excess supply function $J^s - J^d$, where J stands for exportables. The demand for tradables T^d is equal to $I^d + J^d$, and the supply of tradables T^s equals $I^s + J^s$.

Thus, the question of where the 600 of foreign exchange came from in order to meet the project's demand has two equally correct answers. One is that 520 came from reduced demand for tradables and 80 from increased tradables supply. Alternatively, it can be said to have come from a displacement in other imports of 400 and an increase in actual exports of 200. Both responses are correct, and if the calculations are done correctly, one answer will never contradict the other.

b) Introducing Import Tariffs

Suppose now that the only distortion present in this economy is a uniform import tariff (τ_m) of 12 percent. Given the shifts depicted in Figure 9.6, the reduction in other imports (400) is twice as large as the increase in export supply. The calculation of the EOCFX (E_e) would be:

$$E_e = 0.67\ E_m(1.12) + 0.33\ E_m = 1.08\ E_m$$

The shifts depicted in Figure 9.6 are due to the way in which the money for the project was obtained (or "sourced") or is deemed to have been sourced. The assumption here is that the standard source of funds at the margin is the capital market. When funds are withdrawn from the capital market, it is assumed that they came either from displaced domestic investment or from newly stimulated domestic saving (displaced consumption). A third source — capital flowing in from abroad — will be introduced subsequently to complete the picture.

Figure 9.6 shows how this displacement of spending through the "sourcing" of the project's funds is reflected in the demand for tradables taken as an aggregate (Figure 9.5A), with the demand for imports and the supply of exports considered separately (Figure 9.6C). Figure 9.5A is built on the assumption that the "sourcing" of 600 of project funds displaces tradables demand by 400 and non-tradables demand by 200. The reduction of 400 of demand for tradables is broken down into 300, affecting the demand for importables I^d, and 100, affecting the demand for exportables J^d (see panels A and B of Figure 9.6). In turn, these moves are reflected in a leftward shift of the demand for imports ($M^d = I^d - I^s$) and in a rightward shift in the supply of exports ($X^s = J^s - J^d$). Because of these relations — imports being one of excess demand, exports one of excess supply — there is no reason why the slope of the X^s curve should be the same as that of the T^s curve, nor why there should be any similarity between the slope of T^d and that of M^d. Thus, no contradiction is involved when the residual "gap" of 200 is filled 40 percent by a movement forward along T^s and 60 percent by a movement backward along T_0^d, while at the same time the filling of the same gap entails movements of equal amounts (100 each) forward along X_0^s and backward along M_0^d.

c) Introducing Value-Added Taxation

For the most part, the literature on cost–benefit analysis has ignored value-added taxation, and even indirect taxation in general, in its methodology for calculating the EOCFX and/or related concepts. Perhaps this is because value-added taxes did not exist before 1953, while the methodology of cost–benefit analysis has roots going back much further. Furthermore, many expositions of VAT treat it as a completely general tax that applies equally to all economic activities. This may have led cost–benefit analysts to assume that all sorts of resource shifts could take place as a consequence of a project, without causing any net cost or benefit through the VAT, because the same rate of tax would be paid (on the marginal product of any resource) in its new location as in its old.

However, real-world experience suggests that this assumption is grossly unrealistic. In the first place, value-added taxes never cover anywhere near 100 percent of economic activities; education, medical care, government services in general, the imputed rent on owner-occupied housing, plus all kinds of casual and semi-casual employment, all typically fall outside the VAT net, even in countries that pride themselves on the wide scope of their value-added taxes. In the second place, and partly for the reason just given, the effective average rate of value-added taxation is typically much higher for the tradable goods sector than it is for non-tradables. Our work in Argentina and Uruguay, both of which at the time had "general" value-added taxes of around 22 percent, suggested that actual collections are compatible with "effective" VAT rates of about 20 percent for tradables and of about 5 percent for non-tradables. In the exercise that follows these VAT rates will be used, together with an assumed general import tariff of 12 percent, to recalculate the EOCFX plus a related concept, the SPNTO.

The formal exercise to be performed is already illustrated in Figure 9.5. It is assumed that 600 is to be raised in the domestic capital market and spent on tradable goods. In the process, 400 of other (non-project) imports is displaced, on which the tariff is 12 percent. The result is a distortion "cost" of 48 ($= 0.12 \times 400$). In addition, account must be taken of what is happening with respect to the VAT. In the tradables sector, non-project demand is displaced to the tune of 520: 400 from the leftward shift of demand due to the sourcing of project funds in the capital market and 120 from the movement back along T_0^d, which should be interpreted as a demand substitution away from tradables and toward non-tradables. The net result of all of this is a distortion cost of 104 ($= 0.2 \times 520$).

Finally, we turn to the non-tradables sector, the movements of which are depicted in Figure 9.5B. The initial downward shift in the demand for non-tradables can be inferred to be 200, because 600 of funds was assumed to be raised in the capital market, with 400 of this coming from a downward shift of tradables demand. On the substitution side, there is a reflection of the downward movement of 120 in tradables demand (along the demand curve T_0^d). As this substitution is away from tradables, it must be toward non-tradables. This leaves a net reduction of demand of 80 in the non-tradables market. The distortion cost here is 4 ($= 0.05 \times 80$), reflecting the effective VAT rate of 5 percent.

To complete the exercise, a simple consistency check is performed. It has been seen that, for tradables, other demand is down by 520 and supply is up by 80. The difference here is represented by the project's own demand of 600, assumed to be spent on tradables. Hence, supply is equal to demand, in the post-project situation, in the tradables market. Similarly, the supply of non-tradables is down by 80 (reflecting the release of resources to the tradables sector), matched by a decline of 80 non-tradables demand, as shown in the previous paragraph.

To find the foreign exchange premium, the three types of distortion costs are added up ($156 = 48 + 104 + 4$) and the result expressed as a fraction of the 600 that the project is spending on tradable goods and services. Thus, there is a premium of 156/600, or 26 percent. Hence, $E_e = 1.26\ E_m$.

The related concept that must now be explored is the SPNTO. To obtain this, a similar exercise to the one above is performed, with a simple alteration in the assumption about how the money is spent. Figure 9.7 can be used to describe this case. Instead of assuming that project demand of 600 enters in the tradables market to bid up the real exchange rate to E_1, there is zero project demand for tradables, but the same "sourcing" shifts as before. The demand for non-tradable goods shifts from NT_1^d to NT_2^d. At the exchange rate E_0, there is an excess supply of tradable goods of 400 $(Q_0^T - Q_1^T)$ and an excess demand for non-tradable goods of 400 $(Q_2^{NT} - Q_0^{NT})$. This will cause the market exchange rate to fall to E_2, resulting in an increase in the demand for tradable goods by 240 and a decrease in the demand for non-tradable goods by 240. At the same time, there will be a reduction in tradable goods supply by 160, these resources being released in order to expand the production of non-tradables (to meet the incremental demand owing to their relative price decline).

Figure 9.7: Impact of Domestically Sourced Funds Used to Purchase Non-tradable Goods

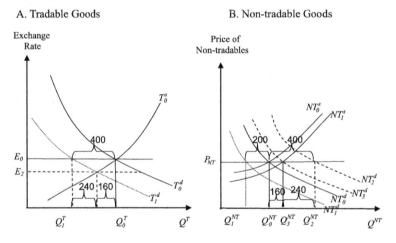

The move from the initial equilibrium at E_0 to the new one of E_2 entails a net reduction of 100 in total imports (and also in non-project imports because the project is here demanding only non-tradables). On this, the distortion cost is 12 $(= 100 \times 0.12)$ from the 12 percent import tariff. In the tradables market, the gap of 400, which exists at E_0 between T_0^s and T_1^d, must be closed by moving along both curves.[59] Starting from the initial point at E_0, the gap of 400 will be met by an increase of 240 along T_1^d and by a decline of 160 along T_0^s. With a VAT of 20 percent on tradables demand, there is a distortion cost of 32 (= 160 × 0.2). (Tradables demand has shifted to the left by 400 and moved to the right along T_1^d by 240.)

In the non-tradables market, there is a shift to the left of demand equal to 200 (from sourcing 600 in the capital market) plus the introduction of a new demand of 600. At the original real exchange rate E_0, this means that a gap of 400 will be opened between supply and demand. The elimination of that gap entails the movement of the real exchange rate down to E_2. In the process, "old" non-tradables demand will decline by 240 (the counterpart of the movement from E_0 to E_2 along T_1^d), and non-tradables supply will increase by 160 (the counterpart of the movement along T_0^s between E_0 and E_2). So overall, we have a reduction of old non-tradables demand by 440. Applying the VAT rate of 5 percent to this decline, we have a distortion cost of 22 (= 0.05 × 440).

The total distortion cost in the case of project demand for non-tradables is thus 66 (= 12 + 32 + 22). Distributing this over a project demand for non-tradables of 600, there is a distortion of 11 percent and a shadow cost of project funds spent on non-tradables equal to 1.11 times the amount actually spent.

Consistency checks can now easily be made for this case. In the tradables market, supply has dropped (from the initial point E_0) by 160, moving along T_0^s, and demand has dropped by an equivalent amount (a "sourcing" shift downward by 400, plus an increase along T_1^d of 240). In the non-tradables market, there is 160 of extra resources, plus displaced demand of 440 (200 from the downward shift of non-tradables demand owing to "sourcing" of the funds to be spent, plus 240 of reduced non-tradables demand as the real exchange rate has moved downward from E_0 to E_2 along T_1^d). Together, these are sufficient to free up the 600 of non-tradables output that the project is here assumed to be demanding.

d) Introducing VAT Exclusions (Credits) for Investment Demand

In the real world, most value-added taxes are of the consumption type and are administered by the credit method. In calculating its tax liability, a firm will apply the appropriate VAT rate to its sales, and then reduce the resulting liability

---

[59] The example of the movements along T_1^d and T_0^s, between E_2 and E_0, shows that this gap

of 400 will be closed by a movement of 240 along T_1^d and of 160 along T_1^s.

by the tax that was already paid on its purchases. In the consumption type of tax, this credit for tax already paid applies both to current inputs and to purchases of capital assets. In this way, investment outlays are removed from the base of the tax.

At first glance, it would appear easy to correct our previous figure to accommodate this additional nuance simply by scaling down the distortion costs that were originally attributed to the VAT. However, the matter is not quite as simple as this, since investment and consumption are likely to be affected very differently by, on the one hand, the act of raising funds in the capital market, and on the other, the process of demand substitution in response to real exchange rate adjustments. In particular, one should expect a large fraction (75 percent is assumed here) of the funds raised in the capital market to come at the expense of displaced investment, while a considerably smaller fraction would seem to be appropriate when a standard, price-induced substitution response is considered (an investment fraction of one-third is used here). Thus, rather than a single adjustment to account for the crediting of tax paid on investment outlays, two adjustments need to be made — one adjusting downward by 75 percent the distortion costs linked to the VAT in response to the raising of project funds in the capital market, and the other adjusting downward by one-third the distortion costs (or benefits) associated with the readjustment of relative prices so as to reach a new equilibrium.

Tables 9.1 and 9.2 provide a very convenient format in which to make these adjustments. At the same time they can be used to show how EOCFX and SPNTO are modified as additional complications are introduced. The values in the table correspond exactly to those underlying Figures 9.5 to 9.7 and embodied in earlier calculations. There are three columns under the general rubric of distortion cost. In the first of these, only a 12 percent import tariff is considered. The point to be noted here is that even with this "super-clean" and simple assumption, there is a need to allow for a SPNTO (see the first column under distortion costs in Table 9.2). In the second column, a VAT of 20 percent on tradables ($v_t = 0.2$) and of 5 percent on non-tradables ($v_h = 0.05$) is introduced. This yields precisely the numbers that emerged from the two exercises already conducted incorporating a VAT.

Table 9.1: Calculation of the EOCFX: 600 of Project Funds Sourced in the Capital Market and Spent on Tradables

			Applicable Distortions		
		Applicable Distortions	τ_m *Alone*	τ_m v_t v_h	τ_m v_t v_h e_{is} e_{ia}
Change Due to Capital Market Sourcing	Impact on Demand and Supply	(Exclusion for Investment $e_{is}= 0.75$)			
Tradables demand	−400	$v_t = 0.20$	n.a.	−80	−20
Import demand	−300	$\tau_m = 0.12$	−36	−36	−36
Export supply	+100	–	n.a.	n.a.	n.a.
Non-tradables demand	−200	$v_h = 0.05$	n.a.	−10	−2.5
Change Due to Real Exchange Rate Adjustment		(Exclusion for Investment $e_{ia}= 0.33$)			
Tradables demand	−120	$v_t = 0.20$	n.a.	−24	−16
Tradables supply	+80	–	n.a.	n.a.	n.a.
Import demand	−100	$\tau_m = 0.12$	−12	−12	−12
Export supply	+100	–	n.a.	n.a.	n.a.
Non-tradables demand	+120	$v_h = 0.05$	n.a.	+6	+4
Non-tradables supply	−80	–	n.a.	n.a.	n.a.
Total Distortion Costs (−), Benefit (+)			−48	−156	−82.5
Distortion Cost/Project Expenditure = Premium on Tradable Outlays			0.08	0.26	0.1375
Ratio of Economic to Market Exchange Rate			1.08	1.26	1.1375

Table 9.2: Calculation of the SPNTO: 600 of Project Funds Sourced in the Capital Market and Spent on Non-tradables

			Applicable Distortions		
		Applicable Distortions	τ_m Alone	τ_m v_t v_h	τ_m v_t v_h e_{is} e_{ia}
Change Due to Capital Market Sourcing	Impact on Demand and Supply	(Exclusion for Investment $e_{is} = 0.75$)			
Tradables demand	−400	$v_t = 0.20$	n.a.	−80	−20
Import demand	−300	$\tau_m = 0.12$	−36	−36	−36
Export supply	+100	−	n.a.	n.a.	n.a.
Non-tradables demand	−200	$v_h = .05$	n.a.	−10	−2.5
Change Due to Real Exchange Rate Adjustment		(Exclusion for Investment $e_{ia} = 0.33$)			
Tradables demand	+240	$v_t = 0.20$	n.a.	+48	+32
Tradables supply	−160	−	n.a.	n.a.	n.a.
Import demand	+200	$\tau_m = 0.12$	+24	+24	+24
Export supply	−200	−	n.a.	n.a.	n.a.
Non-tradables demand	−240	$v_h = 0.05$	n.a.	−12	−8
Non-tradables supply	+160	−	n.a.	n.a.	n.a.
Total Distortion Costs (−), Benefit (+)			−12	−66	−10.5
Distortion Cost/Project Expenditure = Premium on Non-tradable Outlays			0.02	0.11	0.0175
Shadow Price of Non-tradable Outlays			1.02	1.11	1.0175

Finally, in the third column, under distortion costs, the exclusions (credits) for investment outlays are built in. It is for this purpose that the changes have been segmented into two sets — the first associated with the sourcing of project funds in the capital market and the second linked with the substitution effects emanating from the real exchange rate adjustment corresponding to each case. Readers can verify that in the upper panels of Tables 9.1 and 9.2, the distortion costs linked to "tradables demand" and to "non-tradables demand" are reduced by 75 percent as one moves from the second to the third distortion cost column.

Likewise, in the lower panels of these tables, the corresponding distortion costs are reduced by just one-third as one moves from the second to the third distortion cost column.

This simple process of accounting for the crediting of investment outlays under VAT has a major effect on the calculation of EOCFX and SPNTO. The former moves from $1.26\ E_m$ to $1.1375\ E_m$, while SPNTO moves from 1.11 to 1.0175.[60]

9.4.2 Sourcing of Funds in the Foreign Capital Market

The analysis in this section is built on the assumption that all of a project's funds are drawn from the external capital market. We do not consider this to be a realistic assumption, except in rare cases (a point that will be considered below), but it is an extremely useful expository device. In this section the premia on tradables and non-tradable outlays will be calculated on the assumption of sourcing in the external market, and a weighted average then produced in which the premia applying to domestic sourcing and foreign sourcing are combined, using weights designed to simulate the way in which natural market forces would respond to an increased demand for funds by the country in question.

Table 9.3 is presented in the same format as Tables 9.1 and 9.2. It differs only in that the project funds are assumed to be sourced in the external capital market instead of the domestic market. The first point to note is that no table is included that deals with the premia that apply when funds that are raised abroad are spent on tradables. The reason is that in such a case, there should be no repercussion in the domestic market. If the funds are spent on imports, this simply means that an extra truck, electricity generator, or ton of coal arrives at the country's ports. If the funds are spent on exportables, this means that at the prevailing world prices of those exports (assumed to be determined in the world market and beyond the influence of the country in question), the country's exports will be reduced by the amount of the project's demand. Hence, there is no variation of any distorted local market incidental to the spending of foreign-sourced funds on tradable goods.[61]

---

[60]The general formulae for calculating the economic values of EOCFX and SPNTO are presented in Appendix 9A. This appendix covers the cases of both domestic and foreign sourcing.

[61]Readers should be aware that in developing EOCFX and SPNTO we have not incorporated the distortions that apply to the products on which project funds are spent. These are taken into account as aspects of a project's budgeted spending on specific items. Even with a uniform tariff, project imports often enter the country duty-free (especially when imported by government agencies). More generally, the specific imports of a project must be known before it is determined what tariff rate applies. The case is similar for value-added and other indirect taxes. All relevant distortions are taken into account at some point in the analysis. The question is not whether they are counted, but where. The whole concept of economic opportunity costs and shadow prices presupposes that essentially the same pattern of distortions is involved each time a certain operation (e.g., spending project funds on tradables or non-tradables) takes place. The use of E_e and SPNTO represents a shorthand way of taking into account such repetitive patterns of

The situation is quite different when money from abroad is allocated to the purchase of non-tradables. As shown in Figure 9.8, this would be reflected in an excess supply of foreign exchange, together with an excess demand of 600 in the non-tradables market. This situation is quite analogous to that at E_2 in Figure 9.7, which represents an excess demand for non-tradables of 400. Hence, the situation is similar to that depicted in Table 9.2, except that here we do not have the distortion costs stemming from sourcing in the domestic capital market (and shown in the upper panel of Table 9.2). Moreover, the story of the bottom panel of Table 9.2 has to be augmented by 50 percent to reflect an excess non-tradables demand of 600 rather than 400. To meet this demand in the non-tradables market, 600 of foreign exchange must be converted to local currency. This entails stimulating imports by 300 (along the demand curve for imports) and displacing exports by an equivalent amount (along the supply curve of exports). These movements are shown under import demand and export supply in Figure 9.8C. The real exchange rate moves to level E_3, the same as shown in Figure 9.8A, which entails a movement of 360 forward along the demand curve for tradables and one of 240 downward along the supply curve of tradables.

---

distortions. Hence, in calculating them, we want to include all relevant parts of such a repetitive pattern. But we do not want to take into account idiosyncratic distortions, i.e., those that depend on the particular pattern in which project funds are spent. These come into the cost–benefit calculus at the point where these specific outlays are treated.

Table 9.3: Calculation of the SPNTO: 600 of Project Funds Sourced Abroad and Spent on Non-tradables

	Impact on Demand and Supply	Applicable Distortions	τ_m Alone	τ_m v_t v_h	τ_m v_t v_h e_{is} e_{ia}
					Applicable Distortions
Change Due to Capital Market Sourcing		(Exclusion for Investment $e_{is}=0.75$)	n.a.	n.a.	n.a.
Change Due to Real Exchange Rate Adjustment		(Exclusion for Investment $e_{ia}=0.33$)			
Tradables demand	+360	$v_t=0.20$	n.a.	+72	+48
Tradables supply	−240	–	n.a.	n.a.	n.a.
Import demand	+300	$\tau_m=0.12$	+36	+36	+36
Export supply	−300	–	n.a.	n.a.	n.a.
Non-tradables demand	−360	$v_h=0.05$	n.a.	−18	−12
Non-tradables supply	+240	–	n.a.	n.a.	n.a.
Total Distortion Costs (−), Benefit (+)			+36	+90	+72
Distortion Cost/Project Expenditure = Premium on Non-tradable Outlays			−0.06	−0.15	−0.12
Shadow Price of Non-tradable Outlays			0.94	0.85	0.88

Figure 9.8: Impact of Funds Borrowed from Abroad and Used to Purchase Non-tradable Goods

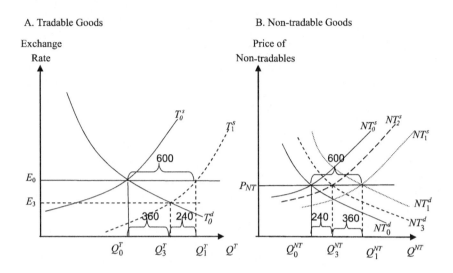

A. Tradable Goods

B. Non-tradable Goods

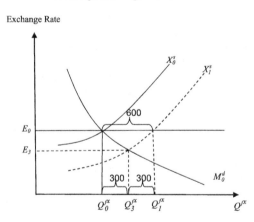

C. Foreign Exchange Market

Thus, there is 240 less of tradables being produced, and hence, 240 more of non-tradables, and 360 more of tradables is being demanded. This uses up 360 of the 600 of foreign exchange that came in to finance the project. The other 240 replaces the aforementioned reduction in tradables supply.

The 600 of project demand for non-tradables is met from the 240 of increase in their supply, plus the 360 induced reduction in their demand (the counterpart of the increase in demand for tradables induced by the fall in the real exchange rate from E_0 to E_3). The same gap of 600 that is closed by an increase of 300 in imports and a fall of 300 (Figure 9.8C) in exports is reflected in an increase of

360 in total tradables demand and a fall of 240 in total tradables supply, as shown in Figure 9.8A. As these are substitution effects, they are reflected in moves of equal magnitude and opposite sign for the non-tradables (Figure 9.8B).

Table 9.3 follows exactly the same principles as Tables 9.1 and 9.2. The only notable feature of Table 9.3 is that, rather than presenting distortion costs, in each case an external benefit is obtained from the use of foreign-sourced funds in order to purchase non-tradables. The external benefit is then 6 percent of the expenditure on non-tradables when there is only a 12 percent tariff, a 15 percent benefit with that tariff plus a VAT ($v_t = 0.20$; $v_h = 0.05$) with no credit in investment goods purchases, and a 12 percent benefit in the final case, when such a credit is given. All this comes from the fact that: a) there is no external effect linked with the actual sourcing of the (foreign) funds in this case; b) there is an unequivocal benefit (tariff externality) from the increase in imports that this case entails; and c) the demand substitution involves more spending on tradables with a higher VAT ($v_t = 0.20$) and less (substitution-induced) spending on non-tradables with a lower VAT ($v_h = 0.05$).

9.4.3 Sourcing of Funds from Both Domestic and Foreign Capital Markets

In Table 9.4, Tables 9.1, 9.2, and 9.3 are combined, and weighted average premia calculated for tradable and non-tradable outlays. Weights $g_d = 0.7$ and $g_f = 0.3$ are used, indicating a 70/30 split between domestic and foreign sourcing of funds. These weights may appear arbitrary, but in principle, can be thought of as market-determined. A simple supply and demand exercise, with many suppliers meeting a total demand, leads to the prediction that an increment of demand may in the first instance fall on one supplier or another, but market equilibrium requires that, in the end, all suppliers will move upward along their supply curves from the old to the new equilibrium price. The distribution of the increased quantity among the different suppliers thus depends on the slopes of the supply curves from different sources.

Table 9.4: Weighted Average Premia with "Standard" Capital Market Sourcing

Applicable Distortions	Project Funds Sourced From		
	Domestic Capital Market	*Foreign Capital Market*	*Both Markets $g_d = 0.7$, $g_f = 0.3$*
$\tau_m = 0.12$			
Project funds spent on:			
Tradables	0.08	0	0.056
Non-tradables	0.02	–0.06	–0.004
$\tau_m = 0.12$, $v_t = 0.20$, $v_h = 0.05$			
Project funds spent on:			
Tradables	0.26	0	0.182
Non-tradables	0.11	–0.15	0.032
$\tau_m = 0.12$, $v_t = 0.20$, $v_h = 0.05$, $e_{is} = 0.75$, $e_{ia} = 0.33$			
Project funds spent on:			
Tradables	0.1375	0	0.09625
Non-tradables	0.0175	–0.12	–0.02375

Notes: g_d: fraction of project funds effectively sourced in the domestic capital market; $g_f(=1-g_d)$: fraction of project funds effectively sourced in the foreign capital market.

The same logic can be followed for thinking of the distribution of sourcing between the domestic and the foreign capital markets. We profoundly reject the idea that developing countries face an infinitely elastic supply curve of funds at the world interest rate (or at the world interest rate plus a specified country-risk premium). The implications of such a set-up are far too strong for us (and for most economists familiar with developing countries) to accept. For example: a) even government investments financed in the first instance by borrowing in the domestic capital market will in the end be effectively financed from abroad; this means no crowding out of domestic investment from the local capital market; b) any new increment to public or private saving will end up abroad; c) any new increment to public or private investment will end up being financed from abroad; d) the economic opportunity cost of public funds is simply the world interest rate (plus a country-risk premium, where applicable).

Rather than settling for the above unrealistic implications of a flat supply curve of funds facing the country, we postulate an upward-rising curve. This means that funds drawn from the capital market are effectively sourced from: a) displaced other investments, b) newly stimulated domestic savings (displaced consumption), and c) newly stimulated "foreign savings" — i.e., extra foreign funds obtained by moving forward along the supply curve of such funds — facing the country.

Items a) and b) were incorporated into the analysis of Tables 9.1 and 9.2. The effects of item c) are traced in Table 9.3. Table 9.4 joins the two types of sourcing on the assumptions indicated.[62] It is interesting to note that in each column of Table 9.4, the difference between the premia on tradables and non-tradables remains the same as one moves from one type of sourcing to another. This makes perfect sense. In the middle column there are the polar cases, of 600 being spent on tradables or on non-tradables, with no distortion costs associated with the sourcing of project funds. The benefits appearing there (as negative premia for non-tradable outlays) represent the net externality linked to closing an excess demand gap of 600 in the non-tradables market. This same gap is split, in the cases of Tables 9.1 and 9.2, between an excess supply of 200 in the first case and an excess demand of 400 in the second.

9.5 Country Studies: Shadow Price of Foreign Exchange and Non-tradable Outlays for South Africa

South Africa is a small, open, and developing country. This section provides the empirical estimation of the shadow price of foreign exchange and non-tradable outlays for South Africa using the general equilibrium framework developed in the previous section.[63] The key parameters used in the estimation include:

- Project funds sourced in capital markets: domestic market (g_d) = 74 percent, foreign market (g_f) = 26 percent.

- Of funds sourced in the domestic market, 61.4 percent comes from displaced demand for tradables and 38.6 percent from the displacement of non-tradables demand.

- In the capital extraction, the fraction of the displaced goods that come at the expense of displaced investment (e_{is}) is 84.4 percent. In the case of the substitution effect that is due to change in relative prices between tradables and non-tradables, the corresponding fraction that belongs to investment goods (e_{ia}) is 19.6 percent.

- Distortions:
  Effective tariff rate (τ_m) = 3.60 percent;
  VAT rates: tradables (v_t) = 11.36 percent, non-tradables (v_h) = 6.54 percent;
  Excise duty rates: tradables = 5.63 percent, non-tradables = 0 percent;

---

[62] An added implication of an upward-rising foreign supply curve of funds is that the marginal cost of funds lies above the average cost, i.e., above the interest rate actually paid. It is this marginal cost that is averaged in, along with the estimated marginal productivity of displaced investment and the marginal rate of time preference applicable to newly stimulated saving, in order to obtain the economic opportunity cost of capital — i.e., the appropriate rate of discount for public sector projects.

[63] The empirical results in this section are obtained from Harberger et al. (2003).

Subsidy rate as a percentage of gross value added = 0.60 percent.

The values of the externalities created by project funds spent on tradables and non-tradables depend on the weights at margin given to various sources of funds. They are summarized in Table 9.5. Using 74 percent as the fraction of project funds sourced in the domestic capital market and 26 percent as the fraction sourced in the foreign market, EOCFX is estimated to be approximately 6 percent higher than the market exchange rate. The corresponding SPNTO is about 1 percent. This suggests that the additional cost of using, or the benefit from generating, foreign exchange in South Africa would be approximately 6 percent of the market value of tradable goods. At the same time, there is a 1 percent premium on the expenditures or receipts of non-tradable goods. These figures represent the value of the generalized distortions that are created by differences between the economic and the market value of expenditures on tradable and non-tradable goods, respectively.

Table 9.5: Premia for Tradable and Non-tradable Outlays in South Africa (percentage)

Funds Drawn From	Funds Spent on Tradables	Funds Spent on Non-tradables
Domestic capital market	8.21	3.06
Foreign capital market	0.00	−5.15
Both markets (weighted average)	6.08	0.93

9.6 Conclusion

This chapter has provided an analytical framework and a practical approach to the measurement of the EOCFX. Because of the existence of indirect taxes on domestic and trade transactions, the EOCFX differs from the market exchange rate.

Thus, when moving from the financial to the economic flows of costs and benefits of a project deriving from the tradables sector, adjustments must be introduced to account for the difference between the EOCFX and the market exchange rate. At the same time, the cost and benefit flows related to non-tradables must be adjusted so as to reflect the SPNTO.

The analysis in this chapter began with a summary of the traditional partial equilibrium framework, in which the demand and supply for the tradable goods or services are not affected by the way in which project funds are raised. It then moved to a general equilibrium analysis, which also took into account the sourcing of the funds to finance the project's purchases. In the process, it became clear that adjusting for the sourcing of funds entails premia (or discounts), not only for the economic value of foreign exchange but also for non-tradable outlays.

This general equilibrium framework was illustrated by examples in which import tariffs, value-added taxes, and investment credits were sequentially introduced. In addition, two types of sourcing (domestic and foreign) of project funds were examined. These illustrations showed how the adjustments needed vary from case to case. Finally, this framework was applied to the estimation of EOCFX for South Africa. The resulting estimate of the foreign exchange premium was approximately 6 percent of the market value of tradable goods. The corresponding premium for non-tradable outlays was about 1 percent. These figures represent the value of the generalized distortions in South Africa that are created by differences between the market and the economic value of expenditures on tradable and non-tradable goods, respectively, when the funds used to make these expenditures are sourced from the capital market, with 26 percent of the funds coming (directly or indirectly) from abroad.

Appendix 9A: A General Form for Estimating the Economic Value of Foreign Exchange and Non-tradable Outlays

General expressions for estimating the EOCFX (E_e) and non-tradable outlays (SPNTO) have strong advantages over numerical exercises. Hence, they are presented here, together with numerical checks based on the exercises of Tables 9.1 and 9.2.

Definitions:

s_1: share of project funds sourced by displacing the demand for importables;

s_2: share of project funds sourced by displacing the demand for exportables;

s_3: share of project funds sourced by displacing the demand for non-tradables;

f_1: fraction of the gap between the demand for imports and the supply of exports that is closed by a movement along the demand function for imports as the real exchange rate adjusts to bring about equilibrium;

δ_1: fraction of the gap between the demand and the supply of tradables that is closed by a movement along the demand function for tradables as the real exchange rate adjusts to bring about equilibrium;

c_1: fraction of the change in value added, stemming from a capital market intervention, that takes the form of consumption goods and services;

c_2: fraction of the change in value added, stemming from an equilibrating real exchange rate adjustment, that takes the form of consumption goods and services.

The first section summarizes the general expressions for the premia on tradable and non-tradable outlays when project funds are sourced in the domestic market. This follows the same sequence as Tables 9.1 and 9.2. First, the case of a uniform tariff (τ_m) as the only distortion is treated. Second, the value-added taxes v_t and v_h on tradables and non-tradables are added to τ_m, but with no credit for outlays on investment goods. Finally, the credit for such outlays is added, with the realistic assumption that investment goods will represent a higher fraction of the spending that is displaced by sourcing in the capital market than they will of spending that is displaced or added through price-induced substitution effects.

Expressions for Premia on Tradables and Non-tradables (Project Funds Sourced 100 Percent in Domestic Capital Market)

With Uniform Import Tariff (τ_m) Alone:

Premium on Tradables. $= (s_1 + f_1 s_3)\tau_m$
Numerical Check. $0.08 = [0.5 + 0.5(0.33)](0.12)$

Premium on Non-tradables $= [s_1 - f_1(s_1+s_2)]\tau_m$
Numerical Check: $0.02 = [0.5 - 0.5(0.67)](0.12)$

With Uniform Import Tariff (τ_m) Plus Value-Added Taxes (v_t and v_h)
(No Credit for Investment Goods)

Premium on Tradables $= (s_1 + f_1 s_3)\tau_m + (s_1+s_2)v_t + s_3 v_h + \delta_1 s_3(v_t - v_h)$
Numerical Check: $= 0.08 + (0.67)(0.2) + 0.33(0.05) + 0.6(0.33)(0.15)$
          $0.26 = 0.08 + 0.1333 + 0.0167 + 0.03$

Premium on Non-tradables $= [s_1 - f_1(s_1+s_2)\tau_m] + (s_1+s_2)v_t + s_3 v_h - \delta_1(s_1+s_2)(v_t - v_h)$
Numerical Check $= 0.02 + 0.1333 + 0.0167 - (0.6)(0.67)(0.15)$
          $0.11 = 0.02 + 0.133 + 0.0167 - 0.06$

With Uniform Import Tariff (τ_m) Plus Value-Added Taxes (v_t and v_h)
(With Credit for Investment Goods)

Premium on Tradables $= [(s_1+f_1 s_3)\tau_m] + c_s[(s_1+s_2)v_t + s_3 v_h] + c_a[\delta_1 s_3(v_t - v_h)]$
Numerical Check: $= 0.08 + (0.25)[0.1333 + 0.0167]] + (0.67)(0.03)$
          $0.1375 = 0.08 + 0.0375 + 0.02$

Premium on Non-tradables $= [s_1 - f_1(s_1+s_2)]\tau_m + c_s[(s_1+s_2)v_t + s_3 v_h] - c_a[\delta_1(s_1+s_2)(v_t - v_h)]$
Numerical Check: $= 0.02 + (0.25)(0.1333 + 0.0167) - 67[0.6(0.67)(0.15)]$
          $0.0175 = 0.02 + 0.0375 - 0.04$

Note: $c_s = (1 - e_{is}); c_a = (1 - e_{ia}).$

Expressions for Premia on Tradables and Non-tradables (Project Funds Sourced 100 Percent Abroad)

This section simply codifies the results of Table 9.3, presenting general expressions for the premia together with numerical checks to link the results to Table 9.3.

With Uniform Import Tariff (τ_m) Alone

    Premium on Tradables.   = zero
    Premium on Non-tradables $= -f_1\tau_m$
    Numerical Check: $-0.06 = -(0.5)(0.12)$

With Uniform Import Tariff (τ_m) Plus Value-Added Taxes (v_t and v_h)
(No Credit for Investment Goods)

    Premium on Tradables.   = zero
    Premium on Non-tradables. $= -f_1\tau_m - \delta_1(v_t - v_h)$
    Numerical Check: $-0.15 = -(0.5)(0.12) - (0.6)(0.15)$

With Uniform Import Tariff (τ_m) Plus Value-Added Taxes (v_t and v_h)
(With Credit for Investment Goods)

    Premium on Tradables.   = zero
    Premium on Non-tradables. $= -f_1\tau_m - c_a\delta_1(v_t - v_h)$
    Numerical Check: $-0.12 = -(0.5)(0.12) - (0.67)(0.6)(0.15)$

Note: $c_s = (1 - e_{is})$; $c_a = (1 - e_{ia})$.

References

Bacha, E. and L. Taylor. 1971. "Foreign Exchange Shadow Prices: A Critical Review of Current Theories", *Quarterly Journal of Economics* 85(2), 197–224.

Balassa, B. 1974. "Estimating the Shadow Price of Foreign Exchange in Project Appraisal", *Oxford Economic Paper* 26(2), 147–168.

Blitzer, C., P. Dasgupta, and J. Stiglitz. 1981. "Project Appraisal and the Foreign Exchange Constraints", *Economic Journal* 91(361), 58–74.

Boadway, R. 1975. "Benefit-Cost Shadow Pricing in Open Economics: An Alternative Approach", *Journal of Political Economy* 83(2), 419–430.

— 1978. "A Note on the Treatment of Foreign Exchange in Project Evaluation", *Economica* 45(180), 391–399.

Dasgupta, P. and J. Stiglitz. 1974. "Benefit-Cost Analysis and Trade Policies", *Journal of Political Economy* 82(1), 1–33.

Dinwiddy, C. and F. Teal. 1996. *Principles of Cost-Benefit Analysis for Developing Countries*, Chapter 6. Cambridge: Cambridge University Press.

Fane, G. 1991. "The Social Opportunity Cost of Foreign Exchange: A Partial Defence of Harberger et al.", *Economic Record* 67(199), 307–316.

Harberger, A.C. 1965. "Survey of Literature on Cost-Benefit Analyses for Industrial Project Evaluation", United Nations Inter-Regional Symposium in Industrial Projects Evaluation, Prague.

Harberger, A.C. and G.P. Jenkins. 2002. "Introduction", in A.C. Harberger and G.P. Jenkins (eds.), *Cost-Benefit Analysis.* Cheltenham: Edward Elgar Publishing.

Harberger, A.C., G.P. Jenkins, C.Y. Kuo, and M.B. Mphahlele. 2003. "The Economic Cost of Foreign Exchange for South Africa", *South African Journal of Economics* 71(2), 298–324.

Jenkins, G.P and C.Y. Kuo. 1985. "On Measuring the Social Opportunity Cost of Foreign Exchange", *Canadian Journal of Economics* 18(2), 400–415.

— 1998. "Estimation of the National Parameters for Economic Cost-Benefit Analysis for the Philippines", Harvard Institute for International Development, Harvard University, Development Discussion Paper No. 653 (September).

United Nations Industrial Development Organization (UNIDO). 1972. *Guidelines for Project Evaluation.* New York: United Nations Publications.

Warr, P. 1977. "Shadow Pricing with Policy Constraints", *Economic Record* 53(142), 149–166.

Chapter Ten

Economic Prices for Tradable
Goods and Services

10.1 Introduction

In the integrated financial and economic analysis, there is a need to choose a numeraire in which all costs and benefits are expressed. The most common practice has been to express all costs and benefits in terms of domestic currency at a domestic price level.[64] This is the natural rule to follow for the construction of the financial cash flow statement of a project that includes all the financial receipts and all the expenditures in each period throughout the duration of the project. However, when this numeraire is chosen to carry out the economic appraisal of the project, it is necessary to adjust the values of the transactions in the financial cash flow that involve internationally tradable goods because of distortions associated with the transactions of these goods and those that affect the market for foreign exchange.

Tradable goods and services can be either importable or exportable. In the case of importable goods that are transported from a border to a project site, additional non-tradable service charges for the project will undoubtedly be involved, such as handling charges and transportation costs, which are usually distorted in the market; thus, their values must be adjusted in the economic evaluation. Likewise, for exportable goods, where a project is considering producing its products for the export markets or using an exportable good as a project input, the financial value of the product (at factory gate) presented in the financial cash flow statement is generally determined in the world market and then net of port charges and transportation costs from the port to the domestic market. The costs of these non-tradable services are also distorted in the markets, and adjustments must be made when deriving the net economic value of the project output or project input. The evaluation of these non-tradable services from the project site to the border will be dealt with in Chapter 11.

Section 10.2 identifies the key economic characteristics of tradable and non-tradable goods. Section 10.3 describes how the financial values and various distortions should be integrated into the economic evaluation of tradable goods. Section 10.4 provides a practical example of how the economic values of various

---

[64]Some authors are concerned that undertaking the analysis in terms of domestic prices might not provide a sound evaluation of the projects. See Appendix 10A.

tradable project outputs and inputs can be measured. Conclusions are made in the final section.

10.2 Identification of Tradable Goods

The first step is to define the relationship between imported and importable goods, between exported and exportable goods, and between non-traded and tradable goods.

10.2.1 Imported and Importable Goods

Imported goods are produced in a foreign country but sold domestically. Importable goods include imports plus all goods produced and sold domestically that are close substitutes for either imported or potentially imported goods. The relationship between importable and imported goods can be seen in Figure 10.1, for the case of an item such as power hand tools used as a project input. Suppose the items purchased by a project are manufactured locally. At the same time, a significant quantity is also being imported. The demander's willingness to pay for this item is shown by the demand curve AD_0, while the domestic marginal cost of production is shown by the supply curve BS_0. If all imports were prohibited, then the equilibrium price would be at P_0, and the quantity demanded and supplied would be at Q_0.

Imported goods can be purchased abroad and sold in the domestic market at a price of P^m, which is equal to the cost, insurance, and freight (CIF) price of imports converted into local currency by the market exchange rate, plus any tariffs and taxes levied on imports. This price will place a ceiling on the amount that domestic producers can charge and will thus determine both the quantity of domestic supply and the quantity demanded by consumers. When the market price is P^m, domestic producers will maximize their profits if they produce only Q_0^s because at this level of output, they will be equating the market price with their marginal costs. On the other hand, demanders will want to purchase Q_0^d because it is at this quantity that their demand price is just equal to the world-market-determined price of P^m. The country's imports of the good measured by the amount $(Q_0^d - Q_0^s)$ are equal to the difference between what demanders demand and domestic producers supply at a price of P^m.

Figure 10.1: Imported and Importable Goods (the Case of Power Hand Tools Used as Project Input)

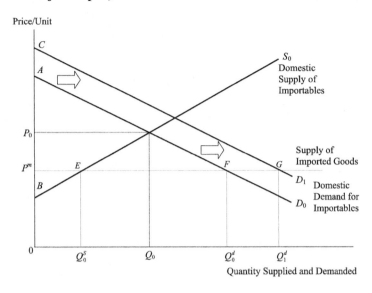

If a project now purchases the item as an input, this can be shown as a shift in its demand from AD_0 to CD_1. Unlike a situation in which there are no imports, the increase in demand does not cause the market price to rise. This is because a change in the demand for such a traded good in one country will in virtually all cases not lead to a perceptible change in the world price for the commodity. As long as the price of imports remains constant, the increase in the quantity demanded leaves the domestic supply of the good unaffected at Q_0^s. The ultimate effect of an increase in the demand for the importable good is to increase the quantity of imports by the full amount ($Q_1^d - Q_0^d$). Thus, in order to evaluate the economic cost of an importable good, we need only estimate the economic cost of the additional imports.

Likewise, the value of the benefits derived from a project that increases the domestic production of an importable good should be based entirely on the economic value of the resources saved by the decrease in purchases of imports. In Figure 10.2, the starting point is the initial position shown by Figure 10.1 prior to the project's purchase of the item. A project to increase the domestic production of these goods will shift their domestic supply from BS_0 to HS_T. This increase in domestic supply results not in a fall in price, but rather in a decrease in imports, as people now switch their purchases from imported items to domestically produced ones.

Figure 10.2: Imported and Importable Goods (the Case of Power Hand Tools Produced Domestically)

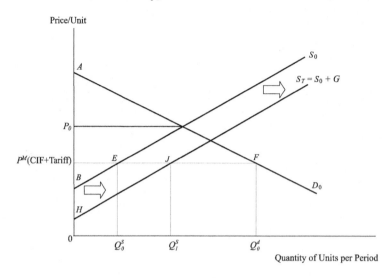

Unless the project is big enough to completely eliminate all imports of the item, the domestic price will be pegged to the price of imports, and thus the domestic demand for the input by other domestic consumers will not be changed. Imports will fall from ($Q_0^d - Q_0^s$) to ($Q_0^d - Q_1^s$), an amount equal to the output of the project ($Q_1^s - Q_0^s$). As domestic production serves as a one-for-one substitute for imported goods, the economic value of the resources saved by the reduction in the level of imports measures the economic value of the benefits generated by the project.

10.2.2 *Exported and Exportable Goods*

Exported goods are produced domestically but sold abroad. Exportable goods include both exported goods and the domestic consumption of goods of the same type or close substitutes to the goods being exported. The relationship between exportable and exported goods is very similar to that between importable and imported goods. In Figure 10.3, the demand for an exportable good is shown as KD_0, and the domestic supply of the exportable good is denoted by LS_0.

Figure 10.3: Exported and Exportable Goods (the Case of Timber Used by a Project)

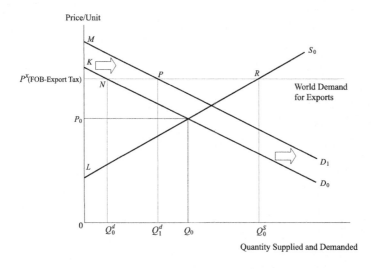

If the domestic production of timber in the country cannot be exported, domestic supply and demand (Q_0) will come into equilibrium at a price of P_0. However, the commodity will be exportable so long as the domestic market price P^x (i.e., the free on board (FOB) price multiplied by the market exchange rate less export taxes), which domestic suppliers receive when they export, is greater than P_0. If, for example, producers receive a price of P^x (see Figure 10.3), timber production will amount to Q_0^s. At this price, domestic demand for timber is only Q_0^d; hence, a quantity equal to $(Q_0^s - Q_0^d)$ will be exported.

We now introduce a project that requires timber as an input, shifting the demand for this exportable good from KD_0 to MD_1. Total domestic demand will now be equal to Q_1^d, leaving only $(Q_0^s - Q_1^d)$ available to be exported. P^x will remain constant so long as the world price is not altered by the change in demand resulting from the project. No changes in incentives have been created that would lead to an increase or decrease in domestic supply. The measurement of the economic cost of this input to the project should be based on the economic value of the foreign exchange that is forgone when the ($Q_1^d - Q_0^d$ units of timber are no longer exported.

As the market price is fixed by the world price, the benefit of a project that produces such an exportable good should be measured by the value of the extra foreign exchange that is produced when the project's output is reflected in increased exports, while the costs entailed in a project's demanding more of the exportable will be measured by the economic opportunity cost (value) of the foreign exchange forgone.

Chapter Ten   *245*

All importable and exportable goods should be classified as tradable goods. Although an input might be purchased for a project from a domestic supplier, as long as it is of a type similar to ones being imported, it is an importable good and should be classified as tradable. Likewise, goods, if domestically produced and used as project inputs, and if similar to exported goods,[65] are exportable goods and are also included in tradable goods.

10.3 Economic Value of Tradable Goods and Services

10.3.1 Essential Features of an Economic Analysis

The distinguishing feature of tradable goods is that changes in their demand or supply end up being reflected in the demand for or supply of foreign exchange. A project that produces more of an importable good will reduce the demand for (and therefore the amount of) imports of that good, thus reducing the demand for foreign exchange. Similarly, a project that produces more of an exportable good will ultimately add to the supply of exports and hence of foreign currency. Thus, the principal benefit of either type of project is to make additional foreign exchange available "for general use". In order to value this foreign exchange, we use the concept of the economic opportunity cost of foreign exchange (EOCFX), which states, in terms of a domestic-currency numeraire, the real economic value (in, for example, a peso or rupee country) of an incremental real dollar of foreign exchange.

We dealt with the precise measurement of EOCFX in Chapter 9. Here it is sufficient to note that: a) it is different from the real exchange rate E_m, which is reflected in the market foreign exchange; b) part of the difference reflects the tariff and indirect tax revenue that is given up when additional foreign exchange is extracted from the market; and c) another part of the difference reflects the tax and tariff revenue that is given up when raising the pesos or rupees that are spent in acquiring that foreign exchange.

For the present, it will be assumed that the EOCFX exceeds E_m so that there is a positive premium on foreign exchange. The present task is to investigate the

---

[65]It is reasonable to ask whether one should not also include an in-between category of "semi-tradables". These would, by and large, be goods whose price is influenced but not totally determined by external world-market forces. Product differentiation between imports and import substitutes, and between exports and export substitutes, would, of course, be the principal element defining the in-between category. It is our view that the insertion of a category of semi-tradables would further substantially complicate an analytical framework that is a daunting challenge to most countries (to develop a large cadre of practitioners capable of seriously applying it in practice). Our preference, therefore, is to stick with a sharp distinction between tradables and non-tradables. The aim would be to classify some semi-tradables as full tradables, thus committing errors in one direction, which it is hoped would tend to be substantially offset by classifying other semi-tradables as non-tradables, thus committing errors in the opposite direction.

ways in which tariffs, taxes, and other possible distortions that are in some sense "specific" to the project under analysis should be dealt with.

A good way of thinking about this subject is to consider a case in which the project authority has borrowed rupees in the capital market and is then going into the foreign exchange market to buy dollars, only to have those dollars incinerated in an accidental fire. As a consequence of that accident, the economy has lost the EOCFX. This should be obvious.

However, we can also learn something from this example that is not so obvious. The EOCFX does not include any item that has something to do with the use or uses to which that foreign exchange may be put (e.g., by importing goods with high, medium, low, or zero import duties), or with the specific distortions that might affect projects that end up generating foreign exchange (e.g., by producing export goods that are subject to either export taxes or subsidies).

If, then, foreign exchange is used to buy an import good M_j that is subject to a tariff T_j, the extra tariff revenue should be considered to be a project benefit (i.e., a financial but not an economic cost). This is also the case if the same type of good is bought from a domestic producer of it, because in the end, the demand will lead to someone else increasing imports of M_j by an equivalent amount.

If the project generates foreign exchange by producing an export good X_i that is subject to an export tax T_i, the extra tax revenue generated from these exports should be considered as an economic benefit, on top of the economic premium on the foreign exchange that the project generates. Here again, the benefit calculation would be the same if the project produced an equivalent exportable good that happened to be sold to domestic demanders. In this case, too, the fact that those demanders turn to the project to meet their demand implies that an equivalent amount that would have been taken by these demanders in the scenario "without" the project will now be available for export.

Import tariff rates applied to project inputs of importable goods, and export tax rates applied to the project outputs of exportable goods, are thus to be explicitly counted as project benefits. In the former case, the financial cost is greater than the economic cost by the amount of the tariff, but the economic cost must be calculated inclusive of the cost of the foreign exchange premium. In the case of the exportable output, its economic value as reflected by its FOB price is greater than the financial price by the amount of the tax. In this case, the economic price must be calculated inclusive of the foreign exchange premium. The story is reversed when it comes to project inputs of exportable goods or project outputs of importable goods. This is because when an exportable good is used by the project, less is exported, and the government loses the potential export tax. When an importable good is produced by the project, the natural consequence is that less of that good will be imported, with a corresponding loss of tariff revenue.

Another way of stating the same case is that when an import good is used, the domestic financial price paid is probably equal to the world price plus the tariff. However, the tariff part is simply a transfer to the government, and hence should be eliminated as a component of the cost. Likewise, when an export good subject to export tax is produced, financial accounts will incorporate the receipts net of tax, but the tax is not a cost from the standpoint of the economy. As a whole, the import tariff or the export tax should be eliminated (as a cost) when moving from the financial to the economic cost–benefit exercise.

10.3.2 Valuation of Tradable Goods at the Border and the Project Site

The economic evaluation of traded outputs and inputs is a two-stage process. First, the components of the financial cost of the import or export of the good that represent resource costs or benefits are separated from the tariffs, taxes, subsidies, and other distortions that may exist in the market for the item. Second, the financial value of the foreign exchange associated with the net change in the traded goods is adjusted to reflect its economic value and is expressed in terms of the general price level (the numeraire).[66] The evaluation of projects expressed in terms of the domestic level of prices is also for the comparability of the results between the financial and the economic appraisal.

The discussion that follows starts with the analysis for a country where there is no premium on foreign exchange. The economic evaluation of tradable goods is then carried out for the case where there is a premium on foreign exchange. These adjustments are built into the calculation of the economic value of the tradable goods and services. Following these estimations, commodity-specific conversion factors are constructed for transforming financial prices into economic values at the border.

---

[66]Alternatively, an international price level (P^w) could be used as the numeraire. This would require the value of non-tradable goods to be adjusted by the reciprocal of the same factor that is used to express the foreign exchange content of the project in terms of the general price level. Although some authors (such as Little and Mirrlees, 1974) have advocated carrying out the full analysis of a project's costs and benefits in terms of foreign currency (e.g., US dollars or euros), practitioners have found it very awkward to generate international prices for commonplace items such as haircuts, taxi rides, and gardeners' services. If two projects from different countries (e.g., Argentina and India) have to be compared to each other, it is easy to bring them to common terms by taking the net present value (NPV) of the Argentinian project (in real pesos) and multiplying it by the real exchange rate measure (real dollars per real peso). Similarly, one would convert the Indian project's NPV (in real rupees) into real dollars by multiplying it by a measure of real dollars per real rupee. Once both NPVs are thus converted to real dollars, they are fully comparable. However, the need for such comparison is rare. It is insignificant compared to the desirability of carrying out the actual computations in real terms, in domestic currency, a procedure that is virtually a necessity if a serious analysis of stakeholder interests is to be undertaken.

a) Importable Goods

The financial cost of an importable input for a project can be equated to the sum of four components of the cost of an imported good, i.e., the CIF price of the imported good, tariffs/taxes and subsidies, the trade margins of importers, and the costs of freight and transportation costs from the port to the project. The sum of these four items will be approximately equal to the delivered price of the input to the project, both when the good is actually directly imported and when it is produced by a local supplier. This is illustrated in Figure 10.4. The ultimate effect of an increase in the demand for an importable good by a project is to increase imports by $(Q_1^d - Q_0^d)$. The domestic value of the foreign exchange required to purchase these goods is equal to the CIF price, P_1, multiplied by the quantity $(Q_1^d - Q_0^d)$, as denoted by the shaded area $Q_0^d HIQ_1^d$. This is part of the economic resource cost of the input because the country will have to give up real resources to the foreign supplier in order to purchase the good.

Tariffs are often levied on the CIF price of the imported good by the importing country. These tariffs are a financial cost to the project but are not a cost to the economy because they involve a transfer of income only from the demanders to the government. Therefore, tariffs and other indirect taxes levied on the imported good should not be included in its economic price.

The importer and perhaps the traders are involved in the process that brings the item from the foreign country to the final delivery at the project site. There are a number of tasks, including handling, distribution, and storage, for which the traders receive compensation. These are referred to as the trading margin. Over and above the trading margin, there are the freight costs incurred by the importer or traders to bring the item from the port or border entry point to the project.

Figure 10.4: Economic Cost of Importable Goods (the Case of Power Hand Tools Used by a Project)

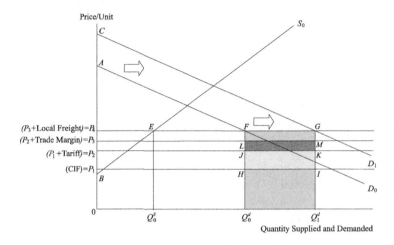

The trading margins are part of the economic costs of the imported good. The financial value of the trading margin may in some cases be larger than the economic cost of the resources expended. The most obvious case of this occurs when the privilege to import a good is restricted to a few individuals through the selective issuing of import licences. In this case, the importer may be able to increase the price of the imported good significantly above the costs incurred in importing and distributing the item. These excess profits are not a part of the economic cost to the country of the imported good as they represent only income transfers from the demanders of the imports to the privileged people who obtained the import licences. Therefore, while the financial value of the trading margins of the traders is shown as the difference in the prices $(P_3 - P_2)$ or the area $JLMK$ in Figure 10.4, the economic cost may be less than this by the proportion of the total trade margin, which is made up of "monopoly profits".

Freight costs may vary greatly with the location of the project in the country, so it is advisable to treat these costs as a separate input. As this sector uses items that are often heavily taxed – such as petroleum products and motor vehicles – as inputs, its economic costs might be significantly less than its financial cost.[67] If the economic cost of an importable input is to be compared with its financial price, the former will consist of the CIF price plus the economic cost of the traders' services, plus the economic cost of the freight and transportation required to bring an importable good from the port to the project.

Table 10.1 shows the breakdown of the financial cost of an imported car. In this case, the economic cost of the car is $24,400, while its financial cost is $37,600. This same evaluation of the economic price of a car also holds if instead it is the economic benefit of producing cars locally that is to be measured.

---

[67]It is more accurate to break the local freight costs down into different component costs and then calculate their economic costs.

Table 10.1: Economic Cost of Importable Input: the Case of Cars

Financial Cost of Imported Car ($)		Economic Cost of Imported Car ($)	
CIF price	20,000		20,000
Tariff (45.0% of CIF)	9,000		-
Sales tax (10.0% of CIF)	2,000		-
Trade margin (30.0%)	6,000	(66.7% of financial cost)	4,000
Freight	600	(66.7% of financial cost)	400
Total	**37,600**	**Total**	**24,400**

We find that the ultimate effect of increasing the domestic production of a traded input is to reduce imports. The economic benefit of such an endeavour is the economic resources saved from the reduced imports. In the above example, the expectation is that a domestic producer of cars will be able to charge a price for a car of $37,600 including taxes and freight. However, the economic resources saved are equal to only $24,400. It is this amount that is equal to the economic value of a unit of domestic car production. Note that a domestically produced car, with costs equal to, say, $30,000, would be a great financial success, but in order to make it economically advisable to produce cars domestically, the cars should (in this example) have economic costs less than or equal to $24,400. If a car that was domestically produced at the project site had costs of $24,000, it would be able to compete with the imported model, even if subject to an excise tax of 45 percent on its full economic cost of $24,000, plus a sales tax of 10 percent on the same base. These together would lead to a financial "price" of $37,200. This example shows how a protective tariff can lead to inefficient domestic production (the case of a car with economic costs of $30,000) and how such inefficiency would be avoided with an equivalent tax treatment of cars, regardless of where they are produced.

The general rule is that before adjusting for the economic price of foreign exchange, the economic value of importable good production at the factory site is equal to the CIF price plus the economic cost of local freight from port to national market and then minus the economic cost of local freight from the project site to the market. By way of comparison, the economic cost of imported inputs is calculated as the sum of the CIF price at the port plus the economic cost of freight from the port to the project site.

b) Exportable Goods

Exportable goods that are used as inputs in a project typically have a financial price that is made up of the price paid to the producer, taxes, and freight and handling costs. However, it is not these items that are adjusted to measure the economic cost of the item: it is the economic benefits forgone by reduced exports that are the measure of economic cost for such an input. The country forgoes the world price (FOB at the port) when a new project buys items that would otherwise be exported. This part of the cost is not altered by the presence of export taxes or subsidies — these simply create differences between the internal price and the FOB price, the domestic selling price at the port being higher than the FOB price in the case of an export subsidy, and lower in the case of export tax.

However, adjustments should be made for freight and handling charges. To obtain the economic benefit forgone by using an exportable good domestically, we begin with the FOB price and deduct the economic costs of the freight and the port handling charges, as these are saved when the goods are no longer exported. We then add the economic costs of freight and handling charges incurred in transporting the goods to the project. This is illustrated for the case of timber in Table 10.2.

As shown in Table 10.2, the financial cost of the timber to the project site is $495, which is made up of a $500 producer price (FOB price of $400 plus export subsidy of $100) less a financial cost differential for transportation of $50 ($125 saved plus $75 newly incurred) plus a domestic sales tax of $45. Any use of this exportable timber as an input to a local project has an economic cost of $360: this is the FOB price of $400 less the economic cost of the freight and handling charges saved of $100 on the forgone timber exports, plus the economic cost of the freight and handling in shipping the timber to the project site of $60. The assumption here is that the economic cost of freight and handling is 80 percent of its financial cost.

Table 10.2: Economic Cost of Exportable Good: the Case of Timber Used by a Project

Financial Cost of Timber ($)		Economic Cost of Timber ($)	
FOB price	400	FOB price	400
Plus export subsidy	100		
Producer price	**500**		
Less freight and handling, market to port	125	Less economic cost of freight and handling, market to port	100
Plus freight and handling, market to project	75	Plus economic cost of freight and handling, market to project	60
Sub-total	**450**		
Plus domestic sales tax 10%	45		
Total	**495**	**Total**	**360**

Moreover, the economic prices for tradable goods at the port should include adjustment for foreign exchange premium, while at the project they should also include the premium on outlays made to non-traded goods and services such as handling charges and transportation costs.

10.3.3 Conversion Factors for Tradable Goods at the Border and the Project Site

The economic prices of tradable goods account for the real resources consumed or products produced by a project and hence are not the same as the prices (gross of tariffs and sales taxes) paid by demanders, or the prices (gross of subsidies and net of export taxes) received by suppliers. These latter "paid or received" prices are what are designated financial prices. However, import tariffs and sales taxes, or export taxes and subsidies, associated with the importable or exportable goods are simply a transfer between the government and importers or exporters; they are not part of the economic cost or benefit.

A conversion factor (CF) is defined as the ratio of a commodity's economic price to its financial price. The value of the conversion factor for the importable good i (CF_i) at the port is the commodity's economic price (EP_i) at the port divided by its financial price (FP_i) at the port. Suppose that there are tariffs and other indirect taxes such as VAT levied on the ith good at the rates of t_i and d_i, respectively. In addition, the foreign exchange premium for the country in question is FEP. The CF_i can then be calculated and expressed as:

$$CF_i = EP_i / FP_i$$
$$= (1 + FEP)/[(1 + t_i)(1 + d_i)] \qquad (10.1)$$

A similar formula can also be used for exportable goods in which exports are exempt from indirect taxes. Thus, CF_j for the jth exportable good can be calculated as follows:

$$CF_j = EP_j / FP_j$$
$$= (1 + FEP)/(1 + k_j) \qquad (10.2)$$

where k_j stands for the subsidy (or a negative value for export tax) rate of the FOB price.

One feature of the conversion factor is its convenience, in that these ratios can be applied directly to convert a financial cash flow into an economic cost or benefit in the move from a project's financial cash flow statement to its economic benefit and cost statement. It should be noted that the above conversion factor does not incorporate any location-specific domestic handling or transportation costs from the port to the project site. When the adjustment for the impact on the economic costs of these non-tradable services for the item is made, one can obtain the economic value and the conversion factor for the tradable goods at the project site, and these can be easily incorporated as part of the total economic costs or benefits of the project.

10.4 An Illustrative Example

There are four possible cases that can be applied to measuring the economic values of tradable goods: a) an importable good is used as an input to a project; b) an importable good is produced by a domestic supplier; c) an exportable good is produced by a domestic supplier; and d) an exportable good is used as an input by a project. Examples provided below illustrate how each of the economic values and the corresponding conversion factors of various outputs and inputs of an irrigation project in the Visayas, Philippines, are estimated (Jenkins et al., 1994). The goal of the project was to alleviate poverty while improving the environmental sustainability of the region. The foreign exchange premium was estimated at 24.60 percent.

a) Project Uses an Importable Input (Pesticides)

In order to improve a farm's productivity, the project requires pesticides, which are importable. The financial prices of pesticides at the border include the CIF cost of the imported item plus additional costs levied on the item, such as a tariff. The CIF border price is $166.00 per 1,000 litres, which is equal to 4,038 pesos when converted by the market exchange rate. This plus the tariff imposed on the item upon arrival at the port of Manila determines the financial prices. There is a 5 percent tariff rate on imported pesticides. Thus, the financial cost in Manila will become 4,239 pesos at the port. However, the economic cost of this imported item will include only the CIF cost, which must be adjusted by the foreign exchange premium to reflect the true cost of this input. The tariff is considered a transfer within the economy and does not represent the real economic resources used. The conversion factor for pesticides in this case is 1.19 at the port, which is calculated either by the ratio of the economic costs to the financial costs of the pesticides, as presented in Table 10.3, or by equation (10.1).

In order to find the cost of pesticide delivered to the farm gate, account must be taken of the additional costs incurred by farmers for trading, handling, and transportation from the port to Manila, the main trading centre, from Manila to the local market, and then to the project site. Adding all these costs, as presented in the second column of Table 10.3, shows that farmers will pay a total of 6,054 pesos to import 1,000 litres of pesticides to their farm gate.

The economic cost of each of the above domestic services differs from its financial cost because of various distortions involved. The estimation of these non-tradable services will be discussed fully in Chapter 11. At present, the conversion factor is assumed to be 0.70 for traders' margins and 0.90 for handling charges. In the case of transportation services, the conversion factor is assumed to be 1.20 owing to a subsidy provided to the transportation producers. As a result, the economic cost of receiving 1,000 litres of pesticides at the project site amounts to 6,767 pesos, and the conversion factor is estimated at 1.12 for pesticides. This indicates that, at the farm gate, the true economic cost of pesticides is 12 percent greater than the financial price suggests.

Table 10.3: Project Uses Importable Pesticides

	Financial Price	Conversion Factor for Non-tradable Services	Value of FEP	Economic Value
CIF world price per 1,000 litres of pesticides				
US$	166.00			
Local currency	4,038.00		993.35	5,031.35
PLUS				
Tariff	201.00			0.00
Price at port	4,239.00			5,031.35
CF at port	**1.19**			
PLUS				
Handling/transportation from port to Manila				
Handling	540.00	0.90		486.00
Transportation	225.00	1.20		270.00
PLUS				
Traders' margin	200.00	0.70		140.00
PLUS				
Handling/transportation from Manila to farm gate				
Handling	600.00	0.90		540.00
Transportation	250.00	1.20		300.00
Price at farm gate	6,054.00			6,767.35
CF at project site	**1.12**			

b) Project Produces an Import-Substitute Output (Rice)

Rice is one of the two major traded crops produced under the project for consumption in the Philippines. The project's production is a substitute for imported rice. The price that the farmers receive for their product depends on the world rice price. Suppose that the CIF price for rice is $314.80 per metric ton at Manila's port. Expressed in units of domestic currency, it becomes 7,659 pesos per metric ton of rice. In this case, no import tariff or taxes are levied on rice. Thus, the rice produced by the farmers could not be sold at the port for more than 7,659 pesos per metric ton, while the economic value will be measured by the economic foreign exchange saved, at 9,543 pesos. Thus, the conversion factor for rice is 1.25.

The traders' margins and handling and transportation costs from the port to the market in Manila will be added, and the corresponding costs for local production subtracted, in order to arrive at the farm gate price. Since rice is a substitute good, merchants in the Manila market would not pay more for the rice produced domestically from the farmers than they pay for imported rice, which is 8,281 pesos per metric ton. To find the financial price of the paddy the farmers produce, it is necessary to take into account the additional expenses they incur for milling, trading, and handling and transportation, as shown in the second column of Table 10.4. In addition, it should be noted that the value of paddy is about 65 percent that of rice. As a consequence, the financial price of paddy at the farm gate will be 4,501 pesos.

To derive the economic value of paddy that the farmers produce, the financial costs of the above services must be adjusted using the respective conversion factors estimated. After all these adjustments have been made, the total economic value of paddy will be 5,601 pesos per metric ton, and the conversion factor for import-substituted rice will be 1.24. Thus, the economic analysis indicates that at the farm gate, the true economic value of paddy is worth about 24 percent more than the financial price suggests.

Table 10.4: Project Supplies Domestically Importable Rice

	Financial Price	Conversion Factor for Non-tradable Services	Value of FEP	Economic Value
CIF world price per ton of rice				
US$	314.80			
Local currency	7,659.00		1,884.11	9,543.11
CF at the port	**1.25**			
PLUS				
Handling/transportation from port to Manila				
Handling	50.00	0.90		45.00
Transportation	100.00	1.20		120.00
Traders' margin	472.00	0.70		330.40
Wholesale price in Manila	8,281.00			10,038.51
LESS				
Transportation from rice mill to Manila	515.00	1.20		618.00
Ex-mill price of rice	7,766.00			9,420.51
LESS				
Milling cost	345.00	1.10		379.50
Pre-milled value	7,421.00			9,041.01
Paddy equivalent (65%)	4,823.65			5,876.66
LESS				
Grain dealers' margin (4%)	192.95	0.70		135.06
Handling/transportation from farm to mill				
Handling	50.00	0.90		45.00
Transportation	80.00	1.20		96.00
Price of paddy at farm gate	4,500.70			5,600.60
CF at project site	**1.24**			

c) Exportable Good (Seeds)

Seeds are produced domestically at the International Rice Research Institute (IRRI) in Manila. Suppose that the IRRI is considering increasing its production of seeds and exporting them to foreign markets. The financial price in domestic currency of seeds will be determined by the FOB price of seeds at the port of Manila, which is the world price of $410, or 9,975 pesos per ton. If the government provides an export subsidy on seeds, its financial revenue for seeds will increase by an equivalent amount. Suppose in this case there is an export subsidy of 10 percent of the sale price of those seeds sold abroad. The IRRI will not sell seeds to domestic buyers for less than the FOB price plus the subsidy of 998 pesos per ton, or 10,973 pesos net of port charges and transportation cost from the port of Manila to the IRRI.

The economic price of the exported product is determined by the FOB price and augmented by the foreign exchange premium to reflect the true value of this output. Thus, the economic value of exportable seeds equals 12,429 pesos at the border. As a result, the conversion factor of the exportable seeds at the port is estimated at 1.13, as presented in Table 10.5.[68]

Suppose that the output of the IRRI increases and the additional output does not affect the world price of the seeds; their economic price delivered to the port is measured by the FOB price of the good multiplied by the market exchange rate. The FOB price will be equal to the price received by the producer plus the financial costs of handling and transportation from the IRRI to the point of export. The economic price of seeds at the IRRI will be the FOB price minus the economic costs of handling and transportation from the port to the IRRI. To arrive at the economic values of these costs, the transportation and handling charges are adjusted for the distortions using the respective conversion factors estimated. The total adjusted economic value of exportable seeds at the factory gate of the IRRI is equal to 12,261 pesos, and the conversion factor becomes 1.14.

---

[68]If the government instead levied an export tax on seeds of 10 percent of the FOB price, the domestic price at the port would fall to 8,977 pesos. The conversion factor would have become 1.38, according to equation (10.2).

Table 10.5: Project Supplies Exportable Seeds (Assuming Export Subsidy of 10 percent)

	Financial Price	Conversion Factor for Non-tradable Services	Value of FEP	Economic Value
FOB price per ton of seeds				
US$	410.00			
Local currency	9,975.00		2,454.00	12,429.00
PLUS				
Export subsidy (10% of FOB price)	998.00			
Price at port	10,973.00			12,429.00
CF at port	**1.13**			
LESS				
Handling/transportation from IRRI to port				
Handling	120.00	0.90		108.00
Transportation	50.00	1.20		60.00
Price at IRRI gate	10,803.00			12,261.00
CF at project site	**1.14**			

d)   Project Uses an Exportable Good (Seeds) as a Project Input

Suppose that seeds produced domestically are an exportable good and are purchased as an input to the project rather than exported abroad. If seeds can be sold for $410 a ton on the world market, the financial price in domestic currency at the port will be 9,975 pesos per ton. Suppose in this case there is an export subsidy of 10 percent on the sale price of those seeds sold abroad. In this case, seeds will not be sold to domestic buyers for less than 10,973 pesos.

As the seeds are used by the farmers, rather than exported, the amount of foreign exchange gained by exporting the seeds is lost, and thus the economic cost will be the cost of foreign exchange earnings forgone. The economic value must be adjusted for the foreign exchange premium to become 12,429 pesos, which results in a conversion factor of 1.13, as shown in Table 10.6.

Table 10.6: Project Uses Exportable Seeds (Assuming Export Subsidy of 10 percent)

	Financial Price	Conversion Factor for Non-tradable Services	Value of FEP	Economic Value
FOB price per ton of seeds				
US$	410.00			
Local currency	9,975.00		2,454.00	12,429.00
PLUS				
Export subsidy (10% of FOB price)	998.00			
Price at port	10,973.00			12,429.00
CF at port	**1.13**			
LESS				
Handling/transportation from IRRI to port				
Handling	120.00	0.90		108.00
Transportation	50.00	1.20		60.00
PLUS dealers' margin	370.00	0.70		259.00
PLUS transportation from IRRI to farm	635.00	1.20		762.00
Price at farm gate	11,808.00			13,282.00
CF at project site	**1.12**			

Seeds can be sold on the world market for an FOB price of 9,975 pesos. However, the IRRI receives 10,803 pesos, since it incurs 170 pesos for the transportation and handling charges from the IRRI to the port, and receives 998 pesos for the export subsidy. The IRRI will not sell rice to the farmers for less than this amount. In addition, it will have to pay the local dealer's margin (370 pesos), plus transportation costs from the IRRI to the farm (635 pesos). There are no taxes levied on seeds in the Philippines, so the total cost that the farmers pay for their seeds amounts to 11,808 pesos per ton at the farm gate.

The total economic value of seeds at the farm gate needs to be measured in terms of the cost of the resources used in handling, transporting, and marketing the good. As these activities are non-tradable services, the economic value must be adjusted from the financial cost using the respective conversion factor. The final economic cost of 13,282 pesos for exportable seeds results in a conversion factor of 1.12.

Expressing the relationship between the economic and financial prices of an item in this way is convenient as long as the underlying tariff, tax, and subsidy distortions do not change in percentage terms; the value of the conversion factor will not be affected by inflation. Similarly, if a series of project evaluations is carried out, some of the conversion factors used for the analysis of one project may be directly applicable to others.

10.5 Conclusion

This chapter began with the identification of the key distinct characteristics of tradable and non-tradable goods. It is important to point out that the fundamental forces for determining their financial price and their economic price are different. In the case of tradable goods, they are defined as including not only exported or imported goods, but also domestically consumed or produced goods, so long as they are close substitutes for exported or imported goods.

We then identified the various distortions associated with tradable goods, such as import tariffs, non-tariff barriers, export taxes, subsidies, VAT, and other indirect taxes. These distortions will have a considerable influence on the financial prices of the goods in the market. However, determining the economic prices of tradable goods and services is their world price, since the world price reflects their economic opportunity cost, or resources saved by the economy.

The economic prices of tradable goods can be estimated from the corresponding financial prices, shown in the financial cash flow statement, multiplied by the applicable commodity-specific conversion factors. The magnitudes of these conversion factors at the border depend on the size of various distortions associated with the goods in question as well as the foreign exchange premium. When the tradable goods used or produced by the project are located away from the border, non-tradable services such as handling and transportation costs, trading margins, etc. are required by the project, and their conversion factors must be estimated and incorporated into the analysis. Both their financial and their economic costs at the project site should be properly assessed and estimated in the financial and economic appraisal of the project.

Appendix 10A: Evaluating Projects Subject to Trade Protection

One of the reasons why some authors (especially Little and Mirrlees, 1974) chose to recommend that the evaluation of development projects be conducted in terms of foreign currency and at "world" prices was their fear that carrying out the analysis in terms of domestic prices would lead to the likely approval of projects that were economically unsound and that were made financially viable only as a result of protectionist measures. In this appendix we show, using numerical examples, that our analytical framework is not subject to this criticism: it will detect unsound projects without fail.

Consider first a project to produce an import substitute for men's shirts that have an external price of $20. The market exchange rate is 10 rupees to the dollar, and the foreign exchange premium is 10 percent. With a 30 percent tariff on men's shirts, the internal price of shirts will be 260 rupees. We assume here that our project is able to produce equivalent shirts domestically for 240 rupees (including a normal return to capital). The project is thus viable from a financial point of view. However, it does not pass the test of an economic evaluation.

Selling price	= Rs. 260
Reduced by 30% tariff (lost revenue to government)	−60
	Rs. 200
Augmented by 10% FEP	+20
Economic benefit	= Rs. 220
Actual cost of domestic production	Rs. 240
Net economic gain (+) or loss (−)	−Rs. 20

Consider next the case of an item subject to a 30 percent export subsidy, under the same conditions.

World price (= $20) at market exchange rate	= Rs. 200
Selling price with 30% export subsidy	= Rs. 260
Reduced by 30% export subsidy (extra outlay by government)	−60
	Rs. 200
Augmented by 10% FEP	+20
Economic benefit	= Rs. 220
Actual cost of domestic production	Rs. 240
Net economic gain (+) or loss (−)	−Rs. 20

The above examples are cases in which ill-advised protectionist measures create incentives for activities to be profitable financially, even though they represent net losses from an economic point of view. The following is an example of a project that is in fact worthwhile economically, but that will not be undertaken because an unwise export tax has made it financially unviable.

World price (= $20) at market exchange rate	= Rs. 200
Selling price net of 30% export tax	
(=financial return)	Rs. 140
Assumed financial cost	Rs. 180
Net financial return	−Rs. 40

Economic return	
World market price ($20) at market exchange rate	Rs. 200
Augmented by FEP	+20
	Rs. 220
Actual cost of domestic production	Rs. 180
Net economic gain (+) or loss (−)	+Rs. 40

References

Boardman, A.E., D.H. Greenberg, A.R. Vining, and D. Weimer. 2001. *Cost-Benefit Analysis: Concepts and Practice*, 2nd edition. Englewood Cliffs, NJ: Prentice Hall.

Curry, S. and J. Weiss. 1993. *Project Analysis in Developing Countries*. New York: St. Martin's Press.

Dinwiddy, C. and F. Teal. 1996. *Principles of Cost-Benefit Analysis for Developing Countries*, Chapter 6. Cambridge: Cambridge University Press.

Dreze, J. and N. Stern. 1990. "Policy Reform, Shadow Prices, and Market Prices", *Journal of Public Economics* 42(1), 1–45.

Harberger, A.C. and G.P. Jenkins. 2002. "Introduction", in A.C. Harberger and G.P. Jenkins (eds.), *Cost-Benefit Analysis*. Cheltenham: Edward Elgar Publishing.

Jenkins, G.P. and M.B. El-Hifnawi. 1993. *Economic Parameters for the Appraisal of Investment Projects: Bangladesh, Indonesia and the Philippines*. Report prepared for Economics and Development Resource Center, Asian Development (December).

Jenkins, G.P., L. Pastor, and P. Therasa. 1994. "Farmer Participation, a Key Input to Success: The Visayas Communal Irrigation Project", Harvard Institute for International Development (December).

Little, I.M.D. and J.A. Mirrlees. 1974. *Project Appraisal and Planning for Developing Countries*. London: Heinemann Educational Books.

— 1991. "Project Appraisal and Planning Twenty Years On", *Proceedings of the World Bank Annual Conference on Development Economics, 1990*. Washington, DC: World Bank.

Mishan, E.J. and E. Quah. 2007. *Cost-Benefit Analysis*, 5th edition, Chapter 14. London and New York: Routledge.

Overseas Development Administration (ODA). 1988. *Appraisal of Projects in Developing Countries: A Guide for Economists*, 3rd edition. London: Stationery Office Books.

United Nations Industrial Development Organization (UNIDO). 1972. *Guidelines for Project Evaluation.* New York: United Nations Publications.

Chapter Eleven

Economic Prices for Non-tradable Goods and Services

11.1 Introduction

Non-tradable items are those that are not traded internationally. They include items such as services for which the demander and producer are in the same location, and commodities that have low value in relation to either their weight or their volume. In such cases, the transportation charges prevent producers from profitably exporting their goods. Typically, non-tradables include such items as electricity, water supply, all public services, hotel accommodation, real estate, construction, and local transportation; goods with very high transportation costs, such as gravel; and commodities produced to meet special customs or conditions in a particular country.

The key element to be borne in mind when considering the tradable or non-tradable classification is where the price for the good (or service) in question is determined. If this determination takes place in the world market, the good should be considered tradable. If the setting of the price takes place through supply and demand in the local market, the good should be considered non-tradable.

High rates of protection can easily cause a good that is internationally tradable to end up being properly classified as non-tradable. One example is rice in Japan, where until recently imports were explicitly forbidden and where the internal price has typically been more than double the international price. Another is grocery items from advanced countries, which often sell in developing-country markets for significant multiples of their free on board (FOB) price. Such high prices, whether caused by tariffs or by the low-volume, high-markup characteristics of the imported good, lead to situations in which "similar" items produced locally have their prices determined by supply and demand in the local market, well under the "umbrella" price of the imported counterpart, but are still not exported. When the price of locally produced merchandise is well below the "corresponding" local price of imported items, it is quite appropriate to treat local production as non-tradable, despite the anomalous price relationship.

If the cost, insurance, and freight (CIF) price, adjusted to include tariffs, taxes, and import subsidies, is greater than the market price, and no imports of the good are present in the country, then it is clearly a non-tradable good from the point of view of that country, or region of the country. Imports cannot compete with domestic production, at least with the existing level of tariff protection. Alternatively, if the FOB price, excluding export duties but including any export subsidies, is less than the domestic market price of the item, and no exports of the commodity are taking place, then again it is non-tradable. The standard relationships between the adjusted CIF, adjusted FOB, and market prices are illustrated in Figure 11.1 for the case of limestone.

Figure 11.1: World Prices, Domestic Price, and Non-tradable Goods (the Case of Limestone)

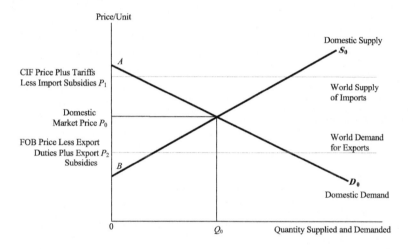

As the CIF price, plus tariffs less import subsidies (P_1), on limestone is above the domestic market price (P_0), the domestic demanders will be unwilling to purchase imported limestone. Similarly, since the FOB price, less export duties plus export subsidies (P_2), is less than the market price, domestic producers will be unwilling to sell abroad for a lower price than they can sell to domestic demanders.

In Chapter 9 the externalities associated with sourcing of funds in the capital market are quantified through the estimation of the foreign exchange premium (FEP) and the premium for expenditures on non-tradable goods and services (NTP). The estimated NTP captures the value of the externalities lost or gained when funds are raised from the capital market and the proceeds used to buy non-tradable goods. The converse is also true. The value of NTP also measures the value of the externalities gained or lost per dollar of output produced when the project sells a non-tradable output. These values do not consider the externalities on the particular tradable or non-tradable item that is purchased with the funds. They are solely associated with the sourcing or disposal of funds in the capital market. It is the objective in this chapter to develop a practical framework for the evaluation of the economic prices for the purchase or sale of a specific non-tradable.

If the project produces or demands a standard non-tradable good with an upward-sloping supply curve and downward-sloping demand curve, the economic value of the good is determined by its demand and supply as well as the impact of the act on the rest of the economy. These cases are discussed in detail in the following sections.

The process of estimating the economic costs or benefits of tradable goods is simplified by the assumption that world prices of these goods and services can be taken as given. Unfortunately, the analysis is more complicated for non-tradable goods. However, it is similar to the tradable case when supplies of the non-tradable good in question are highly elastic.

Section 11.2 describes the way in which the economic value of non-tradable outputs can be measured in the case of an infinite supply elasticity. Section 11.3 considers the case of a non-tradable good in the standard supply and demand framework. Section 11.4 identifies some unique features of applying economic prices to the measurement of net economic benefits of a project. Section 11.5 provides an example of how the economic value of a non-tradable project input can be measured. Conclusions are made in the final section.

11.2 The Case of Infinite Supply Elasticity

The simplest case is for a project producing non-tradable outputs, the market supply function of which is infinitely elastic.[69] Electricity projects make an almost ideal case in point, for a number of reasons. First, the true, intrinsic value of electricity to its demanders is quite hard to gauge. Second, electricity projects can take many forms: run-of-the-stream hydro projects, daily reservoirs, seasonal dams, inter-annual storage dams, and many others. Trying to measure the benefits of each such project (heterogeneous even within any one of the listed types) might seem to be a hopeless task. However, such qualms should be allayed once it is realized that the true measure of the benefits of almost any type of electricity project is the alternative cost of generating a similar flow of energy by some more "standard" means.

Standard alternatives exist, and they are in highly elastic supply. They consist of thermal generators of different types, which can closely approximate the type of energy flow that is likely to come from any given "idiosyncratic" project (with its own pattern of costs). The use of data on different types of thermal-generating facilities enables us to give an alternative cost (= economic price) of energy of any given description (base load, peaking capacity, etc.). The economic cost of

---

[69]For the supply of the output to be in perfectly elastic supply, it will also require that all the inputs used in producing the output are in perfectly elastic supply. The infinite elasticity assumption is a good approximation of the economic value of a non-tradable good, especially in the long run, which is most relevant for the present analysis.

approximately replicating the energy output of any given new project can then be calculated. When the project is undertaken, its benefit is measured by the alternative cost of generating an equivalent flow of energy by standard thermal means. Such costs would be largely for tradable inputs: the generators themselves, the fuel that would be used, etc. Consequently, the foreign exchange costs of the alternatives will have to be inflated to take into account the existence of a FEP. In addition, non-tradable outlays will have to be adjusted to reflect the shadow price applying to them.

The end result of such an exercise would be the economic opportunity cost of providing the same amount of energy as that produced by the project, but by standard thermal means. The new plant, producing output x, would be worthwhile if its cost, appropriately adjusted to reflect economic rather than financial considerations, was less than (or at most equal to) that of its standard thermal alternative.

In this situation, the value assigned to the electricity generated by the new plant is the value of the resources saved by not needing to generate the electricity by alternative means. In the terminology of the three basic postulates of applied welfare economics (Harberger, 1971), this economic value P_x^e is equal to the supply price of the alternative electricity service, P_x^s. In some situations, the market price P_x^m of this alternative-generation technology may not reflect its true economic price. For example, this economic price would exclude any taxes that might exist on the fuel used by the alternative source of supply. These taxes might include such items as tariffs, excise and non-creditable sales taxes on tradable goods, and excise taxes and non-creditable sales taxes on non-tradable goods and services.[70] Such taxes on inputs are not a resource saving or cost, but are transfers to the government. This adjustment is equal to $\sum\limits_{i} a_{ix}^o P_i^m d_i$, where a_{ix}^o is the input–output coefficient of the input i used to produce a unit of x, while P_i^m is the price of a specific input i, and d_i is the tax wedge associated with the use of input i in the production of x. In this case, the economic price of electricity is:

$$P_x^e = P_x^m - \sum_i a_{ix}^o P_i^m d_i \qquad (11.1)$$

Note that d_i expresses the tax or subsidy wedge as a fraction of the market price P_i^m.

Suppose the inputs used in the production of electricity by the other electricity suppliers are made up of tradable inputs equal to a proportion (T_x) of

---

[70]When the final output, in this case good x, is subject to a VAT then any VAT paid on inputs will be creditable against the VAT due on the sales of x, hence, there will be no need to make an adjustment for the VAT paid on inputs.

the total costs of production and non-tradable inputs equal to a proportion (NT_x) of total costs. In deriving the economic value of a unit of electricity produced by the project, a final adjustment must be made because of the externalities (FEP and NTP) that are associated with the sourcing or disposal of funds in the capital market due to changes in the quantities purchased or sold of tradables and non-tradables, respectively. In the case of thermal electricity supply, we would expect T_x to be close to 1 and NT_x to be quite small. Of course, $T_x + NT_x = 1$, by definition.

This adjustment is an additional benefit that arises as tradable and non-tradable resources, which are now made available to the economy as a consequence of the new plant's increase in supply. It measures the value of the generalized economic externalities enjoyed by the economy when resources are released as a consequence of the project. The opposite situation would exist if the project were demanding additional electricity that would be entirely supplied by these alternative-generation facilities. Now the generalized externality would be counted as an additional economic cost of the input purchased. To summarize, in this special case of an infinitely elastic supply of alternative production, the economic value of a unit of good x being produced by the project is equal to:

$$P_x^e = P_x^m - \sum_i a_{ix}^o P_i^m d_i + \left[P_x^m \times T_x \times FEP \right] + \left[P_x^m \times NT_x \times NTP \right] \quad (11.2)$$

11.3 A Non-tradable Good in the Standard Supply and Demand Framework

Many markets for non-tradables (whether these are items that are produced by a project or goods and services that are purchased to build or operate a project) are characterized by upward-sloping supply curves. This section will first consider the steps in the economic evaluation of an output of a project that changes the price of the good or service. It will then describe the way in which this mechanism can be used to value the economic cost of non-tradable inputs purchased by a project.

11.3.1 Economic Value of a Non-tradable Output of a Project

For some non-tradable goods, the increase in output of a new project will lower the price of the good and hence cause some displacement of alternative sources of supply. At the same time, the lower price will create some incremental demand. This is a natural outcome of the standard supply and demand framework with upward-rising supply and downward-sloping demand curves.[71]

---

[71]Some of the concepts for measuring economic welfare changes are further elaborated in Appendix 11A.

In this case, some fraction of the output of the new project will be reflected in a movement backward along the supply curve of the other sources of supply of the same goods, plus a movement forward along the total market-demand curve for the good in question. The fractions applying to supply and demand (W^s and W^d) can be calculated using the price elasticity of supply (ε^s) and demand (η^d) for the goods[72] as $W^s = \varepsilon^s / (\varepsilon^s - \eta^d)$ and $W^d = -\eta^d / (\varepsilon^s - \eta^d)$.

The economic prices associated with the changes in supply and demand as a result of a project are measured using the principles of applied welfare economics. Let P_x^s be the supply price per unit produced by those suppliers other than the project, and P_x^d be the demand price per unit by domestic demanders of the good in question (project output plus other supply). The economic price (P_x^e) per unit of a non-tradable good x produced by a project can be measured by a weighted average of its supply price (P_x^s) and the demand price (P_x^d). The weights reflect the responsiveness of existing suppliers and demanders to changes in the price of the non-tradable good. That is:

$$P_x^e = W_x^s P_x^s + W_x^d P_x^d \tag{11.3}$$

where $W_x^s + W_x^d = 1$.

Let us now introduce distortions in the output market for the item. Suppose there is a production subsidy k_x expressed as a proportion of the net-of-subsidy price.[73] In our terminology, the marginal cost of production is defined as the good's supply price P_x^s. In addition, there is a value added tax levied at the rate of t_x^v on the market price P_x^m| This is the price that the supplier receives excluding any taxes that might have been paid by the final consumer. Thus, the supply price and demand price are $P_x^s = P_x^m (1 + k_x)$ and $P_x^d = P_x^m \times (1 + t_x^v)$, respectively.[74] Equation (11.3) can then be expressed as follows:

$$P_x^e = P_x^m (1 + W_x^s k_x + W_x^d t_x^v) \tag{11.4}$$

---

[72]The relevant elasticities are those that would characterize the markets in reaction on average over the life of the project.

[73]If instead, and perhaps more realistically, the subsidy could be provided as a proportion, k_x', of the total resource costs, then $P_x^s (1 - k_x') = P_x^m$, hence $P_x^s = P_x^m / (1 - k_x')$.

[74]In determining the demand price for x, all taxes on output including VATs, single stage sales taxes or excise taxes are treated in a similar fashion.

The conversion factor, obtained by dividing the economic value per unit of output, shown in equation (11.4), by its financial price exclusive of tax and subsidy, is equal to 1 plus a weighted average of the distortions in the product in the market, i.e., $P_x^e / P_x^m = (1 + W_x^s k_x + W_x^d t_x^v)$. However, if the financial price is inclusive of tax, the conversion factor will be equal to $P_x^e / [P_x^m (1 + t_x^v)]$. This may seem to be similar to the tradable case, but the issue is more complicated owing to the impact that the project's output has on other distorted markets and the reallocation of resources in the economy.

In a standard supply and demand framework with upward-rising supply and downward-sloping demand curves, the economic price (P_x^e) of a non-tradable good x can be estimated in a partial equilibrium analysis as a weighted average of the supply price (P_x^s) and the demand price (P_x^d), as expressed in equation (11.4). The supply price of the product is measured by what producers actually receive (i.e., gross of any subsidy and net of any tax). The demand price is measured by what demanders actually pay (gross of tax). Suppose the good x is a telephone service produced by mobile telephones. The supply that the mobile telephone project displaces is likely to be communications services produced by the existing land-line telephones. The existing supply from all sources is assumed to receive a direct subsidy from the government equal to a fraction (k_x) of all their financial costs. Including the items discussed so far, the economic value of good x is shown by the shaded areas of Figure 11.2.

Figure 11.2: Economic Benefits of a Project (When an Output Tax and a Production Subsidy are Present)

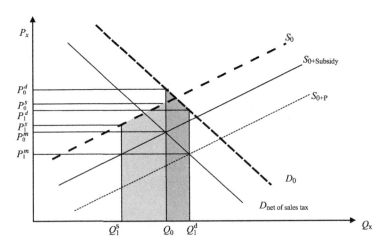

On the demand side of equation (11.4), the amount of income spent on the incremental increase in the quantity of x demanded, measured by $W_x^d P_x^d$, will

Economic Prices for Non-Tradable Goods and Services

no longer be spent on other goods and services in the economy. In general, we would expect that some taxes would have been paid on these goods and services that are no longer being purchased. This effect should be captured by adding an economic cost (reducing the benefit) as the taxes associated with purchases of those goods and services are now forgone. Since it is not known precisely where those goods and services would be forgone, an average indirect tax distortion rate (d^*) on these items is assigned. Hence, the offsetting loss in taxes as a result of the diversion of demand toward good x will be $W_x^d P_x^m d^*$ The second term on the right-hand side of equation (11.4) now becomes $W_x^d P_x^m (1 + t_x^v - d^*)$.

If it was known that the additional quantity of the non-tradable good demanded was being drawn from a specific substitute good or service, y, we would want to subtract the tax t_y lost as a result of the reduction in the purchase of this good from that of the additional tax paid, t_x^v. In this case, the second term on the right-hand side of equation (11.4) would become $W_x^d P_x^m (1 + t_x^v - t_y)$.

Adjustments must also be made to the supply price of producing the good x. However, because different adjustments are required for different types of intermediate inputs used to produce the good x, they will be dealt with in the following subsections.

a) Intermediate Inputs with Infinite Supply Elasticity

Two further adjustments need to be made to the market price of the supply price of this good x in order to derive the value of the resources released by the non-project suppliers of the project output x. First, the supply price in equation (11.4), $[P_x^m(1 + k_x)]$, does not take into consideration any tax distortions (d_i) levied on the intermediate inputs used to produce the existing supply of x that is being partially replaced by the project. These inputs will now go elsewhere in the economy to produce other goods and services. However, the value of the resources saved should not include any non-creditable taxes that will no longer be paid by the non-project suppliers. The composition of these intermediate inputs may differ depending on whether the replaced supply of x was using an identical technology. Often, the technology will be different from that used by the project.

Certainly, the inputs released do not need to be of the same composition as those used by the project (i.e., $\sum_i a_{ix} P_i^m$). Suppose they are $\sum_i a_{ix}^o P_i^m$. In the case in which there are many such intermediate inputs, the adjustment made to the supply side of the economic price of good x of equation (11.4) is $W_x^s [\sum_i a_{ix}^o P_i^m d_i]$

. This adjustment[75] is shown in the lower part of the shaded area as $\sum_i a^o_{ix} P^m_i d_i$ in Figure 11.3.

The second adjustment that has not been accounted for is the FEP and the NTP associated with tradable and non-tradable components, respectively, of the non-tradable good. These premiums arise because with the reduction in production on the part of the non-project suppliers of this good, the demand for tradable inputs will be lower, and hence there is a saving of the FEP associated with this tradable component. The same sort of externality arises when the non-tradable inputs are released by the non-project sources of the supply of the good. In this case, it is the externality measured by the premium associated with the estimated value of SPNTO.

Figure 11.3: Economic Benefits of a Project (When There are Non-Creditable Taxes on Intermediate Inputs are Present)

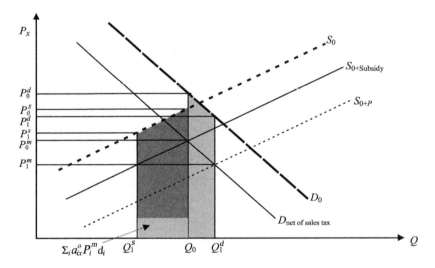

It is likely that when the final equilibrium is re-established after the project has been implemented, the ultimate uses of tradable and non-tradable components of intermediate inputs would not be the same as the initial purchases of the

---

[75]The value of this tax adjustment, $W^s_x \sum_i a^o_{ix} P^m_i d_i$, is exactly correct only if the tax and subsidy distortions are on tradable inputs or on non-tradable inputs that are in perfectly elastic supply. Furthermore, the value of the distortion d_i will not include any VAT paid on inputs used to produce an output that is subject to VAT. It will consist mainly of tariffs, excise taxes and subsidies on inputs. These issues will be discussed later in this chapter.

Economic Prices for Non-Tradable Goods and Services

intermediate inputs employed to produce the non-tradable good x.[76] However, it is difficult to foresee the final uses of tradable and non-tradable components of intermediate inputs. For all intents and purposes, it is assumed that the composition of tradable and non-tradable components of intermediate inputs remains unchanged. The economic value of the non-tradable good produced would then be adjusted by increasing the cost of the tradable component of the non-tradable intermediate inputs required to produce the good x by the FEP, and the cost of the non-tradable component of the non-tradable intermediate inputs by the NTP. That is:

$$+ (P_x^m \times T_x \times FEP) + (P_x^m \times NT_x \times NTP) \tag{11.5}$$

After taking into account all the repercussions of producing the non-tradable good x in the economy, the economic price of the non-tradable good x can be measured as:

$$P_x^e = W_x^s P_x^m (1 + k_x) + W_x^d P_x^m (1 + t_x^v - d*)$$
$$- W_x^s \sum_i a_{ix}^o P_i^m d_i + (P_x^m \times T_x \times FEP) + (P_x^m \times NT_x \times NTP) \tag{11.6}$$

Since the financial receipts of the non-tradable good x are $P_x^m (1 + t_x^v)$, the conversion factor of this product will be:

$$CF_x = P_x^e / P_x^m (1 + t_x^v) \tag{11.7}$$

b) Intermediate Inputs with Finite Supply Elasticity

Up to this point the assumption has been that the only distorted inputs being used in the production of good x by its non-project suppliers were either internationally traded, or, if non-tradable, in perfectly elastic supply. For those intermediate inputs that are neither internationally traded nor in perfectly elastic supply, a different adjustment is required to eliminate the value of the input distortions from the value of the resources released. In this case the price of the input will be lower as the demand for the input is decreased. As a consequence, both the demand and the supply of the input j will be affected, and the objective here is to measure any distortions associated with the supply and demand sides of the non-tradable intermediate inputs j caused by the additional supply of the project's non-traded good x.

---

[76]The interaction and the composition of tradable and non-tradable components are further discussed in Appendix 11B.

As the project produces more good x, the other producers of x will reduce their supply and hence their purchases of input j. The financial cost of the input j will be $P_j^m(1 + t_j^e)$ where t_j^e is the rate of non-creditable taxes (e.g., excise taxes) on input j. Following the standard supply and demand framework with upward-rising supply and downward-sloping demand curves, because their price of j is now allowed to change, the effect will be a cutback in the supply of j. The economic cost of the input j that is due to its supply response will be measured by the response of the input supply W_j^s multiplied by the price of the input P_j^m, or $W_j^s(a_{jx}^o P_j^m)$, where a_{jx}^o is the input-output coefficient of the input j used to produce a unit of x. Suppose there is a subsidy on the production of j, where k_j stands for the subsidy rate, and at the same time there may be import duties plus excise taxes combined to a rate of g_j on the inputs used to produce j. These duties and taxes will increase the financial price of j and must be removed to arrive at the economic cost of j. If we denote these input distortions as g_j then the economic value of the input can be expressed as $W_j^s[a_{jx}^o P_j^m(1 + k_j - g_j]$.

At the same time, owing to the drop in the price, more of the input j will be demanded by other users of the input. We therefore want to estimate the economic value of the input j to these other demanders. In measuring the value of input j to other demanders let t_j^v be the rate of VATs and t_j^e be the rate of non-creditable taxes. At the same time there will be an offsetting adjustment owing to the diversion of expenditures away from other goods to good j. It is assumed that $d*$ is the average rate of indirect taxes that would have been paid on these diverted expenditures[77]. With this adjustment, the net economic value of the input j in the demand response should be measured by $W_j^d[a_{jx}^o P_j^m(1 + t_j^v + t_j^e - d*]$, where the gap between the economic value and the market price is reflected by the term $(t_j^v + t_j^e - d*)$.

To summarize the above discussion, when the non-tradable input j with a finite supply elasticity is used to produce a non-traded good x, the adjustment to the supply side for the distortions on input j can be measured by the excess of the financial cost of the input j over and above its corresponding economic cost. That is: $(t_j^v + t_j^e - d*)$

$$-W_s^x\left\{a_{jx}^o\left[P_j^m(1 + t_j^e) - [W_j^s P_j^m(1 + k_j - g_p) + W_j^d P_j^m(1 + t_j^v + t_j^e - d*]\right]\right\}$$

(11.8)

---

[77]Empirically d* is estimated as the sum of all indirect taxes paid expressed as a proportion of private consumption during the same period.

Simplifying equation (11.8) by replacing $P_j^m(1+t_j^e)$ with $P_j^m(W_j^s+W_j^d)(1+t_j^e)$, the total distortion of taxes and subsidies for the non-tradable input j will become:

$$-W_s^x\{a_{jx}^o[W_j^s P_j^m(t_j^e+g_j-k_j)+W_j^d P_j^m(d^*-t_j^v)]\} \quad (11.9)$$

Both k_j, the subsidy on the non-tradable supply of input j, and t_j^v, the value added tax on j paid by the new consumers of j, enter negatively. They will thus increase the economic cost of the final non-tradable good x. On the other hand, t_j^e, g_j, d^* are positive, and their effect will be to reduce the economic cost of the final non-tradable good x.

Let the symbol d_j denote $t_j^e+g_j-k_j$ which is the sum of the distortions associated with the supply of non-tradable intermediate input j. Thus, equation (11.9) can be written as:

$$-W_s^x\{a_{jx}^o[W_j^s P_j^m d_j+W_j^d P_j^m(d^*-t_j^v)]\} \quad (11.10)$$

After making the adjustments for the distortions in the markets for intermediate inputs i and j, the measurement of P_x^e for equation (11.6) becomes:

$$P_x^e = W_x^s P_x^m(1+k_x)+W_x^d P_x^m(1+t_x^v-d^*)$$
$$-W_x^s\{\Sigma_i a_{ix}^o P_i^m d_i+\Sigma_i a_{jx}^o[W_j^s P_j^m d_j+W_j^d P_j^m(d^*-t_j^v)]\}$$
$$+(P_x^m \times T_x \times FEP)+(P_x^m \times NT_x \times NTP) \quad (11.11)$$

The input–output coefficients in equation (11.11) relate to the factors and factor mix used by the non-project producers of x whose markets are being affected by the project.

11.3.2 Economic Value of a Non-tradable Input Purchased by a Project

Figure 11.4 illustrates a situation in the market for an input z. This input receives a direct subsidy equal to k_z of its production cost, and when it is sold, this input is subject to a value added tax of t_z^v. When the project demands more of this input, its market-demand curve will be shifted from ND_n to CD_{n+p}. This will stimulate additional supply of $(Q_1^s - Q_0)$ and will cause the previous consumers of z to reduce their purchases by $(Q_0 - Q_1^d)$.

Figure 11.4: Economic Costs of a Project Input (When a Production Subsidy and a Sales Tax Are Present)

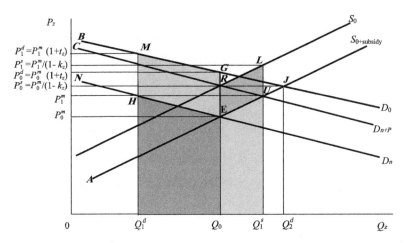

The first step in estimating the unit economic cost (P_z^e) of this non-tradable input z that is purchased by the project is to consider cost from the value of the additional resources used by producers to supply more of z and the value placed on the demand from others that has been given up because the price of z has been raised. These two costs are measured by a weighted average of its supply price (P_z^s) and its demand price (P_z^d), respectively. The weights reflect the responsiveness of existing suppliers and demanders to changes in the price of the non-tradable input. That is:

$$P_z^e = W_z^s P_z^s + W_z^d P_z^d \qquad (11.12)$$

where $W_z^s + W_z^d = 1$.

If we account for the market distortions explicitly, then $P_z^s = P_z^m(1 + k_z)$ and $P_z^d = P_z^m(1 + t_z^v)$; hence, equation (11.12) can be written as:

$$P_z^e = W_z^s P_z^m(1 + k_z) + W_z^d P_z^m(1 + t_z^v) \qquad (11.13)$$

The adjustments to account for the distortions in the prices of the additional inputs used to supply z, or in the price of z when it was previously being
276   *Economic Prices for Non-Tradable Goods and Services*

purchased elsewhere, are of the same form as in the case of an output x in equation (11.11). Similarly, the adjustments are made for the generalized distortions of the FEP, when there is an impact on the demand or supply of tradable goods, and for the NTP. That is, the term $(P_z^m \times T_z \times FEP)$ measures the additional cost associated with the additional tradable inputs that are now demanded because of the project demands for the input z. Likewise, the term $(P_z^m \times NT_z \times NTP)$ measures the additional cost arising from the increased use of non-tradable inputs as a consequence of the project's purchase of this non-tradable input. The final expression for the estimation of the economic price of input z in its generalized form is identical in form to the estimation of the economic price of an output. It is shown as follows:

$$P_z^e = W_z^s P_z^m (1 + k_z) + W_z^d P_z^m (1 + t_z^v - d*)$$
$$- W_z^s \left\{ \sum_i a_{iz}^o P_i^m d_i + \sum_j a_{jz}^o [W_j^s P_j^m d_j + W_j^d P_j^m (d* - t_j^v)] \right\}$$
$$+ (P_z^m \times T_z \times FEP) + (P_z^m \times NT_z \times NTP) \qquad (11.14)$$

It is important to note that exactly the same structure and terms are present in equation (11.14) as in equation (11.11). It does not matter whether a particular good is an input being purchased or an output being produced; its economic value is the same.

11.4 Application of Economic Prices to Estimate the Economic Net Benefits of a Project

Where market distortions take the form of taxes and subsidies that are expressed as a proportion of a price, the natural way to introduce this conversion of financial values into economic values is through the use of commodity-specific conversion factors. In such case, if the rates of distortion do not change, there is a fixed relationship between the real or nominal unit economic value of an item and its financial unit cost to the project. For example, consider a project input, such as electricity or construction services, that will be used over and over again in many projects. If the distortions in the output and input markets can all be expressed as a proportion of P^m, P^d, or P^s, then any one of these prices can be expressed in terms of one of the other prices and the relevant distortions that make them not equal. Hence, it is also the case that, as shown by equation (11.11), the economic price P^e of any good i can be expressed simply as a constant factor multiplied by the financial demand price of the same item. The constant factor will be a function of all the distortions and weights that determine the economic price of the item. This commodity-specific conversion factor CF_i

is the ratio of the economic price of i to its tax-inclusive financial price, or its demand price:

$$CF_i = P_i^e / P_i^m (1 + t_i^v)$$ (11.15)

For inputs and outputs where these conditions hold, the economic benefits and costs can be estimated period by period by simply multiplying the financial line items of financial analysis from the total investment point of view by the corresponding commodity-specific conversion factor for that line item. The result is the value of the economic benefit or the value of the cost item for that period. When all the line items of a financial cash flow analysis are converted to their economic values, it is a relatively simple procedure to subtract the costs from the benefits in order to derive the periodic economic net benefits and the economic net present value of the project.

Of course, when there are distortions such as rationing, quantitative restrictions, and consumer surplus arising from new market entrants, the economic value of the additional consumption will be divorced from the particular financial prices charged. The value of the output of a road, when no tolls are being charged, is a classic example of where the output of the road needs to be evaluated based on the fundamental items that measure the consumers' willingness to pay and the economic value of the resources saved; in this case, these values are completely divorced from what the user of the road pays for the service.

The items where conversion factors cannot be used are usually associated with the outputs of projects. Examples include the benefits of improving a road, of providing access to potable water supplies, and of increasing the reliability of the electricity service. In all these cases, the engineers and sector specialists will often have the professional training required to know how to measure the economic value of the output produced by the project.

A major hurdle to the widespread implementation of economic cost–benefit analysis is the dozens, and sometimes hundreds, of inputs for a single project; the sector specialist often has neither the inclination nor the time to estimate the economic prices of each of these commodities and services. The major advantage of expressing the relationship between the unit economic value and the unit financial value as a conversion factor is that as long as the rates of the distortions do not change, the same conversion factor can be used for the same good across many projects in the country. In addition, the conversion factor is not affected by the rate of inflation. Hence, it can be applied to the nominal financial values of a particular item over time to obtain its nominal economic values through time, or it can be applied to the real values of the same item, and the result will be the real economic value of the item over time.

Furthermore, the nature and magnitudes of the distortions that determine the size of the conversion factor for a particular good or service can be clearly written as a formula using the relationship shown in equations (11.11) and

(11.14). Hence, when it is known that the rate of tax or subsidy has changed, then the conversion factors for the items affected can be readily updated.

11.5 An Illustrative Example

Consider a project in South Africa using bricks as an input, where there are distortions in the markets of bricks, and where, in the markets, two inputs, clay and furnace oil, are used to produce brick.

Assume that the market for bricks is competitive, the market price is subject to a 14 percent general VAT of an invoice tax credit type, and brick producers receive a 15 percent subsidy (k_z) on their total production cost. In this case, the supply price is expressed as $P_z^s = P_z^m /(1 - k_z)$ because the subsidy is a fraction of the supply price. Without the project, the quantity demanded and supplied in the market is 7 million bricks per month at a market price (P_z^m) of R0.2 (rand) per brick. Now we introduce a project that requires 300,000 bricks per month. Two of the inputs used in the production of bricks have distortions in their markets: (a) clay, a non-tradable good, has a 14 percent VAT levied on its market price (P_{clay}^m) of R7 per ton,[78] while (b) furnace oil, an import good, has a subsidy (k_{oil}) of 20 percent on its CIF price of US$240 per ton. The input–output coefficient for furnace oil (a_{oil}) is 180 kilograms of oil per 1,000 bricks and that of clay (a_{clay}) is 3.5 tons of clay per 1,000 bricks. The market exchange rate is R9.85 per US dollar.

The weighted-average excise and other indirect tax rate on tradable and non-tradable goods and services in the economy ($d*$) is 9 percent.

The economic cost per brick can be estimated using equation (11.14). Data requirements for estimating the economic price (P_z^e) of a brick used by the project as an input are described below.

a) Brick

Step 1: Price Estimation

Since $P_z^m = $ R0.2, thus $P_z^s = P_z^m /(1 - k_z) = 0.2 / (0.85) = $ R0.2353

and $P_z^d = P_z^m \times (1 + t_z) = 0.2 \times (1.14) = $ R0.2280

---

[78]It is assumed that the change in the market price of clay on account of the project's demand is relatively small, thus justifying the use of without-the-project prices, rather than an average of the prices with and without the project.

Step 2: Estimation of the Supply and Demand Weights (W_z^s) *and* (W_z^d)

For such a production activity, the expected supply response will be small in the short run as most brick-making kilns are usually operating close to capacity. The supply response will be greater in the longer run, and it is expected that a larger proportion of the bricks required by the project will be obtained from additional supplies by existing producers rather than at the expense of existing demanders, who will divert to other sources. Hence, assigning a weight of 0.33 to the demand side (W_z^d) and a weight of 0.67 to the supply side (W_z^s) seems plausible.

Step 3: Tradable, Non-tradable Good Component in Brick Production

In examining the cost components used in the production of bricks, it is assumed that the tradable and non-tradable good components account for 60 percent and 40 percent, respectively, of the market price of bricks. The FEP is equal to 6 percent, and the premium on the purchase or sale of non-tradable goods and services is 1 percent.

Step 4: Product Distortions

The supply price of the newly stimulated supply of brick, as calculated above, is equal to:

$$P_z^s = P_z^m /(1 - k_z) = 0.2 / (0.85) = R0.2353$$

On the demand side, the tax on good t_z that other demanders will not be paying because they are now buying other goods is partially offset by the taxes they will now pay, $d*$. Hence, the opportunity cost of the forgone consumption of others is equal to:

$$P_z^m[1 + (t_z^v - d^*)] = 0.2(1 + 0.14 - 0.09) = R0.21$$

b)   Furnace Oil

Since furnace oil enjoys a subsidy, its financial market price is different from its economic price, and so an adjustment for this input will have to be made when estimating the economic cost of bricks.

Step 1: Estimating the Market Price

$$P_{oil}^m = \text{CIF price} \times E^m \times (1 - s_{oil})$$
$$= 240 \times 9.85 \times (1 - 0.2)$$
$$= R1,891 \text{ per ton}$$

Step 2: The Economic Cost of Furnace Oil (P_{oil}^e)

$$P_{oil}^e = \text{CIF price} \times E^m$$
$$= 240 \times 9.85$$
$$= \text{R2,364 per ton}$$

The value of the subsidy per ton of furnace oil is estimated below.

The value of the subsidy $= P_{oil}^m - P_{oil}^e$
$$= - \text{CIF price} \times E^m \times s_{oil}$$
$$= -240\,(9.85)\,(0.2)$$
$$= -\text{R472.8 per ton}$$

Thus, the value of the distortion per brick is −R0.0851
$$(= - a_{oilk} \times \text{R472.8}/1{,}000 = - 0.18 \times \text{R0.4728})$$

c) *Clay*

As clay is subject to 14 percent VAT that is creditable when it is purchased against the VAT owed on the output. However, its demand price will be different from its market price, and an adjustment for this input is necessary when estimating the economic cost of bricks.

Step 1: Estimating the Demand and Supply Prices for Clay

Since $P_{clay}^m = \text{R7 per ton}$, thus $P_{clay}^d = P_{clay}^m \times (1 + t_{clay}^v) = 7 \times (1 + 0.14)$
$$= \text{R7.98 per ton}$$
and $P_{clay}^s = P_{clay}^m \times (1 + k_{clay}) = 7 \times (1 - 0) = \text{R7 per ton}$

Step 2: Estimation of the Supply and Demand Weights (W_{clay}^s *and* W_{clay}^d *)*

If clay is not in short supply, it can reasonably be asserted that the demand for clay derived from the project's demand for bricks will be mostly met from additional supply. Accordingly, a demand weight (W_{clay}^d) of 0.33 and a supply weight (W_{clay}^s) of 0.67 are assigned.

Step 3: The Economic Cost of Clay (P_{clay}^e *)*

Using clay as an input will lead to additional supply as well as displaced demand for some existing demand. Thus, the value of the distortion created after taking into account all the repercussions of the demand for clay in the economy can be estimated as:

$$P_{clay}^m\{a_{clayk}[W_{clay}^s(g_{clay}-k_{clay})]+W_{clay}^d(d^*-t_{clay}^v)\}$$

$= 7\{0.0035\times[0.67\times(0-0)+0.33\times(0.09-0.14)]\}$
$= 7*(0.0035)(.33)(-0.05)$
$= -0.0004$ R/brick

Taking into account the distortions in the product and input markets, the economic price per brick by substituting in equation (11.14) yields:

$$P_z^e = W_z^s P_z^m/(1-k_z)+W_z^d P_z^m(1+t_z^v-d^*)$$
$$-W_z^s\{\textstyle\sum_i a_{iz}^o P_i^m d_i + \sum_j a_{jz}^o[W_j^s P_j^m d_j + W_j^d P_j^m(d^*-t_j^v)]\}$$
$$+(P_z^m\times T_z\times FEP)+(P_z^m\times NT_z\times NTP)$$

$= 0.67\times(0.2353)+0.33\times(0.2100)-0.67\times(-0.0851-0.0004)$

$+ 0.2\times0.6\times0.06+0.2\times0.4\times0.01$

$= 0.1577+0.0693+0.0573+0.0080$

$= 0.2923$ R/brick

To estimate the commodity-specific conversion factor for bricks used by the project, we divide the economic price by the financial demand price. Recall that the demand price is inclusive of sales tax. That is:

$CF = 0.2923/0.228 = 1.28$

The same methodology can be used to estimate the conversion factors for a series of non-tradable goods and services involved in projects. Project supply or project demand for tradable goods often requires non-tradable services, such as truck transportation services and handling charges, in order to move the goods between the port and the project site. The financial costs of these services must be converted using the respective conversion factors to the economic costs in the economic appraisal.

As mentioned in Chapter 10, for example, the irrigation project in the Visayas of the Philippines is required to import pesticides to improve the farm's productivity. The project will also incur handling charges, dealers' margins, and transportation costs in moving pesticides from the port to the farm. Thus, in addition to 4,239 pesos paid for the duty-paid value of the item, the project will also pay a total of 1,140 pesos for handling and port charges, 475 pesos for transportation costs from the port to the farm gate, and 200 pesos for dealers' services. Each of these non-tradable service costs presented in the financial cash flow statement must be converted to the economic costs in the economic resource flow statement using their corresponding conversion factors, calculated as outlined in this chapter.

11.6 Conclusion

This chapter describes the analytical framework for estimating the economic prices of non-tradable goods and services. Unlike the case of tradable goods, there will be no direct world price, although an equivalency to the world market can be derived. The analysis begins with the case in which a project produces non-tradable outputs, where its market supply function is perfectly elastic, and then moves to the standard case with upward-rising supply and downward-sloping demand curves. The analysis takes into account all repercussions of the project in the economy by capturing all distortions in the direct product and indirect input markets.

Appendix 11A: Choosing the Relevant Distortion

This appendix provides readers with the basic toolbox for analysing very basic supply and demand relationships. We start with a commodity that is subject to both an excise tax and a value-added tax (VAT). We assume that the posted market price is inclusive of VAT (as is the practice in most VAT countries) and that the excise tax is added to the market price as an extra item on the buyer's bill. In short, in this presentation we assume that the VAT is institutionally paid by the supplier, while the excise tax is paid by the demander. The ultimate incidence of these taxes is a separate issue.

This yields the supply and demand scenario shown in Figure 11A.1. Here, the VAT is 25 percent (on a base price of 0.80), while the excise tax is 40 percent on a base price of 1.00. When a new demand is introduced, say by the project, 70 percent of that demand is met by displacing other demand and 30 percent by generating new increments of supply. In this case, the economic opportunity cost of meeting new demand for this good will be $(0.7 \times 1.40) + (0.3 \times 0.80) = 1.22$.

Figure 11A.1

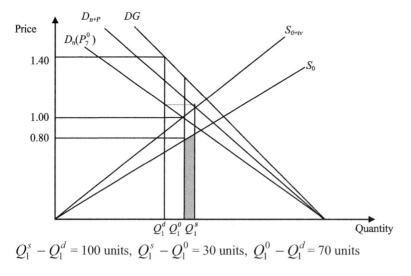

$Q_1^s - Q_1^d = 100$ units, $Q_1^s - Q_1^0 = 30$ units, $Q_1^0 - Q_1^d = 70$ units

One way to visualize this opportunity cost is to consider that we do not know whether or not the project will be required to pay tax on its purchases. Perhaps, as a government project, it will be exempt from the excise tax, or even from both taxes. As a private project producing for export, it might be exempt from both taxes. The point is that as we try to establish the economic opportunity cost of the product Q_1, we do not know what taxes the buyer will be required to pay. However, we do know that suppliers will incur a resource cost of 0.80 on the incremental supply and that demanders will be forgoing units of Q_1 that value at (or a bit above) 1.40 on 70 percent of the amounts that the project takes. Thus it is unambiguously established that the economic opportunity cost of Q_1 is a weighted average of supply and demand prices.

Let us now consider another problem relating to the same market, but with the project in a different area. Its output is a non-tradable good or service Q_7, and, as a consequence of the project, the total demand for Q_7 increases. A likely scenario is that the price of good Q_7 falls from P_7^0 to P_7^1. Because good Q_7 is a substitute for Q_1, when the quantity demanded of Q_7 increases, the demand declines for Q_1.

Figure 11A.2 illustrates this case for an induced shift in demand (away from Q_1 and toward Q_7) of 100 units. Note in Figure 11A.2 that we can still say (if we want to) that the economic opportunity cost of those 100 units of shifted demand is $(0.3 \times 0.80) + (0.7 \times 1.40) = 1.22$, as before.

Figure 11A.2

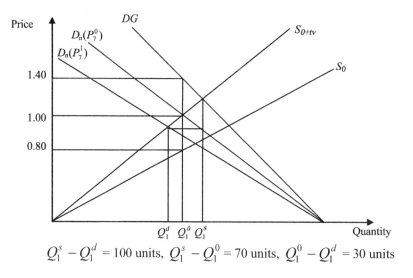

$Q_1^s - Q_1^d = 100$ units, $Q_1^s - Q_1^0 = 70$ units, $Q_1^0 - Q_1^d = 30$ units

However, this is not an effective way to summarize what is going on. What actually happens is simply a reduction of the equilibrium quantity of Q_1 by 30 units. In the exercise depicted in Figure 11A.2, certain demanders (call them the shifters) shift 100 units of demand away from Q_1. In order to buy more of Q_7, they induce a group of other demanders of Q_1 (call them the stayers) to augment their demand by 70 units. But that change of +70 units by the stayers is more than cancelled out by the −100-unit change produced by the shifters. The end result is a net reduction in demand for Q_1 of 30 units, which necessarily also equals the reduction in supply.

Figure 11A.3 shows a clearer picture of what happens in the market for Q_1 as a consequence of a project-induced increase in demand in the market for Q_7 (the project good). This scenario allows for the induced increase in demand of 70 (by the stayers) to be fully cancelled out by the project-generated reduction in demand for Q_1 of 100 (by the shifters). The net result is a reduction of -30 in the equilibrium quantity of Q_1, to which a distortion of 0.60 ($= 1.40 - 0.80$) applies. In this case, the distortion effects are not split between a supply change in one direction and a demand change in the other, but are combined into a simple grand distortion ($=$ demand price minus supply price), which applies to the net change in the equilibrium quantity of the good in question (here Q_1).

Figure 11A.3

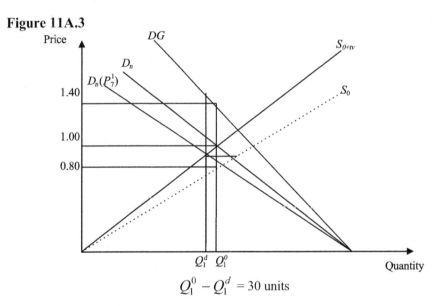

$$Q_1^0 - Q_1^d = 30 \text{ units}$$

Note that this example is relevant for all kinds of external effects that take place outside the purview of the project under analysis. In dealing with the current project's demand, we want to separately consider the distortions applying to increased supply and decreased demand (or vice versa). However, in cases where we are examining induced effects in other markets, those effects are necessarily shifts (up or down) in the equilibrium quantity of good Q_j, in whatever market that might be.

The important corollary of this simple lesson is that when there is an increase in demand of, say, 400 for the project good Q_{j7}, 100 is the result of the shifters substituting away from good 1 and toward Q_7 as a consequence of the project. We do not want to assign an externality of $(1.22 - 1.00) \times (-100)$ of shifted demand for Q_1. This would equal -22. Nor do we want to assign an externality of $(1.22 - 0.80) \times (-100)$, which would equal -42. The correct externality assignment is of $(1.40 - 0.80) \times (-30) = -18$.

Economic Prices for Non-Tradable Goods and Services

Unfortunately, this simple lesson is not widely understood, even among experienced project economists. It follows directly from the standard expression for measuring external effects $\sum_i D_i \Delta Q_i$, where D_i is the distortion affecting activity i and ΔQ_i is the amount by which the equilibrium quantity of Q_i changes as a consequence of the event being analysed (in this case, our project in the market for Q_7).

Thus, when we consider increases in demand for project output, even if all the increase in demand were to come from Q_1, that does not mean that a Q_1 distortion should be assigned to that full increase of 400 in demand for Q_7. In this case, the full Q_1 distortion of 0.60 per unit would be assigned to a shift in equilibrium quantity of Q_1, equal to -120 [$= 0.3 \times (-400)$]. That is, the externality $D_i \Delta Q_i$ would equal $(0.60) \times (-120) = -72$.

In dealing with the Q_7 market, the project output would be 1,000, of which 600 would be reflected in reduced supply by others and would be assigned a distortion equal to $d*$ (as those resources find their new equilibrium locations elsewhere). Then we would have 400 of increased output of Q_7, to which the tax T_7 would apply (i.e., our project's output would be valued at its demand price). Finally, on the externality applying in the market for Q_1, there would be a Q_1 externality equal to $D_i \Delta Q_i = -72$ ($= -120 \times 0.60$), plus an additional externality of $+120 \times d*$, as the resources released from Q_1 would be absorbed elsewhere in the economy.

Appendix 11B: Relationship between Tradable and Non-tradable Goods

The distinction between tradable and non-tradable goods is quite naturally right at the core of the field of international economics, and it carries over well to the field of cost–benefit analysis. However, in this area a special case arises with regard to items that have no market prices, but must nevertheless be assigned a value for project evaluation purposes. Examples are the value of time saved as a result of a highway improvement, or the amenity values created by a public park, or other cases in which consumer surplus benefits are assigned on top of actual market prices paid. Such items, as they are not actual outlays (or receipts), are not subject to shadow pricing. However, all actual cash outlays and receipts should in principle be classifiable as referring to one of the two broad categories, tradables and non-tradables.

In order to see how this distinction arises, and how it works, it is useful to describe the development of our professional thinking about project evaluation. The first step in this process involved focusing on the actual imports that were made by a project and the actual exports of its products. The cost of the imports was reduced to the cost of acquiring the foreign exchange needed to buy them, and the value generated by the project's exports was the value of the foreign exchange that they produced. Even at this early stage, there was a clear need to calculate an economic opportunity cost of foreign exchange (EOCFX) in order to accurately reflect the true economic costs (in local currency) of the project's imports and the corresponding true economic benefits of its exports.

However, this was only the first step. It soon became clear that there was also domestic production of many of a country's imported goods and, similarly, domestic use of many of its export products. In these cases, it really did not matter whether the copper bought by a project was domestically produced or imported; copper bought from a domestic source in the United States would simply lead to somebody else importing an equivalent amount, and wheat demanded by a Canadian project would leave that much less wheat to be exported. Using T_i^d and T_i^s to represent the country's own demand and supply of importable good i, we find that imports of i (M_i) are equal to $T_i^d - T_i^s$. Similarly, using T_j^d and T_j^s to represent the country's own demand and supply for exportable good j, we see that exports of that good (X_j) are equal to $T_j^s - T_j^d$.

Now the country's total imports (M) can be represented as:

$$M = \sum_i M_i = \sum_i T_i^d - \sum_i T_i^s$$

Similarly, its total exports (X) can be represented as:

$$X = \sum_j X_j = \sum_j T_j^s - \sum_j T_j^d$$

The country's balance of trade is accordingly:

$$X - M = \sum_j T_j^s - \sum_j T_j^d - (\sum_i T_i^d - \sum_i T_i^s)$$

$$= (\sum_j T_j^s + \sum_i T_i^s) - (\sum_j T_j^d + \sum_i T_i^d) = T^s - T^d$$

Here T^s represents the sum of a country's total supplies of all tradables $(\sum_j T_j^s + \sum_i T_i^s)$ and T^d the sum of its total demands for all tradables $(\sum_j T_j^d + \sum_i T_i^d)$.

From here, it follows that when there is equilibrium in a country's trade balance, there is also equilibrium between that country's total demand and supply for tradables. Similarly, a given deficit $(M - X)$ in a country's trade will reflect an excess demand of equal size $(T^d - T^s)$ for that country's total tradables.

These ideas and procedures can then be developed further. It is certainly not enough just to look at the project's own actual imports and actual exports (step one). Nor is it enough to extend this by simply considering the project's direct demand for and supply of tradable goods (step two). What is needed is a further extension to include the project's overall impact on the country's demand and supply of tradable goods (step three).

Although in principle a project may have more reverberations than can be conveniently captured, the basic procedure suggested concentrates on the flows of "receipts" (sales of project output) and expenditures (project outlays for investment activities plus operating costs) over the course of a project's economic life.

The division of project outlays is represented in Table 11B.1. When the project purchases tradables directly, the purchases are classified under item 1. This is the case regardless of whether the goods bought were actually imported, or domestically produced items falling into the "importable" category, or domestically consumed but falling in the "exportable" category. It is deemed that all three of these categories put pressure on the foreign exchange market, through (a) direct demand, (b) indirect demand, in which others do the importing, or (c) reduced export supply.

When the project purchases non-tradables, the situation is slightly more complicated because there are various ways in which this type of purchase can eventually be reflected in incremental demand for tradables. We first look at that part of the project's non-tradables purchased (d) that ends up as increased output of the goods or services in question. This increased output will be reflected in either increased value added (d_1), or increased tradable inputs (d_2), or increased non-tradable inputs (d_3).

However, this case tells the whole story only when the project's entire demand for non-tradables is met through increases in their supply. In the typical case, some fraction f_k^d of the project's demand will be met by squeezing out other demanders for the non-tradable goods and services in question. In looking for the consequences of this process, we must ask about the activities that are stimulated as some of the previous demanders of H_k reassign that demand to other activities. In particular, it must be recognized that some of the relevant substitutes for H_k will themselves be tradable items, while others will, though non-tradable themselves, have tradable inputs. This is why, in Table 11B.1, there are two items (e_1 and e_2) representing increases in tradables demand arising from what happens when the project satisfies some of its extra demand for non-tradables by displacing other demands for them.

Table 11B.1: Classification of Project Outlays

	Final Classification	
	Tradable (T)	Non-tradable (H)
1. Project purchases of tradables		
a. Actual imports by project (M_i)	X	
b. Importable goods produced in the country (T_i^s)	X	
c. Exportable goods consumed in the country (T_j^s)	X	
2. Project purchases of non-tradables (H_k^p)		
d. Project demand met through increased domestic supply $(f_k^s H_k^p) = \Delta H_k^s$		
d_1 value added in activity $k = (v_k \Delta H_k^s)$		X
d_2 tradable inputs into activity $k = a_{tk}(\Delta H_k^s)$	X	
d_3 non-tradable inputs into activity $k = a_{hk}(\Delta H_k^s)$		X
e. Project demand for (H_k^p) met through displacing other demanders $(f_k^d H_k^p) = (-\Delta H_k^d)$		
e_1 demand displaced into tradable substitutes $b_{tk}(-\Delta H_k^d)$	X	
e_2 demand displaced into non-tradable substitutes $b_{hk}(-\Delta H_k^d)$		
value added $e_{2v} = v_{hk}b_{hk}(-\Delta H_k^d)$		X
tradable inputs $e_{2t} = c_{tk}b_{hk}(-\Delta H_k^d)$	X	
non-tradable inputs $e_{2h} = c_{hk}b_{hk}(-\Delta H_k^d)$		X

Table 11B.2 presents a numerical example that may help to demonstrate that the framework presented here is relatively simple and straightforward. Here the direct outlays of the project are assumed to be divided 40–60: 40 on direct purchase of tradables and 60 on direct purchase of non-tradables. All of the amount spent on tradables stays there, on the basis that there is presumably no incremental domestic production of tradables arising out of our project's demand.

Table 11B.2: Classification of Project Outlays (Numerical Example)

	Final Classification	
	Tradable (T)	Non-tradable (H)
1. Project Buys Tradable Goods (40)		
a. Actual imports of vehicles	20	
b. Petroleum (an importable) from local sources	15	
c. Cotton (an exportable) from local sources	5	
Sub-total for tradable outlays	40	0
2. Project Buys Buildings (non-tradables) (60)		
d. Project demand met through net increase in construction (28)		
d_1 value added in this increase in construction		14
d_2 tradable inputs used in same (materials)	6	
d_3 non-tradable inputs used in same (purchased services)		8
e. Project demand met through displacing other construction (32)		
e_1 demand displaced into tradable substitutes (machinery and equipment)	7	
e_2 demand displaced into non-tradable substitutes (maintenance and repair)		
e_{2t} (materials)	9	
e_{2h} (purchased services)		6
e_{2v} (value added in maintenance & repair)		10
Sub-total for non-tradable outlays	22	38
Totals for project	62	38

The situation is different when it comes to the project's demand for non-tradables. In this case there is every reason to believe that some increased production will be stimulated, but that this will involve greater value added plus greater use of both tradable and non-tradable inputs. Thus, in the example of Table 11B.2, we have 60 spent on construction of buildings by the project, of which 28 represents a net increase in construction and 32 represents a displacement of the demand of others. Of the 28 of net increase, 6 is assumed to reflect increased demand for tradable inputs (d_2), while 22 reflects either increased value added in construction (14) or increased use of non-tradable inputs (8).

We now turn to the items representing project demand met through displacing other construction. The issue here is not what resources were used to satisfy the demand before it was displaced. These resources are assumed now to be satisfying the project's demand. The key question is what resources will be used in other places to satisfy the demand of others, which the project has managed to displace.

In item (e) it is assumed that part of this displaced demand (7) moves directly to the purchase of tradable substitutes. The remaining 25 is assumed to be shifted to non-tradable substitutes. However, here it contains three components: tradable inputs (materials) taking 9, non-tradable inputs (purchased services) taking 6, and value added taking 10. Hence, the correct division of the project outlays of 100 is 62 to tradables and 38 to non-tradables, almost the reverse of the initial 40–60 division of the direct expenditures.

With regard to the 60 of non-tradables purchased, the tradable content as a proportion of the total purchased is $T = 22/60 = 0.36$, while for the non-tradable content the proportion is $NT = 38/60 = 0.64$.

References

Curry, S. and J. Weiss. 1993. *Project Analysis in Developing Countries*. New York: St. Martin's Press.

Dinwiddy, C. and F. Teal. 1987. "Shadow Prices for Non-traded Goods in a Tax-distorted Economy: Formulae and Values", *Journal of Public Economics* 33(2), 207–221.

— 1996. *Principles of Cost-Benefit Analysis for Developing Countries*, Chapter 6. Cambridge: Cambridge University Press.

Harberger, A.C. 1971. "Three Basic Postulates for Applied Welfare Economics", *Journal of Economic Literature* 9(3), 758–797.

— 1972. "Marginal Cost Pricing and Social Investment Criteria for Electricity Undertakings", *Project Evaluation: Collected Papers.* Chicago: The University of Chicago Press.

Harberger, A.C. and G.P. Jenkins. 2002. "Introduction", in A.C. Harberger and G.P. Jenkins (eds.), *Cost-Benefit Analysis.* Cheltenham: Edward Elgar Publishing.

Jenkins, G.P. and M.B. El-Hifnawi. 1993. *Economic Parameters for the Appraisal of Investment Projects: Bangladesh, Indonesia and the Philippines*, report prepared for Economics and Development Resource Center. Manila: Asian Development Bank (December).

Mishan, E.J. and E. Quah. 2007. *Cost-Benefit Analysis*, 5th edition. London and New York: Routledge.

Overseas Development Administration (ODA). 1988. *Appraisal of Projects in Developing Countries: A Guide for Economists*, 3rd edition. London: Stationery Office Books.

Powers, T.A. 1981. *Estimating Accounting Prices for Project Appraisal.* Washington, DC: Inter-American Development Bank.

Scott, M.FG., J.D. MacArthur, and D.M.G. Newbery. 1976. *Project Appraisal in Practice.* London: Heinemann Educational.

Warr, P.G. 1982. "Shadow Pricing Rules for Non-traded Commodities", *Oxford Economic Papers* 34(2), 305–325.

Chapter Twelve

Economic Opportunity Cost of Labour

12.1 Introduction

The concept of economic opportunity cost is derived from the recognition that when resources are used for one project, opportunities to use these resources are sacrificed elsewhere. Typically, when workers are hired by a project, they are giving up one set of market and non-market activities for an alternative set. The economic opportunity cost of labour (EOCL) is the value to the economy of the set of activities given up by the workers, including the non-market costs (or benefits) associated with the change in employment (Harberger, 1980).

When determining the EOCL, it is important to remember that labour is not a homogeneous input. It is perhaps the most diverse factor of production in any economy. In this chapter, we will examine how the EOCL is estimated in an economy that contains markets for many different types of occupation, with variations by region and by quality of employment opportunities (e.g., pleasant, unpleasant, permanent, temporary, etc.) that affect the EOCL for a project. The focus is primarily on the conditions and distortions in the labour market; the discussion at this point will not concern the potential impacts that employment of domestic labour might have on the market for savings or foreign exchange.[79]

---

[79] In the evaluation of the EOCL, we do not take into account the potential impact on national savings of changes in the amount of income received by labour. This decision is based on three observations. First, most of the labour hired by a particular project would have been employed elsewhere in the absence of the project. Second, the overall level of national savings is fundamentally determined by macroeconomic and public sector budgetary conditions. Third, the level of uncertainty surrounding the quantitative estimates of the size of the distortion attributed to savings, and the impact on national savings of labour receiving more or less income from a project, warrants considerable caution. If, however, a particular project is deemed to have a measurable impact on savings, and there is an externality associated with this impact, then the value of this externality should be included in the evaluation of the economic net present value (NPV) of that project. In a similar manner, we do not take into consideration the indirect effects on distorted markets, such as foreign exchange, that are due to the movements of labour from other activities to the project. If the quantitative impact of the indirect effects that occur through the foreign exchange market or any other distorted market is known, the value of this externality should be included in the evaluation of the economic benefits and costs of the project.

A labour externality (LE_i) is created for any project when the economic opportunity cost of labour $(EOCL_i)$ differs from the wage rate (Wp_i) paid to the labour by the project. This externality can be expressed for a specific type of labour (i) as:

$$LE_i = Wp_i - EOCL_i \qquad\qquad (12.1)$$

When LE_i is positive, the financial cost of labour will be greater than its economic cost and vice versa. As this analysis will show, the magnitude of this externality is a function of more variables than simply the rate of unemployment in the relevant labour market for this class of workers. It will also depend on other distortions in the labour market, such as taxes, unemployment insurance, and protected labour market segments. Furthermore, it will be affected by the quality of the job created. The magnitude of this externality is one factor that causes the economic performance of a project to diverge from its expected financial outcome.

12.2 Alternative Approaches to Estimating the Economic Opportunity Cost of Labour

In estimating the EOCL, two alternative starting points for analysis may be chosen: a) the value of the marginal product of labour forgone; and b) the supply price of labour. It should be noted that calculating the EOCL using either method will theoretically produce the same result. However, these two approaches have different data requirements, levels of computational complexity, and, hence, different degrees of operational usefulness.

12.2.1 Value of Marginal Product of Labour Forgone

The value of marginal product of labour forgone for labour hired by a project is determined by starting with the gross-of-tax alternative wage (W_a) that the labour hired for that project would have earned in its absence. In most cases there will, at any future point in time, be an estimated distribution of the labour activities in the presence of the project and an alternative distribution in its absence. The differences between these two allocations will usually sum to zero, especially if leisure and involuntary unemployment are counted among the relevant activities. This means that the net reductions in labour allocated to other activities must add up to the amount of employment provided by the project. If one works strictly with forgone marginal product, the EOCL for the project would simply be the weighted sum of the forgone marginal products of labour of all different types sourced from the various activities.

This method is not well adapted for reflecting differences in the underlying working and living conditions that do not directly reduce output elsewhere in the economy (Little and Mirrlees, 1974). Historically, some economists have argued that the value of the marginal product of unskilled agricultural workers in developing countries was zero because it was believed that there was a large surplus of labour in the countryside. However, empirical studies of subsistence farmers have demonstrated that their labour does have a positive marginal value, both in farming and in a variety of other productive activities. Using the assumption that the value of the marginal product forgone is zero when hiring unemployed workers, this approach leads to an underestimation of the EOCL, and the estimate does not reflect the true economic costs of the project using the labour.[80]

12.2.2 Supply Price of Labour

An alternative method that is based on the supply price of labour is more straightforward and easier to use under a wide variety of conditions (Harberger, 1971). The starting point is the market wage (the supply price) required to attract sufficient people of the required skill level to work on the project. The supply price of labour to a project is the minimum wage rate that the project needs to pay in order to obtain sufficient supplies of labour with the appropriate skills. That wage will account for the workers' preferences regarding the location, working conditions, or any other factors that affect the desirability of working for the project. For example, if a very high local market wage is required to attract skilled labour to a project where the living conditions are bad, that wage already includes both the value of the forgone wage and the compensation for the economic costs inflicted by the relatively bad living conditions. Of course, the supply price should be adjusted further to account for other distortions, such as taxes, to arrive at the EOCL. But unlike the marginal product forgone approach, where one must measure both of these components separately, the local supply price directly captures in a combined package the wage and non-wage costs of employing labour on the project.

In practical terms, the supply price of labour can be determined by establishing the minimum wage the project must pay in order to attract an adequate number of applicants to work on the project with an acceptable turnover rate. This can often be done by informally surveying workers near the location of the project or using a more formal assessment of the prevailing wage in that activity. To test whether the wage rate being paid by a project is the minimum supply price, one should compare the number of applications by qualified people with the number of positions available. If the number of acceptable applications per job available is very high, and the turnover rate for the project is abnormally low, it is likely that the wage rate paid by the project is

---

[80]For a summary of this debate, see Marglin (1979, pp. 10–23).

above the minimum supply price. However, if the ratio of qualified applicants to positions available is low, this indicates a fairly tight labour market, and the turnover rate is high for the type of skill required. In this case it can be assumed that the project wage is close to the minimum supply price of labour.

Once the minimum supply price of labour has been determined, the EOCL is calculated by adjusting that value to account for relevant distortions (such as income taxes or subsidies). Care must be taken at this point to ensure that all of the market distortions that drive a wedge between the supply price and the EOCL are properly accounted for when estimating the EOCL for the project. The evaluation of a number of these distortions is covered in the following sections of this chapter.

To compare these two methods of calculating the EOCL, let us consider the example of unskilled farm workers who have decided to move from their jobs cutting sugar cane (c) to work on a new project in a more pleasant place (o), harvesting oranges.

The starting point for calculating the EOCL using the marginal product forgone approach would be the alternative wage on the sugar cane plantation farms (W_c), while the supply price approach would begin with the market wage for working in the orange groves (W_o). It is assumed that these workers do not pay income taxes or face any other significant distortions in their labour market. Other factors, however, could influence their decision to relocate to the new project. For example, the more pleasant climate of the orange-growing region might translate into a reduced cost of living (C), which would allow the workers to maintain the same level of well-being with lower wages. Another factor might be a preference (S) on the part of workers to work in a more pleasant region.

For the purpose of this example, it is assumed that values of the wage and the other factors are as follows:

W_o = $15.00 per day, W_c = $20.00 per day,
C_o = $3.00 per day, C_c = $6.00 per day,
S_o = $2.00 per day (value of the preference for the warmer region)

Using the marginal product approach, the EOCL can be calculated for the new project as follows:

$EOCL$ = prior wage − change in cost of living − worker preferences
= $W_c - (C_c - C_o) - S_o$
= $20 − ($6 − $3) − $2
= $15.00 per day

Using the supply price approach, it is possible to arrive at the same value directly because it is known that the market wage necessary to induce the workers to move to the new project in the orange-growing region (W_o) already accounts for the cost of living difference $(C_c - C_o)$ and the workers' regional preference for the better climate (S_o). Therefore, the EOCL is simply equal to the market wage in the region where the new job is located:

$$EOCL = W_o = \$15.00 \text{ per day}$$

This highly simplified example demonstrates that both methods for calculating the EOCL should produce the same result. However, in most circumstances it is difficult to place values upon complex factors such as cost of living differentials and workers' regional preferences. Uncertainties in the value of those factors make the marginal product forgone approach cumbersome to use when information is scarce. Consequently, the straightforward supply price approach is usually an easier way to determine the EOCL.

12.3 Structure of Analysis in the Labour Market

The analysis of the EOCL presented here is structured around five sets of factors, which are primary determinants of the cost of labour to a project. Labour prices can vary greatly from one project to the next, so the following classifications are used to help to identify which of the determinants may have an effect on the labour costs of the project being evaluated:

- Type of labour (skilled vs. unskilled)
- Regional variations and domestic migration
- Type of job (permanent vs. temporary)
- International migration
- Type of labour market (protected vs. unprotected)

First, an analytical distinction is made between different skills and occupations. Classifying workers into relevant occupational categories is essential because of the enormous heterogeneity of the labour factor. In general, the lower the skill, the greater the likely homogeneity of labour within the skill or occupational category. Estimating the economic opportunity cost of unskilled labour is also made more straightforward by the frequent absence of distortions such as taxation and unemployment insurance in that part of the labour market. The skilled labour market, on the other hand, displays much greater heterogeneity and is frequently subject to multiple distortions, which must be identified and accounted for in the estimation of the EOCL.

Second, regional migration induced by differences in wages, cost of living, and access to consumer goods and amenities also affects the EOCL for a project. Regional wage differentials are a key consideration in the labour market, where a rise in project employment in an urban setting has as its counterpart reductions in employment in rural areas that are traditional sources of migration. In such cases, distortions in the economy related to that migration must be accounted for when estimating the EOCL.

Third, it may also be necessary to take international migration into account. This includes the case in which the creation of jobs will retain workers who would otherwise have gone abroad or, alternatively, the case in which foreign skilled workers are brought into the country to perform certain services.

Fourth, the estimation of the EOCL for a project must consider whether permanent or temporary employment will be created. Temporary positions in sectors such as tourism and construction lead to greater turnover in the labour market and create conditions for voluntary unemployment. This churning effect in the labour market results in additional costs to the economy, which the EOCL should take into account.

Fifth, the rigidities imposed on the labour market through minimum wage laws, restrictive labour practices, and high-wage policies of state and multinational enterprises in some countries tend to create "protected sectors" in the labour market. In such situations, quasi-voluntary unemployment and seasonal unemployment are common. Under these circumstances the evaluations of the EOCL used by a project should reflect these special labour market conditions.

These five classifications within a labour market provide a framework for analysing the complex concept of EOCL. In this chapter, the EOCL will be analysed for the simplest case, i.e., unskilled rural labour. Additional elements will then be brought into the analysis as they are needed in order to estimate the EOCL for progressively more complex cases encountered in the appraisal of actual projects.

12.4 Economic Opportunity Cost of Unskilled Rural Labour

Some well-known growth models of underdeveloped countries have often taken the most extreme interpretation of the marginal product forgone hypothesis by placing a value of zero on the EOCL of unskilled labour in rural areas (Todaro, 1989). As previously explained, those theories rely upon the assertion that because of the large number of unskilled rural workers, there is no economic opportunity cost to filling additional jobs (Marglin, 1979, pp. 10–23). However, there is a lack of empirical evidence for the existence of a surplus of idle rural labour. In fact, research into rural economies provides a persuasive body of evidence indicating that when unskilled workers are not employed in the formal agricultural sector, they spend a large proportion of their time on other productive household and family-farming activities. In this circumstance, the prevailing daily or weekly wage rate (the supply price of unskilled labour) is a reflection of the marginal productivity of this type of activity. Hence, the market wage can be used as an effective measure of the value of the forgone marginal product of unskilled labour (Harberger, 1971).

A series of steps serves as a guide to the estimation process when the supply price of labour approach is used to calculate the EOCL. The first step is to determine the minimum gross-of-tax wage (W) needed to attract sufficient unskilled labour to the positions available on the project. The second is to identify distortions in the labour market, such as income taxes or unemployment insurance benefits. The final step is to determine the EOCL by adjusting the market wage to compensate for such distortions.

To demonstrate this process, two cases will be considered. In the first case there are no seasonal variations in either the market wage rate or the demand for unskilled workers. The second example demonstrates the way in which EOCL can be estimated when there are seasonal variations in the market wage rate and in the project's demand for unskilled labour over the year.

In the first case it is assumed that there are no distortions in the unskilled labour market, i.e., there are no taxes paid by the employer (demand side) and no income taxes paid by the worker (supply side). It is also assumed that there are no fluctuations in wages or labour demand over time. It follows that the supply price of labour (W^s) is always equal to the prevailing market wage (W). Since there are no distortions, there is no need to make further adjustments to the market wage to estimate the EOCL. Consequently, the market wage rate for unskilled labour is the supply price of labour, which in turn is the EOCL, as shown in equation (12.2).

$$EOCL = W = W^s \qquad\qquad (12.2)$$

Note that the EOCL is estimated using the market supply price (W^s) rather than the project wage (W_p). The project wage is the demand price and measures the financial cost of labour for a particular project, while the market wage measures the opportunity cost to the economy of the unskilled labour. If the demand price is higher than the market wage, the difference is an economic externality that arises from the employment of this type of labour.

In the second case, the estimation of the EOCL of unskilled labour is carried out for a project that demands workers throughout the year, while the market wage varies as a result of demand and supply factors affecting the local labour market. Using the supply price approach, we begin again with the market wage of unskilled labour for this type of project. There are no tax distortions. Owing to the seasonal fluctuations in the market wage, the EOCL at any point in time will be calculated by the market wage rate (W_t) that corresponds to the period of time in which labour is hired by the project.

For example, if a region growing rice and sugar cane has a wage rate of $5 per day during the off-season, it is possible that the wage could be many times higher during the harvesting seasons if these coincide. If a project is built based on the assumption that labour will be steadily available at $5 per day, but instead it must compete for labour at a much higher rate during the harvest season, the financial and economic viability of the project may be threatened.

These higher seasonal labour costs must be accounted for in arriving at an accurate estimate of the EOCL for a project. Furthermore, seasonal variations in the size of the employed workforce should also be reflected in the calculation of the wage. It is a common condition in rural areas that both the demand for unskilled labour and the market wage rate have pronounced seasonal patterns, as illustrated in Figure 12.1. Equation (12.3) deals with this situation by defining the total EOCL used by a project over a year as the product of the quantity of labour hired in each season or wage period multiplied by the corresponding market wage rate (supply price) for the period. This is equal to the sum of the unskilled wage rate for each particular season or wage period (W_t) multiplied by the total amount of unskilled labour employed by the project in that period (L_t):

$$EOCL = \sum_{t=1}^{n}(L_t W_t) \tag{12.3}$$

where t denotes the period of time and n denotes the total number of periods.

Figure 12.1: Effect on the Economic Opportunity Cost of Labour of Seasonal Variations in Wages and Labour Demand in Rural Regions

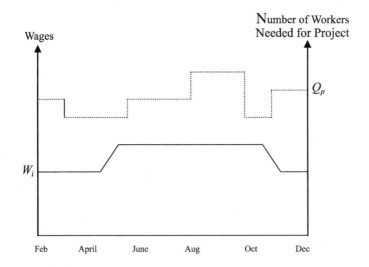

where:

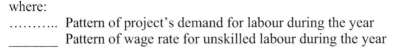

.... Pattern of project's demand for labour during the year
_____ Pattern of wage rate for unskilled labour during the year

If the project's demand for labour is relatively high in the off-season, the total EOCL will be lower than if the project's demand for labour coincides with the seasonal peak demand for this labour.

Consider the case of a labour-intensive sugar project.[81] The project requires unskilled workers on a temporary basis and pays a wage of $180 per month (W_p). The working conditions are identical to those prevailing in the labour market. Table 12.1 shows the project's monthly requirements for workers in Column (3), and the monthly market wage rates that labour would be willing to work for on this project in Column (2).

Table 12.1: Market Wages and Project Demand for Seasonal Labour

Month	Market Wage ($/month)	Person-Months Required by Project	EOCL for Period ($)
(1)	(2)	(3)	(4)
January	120	18	2,160
February	100	18	1,800
March	180	18	3,240
April	180	9	1,620
May	100	9	900
June	150	0	0
July	180	0	0
August	120	0	0
September	150	0	0
October	110	0	0
November	150	9	1,350
December	180	9	1,620
Total	-	**90**	**12,690**

In this case, the monthly market wage rates are the supply prices of unskilled labour to the sugar project. Using equation (12.3), the EOCL is then calculated as follows:

$$EOCL = \sum_{t=1}^{n=12}(L_t W_t)$$
$$= 120 \times 18 + 100 \times 18 + \ldots + 150 \times 9 + 180 \times 9$$
$$= \$12,690$$

[81] Examples are based upon work done by Jenkins and El-Hifnawi (1993).

The project wage (W_p) paid does not play a direct role in the estimation of the EOCL. The wage paid by the project is the financial cost to the project. The difference between the financial cost and the EOCL is the value of the labour externality.

12.5 Economic Opportunity Cost of Skilled Labour

Skilled labour is not a homogeneous factor, nor are the financial cost and the EOCL going to be the same for all types of such labour. There is no doubt that securing adequate supplies of labour with the appropriate skills is a key determinant of the success of most projects. Post-evaluations of development investments have demonstrated that projects are often seriously delayed or even abandoned because of an inadequate supply of labour with specific skills. Hence, special attention needs to be paid to determining the sources of supply, levels of compensation, and potential distortions in these labour markets.

To meet a project's requirements, labour is often induced (with higher wages and a better living environment) to migrate from other areas. For example, skilled workers in urban areas are able to obtain many goods and services, such as better education for their children, that are more readily available in the city. If called upon to move from an urban to a rural area, they may well require a wage premium to be paid, in spite of the fact that simple food items are cheaper in the countryside.

The supply price approach for determining the EOCL for skilled occupations follows the same basic procedure as the unskilled case. The first step is to determine the market supply price of labour (W^s) needed to attract workers to the project. Distortions to that wage are then identified and quantified. The EOCL can be estimated by adjusting W^s to account for those distortions.

To demonstrate this approach, the EOCL is estimated for three situations. The first example is simplified by using the somewhat unrealistic assumptions that there are no distortions in the market for labour and that the project provides jobs with the same working conditions as other employers of these occupations in the area. Furthermore, no workers need to (or can) be attracted from outside the area. The second case drops these assumptions and considers a situation in which labour must be induced to move from alternative projects or regions where there are market distortions. The final case is one that demonstrates how employment that lasts for less than a full year can be a factor in determining the value of the EOCL of any particular type of skilled labour.

12.5.1 Labour Market Without Distortions or Regional Migration

If there are no distortions in the market, such as income tax on the wages for a given occupation, and if the employment provided by the project has the same

Economic Opportunity Cost of Labour

working conditions as alternative employment in the region, it does not matter whether the new workers come from other employment (reduced demand) or from non-market activities (new supply). In both cases, the EOCL is equivalent to the local market wage (W), which is the supply price (W^s).

This is exactly the same result as in the case of the unskilled rural labour. In fact, the analysis of the EOCL is differentiated not so much by the skill level of the worker as by the nature of the distortions in the labour market. In the case of skilled occupations, it is more realistic to assume that a higher wage will have to be paid to attract such labour away from other jobs that have different working conditions and/or are located in other regions that have distorted labour markets.

12.5.2 Workers Migrate to Project from Distorted Regional Labour Markets

Suppose a project hires labour and some of the workers are induced to migrate from alternative employment in other labour markets. For each occupational type, the project pays a wage equal to or higher than the gross-of-tax supply price (W_g^s) to attract an adequate number of workers. As demonstrated by Figure 12.2, the migration of workers from the other regions to the project will shift the labour supply curve leftward to the new position $S'S'$ from SS. This shift intersects the demand curve (DD) at the higher equilibrium wage rate at B from A, causing a decrease in the demand for the current employment from Q_0 to Q_2.

At the same time, the higher wage rate may induce some skilled workers to enter the formal labour force, or may result in more overtime being worked, thereby increasing the quantity of skilled labour supplied from Q_1 to Q_2. The net effect is that even if all of the labour for the project migrates from the sending regions, a proportion of the labour (H_s) ultimately comes from the newly induced supply, and a proportion (H_d) comes from the reduced demand for workers elsewhere.[82]

---

[82]For a further development of some of these issues, see Bell (1991) and Gemmel and Papps (1991).

Figure 12.2: Regional Interaction among Skilled Labour Markets

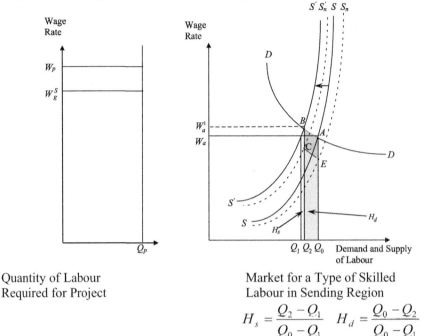

Quantity of Labour
Required for Project

Market for a Type of Skilled
Labour in Sending Region

$$H_s = \frac{Q_2 - Q_1}{Q_0 - Q_1} \quad H_d = \frac{Q_0 - Q_2}{Q_0 - Q_1}$$

The reduction in the quantity of labour employed elsewhere (i.e., $Q_0 - Q_2$) results in a loss of personal income taxes to the government, and this is shown as the area bounded by $ABCE$; this is also the same as the area measured by the vertical difference between the gross-of-tax supply curve, SS, and the net-of-tax supply curve, $S_n S_n$, multiplied by the change in employment $(Q_0 - Q_2)$. When calculating the EOCL, only the tax loss resulting from the reduced demand (H_d) need be accounted for because it is assumed that the increased supply (H_s) of labour is coming from market or non-market activities where there are no taxes or other distortions. Thus, the EOCL for the project in such cases is the gross-of-tax supply price (W_g^s) of workers induced to move to the area minus the difference between the income taxes the workers would pay on this gross-of-tax supply price of labour $(W_g^s T)$, which are gained by the government, and the income taxes previously paid by the workers in their alternative employment $(H_d W_a T)$, which are lost by the government. For simplicity's sake, it is assumed that the tax rates these workers pay on the supply price and alternative wage in the sending region are the same, although this is not necessarily the case.

The EOCL of skilled labour hired by the project in the area can be expressed as follows:

Economic Opportunity Cost of Labour

$$EOCL = W_g^s - (W_g^s T - H_d W_a T) \qquad (12.4)$$

where: H_d denotes the proportion of the project's demand for labour obtained from taxed employment activities in the alternative labour market;

W_a denotes the gross-of-tax wage of labour from alternative sources;

W_g^s denotes the gross-of-tax supply price of labour; and

T denotes the income tax rate levied on workers in all regions.

In this situation, $H_s = (1 - H_d)$ includes both the supply of labour coming to the region from untaxed market and non-market activities and increases in labour force participation and the number of hours worked. While it is theoretically possible for a project to change the level of labour force participation or the number of hours worked, over the lifetime of a project this effect is likely to be small, depending on the type of skill and the market at the time of recruitment to the project.

Let us consider again the sugar project discussed above. In addition to the unskilled workers hired for the project, the project requires 1,000 person-months of labour in skilled occupations each year. Owing to a shortage of such workers in this region, the project will have to attract them from the urban areas surrounding the region in which the project is located. It is assumed that despite their monthly gross-of-tax salaries (W_a) of $900 in the urban area, these workers will not work for the project for less than $1,200 gross of tax ($W_g^s$). These wage rates reflect the gross-of-tax supply prices of the workers in the two markets, respectively. Suppose there is a policy of encouraging more workers in these occupations to migrate to the rural areas; in this case the project is required to pay a higher salary (W_p) of $1,500 per month for such labour, or $300 more than the supply price. All skilled workers pay 20 percent of their wages in income taxes.

Using equation (12.4), we can estimate the EOCL of this labour to the project by determining: a) the taxes to be paid on the supply price of skilled labour for the project and b) the taxes forgone by the workers in their alternative employment.

a) Taxes on the Supply Price of Labour

$$W_g^s T = 1,200 \times (0.20) = \$240/\text{month}$$

b) Taxes Forgone in Alternative Employment

Let us assume that the supply of labour in these occupations in the economy is relatively inelastic compared with the demand for that labour, and let $H_d = 0.90$

and $H_s = 0.10$. Hence, we can anticipate that approximately 90 percent of the project's labour requirements will ultimately be sourced from the decrease in the quantity of labour employed elsewhere, while the remaining 10 percent of the project's needs will be met through increased labour force participation owing to the new project's higher wage. The forgone taxes from the previous employment of the workers are calculated as follows:

$$H_d W_a T = 0.90 \times 900 \times 0.20 = \$162/\text{month}$$

Combining those two parts with the supply price, the EOCL of the labour used by the project in this rural area is calculated from equation (12.4) as follows:

$$
\begin{aligned}
EOCL &= W_g^s - (W_g^s T - H_d W_a T) \\
&= 1{,}200 - [(1{,}200 \times 0.20) - (0.90 \times 900 \times 0.20)] \\
&= \$1{,}122/\text{month}
\end{aligned}
$$

The difference between the EOCL and the project wage represents the value of the project's labour externality per month of labour employed. Following equation (12.1), the labour externality for the above case can be expressed as:

$$
\begin{aligned}
LE_i &= W_p - W_g^s + (W_g^s T - H_d W_a T) \\
&= W_p(1-T) - W_g^s(1-T) + W_p T - H_d W_a T
\end{aligned}
$$

Carrying this analysis one step further, we can determine how these labour externalities are distributed between the workers and the government. The benefits to each can be calculated as follows:

Labour benefits
$$
\begin{aligned}
&= W_p(1-T) - W_g^s(1-T) \\
&= 1{,}500 \times (1-0.20) - 1{,}200 \times (1-0.20) \\
&= \$240/\text{month}
\end{aligned}
$$

Government benefits
$$
\begin{aligned}
&= W_p T - H_d W_a T \\
&= 1{,}500 \times (0.20) - (0.90 \times 900 \times 0.20) \\
&= \$138/\text{month}
\end{aligned}
$$

Thus, of the total of externalities created per month by the employment of labour by a project, the workers will gain an additional $240 per month, while the government will capture $138 per month in additional taxes. The distributional analysis provides a means of evaluating the financial gains and losses affecting groups in the economy other than the owners of the project.

12.6 Economic Opportunity Cost of Labour When Labour is Not Employed Full-Time

In this analysis, workers are not divided between those who are working in the formal labour market and those who are not. Instead, it is postulated that each worker could spend part of each year in non-market activities or unemployment. In this case, workers can expect to be employed in market activities for a proportion (P_p) of the year if they work for the project. If they are not associated with the project, they will be employed for a different proportion (P_a) of the year. When they are not working in the formal labour market, they will be engaged in non-market activities outside the project or in alternative regions, i.e., $(1 - P_p)$ and $(1 - P_a)$ proportions of their labour force time, respectively.

The gross-of-tax supply price of skilled labour in the area of the project is again denoted as W_g^s and the alternative wage, which reflects this labour's other opportunities, as W_a. From the supply price approach, the EOCL is equal to the gross-of-tax expected supply price for labour (W_g^s), but only working a portion of the year on the project (P_p), minus the additional tax payments that the workers would incur if earning their supply price wage W_g^s on this project.

This additional tax is the difference between the tax paid on the project $(P_p W_g^s T)$ and the tax previously paid in the alternative mix of market activities $(H_d P_a W_a T)$. The taxes lost in alternative market activities arise because there is a net reduction in employment of this type of worker elsewhere. We assume that workers do not pay taxes on non-market activities. Using the supply price approach, the EOCL of these workers is the expected gross-of-tax supply price less the expected net change in tax payments. It can be expressed as equation (12.5):

$$EOCL = P_p W_g^s - (P_p W_g^s T - H_d P_a W_a T) \tag{12.5}$$

Suppose in this case that the alternative wage rate for skilled labour is $W_a =$ \$600/month and the project wage is equal to the gross-of-tax supply price paid to induce labour to move to the project area ($W_g^s = W_p =$ \$800/month). The tax rate on skilled labour in all locations is 20 percent. All of the labour is obtained from alternative employment ($H_d = 1$), and the proportion of time employed in the alternative areas is $P_a = 0.8$. Assuming that a skilled worker expects to be employed in the project and the project region is $P_p = 0.9$, the EOCL on this rural project would be:

$$EOCL = 0.9 \times 800 - (0.9 \times 800 \times 0.20 - 1.0 \times 0.8 \times 600 \times 0.20)$$
$$= 720 - (144 - 96)$$
$$= \$672/\text{month}$$

While the financial cost of labour to fill a job (which employs someone for 90 percent of the year) is estimated on average to be \$720 $(= P_p W_p)$ per month, the EOCL is only \$672 per month, or \$48 less than the financial cost. This difference is the net tax gain to the government.

We now extend the analysis to examine a scenario in which workers are employed less than full-time in market activities during a typical year. This is especially important in the case of countries with high unemployment compensation payments, such as Canada and the countries of northern Europe.[83] We differentiate between those engaged in full-time employment and those who have a work history characterized by a succession of work experiences interspersed with unemployment. Because of their choice of occupation or their level of seniority, people in the permanent (or full-time) employment sector are almost never unemployed. On the other hand, workers employed in temporary sectors such as tourism and construction are in jobs that are not expected to be associated with continuous employment. For this analysis, individuals who are expected to experience periodic spells of unemployment or non-market time are included in the temporary labour force, both when they are working and when they are unemployed.

When evaluating projects, one further issue for consideration is the quality of the jobs being created (Jenkins and Kuo, 1978). Jobs need to be classified by the type of employment they provide. Are the jobs full-time for the entire year (i.e., permanent sector), or will they employ a given worker for only part of the year (i.e., temporary jobs)? Temporary jobs are those that do not retain the workers for a full year but intersperse employment with spells of unemployment or non-market activities. Permanent jobs provide full-time employment all year round.

Identifying the type of employment being created is important because temporary jobs can have a high economic cost when unemployment insurance payments (or other forms of social security) are paid to such workers when they are engaged in non-market activities, including being unemployed (Boadway and Flatters, 1981). Hence, account needs to be taken of unemployment insurance in the appraisal of a project that creates these jobs.

Let us consider first the creation of permanent jobs. When a project creates new permanent jobs, they will generally be filled by individuals already working in alternative permanent sector jobs or other temporary sector jobs; some individuals will be hired who are currently out of the labour force. These

---

[83]In these countries, the unemployment benefits vary from 55 percent and 75 percent of lost wage in Canada and Sweden, respectively, to as high as 90 percent of the previous daily wage in Finland.

proportions are denoted as H_d^p, H_d^t, and H^s, respectively, where $H_d^p + H_d^t + H^s = 1$. For those being sourced from alternative jobs in the permanent sector, there will be an externality arising from the loss in income tax receipts from the reduction of employment in these activities. For those sourced from the temporary sector, there will be a saving in the unemployment insurance being paid to the temporary sector workers when they are unemployed. At the same time, there is a loss of any taxes they would have paid while working. For those jobs that are filled by people who were previously out of the labour force, no externalities need to be included. Therefore, the EOCL of a permanent job can be expressed as follows:

$$EOCL^P = W_g^s(1-T) + H_d^p W_p T + H_d^t [P_t W_t T - (1-P_t)fU(1-T)]$$

(12.6)

where: W_g^s denotes the gross-of-tax supply price of labour to the project;

W_p denotes the gross-of-tax wage earned in alternative jobs in the permanent sector;

W_t denotes the gross-of-tax wage earned in the temporary sector;

P_t denotes the proportion of time a temporary sector worker expects to be employed during a calendar year;

T denotes the personal income tax rate;

f denotes the proportion of time an unemployed worker expects to collect unemployment benefits; and

U denotes the unemployment insurance benefits.

In countries where there is no unemployment insurance, such as Indonesia and Vietnam, then $f = 0$. Equation (12.6a) will then measure the EOCL to fill a permanent job as:

$$EOCL^P = W_g^s(1-T) + H_d^p W_p T + H_d^t P_t W_t T$$

(12.6a)

On the other hand, when a year's worth of additional employment is created in the temporary sector of a labour market, these workers will be sourced from the permanent sector, from the temporary sector, and from those previously out of the labour force, in the proportions H_d^p, H_d^t, and H^s, respectively. In this situation, suppose P_t is the proportion of time that any one person actually works in a temporary sector job during a year. As temporary jobs are created, and people are attracted to them from the permanent sector, these people will experience periods of unemployment and collect unemployment insurance. Each period of labour services sourced from the permanent sector will have associated with it $1/P_t$ individuals and $(1-P_t)/P_t$ periods of unemployment. This will give rise to $(1 - P_t)/P_t$ periods of paid unemployment insurance compensation. For labour services sourced from those already in the temporary sector, the loss in taxes will be for the same length of time as the time working on the project, and the amount of unemployed time and unemployment insurance compensation will also be the same as before. The EOCL that relates to a year's worth of temporary sector jobs will then be equal to:

$$EOCL^T = W_g^s(1-T) + (H_d^p/P_t)\big[W_pT + (1-P_t)fU(1-T)\big]$$
$$+ H_d^tW_t(T) + H^s\big[(1-P_t)/P_t\big]fU(1-T) \qquad (12.7)$$

In the case where the wage rates paid for temporary and permanent jobs are the same, the economic cost of 12 months of temporary jobs would be greater than for a year in a permanent job because of the higher amount of taxes that would be lost and the higher amount of unemployment insurance payments associated with these jobs.

12.7 International Migration and the Economic Opportunity Cost of Labour

Until recently, labour has been considered a non-internationally traded service. However, this is changing as more and more workers are relocating to other countries to sell their skills and services. There are two scenarios: retention, or returned migrants, and foreign workers.

12.7.1 Retained or Returned Migrants

This is particularly relevant for countries such as the Philippines, Egypt, and Sri Lanka, where large numbers of skilled and semi-skilled workers are regularly employed abroad for substantial periods of time. In such a situation, when a project is created inside the country and additional labour in certain occupations is hired, we would expect to find a part of this labour to be sourced from a reduction in the outflow of international migration. When this occurs, the EOCL must take into consideration not only the adjustment of the demand and supply of labour in the local markets, but also any distortions associated with the retention or return of migrants who would have been employed abroad.

It is quite common for a country's citizens who are working abroad to send back a stream of payments in the form of personal savings or remittances to relatives. Following the supply price approach to the EOCL, reductions in remittances are not an economic cost as they will be factored into the worker's supply price to the project. However, an adjustment needs to be made to the supply price because the remittances are made in foreign exchange, in which a foreign exchange premium exists in most countries. Taking into account the adjustments to both the local and the international labour markets, the expression for the EOCL becomes:

$$EOCL = W_g^s(1 - T) + H_d W_a T + H_f R(\frac{E^e}{E^m} - 1) \qquad (12.8)$$

where: H_d denotes the proportion of the project's demand for a given type of labour obtained from taxed employment activities in the domestic market;

H_f denotes the proportion of the project's demand for a given type of labour sourced from reduced international out-migration;

R denotes the average amount of remittances (measured in local currency) that would have been made per period if this type of worker had been employed abroad; and

$(\frac{E^e}{E^m} - 1)$ denotes the rate of foreign exchange premium as a fraction of the value of the amount that would otherwise have been remitted.

When some of the sourcing of labour for a project is through an adjustment in the international migration of workers, it is recognized that a share of this labour is being sourced from alternative domestic activities ($H_d = 0.6$) and a share from changes in international flows of labour $H_f = 0.3$. Let us also assume that the VAT rate is 15 percent, that these workers would have remitted $500 on average per month, and the foreign exchange premium is 6 percent. Applying equation (12.8), the EOCL is as follows:

$$EOCL = W_g^s(1 - T) + H_d W_a T + H_f R(\frac{E^e}{E^m} - 1)$$
$$= 1,200 \times (1 - 0.2) + 0.6 \times (900) \times 0.2 + 0.3 \times (500) \times (0.06)$$
$$= \$1,077$$

The difference between the EOCL and the project wage represents the value of the project's labour externality including the premium of foreign exchange that is no longer remitted to the project country.

12.7.2 Foreign Labour

In countries where the labour shortage is particularly acute, it may be necessary to import foreign workers to work on projects. Examples of this practice can be seen in both developing and developed countries where the demand for labour exceeds the supply. Often, foreign workers are brought into the country by corporations or governments to work on projects requiring their skills. In developing countries, this often takes the form of skilled advisers or technical staff, while in developed countries, guest workers or unskilled labourers are imported to fill gaps in the labour pool. There is an EOCL associated with this foreign labour ($EOCL^f$), which should be included in the project assessment.

$EOCL^f$ is the net-of-tax wage paid to the foreign workers plus adjustments to the amount of foreign exchange associated with the repatriated portion, and adjustments to the amount of VAT associated with consumption by the foreign workers using the non-repatriated portion of that wage, plus any subsidies the foreign workers may benefit from while in the country. The repatriated portion of the wage should be adjusted to account for the true cost of the foreign exchange to the economy rather than just its market value. This is necessary because the value of the foreign exchange may be distorted. While living in the country, foreign workers have to use a portion of their wage for consumption. The incremental amount of VAT revenue paid as a result of the foreign workers' consumption in the country should be accounted for as an economic benefit to the country, as the country gains from the local consumption of the foreign workers. At the same time, foreign workers may benefit from government subsidies on a variety of items, such as food, fuel, housing, and health care. The amount of benefit received by foreign labour from those subsidies should be accounted for as an economic cost to the country. The EOCL of foreign labour can be expressed as:

$$EOCL^f = W^f(1-T_h) - W^f(1-T_h)(1-R)t_{VAT}$$
$$+ W^f(1-T_h)R(\frac{E^e}{E^m}-1) + N \tag{12.9}$$

where: W^f denotes the gross-of-tax wage of foreign labour;

T_h denotes the personal income tax levied by the host country on foreign labour;

t_{VAT} denotes the VAT rate levied on consumption;

R denotes the proportion of the net-of-tax income repatriated by foreign labour;

E^e denotes the economic cost of foreign exchange;

E^m denotes the market exchange rate; and

N denotes the value of benefits gained by foreign workers from subsidies.

If $EOCL^f$ is greater than the financial cost of labour to the project, the second term must be smaller than the sum of the third and fourth terms; this implies that the economic benefit created by foreign consumption in the country cannot offset the foreign exchange premium related to the remitted portion of the wage and the cost of government subsidies. In this case, the EOCL of hiring foreign labour will be greater than the project wage. However, if the second term is greater than the third and fourth terms, the EOCL of foreign labour will actually be lower than the market wage; this means that the country is benefiting economically from the presence of foreign labour.

Suppose a multinational corporation considers an electronic-assembly project in an urban area and discovers that there is insufficient local labour. It decides to import skilled workers from a nearby country to operate the project until enough local workers can be trained for the production requirements. The shortfall is estimated to be equivalent to 50 workers, who will be paid $2,000 per month. That wage will be subject to a 25 percent personal income tax. Workers are expected to repatriate 30 percent of their net-of-tax income to support family members at home. The VAT rate is 15 percent. The market exchange rate is held constant by the government, while the economic exchange rate is estimated to be 6 percent higher than the market value. In this case, it is assumed that no subsidies are paid by the government with respect to these workers, i.e., $N = 0$.

Applying these values to equation (12.9), the EOCL of foreign labour is:

$$EOCL^f = 2,000 \times (1 - 0.25) - 2,000 \times (1 - 0.25) \times (1 - 0.30) \times \quad (0.15) +$$
$$2,000 \times (1 - 0.25) \times (0.30) \times (0.06)$$
$$= \$1,369.50/\text{month}$$

This analysis shows that the EOCL of each worker will be $630.50 less than the gross-of-tax wage of $2,000. Hence, a substantial external benefit is generated by this use of foreign labour.

12.8 Effects of a Protected Sector on the Economic Opportunity Cost of Labour

The focus so far has been on estimating the EOCL in competitive labour markets. In many countries, however, the urban labour market is segmented into a protected sector and an unprotected, or open, sector.[84]

The protected sector is usually made up of the government agencies, foreign companies, and large local firms that provide wages (W^P) above the market-clearing wage. The higher wages offered by these types of employers are often the result of stricter compliance with minimum wage laws, powerful unions that are able to demand and receive significantly higher wages, government policies that give higher wages to civil servants, or foreign companies that pay high

---

[84]The discussion of the EOCL for the protected sector starts from the approach followed by Edwards (1989). See also Bicak et al. (2004).

wages to decrease possible resentment by workers and politicians in the host country. Consequently, employment in the protected urban labour force is highly attractive, with a variety of rationing methods being used to select the people to fill the limited number of positions.

The open labour market is typically affected by fewer distortions to the supply price of labour (W^O). Wages are determined competitively in the marketplace, where there are fewer barriers to entry, lower wages, and less security of employment. While workers may be initially attracted to this labour market by the prospect of finding a job in the protected sector, they often end up working in the open labour market.

The phenomenon of chronic unemployment, at rates far in excess of what might be explained in terms of normal friction in the economy, has been attributed, in part, to the existence of a protected labour market. A portion of those chronically unemployed workers are attempting to gain access to the protected sector but, at the same time, are unwilling to work for the lower wages offered by the open labour market. This unwillingness to work for the open market wage creates sub-sectors in the labour market in which quasi-voluntary and search unemployment exists.

12.8.1 The Protected Sector and No Migration

The characteristics of unemployment in this situation are shown in Figure 12.3A. If the overall supply of labour to the market is given by the supply curve (SS^T), the total number of workers making themselves available for work at the protected sector wage of W_1^P is shown as point C. The number of protected sector jobs available is much more limited at Q^P (i.e., BC).

Figure 12.3: Estimating the Economic Opportunity Cost of Labour for Protected Sector Jobs (One Protected Sector and $\eta = \infty$)

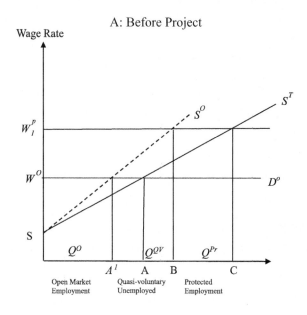

A: Before Project

B: After Project

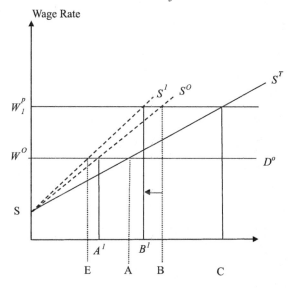

Hence, there is an excess supply of labour available at the protected sector wage, as shown by the quantity B. If the selection of workers for employment in the protected sector is carried out in a random fashion from the available workers, independent of their supply prices, it follows that the supply of labour available to the open market will be a fraction (B/C) of the total labour supply SS^T at each wage rate. This labour supply is shown as the curve SS^O.

To simplify the analysis for this case, it is assumed that the demand for labour in the open sector is perfectly elastic at a wage rate of W^O and that the intersection of the demand for labour in the open sector $(W^O D^O)$ with the supply (SS^O) determines the quantity employed in the open market. This quantity is indicated by point A^1. The quantity of labour classified as unemployed (Q^{QV}) is determined by the difference between points A^1 and B. These quasi-voluntary unemployed are those workers who will choose not to take jobs in the open market sector because their basic supply price of labour is above the open market wage (W^O). They actively seek jobs in the protected sector and will consider themselves involuntarily unemployed. They are seeking work that will pay the protected sector wage (W_1^P), but are unable to find it.

If a project is added to the protected sector, then, as shown in Figure 12.3B, the size of the protected sector increases from $(C - B)$ to $(C - B^1)$. If, again, these additional workers $(B - B^1)$ are selected randomly from those remaining who want to work in the protected sector, the supply of labour to the open market will shift to the left, from SS^O to SS^1. The number of workers willing to take jobs in the open sector will fall from A^1 to E. When workers are attracted from the unemployed and open sectors in proportion to their numbers in the labour pool, in the absence of any distortions, the EOCL of this project is a weighted average of the open sector wage (W^O) and the average supply price of the quasi-voluntary unemployed $[(W^O + W_1^P)/2]$. The relevant weights are the proportions in which workers in each of those categories will be chosen for the protected sector jobs. Under a random selection method, the weights are the fraction of the open sector employment as a share of the total supply of labour not working in the protected sector (A^1/B) and the fraction of the quasi-voluntary unemployed as a share of the total labour force not working in the protected sector, $[(B - A^1)/B]$. Hence, the EOCL for protected sector jobs is given by the expression:

$$EOCL^P = (W^O) \times (A^1 / B) + \left[(W^O + W_1^P)/2\right] \times \left[(B - A^1)/B\right] \quad (12.10)$$

If Q^O denotes the quantity employed in the open market and Q^{QV} the amount of quasi-voluntary unemployment before the creation of these additional protected sector jobs, the expression for the EOCL of protected sector jobs can be written as:

$$EOCL^P = W^O \times \left[Q^O /(Q^O + Q^{QV})\right] + \left[(W^O + W_1^P)/2\right]$$
$$\times \left[Q^{QV} /(Q^O + Q^{QV})\right] \qquad (12.10a)$$

When income taxes are levied on wages in both the protected and the open sectors, the economic cost of hiring workers from the open sector is the gross-of-tax wage they were earning in the open sector W^O, because the taxes on this labour will now be lost. In the case of the quasi-voluntary unemployed hired by the protected sector, their EOCL is still the average of the net-of-tax open and protected sector wages because they pay no taxes when unemployed. To account for these lost taxes, equation (12.10a) can be rewritten as follows:

$$EOCL^P = W^O \left[Q^O /(Q^O + Q^{QV})\right]$$
$$+ \left[(W^O + W_1^P)/2)(1-T)\right]\left[Q^{QV} /(Q^O + Q^{QV})\right] \qquad (12.10b)$$

12.8.2 Two Protected Sectors

It is more realistic to think of the protected sector as containing a series of segmented markets, with different protected sector wages: W_1^P, W_2^P, ... , W_i^P. Figure 12.4A portrays the same labour market as the one dealt with above, with one protected sector. To simplify the analyses somewhat, it is assumed that the demand for labour in the open sector is perfectly elastic. Furthermore, it is assumed that there are no distortions (i.e., taxes or subsidies) in the labour market.

Figure 12.4: Estimating the Economic Opportunity Cost of Labour for Protected Sector Jobs (Two Protected Sectors and $\eta = \infty$)

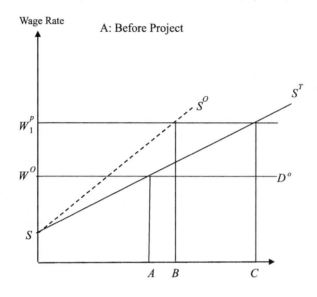

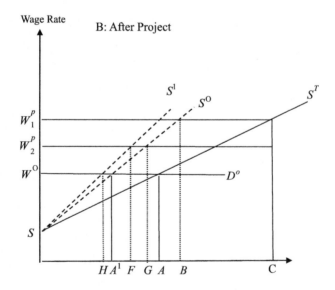

As shown previously, when the first protected sector is introduced at a wage of W_1^P, the total number of workers making themselves available for work at the protected sector wage will be given at point C. After the jobs in the first protected jobs are filled, the total number of workers employed in the open sector is given by point A^1 in Figure 12.4B. Suppose that additional protected sector jobs are then created, where the wage (W_2^P) paid is above the open wage but below that of the first protected sector. For the moment, it is also assumed that there are no income taxes. Given the existence of $(C - B)$ jobs in the first protected sector, now a total of G workers would be willing to work in the second protected sector. This is shown in Figure 12.4B by the intersection of the labour supply curve SS^O and the wage of W_2^P.

The quantities of labour working in the first and second protected sectors are given by $(C - B)$ and $(G - F)$ respectively. With the introduction of the second protected sector, which hires workers in a random fashion from those willing to work at the wage offered, the quantity of workers employed in the open sector falls from A^1 to H. This contraction comes about because some open sector workers are fortunate enough to be selected for a protected sector job. Similarly, the number of quasi-voluntarily unemployed falls from $(B - A^1)$ to $(B - G) + (F - H)$. The quantity of workers $(B - G)$ would be willing to work for the protected wage of W_1^P, but none of this group would be willing to work for anything less than W_2^P. Thus, the quantity of workers $(F - H)$ would be willing to work for a wage of W_2^P, but none would work for the open market wage of W^O.

In these circumstances the EOCL in the second protected sector is the weighted average of the open wage (W^O) for those sourced from the open sector and the average of the open sector wage and the second protected sector wage [($W_2^P + W^O$)/2] for those sourced from the quasi-voluntarily unemployed who are willing to work in this sector. The weights are the number of open sector workers as a share of the total quantity of labour available at a wage of W_2^P (i.e., A^1/G), and the number of quasi-voluntarily unemployed as a share of the same total quantity available (i.e., $(G - A^1)/G$). Hence, the EOCL of the second protected sector jobs can be expressed as:

$$EOCL_2^P = W^O(A^1 / G) + \left[(W_2^P + W^O)/2\right]\left[(G - A^1)/G\right] \qquad (12.11)$$

When income taxes are levied on wages in both the protected and the open sectors, the same adjustment as that made in equation (12.10b) is needed in order to recognize the loss of income tax revenue from the net reduction in employment in the open sector when protected sector jobs are created. Hence, equation (12.11) becomes:

$$EOCL_2^P = W^O(A^1 / G) + \left[((W_2^P + W^O)/2)(1 - T)\right]\left[(G - A^1)/G\right]$$
$$(12.11a)$$

On the basis of the assumptions used in the above example, similar expressions can be derived to measure the EOCL for any number of protected sector jobs, each with their own wage rate. If the total supply function of labour to the market is a linear function of the wage rate (i.e., the quantity of labour supplied at a given wage is $Q_i = S^T\{W_i\}$), then from Figure 12.4B the following relationship can be defined:

$$A/C = S^T\{W^O\}/S^T\{W_1^P\} \text{ and } A^1/G = S^O\{W^O\}/S^O\{W_2^P\}$$

As $(C - A)/C = \left[S^T\{W_1^P\} - S^T\{W^O\}\right]/S^T\{W_1^P\}$, it follows from the geometric properties of similar triangles and parallel lines that:

$$(G - A^1)/G = \left[S^O\{W_2^P\} - S^O\{W^O\}\right]/S^O\{W_2^P\}$$

The EOCL in the first protected sector can be calculated as follows:

$$EOCL_1^P = W^O\left[S^T\{W^O\}/S^T\{W_1^P\}\right]$$
$$+ (W_1^P + W^O)/2\left[(S^T\{W_1^P\} - S^T\{W^O\})/S^T\{W_1^P\}\right]$$
$$(12.12)$$

Likewise, the EOCL in the second protected sector can be expressed as follows:

$$EOCL_2^P = W^O\left[S^O\{W^O\}/S^O\{W_2^P\}\right]$$
$$+ \left[(W_2^P + W^O)/2\right]\left[(S^O\{W_2^P\} - S^O\{W^O\})/S^O\{W_2^P\}\right] \quad (12.13)$$

In general, it follows that under these conditions (i.e., linear supply curve and a perfectly elastic demand for labour at the open wage of W^O) the EOCL for any protected sector paying a wage W_i^P can be expressed as:

$$EOCL_i^P = W^O\left[S^T\{W^O\}/S^T\{W_i^P\}\right]$$
$$+ \left[(W_i^P + W^O)/2\right]\left[(S^T\{W_i^P\} - S^T\{W^O\})/S^T\{W_i^P\}\right] \quad (12.14)$$

The EOCL for any protected sector is simply a weighted average of: a) the open sector wage W^O and b) the average of the specific protected sector wage

Economic Opportunity Cost of Labour

and the open sector wage. The weights can all be expressed as functions of the original total market supply of labour $S^T\{W_i\}$.

When income taxes are levied on wages in both the protected and open sectors, the same adjustment as that made in equation (12.10b) is needed in order to recognize the loss of income tax revenue from the net reduction in employment in the open sector when protected sector jobs are created. Hence, equation (12.15) becomes:

$$EOCL_i^P = W^O\left[S^T\{W^O\}/S^T\{W_i^P\}\right]$$

$$+ \left[(W_i^P + W^O)/2\right]\!\left(1-T\right)\!\left[(S^T\{W_i^P\} - S^T\{W^O\})/S^T\{W_i^P\}\right]$$

(12.15)

12.8.3 Search Unemployment with No Migration

This analysis of unemployment assumes that all workers, whether they are employed in the open market or are quasi-voluntarily unemployed, have an equal chance of obtaining the protected sector jobs. However, in practice, some workers will have more to gain (by their own assessment) from the protected sector jobs than others and, therefore, can be expected to go to greater lengths to obtain those positions. Some of this extra effort is likely to be reflected in search unemployment, which is a particular type of voluntary unemployment. Search unemployment can be thought of as a category in which the worker voluntarily accepts unemployment with the intention of enhancing the probability of obtaining a protected sector job.

Figure 12.5A depicts a labour market in which search unemployment and the standard type of quasi-voluntary unemployment coexist. We also introduce a less than infinite elastic demand for labour in the open sector (LD^O). The curve W^mS^O is the supply curve of all those willing to work in the open market. This supply curve has been adjusted for the effect that searching has on the supply of labour available to the open market. The interaction of the demand function for open market workers LD^O with that supply of open market workers W^mS^O determines the initial open market wage W^O. The lateral distance between this new supply curve W^mS^O and the prior supply curve SS^O is the quantity of search unemployment corresponding to any given open market wage. When the wage is W^m, the number of workers who opt for search unemployment is equal to the distance W^mE, whereas it is the difference between F and G at the open market wage W^O. This distance is greatest at wage W^m. At this wage, all those not working in the protected sector would prefer to remain unemployed in order to search for protected sector jobs instead of accepting jobs in the open market. As the open market wage rises, fewer and fewer workers are willing to forgo open market earnings in order to seek protected sector jobs until, finally, as the open market wage approaches the protected sector wage W^P, the quantity of search unemployment approaches zero.

When additional protected sector jobs are introduced into the protected sector under these conditions, a proportion of the new positions will be filled from each of the three labour pools: search unemployed, quasi-voluntary unemployed, and those currently employed in the open sector.[85] The EOCL will be the sum of the supply price multiplied by the proportions of new hires that come from each of these sectors. Workers who opt for search unemployment are voluntarily accepting a gamble, in which one outcome is to be unemployed and the other is to have a protected sector job. The value of that gamble to them is precisely the open market wage at which they would willingly withdraw from the search process. Therefore, the supply price of the search-unemployed workers (W^S) will be given by equation (12.16):

$$W^S = P_1(0) + P_2(W^P) \qquad\qquad\qquad (12.16)$$

where P_1 denotes the probability of earning zero income and P_2 denotes the probability of finding a protected sector job. W^S will necessarily be higher than W^O because the open market wage is available with certainty, but these individuals refuse to work at this wage in preference to searching for a protected sector job that pays W^P.

---

[85]To simplify the analysis, the reaction of the open market wage to the decrease in the workers now available to the open market will be ignored. This analysis is shown in Figure 12.5B.

Figure 12.5: Estimating the Economic Opportunity Cost of Labour with Quasi-Voluntary and Search Unemployment

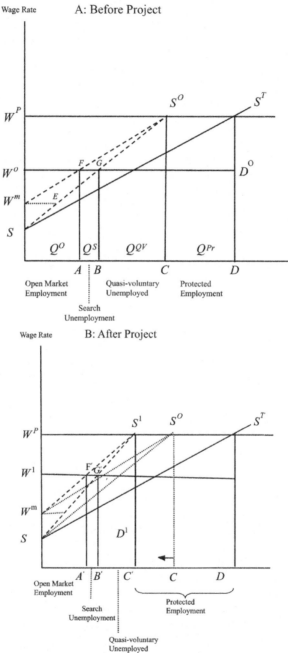

The quasi-voluntary unemployed are unwilling under any circumstances to work at wage W^O, requiring a higher wage in order to re-enter the workforce.

Workers sourced from quasi-voluntary unemployment for jobs at the protected sector wage (W^P) will (with linear supply curves) have a supply price averaging $[(W^O + W^P)/2]$. Finally, the supply price for workers already employed in the open sector will simply be the open market wage W^O because they have already shown a willingness to accept work at that wage rate. Hence, the EOCL for the protected sector project can be estimated by combining those supply prices and the proportions of labour from each sector as follows:

$$EOCL^P = W^S H^S + \left[(W^O + W^P)/2\right]H^{QV} + W^O H^O \qquad (12.17)$$

where H^S, H^{QV}, and H^O stand for the proportion of labour sourced from each of the labour pools: search unemployed, quasi-voluntary unemployed, and those currently employed in the open market sector.

If individuals obtain the permanent jobs in a manner unrelated to their supply prices, then:

$$H^S = Q^S /(Q^S + Q^{QV} + Q^O)$$
$$H^{QV} = Q^{QV} /(Q^S + Q^{QV} + Q^O)$$
$$H^O = Q^O /(Q^S + Q^{QV} + Q^O)$$

Comparing this value with the EOCL when there is only quasi-voluntary unemployment, the addition of the economic cost of search unemployment $(W^S H^S)$ will tend to raise the open sector's wage (W^O) and, hence, raise the EOCL for the project in the protected sector.

12.8.4 No Open Sector and Labour Market Supplied by Migrants

In some circumstances, no open sector has been allowed to develop, because of either the strict enforcement of minimum wage laws or the nature of the development in the area (e.g., there is a one-company town, or the only sources of employment available are protected sector jobs). In this case it is assumed that it is the migration of labour from other regions that is the source of additional workers. Workers will be attracted to the region because the protected sector wage is greater than their supply price of labour for that place. Not all potential workers will find employment; some who come to the area in search of a protected sector job will end up being unemployed.

In this case it is necessary to differentiate between the supply price of an additional potential worker (a migrant) and the EOCL required to fill a job. Potential migrants evaluate their prospects in the region where there are protected sector jobs against the opportunities available around them. If they

Economic Opportunity Cost of Labour

migrate, there is a probability of finding a protected sector job (P^P) and also a probability of being unemployed $(1 - P^P)$. Hence, from the perspective of a potential migrant, if the protected sector wage is W^P, the expected wage from migrating $(E(W))$ is equal to the product of the protected sector wage (W^P) and the probability of being employed in the protected sector (P^P), i.e., $E(W) = P^P W^P$.

When there is no open sector, it is the unemployment rate $(1 - P^P)$ that brings about the equilibrium between the supply price of a migrant and the protected sector wage. Suppose the supply price for a migrant to move to the region where there are protected sector jobs is W^m. As this supply price is less than the protected sector wage of W^P, there is incentive for more migrants to move to seek protected sector employment than there are jobs available. This migration process will continue until the probability of finding a protected sector job falls to the point where:

$$P^P = (W^m / W^P) \text{ and } W^m = E(W) \tag{12.18}$$

At this point, the potential migrant's expected wage from moving to the protected sector is just equal to his or her supply price. Furthermore, when more protected sector jobs are created, the number of migrants to the region in pursuit of these jobs will always be greater than the number of jobs. Hence, when the full adjustment has taken place, the equilibrium unemployment rate will be maintained and the number in the pool of unemployed labour will be increased.

To estimate the EOCL for protected sector jobs, we need to account for the opportunity cost of all migrants, both employed and unemployed, who were induced to move in pursuit of these new jobs. If the equilibrium unemployment rate is $(1 - P^P)$, for every new protected sector job created there will have to be $(1/P^P)$ migrants. The economic opportunity cost of each of these migrants is equal to $W^P P^P$ when the labour market is in equilibrium. Hence, the EOCL to fill a protected sector job is expressed as:

$$EOCL^P = (W^P P^P)(1/P^P) = W^P \tag{12.19}$$

In this case, where it is the unemployment rate that is the equilibrating force between the protected sector and the rest of the economy, the $EOCL^P$ is equal to the protected sector wage. There is no net economic externality from the creation of protected sector jobs. The additional unemployment created by those searching for a protected sector job inflicts an economic cost on society equal to the difference between the supply price of a migrant and the protected sector wage. As a consequence, when there is no open sector and no other distortions such as taxes, the EOCL for protected sector jobs is the protected sector wage.

When there are taxes levied on the protected sector wage, and taxes are levied on the wages paid in the sending region, the $EOCL^P$ will need to be adjusted to reflect the net change in tax revenues. The gross-of-tax wage rates in the protected sector and in alternative employment are denoted as W^P and W^a, respectively. Further, if the proportion of migrants from the sending region who would have been employed in that region is expressed as H_a, and T is the tax rate, the $EOCL^P$ can be expressed as:

$$EOCL^P = W^P(1-T) + H_a W_a T(1/P^P) \tag{12.20}$$

In this situation, the amount of taxes lost from reduced activities in the sending regions must account for the fact that not all the adjustment comes from reduced employment. Further, for every new protected sector job, there will be more than one migrant moving to the labour market where the protected sector jobs are located.

12.9 Conclusion

In this chapter, the EOCL has been estimated using the supply price approach under a wide variety of labour market conditions and types of jobs. This approach is shown to be equivalent to the value of the marginal product of labour forgone approach when the latter can be estimated accurately. The primary reliance of the supply price approach greatly facilitates the estimation of this economic parameter for use in the economic valuation of projects.

A methodology has been outlined in detail to account for several adjustments that may need to be made to this supply price to reflect special labour market characteristics and distortions. Most of these factors, such as income taxes and unemployment insurance compensation, are straightforward and easy to estimate. Others, such as those dealing with inter-regional and international migration, as well as imperfections in the labour market, including phenomena such as migration-fed, quasi-voluntary unemployment and employment created in protected sector jobs, require a more detailed examination of the labour market. In all these cases, the special features in question give rise to the need for further specific adjustments in the calculation of the EOCL for a specific skill on a particular project.

References

Bell, C. 1991. "Regional Heterogeneity, Migration, and Shadow Prices", *Journal of Public Economics* 46(1), 1–27.

Bicak, H.A., G.P. Jenkins, C.Y. Kuo, and M.B. Mphahlele. 2004. "An Operational Guide to the Estimation of the Economic Opportunity Cost of Labour in South Africa", *South African Journal of Economics* 72(5), 1057–1068.

Boadway, R.W. and F. Flatters. 1981. "The Efficiency Basis for Regional Employment Policy", *Canadian Journal of Economics* 14(1), 58–77.

Edwards, A.C. 1989. "Labor Supply Price, Market Wage, and the Social Opportunity Cost of Labor", *Economic Development and Cultural Change* 38(1), 31–43.

Gemmel, N. and I. Papps. 1991. "The Shadow Wage in Economies with Migrant Labor: The Case of Labor as a Traded Good", *The Manchester School* 60(1).

Gupta, M.R. 1988. "Migration, Welfare, Inequality and Shadow Wage", *Oxford Economic Papers* 40(3), 477–486.

Harberger, A.C. 1971. "On Measuring the Social Opportunity Cost of Labor", *International Labor Review* 103(6), 449–479.

— 1980. "The Social Opportunity Cost of Labor: Problems of Concept and Measurement as Seen from a Canadian Perspective", *Report for the Canadian Immigration and Employment Commission, Task Force on Labor Markets.* Ottawa.

Harris, J.R. and M.P. Todaro. 1970. "Migration, Unemployment, and Development", *American Economic Review* 60(1), 126–142.

Heady, C.J. 1981. "Shadow Wages and Induced Migration", *Oxford Economic Papers* 33(1), 108–121.

Jenkins, G.P. and M.B. El-Hifnawi. 1993. *Economic Parameters for the Appraisal of Investment Projects: Bangladesh, Indonesia and the Philippines*, report Prepared for Economics and Development Resource Center. Manila: Asian Development Bank (December).

Jenkins, G.P. and C.Y. Kuo. 1978. "On Measuring the Social Opportunity Cost of Permanent and Temporary Employment", *Canadian Journal of Economics* 11(2), 220–239.

Jenkins, G.P. and C. Montmarquette. 1979. "Estimating the Private and Social Opportunity Cost of Displaced Workers", *The Review of Economics and Statistics* 61(3), 342–353.

Little, I.M.D. and J.A. Mirrlees. 1974. *Project Appraisal and Planning for Developing Countries.* London: Heinemann Educational Books.

Marglin, S.A. 1979. *Value and Price in the Labor-Surplus Economy.* Oxford: Clarendon Press.

Sah, R.K. and J.E. Stiglitz. 1985. "The Social Cost of Labor and Project Evaluation: A General Approach", *Journal of Public Economics* 28(2), 135–163.

Todaro, M.P. 1989. *Economic Development in the Third World*, 4th edition. New York: Longman, 62–113.

Chapter Thirteen

Evaluation of Stakeholder Impacts

13.1 Introduction

The social analysis of a project can be carried out in two ways. One is to estimate how the income changes caused by the project are distributed, a method known as distributive analysis. This includes the reconciliation of financial, economic, and distributional appraisals. It also identifies the impact of the project on the principal objectives of the society concerned. This chapter covers the way in which the benefits and costs associated with a project are distributed among different stakeholder groups.

A distributive analysis of a project asks the following questions: Who will benefit from the project and by how much? Who will pay for the project, and how much will they pay? The sustainability of any project is heavily impacted by which parties in the project's sphere of influence gain or lose because of it. If an influential group is expected to bear the burden of losses, then the successful implementation of the project may be hindered. The risk of a strong political opposition to the project being mobilized by the losing party is a contingency that the project's implementers should be prepared to tackle.

Another aspect of the social analysis is concerned with how the project will help or hinder society to address its basic needs. For example, a road project may not only reduce transportation costs, but also increase the level of security in a village, or allow more children to attend school, both of which are viewed positively by society. In such cases, society may want to credit an extra net benefit (a social externality) to the project. This basic needs externality will be dealt with in Chapter 14.

This chapter begins with a discussion of distributive analysis and the impact of a project on poverty alleviation. It is followed by the description of the methodology for reconciling economic and financial values in different cases. These include: a) the case of a major expansion in the supply of a non-traded good in an undistorted market, b) the case of a non-traded good sold to a market with a unit tax, and c) the case of an importable input that is subject to a tariff. The next section provides an illustration of integrated financial, economic, and distributional analysis using three cases — a workers' transportation project, a tomato paste production project, and the Jamuna Bridge project in Bangladesh. Concluding remarks are made in the final section.

13.2 Nature of Distributive Analysis

A traditional financial analysis examines the financial feasibility of a project from the owners' perspective and the total investment point of view. Economic analysis evaluates the project's feasibility in terms of the whole country or economy. A positive economic net present value (NPV) implies a positive change in the wealth of the country, while a positive financial NPV from the point of view of any particular stakeholder group indicates a positive expected change in the wealth of that group's members.

The difference between the financial and economic values of an input or output of a project represents a benefit or a cost that accrues to some party other than the financial sponsors of the project. Such differences can be analysed by undertaking a distributive analysis, which allocates these externalities (differences between economic and financial values) to the various parties affected. For example, a project that causes the price of a good to fall will create economic benefits that are greater than its financial revenues. This difference between the financial and economic values will represent a gain to the consumers of the output and a loss to the other producers of the good or service who are competing in the market with the project. The differences between the financial and economic values of other inputs and outputs may also arise as a result of a variety of market distortions, such as taxes and subsidies, or because the item sold to consumers is at a price that is different from the marginal economic cost of additional supply.

Tariffs, export taxes, sales and excise taxes, production subsidies, and quantitative restrictions create common market externalities. Public goods are normally provided at prices different from their marginal economic costs. The economic values of common public services such as clean water and electricity are the maximum amounts people are willing to pay for these services. These values are often significantly higher than the financial prices people are required to pay for the services. Any of these factors will create divergences between the financial and economic prices of goods and services consumed or produced by a project.

A distributive analysis is composed of six distinct steps:

1. Identify the externalities.
2. Measure the net impact of the externalities in each market as the real economic values of resource flows minus the real financial values of resource flows.
3. Measure the values of the various externalities throughout the life of the project and calculate their present values using the economic opportunity cost of capital (EOCK).
4. Allocate the externalities across the various stakeholders of the project.
5. Summarize the distribution of the project's externalities and net benefits according to the key stakeholders in society.

6.   Reconcile the economic and financial resource flow statements with the distributional impacts.

In essence, a distributive analysis seeks to allocate the net benefits/losses generated by a project. Such an analysis is important to decision-makers as it allows them to estimate the impact of particular projects on segments of society, and to predict which groups will be net beneficiaries and which will be net losers.

For example, a project is especially designed to address poverty alleviation.[86] When the project reduces the price of a good or service, the demanders of the output can acquire the good at a lower price. The net benefit will be identified and quantified in the distributive analysis. If the poor are the demanders, this project will have a poverty alleviation impact. In the case of water, the willingness of the poor to pay water vendors is often fairly high because water is a necessity. Often the poor, with limited access to water, are paying more than the better-off demanders for marginal supplies of water. Thus, a new project that increases the supply of potable water may end up providing it at a lower price for everyone. But the benefit brought by this lower price may be deemed to be greater to the degree that it accrues to the poorer strata of the society, thus contributing to poverty alleviation. In order to be able to quantify this impact, it is necessary to evaluate the differences between the economic value and financial cost of the water being demanded by the various income groups.

Another channel through which a project can have an impact on the incidence of poverty is the labour market. When the lower-income groups sell their services to projects that pay a wage rate significantly above the workers' supply prices for their labour, they are likely to be made better off by the project. The difference between the supply price of labour and the financial wage paid by the project will be measured as an externality, and this can be allocated according to the various income groups to determine whether the project has a direct impact on poverty alleviation.

13.3 Reconciliation of Economic and Financial Values of Project Inputs and Outputs

When the economic and corresponding financial values of variables are expressed in terms of the same numeraire, we wish to show for each variable that the economic value can be expressed as the sum of its financial value and the total of the externalities that cause the financial and economic values to differ.[87] These externalities may be reflecting things such as taxes, subsidies, changes in consumer and producer surplus, or public good externalities.

---

[86]This issue has been identified as a major reason for development assistance by the World Bank. See Wolfensohn (1997).

[87]Details of various cases can be found in Harberger (1987).

If each of the variables is discounted using any common discount rate (in this case, the EOCK), it must be the case that the NPV of the economic net benefits is equal to the NPV of the financial net cash flows plus the present value of the externalities. This relationship can be expressed as shown in equation (13.1):

$$NPV^e = NPV^f + \sum PV(EXT_i) \tag{13.1}$$

where NPV^e is the NPV of the economic net benefits, NPV^f is the NPV of the financial net cash flows, and $\sum PV(EXT_i)$ is the sum of the present value of all the externalities generated by the project; all are discounted using the same EOCK.

The following cases illustrate how this relationship holds for non-tradable and tradable goods.

13.3.1 Expansion in the Supply of a Non-tradable Good in an Undistorted Market

Figure 13.1 illustrates the market for a good that is the output of a project. The project results in an increase in the supply of a non-tradable good in a market with no tax or subsidy distortions. One example would be a project that increases the supply of drinking water at a lower cost, hence expanding total consumption while also reducing the quantity generated by higher-cost plants.

Figure 13.1: Financial and Economic Values for Production of a Non-tradable Good

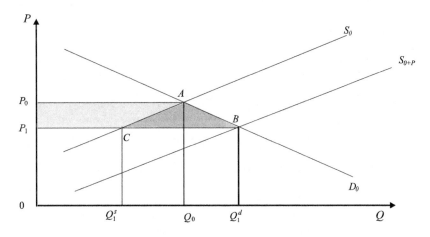

Before the project is introduced, the equilibrium price and quantity are P_0 and Q_0, respectively. P_0 represents the price paid for drinking water prior to the project. Introducing the project causes the supply curve to shift to the right. The price falls to P_1, which is the price of drinking water after the project; total demand increases to Q_1^d, and the quantity supplied by others is reduced to Q_1^s. The financial value of the output is $Q_1^s CBQ_1^d$, and the economic value is $Q_1^s CABQ_1^d$. The difference between the economic and financial values is CAB, which is the sum of two distributional impacts: the demanders' gain, $P_0 ABP_1$, and other producers' loss, $P_0 ACP_1$.

In summary, when there are no distortions in a market, the gross value of a non-tradable good or service from a project that causes a change in the price of the good or service can be disaggregated as follows:

Economic value of output   = financial value of output
                                  + gain in consumer surplus
                                  − loss in producer surplus

While the example assumes that there is a market-determined price before and after the project, this could just as easily be an illustration of a public service, such as a road, before and after it has undergone a major improvement. In such a case, P_0 would reflect the time and operation costs (per vehicle-mile) before the project, and P_1 would be the sum of these costs per vehicle-mile after the project.

13.3.2 Non-tradable Good Sold into a Market with a Unit Tax[88]

In this case, a distortion is introduced into the market. Figure 13.2 demonstrates the case of a non-tradable good with a unit tax. As a result of the unit tax, the demand curve facing the producer will shift downward to D_n. Before the project is introduced to the market, the equilibrium quantity is Q_0, the supply price is P_0^s, and the demand price is P_0^d, which is equal to the supply price plus the unit tax. Following the introduction of the project, the quantity demanded increases to Q_1^d, the quantity supplied by producers other than the project falls to Q_1^s, and the supply and demand prices fall to P_1^s and P_1^d, respectively. The financial value of the output is shown as $Q_1^s CBQ_1^d$. The economic value is shown as $Q_1^s CAQ_0$, the value of resources saved through the contraction or postponement

---

[88]The illustration in this case is for a unit tax, but the same results also hold for an ad valorem tax imposed on goods or services.

of supply by others, in addition to ($Q_0 ABQ_1^d + AEFB$), which is the value to consumers of the increase in the quantity demanded.

Figure 13.2: Financial and Economic Values for Production of a Non-tradable Good with a Unit Tax

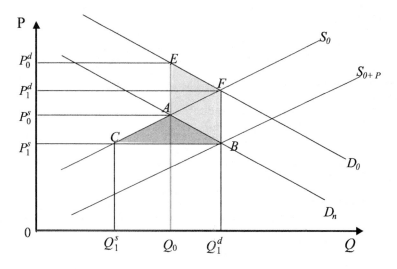

The difference between the economic and financial appraisal of the project's output in this case is equal to ($CAB + AEFB$). Here again, CAB represents the gain in consumer surplus $P_1^d P_0^d EF$ minus the loss in producer surplus $P_1^s P_0^s AC$. This is easy to see in the case of a unit tax because ($P_0^s - P_1^s$) must equal ($P_0^d - P_1^d$). Hence, the area $P_1^d P_0^d EF$ must equal $P_1^s P_0^s AB$.

The area $AEFB$ is equal to $T(Q_1^d - Q_0)$, where T stands for a unit tax, or the net gain in government revenue that results from the increased demand. The gross economic value of the output is therefore equal to the financial value ($Q_1^s CBQ_1^d$) plus the change in government tax revenues ($EFBA$) plus the increase in the consumer surplus ($P_0^d EFP_1^d$ or $P_0^s ABP_1^s$) minus the loss in producer surplus ($P_0^s ACP_1^s$). Consumers gain as a result of the lower price of the good. Producers lose because of the fall in price and reduced production, and the government collects more tax revenues because of the expansion in the quantity demanded as a result of the lower price.

In summary, when the market is distorted only by a unit tax, the gross economic value of the output of a project can be expressed as:

Economic value of output	= financial value of output
	+ change in government tax revenues
	+ increases in consumer surplus
	− loss in producer surplus

13.3.3 Importable Input Subject to Tariff

Figure 13.3 illustrates the case of an importable good for which the inputs are subject to a tariff at a rate of t. The price of cost, insurance, and freight (CIF) is P^w, and the domestic price is $P^w(1+t)$. The initial market equilibrium is found at the domestic price of $P^w(1+t)$, where the quantity demanded is Q_1^d and the quantity supplied by domestic producers is Q_1^s. The quantity imported is ($Q_1^d - Q_1^s$). A new project now demands an additional quantity of this item as input. This addition to demand is shown as a shift in the market-demand curve from D_0 to D_{0+P}.

Because it is an importable good, this increase in demand will lead to an equal increase in the quantity of the item imported of ($Q_2^d - Q_1^d$). The financial cost of the additional imports is $P^w(1+t)(Q_2^d - Q_1^d)$, while the economic cost is $P^w(Q_2^d - Q_1^d)(E^e / E^m)$, where E^e is the economic exchange rate and E^m is the financial market exchange rate.

The difference between the economic and financial costs of the importable good can be expressed as:

$$[(E^e / E^m) - 1] P^w(Q_2^d - Q_1^d) - tP^w(Q_2^d - Q_1^d).$$

The first term of this expression is the rate of foreign exchange premium (FEP), $[(E^e / E^m) - 1]$, multiplied by the cost of the inputs purchased at world prices, P^w. This measures the externality, usually the tariff and other tax revenues forgone, from the use of foreign exchange to purchase the input. The tariff and taxes would have been paid if the foreign exchange required for this purchase had been used to purchase other imports. The second expression is the tariff revenues paid by the project when it imports these inputs.

Figure 13.3: Measuring the Financial and Economic Values of Inputs with Tariffs

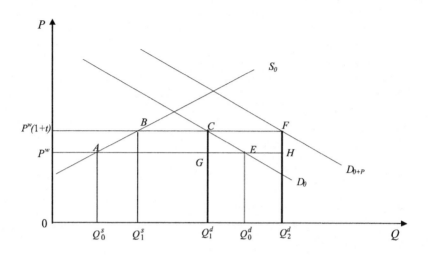

The net distributional impact on the government is the difference between the two effects. The government gains revenue as a result of the imposition of the tariff on the imported good in question, while it loses because the foreign exchange would otherwise have yielded some tariff revenues elsewhere. These losses are captured by the FEP, $[(E^e / E^m) - 1]$.

In summary, for the case of an importable good subject to a tariff, the economic cost of the item can be expressed as follows:

Economic cost of importable input = financial cost
            − gain to government from tariff revenues paid on purchase of item
            + loss in government revenues as a result of FEP on foreign exchange used to purchase this input

13.4 Case Illustrations of Integrated Financial, Economic, and Distributional Analysis

If each of the values for the input and output variables that make up a project are broken down into their economic, financial, and distributional components, the result can be expressed as in equation (13.1), where the economic NPV is equal to the NPV of the financial outcome of the project plus the present value of a series of distributional impacts on the various stakeholders of the project. The three projects described below illustrate the use of distributional analysis in determining the ultimate outcome of a project.

Chapter Thirteen 337

The three cases illustrate the way in which stakeholder impacts are estimated. The output of an integrated analysis identifies the key stakeholders to determine whether the project promoters are likely to face difficulties in project implementation, whether the authorities are likely to be pressured to accept a bad project, and whether the project is likely to face risks to its future sustainability. Identifying the stakeholders and the ways in which they are affected will produce project-specific results. However, the economic analysis of what affects the economic values of inputs and outputs will provide the basic data for estimating the specific stakeholder impacts. For each of the cases there is a financial cash flow table, an economic resource flow table, and a table of externalities for illustrative purposes.

13.4.1 Case A: Workers' Transportation Project

Suppose a public enterprise is considering the purchase of a bus to transport its low-wage workers to and from work. The enterprise is located far away from the residential areas and, as a result, is having difficulty recruiting workers.

a) Basic Facts about the Workers' Transportation Project

- The factory currently employs 20 workers.
- Workers currently use taxis at a cost of $1 each way, to and from the factory.
- The factory wants to employ a total of 40 workers, but cannot recruit any additional workers without either subsidizing transportation or paying higher wages.
- In order to attract the additional 20 workers that the enterprise wants to employ, it will have to either pay the workers more or provide a bus, for which the workers would be charged only $0.40 per trip.
- The proposal is to import a bus at a cost of $50,000. This price consists of the CIF price of $40,000 plus a tariff of 25 percent. The bus is expected to have a residual "in-use" value of $20,000 in Year 5.
- The bus will operate for 250 days per year.
- It will be necessary to employ a driver to operate and maintain the bus at a wage of $20 per day. No taxes would be paid by the driver, but it is estimated that the economic opportunity cost of employing the driver is equal to approximately 80 percent of his or her wage.
- The cost of oil and gas will be $4 per day. The conversion factor for oil and gas is estimated to be 0.60 because of the high taxes imposed on their purchase price.
- The spare parts bill is expected to be $200 per year. The tariff and taxes on spare parts are equal to 25 percent of their CIF price. The spare parts conversion factor is thus 0.80.
- The ratio of the economic exchange rate to the market exchange rate is 1.

- No income taxes are levied on the income of this public enterprise.
- The financial cost of capital to the public enterprise is 6 percent, and the EOCK is 10 percent.

b) Project Outcome

A financial, economic, and distributive appraisal of the project is conducted to determine whether the project is feasible financially and economically, and who would gain from the investment. The first step is the financial appraisal, in which the financial cash flow from the total investment point of view is compiled (see Table 13.1). The company will obtain receipts of $8,000 per year as a result of running the bus service. This is calculated by multiplying together the price to be charged ($0.40), the number of workers who will be transported per day (40), the number of trips per day (2), and the days of operation per year (250). The final in-use value of the bus ($20,000) is given in the problem. The cash inflow over the five-year period consists of the annual receipts plus the final in-use value of the bus.

Table 13.1: Financial Cash Flow for Workers' Transportation Project (dollars in Year 0)

	NPV @ 10%	Year 0	Year 1	Year 2	Year 3	Year 4	Year 5
Cash inflow							
Receipts	33,359	8,000	8,000	8,000	8,000	8,000	
Final in-use value	12,418						20,000
Total cash inflow	45,777	8,000	8,000	8,000	8,000	8,000	20,000
Cash outflow							
Capital expenditures							
- Bus purchase	40,000	40,000					
- Tariff on bus	10,000	10,000					
Operating expenses							
- Labour	20,849	5,000	5,000	5,000	5,000	5,000	
- Fuel	4,170	1,000	1,000	1,000	1,000	1,000	
- Spare parts	834	200	200	200	200	200	
Total cash outflow	75,853	56,200	6,200	6,200	6,200	6,200	
Net cash inflow	−30,076	48,200	1,800	1,800	1,800	1,800	20,000
NPV financial @ 6%	−27,018						

The financial cost of the bus is the $40,000 CIF price plus the $10,000 tariff charge. The cost of employing the worker to operate and maintain the bus is $20 per day. Multiplying this sum by the 250 days of operation per year gives $5,000 as the annual cost of operating labour. Fuel costs are obtained by multiplying the $4 per day charge by the 250 days, which gives $1,000 per year. The $200 annual cost of spare parts was given in the problem. Adding up these items produces the cash outflow for each of the five years. The net cash flow is obtained by subtracting the cash outflow from the cash inflow.

The present value of inflows, outflows, and net cash flows is obtained by discounting the respective items. The NPV of the project will be required at both the financial and economic discount rates in order for the distributive analysis to be undertaken. Therefore, both these amounts are calculated as part of the financial appraisal. The financial NPV at the financial discount rate of 6 percent is −$27,018, and the financial NPV at the economic discount rate of 10 percent is −$30,076. Note that the financial NPV at the economic discount rate is a larger negative number because the economic discount rate is higher than the financial discount rate.

The second step in the analysis is the economic appraisal, represented by the economic resource statement, as shown in Table 13.2. The economic value of the bus service to the workers is a combination of the economic benefit to previous workers plus the economic benefit to new workers. The 20 existing workers were willing to pay $1 for a one-way trip. Therefore, their economic benefit from the bus service is the same as it was previously. This amount is obtained by multiplying together the price ($1), the number of trips per day (2), the number of existing workers (20), and the number of working days per year (250), to give a total of $10,000.[89]

Table 13.2: Economic Resource Statement for Workers' Transportation Project (dollars in Year 0)

	CF*	PV @ 10%	Year 0	Year 1	Year 2	Year 3	Year 4	Year 5
Economic benefits								
Receipts	2.125	70,887	17,000	17,000	17,000	17,000	17,000	
Final in-use value	0.8	9,935	0	0	0	0	0	16,000
Total benefits	-	80,822	17,000	17,000	17,000	17,000	17,000	16,000
Economic costs								
Capital expenditures								
- Bus purchase	1.0	40,000	40,000					
- Tariff on bus	0	0	0					
Operating expenses								
- Labour	0.8	16,679	4,000	4,000	4,000	4,000	4,000	0
- Fuel	0.6	2,502	600	600	600	600	600	0
- Spare parts	0.8	667	160	160	160	160	160	0
Total costs	-	59,848	44,760	4,760	4,760	4,760	4,760	0
Net economic benefits	-	20,974	−27,760	12,240	12,240	12,240	12,240	16,000

*Conversion factor.

The value of the bus trip to the new workers varies. Some on the margin would have taken the trip if the price charged had been $0.99, while at the other end of the scale, some would not have taken the trip at a price of $0.41. In order to take all the new workers into account, a weighted average of their valuations is taken to find the average price that these workers would have been willing to pay. Assuming a linear (rectangular) distribution of demand prices of these new workers, this amounts to $0.70 per trip (($1.00 + $0.40)/2). Therefore, the benefit to the additional workers of the bus service is calculated by multiplying together the price of $0.70, the number of daily trips (2), the number of new workers (20),

---

[89]Existing workers' benefit is a cash saving of $0.60 per trip per individual; hence, the total saving for all workers is $6,000 per year.

Evaluation of Stakeholder Impacts

and the 250 days of operation, which gives a total of $7,000.[90] Adding up the economic benefit to previous workers ($10,000) and the economic benefit to additional workers ($7,000) gives us $17,000 as the gross economic benefit of the bus service.

The residual value of the bus in economic terms is $16,000. This is because the tariff has to be allocated to the entire life of the bus. Therefore, the residual tariff value of $4,000 has to be subtracted from the financial final in-use value of the bus of $20,000.[91] By the same token, the CIF price of the bus ($40,000) is the same from the financial and economic points of view. The tariff paid on the bus is only a transfer of income from the enterprise to the government, and it is thus not included in the economic appraisal.

The economic value of labour is 80 percent of its financial value. This means that labour has a shadow price that is 80 percent of its private opportunity cost. Therefore, the economic value of labour is $4,000 per year. Fuel has a conversion factor of 0.6, so the economic price of the fuel is $600. The difference between the financial and economic prices of fuel is due to taxes that were paid on the purchase of fuel. These taxes are a transfer within the economy and are therefore not accounted for in the economic appraisal. The 0.8 conversion factor for spare parts is multiplied by the financial value ($200) to give the economic value of $160. Here again, the difference between financial and economic values can be attributed to taxes paid.

Subtracting the economic costs from the economic benefits yields the economic net benefits. Discounting these values using the economic cost of capital gives $20,974 as the present value of net economic benefits.

The final step is an appraisal of the distributional effects of the project, as presented in Table 13.3. The distributive appraisal looks at net transfers in the economy as a result of the project. The object is to determine how the net benefits of having the bus service are distributed among the various participants. In this case, the relevant impacts are on the government, the consumers (i.e., the workers who will use the service to travel to and from work), and the labour that will be hired to operate the bus. First, the present value of net benefits to consumers is calculated, which is the same as saying that the change in consumer surplus is being determined. It should be remembered that the formula developed earlier requires that the present value of externalities at the economic discount rate be obtained. To calculate the present value of this benefit it is necessary to subtract the financial receipts ($8,000) from the economic receipts ($17,000) for each of the five years, giving a result of $9,000 per year. Discounting this cash

---

[90]Consumer surplus to new workers is equal to the amount by which $7,000 exceeds $4,000, i.e., $3,000 per year.

[91]A conversion factor of 0.8 was used to calculate the final economic in-use value of the bus. This conversion factor was calculated by dividing the economic value of the bus by its financial value (i.e., CF = 40,000/50,000). Since the difference between the financial and economic value is $4,000, we know that this is the residual tariff value.

flow stream using the economic cost of capital gives a present value of $37,528. This positive externality goes to bus riders.

Table 13.3: Allocation of Net Benefits for Workers' Transportation Project (dollars in Year 0)

	Sum of Total Externalities	Government	Workers	Driver
Benefits				
Receipts	37,528		37,528	
Final in-use values	−2,484	−2,484		
Total benefits	35,044			
Costs				
Expenditures				
- Bus purchase				
- Tariff on bus	10,000	10,000		
Operating expenses				
- Driver	4,170			4,170
- Fuel	1,668	1,668		
- Spare parts	167	167		
Total costs	16,005			
Net resource flows	51,050	9,351	37,528	4,170

The transfer to the government of tariff revenue from the bus purchase is $10,000 in Year 0. However, in Year 5 the project effectively releases the bus back into the economy and recaptures $20,000, but the economy values the bus at only $16,000. This increase in the value of the bus to the economy causes a loss of tariff revenue to the government that has a present value of −$2,484. Therefore, the net tariff revenue received by the government is calculated by subtracting $2,484, the loss in tariff revenues in Year 5, from the $10,000 received in Year 0.

The transfer to labour (the bus driver) is calculated in the same way as the calculation of the present value of net benefits to consumers. The economic wage received ($4,000) is subtracted from the financial wage ($5,000) for each of the five years. Discounting this cash flow at the 10 percent economic discount rate gives a present value of $4,170. This is a positive transfer to labour, since it was included in the financial costs, but not in the economic costs.

There is also a transfer to the government as a result of taxes paid on the purchase of fuel and spare parts. In both these cases, the economic costs are lower than the financial costs. The difference between the financial and economic costs of fuel is $400 per year. The present value of this stream is $1,668. The difference for spare parts is $40 per year. This cash flow stream has a present value of $167.

To determine the overall distributive impact of the project we need to calculate the net effects on each of the affected groups. Adding up the impacts on the government shows that it gains $9,352 as a result of the project. The workers who will use the bus gain $37,528, and the labour hired to operate the bus gains $4,170. The sum of these externalities is $51,050.

c) Reconciliation of the Project

Using equation (13.1), the previous tables can be summarized as follows:

$$NPV^e = NPV^f + \sum PV(EXT_i)$$

$$20,974 = -30,076 + 51,050$$

From the point of view of the bus company, this is an unfavourable project, though it appears to be favourable economically. The decision on whether or not to pursue a project where the financial and economic appraisals produce such different results will depend on whether or not there are ways to make the project attractive. It may be that the value of the marginal product of the additional workers is sufficiently greater than the wage they are paid to make it attractive for the factory owner to underwrite the financial losses of the bus. Alternatively, the government may levy taxes on the whole community to subsidize the operation of the bus because of the distributional benefits the workers who now obtain this service will receive.

13.4.2 Case B: Tomato Paste Production Project

This is a project undertaken in the Philippines that appears attractive on the basis of the results of the integrated financial and economic analysis. The plant was built in a rural area that has a suitable climate for growing tomatoes. A co-operative of small farmers was organized to grow the tomatoes under contract with the processing plant. The financial and economic analysis shows that the economic NPV of the project is much higher than its financial NPV. The stakeholder analysis indicates that the government, the farmers, and the domestic consumers will be the main beneficiaries of this project.

a) Basic Facts about the Tomato Paste Production Project

The main features of the project are summarized below:

- The tomato paste project has an economic life of 15 years. The project is able to produce 20,200 tons of tomato paste per year. Under a contractual arrangement with the plant, 3,000 farmers are organized into co-operatives for the supply of fresh tomatoes to the plant; supply will reach about 109,000 tons at the peak of the plant's production.

- The project mainly targets the domestic market. The demand for tomato paste was projected to grow at a rate of 7.7 percent during the coming ten years. Part of the project's output is exported. Exports were expected to vary from 46 to 20 percent of the total sales from 2003 to 2010 and progressively decline to a level of about 3.5 percent of the total production in later years, as domestic consumption increased.
- At the production output level of 20,200 tons per year, the project will cause the tomato paste to shift from the import to the export category. This in turn will cause its internal price to be determined by its free on board (FOB) price instead of its CIF price plus tariff and transport costs.
- The project cost was estimated at $22 million, with a foreign exchange component of $9.2 million.
- The project's main items of expenditure are raw tomatoes, direct labour, energy, processing overhead costs, packaging materials, selling and administrative expenses, maintenance, and staff costs. The project employs 370 permanent staff, plus temporary staff during the high season. Payroll costs are the most significant component of the project's operating costs.
- The tomato paste plant will enjoy a six-year tax holiday and then be subject to income taxation.
- The financial real cost of capital was estimated to be 10 percent.
- The economic benefits of the project's output fall into four categories:
  o the economic benefits of the quantity exported, which include:
    - the FOB value of the exports, plus
    - the FEP on the FOB value, minus
    - the transportation costs from the factory to the port;
  o the benefits of additional consumption by the new domestic consumers;
  o the benefit of the reduction in quantity imported, which is the benefit of import substitution; its economic value equals the CIF value of the previously imported quantity, plus the FEP, minus the transportation costs from the factory to the port;
  o the benefits of the cutback in production by other producers, which are the savings in production inputs or resource savings for the economy.
- The market exchange rate is 45 pesos per US dollar.
- The FEP is assumed to be 6 percent of the financial cost of foreign exchange.
- The EOCK is assumed to be 11 percent real.

b) Project Outcome

Tables 13.4, 13.5, and 13.6 summarize the financial, economic, and distributive analysis of this project. The economic outcome of the project is reconciled with the financial outcome and the expected distributional impact. All values in these tables are expressed in real pesos.

As shown in Table 13.4, the financial NPV discounted at a 10 percent rate is 74.6 million pesos. The cash flow after the project was built was projected to be positive in 2002 and to continue to be positive through to the end of the project in 2017. All cash flow values presented in the table below are expressed in real prices at the price level of 2000.

Table 13.4: Financial Cash Flow for the Tomato Paste Production Project (million pesos, in 2000 prices)

Category	2000	2001	2002	2003	...2007	...2012	...2017
Revenue							
Net sales							
- Domestic			74.45	92.00	158.06	189.86	16.44
- Exports			0.00	84.60	41.14	7.76	0.00
Change in accounts receivable			−6.20	−8.97	−1.20	−1.20	15.25
Leasing receipts			4.85	4.85	0.00	0.00	0.00
Salvage value							6.27
Total cash inflow			73.10	172.45	198.00	196.42	37.96
Investment cost							
Project cost	145.55	80.20					
Initial working capital							
Cash balance		6.50					
Advances to farmers		58.40					
Operating costs							
Raw tomatoes			28.55	78.95	85.60	85.60	
Direct labour			0.35	1.00	1.15	1.25	
Energy			4.60	12.75	13.80	13.80	
Processing overhead costs			0.90	2.50	2.70	2.70	
Packaging materials			6.25	18.35	10.50	4.85	
Selling and administrative expenses			13.50	16.45	16.45	16.45	
Change in accounts payable			−2.45	−4.55	−0.40	−0.50	6.00
Change in cash held as working capital			1.05	10.00	0.95	1.15	−14.45
Change in advances to farmers							−17.05
Corporate income tax						25.20	2.85
Total cash outflow	145.55	145.05	52.76	135.40	130.74	150.53	−22.64
Net cash flow	−145.55	−145.05	20.35	37.05	67.26	45.87	60.60
NPV financial @ 10%	74.60						
NPV financial @ 11%	52.14						

It can be seen from Table 13.5 that the economic appraisal of the project indicates that the project is favourable for the country. The NPV of the economic benefits is 372.37 million pesos, discounted at a real economic cost of capital of 11 percent. From an economic point of view, this project is expected to contribute positively to the overall welfare of the economy.

Table 13.5: Economic Resource Statement for the Tomato Paste Production Project (million pesos, in 2000 prices)

Category	CF*	2000	2001	2002	2003	...2007	...2012	...2017
Revenue								
Net sales								
Domestic	0.884			65.86				
Domestic and exports	1.081				190.89	215.35	213.63	17.76
Change in accounts receivable	1.081			−6.70	−9.69	−1.28	−1.31	16.50
Leasing receipts	1.000			4.85	4.85			
Salvage value	1.112							6.45
Total economic benefits				63.99	186.04	214.04	212.31	40.71
Investment cost								
Project cost	1.029	149.77	82.52					
Initial working capital								
- Cash balance	1.000		6.50					
- Advances to farmers	1.000		58.40					
Operating costs								
Raw tomatoes	0.651			18.56	51.36	55.69	55.69	
Direct labour	1.000			0.35	1.00	1.15	1.25	
Energy	1.070			4.92	13.63	14.78	14.78	
Processing overhead costs	1.009			0.91	2.52	2.72	2.72	
Packaging materials	0.817			5.11	14.98	8.56	3.95	
Selling and administrative expenses	1.000			13.5	16.45	16.45	16.45	
Change in accounts payable	0.727			−1.70	−3.30	−0.29	−0.35	4.37
Change in cash held as working capital	1.000			1.05	10.00	0.95	1.15	−14.45
Change in advances to farmers	1.000							−17.05
Corporate income tax								
Total economic costs		149.77	147.38	42.64	106.61	100.00	95.68	−27.10
Net economic benefits		−149.77	−147.38	21.35	79.43	114.03	116.62	67.81
NPV economic @ 11%		372.37						

*Conversion factor.

c) Allocation of Externalities among Stakeholders

Table 13.6 shows the distributional impacts of this project. The values in this table are calculated by taking the differences between the economic values and their financial values. These differences are obtained by subtracting the present value of the rows in Table 13.4 (financial appraisal from total investment point of view) from the corresponding present values of the rows in Table 13.5 (economic appraisal) and separating the differences into the various distributional impacts (among the main stakeholders). The NPV discounted at the economic cost of capital of the externalities generated by the project is 320.23 million pesos.

Table 13.6: Allocation of Net Benefits for the Tomato Paste Production Project (million pesos, in 2000 prices)

Category	Sum of Total Externalities	Govt.	Farmers	Consumers	Existing Producers
Benefits					
Net sales					
- Domestic in 2002	−6.99	−6.99			
- Domestic and exports (2003–17)	90.08	51.21		56.01	−17.14
Change in accounts receivable	−1.31	−1.31			
Leasing receipts					
Salvage value	0.03	0.03			
Total benefits	81.81	42.94		56.01	−17.14
Investment cost					
Project cost	6.36	−6.36			
Initial working capital					
- Cash balance					
- Advances to farmers					
Operating costs					
Raw tomatoes	175.87		175.87		
Direct labour					
Energy	−5.68	−5.68			
Processing overhead costs	−0.14	−0.14			
Packaging materials	11.78	11.78			
Selling and administrative expenses					
Change in accounts payable	−1.82	−1.82			
Change in cash held as working capital					
Change in advances to farmers					
Corporate income tax	64.78	64.78			
Total costs	238.42	62.54	175.87		
Stakeholder impacts	320.23	105.48	175.87	56.00	−17.14

These externalities can be summarized as follows:

- The farmers will realize an additional income of 175.87 million pesos, which is the difference between the price the farmers actually receive and the economic cost of production. This higher income will be earned by the farmers from the prices they will receive for supplying fresh tomatoes to the project.
- The existing tomato paste producers will lose part of the market as a result of a decrease in the tomato paste price in the domestic market. When the project starts selling its product, this will result in a reduction in the price of tomato paste. The fall in the price will create a negative externality on existing producers by making them worse off. Therefore, the existing producers of tomato paste will lose 17.14 million pesos, which is what they would have earned from their production, once the new project entered the market.
- Consumers of tomato paste will realize a positive externality of 56.01 million pesos. This positive net benefit will be generated by the

reduction in the price of tomato paste and hence an increase in consumption by consumers. This is due to the fact that consumers will save money as a result of paying less for the tomato paste, which they previously paid more for, and new consumers (i.e., those who could not afford to buy before) will create additional consumption as a result of the lower price.

- On the one hand, the government will lose VAT and tariff revenue from imports as a result of the import substitution by the consumers. On the other hand, the government will gain positive benefits in the form of the FEP on the foreign exchange generated from additional exports and replaced imports, plus the VAT revenue on the expansion of domestic consumption after the project's introduction. Overall, the government will gain a net benefit of 105.48 million pesos.

d) Reconciliation of the Project

Using equation (13.1), the tables can be summarized as follows:

$$NPV^e = NPV^f + \sum PV(EXT_i)$$

$$372.37 = 52.14 + (105.48 + 175.87 + 56.00 - 17.14)$$

where NPV^f is obtained from Table 13.4 but discounted at the EOCK.

13.4.3 Case C: Jamuna Bridge Project

The Jamuna, the Meghna, and the Padma constitute a system of rivers that physically divides Bangladesh into eastern, southwestern, and northwestern regions. Most of the major centres within each region are connected by road or rail. All the connections between regions depend on the inland waterway transport system. The services provided at the river crossings are of poor quality, are subject to many interruptions owing to the adverse geographical and meteorological conditions, and can involve waiting times of many hours or days for freight traffic. In 1994, the Bangladesh government proposed to build a bridge over the Jamuna River to link eastern and western Bangladesh.[92] The bridge was expected to facilitate economic growth within the country by improving the links between the relatively more developed region east of the Jamuna River and the agricultural region to the west. The project would also allow transmission of electricity and transfer of natural gas between the eastern and the western regions.

---

[92]Detailed analysis can be found in Jenkins and Shukla (1997).

Evaluation of Stakeholder Impacts

a) Basic Facts about the Jamuna Bridge Project

The main features of the project include the following:

- The previous ferry services were poor, threatening the stability of the inter-regional transportation system. The whole ferry system had reached its capacity limits, creating delays ranging from 1–8 hours for light vehicles to 30–40 hours for heavy vehicles.
- The bridge would be about 4.8 km long and 18.5 metres wide to carry four road lanes with pedestrian walkways. Two bridge-end viaducts were to be constructed, each about 128 metres long, connecting the bridge to the approach road.
- The project was expected to cost approximately $696 million, including provision for physical and price contingencies.
- Approximately $600 million in loans was to be given by bilateral and multilateral agencies to the government of Bangladesh at a nominal interest rate of 1 percent. The rest of the financing would be provided as a grant by the government.
- Implementation of the project began in 1996. The project life, for financial and economic evaluation purposes, was considered to be 50 years from 1998, when it opened to traffic.
- The average daily traffic in 1993 on the two relevant crossing channels (Aricha–Nagarbari and Bhuapur–Sirajganj) consisted of 271 buses, 140 light vehicles, and 770 trucks. The average annual growth rate of traffic in the bridge corridor was about 7.5 percent during the period 1986–1993. The annual traffic growth rates from 1993–1998 were estimated at 6.6 percent for buses and trucks and 8.2 percent for light vehicles. From 1998–2025, it was estimated that the bridge traffic would grow at 5 percent per year. It was assumed that there would be no further traffic increases from 2025 until the end of the 50-year period.
- The economic benefits consisted of the savings in vehicle operating costs and reduced waiting times, as well as the willingness to pay (in the form of tolls) on the part of newly generated traffic. Financial revenues would arise from the tolls charged. This bridge would not only facilitate the transport of passengers and freight, but also enable natural gas, electricity, and telecommunication links to be made across the river.
- The FEP was estimated to be 30.4 percent as a result of high tariff rates in Bangladesh (Jenkins and El-Hifnawi, 1993).
- The financial real cost of capital was estimated to be 10 percent, while the EOCK was estimated to be 12.1 percent (Jenkins and El-Hifnawi, 1993).
- As part of the financial and economic analysis, the option of improving the existing ferry service was considered.

b) Project Outcomes

The estimation of the distributional impacts of the Jamuna Bridge project was derived from the financial and economic analysis in the same way as for the tomato paste production project mentioned above. Only a summary of the background analysis for this case will be presented here.

A comparison of the financial profitability of the bridge project (with the specified set of tolls) with the existing ferry system indicated that the financial NPV of the bridge project would be a positive 1.07 billion takas ($27 million).[93]

An economic analysis was performed to determine whether the project would be beneficial to the overall economy of Bangladesh. The analysis revealed that compared to the existing ferry system, the real economic NPV of the bridge project was 7.77 billion takas ($195 million).

When comparing the economic and financial analysis of this project, it was found that the major net beneficiaries were the truck operators, the producers and consumers of cargo, the power company, and the bus passengers. On the other hand, both the government and the aid agencies would lose, as would the ferry operators. Truck operators, shippers, and consumers would realize savings of about 31.09 billion takas, while bus passengers and light vehicle owners and passengers would gain only 1.95 and 0.63 billion takas, respectively. The existing ferry operators would incur a negative financial impact amounting to 1.84 billion takas as the ferry services were replaced by the bridge.

Table 13.7 summarizes the allocation of externalities of this project among stakeholders, all discounted at the EOCK.

Table 13.7: Allocation of Net Benefits for the Jamuna Bridge Project (million takas, in 1994 prices)

Total Net Benefits	Light Vehicles Passengers	Bus Passengers	Truckers, Producers, and Consumers of Cargo	Power Company	Government and Aid Agencies	Locality	Ferry Operators
7,132.3	627.0	1,951.6	31,094.1	2,544.3	−27,700.7	456.9	−1,840.8

c) Reconciliation of the Project

Using equation (13.1), the analysis of this project can be summarized as follows:

$$NPV^e = NPV^f + \sum PV(EXT_i)$$

$$7,774.9 = 642.5 + 7,132.3$$

---

[93]The taka is the unit of currency of Bangladesh. In 1994, the exchange rate was 39.8 takas/US$.

A key feature of this project is the large amount of subsidized financing it received. The distributional analysis shows that as a consequence, the total subsidies amounted, in present value terms, to −27,700 million takas. This is the sum of the interest subsidy on the loan (19,851 million takas), the government grant (2,455 million takas), and the premium lost on the foreign exchange used to purchase tradable goods on the investment cost of the bridge (5,358 million takas).

However, the estimated benefits to truck operators, shippers, and consumers would amount to 31,094 million takas, which is more than the entire investment cost of the bridge.

These results indicate that if a tariff structure were designed that would capture the benefits received by the consumers and producers of the cargo, little or no subsidy would have been needed. Perhaps it would be desirable, for economic development and distributional reasons, to allow the users of the bridge to receive a substantial portion of the benefits from the bridge. However, in a country like Bangladesh there are many pressing social and economic needs that are not being met owing to a scarcity of resources. It is possible that the overall development impact of the $600 million in low-cost loans might have been greater if a somewhat smaller subsidy had been provided to the Jamuna Bridge project. For example, the funds might have been better used to subsidize other public investments, such as education and health, where the application of user fees may be more difficult to implement than in the case of a bridge.

When considering the potential sustainability of this bridge, in terms of maintenance and construction of access roads, it is clear that sufficient funds could be generated by tolls to cover these costs. For this bridge, the maintenance of the river infrastructure and the construction of access roads will be critical for the success of its long-term operation.

13.5 Conclusion

The type of integrated financial, economic, and distributive analysis proposed in this chapter has a number of advantages for evaluating both public and private sector investments. First, it ensures that the economic and financial analyses are carried out in a consistent manner. If the economic and financial analyses are done correctly, the differences will be a series of distributional impacts that can be identified and measured. If the process presented in this chapter is followed, the possibility of error in completing the analysis will be substantially reduced.

Second, the clear identification of the stakeholders and how they will fare as a consequence of a project is a key ingredient in determining the likelihood of its successful implementation, as well as in prompting the authorities to consider redesigning the project so that the impact on stakeholders is more favourable. Although most projects will have negative impacts on some segments of the population, if these are clearly identified and their political strengths assessed, the likelihood of unforeseen challenges and stalled implementation may be substantially reduced.

Third, this analysis can also be used to identify the likely impact that a project will have on the incidence of poverty in particular groups. In the case of the workers' transportation project, the employees who will benefit are likely to be from the lower end of the income distribution. In the case of the tomato paste factory, the major beneficiaries are the farmers who produce the tomatoes. As small-holders, they will tend to be from the poorer segments of society. Likewise, bus passengers, truck operators, producers, and consumers of cargo services have gained substantial benefits from the implementation of the Jamuna Bridge project.

This analysis may not address all the political economy questions relating to what projects should be selected and implemented, but it does at least provide a quantitative basis for making judgments as to the attractiveness of a project, and helps to identify the sources of support and opposition that the project is likely to receive.

If projects are to be sustainable, they should not be subject to continued political pressure for their suspension. The stakeholder analysis, which is undertaken through the comparison of the economic and financial outcomes, provides a clear signal of the groups that are likely to promote, and those that will not support, a project. Through the identification of the fiscal and stakeholder impacts of the project, it is possible to make a more realistic assessment of successful implementation. In addition, if the project inflicts a continuous fiscal drain on the public sector budget, it is likely to be at some risk of losing this financial support in the future. Hence, such subsidies put a project's long-term sustainability at risk.

Appendix 13A: Economic Aspects of Foreign Financing

13A.1 Introduction

Large-scale, capital-intensive projects frequently rely on foreign financing, and, as a result, the foreign-owned segment of many sectors has grown considerably. New projects either reallocate the existing foreign investment within an economy or draw incremental foreign investment into the country. Conventional methodologies for the economic appraisal of projects have usually recommended that the source of the funds used for financing of project, either domestic or foreign, be ignored. This assumption is increasingly being called into question as foreign investors and operators have increasingly dominated the private provision of public services. Many of these build–operate–transfer and build–operate–own contracts are far from being transparent capital market transactions. Hence, the form of any arrangement will have a different economic cost as it involves different flows of resources in and out of the host country. This appendix outlines a methodology for estimating the nature and magnitude of the net economic benefits that may result from the foreign financing of new investments; such net benefits should be included in the overall economic evaluation of a project.

Public concern over foreign ownership has often focused on the issue of possible foreign control of a country's economy and interference with decision-making that would otherwise have been in the domestic economy's best interests.[94] Although the importance of such issues is recognized, the current examination will be limited to estimating the net economic benefits (costs) resulting from changes in the pool of capital resources available to a country owing to the use of foreign financing for the project. Negative political externalities resulting from foreign control could also add to the economic costs arising from changes in foreign investment, as they may cast a shadow over a project that would otherwise have created substantial net economic benefits for the country.

The economic benefits and costs of a project should initially be examined regardless of the source of financing. The EOCK should be used as the economic discount rate for evaluating the economic costs and benefits that accrue to the project over time. The EOCK is the measure of the real opportunity cost of the funds that are drawn out of the pool of capital available to the country to finance investments. This pool of capital will include both domestic and foreign-owned funds.

From a global perspective, if a new investment opportunity is financed from foreign sources, the net economic benefits from the project (discounted by the EOCK) are going to be shared not only by the government (g) and the other

---

[94]For an excellent discussion of some of the historical experience of conflict between foreign investors and sovereign governments, see Wells and Gleason (1995).

residents of the country (p) but also by foreigners (f). Thus, in NPV (NPV^e) terms:

$$NPV^e = B_g + B_p + B_f - C_g - C_p - C_f \qquad (13A.1)$$

where B and C represent gross benefits and costs, respectively. Benefits realized by the government (B_g) take the form of such items as taxes and fees paid to the treasury. Benefits realized by the foreign investors (B_f) comprise the debt-repayment, interest, and dividend payments. B_p denotes the benefits accruing to the non-government sectors of the host country. All values are expressed as present values. Since the intention is to evaluate the economic performance of the project from the perspective of the host country only, it is necessary to adjust the net economic benefits for the benefits and costs realized by foreigners.

However, in order to make this adjustment in the appropriate manner, it is also necessary to ascertain whether the project has simply reallocated the existing foreign capital in the country, or whether it has attracted incremental foreign investment into the country. A normal supply function of foreign financial capital to any country has a finite elasticity. The implication is that the use of foreign-owned capital for a specific project makes additional foreign investment more expensive to attract. Some fraction of the foreign investment for the project will thus result in a move away from foreign financing of other projects, and some fraction is likely to be an incremental addition to the total quantity of foreign financing obtained by the country. The normal cost of these funds as measured by the capital market is included in the EOCK for a country. However, the estimate of the EOCK does not capture the net economic benefits (costs) resulting from foreign investment that arise as a result of the special characteristics of the project and the idiosyncratic nature of the financial agreements that determine the ultimate return to the foreign investors.

13A.2 Measurement of the Benefits from Incremental Foreign Investment

Foreign investment can be considered incremental to a host country when it is specific to a project and when the project would not be undertaken unless the foreign capital was available. Furthermore, the attraction of foreign investment to the project should not affect the ability of the country to service its other foreign-owned financial obligations. This suggests that the project is not available to other foreign investors and that the project itself will generate enough incremental foreign exchange to service this investment. In economic terms, the combination of this project and its funding causes the supply curve of foreign financing to the country to shift by an equal amount to the right. In this sense, foreign financing of the project is incremental to the amount that foreigners would otherwise invest in the host country.

If the foreign investment is incremental, the host country should not be concerned over how much the foreigners put into or take out of the project. However, it should ensure that the resources it employs in the project along with the foreign capital earn an economic rate of return at least as high as they could have earned in alternative uses. This is accomplished by evaluating all resources at their economic opportunity cost and by discounting all relevant costs and benefits by the EOCK. Since our evaluation of a new investment opportunity adopts a host country point of view, we simply want to exclude C_f and B_f from equation (13A.1) by adding $(C_f - B_f)$ to it, as follows:

$$NPV = NPV^e + (C_f - B_f) = B_g + B_p - C_g - C_p \quad (13A.2)$$

Since the incremental foreign capital (C_f) also provides incremental foreign exchange, the additional foreign investment carries an additional premium (FEP) to reflect the difference between the economic opportunity cost of foreign exchange and the market exchange rate (Harberger and Jenkins, 2002; Harberger et al., 2003). By the same token, dividends, interest, and loan repayments made to foreign investors (B_f) entail a loss of foreign exchange, which also results in a loss of the FEP. Foreign owners of the capital in turn do not capture the net foreign exchange externality that accrues to the host country as a result of foreign investment. As the foreign exchange externality from foreign financing is not included in the NPV^e of net benefits from the project, it is necessary to add $(FEP)(C_f - B_f)$ to both sides of equation (13A.2) to yield the adjusted economic NPV (NPV_a^e):

$$NPV_a^e = B_g + B_p - C_g - C_p + (FEP)(C_f - B_f) \quad (13A.3)$$

The total adjustment to equation (13A.1) made necessary by incremental foreign investment, $(1 + FEP)(C_f - B_f)$, will raise or lower the present value of net economic benefits to the host country depending on whether $(1 + FEP)(C_f - B_f)$ is positive or negative. If $B_f > C_f$, for example, the stream of dividends (net of withholding tax) plus interest and debt repayment is sufficient, when discounted at the EOCK, to permit foreigners to recapture their investment and to earn a rate of return greater than the EOCK. The result is that the economic NPV from the point of view of the host country will be less after making the adjustment for the cost of incremental foreign investment than before the adjustment is made. If, after making the adjustment, it is found that the economic NPV (NPV_a^e) is greater than zero, the host country should permit the project. If, on the other hand, NPV_a^e is less than zero, the project is going to make the country worse off, and it should not go ahead.

13A.3 The Benefit from Reallocating Foreign Investment Already Present in the Host Country

As noted above, a normal supply function of foreign financial capital to a host country has a finite elasticity. The previous section adopted the extreme assumption of allowing all the foreign investment for a project to be incremental to the host country. This section deals with the opposite extreme by assuming that foreign investment for a project results only in a reallocation of foreign investment away from other projects in the host country. If it is assumed that the project will go ahead even without the foreign investment, we then need to know whether the country is better off using the foreign capital for this specific project rather than for alternative projects.

When none of the foreign investment for the project is incremental to the host country, but only reallocates the existing pool of foreign capital resources away from other projects, equation (13A.1) must be adjusted in a different fashion. As before, the present value of the benefits foreigners receive from their investment (B_f) is the stream of dividends, interest, and loan repayments, discounted at the EOCK that actually flows from the project. The relevant opportunity cost of the investment for foreigners is the stream of benefits that they would have received from the alternative investment forgone (B_f^a).

The benefit to foreigners from alternative investment in the host country is equal to the present value of the real (net of inflation) returns that these investments would have earned. Since foreign-owned capital is part of the host country's capital stock, it is reasonable to expect that foreign investors would earn a rate of return roughly equal to that earned on the total capital stock in the host country. The private discount rate, which makes the present value of the net-of-tax net cash flow to total capital equal to zero, is denoted by r_f.[95]

In the case in which the foreign investment is non-incremental, a greater-than-normal return to foreigners represents a net cost to the economy. In contrast, a foreign investor may be willing to make an investment and receive a lower-

---

[95]For example, in the Philippines the value of r_f has been estimated to be approximately 9.75 percent (Jenkins and Kuo, 1998).

Evaluation of Stakeholder Impacts

than-normal rate of return (for example, if the investment is of great strategic importance to the firm). In this case, the participation in the financing by this particular foreign investor will increase the economic NPV of the project.

The level of political risk that foreign investors face with a particular project may mean that they will require a higher- or lower- than-normal rate of return from a particular project (Wells and Gleason, 1995). There is strong evidence that foreign investors considering investing in electricity projects in some countries have required higher-than-normal rates of return owing to the perceived political risk they are likely to face in the future with such projects (Jenkins and Lim, 1998). In other cases, foreign investors might face restrictions on the length of the term of debt financing available for a project. This may mean that the price of the project's service has to be set very high initially in order to fulfil the debt service obligations. Over time, the debt will be repaid, but the continuation of such pricing policies might cause the foreign equity holders to earn an extraordinarily high rate of return.

In either of these circumstances, the project might still have a positive economic NPV from the host country's point of view after making the adjustment for the higher-than-usual returns that have to be paid to these particular foreign investors. In such a situation, the host country evaluators of the project should first consider alternative methods of managing the risks, or consider alternative financial structures, before giving final approval to the project.

If by investing in a specific project foreigners earn a real return just equal to the average of r_f, the ratio (Z) of the present value (discounted at r_f) of the stream of foreign equity and debt invested in the project over the present value (discounted at r_f) of the foreign dividends, debt repayment and interest received (equation 13A.4) would equal 1. If this ratio (Z) were greater than 1, foreigners would be earning less than an r_f return by investing in the project; if the ratio were less than 1, then foreigners would be earning more than an r_f real return.

$$Z = \left[\frac{PV\,(foreign\,equity + foreign\,debt)\,at\,r_f\,discount\,rate}{PV\,(foreign\,dividend + foreign\,interest + foreign\,repayment)\,for\,project\,at\,r_f\,discount\,rate} \right] \quad (13A.4)$$

By multiplying together this ratio and the actual stream B_f^t (where $t = 0,...,n$) of dividends, debt repayment, and interest received from foreigners from the project, it is possible to determine the stream of payment to foreigners, which is below, above, or equal to what the normal stream would be, B_f^{at} (where

$t = 0,...,n).$[96] Discounting the difference between these two streams ($B_f^{at} - B_f^{t}$) by the EOCK for the country yields an estimate of the present value of the externality E_f enjoyed by (or imposed on) the country because the foreign investment in this specific project will demand a return that is lower (or higher) than what is normal in the market.

Following the reasoning used in Appendix 13A.2, the total adjustment to be made in this case is to add $(1 + FEP)E_f$ to equation (13A.1). Hence, equation (13A.1) becomes:

$$NPV^e = B_g + B_p + B_f - C_g - C_p - C_f + (1 + FEP)E_f \qquad (13A.5)$$

When the ratio of the present values, Z, is equal to 1, the project yields foreign investors just a normal return, and no adjustment to equation (13A.1) is necessary.

However, if Z is greater than 1, $E_f > 0$, and therefore $(1 + FEP)E_f > 0$. This suggests that the project should receive a net benefit for paying out less to foreigners than the country would have if it had used the foreign financing for alternative investments. Since this case also implies that private investors earn less than a normal real rate of return of r_f, it is necessary to consider some other factors before adding this net benefit to the economic externalities attributable to the project.

A critical factor in determining the rate of return that a foreign investor demands before making the investment is the economic cost of any explicit and implicit guarantees that the project or the investor receives from the country (usually the government) (Vega, 1997). The guarantees that are designed to remove risk from the perspective of the foreign investor may cover a wide range of issues. Examples include completion guarantees, loan guarantees, and the contractual allocation of the foreign exchange rate risk to either the government or consumers.[97] These guarantees have real economic costs associated with them that are usually not explicitly accounted for in the cash flows of the project (Mason et al., 1983). Hence, while it may appear that the foreign investor is willing to make funds available at an abnormally low required rate of return, it

---

[96]The stream of dividends, debt repayment, and interest received are all measured in constant dollars.

[97]A good example of the allocation of foreign exchange rate risk to consumers can be found in the concession agreement between Metropolitan Waterworks and Sewerage System and the private contractor in the case of the privatization of the water systems in Manila. In this case, any movement in the nominal exchange rate between the peso and the currency of the loans that was greater than 2 percent from the date of the agreement would be built into the adjustment for the price of water. It is not surprising that the concessionaires borrowed large amounts of funds in Japanese yen, the currency that was likely to appreciate the most with respect to the peso.

Evaluation of Stakeholder Impacts

might simply be that the government is bearing a larger proportion of the financial risks than is normal for such investments.

Another factor that is often present in the foreign financing of investment projects is financing subsidies given by foreign governments to promote certain types of investments abroad. If these subsidies are included, it might appear that a host economy is receiving a substantial benefit because the project attracts this subsidized financing.

It is generally incorrect to include any foreign (or domestic) financing subsidies as a benefit (or a reduction in financing costs) to any single project. Usually, such financing subsidies are provided to countries through a quota system, whereby a country will not be able to receive more than a given amount of such subsidies over a period of time. From the point of view of the promoter of any single investment in the host country, it might appear that these foreign financing subsidies are either bringing in incremental foreign financing or are at least a reduction in the cost of foreign financing that would have been available to the host country. In both cases, it is incorrect to credit the financing subsidy provided to any single project within a country.

13A.4 Concluding Remarks

The central issue in the evaluation of the benefits or costs to an economy from the foreign financing of investments is determining the proportion of the inflow of foreign financing to a project that is simply a substitute for other foreign capital inflows and the proportion that represents an increase in the productive resources available to the host country. Because the economic cost of incremental and non-incremental foreign investment may be quite different, the relative size of this parameter can be a critical determinant of the economic NPV of a project.

A difficulty that plagues the empirical estimation of the proportions of the foreign investment that are incremental and non-incremental arises because the impact of today's foreign investment on the demand and supply of foreign savings need not be completed within a given period of time. In addition, the nature of the various types of financial obligations undertaken by a country will alter the impact of the inflow of foreign savings on the investment and saving decisions in the country over extended periods of time.

Because of the serious statistical problems that arise in the derivation of reliable estimates of the long-term effects of foreign investment on capital formation, and the plethora of unaccounted-for implicit and explicit guarantees associated with many projects, caution is warranted before crediting a project either with inducing incremental foreign investment or with securing low-cost foreign financing. In the vast majority of cases, a project that is being financed from foreign sources will simply be reallocating the total amount of foreign investment available to the country. This arises due to the constraints on a country's ability to repay its foreign financial obligations. In such a situation, the main concern of the project evaluator is to determine whether the project is being structured in such a way (or is attracting the type of foreign investor) that will require a greater-than-normal rate of return to participate in this project. In this case, the economic analysis should reflect this higher cost and the particular financial design of the project be appropriately penalized.

Factories that are being set up in an export-processing zone can illustrate a scenario in which a project is likely to create incremental foreign investment. In such a case, the primary concern of the project analyst is to see that the domestic resources being used to accommodate this foreign investment are yielding a net return that is at least equal to the EOCK. The foreign investment coming in to finance the factory is a benefit to the country, and the flow of interest, dividends, and loan repayments are costs. The question here is whether the domestic labour and capital being employed earn a return greater than their economic opportunity cost.

Probably the most important reason for not giving a benefit to a project for non-incremental foreign investment that appears to have been made available at lower-than-normal costs is the existence of complex guarantee provisions, which are at the heart of all project financing arrangements. In such a situation, the costs of financial risk may be reflected in other charges to the project separate from the rate of interest and expected dividends. Often, the costs of risk management are being borne by the government and are not allocated in any way to the project. It is the economic costs of these guarantees that need to be the focus of the analyst's attention.

Guarantees that are provided by a government to domestic investors may alter behaviour and damage or help a project, but the triggering of the guarantee is essentially a transfer from the government to the domestic financial institutions within the country. This could have little or no economic cost. This is not the case with guarantees made to foreign investors. When such a guarantee is exercised, the flow of funds is an outflow of economic resources. In this case, the expected economic cost to the economy is increased above the level it would be if no guarantee were given.

References

Harberger, A.C. 1987. "Reflections on Social Project Evaluation", in G.M. Meier (ed.), *Pioneers in Development*, Vol. II. Washington, DC: The World Bank and Oxford: Oxford University Press.

Harberger, A.C. and G.P. Jenkins. 2002. "Introduction", in A.C. Harberger and G.P. Jenkins (eds.), *Cost-Benefit Analysis*. Cheltenham: Edward Elgar Publishing.

Harberger, A.C., G.P. Jenkins, C.Y. Kuo, and M.B. Mphahlele. 2003. "The Economic Cost of Foreign Exchange for South Africa", *South African Journal of Economics* 71(2), 298-324.

Jenkins, G.P. 1999. "Evaluation of Stakeholder Impacts in Cost-Benefit Analysis", *Impact Assessment and Project Appraisal* 17(2), 87-96.

Jenkins, G.P. and M.B. El-Hifnawi. 1993. *Economic Parameters for the Appraisal of Investment Projects: Bangladesh, Indonesia and the Philippines*, Harvard Institute for International Development (November).

Jenkins, G.P. and C.Y. Kuo. 1998. "Estimation of the National Parameters for Economic Cost-Benefit Analysis for the Philippines", Development Discussion Paper, Harvard Institute for International Development, Harvard University (May).

Jenkins, G.P. and H.B.F. Lim. 1998. "An Integrated Analysis of a Power Purchase Agreement", Development Discussion Paper, Harvard Institute for International Development, Harvard University.

Jenkins, G.P. and G.P. Shukla. 1997. "Linking East and West Bangladesh: The Jamuna Bridge Project", *The Canadian Journal of Program Evaluation*, Special Issue (September), 121–145.

Jenkins, G.P., P. Lorenzo Jr., and G.P. Shukla. 1996. "Poverty Reduction: Integrated Agricultural Development", paper prepared for Harvard Institute for International Development (February).

Mason, S., C. Baldwin, and D. Lessard. 1983. "Budgetary Time Bombs: Controlling Government Loan Guarantees", *Canadian Journal of Public Policy* 9(3), 338-346.

Vega, A.O. 1997. "Risk Allocation in Infrastructure Financing", *The Journal of Project Finance* 3(2), 38-42.

Wells, L.T. and E.S. Gleason. 1995. "Is Foreign Infrastructure Investment Still Risky?", *Harvard Business Review* (September-October).

Wolfensohn, J.D. 1997. "The Challenge of Inclusion," address to the Board of Governors by the President of the World Bank Group, Hong Kong, China (September 23).

Chapter Fourteen

Shadow Price of Government Funds, Distributional Weights, and Basic Needs Externalities

14.1 Introduction

There is always a question, in cost–benefit work, of how far to go in incorporating additional externalities into a formal system of professional analysis. One consideration is the importance of the class of externalities in question; the alternative consideration is the degree of uncertainty that surrounds any estimate of the size of the externality. Thus, even important externalities (such as those dealing with national defence) can be too difficult to quantify for them to be incorporated directly into a cost–benefit analysis. In such cases, the best advice is to calculate the net present value (NPV) of the project using standard cost–benefit analysis and present the policy-makers with a statement like, "This project has a net economic cost (in present value terms) of $3.5 billion. This does not incorporate its national defence benefit. Your decision concerns whether the cost of $3.5 billion is worth incurring as the price for achieving the national defence benefits of this project." A similar approach would very likely apply to projects dealing with offsetting some of the forces leading to long-term climate change and to many (though probably not all) cases of projects that deal with air or water pollution.

Our judgment in this matter is simple. When our information about the size of an item is so uncertain that some valuations, well within the plausible range, would make the project acceptable, while others, also well inside the plausible range, would lead to its rejection, then the final call in that project is not within the purview of professional cost–benefit analysis.

Of course, the constant challenge facing the profession is that of developing analytical and research techniques that will constantly narrow the ranges of uncertainty that we have to deal with. Thus, there have been impressive advances in developing methods of quantifying the value of travel time (by commuters and others) and the amenity value of local parks and other neighbourhood improvements. Moreover, we can certainly expect additional advances that will further narrow the margins of uncertainty that apply in different fields. But at the same time, we can be confident that in many major areas, the level of uncertainty will continue to be high for a long time to come. Our advice here focuses on the key word – professionalism. We should incorporate into our analysis whatever we can claim to be based on solid professional results and judgments and leave to others those items on which we have no serious professional expertise.

In the cases of some externalities, there may be a sort of middle ground. There are cases in which an externality of a given type can be summarized in one or a few key parameters, which themselves can then be fit quite easily into our professional cost–benefit framework. In this chapter we will consider three candidates that fall into this category: a) the shadow price of government funds, b) the distributional weights that might be applied to the benefits and costs of different groups, and c) the premia that might be attached to the successive steps of increased fulfilment of the basic needs of disadvantaged members of a society.

14.2 Shadow Price of Government Funds

Cost–benefit analysis has traditionally been carried out on the assumption that the funds involved are being sourced in the capital market. This indeed is the assumption made in this book (see Chapter Eight on the economic opportunity cost of capital, or EOCK). This assumption is easy to rationalize when the projects involved yield their full benefits in the form of cash accruing to the public treasury (e.g., an electricity or potable water project, with electricity rates and water charges set on the basis of economic principles). However, how does one deal with public projects that yield no revenue in the form of cash? In such cases, the standard assumption of obtaining the money from the capital market seems to lead to a debt, then grows year after year, compounded at a rate equal to the EOCK. If the latter rate is 10 percent (in real terms), it means that a project for an ordinary highway (not a toll road) that cost $20 million would compound to a debt of $40 million after seven years, $80 million after 14 years, $160 million after 21 years, and $320 million after 28 years. If the EOCK were 7 percent, the debt would reach $40 million after ten years and $320 million after 40 years. In light of these numbers, it is pretty clear that something should be done to tie up this loose end in the cost–benefit framework.

The answer is quite straightforward and logical. Somewhere, somehow, the framework should make provision for such debts to be paid. Furthermore, the natural source for paying them should be taxes. This would require no adjustment if obtaining extra dollars using the tax route implied an economic opportunity cost of one dollar for every additional dollar raised. However, this is far from being the case in reality. Figure 14.1

shows why. In the upper panel, the tax T_0 originally yields revenue of R_0. When this tax is raised to $T_0 + \Delta T$, revenue goes up by $A-B$. There is also an increment to efficiency cost, which can be approximated by B. Thus, the extra efficiency cost, per dollar of additional tax revenue, is $B/(A-B)$. In the lower panel, we have an upward-sloping supply curve. The rate now goes up from T_0

to $(T_0 + \Delta_1 T + \Delta_2 T)$, and tax revenue goes up by $A_1 + A_2 - B$. Efficiency cost per dollar of extra revenue is in this case $B/(A_1 + A_2 - B)$.

For small changes in the tax rate, the increment of efficiency cost is $-\tau(\partial q/\partial t)dt$, and the increment to tax revenue is $qdt + t(\partial q/\partial t)dt$. The ratio of these is simply $-e_{qt}/(1+e_{qt})$, where e_{qt} is the elasticity of quantity with respect to the tax rate and is a negative number. Thus, if e_{qt} is -0.20, the marginal cost of extra revenue is 25 cents $[=0.20/(1-0.20)]$ per dollar. If e_{qt} is -0.25, this marginal cost is 33 1/3 cents $[=0.25/(1-0.25)]$ per dollar. If e_{qt} is -0.333, the marginal cost of extra tax dollars is 50 cents $[= 0.333/(1-0.333)]$ per dollar.

The expression for the marginal economic opportunity cost of extra tax revenue is simple enough. The problem is that this number is likely to be different for every single tax in the system. Indeed, for complicated taxes such as the personal income tax, there are literally hundreds of different adjustments that could be made to the tax law, each of which would carry a different efficiency cost per extra dollar of revenue. We see no way of predicting what form the next change in tax law will take; hence, there is no way to select, from among all the possible ways, a particular one that we would want to call the "standard" way of raising extra tax revenue.

Figure 14.1: Estimating Marginal Cost of Government Funds

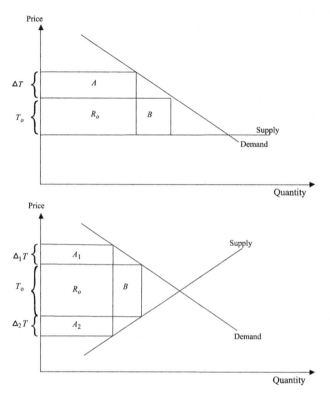

Now we face a problem. We do not want to choose a standard route for raising extra revenue, yet if we do nothing, we are implicitly assuming that the marginal efficiency cost of extra tax revenue is zero. This, of course, is also unacceptable.

Our solution is for the country's project evaluation (cost–benefit) authority to make that choice. Our recommendation is for the choice to lean toward the conservative side so that the chance of its marginal cost of tax revenue being too high would be smaller than the chance of it being too low. In order to have a specific number to deal with, we will use a marginal cost of funds equal to 1.20, which implies an elasticity of the tax base (quantity) with respect to the tax rate of $-1/6$ (see above). It should also be noted that when this assumption is applied to real-world cases, the tax-base elasticity should incorporate increases in evasion as tax rates are raised, as well as the simple substitution of other items for the taxed item. Moreover, real-world efficiency costs of taxation should be defined to include the incremental costs of administration and compliance that are induced when a given tax rate is raised.[98]

14.3 Distributional Weights

In discussions of issues of how public policy should treat different groups of citizens, a particular approach, that of distributional weights, has enjoyed some degree of prominence. This approach applies different weights to the benefits and costs perceived by different groups of participants in the economy. Normally, higher weights apply to the poor and disadvantaged, lower weights to wealthier groups. The idea of such weights is appealing to most people because they instinctively feel that an incremental dollar going to a richer person should be thought of as being less valuable, from the point of view of society as a whole, than the same dollar going to a poorer person. Sometimes this idea is embodied in the concept of a representative utility function, in which the marginal utility of extra money is calculated to decline as people's income or wealth increases.

Traditional applied welfare economics did not incorporate distributional weights, even while recognizing the likelihood that each individual's or family's marginal utility of income may decline as income or wealth increases. It did not require any complex analysis to reach this point. Actually, it followed directly from the choice of a numeraire in which real economic values were expressed. The standard numeraire for most real-world applications is either the consumer price index or the gross domestic product (GDP) deflator of the country under study. Thus, real economic magnitudes are expressed in either "consumer baskets" or "producer baskets". When economic costs and benefits are expressed in terms of one or the other of these two numeraires, the translation from individual utility into units of the numeraire basket is implicitly made at the individual level. Individual A's utility is translated into numeraire baskets using A's marginal utility of the basket. B's translation occurs using B's marginal utility of the basket, etc. for all the relevant individuals. There is no need for utility units even to be comparable across individuals in order for this process to work.

Distributional weights can still be introduced into this framework, not being thought of as measures of the utility of each relevant individual, but instead as reflections of a societal decision of the importance of incremental purchasing power as it flows into or out of the hands of particular individuals and groups. This way of framing the concept helps to avoid what was a particularly gnawing problem, when the weights were interpreted as directly measuring utility.

---

[98]Some empirical results for the efficiency costs of tax on labour income are Dahlby (Canada), 1.38; Futm and Lacross (Quebec), 1.39–1.53; Jorgenson and Yun (US), 1.35–1.40; Gruber and Saez (US), 1.28; Klever and Kremer (UK), 1.26; (Italy), 1.72; (Germany), 1.85; Hansen and Stuart (Sweden), 1.69. See, e.g., Dahlby (2008). Typically, studies such as these provide no allowance for evasion or for costs of administration.

That problem is most easily illustrated by a case of constant supply price of, say, construction labour. The constant supply price means zero producer surplus is generated as additional labour is hired for a public project, yet the families involved may indeed increase their cash income by part or all of the cash wages paid out by the government. Actual practice would normally assign these cash wages, adjusted by the relevant distributional weight as a benefit, and consider the supply price of the labour (its cash wage) as an economic cost. This is not correct if the relevant "base" for the distributional weight is the utility gain linked to the increased employment. But it is justifiable if the relevant base is the purchasing power in the hands of the workers or their families.[99]

In our opinion, the principal weakness of the distributional weights approach derives not from the idea of these weights as such, but rather from the patterns of weights that have typically been assumed in the expositions and applications that appear in the economics literature. To make our point very briefly: modest differences in weights do not cause serious problems, but large differences in weights do indeed entail such problems.

Any actual or implicit transfer of purchasing power from richer (low-weighted) persons to poorer (higher-weighted) persons can be thought of as an implicit approbation of economic waste, in an amount whose magnitude is governed by the size of the differences between the weight of the "donor" and the weight of the "recipient". Thus, a project or other operation that reduces the income of A by 1,000 would have a weighted cost of 500 if A had a distributional weight of 0.5. If that project also caused the income of B to increase by 300, there would be a weighted benefit of 600 if B had a weight of 2. We could thus have:

Efficiency benefits (measured without regard to distribution)		3,000
Efficiency costs (measured without regard to distribution)		3,700
Efficiency NPV		−700
Distributional externalities (weighted cost of A is 500 vs. unweighted cost of 1,000)		+500
Distributional externalities (weighted benefit of B is 600 vs. unweighted benefit of 300)		+300
Distributional NPV	+800	
Weighted NPV of project	+100	
Unweighted NPV of project		−700

The assertion of a distributional (or any other) externality really means a willingness to accept (if need be) a net loss, in efficiency terms, of up to the full size of that externality. Of course, it does not require, though nonetheless invites, such an efficiency loss. Put another way, distributional considerations do not modify a decision on a project if efficiency considerations alone would lead to

---

[99]This treatment helps to partially bridge the gap between the distributional weights approach on the one hand and that of basic needs externalities on the other (see below for an exposition of the basic needs approach).

the same answer. Thus, to the extent that a distributional externality has an impact on the result, it necessarily must be operating to offset an efficiency cost, up to the full size of the externality.

This line of thinking has extremely powerful implications. Let us simply consider two groups, those (A) with distributional weights less than 0.5 and those (B) with weights greater than 2. Clearly, it would "pay", in the sense of being acceptable from society's point of view, to undertake every independent project or programme that brings about transfers from Group A to Group B so long as the efficiency cost linked to that project was less than 75 percent of its budget. Hearing this usually bothers listeners, and their instinctive reaction is to ask whether the same transfer could be obtained at much lower cost than that. If a lower cost is indeed possible, the answer is to narrow the range — say, by taking from those with weights less than 2/3 and transferring to those with weights greater than 1.5. Under this rule, the weighted cost of taking 900 from Group A would be 600, and the weighted benefit of giving 400 to Group B would be 600. Thus, an efficiency cost of up to 500 (= 5/9 of the amount taken from the "donors") would be "invited" by the scheme.

Following these general lines, which are implied by a distributional weights approach, would typically lead to huge transfers, so that in the end, hardly anyone would be left with incomes under a lower bound and hardly anyone would be left with incomes above an upper bound. The exceptions would probably be upper-income individuals from whom taking money would be very expensive in efficiency terms (e.g., high earners who would simply move to another country in response to a given scheme of transfer). But those who would simply reduce their effort modestly, or who would actually increase their effort in response to a fall in their net take-home income, would be easy targets for a "taking".

The Achilles heel of a distributional weights approach arises when large differences in weights are associated with differences in income that appear to most people to be within a quite "normal" range. We do not see such a problem if all we do is give the bottom decile a weight of 1.3, the second decile a weight of 1.2, and the third decile a weight of 1.1, leaving everyone else with a weight of 1.0. But the optimal tax literature is full of applications in which the distributional weights are inversely proportional to income. In such a case, one might have a weight of 1.0 applying to a family income of $60,000, a weight of 2 applying to an income of $30,000, and a weight of 0.5 applying when income is $120,000. Here a transfer from someone with an income slightly above $120,000 to someone with an income slightly below $30,000 would be acceptable, so long as its efficiency cost did not exceed 75 percent of the amount "taken". If good diligence then uncovered ways of taking and transferring that had efficiency costs of "only" 5/9 of the amount taken, then most incomes above $90,000 would one way or another be taken, and most people starting below $40,000 would have their incomes supplemented up to that point.

It is not the case that a distributional weights framework can be used, say, only for the purpose of setting an income tax schedule and then put to one side and forgotten, as it were, when evaluating other taxes, tariffs, agricultural price schemes, price controls, and rationing schemes, generally and, of course, the whole range of public expenditures (on both current and capital accounts). On the contrary, the spirit of cost–benefit analysis is that we apply it to each and every decision that comes along, in a context in which prevailing distortions are, as a first approximation, taken as given.

Weights that are inversely proportional to income "invite" too many transfers, and transfers that are too costly, for most people to accept. Inverse proportionality implies a weighting scheme in which the elasticity of the weight with respect to the income level of the subject is -1. Most of the examples in the tax literature deal with assumed elasticities in the range of -0.5 to -2. The case of an elasticity of -2 is even more exaggerated than that of -1. An elasticity of -0.5 would be more generous. Here the weight of 0.5 would apply to incomes of \$240,000, and the weight of 2 would apply to incomes less than \$15,000, but between these limits, efficiency losses of up to 75 percent of the amount "taken" from the upper-income group would still be acceptable under a weighted cost–benefit test.

Pursuing the implications of exponential weighting patterns with elasticities in the indicated range leads to implied distributions of after-tax income that are far narrower than are observed in reality, and quite beyond what most people would regard as plausible. But distributional weights, where the highest weight is, say, 1.5 or even 2 times the lowest, would be much less vulnerable to this sort of critique.

14.4 Basic Needs Externalities

Our thinking in terms of basic needs began during a period (1970s and early 1980s) when the terms *distributional weights* and *basic needs externalities* were widely used, often being treated as alternative labels for the same general approach. We reacted against this, particularly since at that time, our own vision of distributional weights was the classical one, in which the focus was directly on the utility level of each relevant economic agent. We thought quite naturally of the example from economics texts and classrooms, which shows that if the utility of a recipient is the objective, then the most efficient way to enhance that utility is by giving money, which that person can then use to buy whatever bundle of goods and services (from among those thus rendered affordable) brings the greatest satisfaction. We noted, however, that the great bulk of transfers carried out by the public sector (worldwide, looking at all countries) turn out to be accomplished *in kind* rather than in cash. This led us to conclude that some motivation other than the pure utility of the recipients must be involved.

This led us to focus on the idea that the objective of many transfer operations is the welfare, not the utility, of the recipients — *welfare* being defined by someone other than the recipients themselves. This could be thought of as the voters, or the taxpayers, or their legislative representatives, or just the government. The implicit idea is that the recipients' welfare is being defined by someone else, with that someone, in one sense or another, trying to represent the tastes or judgments of "society".

No transfer programme is more widespread, across the entire world, than free primary education. Yet this is invariably, so far as we know, delivered *in kind*. Governments do not give $1,000 per pupil to each child's parents, saying that they can use that money to pay for a year's education for their son or daughter, but they can also use it for a daughter's dowry or to take a trip. On the contrary, educational transfers are delivered in kind. Voucher schemes, which are still quite rare, give parents money that they can freely use, but only to pay for their child's education. The freedom of choice is restricted to the educational realm, where, in our opinion, it meets an important basic need.

The situation is quite similar with respect to public programmes for other basic needs. Medical care is quite clearly delivered in kind. So too is housing. Nutrition, yet another basic need, is sometimes delivered through soup kitchens or similar establishments (in which case it is clearly in kind), but sometimes through subsidized prices or food stamps. These latter cases differ from those of education and medical care in that they are more readily subject to abuse by the recipients. In the United States, for example, food stamps are often accepted by retailers in payment for non-food items. More blatantly, they are quite openly sold for cash in many places.

If such evasion of the labelled intent of the subsidy is widespread, it effectively nullifies the basic needs justification and turns the policy into one that is better supported by distributional weights arguments. We believe, however, that the basic needs motivations for food and housing programmes are only partially frustrated. In addition, we believe that, to the extent that food stamps are sold, and subsidized quarters are rented out to non-family members (with the proceeds then being used for general purposes, unlinked to basic needs), most citizens and taxpayers who support these programmes become quite annoyed, so much so that if they felt that these evasive measures were widespread, they would probably no longer favour the programmes.

The basic needs approach, then, says that society is willing to pay a premium in order to more fully meet the basic needs of disadvantaged people — to leave them more adequately fed, and with improved housing facilities, and better cared for medically, and/or with their children better educated. This premium reflects a willingness to pay more than the normal price, to bear more than the normal cost, to deliver elements that add to the fulfilment of the basic needs of the disadvantaged. Put another way, and as a direct reflection of what was said concerning the distributional weights approach, society is willing to put up with certain amounts of extra cost, or economic inefficiency, if this makes possible the fulfilment of some unmet basic needs. The size of the premium assigned for a given basic need, and the definition of the base to which that premium applies, defines the precise trade-off involved — i.e., how much society is willing to pay for a specific sign of improvement.

Let us start with a rather idealized picture — one that best displays the underlying rationale for basic needs externalities. This would be similar to using an idealized standard utility function, or a continuously declining relationship giving distributional weights as a function of real income, in a distributional weights approach. The counterpart in a basic needs setting is a function in which the horizontal axis measures an index of nutrition, medical care, housing, or education, and the vertical axis displays the premium that society is willing to pay for each successive increment of that index (see Figure 14.2).

Figure 14.2: Measuring Basic Need Externalities

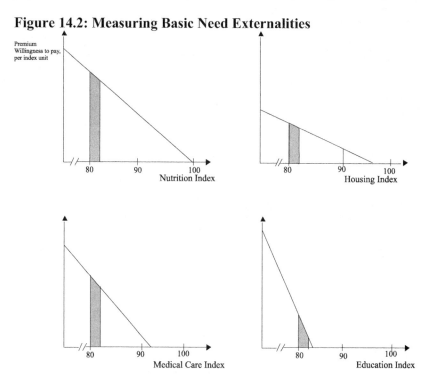

Figure 14.2 reveals several points. First, society may have different attitudes with respect to different basic needs. These are expressed (with linear curves) in the two intercepts. Both intercepts are highest for nutrition. In this case, society is willing to pay more for a 1-point gain in the nutrition index than for a similar gain in any other index at the same level, and it is willing to keep paying up to an index level 100 (which we might take to be the national per capita median level). The education picture reveals a high willingness to pay at low levels of the index, but this willingness disappears long before the median level is

reached. This might reflect a situation in which society places a high value on universal primary education, but is unwilling (or unable) to pay premia for secondary and higher education. To display the differences in another way, the shaded bars in the four graphs indicate the amount society would be willing to pay to lift one individual from index level 80 to index level 82 for each of the four basic needs categories. This clearly shows how substantial differences or priorities can exist among the categories.

We believe that the framework shown in Figure 14.2 is important in laying the groundwork for a basic needs approach. Few would argue that the move from index level 90 to 92 should be valued as highly by society as the move from level 80 to 82. It is also quite reasonable that the "true" premia, representing society's true willingness to pay, should decline continuously with each additional step of fulfilling a given basic need.[100]

Figure 14.3 illustrates how the idealized vision of Figure 14.2 can be modified as one attempts to be practical. Depending on the circumstances, one might have a single premium (Panel A) applying to all basic needs improvements up to a point. Or one could distinguish between two (Panel B) or among three (Panel C) levels, reflecting declining premia as needs are more fully met.

---

[100]Economists have a technical concept of a public good, whose benefits are available to the public at large. A's enjoyment of the national parks, for example, is not diminished by B and C also enjoying them (at least up to a given point of congestion). Thus, their individual utilities can be summed in reaching society's valuation of the parks. In the same way, many members of society are willing to pay to reduce the incidence of malnutrition and disease among poor children (and poor people generally). A society's total willingness to pay, under this concept, would be the sum of all that society's members, some of whom, of course, could have zero willingness to pay. Dealing with basic needs through public sector actions, as against (or in addition to) private charity, is motivated by the fact that many people's willingness to pay is very likely to be contingent on others also paying. They are willing to pay as long as others do also. We present this discussion of public goods as a link to economic theory. However, the basic needs approach can alternatively be thought of as simply reflecting a country's policy, without seeking deeper roots for its justification.

Figure 14.3: Basic Needs Premiums in Practice

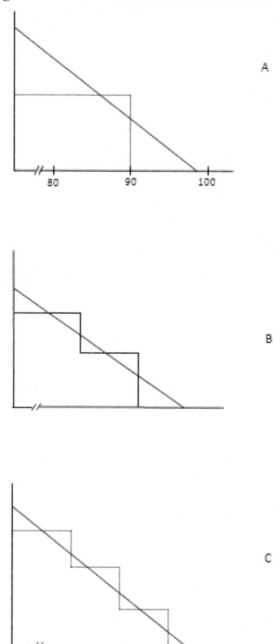

We believe that it is worthwhile for people to think in these terms because doing so really helps them to understand their own values. Most people instinctively respond positively to the question of whether food should be exempted from a sales or value-added tax. Yet they tend to modify that view when they think of expensive meals in luxury restaurants or gourmet foods bought in upscale stores. Many would end up preferring to tax most foods and to explicitly subsidize a few items (rice, beans, fresh vegetables, milk) that are important or valuable components of the diets of the poor. Trying to quantify basic needs according to an index encourages people to think seriously about details such as this; the end result is a pattern of premia that better reflects society's preferences and values.

However, it is certainly possible to implement a basic needs approach without the concept of an index. Thus, one can be willing to incur greater costs (e.g., up to 50 percent above the national average) to bring about good results in primary schools in poor neighbourhoods. Or one could simply not consider as costs the standard amounts spent giving prenatal care to poor mothers or the necessary shots and vaccines for poor children.

The big picture, so far as the basic needs framework is concerned, is that most societies are not ready to give tuition money to parents and then let them choose to spend it on something other than educating their children. It is exactly similar, of course, for societies' outlays on medical care, public housing, and nutrition-oriented programmes. In short, most societies are paternalistic in the way they provide and distribute public services. It is this element that points to a system built on basic needs externalities rather than distributional weights.

14.5 Basic Needs Externalities (Type B) Linked to Income

The gap between the basic needs approach and that of distributional weights may be substantial at a philosophical level, but it may be quite easy to bridge at a practical level. The bridge consists of recognizing that individuals' or families' basic needs are progressively better met as one moves from the first to the second, then from the second to the third, then from the third to the fourth deciles in the income distribution. Furthermore, it is often the case that a project will have the effect of actually lifting significant numbers of families to higher income levels in this fashion. This is quite commonly true for projects that involve incorporating workers into the so-called formal, or modern, sector of the economy, when those workers would otherwise be in the much lower-paid informal, or traditional, sector. When workers make this sort of transition, their family incomes may jump, say, from the first to the third decile. Quite rationally, then, and without any particular government or other external stimulus, the families will move to a better diet, take better medical precautions, fix the roof or windows or floors of their home, and raise the school-leaving age and grade of their children. In short, they move forward in better meeting all four categories of basic needs.

One simple but also quite crude way of incorporating such considerations into a cost–benefit framework would be to assign a premium of, say, 40 percent to extra income within the first decile, 30 percent to extra income within the second decile, 20 percent to extra income within the third decile, and 10 percent to extra income within the fourth decile. This could certainly be justified on basic needs grounds, but an analyst would find it hard to answer the question of precisely what is being paid for.

A better approach would be to operate with the average family budgets (in the project's region) of people in the successive deciles of the income distribution. Then, at least, one could detail how much more they are spending on food, housing, medical care, etc. and assign basic needs premia to these added expenditures. It would be still better to analyse what these added expenditures are typically spent on and assign greater premia, for example, to potable water than to curtains and greater premia to extending the school-leaving age of the children than to making extra trips back to the family's native village.

Sometimes the assignment of a basic needs premium to a particular item will be straightforward. For example, installing running water and plumbing in a house might warrant a premium equal to all or nearly all of its standard full costs. But other things might be more difficult to value. For example, in most countries public education is free, at least up to a certain grade level. The fact that it is free is already a reflection of the societies' willingness to pay, and keeping children in school longer may, as a result, not necessitate any obvious extra educational expenditures in the family budget. Yet one might want to recognize a basic needs externality in the case where a new job in the formal sector causes a family's children to stay in school longer.

To illustrate, consider a case where a formal sector project is expected to lift 1,000 families from the first to the third deciles of income. We do not know who they are at the moment of analysing the projects. So we go to a recent census or sample survey in order to find the distribution of children of households in each decile. We should at least be able to determine what fraction of each decile's children are in school at each age. Perhaps 1,000 families in the first decile have 20 children in the ninth grade, while 1,000 in the third decile have 50 children in that grade. Making such calculations across all grades, one could estimate ΔN_g, the increase in the number of children in Grade g that we can expect as a consequence of the income improvement of the 1,000 families. We should also be able to estimate the approximate cost (borne by the state) of a student year at each grade level. If we call this cost C_g, we can then think of a basic needs premium that should apply to poor children reaching that grade level. That premium could be a general one, Π^*, in which case the total education externality would be $\Pi^* \Sigma C_g \Delta N_g$. Or it could be a premium Π_g that varies with grade level, in which case, the total education externality would be

$\Sigma \Pi_g C_g \Delta N_g$. This number, in turn, need not necessarily be calculated for each project, but may simply serve as one component of a broad income premium that applies to the transition from the first to the third decile of the income distribution.

References

Becker, G.S. 1976. *The Economic Approach to Human Behavior.* Chicago: The University of Chicago Press.

Boardman, A.E., D.H. Greenberg, A.R. Vining, and D.L. Weimer. 2001. *Cost-Benefit Analysis: Concepts and Practice,* 2nd edition. Englewood Cliffs, NJ: Prentice Hall.

Bouis, H. 1994. "The Effect of Income on Demand for Food in Poor Countries: Are Our Food Consumption Databases Giving Us Reliable Estimates", *Journal of Development Economics* 44(1), 199–226.

Browning, E.K. and W.R. Johnson. 1984. "The Trade-off between Equity and Efficiency", *Journal of Political Economy* 92(2), 175–203.

Collier, P. 1998. *Social Capital and Poverty.* Washington, DC: World Bank.

Dahlby, B. 2008. *The Marginal Cost of Public Funds: Theory and Applications.* Cambridge MA: MIT Press Books, 1.

Gramlich, E.M. 1997. *A Guide to Cost-Benefit Analysis.* Englewood Cliffs, NJ: Prentice Hall.

Harberger, A.C. 1978. "On the Use of Distributional Weights in Social Cost-Benefit Analysis", *Journal of Political Economy* 86(2), Part 2: Research in Taxation, S87–S120.

— 1984. "Basic Needs Versus Distributional Weights in Cost-Benefit Analysis", *Economic Development and Cultural Change* 32(3), 455–474.

— 1985. "Reflections on Social Project Evaluation", paper prepared for *Pioneers in Development*, Vol. II. Washington, DC: World Bank.

Herrin, A. and R. Racelis. 1994. *Monitoring the Coverage of Public Programs on Low-Income Families: South Africa, 1992,* Integrated Population and Development Planning Project, National Economic and Development Authority.

Johansson-Stenman, O. 2005. "Distributional Weights in Cost-Benefit Analysis – Should We Forget about Them?" *Land Economics* 81(3), 337–352.

Lanzona, L. 1997. "Measurement of Basic Needs Externalities: Education and Nutrition", report submitted to the Public Investment Staff, NEDA.

Layard, R. 1980. "On the Use of Distributional Weights in Social Cost-Benefit Analysis", *Journal of Political Economy* 88(5), 1041–1047.

Little, I.M.D. and J.A. Mirrlees. 1974. *Project Appraisal and Planning for Developing Countries.* London: Heinemann Educational Books.

McConnell, K.E. 1997. "Does Altruism Undermine Existence Value?" *Journal of Environmental Economics and Management* 32(1), 22–37.

Perkins, F. 1994. *Practical Cost-Benefit Analysis: Basic Concepts and Applications.* South Melbourne: Macmillan Education Australia.

Sjaastad, L.A. and D.L. Wisecarver. 1977. "The Social Cost of Public Finance", *Journal of Political Economy* 85(3), 513–547.

Schwartz, H. and R. Berney. 1977. *Social and Economic Dimensions of Project Evaluation*. Washington, DC: Inter-American Development Bank.

Squire, L. and H.G. van der Tak. 1975. *Economic Analysis of Projects*. Baltimore: The John Hopkins University Press.

Woolcock, M. and D. Narayan. 2000. "Social Capital: Implications for Development Theory, Research, and Policy", *The World Bank Research Observer* 15(2), 225–249.

Yitzhaki, S. 2003. "Cost-Benefit Analysis and the Distributional Consequences of Government Projects", *National Tax Journal* 56(2), 319–336.

Chapter Fifteen

Cost–Effectiveness Analysis

15.1 Introduction

Students of cost–benefit analysis are often confronted with the problem of placing a monetary value on a project's benefits. This problem is not present when the project's output is directly priced in the market, and when the output itself is relatively homogeneous and well-defined. At the other extreme the benefit stream itself can be hard to pin down in quantitative terms (e.g., in areas such as national defence or hospital services), and putting monetary values on its components (where are the services of an army division or a hospital wing?) can be even harder.

For many decades, cost–effectiveness analysis has been put forward as a potential alternative to cost–benefit analysis, precisely for cases in which benefits are hard to value. The idea is very simple. Consider a set of alternative projects, each of which will produce the same benefit stream, and then choose the least expensive among them. The idea sounds good, but in practice it has significant limitations. For most of the time each project has different characteristics. It is not always wisest to buy the cheapest car, truck, bicycle, or TV set; others in the comparison set may be preferred for being larger, more durable, more comfortable, etc. The fact the two projects are similar in producing benefits does not preclude them from being quite different in many other dimensions.

Hence, this discussion begins with a warning to be wary of the temptation to think of cost–effectiveness analysis as an analytical tool of simple and wide application. It can fit this bill sometimes, though not universally.

Having said that, there are two ways of computing cost–effectiveness ratios. One way to calculate effectiveness is to estimate a ratio of a project's costs to its benefits. An alternative method is to calculate effectiveness in terms of its cost. When several alternative options for an existing situation are evaluated, there is a need to compute incremental or marginal cost–effectiveness ratios.

In addition, the costs incurred in interventions or alternative options may involve capital or operating expenditures that are spread over many years. Capital projects usually have large investment outlays at the beginning, with their recurrent costs and their benefits spread over many subsequent years. The costs and benefits should both be discounted to a common time period in order to make a comparison of alternative options. Because the benefits are measured in physical units, the effectiveness in quantity should be discounted by the same rate as the costs. The proper cost–effectiveness ratio for each option is then computed as the ratio of the discounted costs to the discounted benefits over the life of the project.

The following sections of this chapter describe how cost–effectiveness analysis can be applied to projects in education, power, health, and water. Conclusions are presented in the final section.

15.2 Education Projects

The following case, which deals with the strategy of expanding the supply of schoolrooms in rural parts of South Africa, represents a sound application of cost–effectiveness analysis. What makes this project a good candidate for cost–effectiveness analysis is that it has been fairly well established that the needs identified can be met most effectively by building standard structures (blocks), each consisting of four schoolrooms. Thus, there is no need to deal with the issue of benefit heterogeneity arising from this source.

However, there is another important respect in which the benefits of identical new school blocks differ greatly across projects. The heterogeneity here stems from the fact that the number of pupils varies greatly across potential project sites. This problem is solved by defining project output as the reduction in the number of students per classroom, applied to each affected student. In the exercise that follows, the number of students in each school district at any given time is the result of demographic forces, and is not influenced by the project. It is assumed that, for the year 2015, the number of pupils in a district is 400, and that the number of classrooms is four without the project and eight with it. The ratio of students per classroom would then fall from 100 to 50 as a consequence of the project, and its benefits for 2015 would be calculated as $50 \times 400 = 20,000$. Similarly, if the number of pupils was projected to be 440 by 2020, the ratio of students per classroom would fall from 110 to 55, and project benefits for that year would be calculated as $55 \times 440 = 24,200$.

Projecting the growth of the student population further into the future, along with the depreciation of already existing classroom blocks, creates a potential problem, namely that the benefits attributed to a new project by the methods described above would keep growing indefinitely, causing almost any current project to look good. This is a standard problem in cost–benefit analysis, and it has a standard answer. When an investment to be made now (or in the near future) is evaluated, the assumption should be that future investments will be made, following sound cost–benefit criteria, similar to those used currently. So, if the growth of enrolments and/or the demise of old structures reaches a point in the future where investment in an additional classroom block is warranted, that investment should be built into the future projects on which today's expansion decision is based.

In the final analysis, the criterion for investment in additional schoolroom blocks is quite straightforward. As is the case with highway improvements, the fact that the benefit stream from a new investment is expected to grow through time turns the choice problem into one of when, rather than whether, an investment should be made. The resulting criterion is surprisingly simple: time the investment so that the first-year benefit is for the first time greater than or equal to the economic opportunity cost of capital (i.e., its percentage yield on the project's accumulated costs). If the budgetary funds available are insufficient to meet this criterion and the competing projects are independent of each other, the limited funds should be allocated to the subset of projects with the highest first-year yields.

The school block investment problem turns into one of cost-effectiveness when it is recognized that it is difficult to place a monetary value on the annual benefits of an investment in new classrooms. Indeed, it is not easy even to describe precisely what these benefits are. For the specific case of the province of Limpopo, South Africa, it was recognized that there was a genuine shortage of classroom space in the province's school districts, with nearly all districts having well above the official target ratio of 40 students per classroom. This suggested that the measure of project benefits should be related to a) the degree by which a project reduced the student–classroom (N/C) ratio, and b) the number of students (N) affected by this reduction.

Although a monetary value (V) cannot be put on this measure, it is recognized that if funds are allocated according to the ratio of first-year benefits to project investment cost (I), the ranking of quantitative benefits per rand of investment costs will be the same as the ranking of monetary benefits per rand. This is simply because monetary benefits are equal to quantitative benefits multiplied by the (unknown) monetary value (V). All this works well as long as the measure of quantitative benefits is appropriate, and as long as any ancillary benefits that are not counted are either a) only minor ones, or b) if not minor, then similarly distributed across the set of projects, so as not to seriously affect their ranking.

Table 15.1 indicates how these considerations can be implemented.[101] Column (1) shows each district's enrolment for next year. Column (2) shows the existing number of classrooms. Column (3) is the ratio of (1)/(2), which applies if no project is undertaken. Column (4) shows this same ratio if one classroom block (four classrooms) is added. Column (5) shows the reduction in this ratio ((3) − (4)), while Column (6) weights this reduction by the number of students affected. This weighted measure is an estimate of quantitative benefits of the project. Assume that the investment costs of each additional classroom block was R420,000 (rand) in 2004 prices and that these did not vary significantly from one school district to another. Column (7) shows the incremental project costs of one classroom block. These benefits are expressed as a ratio of the project benefits to project costs in Column (8).

The schools should be funded according to Column (8) of Table 15.1, with the highest first-year benefit per rand of costs first, the second highest second,

---

[101] The data in Columns (1) to (2) were obtained from Zeinali (2010).

Cost-Effectiveness Analysis

and so on. However, each additional school block will alter the current cost–effectiveness ratio, and the ranking of schools will therefore need to be recalculated after each new addition of classrooms. The selection process is intended to allocate limited funds in the most efficient manner. The results are presented in Table 15.2 for funding priority of the top 15 schools based on the descending order of the benefit–cost ratios. The final column shows accumulative construction costs of schools until the capital budget for new school blocks, say, R6.0 billion, has been exhausted.

Readers will note that the Legadimane, Pienaarsrivier, Badimong, and Muchuchi school districts appear twice in Table 15.2. The reason is that in each of these cases it is found to be cost-efficient to add two blocks of four classrooms each to the present levels of five classrooms in Legadimane, Pienaarsrivier, and Muchuchi and nine classrooms in Badimong. The analysis of whether a second block should be added should, of course, be done as a second and separate step, once investments in the first block have passed the test. This should be done, in principle at least, for all the school districts for which investments on one additional classroom block have been shown to be warranted. In the case of the Limpopo province exercise, only the four districts listed passed this second test before all the available funds were accounted for.

Table 15.1: Calculation of the Incremental Benefit–Cost Ratios for 20 School Districts in Limpopo, South Africa, 2004

School Name	Next Year's Enrolment N	Existing Number of Classrooms C	Next Year's (N/C) Without Project	Next Year's (N/C) With Project	Reduction in (N/C) [(3)−(4)]	First-Year Benefits of Project [(5)×(1)]	Project Investment Costs (R thousand)	First-Year Benefits/Project Costs [(6)/(7)]
	(1)	(2)	(3)	(4)	(5)	(6)	(7)	(8)
1. Legadimane Primary	685	1	685	137	548	375,380	420	0.8938
2. Pienaarsrivier	567	1	567	113	454	257,418	420	0.6129
3. Mantsha Primary	876	9	97	67	30	26,280	420	0.0626
4. Muchuchi Primary	531	1	531	106	425	225,675	420	0.5373
5. Badimong Primary	1,028	5	206	114	92	94,576	420	0.2252
6. Marotobane Primary	439	1	439	88	351	154,089	420	0.3669
7. Thomas Ntshaveni	396	2	198	66	132	52,272	420	0.1245
8. Nakgwadi Secondary	780	12	65	49	16	12,480	420	0.0297
9. Segopotje Secondary	347	5	69	39	30	10,410	420	0.0248
10. Mpapalati Primary	772	16	48	39	9	6,948	420	0.0165
11. Mashaha Secondary	333	1	333	67	266	88,578	420	0.2109
12. Rootse Primary	450	3	150	64	86	38,700	420	0.0921
13. Mokwasele	847	10	85	61	24	20,328	420	0.0484
14. Madikoti Putsoa	704	15	47	37	10	7,040	420	0.0168
15. Kulani Primary	275	4	69	34	35	9,625	420	0.0229
16. Nkotobona High	474	3	158	68	90	42,660	420	0.1016
17. Mookamedi Secondary	280	5	56	31	25	7,000	420	0.0167
18. Paulos Primary	852	11	77	57	20	17,040	420	0.0406
20. Sefufule Primary	372	4	93	47	46	17,112	420	0.0407
21. Lefakomo Secondary	901	12	75	56	19	17,119	420	0.0408

Source: The data in Columns (1) and (2) were obtained from Zeinali (2010).

Table 15.2: The 15 Schools with the Highest Incremental Benefit–Cost Ratios in Limpopo, South Africa, 2004

School Name in Ranking	Next Year's Enrolment N	Existing Number of Classrooms C	Next Year's (N/C) without Project	Next Year's (N/C) with Project	Reduction in (N/C) [(3)−(4)]	First-Year Benefits of Project [(5)×(1)]	Incremental Benefit–Cost Ratio	Accumulative Project Costs (R thousand)
	(1)	(2)	(3)	(4)	(5)	(6)	(7)	(8)
1. Legadimane Primary	685	1	685	137	548	375,380	0.8938	420
2. Pienaarsrivier	567	1	567	113	454	257,418	0.6129	840
3. Muchuchi Primary	531	1	531	106	425	225,675	0.5373	1,260
4. Marotobane Primary	439	1	439	88	351	154,089	0.3669	1,680
5. Badimong Primary	1,028	5	206	114	92	94,576	0.2252	2,100
6. Mashaha Secondary	333	1	333	67	266	88,578	0.2109	2,520
7. Thomas Ntshaveni	396	2	198	66	132	52,272	0.1245	2,940
8. Nkotobona High	474	3	158	68	90	42,660	0.1016	3,360
9. Legadimane Primary*	685	5	137	76	61	41,785	0.0995	3,780
10. Rootse Primary	450	3	150	64	86	38,700	0.0921	4,200
11. Badimong Primary*	1,028	9	114	79	35	35,980	0.0857	4,620
12. Pienaarsrivier*	567	5	113	63	50	28,350	0.0675	5,040
13. Mantsha Primary	876	9	97	67	30	26,280	0.0626	5,460
14. Muchuchi Primary*	531	5	106	59	47	24,957	0.0594	5,880
15. Mokwasele	847	10	85	61	24	20,328	0.0484	6,300

Note: * indicates schools that appear a second time in the table.

15.3 Electric Power Projects

In the Limpopo school analysis, the monetary costs of a classroom block did not differ significantly from one school district to another. The differences were on the benefit side, where the benefits of adding a classroom block in Legadimane were 15 times greater than those in Muchuchi when it appears a second time (see Table 15.2). The key to that analysis was finding a quantitative measure of benefits (Column (6) of Table 15.2) that could be estimated for each project and then compared across projects.

Electric power projects are different, since cost-minimization plays a central role throughout. In the simplest case – that of bringing power to an area that does not currently have a service – one simply seeks the most cost-effective option. But in most cases, there is not even a common unit in which to measure benefits. As will be shown in Chapter 18, the economic value of electrical energy varies widely according to the time of day, the season, and other factors. How, then, can a basis of comparison be found between, say, winter peak and summer off-peak electricity? The process of cost-minimization itself can provide an answer. The aim is to find the cheapest way of satisfying peak-time and off-peak demands, and there may be many layers in between. The standard methodology starts from the load duration curve, which shows how the hourly demand for energy varies throughout the year.[102]

The task becomes one of finding the pattern of current and likely future investment that minimizes the costs of meeting the demands given by sequence of load duration curves now until some future time horizon. This task can usually be broken down into finding the cheapest ways of generating baseload demand, peak-time demand, and various intermediate demand levels. In the relatively easy case used as an example in Chapter 18, this problem is solved by investing in big thermal for baseload demand, gas turbines for peak-time demand, and combined cycle for all the demands in between. Chapter 18 shows how the ideal mix of these types of generation can be found for a given set of costs. The same chapter also shows how to proceed with new power investments when the existing mix of power sources is different from the optimum.

All through this process the principle of cost-minimization is paramount; even when the electricity systems charge prices that do not reflect costs, investment choices should be based on minimizing the cost of meeting expected demands. The underlying principle is that system marginal cost is always the

---

[102] It is necessary to make assumptions about the prices paid by electricity users in order to build (or conceptualize) such a curve. The ideal case would be one in which the prices facing consumers vary so that at each moment they reflect the highest marginal running cost, among the generating sources that are operating at that moment. With such a system, a single peak-time surcharge is usually called for, in order to cover the capital costs of the equipment (often gas turbines or engines) that is used exclusively (or at least predominantly) to meet demand peaks. Such pricing systems hardly exist in the real world, however, so in real-world cases the estimated load duration curve should be built based on a best judgment as to the schedule of prices that is most likely to be in place for each future year.

marginal cost of the highest-cost plant in operation at that moment, except during peak hours, when a peak-time surcharge must be added.

A case presented in Chapter 19 illustrates how cost–effectiveness analysis has been used to evaluate alternative electricity-generation technologies (i.e., combined-cycle plant and single-cycle plant) when they provided the same amount of electricity with 126 MW of additional capacity to the existing system in Adukki in 2010. The combined-cycle plant is 40% more expensive in terms of capital expenditures than the single-cycle plant, while it is much higher in energy-transformation efficiency. As a consequence, the cost–effectiveness ratio – levellized energy cost – is computed as the present value of the total economic costs incurred over the project's life divided by the present value of the net electricity generation produced by the plant during the same time. The results shown in Table 15.3 indicate that for the base case scenario, the levellized energy cost is 0.146 rupees per kWh for the combined-cycle plant, which is lower than the 0.183 rupees per kWh for the single-cycle plant; thus, the combined-cycle plant should be the one recommended for implementation.

Table 15.3: Levellized Economic Cost of Energy (in 2008 prices)

Category	Combined-Cycle Plant	Single-Cycle Plant
PV of economic costs (million rupees):		
Investment costs	205.57	146.83
Operating and maintenance costs other than fuel	68.95	68.95
Fuel	207.32	388.72
Total	481.84	604.51
PV of net energy generated (MWh)	3,297,471	3,297,471
Levellized cost of energy expressed in rupees/kWh	0.146	0.183

Source: Table 19.15 of Chapter 19.

15.4 The Use of Quality-Adjusted Life-Years (QALYs) for Medical Projects

15.4.1 Nature of Health Projects[103]

Few project areas present more daunting problems than the medical area. Researchers are at best uneasy about placing an economic value on human life, but the problems go beyond that. Even if a medical invention can be shown to

---

[103] Health services are generally subsidized, at least at the primary care level. In almost all situations in the field of health care, patients do not pay a price or fee that reflects the opportunity costs of the resources employed. The levels of knowledge and information held by physicians and patients about sickness or disease are asymmetric. As a result, the supply and demand for health services is not negotiable, and not as well defined as other goods or services regularly bought and sold in markets.

save lives, these lives will not last forever. Those whose deaths from Disease A are prevented by an intervention will eventually die from another cause. Thus, the benefit of the intervention is better described as extending the life span of individuals, rather than preventing their deaths. This sort of reassuring led to the concept of QALYs as a quantitative measure of the weighted benefits of medical projects. The basic idea is a straightforward one, in that one year of perfect-health life expectancy is assigned a value of 1, and one year of less-than-perfect-health life expectancy a value of less than 1; a value of 0 is used for death. This also refers to a cost–utility analysis. The concept can be used in a full benefit–cost analysis if the investigations are willing (or able) to assign an economic price (a value) to the QALY. But it can also be used in cost–effectiveness analyses in cases where one can seek to minimize the cost of a given number of QALYs, or to maximize the number of QALYs that can be generated by using a given budgetary allotment.

Consider a national health care system with a given budget for medicines. Assume, too, that several new medicines have been developed and subjected to high-quality clinical trials. These trials will reveal the survivorship rates of people who do not use the tested medicine compared with those of people who do use it. From these survivorship rates one can predict the number of QALYs likely to be generated if the national health care system "adopts" (i.e., buys) Medicine A, Medicine B, or Medicine C. We assume here that A, B, and C deal with different diseases, have different costs,[104] and have different amounts of likely use, if adopted. Thus, it is possible to choose a cost-efficient allocation of the budget, by choosing first the medicine with the highest ratio of QALYs to its cost, then the one with the second-highest ratio, and so on until the limited budget is exhausted.

Disability-adjusted life-years (DALY) is another concept that is considered to be an overall measure of disease burden on an individual. It combines a years-of-life-lost measure and a years-lived-with-disability measure. It calculates the productive years lost from an ideal lifespan owing to morbidity or premature mortality. The reduction of productive years owing to morbidity is a function of the years lived with the disability and a weight assigned. Like QALYs, this approach also allows morbidity and mortality to be combined into a single measure.

A vast amount of research has been carried out on defining a health status. Usually, health status is defined in terms of a composite index, covering most of the physical and psychological conditions. Every health aspect included in the index is rated on an appropriate scale, from the worst to the best state. A single index can then be constructed from all the aspects. For instance, one of the most comprehensive classifications is based on four dimensions: physical function

---

[104] Given the benefits, the analyst should identify the incremental costs for each alternative option. These include capital expenditures for the hospital, clinic, computers, medical equipment, etc., and operating costs for office supplies, administration, and salaries of physicians, nurses, laboratory technicians, and other staff, and so on. In the economic analysis, the cost should also include the opportunity cost of travel, waiting, and forgone earnings of patients or parents of sick children.

(mobility and physical activity), role function (ability to care for oneself), social-emotional function (emotional well-being and social activity), and health problems (including physical deformity) (Torrance et al., 1982). Hence, the usefulness of the QALY or DALY index in cost–utility analysis depends on the reliability of the methods used to define and measure health status.

15.4.2 An Example of Cost–Utility Analysis

Health projects or programmes typically result in multiple benefits, even if a single objective is originally targeted. Using a simple cost–effectiveness analysis often omits some important side benefits. Hence, such problems can be addressed through cost–utility analysis.

Suppose that policy-makers want to design an immunization programme to maximize improvement in health for a given budget in a particular region.[105] Three alternative options are identified that need to be evaluated. They are DPT (a combination of diphtheria, pertussis, and tetanus vaccines for children), BCG (Bacillus Calmette–Guérin, used to prevent tuberculosis), and a package of DPT and BCG combined.

The effects of these alternative options can be obtained from simulations of an epidemiological model that is devised and based on the number of vaccinations, the efficiency of the vaccines, the incidence of fatality rates, duration of morbidity, and years of life lost based on a life-table for the relevant population. The effectiveness of immunization is measured by the reduction in morbidity and mortality rates, and both can ultimately be translated into years of life.

Let us assume that three individuals were saved with an immunization programme: the first individual has avoided a loss of five life-years, based on his or her life expectancy; the second has gained eight life-years; and the third has saved three life-years. The resulting total mortality prevented by this programme, as measured in life-years, is 16 years. A similar count can be carried out for morbidity, which presumes that a person with a lower health status will eventually live a shorter life, while an individual with higher health status will enjoy more years of life. The epidemiological model makes a projection for the population in the particular region and reports the impact of an immunization programme on total life-years gained. This is the simplest type of cost–utility analysis, as it accounts for mortality and morbidity, both measured in number of life-years saved.

Each of the three alternative options described above will result in different additional numbers of life-years gained. These are summarized in Table 15.4. The option of using DPT alone would result in a reduction of total mortality of 209 years and a reduction in total morbidity of 21,401 years. The cost of this option is $1.97 million. The second option, BCG alone, would reduce mortality

---

[105]This example is adopted from Belli et al. (2001).

by 129 years and morbidity by 2,735 years, at a budget cost of $0.585 million. This option is not cost-effective in terms of total years of mortality and morbidity gained. However, the BCG-only programme is more cost-effective in terms of mortality prevention, while the DPT-only programme is superior in terms of reduction of morbidity. The third option, a combination of the two programmes, simply includes all impacts of each of the individual immunization methods.

Table 15.4: Cost-Effectiveness of Alternative Immunization Programmes

Options	Cost ($000)	Life Saved			Cost of Mortality ($/Year)	Cost of Morbidity ($/Year)	Cost–Utility Ratio ($/Year)
		Mortality (Years)	Morbidity (Years)	Total (Years)			
DPT	1,970	209	21,401	21,610	9,408	92	91.2
BCG	585	129	2,735	2,865	4,521	214	204.2
DPT and BCG	2,555	339	24,136	24,475	7,542	106	104.4

Overall, the DPT programme is the most cost-effective of the alternatives as it is able to save an additional year of life at the lowest cost, $91.2 per life-year. Using the BCG vaccination alone is the most expensive way of gaining additional life-years. A combination of DPT and BCG results in a cost of $104.4 per life-year, which is much lower than the option of BCG alone, and only slightly more expensive than DPT vaccination. If the decision is to be taken strictly on the basis of the cost–utility rule, the strategy of using DPT alone should be chosen because it is the most efficient programme in terms of per unit cost. However, if there is sufficient funding to implement both DPT and BCG at the same time, this option is better simply because it saves more lives than either DPT or BCG alone.

This example takes into consideration two aspects of health status: number of additional life-years (reduction in mortality) and condition of disability (morbidity). Reduction in both mortality and morbidity is expressed in additional years of life gained. It is implicitly assumed that the resulting additional years will have the same health status. However, a more elaborate method can be employed for cost–utility analysis in health care. This is a measure of various forms of health outcomes in terms of healthy years of life gained: QALY.

15.4.3 Issues Relating to the Application

Caution is necessary when using cost–utility analysis. Such analysis overcomes the limitation inherent in cost–effectiveness analysis, that of taking account of only one type of benefit. There are other issues that require attention and further research.

First, although cost–utility analysis includes several key benefits, it relies on the construction of a composite utility index and its underlying relative importance in the index. Assignment of relative weights to different types of benefits is usually based on a survey and consultation with government officials, the local community, and experts in the field of the project. Nevertheless, the weights are not based on marketplaces, or on consumers' willingness to pay. Different methods of utility derivation may result in different weights and generate different results (Hornberger et al., 1992).

Second, caveats must be placed on the process of ranking different types of benefits because of the choice of scale on which the benefits are measured or the interaction among the outcomes. For instance, a programme to treat drug addicts is likely to result not only in their lower mortality and morbidity but also in a reduction in street crime. Because different types of benefits are often measured in different units, the choice of a common ranking scale should be compatible with all the benefits.

A further problem arises when different types of benefits are ranked. If one type of benefit is ranked at 80 on a 100-scale and another benefit is assigned ranked at 40, it does not necessarily mean that the first outcome is twice as preferable.

Another caveat lies in the aggregation of individual preferences. A simple summation may seem to be the right way of combining individual choices into social preferences, but this procedure is not appropriate if there are interactions among individuals that would require another method of compiling their total score (Arrow, 1963).

Third, concerns are often raised regarding the discounting of health status and life-years in health care applications. The discounting of costs is not in question, but concern is sometimes expressed about whether additional years and health status should also be discounted. If costs are indeed discounted, while health benefits are not, the cost–effectiveness ratio becomes smaller and smaller in subsequent years. Timing decisions will be biased toward future dates because the ratios improve (Keeler and Cretin, 1983).

When additional years and health quality are discounted, the rate used for discounting is often debatable. The general consensus is necessary for discounting health improvement and additional years gained in the future because individuals normally prefer having better health now than in the distant future; in addition, a life saved today is more valuable than a life saved tomorrow. Nevertheless, there is still considerable controversy over the theory, the methods of measurement, and the appropriate discount rate (Gafni, 1995).

Currently, a rate of 3 or 4 percent is used by various institutions to discount the stream of benefits and costs in health projects in order to compare alternatives. The rate is based on the rate of time preference alone in terms of present versus future consumption. However, there is serious concern that such a discount rate does not fully capture the value that society forgoes in terms of pre-tax returns on displaced investment. A rate of discount that takes into consideration the opportunity cost of forgone investments will be much higher than the rate of time preference of consumption. Note that in the case of most health interventions, where the costs are spread over the time of the intervention, when the benefits are also being realized, the discount rate may not be too critical. However, the size of discount rates is extremely important when capital expenditures such as the construction of hospitals and clinics or the purchase of expensive machines and other advanced equipment are incurred at the beginning of a project. Hence, a reasonable approach to the discount rate is to use a weighted average of the economic rate of return on private investment and the time preference rate for consumption, as outlined in Chapter 8.

15.5 Water Projects

Cost–effectiveness analysis can also be applied in other areas. For example, the growth in water demand over time by the various water users in Polokwane, Capricorn District, and Sekhukhune Cross Border District in South Africa is rapidly using up all the available water resources.[106] Six groups of water users have been identified: Polokwane, Lebalelo Water User Association (WUA), the mining companies, smaller town centres, irrigation demands, and the rural communities (Shand, 2001).

The Olifants-Sand Water Transfer Scheme (OSWTS), including the building of the Rooipoort Dam, is proposed as a major new source of potable water for the region. Three alternative strategies are under consideration.

- Raise the existing Flag Boshielo Dam by 5 metres, but do not build the Rooipoort Dam.
- Construct the Rooipoort Dam but do not raise the Flag Boshielo Dam.
- Construct the Rooipoort Dam and also raise the Flag Boshielo Dam by 5 metres.

Another important and related issue is the scale of the Rooipoort Dam. Technically, two alternative sites are available: an upstream site (smaller reservoir volume) and a downstream site (larger reservoir volume). Both upstream and downstream sites have three possible wall heights (full supply levels, or FSLs), resulting in different capacities for the reservoir. The upstream dam location has three possible wall heights: FSL724 (lowest), FSL728 (medium), and FSL731 (highest). The downstream site also has three alternative wall heights: FSL720 (lowest), FSL725 (medium), and FSL731 (highest). Since only one dam wall will be built, all six options are mutually exclusive alternatives. The investment costs for each of the six options are different.

---

[106]This section is extracted from Cambridge Resources International, Inc. (2003).

Needless to say, each of the six scale alternatives results in a different capacity for the dam reservoir and a different amount of water available for supply.

The amount of water shortage can be calculated from the amount of available water supply less the total bulk water demand. Table 15.5 summarizes the total water shortages under alternative development strategies and project scales over the period 2002–2020 in terms of the present value of the quantity of the shortage.[107] The amount of water deficit, expressed in million m³, is discounted to 2002, the starting point of the analysis.

Table 15.5: Present Value of Water Shortages under Alternative Development Strategies and Project Scales (million m³, in 2002)

	Rooipoort Site	Upstream			Downstream		
	Height of Rooipoort Wall	FSL724	FSL728	FSL731	FSL720	FSL725	FSL731
A	Flag Boshielo+5m (Rooipoort is not built)	85.7	85.7	85.7	85.7	85.7	85.7
B	Rooipoort (Flag Boshielo is not raised)	56.4	31.9	19.7	56.4	28.7	15.6
C	Flag Boshielo+5m and Rooipoort	12.2	3.6	1.7	12.2	2.8	1.7

The highest water shortage amount is about 85 million m³, occurring when only Flag Boshielo is raised and Rooipoort is not built. The strategy that includes both raising Flag Boshielo and building Rooipoort results in the lowest present value of water shortage, 1.7 million m³. If a minimum level of effectiveness were to be used to rank the three alternative water development strategies, Strategy A would be excluded from further evaluation since it does not provide enough water for users.

However, the analysis of such a project is intended to ensure the minimum level of cost-effectiveness in relation to water supply, in terms of alleviating water shortage over years. Thus, the criterion for selecting the best water development policy and scale of the projects is the project's efficiency in providing certain "basic needs" to the region that are essential for sustainable functioning of the economy. The cost–effectiveness ratios should be calculated as the present value of all investment and operating and maintenance costs of each strategy and each scale of the project, divided by the present value of water delivered to bulk users under the corresponding alternative configuration of the OSWTS:

---

[107] The discount rate used for both the costs and the quantity of water shortage in this project was estimated at 11 percent in real terms for South Africa. See Kuo et al. (2003).

$$\frac{Marginal\ Financial}{Unit\ Cost\ of\ Water} = \frac{PV_{Investment+O\&M}}{PV_{Quantity\ of\ Water\ Delivered}}$$

The criterion represents the marginal financial unit cost of water delivered to bulk users. Table 15.6 shows the resulting water costs, expressed as the number of rand per cubic metre (R/m³) of water for each of the alternatives in question.

Table 15.6: Marginal Financial Unit Cost of Water Delivered to Bulk Users (R/m³ of water, in 2002 prices)

		Rooipoort Site			Upstream		Downstream	
	Height of Rooipoort Wall	FSL724	FSL728	FSL731	FSL720	FSL725	FSL731
A	Flag Boshielo+5m (Rooipoort is not built)	1.47	1.47	1.47	1.47	1.47	1.47
B	Rooipoort (Flag Boshielo is not raised)	3.00	2.49	2.29	3.15	2.50	2.20
C	Flag Boshielo+5m and Rooipoort	2.17	2.06	2.05	2.26	2.10	2.04

We first determine which development strategy is worth pursuing. If a maximum acceptable water shortage amount has been set, Strategy A is not a viable option for economic development simply because it does not provide enough water to the users. With this condition, the analyst would then compare Strategies B and C in terms of their cost–effectiveness ratios. Table 15.6 shows that Strategy C is superior to Strategy B at all scales of the project because the marginal cost of water under Strategy C is lower. Therefore, Strategy C is the "optimal" way of developing water resources. Finally, in choosing the wall height of the Rooipoort site, the design of the Rooipoort Dam at the downstream site with the highest, and the most expensive, dam wall (FSL731) has the lowest marginal financial cost of water, at 2.04 R/m³ in 2002 prices.

We now turn to the economic evaluation of the OSWTS. The marginal economic unit cost of water is calculated as the sum of all the economic costs of the OSWTS including the impact of water deficit on the economy divided by the total quantity of water delivered to bulk users, all being expressed in *PV*:

$$\frac{Marginal\ Economic}{Unit\ Cost\ of\ Water}\ \left(R_{2002}/m^3\right) = \frac{PV\left(Economic\ Costs_{Investment+O\&M}\right) + PV\left(\begin{array}{c}Economic\ Cost\\of\ Water\ Deficit\end{array}\right)}{PV\left(\begin{array}{c}Quantity\ of\ Water\\Delivered\ to\ Users\end{array}\right) + PV\left(\begin{array}{c}Quantity\ of\ Water\\Deficit\end{array}\right)}$$

Assuming the opportunity cost to the country of any water deficit to be 3.0 R/m³, the opportunity cost of water deficit to the economy can be calculated by applying the value to each unit of water that is not delivered to the users. The highest opportunity cost would be incurred if Strategy A were to be undertaken, and this would result in a massive water shortage compared with the other two strategies.

Table 15.7 presents the marginal economic unit cost of water delivered to bulk users resulting from the different development strategies and scales of the project. It is interesting to note that if the cost of water shortages is not accounted for, Strategy A has the lowest water cost per unit delivered to bulk users. However, when the economic cost of water deficit is assumed to be 3.0 R/m³, Strategy A results in the highest water cost compared with the other two strategies. The conclusion from the economic cost–effectiveness analysis of the OSWTS is that the best development strategy is C, comprising the raising of the Flag Boshielo Dam and building the Rooipoort Dam at the wall height of FSL731. The unit cost is the same at both the upstream and the downstream sites of the highest dam option.

Table 15.7: Marginal Economic Unit Cost of Water Delivered to Bulk Users (R/m³, in 2002 prices)

	Rooipoort Site			Upstream			Downstream	
	Height of Rooipoort Wall	FSL724	FSL728	FSL731	FSL720	FSL725	FSL731
A	Flag Boshielo+5m (Rooipoort is not built)	2.19	2.19	2.19	2.19	2.19	2.19
B	Rooipoort (Flag Boshielo is not raised)	3.40	2.43	2.07	3.53	2.39	1.95
C	Flag Boshielo+5m and Rooipoort	2.12	1.91	1.87	2.21	1.94	1.86

15.6 Conclusion

Given the difficulties in quantifying the outcomes in monetary terms for public security, education, health care and other social projects, cost–benefit analysis cannot be used to evaluate their alternative options. This chapter has presented one approach, namely cost–effectiveness analysis, for handling these types of projects including education, power, health, and water. The general procedure requires calculation of the incremental impacts of a particular project associated with the incremental cost. The resulting marginal cost–effectiveness ratios are used to rank the alternative options.

When only one aspect of the benefits of a project matters, cost–effectiveness analysis offers a simple tool for selecting alternative options with technical efficiency. However, the approach does not cover more than one single benefit; other benefits may also be important, and should be accounted for in the selection of the project.

A weighted cost–effectiveness or cost–utility analysis is generally used when multiple benefits need to be included in the assessment. It is measured by a composite index that includes important factors affecting the project selection. The main advantage of this approach is that it can capture a whole host of benefits in a single measure for ranking alternative options. This is especially useful when applied to health or education projects because they usually generate multiple benefits. As regards the costs, they should be measured in resource costs over the life of the project or programme.

While both cost–effectiveness and cost–utility analysis offer practical methods for selecting among alternative projects or programmes, they have limitations because their output is not priced in the market and it is difficult to measure the consumers' willingness to pay for them. As a consequence, some subjective judgments must be made in quantifying a composite effectiveness of alternative options under consideration, even though surveys and consultation exercises with experts in the field are frequently employed to minimize the possible bias. Other questions, such as the appropriate size of the discount rate, are still contentious issues, especially in health projects. Research continues to advance the methodology for practical application of cost–effectiveness analysis in a wide range of fields.

References

Adhikari, R., P. Gertler, and A. Lagman. 1999. "Economic Analysis of Health Sector Projects – A Review of Issues, Methods, and Approaches", Economic Staff Paper. Manila: Asian Development Bank (March).

Arrow, K.J. 1963. *Social Choice and Individual Values.* New York: Wiley.

Belli, P., J.R. Anderson, H.N. Barnum, J.A. Dixon, and J.P. Tan. 2001. *Economic Analysis of Investment Operations: Analytical Tools and Practical Applications*, Chapters 7–9. Washington, DC: The World Bank.

Belli, P., Q. Khan, and G. Psacharopoulos. 1999. "Assessing a Higher Education Project: A Mauritius Feasibility Study", *Applied Economics* 31(1), 27–35.

Cambridge Resources International, Inc. 2003. "Evaluation of the Olifants-Sand Water Transfer Scheme in the Northern Province of South Africa", report prepared for the Northern Province of South Africa. Cambridge, MA (January).

Gafni, A. 1995. "Time in Health: Can We Measure Individuals' Pure Time Preference?" *Medical Decision Making* 15(1).

Garber, A.M. and C.E. Phelps. 1997. "Economic Foundations of Cost-effectiveness Analysis", *Journal of Health Economics* 16(1), 1–31.

Hornberger, J.C., D.A. Redelmeier, and J. Peterson. 1992. "Variability among Methods to Assess Patients' Well-Being and Consequent Effect on a Cost-effectiveness Analysis", *Journal of Clinical Epidemiology* 45(5), 505–512.

Keeler, E.B. and S. Cretin. 1983. "Discounting of Life-Saving and Other Nonmonetary Effects", *Management Science*, 29 (3), 300-306.

Kuo, C.Y., G.P. Jenkins, and M.B. Mphahlele. 2003. "The Economic Opportunity Cost of Capital in South Africa", *South African Journal of Economics* 71(3).

Psacharopoulos, G. 1994. "Returns to Investment in Education: A Global Update", *World Development* 22(9), 1325–1343.

Shand, N. 2001. "Olifants-Sand Water Transfer Scheme: Feasibility of Further Phases", Interim Report, prepared for the Department of Water Affairs and Forestry, Government of the Northern Province, P B500/00/2499.

Torrance, G.W., M.H. Boyle, and S.P. Horwood. 1982. "Application of Multi-attribute Utility Theory to Measure Social Preferences for Health Status", *Operations Research* 30(6), 1043–1069.

Viscusi, W.K. 1993. "The Value of Risks to Life and Health", *Journal of Economic Literature* 31(4), 1912–1946.

Viscusi, W.K. and J.E. Aldy. 2003. "The Value of Statistical Life: A Critical Review of Market Estimates throughout the World", *Journal of Risk and Uncertainty* 27(1), 5–76.

Zeinali, A., 2010. *Infrastructure Choices in Education in South Africa: Location, Build or Repair,* An essay submitted to the Department of Economics in partial fulfilment of the requirements for the degree of Master of Arts.

Chapter Sixteen

Cost–Benefit Analysis of
Transportation Projects

16.1 Introduction[108]

This chapter will focus on the problems of evaluating transportation projects in the context of less-developed countries. Emphasis will be placed on highway projects because these account for the bulk of transport investments in the developing parts of the world, with rail projects being largely limited to the modernization of existing facilities, and air transport and port projects, even when they are basically new, being of small magnitude relative to road investment.

If a project passes a straight financial test, based on the present value of its cash inflows and outflows, projects would be accepted only if the financial net present value (NPV) were outweighed by the present value of the project's various externalities. Road projects, however, carry a special interest compared to other types of transport investments because of the fact that they can only rarely be justified on the basis of strictly commercial considerations. Rail and air fares and port and landing charges constitute direct devices by which the costs of the relevant facilities can, over time, be recouped from the beneficiaries. To a first approximation, therefore, whether such projects are worthwhile can be judged by the strictly commercial criterion of prospective profitability. Except for toll roads, road investments never offer the luxury of such a positive financial NPV. User charges are, of course, present in the road transport field in the form of gasoline taxes, motor vehicle licences and taxes, and the like. But these charges are functions of the general tax structure of the country in question and do not vary depending on whether vehicles are used on one highway or another. They are related neither to the benefits that the users of a particular project may be expected to enjoy nor to the costs of constructing that project.

This means that whereas for other important types of transport projects user charges can be taken as the first-approximation measure of benefits, for road projects we must confront the problem of estimating benefits essentially from scratch. This may be difficult or easy, depending upon the circumstances of the case. By and large, the great bulk of road projects entail improvements of existing roads or, what amounts to much the same thing, linking by a shorter

---

[108]This chapter is largely drawn from the paper by Harberger (1967).

and/or better road population centres that were already linked by the pre-existing network. In these cases, we can in general have access to two key pieces of information of great value in estimating project benefits: a) the actual volume of traffic now flowing between the points to be served by the road improvements, and b) the probable reduction in costs of travel per vehicle-mile that will occur as a consequence of the improvement. It will be seen below that with the aid of these two types of facts, reasonably accurate measurements of the prospective benefits of road improvement projects can normally be made.

Such is not the case with respect to totally new roads that penetrate areas not yet served by the highway network. For these roads, the prospective volume of traffic is much more of an unknown than in the case of road improvements, and the benefit per user, which for the road improvement can be measured quite accurately in terms of cost-reduction per vehicle-mile, now presents more formidable problems of estimation.

16.2 The Case of Road Improvements

It is the nature of the case that road improvement projects do not bring into being possibilities of vehicular transport that did not exist before. They may generate new traffic owing to the fact that they reduce costs of travel, but the bulk of the traffic to be served by the improved road is likely already to have been travelling on the existing one. This means that the bulk of the benefits stemming from the improvement are likely to accrue to traffic that would in any case have passed over the road in its unimproved state.

The direct benefits of a road improvement all involve savings of costs. The better the road, in general, the lower will be the consumption of gasoline and oil, the less the wear and tear on tyres, the lower the incidence of repair and maintenance expenses, and the longer the useful life of the vehicle using it. Traffic engineers have provided us with the technical coefficients relating the quality of the road and the speed travelled to the vehicle operating costs in terms of quantities of inputs required by type of vehicle. For example, fuel consumption will vary with the type of road (earth, gravel, paved) for automobile, bus and size of truck. It will also vary by speed of vehicle, by the rate of rise or fall of the road, and by the degree of curvature of the road. In a similar fashion, for each type of vehicle, engine oil consumption, tyre wear, maintenance costs, and depreciation of vehicles will vary with the type of road and the speed of travel.

Additional savings beyond those connected directly with vehicle costs include the saving of time for occupants of the vehicles, the savings of maintenance expenditures on the road itself, and the possible reduction in the costs of accidents as a result of the road improvement. Of these, the first two are usually the most important. If the time of the occupants of a vehicle is valued at $10 per hour, this amounts to $0.40 per vehicle-mile at 25 mph and $0.25 per vehicle-mile at 40 mph – the saving of $0.15 per vehicle-mile is clearly large in comparison with the likely reduction in direct vehicle costs associated with an improvement from earth to gravel. Of course, the value of this saving is tied to the value placed on the hour of the occupants' time and is therefore sensitive to the level of living in the country. In a very low-income country such as India, the time-saving aspect of road improvements is likely to contribute little to the overall estimate of their benefits, but even at relatively modest income levels, it has an important effect – a saving of $0.01 per vehicle-mile arising from the above-assumed increase in speed at a value of $0.37 per vehicle-hour.[109]

With respect to road maintenance costs, it is clear that improvement can often generate substantial savings. A study based on Venezuelan data estimated that the maintenance costs of a gravel road were equal to those of an earth road at an average traffic level of 100 vehicles per day; beyond this travel level, there was a saving of over $0.02 per vehicle-kilometre when the road was gravel. Similarly, the maintenance costs of paved and gravel roads were estimated to be equal at an average daily traffic of 300 vehicles per day, beyond which there was a saving of over $0.02 per vehicle-kilometre in having a paved as against a gravel road (Soberman, 1966).

We now turn to the basic procedure for evaluating the direct benefits of a particular road improvement. First, we estimate, on the basis of currently observed traffic volume, its past trend, and the likely rate of growth of the economy in the area, a projected time path for the traffic volume of vehicles of each type, assuming that the improvement is not made. This will generate a time-series for each type of vehicle, V_{it}, where V stands for traffic volume, i for type of vehicle, and t for time. We sum these for each year to obtain $V_i \; (= \sum V_{it})$, the volume of traffic that we expect for each year. On the basis of the expected volume, we then project the estimated average speed of traffic on the road in year t. This can be done either by using direct observations of the relationship between average speed and traffic volume on the road in question or, if those are not available, by using functional relationships between speed and traffic volume for the particular type of road. Such relationships have been estimated for many years by the US Bureau of Public Roads and other highway authorities. We thus obtain $S_{it} = f(V_t)$, where S_{it} is the average speed of the ith vehicle type.

The estimates of average speed, together with the characteristics of the road (such as gradient and curvature) enable us to estimate the average cost, c_{it}, per vehicle-mile at time t for vehicles of class i on the unimproved road.

We must next estimate corresponding figures for the improved road. If traffic volumes are expected to be the same whether the road is improved or not, this is an easy task. It simply entails inserting the estimated V_t into the equation setting out the relationship between average speed and traffic volume for roads

---

[109] Note that the average vehicle carries more than one passenger. Suppose there are on average 1.8 passengers per automobile and 1.2 passengers per truck. The saving of $0.01 per vehicle-mile would therefore be reached at a value of time of about $0.37 per hour for occupants of passenger vehicles and about $0.56 per hour for the occupants of trucks.

Cost–Benefit Analysis of Transportation Projects

of the type (such as two-land gravel) being planned. The estimated speeds s'_{it} thus obtained, along with the gradient and curvature characteristics of the proposed improved road, enable us to estimate the prospective average costs c'_{it} of travel on that road for each vehicle class.

Included in c_{it} and c'_{it} should be all costs perceived by the owners and occupants of the vehicles – including fuel, oil, maintenance, repair, depreciation, and the time-costs of the occupants. The benefits accruing in year t to the owners and occupants as a consequence of the proposed improvement are therefore estimated as $\sum_i (c_{it} - c'_{it}) V_{it}$, and the present value of this class of benefits is $\sum_i (1+r)^{-t} \sum_i (c_{it} - c'_{it}) V_{it}$, where r is the rate of discount used for purposes of cost–benefit analysis and the current year is taken as the origin for the purpose of measuring time. To these benefits we must then add the prospective savings in maintenance costs, $M_t - M'_t$, where M_t refers to maintenance costs on the unimproved road and M'_t to those on the improved road. These will be functions of the prospective traffic volumes V_t and should be estimated on the basis of them. The expression for the present value of total direct benefits (accident prevention is assumed to be a negligible component of total benefits) is therefore:

$$\sum_t (1+r)^{-t} \sum_i (c_{it} - c'_{it}) V_{it} + \sum_t (1+r)^{-t} \sum_i (M_t - M'_t) \quad (16.1)$$

When it is anticipated that the traffic volume at time t will increase as a direct consequence of the improvement, the analysis becomes slightly more complicated. First, one must estimate the expected increase in traffic $(V'_{it} - V_{it})$ of different types. Then on the basis of $V'_t (= \sum_i V'_{it})$, one should estimate S'_{it}, using the functional relationship between speed and volume for roads of the improved type. Using these speeds, one then proceeds to estimate the average costs per vehicle-mile, c'_i, under the proposed changes in road characteristics. Using the prospective volumes of traffic V'_{it}, one estimates the projected road maintenance costs M'_t. With these modifications in methodology, equation (16.1) remains valid as a measure of the present value of a large part of total direct benefits, but omits one component thereof – the gain in consumer surplus to the newly generated traffic. This additional traffic can come from more frequent use of the road after it is improved by those who already travel on the road (generated traffic) plus those who now use the improved road but previously travelled on another road (diverted traffic).

This is illustrated in Figure 16.1. Here $D_i D'_i$ represents the demand function for the use of the road by vehicles of type i. On the vertical axis is measured the price that each successive unit of traffic would be willing to pay, per vehicle-mile, for travelling over the road. This price should be interpreted as the maximum total cost per vehicle-mile that this unit of traffic would be willing to bear in order to travel on the road. On the unimproved road, the cost per vehicle-mile is c_{it}, and the corresponding traffic level V_{it} includes all those traffic units willing to bear costs of c_{it} or more. Under the improvement, costs will fall to c'_{it}, and traffic volume will now expand to V'_{it}. The gross benefits received by the incremental traffic are measured by $V_{it}EFV'_{it}$, but the costs they perceive are $V_{it}GFV'_{it}$. Therefore, the triangle EFG measures their net benefit for the year t. They do not receive as much net benefit as the existing traffic because some of the reduction in costs per vehicle-mile is of no relevance to them. If c_{it} is \$0.10 and c'_{it} is \$0.07, a potential traveller willing to pay no more than \$0.08 to use the road obtains no benefit from a reduction in cost from \$0.10 to \$0.08; at that point, he may use the road, but he will be on the margin of indifference between using it and not using it. If the use of the road is now made available to him at a cost of \$0.07 per vehicle-mile, the measure of his net benefit is \$0.01 (= \$0.08 − \$0.07), while those who were already paying \$0.10 to use the road in its unimproved state will perceive a benefit of \$0.03 per vehicle-mile.

Figure 16.1: Direct Benefits of Road Improvement

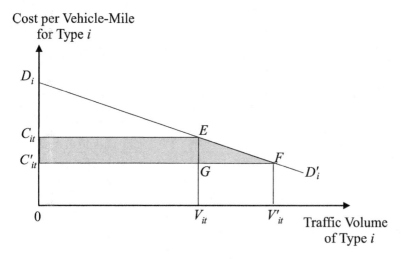

If the demand curve for the services of the road is linear, or if not, taking a linear approximation to that curve, we may express the triangle EFG as $\frac{1}{2}\sum_i (c_{it} - c'_{it})(V'_{it} - V_{it})$. We must therefore add to (16.1) the expression

$$\frac{1}{2}\sum_t (1+r)^{-t}\sum_i (c_{it} - c'_{it})(V'_{it} - V_{it}) \qquad (16.2)$$

in order to capture that component of benefit represented by consumer surplus accruing to traffic generated directly as a consequence of the improvement.

16.3 The Case of Penetration Roads

When a road is built in an area to which access by motor vehicles was previously impossible, the analysis of Section 16.2 remains in principle unchanged, but in practice, significant modifications in approach may be required. The difficulties here stem from the fact that V_t is zero; hence, the component of benefits represented by $C_{it}EGC'_{it}$ in Figure 16.1 simply does not exist. All traffic is newly generated by the presence of the road, and all direct benefits to users, therefore, are in principle of the type represented by the triangle *EFG*. Figure 16.2 represents such a case.

Figure 16.2: Direct Benefits of New Road

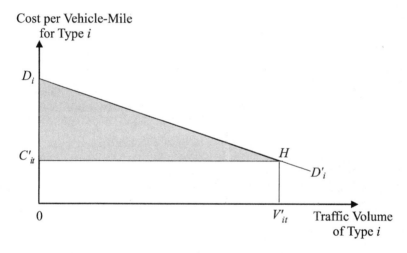

Here the annual net benefit to users of type i is given by the triangle $D_iHC'_{it}$, which corresponds exactly to triangle *EFG* in Figure 16.1. The special problems presented by the present case arise because: a) whereas for improvement of existing roads the increment in volume caused by the improvement $(V'_t - V_t)$ is likely to be relatively small in relation to V_t, this increment represents the entire volume of traffic in the case of a penetration road; and b) whereas, in the case of road improvements, the costs per vehicle-mile c_{it} and c'_{it} of a given amount of traffic on the existing and improved roads can be rather precisely estimated, thus giving us a good estimate of the height of the triangle *EFG*, we do not have any correspondingly precise estimate of the height of the triangle $D_iHC'_{it}$ in the case of a penetration road. A problem is raised by a) because the increment of traffic caused by an improvement, is obviously subject to greater estimation error than the traffic based on the normal expansion of what we observe today; for a road improvement, this error applies to a relatively small part of the total direct annual benefit, while for a penetration road, the error applies to more than the whole (more because from the triangle $D_i HC'_{it}$ we must deduct the annual maintenance costs of the road, M_i). A problem is raised by b) because the existing cost of moving goods and people into an area to be newly penetrated by a road is likely to be high (if not, as, for example, in the case of easy transport by water, the analysis becomes quite similar to that of a road improvement). This cost does not provide a useful estimate of the location of point D_i. Moreover, the assumption of linearity of the demand curve for the services of the road, which is likely to yield a good approximation, when, as in Figure 16.1, the relevant points (E and F) are not too distant from each other, is much more precarious in the case of Figure 16.2, where deviations of the segment $D_i H$ from linearity could have a substantial effect on the area of $D_i HC'_{it}$.

The above-mentioned types of difficulties encountered in the analysis of penetration roads can make it advisable in some cases to use alternative approaches to the estimation of benefits. The simplest case is that of an isolated mine, where the problem of access to the mine should be thought of in the course of deciding whether it is worthwhile to exploit it. If the traffic to be carried over the road is to be exclusively or almost exclusively connected with the operation of the mine, then the enterprise exploiting the mine should also bear the costs of the road. If under these circumstances the mine is not an attractive venture, the implication is that it is not advantageous to the society as a whole to exploit the mine. (Needless to say, this conclusion could be reversed if externalities were present in sufficient amount, but this qualification would apply to any apparently unprofitable investment whatever.)

A more complex case is that of a road that is opening up a new area to agricultural exploitation. Here the essence of the problem can best be seen by assuming that the area to be opened up consists entirely of public lands that have no value at present, owing to their remoteness. The benefits attributable to the road project would then be the total estimated yield that the government could obtain from the sale of the lands once the road was built, assuming that the market for land would be functioning well. If the land already had a value in its existing state, the benefit attributable to the road would be the excess of the prospective sale value of the land over its present market price.

Institutional arrangements and market imperfections, however, can make land-value comparisons fall wide of the mark as estimates of the benefits of penetration roads. To mention the most obvious case, the land (here assumed to be privately held) may have no true economic productivity in the absence of a road, but it may have a positive market price today because its owners anticipate that the government someday will build a road into the area. In this case, the prospective sale value of the land, once the road is built, and not the difference between this and today's market value of the land, is the relevant measure of the road's benefits. A second problem concerns possible improvements of the land. In all uses of land-value comparisons to assess the benefits of a road, the costs

Cost–Benefit Analysis of Transportation Projects

of any improvements in the land (clearing, levelling, irrigating, and so forth) that do not already exist today should be deducted from its prospective future value before attributing any benefit to the road.

Where direct use of land-value comparisons is found to be unwarranted or excessively risky, one may attempt to assess the benefits of a road opening up a new area to agriculture on the basis of prospective agricultural production. Here, once again, care must be taken to deduct from the value of prospective farm output all the relevant associated costs, including those of clearing and improving the land (capital costs) as well as such current costs as labour, fertilizer, and transporting the inputs and outputs of agriculture over the road itself. To the extent that complementary social investments such as the provision of electricity or drinking water are entailed in opening up the area to agriculture, their costs, too, must be deducted from the value of prospective farm output before arriving at the benefit due to the road itself. Or, what amounts to essentially the same thing, the entire set of investments entailed in opening up the area can be evaluated as a "package", weighing the discounted value of expected flows of agricultural output against the discounted sum of all costs — capital and current, public and private — entailed in bringing forth that output.

It is of utmost importance to recognize that the use of changes in land values, the use of the present value of changes in agricultural output less costs, and the estimation of the present value of annual triangles $D_i HC'_{it}$ in Figure 16.2 are three *alternative* ways of achieving essentially the same thing. If land prices initially contain no speculative component anticipating that a road would be built, the rise in land values induced by the road is simply the capitalized value of benefits obtained but not paid for by road users. It may not capture all of $D_i HC'_{it}$ for some users of the road other than farmers who may be capturing part of it, and some road benefits perceived by farmers may not be capitalized into land values. But, in any case, the rise in land values is not additional to the present value of the demand triangles. Similarly, we can represent today's non-speculative value of land as the present value of expected future net output in the absence of the road and relate it to a corresponding value in the presence of the road. This means that the change in land value will be the present value of the increase in output due to the road less the present value of the additional farm-owner capital and current costs of achieving that output. Failure to recognize these three approaches as alternative ways of measuring the same thing has often led to double-counting of benefits and even in some cases to triple-counting!

16.4 Externalities Connected with Road Projects

It is appropriate, in the analysis of any project from the point of view of society as a whole, to take into account external or indirect benefits and costs. These can conveniently be summarized in the formula $\sum_i D_{it}(X'_{it} - X^o_{it})$, where D_{it} is the excess of benefits over costs associated with a unit change of the level of activity X_i at time t, X'_{it} is that level in the presence of the project in question, and X^o_{it} is that level in the absence of the project. Thus, for example, X_{1t} might be the number of unskilled labourers employed in a particular textile plant, and D_{1t} might be the excess of the wage paid to them over opportunity cost of their labour in alternative employments. Similarly, X_{2t} might be the output of a tyre factory, and D_{2t} might be the excise tax collected per tyre, representing the excess of the social benefit (here measured by the market price people pay for tyres) over the resource cost of producing them. If, owing to the existence of a road project, more or less unskilled labour were to be employed in the textile plant, or more or fewer tyres were to be produced in the tyre factory, indirect benefits or costs, as given by the formula presented above, would have to be attributed to the project.

There is nothing in the cases cited above that is unique to road investment projects. If we were considering an electricity project or an irrigation project, we would want to ask how the level of employment of unskilled workers in the textile plant and how the output of the tyre factory would change, if at all, as a consequence of the project, just as we would do in the case of a road project. In principle, the authorities in charge of project evaluation ought to identify all activities X_i for which marginal social benefit differs by a meaningful amount from marginal social cost and to provide project evaluators with estimates of the extent of the corresponding distortions, D_i. The project evaluators would then estimate the changes in the relevant activity levels caused by each particular project, to obtain $\sum_i D_{it}(X'_{it} - X^o_{it})$ for each year of the project's expected life, as a summary measure of the project's indirect benefits or costs.

16.4.1 Externalities Involving Traffic on Other Roads

Although, then, the general procedure for dealing with externalities contains nothing peculiar to road projects, there are nonetheless two types of distortions that are of special interest where road projects are concerned. These are: a) the likely excess of marginal social cost over marginal social benefit for traffic on roads, and b) the likely excess of marginal social benefit over marginal social cost for traffic on railways. Some readers may be surprised by the assertion that an excess of marginal cost over marginal benefit is likely in the case of road traffic, but a little reflection is sufficient to establish the point. All the studies that have been done of the relationship between average speed and volume of traffic on particular roads have shown that the higher the traffic volume, the lower the average speed. This negative relationship applies even at relatively low traffic volumes, long before anything that one might call congestion sets in. The consequence is that an increment of traffic on a road has the effect of slowing down the pre-existing traffic, increasing its cost per vehicle-mile in terms of the time spent by the occupants and possibly in terms of other costs as well.

Let the function relating speed to volume be:

$$S = a - bV \qquad (16.3)$$

and let the value of the occupants' time be H per vehicle-hour. The time-cost perceived by the occupants of a typical vehicle will be H/S per vehicle-mile; this is also the marginal private time-cost as seen by the typical driver. The total time-cost of all users of the road will be VH/S, and the marginal social time-cost will be:

$$\partial(VH/S)/\partial V = H[S - V(\partial S/\partial V)]/S^2 \qquad (16.4)$$
$$= H[a - bV + bV]/V^2 = aH/S^2$$

Thus, marginal social cost exceeds marginal private cost by the percentage:

$$(MSC - MPC)/MPC = [aH/S^2 - H/S]/(H/S) = (a - S)/S \, (16.5)$$

This expression can be easily interpreted as the "percentage speed deficit". If, on the type of road in question, the average speed of travel (a) at very low traffic volumes is 60 miles per hour (mph), and if, at the actual traffic volume, average speed is 40 mph, then marginal social time-cost exceeds marginal private time-cost by 50 percent [$=(60 - 40)/40$].

The presence of this externality suggests the possibility of collecting a tax (a congestion toll), meaning that travellers would face a marginal private cost equal to the marginal social cost entailed in their trips. A gasoline tax operates in a rough way to help offset the discrepancy between marginal private and marginal social cost of travel. But it is at most a very imperfect offset, as the discrepancy between social and private costs varies greatly with the volume of traffic, while the amount of gasoline consumed per mile is almost constant. Table 16.1 shows how the optimum tax (one designed just to offset the discrepancy between marginal social and marginal private costs) would vary for different speeds and different values of the percentage speed deficit, assuming the vehicle-hour to be valued at $1. It is seen there that where average speeds are as low as 20 mph (as is often the case on earth and gravel roads), the optimum tax is likely to be in excess of $0.01 per vehicle-mile. And even at a speed of 40 mph, an optimum tax of $0.01 per mile would not be rare — this would require a speed deficit of 40 percent, meaning a situation in which the average speed of unimpeded traffic would be 56 mph as compared with an actual average speed of 40 mph. It is unlikely, therefore, that gasoline taxes compensate for more than a part of the typical discrepancy between social and private costs — particularly when one realizes that the heaviest volumes of traffic occur at the times when the speed deficit is greatest, the latter being a direct function of traffic volume. We proceed, then, under the assumption that, in general, marginal social costs of travel on roads exceed marginal private cost, even when the offsetting effects of gasoline taxes are taken into account.

Table 16.1: Excess of Marginal Social Cost over Marginal Private Cost per Vehicle-Mile (Based on Assumed Value of Time of $1 per Vehicle-Hour and Gasoline Tax of Zero)

$(a-S)/S$	Miles per Hour			
	20	30	40	50
0.10	$0.005	$0.0033	$0.0025	$0.002
0.20	0.010	0.0067	0.0050	0.004
0.30	0.015	0.0100	0.0075	
0.40	0.020	0.0133	0.0100	
0.50	0.025	0.0167		

We now distinguish two cases in which adjustment is warranted for externalities of the type we have been discussing, the first being a case in which the road improvement in question is a substitute for existing roads, and the second in which the relationship is one of complementarity. Broadly speaking, one can identify substitutability with urban complexes, in which there normally exist many alternative routes to get from one place to another, and complementarity with rural roads, where there is normally only one relevant route between two places. In the case of substitutability, a part of the newly generated traffic on the improved road will have been diverted from other roads. An external benefit appears here, for there is now less traffic on the substitute roads, and such traffic as remains will move faster, implying a saving of time-costs for the occupants of those vehicles. In the case of complementarity, traffic volumes will increase on the roads feeding into and out of the improved segment; travel on these roads will therefore be slower, implying an increase in the cost of travel for using them.

These effects are illustrated in Figure 16.3, which depicts the situation on a road, *B*, either competitive or complementary with the one (Road *A*) on which the improvement is to be made. For the sake of simplicity, the traffic on this road is assumed to be all of one type so that the costs facing each unit of that traffic will be the same for all vehicles. Let *DD'* be the demand curve for travel on road *B*, and let *CC'* be the curve relating private costs of travel per vehicle-mile to the volume of traffic on that road. *CS'*, the curve marginal to *CC'*, represents the marginal social cost of travel on Road *B*. The initial equilibrium, before Road *A* is improved, will be at the traffic volume V_0, where the private cost curve intersects the demand curve.

Figure 16.3: Externalities for Substitute and Complementary Roads

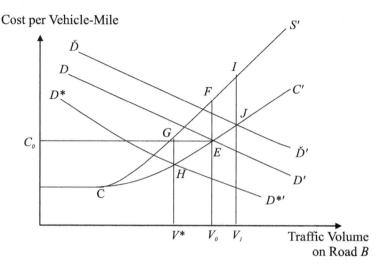

If Road B is competitive with Road A, the improvement of A will cause the demand curve for travel on B to shift to the left, taking the position, say, $D*D*'$ and producing a new equilibrium level of traffic of $V*$. The external benefit caused by the diversion of $(V_0 - V*)$ units of traffic from Road B will be measured by the area $EFGH$.

If Road B is complementary with Road A, the improvement of A will cause the demand curve for travel on B to shift to the right to the position, say, $\check{D}\check{D}'$ and yielding the equilibrium traffic volume V_1. The external cost associated with the increase in traffic volume on B will in this case be measured by the area $EFIJ$.

Unless the change in traffic volume is large in relation to its initial level, the area $EFGH$ or $EFIJ$ can be closely approximated by the formula $C_0 f \Delta V (a - s_0)/s_0$. Here C_0 is the initial cost per vehicle-mile on Road B, f is the fraction of C_0 represented by time-costs, ΔV is the change in traffic volume on Road B induced by the improvement of A, a is the average speed of unimpeded traffic on roads of the same type as B, and s_0 is the initial average speed of traffic on road B. Here C_0 is equal to the height $V_0 E$; $C_0 f$ that part of $V_0 E$ represented by time-costs; and $(a - s_0)/s_0$ is the fraction of $C_0 f$ that represents the excess of social over private costs in the initial situation. Thus, $C_0 f (a - s_0)/s_0$ is equal to the height EF. The approximation involved in the formula, therefore, entails assuming that the vertical distance between CC' and CS' remains constant at EF over the range of the change in traffic volume, rather than increasing to IJ in the case of growing traffic volume or declining to GH in the case of reduced traffic volume.

When traffic on a number of different roads is likely to be affected by the improvement of Road A, the technique outlined above should be applied to each of them. This leads to an expression for the external effects of the improvement of A, which is equal to $\sum_j C_{0j} f_j \Delta V_j (a_j - s_{0j})/s_{0j}$, where the symbols have the meanings defined above and the index j varies over the number of other roads on which traffic volume is affected by the improvement of Road A. Typically, it will be necessary to distinguish, for a given road, between periods with different initial traffic volumes. In this event, we may define several traffic volume intervals V_{jk} on Road j; associated with each such interval will be a level of private costs, C_{0jk}, a fraction f_{jk} of such costs that is represented by time-costs, and an average speed of traffic s_{0jk}. The measure of the external effects of the improvement of Road A then becomes:

$$E = \sum_j \sum_k C_{0jk} f_{jk} \Delta V_{jk} (a_j - s_{0jk})/s_{0jk}$$

This expression should be estimated for each year of the expected life of Project A, and the value $\sum_t (1+r)^{-t} E_t$ should then be subtracted from the estimated present value of direct benefits of A. Note that E will be negative if substitute roads predominate in the set j, so that in this case, net benefits will be algebraically larger after making the adjustment for these external effects.[110]

16.4.2 Externalities Involving Rail Traffic

The problems involved in the relationships between road and rail transport can be complex, owing to the difficulty of isolating the relevant costs of rail transport. The marginal costs of carrying additional passengers or freight on trains that are running in any event are very low indeed; the marginal costs of running additional trains on runs where the track and station facilities will in any event be kept in working condition are at an intermediate level; and the marginal

---

[110]A similar adjustment of the analysis to take account of differing traffic volumes at different times is advisable in the analysis of the direct benefits of a road improvement; this was outlined in Section 16.2. The first term in expression (16.1) would then become $\sum_t (1+r)^{-t} \sum_i \sum_k (c_{itk} - c'_{itk}) V_{itk}$, and expression (16.2) would become $\frac{1}{2} \sum_t (1+r)^{-t} \sum_i \sum_k (c_{itk} - c'_{itk})(V'_{itk} - V_{itk})$. This adjustment allows us to take account of the fact that the benefits of a road improvement are likely to be greater, per vehicle-mile, in periods of high traffic density than in periods of very low volume with essentially unimpeded flow.

Cost–Benefit Analysis of Transportation Projects

costs of providing rail service on a stretch of track as against the alternative of abandoning that stretch are higher still.

In what follows, we shall assume that the basic relationship between road and rail transport is one of substitutability — that is, that a project of road construction or improvement will tend to reduce the volume of rail traffic, if it has any effect at all on it. Consider now a road from B to C, which parallels a railway that runs from A to D. Assume also that the stretch from B to C is but a small fraction of the total distance from A to D, and that all trains on the railway ply the full distance from A to D, at least some of them stopping at B and C.

Under the above assumptions, it is likely that the improvement of the BC road will divert some traffic that otherwise would move by rail between these points. It is unlikely, however, to affect the volume of rail traffic moving between A and B, between C and D, or between A and D. In this case, the diversion of traffic from rail to road will probably not cause a reduction in the number and size of trains moving between A and D; they will just have more excess capacity than before over the stretch from B to C.[111] When traffic is thus diverted from rail to road, we measure the direct gross benefits of the diverted traffic as the area under the demand curve for travel on the road, and the direct costs as the average costs per vehicle-mile in the new situation, multiplied by the number of vehicle-miles of traffic diverted from the railway. What have we neglected here? First, the diverted traffic ceases to benefit from the use of the railway; we measure these forgone benefits by the passenger fares and freight rates that this diverted traffic would have paid to the railway in the absence of the improvement. Second, the railway no longer has to bear the marginal cost of carrying the diverted traffic. These costs are likely to be very low in relation to fares and freight rates in the case we are now examining. The net external effect will therefore almost certainly be negative and will be measured by $\sum_i (F_i - R_i) \Delta X_i$, where F_i is the fare or freight rate for the ith type of rail traffic, R_i is the marginal cost associated with carrying that traffic, and ΔX_i is the change in the volume, induced by the road improvement, of the ith type of traffic on the railway. In some cases of this type, the relevant marginal costs of rail transport may be so low that one can safely neglect them, in which event the measure of the net external effect produced by the road improvement becomes $\sum_i F_i \Delta X_i$, which is equal to the loss of revenue to the railway that the road project has occasioned.

The intermediate case occurs when the diversion of traffic to the road permits the railway to reduce the number and/or size of trains. This can occur on a stretch like BC, if that stretch previously carried the heaviest traffic volumes

---

[111] Some reduction in the size of trains may be occasioned by the road improvement if, before the improvement, the heaviest traffic volumes on the railway were between B and C. In this case, the demand for rail movement between B and C would be the determining factor governing the size and/or number of trains, and a reduction in that demand would permit shorter and/or fewer trains. In the text, we assume that the BC stretch does not have this characteristic.

Chapter Sixteen

on the railway and hence determined the size and number of trains. However, it is more likely to occur where the road project connects one of the principal terminals of the railway with some intermediate point — for example, if the road project is between C and D. In this event, some trains that previously went from A to D can now be turned around at C, thereby reducing the amount of equipment that the railway has to operate and maintain, and the outlays of the railway for operating and maintenance personnel. The savings of these costs must accordingly be added to $\sum_i (F_i - R_i)\Delta X_i$ before arriving at our estimate of the net external effect associated with diversion of traffic from the railway. In practice, however, the added saving is unlikely to be sufficiently large to convert a net diseconomy into a net external benefit.

The final case occurs when the road project permits the abandonment of a segment of track. For this to occur, the road project must almost necessarily connect a terminal point with an intermediate point along the road. The savings here include not only the direct marginal costs of haulage, and the costs of equipment and maintenance that are saved by reduced rail traffic levels, but also the costs of track maintenance and repair, station operation, and so forth over the stretch of track to be abandoned. Usually, moreover, the railway right-of-way and its station and yard properties on the abandoned stretch will have some alternative economic use; the value of these properties in their alternative uses should therefore be counted as an indirect benefit of the road improvement project.

An additional cost is entailed in abandonment, however, which we have not yet discussed. This cost arises from the fact that, so long as the stretch of railway is not abandoned, any diversion of traffic that takes place from rail to road is voluntary, while when abandonment occurs, some traffic for which the railway would have been the preferred mode even in the presence of the road improvement must nonetheless cease to use the rails. The situation is depicted in Figure 16.4 and Figure 16.5.

Figure 16.4 shows the situation on the road before and after improvement. $C_1 C'_1$ represents the private unit costs of travel on the road before the improvement, and $C_2 C'_2$ after improvement. $D_1 D'_1$ is the demand curve for the services of the road on the assumption that the railway is operating and charging the fare level OF (from Figure 16.5); $D_2 D'_2$ is the demand curve for the services of the road assuming the railway has been abandoned. C^*_1 and V_1 are the initial levels of unit costs and traffic volume on the road; C^*_2 and V_2 are the equilibrium levels after the road has been improved and the railway abandoned. In this case, the measure of direct benefits is the area $C^*_1 MNC^*_2$ in Figure 16.4. The rectangle $C^*_1 MRC^*_2$ represents the benefit perceived by traffic that would have used the unimproved road in any event; the triangle MNR represents the net benefit perceived by those who would not have used the road at a unit cost of C^*_1, but who would have used it at a unit cost of C^*_2 even if the railway were still operating. MNR includes the benefits obtained by those who would voluntarily have shifted their traffic from the railway to the road at a road cost of $C*_2$.

Figure 16.4: Direct Benefits for Road Improvement

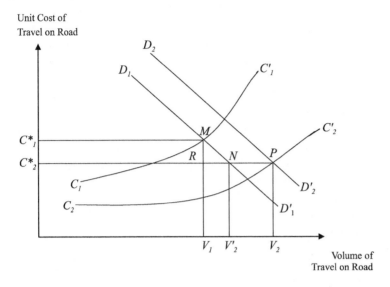

The area $NPV_2V'_2$ represents the costs incurred in travel on the road by traffic that has been involuntarily shifted to the road from the railway because of the abandonment of service on the latter. No net benefit can be attributed to this traffic because of the involuntary nature of its transfer; indeed, a net cost is involved here. This is shown in Figure 16.5, where $D_3D'_3$ represents the demand curve for the services of the railway when the unit costs of travel on the road are $C*_1$, and $D_4D'_4$ represents the same thing under the assumption that the unit costs of travel on the road are $C*_2$. The area *GHIJ* represents the fares paid by those units of traffic that voluntarily shifted from the railway to the road because of the road improvement. These units of traffic shift, as the costs of road travel are reduced, at the point where the cost of travel on the railway barely exceeds the benefit obtained from such travel. Thus, from their private point of view, the benefits forgone when they cease to use the railway are just barely compensated by the fares saved.

Figure 16.5: Impacts of Road Improvement on Railway

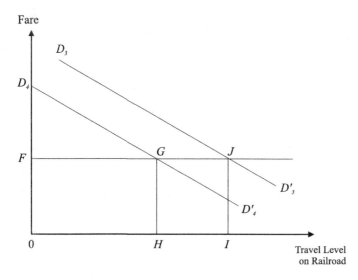

The situation is different for those forced from the use of the railway because of its abandonment. Their benefits from using the railway are measured by the area OD_4GH, while their costs are measured by $OFGH$. From their private point of view, therefore, a loss of the triangle D_4GF is involved in the railway's abandonment.

To summarize, then, the net benefit and cost situation of a road improvement project entailing the abandonment of service on a competing segment of railway would be:

a) the present value of cost savings to the users of the road (represented by $C^*_1 MNC^*_2$);

less b) the present value of those private net costs associated with abandonment of the railway (represented by D_4GH);

less c) the present value of the excess of rail fares over the direct marginal costs of operation;

plus d) the present value of the savings stemming from lower equipment, maintenance, station operation costs, and so forth, for the railway;

plus e) the current market value in alternative uses of the properties to be abandoned.

It is often true that the net benefits of a road improvement, taken together with the abandonment of a competing segment of railway line, are strongly positive. This usually occurs when the railway's total cost of maintaining service on the segment (including d) and e), above) exceed the operating profit represented by c). The heavy and persistent losses of, for example, the Argentine national railway system suggest that such cases are not at all infrequent and that a judicious programme of road improvement could prove to have net external benefits associated with rail line abandonment. Where rail abandonment is not involved, however, there is a strong presumption that the external effects associated with diversion of traffic from rail to road will be negative.

16.5 Some Implications and Generalizations

Up to now, we have set forth the basic principles and procedures to be applied in the analysis of costs and benefits of road projects. In this section, we attempt to present more general conclusions that are suggested or implied by the preceding analysis. We shall discuss, in turn, a) critical traffic levels, b) stage construction, c) the timing problem, d) the problem of segment construction, and e) the road-rail problem.

16.5.1 Critical Traffic Levels

It was shown in Section 16.2 that the principal direct benefit of a road improvement was the reduction in road-user costs for the traffic that would in any event have travelled on the unimproved road. The higher the traffic volume, therefore, the greater will be the presumed benefit. This is true not only because the benefits accrue to more traffic, but also because the cost savings per vehicle, associated with a given improvement, are likely themselves to be greater at higher rather than at lower traffic volumes. This effect stems from the facts that costs per vehicle increase at an increasing rate with volume of traffic and that their rate of increase at any given traffic volume is higher on poorer roads than on better roads. Figure 16.6 illustrates the point. At existing traffic volume V_a, the initial benefit $C_1^a ALC_2^a$ of the road improvement may be too small to justify the project, but if that traffic volume were greater (V_b), the initial benefit $C_1^b BHC_2^b$ would be much greater, with both the base and the height of the trapezoid having increased.

Figure 16.6: Impacts of an Increase in Traffic Volume

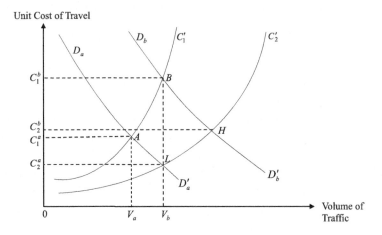

Since benefits are so closely related to traffic volume, it is possible, for any given road, to estimate the critical level of traffic at which it would be worthwhile to upgrade the road, say, from gravel to tar. Moreover, given that the cost situation is basically determined by the type of road and the price and wage structure of the country in question, it should be possible for the highway authorities of a country to develop analyses showing at what critical level of traffic it will normally be worthwhile to upgrade a road from earth to gravel, from gravel to paved, and from two-lane paved to four-lane paved, for example. Such analyses could usefully go into more detail, specifying critical traffic levels for a given type of improvement according to gradient, drainage requirements, nature of subsoil, and so forth.

In any event, critical traffic levels should be used as general guides to policy, not as a substitute for the detailed analysis of benefits and costs on each road. Properly employed, they serve the function of alerting the highway authorities to which stretches of road should be considered as likely candidates for improvement, thus enabling these authorities to employ their project evaluation personnel to better advantage.

One noteworthy aspect of critical traffic levels is that they are likely to vary considerably from country to country. Not only do costs of construction exhibit significant variation across countries, but the benefits associated with a given improvement at given traffic levels are also widely different in different countries — owing in large measure to the extreme differences that exist in the value of time. It is highly likely, therefore, that the critical level of traffic that would justify paving a road would be much higher in India, where the time-saving element of benefits is low, than in the United States, where time saving is likely to be the biggest component of total benefits. One must, accordingly, be extremely wary of "exporting" to other countries critical traffic levels derived on the basis of the situation prevailing in a particular country.

16.5.2 Stage Construction

In light of the foregoing analysis, a strategy of stage construction of roads has a high degree of appeal. Such a strategy would entail upgrading a road from earth to gravel when the traffic level was sufficient to warrant that move, paving the road when traffic had so increased as to justify that move, and adding additional lanes when that investment, in turn, was called for in the light of the traffic level.

Operating against the stage construction strategy is the argument that it is likely to be more costly to go through a series of upgrading investments than to build, once and for all, a higher-quality road than may be merited by present levels of traffic. The problem of timing will be discussed directly in the next section; we therefore concentrate here on the question of the differential cost of stage versus unitary construction.

A World Bank study reappraising a road project in Iran gives estimated costs of two-stage construction of a road — first gravel, then paved. The costs of a 5m-wide gravel road are estimated at 2.77 million rials per kilometre; the incremental costs of paving and widening to 6m are 2.0 million rials per kilometre. The total costs of single-stage construction of a 6m-wide paved road are 4.5 million rials per kilometre. The excess costs of stage construction are therefore estimated to be in the order of 5 percent. Similar estimates for stage construction of a 6m-wide gravel road, later widened to 7m and paved, are 3.46 million rials per kilometre for the first stage and 2.60 million rials for the second stage, compared with 5.77 million rials per kilometre for single-stage construction of a 7m-wide paved road (van der Tak and De Weille, 1969, p. 48).

Obviously, the excess costs of stage construction should be analysed in each particular case and compared with the extra benefits that a higher-quality road will provide. Nonetheless, the Iranian data suggest that stage construction is highly likely to be worthwhile. In the first example, the excess cost of stage construction was 0.27 million rials per kilometre. At a discount rate of 10 percent (certainly not excessive for a less-developed country), the interest savings on postponement would be sufficient to offset this excess cost even if the postponement of the second stage were to be as brief as 1.1 years. For the second set of data, the excess cost of 0.29 million rials per kilometre could once again be offset by the interest saving entailed in the postponement of the second stage for as little as 1.1 years.

Nor are the incremental benefits of single-stage construction likely to be justified unless traffic levels are well above those required to warrant first-stage construction. Let V_1 be the critical traffic level that would justify construction of a gravel road and V_2 be the level that would justify upgrading to a paved road. Suppose that traffic has just now reached the level V_1 and is expected to reach V_2 in t^* years. Let K_1 be the capital cost of constructing the gravel road and K_2 that of the paved road, and let $K*_2$ be the cost of upgrading from gravel to pavement. The present value of cost saving involved in stage construction will then be $(K_2 - K_1) - K*_2 (1 + r)^{-t^*}$. The factor $(1 + r)^{-t^*}$ is equal to approximately 0.6 for $r = 0.10$ and $t^* = 5$ years and to approximately 0.36 for $t^* = 10$ years. If, as suggested by the Iranian data, K_1 is equal to $0.6 K_2$ and $K*_2$ is equal to $0.45 K_2$, the present value of cost saving will be equal to 0.13 K_2 when $t^* = 5$ years and $0.24 K_2$ when $t^* = 10$ years. The cost of the gravel road itself being $0.6 K_2$, this means that the extra benefits of having a paved road instead of a gravel road during the first t^* years would have to cover 22 percent of the total costs of the gravel road in order to warrant single-stage construction if traffic would grow to justify the second stage in five years, and the extra benefits would have to cover approximately 40 percent of the total cost of the gravel road if t^* were equal to 10 years. It should be emphasized that these extra benefits would be just those accruing during the period between construction of the gravel road and its prospective upgrading to a paved road, as subsequent to t^* the benefits of either single-stage or two-stage construction would be the same.

We conclude, therefore, that although each case should in principle be examined on its merits, there is a strong presumption that stage construction will prove to be the optimal strategy in most cases. Moreover, stage construction has the added advantage of permitting investment decisions to be based on the existing observed volumes of traffic, rather than on predictions of future traffic growth, which could be subject to substantial error. In the example just presented, the fact that traffic on an existing earth road has reached the level V_1 would be sufficient to justify the investment in a gravel road so long as traffic was not expected to be reduced in the future. The highway authority, under stage construction, could wait to see when traffic would grow to V_2 so as to justify paving the road. If the highway authority attempts to justify the construction of a paved road now, on the other hand, it must be on the basis of a prediction of how far into the future the traffic level V_2 will be reached. If the highway authority errs in this prediction on the side of underestimating the actual growth of traffic, it may in some cases decide on multi-stage construction when single-stage construction would in fact have been economically justified. The cost of this type of error is likely to be small, however, because of the small excess of multi-stage over single-stage construction costs. If, on the other hand, the highway authority errs in the direction of overstating the actual growth of traffic, the error can be very costly indeed, as traffic may not reach the point at which the next stage of improvement would be warranted for 15 or 20 years, if indeed ever. The asymmetry of the costliness of errors of prediction of the two types should therefore bias the authority's choice in the direction of multi-stage construction.

16.5.3 The Timing Problem

In this section we discuss the problem of the timing of road investments, a problem that is made easy by the typical nature of the benefit streams generated by roads. With relatively minor qualifications, one can say that the traffic volume carried on a road, and hence the benefits of that road, will depend at any time on the quality of the road and not, to any significant degree, on when the road was raised to that level of quality. Moreover, in the great bulk of cases, the normal pattern is for the traffic on a road to grow through time.

These two characteristics — benefits dependent on calendar time, but not on the age of the project, and a rising benefit stream through time — make the timing problem amenable to an exceedingly simple solution. Assume that we have a gravel road and are contemplating paving it. Let B_t represent the undiscounted flow of benefits (road-user savings plus maintenance savings plus net external benefits that will flow from having a paved rather than a gravel road in Year t). Let K be the cost of paving the road.

If, under these assumptions, we face the problem of whether to pave the road in Year 0 or Year 1, we must recognize that regardless of which of these decisions we take, the benefits of having a paved road from Year 2 onward will be obtained. The benefits lost by postponing paving for a year will be those of that year — say, B_1. The gains to be obtained by postponing will be the use of the amount of K of investible funds for one year; this we measure by rK, where r, as before, represents the rate of discount to be used in cost–benefit analysis, reflecting the productivity that investible resources could have in alternative marginal uses.

The answer to the problem is therefore simple: when $rK > B_1$, postpone; when $rK < B_1$, pave. This leads to the rule that construction should be done at the time when benefits in the first year following construction will first exceed the discount rate times the capital cost.

A slight complication is introduced when construction costs themselves are expected to change through time. If construction costs are rising, we gain by constructing in Year 0 not only the benefit flow in Year 1, but also the saving in construction costs $(K_1 - K_0)$ entailed in building now rather than later. The rule is therefore modified to read: when $rK_t > B_{t+1} + (K_{t+1} - K_t)$, postpone; when $rK_t < B_{t+1} + (K_{t+1} - K_t)$, invest in the project. This same rule applies when construction costs are expected to decline; here one saves costs by postponing, thereby making postponement more likely.

The assumption that B_t will increase through time guarantees that if $B_1 > rK$, the discounted value of all future benefits $\sum_t B_t (1 + r)^{-t}$ will be greater than K (here assumed constant through time). This is the only sense in which the characteristic of growing benefits is relevant. If the future stream of benefits is expected to rise for a period and subsequently decline (as competing roads are built, for example), the basic criterion of $B_1 > rK$ remains the valid one as far as timing is concerned. Once this question has been settled, one must then make the further check to assure oneself that $\sum_t B_t (1+r)^{-t}$ is greater than K_0. If so, Year 0 is the optimal time to construct the project.

Similarly, when construction costs are expected to change, the criterion of $B_{t+1} + (K_{t+1} - K_t)$ exceeding rK_t remains a necessary condition for construction at time t. But if expected benefits do not continue to rise indefinitely in the future, the additional condition that the present value of expected future benefits exceeds the capital cost of the project must also be fulfilled to warrant construction. If K is an increasing function of time, the above conditions are sufficient to justify construction; if K is a declining function of time, a further test is necessary: $\sum_{t=0}^{t*} B_t (1+r)^{-t}$ must exceed $K_0 - K_{t*}(1+r)^{-t*}$ for all $t* > 0$.[112]

In this section, we have reached the conclusion that in most cases, decisions regarding the timing of road improvements will be governed by the value of benefits in the first year of operation on the improved road. Since these benefits are closely linked to the existing volume of traffic on the unimproved road, the relevance of using existing and immediately prospective traffic levels when taking investment decisions is established. Benefits in the farther future can be obtained in any event by building later; there is therefore no economic need to "build ahead of demand" where road improvements are concerned.

16.5.4 The Problem of Segment Construction

The preceding analysis also suggests that road improvement ought to be carried to different levels on the different segments of a given road, depending on the volume of traffic they carry. There is no reason why the road from D to G should not contain a paved segment from D to E, a gravel segment from E to F, and an earth segment from F to G, if those are the qualities of road justified by traffic levels on the respective segments. One can be sure that large amounts of investible resources have been wasted (in the sense of yielding less than

---

[112]All criteria derived in this section can be deduced from the basic proposition that the proper time to construct a project is that construction time for which the NPV of the project is highest, when NPV is discounted to the same point in time for all construction times being compared. The NPV of the project constructed at time zero is:

$$\sum_{t=1}^{\infty} B_t (1+r)^{-t} - K_0 \qquad (a)$$

and the NPV, as of time zero, of the project constructed at time $t*$ is:

$$\sum_{t=t*+1}^{\infty} B_t (1+r)^{-t} - K_{t*}(1+r)^{-t*} \qquad (b)$$

The last condition in the text simply states that in order for construction at time zero to be optimal, (a) must exceed (b) for all $t*$. A good general discussion of the timing problem, in which these issues are treated, can be found in Marglin (1963).

economic returns) as a result of the penchant of highway authorities to bring all segments of a road to a given quality level. Unlike the case of stage construction, where some small cost savings may be involved in single-stage construction, construction of a road in segments is likely to be no more costly than its construction as a single project; hence, unitary construction of the whole is not justifiable by cost considerations. We must therefore look to the benefit side to justify bringing the whole length of a given road to the same level of quality. Certainly, cases will exist in which this decision will be warranted; they will have the attribute that each of the distinct segments of the road is carrying approximately the same amount of traffic. But most roads of significant length do not possess this attribute; hence, we must conclude that optimal road investment strategies are probably not being followed in most cases where roads spanning long distances are built to a single standard of quality over their entire length.

A minor qualification to the above judgment must be introduced, however, stemming from the external effects of road improvements. The paving of a stretch of road DE will cause traffic to increase on the unpaved stretch EF as this is the path of access to or egress from DE for some of its additional traffic. The fact that DE is paved, therefore, will increase the benefits to be obtained from paving EF.

Let B_T be the total present value of benefits (direct and indirect) that would accrue from paving the entire road DF; let B_1 be the total present value of benefits of paving the stretch DE only and B_2 the total benefit of paving the stretch EF only. Because of the complementarity between DE and EF alluded to above, we have the result that $B_1 + B_2 < B_T$. Let B_3 be the present value of benefits of paving the stretch EF, given that DE is already paved. $B_1 + B_3$ must equal B_T, since the two projects together amount to paving the entire road DF.

If K_1 represents the cost of paving DE, K_2 the cost of paving EF, and $K(= K_1 + K_2)$ the cost of paving the entire road DF, the possibility thus emerges that it would not pay to pave EF alone $(K_2 > B_2)$, but that if the stretch DE were to be paved, it would also pay to pave the stretch EF $(K_2 < B_3)$. It is even possible that it would not be worthwhile to pave either DE or EF alone ($K_1 > B_1$ and $K_2 > B_2$), but that paving both together would be justified $(K = K_1 + K_2 < B = B_1 + B_3)$.

All of these possibilities are a result of the complementarity relationship between adjacent stretches of the same road. How relevant they are likely to be depends on the difference between the traffic levels on the two stretches DE and EF. If the critical traffic level for paving either stretch alone is 1,000 vehicles per day, and if traffic has reached that level on DE but stands at only 500 vehicles per day on EF, there is no relevant justification for paving EF once DE is paved. Paving DE is warranted, by assumption, even counting the diseconomy involved in increasing the traffic level on EF. But the increase in traffic on EF induced by paving *DE* will be only a part of the increase in traffic on *DE*; it may amount, plausibly, to 50 or 100 vehicles per day, but it would be absurd to assume that paving *DE* would bring traffic on *EF* from 500 to nearly 1,000 vehicles per day. (If 1,000 vehicles per day are required to justify paving *EF* alone, somewhat less than 1,000 would be required to justify paving *EF* when *DE* is also paved because the external diseconomies associated with paving *EF* will be slightly less in the latter case than in the former.) Thus, we conclude that if traffic on *EF* is quite close to the level that would justify paving that stretch alone, paving it may indeed become worthwhile when *DE* is also to be paved. But if traffic on *EF* is significantly below the critical level, it is highly unlikely that paving it will be worthwhile regardless of whether the stretch *DE* is paved or not. Since, in the real world, there are great disparities among traffic levels on given roads, we must maintain, in spite of the above qualification, our general conclusion that normally it will be optimal to upgrade different stretches of a given road at widely separated times and that, at any given time, the typical road should contain stretches of distinctly disparate qualities.

16.5.5 The Road-Rail Problem

It was shown in Section 16.4 that whenever a road project would reduce rail traffic without causing abandonment of some portion of the rail line, the diversion of traffic away from the railway would represent in all probability a negative external effect of the road project. The amount of the external diseconomy would be the fares and freight rates that the railway ceased to collect minus any savings of costs that the railway would have as a consequence of its reduced traffic volume. In such cases of non-abandonment, then, the only issue is to be sure to take the external diseconomy into account when evaluating the road project. If its benefits, thus adjusted, exceed its costs, the road project is justified in spite of its negative effect on rail traffic.

When abandonment of a segment of track is likely as a consequence of a road project, the cost savings to the railway are certain to be greater than in the case of non-abandonment, and it is even possible that these savings will be sufficiently great to convert what would otherwise be an external diseconomy into an external economy of the road project. For this to happen, the present value of the cost savings to the railway, including the value of its abandoned properties in alternative uses, must exceed the present value of the fares and freight charges that would have been paid by traffic on the abandoned line in the absence of the road project. In short, the abandoned stretch of track must have been unprofitable, even in the absence of the road project, in order for abandonment to cause a net external benefit for the road investment. This case is relevant because, for political and other reasons, many segments of track on which trains are run are kept in operation in spite of yielding large net losses. A road project may, therefore, by providing alternative communication facilities of adequate quality, so reduce the political opposition to rail abandonment as to make abandonment possible.

Under the circumstances, then, of a) abandonment of track and b) unprofitability of the abandoned stretch in the absence of the road project, there may be a positive external effect of the road project on the operations of a competing rail line. Whether the effect will be positive or not depends on whether the loss of consumer surplus on that traffic that is involuntarily driven from using the railway by the abandonment decision exceeds the net benefit enjoyed by the railway on account of abandonment.

We have not discussed the case of complementarity between a road project and an existing railway because of its relative unimportance in the modern world. In most countries, the rail facilities were built many decades ago, and the road networks gave adequate access to the rail terminals early. Thus, in principle, the improvement of road access to the railway could stimulate the use of the latter, generating a probable external benefit for the road project in question; however, in practice, the number of such cases and the magnitude of the effects are likely to be very small. We therefore do not enter into a detailed analysis of such cases here; their proper treatment can be inferred from that described in the text for road projects that compete with railways, recognizing that increments in rail traffic where fares and freight rates exceed the relevant marginal costs of haulage will generate net external benefits to a complementary road project.

References

De Weille, J. 1966. *Quantification of Road User Savings*. Washington, DC: IBRD.

Harberger, A.C. 1967. "Cost-Benefit Analysis of Transportation Projects", paper prepared for the Engineering and the Building of Nations conference, Estes Park, CO, August 27–September 1.

Marglin, S.A. 1963. *Approaches to Dynamic Investment Planning*, Chapter 2. Amsterdam: North-Holland Publishing Co.

Soberman, R.M. 1966. "Economic Analysis of Highway Design in Developing Countries", Highway Research Board, *Highway Research Record,* No. 115 (publication 1337).

van der Tak, H.G. and J. De Weille. 1969. *An Economic Reappraisal of a Road Project*, IBRD Report No. EC-147.

Chapter Seventeen

Appraisal of the Upgrading of a Gravel Road

17.1 Introduction

The purpose of this chapter is to describe how a proposed investment in the upgrading of a gravel road to a tarred surface should be evaluated. The project was located in the Limpopo province of South Africa. It involved the upgrading of two existing, mainly gravel, roads to a tar-surfaced road connecting the Sekhukhune and Capricorn districts. The whole route has several sections, starting at Flag Boshielo and running to Mafefe, Sekororo, Ga-Seleka, and finally to Mmatladi. According to Roads Agency Limpopo (RAL), the proposed road consisted of sections D4100, D4250, D4190, D4050, and D1583, with D4100 being an exception, since a section of 25 kilometres (km) had already been tarred. It was estimated that more than 98 percent of the sections of gravel road were considered to be in either poor or fair condition (ARCUS GIBB Ltd., 2004).

The main users of the existing gravel road were minibuses and private vehicles transporting people from local areas to Lebowakgomo and other towns. The predominant economic activity in the region is small-scale agriculture, carried out on a number of irrigation schemes. At the time, no specific tourist sites were operational in the area, but it was anticipated that the Lekgalameetse Reserve might become a tourist attraction in the near future.

The project was expected to serve some 35,000 people living in the immediate vicinity of the route and to provide convenient access to existing and future developments in the agriculture, tourism, and mining sectors.

The section of the proposed road consisting of segments D4100, D4250, and D4190 is about 81 km long.

At the time, this road served a number of communities, including 20 villages located directly along it, including the town of Lebowakgomo and the communities around the Flag Boshielo Dam. Upgrading this link would ensure convenient access for the regional population to the Lebowakgomo and Groothoek hospitals, Jane Furse and Lebowakgomo police stations, and possible future sites of agriculture and tourist projects.

The other component of the proposed road improvement, consisting of segments D4050 and D1583, is about 75 km long. This section already served more than 28 villages located directly on the route, the town of Lebowakgomo, and the Lekgalameetse Reserve. The improved road would facilitate easier access to the hospitals in Lebowakgomo, Groothoek, and Sekororo as well as to police stations in Jane Furse and Lebowakgomo. Once improved, the road would provide a direct link to Tzaneen and Phalaborwa, making it convenient for vehicles to travel across the province.

17.2 Project Costs

It was proposed that the project would take three years to construct, starting in 2005 and ending in 2007. For sections D4100, D4250, and D4190, which pass through relatively flat terrain and comprise about 81 km, an average construction cost of R1.301 million per km was estimated. For sections D4050 and D1583, which are located in a mountainous area and stretch for about 75 km, the estimated costs of upgrading were R1.459 million per km.

It is typical to include some provision for linking roads that would connect the upgraded road with other roads and projects en route. It was estimated that about 15 km of linking roads would be included in this road improvement project. The average construction cost of these linking roads was expected to be R0.700 million per km. Ten small river crossings were also included in the project; their estimated cost was R0.040 million per km (ARCUS GIBB, 2004, p. 3–2).

In addition to the physical construction costs, professional fees would be levied at 12 percent of the total construction expenditures. A provision for contingencies accounted for an additional 10 percent of the total construction costs. In South Africa, value-added tax (VAT) at 14 percent is imposed on the total construction costs, exclusive of professional fees and contingencies.

In terms of timing, sections D4100, D4250, and D4190, located in Sekhukhune district, have a higher traffic volume and would be upgraded in the first phase, starting at the beginning of 2005. The second phase of construction would upgrade sections D4250 and D4190, located in Capricorn district, in 2006. The last phase would upgrade one-third of the 75 km of D4050 and D1583, located in a mountainous area, in 2006 and the remaining 50 km in 2007.[113] It was assumed that the costs of linking roads, river crossings, professional fees, contingencies, and VAT would be evenly spread over the three years.

The total tax-inclusive investment cost of the project over the three years was expected to be R307 million in 2005 prices. The detailed cost breakdown of total investment is presented by road section and time schedule in Table 17.1.

---

[113]In 2005, 34 km of D4100 and 20 km of D4250 would be built, while 7 km of D4250, 20 km of D4190, and 25 km of D4050/D1583 would be built in 2006. Finally, 50 km of D4050/D1583 would be constructed in 2007.

Table 17.1: Breakdown of Project Investment Costs (R million, in 2005 prices)

	2005	2006	2007	Total
Road:				
D4100	44.2	0	0	44.2
D4250	26.0	9.1	0	35.1
D4190	0	26.0	0	26.0
D4050/D1583	0	36.5	72.9	109.4
Sub-total	70.2	71.6	72.9	214.7
Linking roads	3.5	3.5	3.5	10.5
River crossings	0.1	0.1	0.1	0.3
Professional fees	8.9	9.0	9.2	27.1
Contingencies	7.4	7.5	7.7	22.6
VAT	10.3	10.5	10.7	31.5
Total	100.5	102.3	104.1	307.0

17.3 Analytical Framework

The roads involved in this project are owned and operated by RAL. There was no toll imposed on road users at the time, nor would one be imposed after the roads were upgraded from gravel to a tarred surface. Therefore, no financial revenues were expected from road users, and no financial evaluation would be carried out on this project. The financial outlays by RAL would simply follow the time path of project expenditures. The objective of this chapter is to examine whether this investment was expected to increase the economic welfare of South African society as a whole.

To evaluate the economic impact of upgrading a gravel road, it is necessary to measure how its effects differ from those that are likely to have been observed in the absence of the project. This incremental impact analysis entails developing two alternative scenarios: "with" and "without" the proposed road improvement. The "without" scenario, which assumes the absence of the project, assumes that no major rehabilitation or capital outlays will be spent on the existing gravel roads. It does, however, assume that regular, normal maintenance and rehabilitation operations will continue on these roads so that the incremental impact of the proposed project will not be overstated when compared to the "without" project scenario.

The capital expenditures of a tarred surface are typically justified by its lower annual maintenance costs compared to those of a gravel surface. However, several other types of benefit must be accounted for when conducting an evaluation from the economic point of view. They should include the reduction in vehicle operating costs (VOC) for road users because of the improved road surface, time savings for road users resulting from the increased average speed of vehicles, and a possible reduction in the costs of accidents and other fiscal externalities.

Once the road is upgraded, road users will start to travel on the tarred road. Since the total construction phase of this project would take three years, and each section of the road would take approximately six months to upgrade, some improved sections may serve longer than others if the project is terminated at the same time. For the purpose of this evaluation, it was assumed that the project would last at least 20 years until 2027, with no salvage value remaining.

In measuring the economic benefits of transportation projects, it is important to distinguish between those who would use an existing road even in the absence of the improvement and those who would be induced to travel as a consequence of the improvement. The benefits to the first group were measured by the reduction in VOC and time-costs between travelling on the gravel road and travelling on the tarred road. The benefits to the second group were taken to be one-half of such savings in vehicle operating costs and time-costs (see Chapter Sixteen).

In order to ensure consistency, a number of adjustments were made when converting these financial values into their corresponding economic values. This entailed estimating commodity-specific conversion factors for several key project input variables, based on the methodology outlined in Chapters 10 and 11.

Once the annual benefits and costs for the "with" and "without" project scenarios had been estimated, the incremental net benefits were discounted over the project life by the economic opportunity cost of capital for South Africa to determine whether the net present value (NPV) was greater than zero.

In the discussion that follows, we will examine first the traffic forecasts "with" and "without" the project, then the savings in maintenance costs, vehicle operating costs, and time-costs for each type of vehicle. We will then assess the project in terms of its economic feasibility, its impact on the stakeholders affected, and, finally, its level of inherent risk.

17.4 Maintenance Costs

The upgraded road was expected to require substantially less maintenance in terms of costs and frequency compared to the existing gravel surface. In the case of the "without" project scenario, maintenance activities would include the regular and periodic maintenance expenditures and rehabilitation costs of the existing road in compliance with the maintenance standards of RAL. Table 17.2 presents the engineering estimates of maintenance costs of tarred ("with" project) and gravel ("without" project) roads per km by type and frequency of maintenance activity for 2004. These estimates were then updated to 2005, based on the annual inflation rate of 6.5 percent.

As previously mentioned, the construction of the project was to start in 2005 in certain sections of the road and to end in 2027 for the purpose of this evaluation.

Table 17.2: Road Maintenance Costs for Tarred and Gravel Road (R million per km)

Road Surface	Type of Activity	Frequency	Amount 2005
Tarred ("with" project)	Routine	Annual	0.032
	Intermediate	Every 3 years	0.160
	Periodic	Every 10 years	0.533
Gravel ("without" project)	Blading	Annual	0.037
	Wearing Course	Every 2 years	0.213
	Heavy Gravel	Every 5 years	0.373

Source: ARCUS GIBB Ltd. (2004).

Given these estimates of maintenance costs of maintaining and upgrading various road sections, the annual financial maintenance costs were estimated. These are presented in Table 17.3 for "with" and "without" project scenarios over the life of the project. The annual savings in financial maintenance expenditures after roads are upgraded from gravel to tarred surfaces can then be estimated.

Table 17.3: Estimates of Annual Financial Maintenance Costs (R million, in 2005 prices)

Year	Tarred Road ("with" Project)				Gravel Road ("without" Project)			
	Routine	Intermediate	Periodic	Total	Routine	Intermediate	Periodic	Total
2005	3.80	0.00	0.00	3.80	5.81	0.00	0.00	5.81
2006	3.59	0.00	0.00	3.59	5.81	33.23	0.00	39.04
2007	3.39	0.00	0.00	3.39	5.81	0.00	0.00	5.81
2008	4.98	8.63	0.00	13.61	5.81	33.23	0.00	39.04
2009	4.98	8.31	0.00	13.29	5.81	0.00	58.15	63.96
2010	4.98	7.99	0.00	12.97	5.81	33.23	0.00	39.04
2011	4.98	8.63	0.00	13.61	5.81	0.00	0.00	5.81
2012	4.98	8.31	0.00	13.29	5.81	33.23	0.00	39.04
2013	4.98	7.99	0.00	12.97	5.81	0.00	0.00	5.81
2014	4.98	8.63	0.00	13.61	5.81	33.23	58.15	97.19
2015	4.98	8.31	28.76	42.05	5.81	0.00	0.00	5.81
2016	4.98	7.99	27.69	40.66	5.81	33.23	0.00	39.04
2017	4.98	8.63	26.63	40.24	5.81	0.00	0.00	5.81
2018	4.98	8.31	0.00	13.29	5.81	33.23	0.00	39.04
2019	4.98	7.99	0.00	12.97	5.81	0.00	58.15	63.96
2020	4.98	8.63	0.00	13.61	5.81	33.23	0.00	39.04
2021	4.98	8.31	0.00	13.29	5.81	0.00	0.00	5.81
2022	4.98	7.99	0.00	12.97	5.81	33.23	0.00	39.04
2023	4.98	8.63	0.00	13.61	5.81	0.00	0.00	5.81
2024	4.98	8.31	0.00	13.29	5.81	33.23	58.15	97.19
2025	4.98	7.99	0.00	12.97	5.81	0.00	0.00	5.81
2026	4.98	8.63	0.00	13.61	5.81	33.23	0.00	39.04
2027	4.98	0.00	0.00	4.98	5.81	0.00	0.00	5.81

17.5 Demand for Traffic on the Improved Road

The projected demand for traffic is the most important element in the economic analysis of a road project. The traffic forecast model used in the present analysis was based on a study completed for RAL, and most of the parameters and assumptions of its model were kept unchanged. The model was built around six groups of road users, differentiated by vehicle type and purpose of journey: passenger cars, tourist vehicles, minibuses, light goods vehicles (LGVs), agricultural transport, and heavy goods vehicles (HGVs). For practical purposes, we combined LGVs with agricultural transport; thus, our traffic projections were actually carried out for five types of traffic.

The projected demand for traffic must be forecast over the life of the project for each of the five vehicle categories, using both the "with" and the "without" project scenarios.

17.5.1 Traffic Level without the Project

As a result of the generally poor road conditions described above, the volume of traffic on the existing gravel road was low. The main users of the road were minibuses and private vehicles transporting people from local areas to Lebowakgomo and other towns. The predominant economic activity in the region is small-scale agriculture, carried out on a number of irrigation schemes. At the time there were no specific tourist sites in the area, though it was expected that the Lekgalameetse Reserve would become a tourist attraction in the near future. The improved road would also provide direct access for tourists from the Flag Boshielo area to Tzaneen and Phalaborwa. Economic activity in the region was being stimulated by the gradual development of mining resources.

In 2003 the total annual average daily traffic (AADT) was about 285 vehicles on D4100, 380 on D4250, 380 on D4190, and 60 on D4050/D1583. In terms of types of traffic, the proportions on the first three roads were 72 percent minibuses, 26 percent passenger cars, and 2 percent HGVs. On the remaining road sections, D4050/D1583, the total traffic was split equally between minibuses and private passenger cars.

a) Passenger Cars

The initial levels of passenger car traffic in 2003 for sections D4100, D4250, D4190, D4050, and D1583 were calculated using the total AADT counts multiplied by the estimated proportion of traffic type. The average volumes of passenger car traffic on these segments were found to be 75, 100, 100, 30, and 30 vehicles per day respectively.[114] For subsequent years the volume of passenger traffic on each segment was assumed to grow by 4 percent over the life of the project until 2027.[115]

b) Tourists

It was expected that tourist trips would use sections D4050 and D1583 starting in 2005 with an AADT of 6. For subsequent years, the traffic was expected to rise annually by 4 percent.

c) Minibuses

The annual increase in minibus traffic will be linked to the growth of passenger traffic, with volume on all road segments rising by 4 percent per year. The initial AADT counts for sections D4100, D4250, D4190, D4050, and D1583 were estimated at 204, 272, 272, 30, and 30, respectively. The assumed 4 percent

---

[114]For instance, the share of passenger traffic on D4100 was 26 percent, and total AADT was 285. The number of passenger cars was 75.

[115]Since 2001, the annual GDP growth rate in South Africa was about 3.4 percent.

growth rate of passenger and minibus traffic was considered to be a conservative estimate.

d) Light Goods Vehicles and Agricultural Transport

A number of small irrigation schemes are located within reach of the D4100 section. Most of these schemes were expected to become operational within four years as the Department of Agriculture completed rehabilitation and transfer of the affected properties to their farm owners. The improvement of the road would bring about a reduction in transport costs. Agricultural and LGV traffic was expected to start in 2005, with an AADT of 4. The future growth rate of agricultural and LGV traffic on the D4100 section was assumed to be 5 percent. On sections D4190 and D4250, the movement of LGVs and agricultural transport would start in 2005, with an AADT of 4, and then gradually reach an AADT of 6 in 2007; thereafter, a constant growth rate of 5 percent was assumed. No LGV or agricultural traffic was expected on sections D4050 or D1583.

e) Heavy Goods Vehicles

It was expected that most HGV traffic on the proposed road would originate from the irrigation schemes, which would be operational within a few years. Agricultural produce grown on the farms would be transported to the larger towns of Polokwane, Lebowakgomo, and possibly Burgersfort. For the D4100 segment of the proposed road, it was expected that the HGV traffic would consist of agricultural transport, plus a very few mining vehicles. In the absence of firm plans for mining development, it was difficult to predict what the additional mining HGV traffic volume would be. For this particular segment, the traffic volume was expected to grow gradually from an AADT of 6 in 2003 to an AADT of 15 in 2010, after which time an annual growth rate of 5 percent was assumed. The possible construction of the Flag Boshielo Dam wall would bring added traffic to this segment for two years, but no firm decision had been taken in this regard; thus, this traffic was not included in the forecast.

On road sections D4250 and D4190, the 2003 AADT of 8 was modelled to rise by a rate of 5 percent annually throughout the entire period of 2003–2027. No regular HGV traffic was expected on sections D4050 or D1583.

The traffic projections for the "without" project scenario over the life of the project are presented in Table 17.4.

Table 17.4: Projected Traffic by Road Section and Vehicle Type for "Without" Project Scenario (number of AADT)

Year	D4100					D4250/D4190					D4050/D1583				Total
	Car	Minibus	LGV/Agri	HGV	Sub-total	Car	Minibus	LGV/Agri	HGV	Sub-total	Car	Tourist	Minibus	Sub-total	
2003	75	204	0	6	285	100	272	0	8	380	30	0	30	60	725
2004	78	212	0	6	296	104	283	0	8	395	31	6	31	68	760
2005	81	221	4	7	313	108	294	4	9	415	32	6	32	71	799
2006	84	229	4	9	327	112	306	5	9	433	34	6	34	74	833
2007	88	239	4	11	341	117	318	6	10	451	35	7	35	77	869
2008	91	248	5	12	356	122	331	6	10	469	36	7	36	80	906
2009	95	258	5	14	372	127	344	7	11	488	38	7	38	83	943
2010	99	268	5	15	387	132	358	7	11	508	39	8	39	87	982
2011	103	279	5	16	403	137	372	7	12	528	41	8	41	90	1,021
2012	107	290	6	17	419	142	387	8	12	550	43	8	43	94	1,062
2013	111	302	6	17	436	148	403	8	13	572	44	9	44	97	1,105
2014	115	314	6	18	454	154	419	8	14	595	46	9	46	101	1,150
2015	120	327	7	19	472	160	435	9	14	619	48	9	48	105	1,196
2016	125	340	7	20	491	167	453	9	15	644	50	10	50	110	1,245
2017	130	353	7	21	511	173	471	10	16	670	52	10	52	114	1,295
2018	135	367	8	22	532	180	490	10	17	697	54	10	54	118	1,347
2019	140	382	8	23	554	187	509	11	17	725	56	11	56	123	1,402
2020	146	397	8	24	576	195	530	11	18	754	58	11	58	128	1,459
2021	152	413	9	26	600	203	551	12	19	785	61	12	61	133	1,518
2022	158	430	9	27	624	211	573	12	20	816	63	12	63	139	1,579
2023	164	447	10	28	649	219	596	13	21	849	66	13	66	144	1,643
2024	171	465	10	30	676	228	620	14	22	884	68	13	68	150	1,709
2025	178	483	11	31	703	237	645	14	23	919	71	14	71	156	1,778
2026	185	503	11	33	732	246	670	15	25	957	74	14	74	162	1,850
2027	192	523	12	34	761	256	697	16	26	995	77	15	77	169	1,925

17.5.2 Traffic Level with the Project

In addition to the traffic levels for the "without" project scenario projected above, there would also be a moderate volume newly generated traffic as a consequence of the project.

a) Passenger Cars

It was assumed that passenger traffic diverted from other roads would start at a level of 8 AADT on each of sections D4100, D4250, and D4190, and at a level of 4 AADT on sections D4050 and D1583 in 2006. Thereafter, it was assumed that it would increase by 3 percent annually for passenger vehicles.

The generated passenger traffic was expected to start at very low levels: in 2006 with 4 AADT on D4100, in 2007 with 6 AADT on D4250/D4190, and in 2008 with 1.5 AADT on D4050/D1583. The annual growth rate of generated traffic on all sections was also assumed to be 3 percent.

b) Tourists

The diverted tourist traffic was expected to use sections D4050 and D1583. The initial level of such traffic was projected to be 3 AADT in 2006, increasing by 3 percent per year for the rest of the forecast period. It was assumed that generated tourist traffic would develop only on sections D4050 and D1583, with a starting level of 1.5 AADT in 2008. This was projected to grow by 3 percent per year until 2027.

c) Minibuses

It was assumed that diverted minibus traffic would begin at a level of 9 AADT in 2006 on each of sections D4100, D4250, and D4190, and at a level of 6 AADT on sections D4050 and D1583. This traffic volume was expected to rise by 3 percent per annum. There was an assumption that generated minibus traffic would start in 2006 with 7 AADT on D4100, would be 8 AADT in 2007 on D4250/D4190, and 1.5 AADT in 2008 on D4050/D1583. The annual growth rate of generated traffic on all sections was assumed to be 3 percent.

d) Light Goods Vehicles and Agricultural Transport

No substantial diverted traffic was expected on any of the sections for LGVs or agricultural transport, but some users would be induced to use the improved road. This generated traffic would begin in 2006 with 1 AADT on D4100, and in 2007 would also be 1 AADT on D4250/D4190. The annual growth rate of generated traffic on all sections was assumed to be 3 percent.

e) Heavy Goods Vehicles

It was assumed that some diverted HGV traffic would begin in 2006 at a level of 1 AADT on each of sections D4100, D4250, and D4190. This traffic volume was expected to rise by the assumed growth rate of 3 percent per annum. A newly generated flow was expected to begin in 2006 with 1 AADT on D4100 and then gradually increase to 1.75 AADT in 2009, after which it was projected to grow at a rate of 3 percent per annum. On sections D4250 and D4190, the initial level of generated HGV volume was assumed to be 1 AADT, with a subsequent annual growth rate of 3 percent.

The above information was obtained in consultation with local experts. It allowed us to project the yearly average daily diverted and generated traffic over the life of the project resulting from the improvement of the road. The volumes of diverted and generated traffic are presented in Tables 17.5 and 17.6, respectively.

17.6 Savings in Vehicle Operating Costs

Since the conditions of the existing road varied significantly among road sections, vehicle operating costs (VOC) also differed by section, as well as by vehicle type.

VOC includes consumption of gasoline and oil, wear and tear on tyres, and repair expenditures on vehicles. Estimates for this project were based on the Road Economic Decision Model (RED) developed by the World Bank and modified for South Africa by CSIR Transportek in 2003.[116]

---

[116]Archondo-Callao (2001). The model was customized for South African conditions by CSIR Transportek at the request of the Development Bank of Southern Africa (DBSA). Available at http//:www.dbsa.org.

Table 17.5: Projected Diverted Traffic by Road Section and Vehicle Type for "With" Project Scenario (number of AADT)

Year	D4100				D4250/D4190				D4050/D1583				Total
	Car	Minibus	HGV	Sub-total	Car	Minibus	HGV	Sub-total	Car	Tourist	Minibus	Sub-total	
2003	0.0	0.0	0.0	0.0	0.0	0.0	0.0	0.0	0.0	0.0	0.0	0.0	0.0
2004	0.0	0.0	0.0	0.0	0.0	0.0	0.0	0.0	0.0	0.0	0.0	0.0	0.0
2005	0.0	0.0	0.0	0.0	0.0	0.0	0.0	0.0	0.0	0.0	0.0	0.0	0.0
2006	8.0	9.0	1.0	18.0	8.0	9.0	1.0	18.0	4.0	3.0	6.0	13.0	49.0
2007	8.2	9.3	1.0	18.5	8.2	9.3	1.0	18.5	4.1	3.1	6.2	13.4	50.5
2008	8.5	9.5	1.1	19.1	8.5	9.5	1.1	19.1	4.2	3.2	6.4	13.8	52.0
2009	8.7	9.8	1.1	19.7	8.7	9.8	1.1	19.7	4.4	3.3	6.6	14.2	53.5
2010	9.0	10.1	1.1	20.3	9.0	10.1	1.1	20.3	4.5	3.4	6.8	14.6	55.1
2011	9.3	10.4	1.2	20.9	9.3	10.4	1.2	20.9	4.6	3.5	7.0	15.1	56.8
2012	9.6	10.7	1.2	21.5	9.6	10.7	1.2	21.5	4.8	3.6	7.2	15.5	58.5
2013	9.8	11.1	1.2	22.1	9.8	11.1	1.2	22.1	4.9	3.7	7.4	16.0	60.3
2014	10.1	11.4	1.3	22.8	10.1	11.4	1.3	22.8	5.1	3.8	7.6	16.5	62.1
2015	10.4	11.7	1.3	23.5	10.4	11.7	1.3	23.5	5.2	3.9	7.8	17.0	63.9
2016	10.8	12.1	1.3	24.2	10.8	12.1	1.3	24.2	5.4	4.0	8.1	17.5	65.9
2017	11.1	12.5	1.4	24.9	11.1	12.5	1.4	24.9	5.5	4.2	8.3	18.0	67.8
2018	11.4	12.8	1.4	25.7	11.4	12.8	1.4	25.7	5.7	4.3	8.6	18.5	69.9
2019	11.7	13.2	1.5	26.4	11.7	13.2	1.5	26.4	5.9	4.4	8.8	19.1	72.0
2020	12.1	13.6	1.5	27.2	12.1	13.6	1.5	27.2	6.1	4.5	9.1	19.7	74.1
2021	12.5	14.0	1.6	28.0	12.5	14.0	1.6	28.0	6.2	4.7	9.3	20.3	76.3
2022	12.8	14.4	1.6	28.9	12.8	14.4	1.6	28.9	6.4	4.8	9.6	20.9	78.6
2023	13.2	14.9	1.7	29.8	13.2	14.9	1.7	29.8	6.6	5.0	9.9	21.5	81.0
2024	13.6	15.3	1.7	30.6	13.6	15.3	1.7	30.6	6.8	5.1	10.2	22.1	83.4
2025	14.0	15.8	1.8	31.6	14.0	15.8	1.8	31.6	7.0	5.3	10.5	22.8	85.9
2026	14.4	16.3	1.8	32.5	14.4	16.3	1.8	32.5	7.2	5.4	10.8	23.5	88.5
2027	14.9	16.7	1.9	33.5	14.9	16.7	1.9	33.5	7.4	5.6	11.2	24.2	91.2

Table 17.6: Projected Generated Traffic by Road Section and Vehicle Type for "With" Project Scenario (number of AADT)

Year	D4100					D4250/D4190					D4050/D1583				Total
	Car	Minibus	LGV/Agri	HGV	Sub-total	Car	Minibus	LGV/Agri	HGV	Sub-total	Car	Tourist	Minibus	Sub-total	
2003	0.0	0.0	0.0	0.0	0.0	0.0	0.0	0.0	0.0	0.0	0.0	0.0	0.0	0.0	0.0
2004	0.0	0.0	0.0	0.0	0.0	0.0	0.0	0.0	0.0	0.0	0.0	0.0	0.0	0.0	0.0
2005	0.0	0.0	0.0	0.0	0.0	0.0	0.0	0.0	0.0	0.0	0.0	0.0	0.0	0.0	0.0
2006	4.0	7.0	1.0	1.0	13.0	0.0	0.0	0.0	0.0	0.0	0.0	0.0	0.0	0.0	13.0
2007	4.1	7.2	1.0	1.3	13.6	6.0	8.0	1.0	1.0	16.0	0.0	0.0	0.0	0.0	29.6
2008	4.2	7.4	1.1	1.5	14.2	6.2	8.2	1.0	1.0	16.5	1.5	1.5	1.5	4.5	35.2
2009	4.4	7.6	1.1	1.8	14.9	6.4	8.5	1.0	1.0	17.0	1.5	1.5	1.5	4.6	36.5
2010	4.5	7.9	1.1	1.8	15.3	6.6	8.7	1.1	1.1	17.5	1.6	1.6	1.6	4.8	37.6
2011	4.6	8.1	1.1	1.9	15.8	6.8	9.0	1.1	1.1	18.0	1.6	1.6	1.6	4.9	38.7
2012	4.8	8.4	1.2	1.9	16.2	7.0	9.3	1.2	1.2	18.5	1.7	1.7	1.7	5.1	39.9
2013	4.9	8.6	1.2	2.0	16.7	7.2	9.6	1.2	1.2	19.1	1.7	1.7	1.7	5.2	41.0
2014	5.1	8.9	1.3	2.0	17.2	7.4	9.8	1.2	1.2	19.7	1.8	1.8	1.8	5.4	42.3
2015	5.2	9.1	1.3	2.1	17.7	7.6	10.1	1.3	1.3	20.3	1.8	1.8	1.8	5.5	43.5
2016	5.4	9.4	1.3	2.2	18.3	7.8	10.4	1.3	1.3	20.9	1.9	1.9	1.9	5.7	44.9
2017	5.5	9.7	1.4	2.2	18.8	8.1	10.8	1.3	1.3	21.5	2.0	2.0	2.0	5.9	46.2
2018	5.7	10.0	1.4	2.3	19.4	8.3	11.1	1.4	1.4	22.1	2.0	2.0	2.0	6.0	47.6
2019	5.9	10.3	1.5	2.4	20.0	8.6	11.4	1.4	1.4	22.8	2.1	2.1	2.1	6.2	49.0
2020	6.1	10.6	1.5	2.4	20.6	8.8	11.7	1.5	1.5	23.5	2.1	2.1	2.1	6.4	50.5
2021	6.2	10.9	1.6	2.5	21.2	9.1	12.1	1.5	1.5	24.2	2.2	2.2	2.2	6.6	52.0
2022	6.4	11.2	1.6	2.6	21.8	9.3	12.5	1.6	1.6	24.9	2.3	2.3	2.3	6.8	53.6
2023	6.6	11.6	1.7	2.6	22.5	9.6	12.8	1.6	1.6	25.7	2.3	2.3	2.3	7.0	55.2
2024	6.8	11.9	1.7	2.7	23.2	9.9	13.2	1.7	1.7	26.4	2.4	2.4	2.4	7.2	56.8
2025	7.0	12.3	1.8	2.8	23.9	10.2	13.6	1.7	1.7	27.2	2.5	2.5	2.5	7.4	58.5
2026	7.2	12.6	1.8	2.9	24.6	10.5	14.0	1.8	1.8	28.1	2.6	2.6	2.6	7.7	60.3
2027	7.4	13.0	1.9	3.0	25.3	10.8	14.4	1.8	1.8	28.9	2.6	2.6	2.6	7.9	62.1

Estimates were made by type of vehicle and by terrain, depending upon the degree of roughness of road, measured according to the international roughness index. VOC is expressed as a function of the degree of road roughness (see Appendix 17A).

Since the original model's output was expressed in 2003 prices, VOC for "with" and "without" project scenarios for different road sections was estimated according to their degree of road roughness in 2003 prices. These estimates were then adjusted by an annual inflation rate of 6.5 percent over the next two years to 2005 prices. For example, on section D4100, the VOC for private passenger cars was originally estimated from the RED model at R3.261 per vehicle-kilometre in 2003 prices. This estimate is applied to flat terrain in the absence of road improvement with a degree of road roughness measured at 10.0 (see Appendix 17A). The cost was then adjusted for inflation to become R3.699, expressed in 2005 prices. After the road is upgraded from gravel to tarred surface, the road roughness would be improved from index 10.00 to index 2.0. The resulting VOC, re-estimated from the RED model and adjusted for inflation, was R2.500 per vehicle-kilometre in 2005 prices.

The same procedure was used to estimate the average VOC per vehicle-kilometre for other vehicle types and other road sections. Estimates of the average VOC for each vehicle type travelling on each road section before and after the road improvement are presented in Table 17.7. These data provided the basis for subsequent estimates of total project-induced annual savings in VOC.

Table 17.7: Vehicle Operating Costs for "With" and "Without" Project Scenarios (R per vehicle-km, in 2005 prices)

Road Surface	Road Section	Car/ Tourists	Minibus	LGV/ Agricultural	HGV
Tarred ("with" project)	D4100	2.500	3.065	3.770	6.050
	D4250/D4190	2.500	3.065	3.770	6.050
	D4050/D1583	2.833	3.443	4.569	8.160
Gravel ("without" project)	D4100	3.699	4.723	6.299	9.168
	D4250/D4190	3.699	4.723	6.299	9.168
	D4050/D1583	3.922	4.981	6.910	11.155

Source: Details can be found in Appendix 17A.

17.7 Average Speeds of Vehicles

In addition to VOC, the time-cost of occupants travelling on the road can also be an important factor in the economic evaluation of road improvement projects. The time-cost of travellers can be determined by the speed of the vehicle and the time value of travellers. The former will be influenced by the condition of the road and the volume of the traffic, while the latter is related to the wages and salaries of the driver and other occupants of the vehicle.

Since this project was located in a low-traffic-volume region (see Section 17.5), vehicle speed is unlikely to be affected by the volume of traffic. Rather, the average vehicle speed is determined by the roughness of the road. As a consequence, the average vehicle speed measured in this project was based on the RED model, taking into consideration the specific conditions in the Limpopo province of South Africa. The speed estimates were for different vehicle types and for various terrain and road conditions. As with VOC, speed was measured as a function of the degree of roughness.[117] The estimating equations used for each vehicle type were originally estimated for 2003 and are shown in Appendix 17B.

The results are presented in Table 17.8. For example, without the road improvement, the average vehicle speed for passenger cars travelling on gravel road D4100 is 68.8 km per hour, using an international roughness index of 10.0. With the road upgraded to a tarred surface, the roughness index would be reduced to 2.0, and vehicles could reach average speeds of 86.6 km per hour. This increase in vehicle speed, together with the value of time per hour, allowed the value of project-induced time savings per vehicle-kilometre on D4100 to be estimated. The methodology for estimating the value per vehicle-kilometre for each vehicle type is explained below.

Table 17.8: Average Speeds of Vehicles for "With" and "Without" Project Scenarios (km/hour)

Road Surface	Road Section	Car/ Tourists	Minibus	LGV/ Agriculture	HGV
Tarred ("with" project)	D4100	86.61	81.92	75.53	59.63
	D4250/D4190	86.61	81.92	75.53	59.63
	D4050/D1583	69.07	63.86	53.44	35.98
Gravel ("without" project)	D4100	68.76	60.44	53.88	45.07
	D4250/D4190	68.76	60.44	53.88	45.07
	D4050/D1583	60.71	53.64	44.83	31.62

Source: Details can be found in Appendix 17B.

The next step was to estimate the average occupancy of each vehicle type and the time value per hour for its occupants. With regard to average vehicle occupancy, a road-user survey was used to obtain a reliable estimate. The time value for passengers was based on wage rates for skilled and unskilled labour.

The information regarding vehicle occupancy and labour wage rates was obtained from the study by ARCUS GIBB (2004, pp. 4–2 to 4–3). For passenger

---

[117]Passenger cars and tourist traffic corresponded to the "car" class, minibuses were linked to the "light bus" class, LGVs and agricultural transport were presumed to be in the "light truck" class, while HGVs corresponded to the "heavy truck" class. The speeds were estimated on a flat terrain, with a roughness index of 2.0 for tarred roads, and on a flat terrain with an index of 10.0 for gravel roads.

Appraisal of Upgrading a Gravel Road

cars, an average rate of 1.2 skilled occupants was used. For tourist trips it was assumed that there would be, on average, 1.5 tourists per vehicle and also on average 0.5 tourist guides per vehicle, making a total of 2.0 occupants per vehicle. For minibuses, 10.0 unskilled commuters comprised an average travel group. Note that for HGVs, LGVs, and agricultural vehicles, the driver's salary would be a direct cost of transportation and was already accounted for as part of VOC.

The wage rate for unskilled labour was taken as R7.15 per hour, and the rate for skilled labour R18.25 per hour.[118] For tourists, who are likely to belong in the skilled category, the value of time was taken as one-half of their wage rate, R9.13 per hour. For LGVs, HGVs, and agricultural traffic, the value of time saving is dependent on the content and value of cargo and the cost of delivery delays. Because of the wide diversity of agricultural, mining, and other goods that could be being transported on the proposed road, they should be estimated separately, as far as possible. The total time saving for each vehicle type can then be estimated.

For passenger cars, the value of time saving per vehicle-kilometre was equal to the value of time per vehicle-kilometre on the gravel road minus the value of time per vehicle-kilometre on the tarred road. For example, on section D4100, the value of time per vehicle-kilometre for a single occupant of a passenger car with a wage rate of R18.25 per hour and travelling at a speed of 68.8 km per hour was R0.2654 per vehicle-kilometre. With the same value of time, a car travelling at a speed of 86.6 km per hour would have a time-cost of R0.2107 per vehicle-kilometre. The estimated value of time saving for a passenger car with 1.2 occupants would then be about R0.0656 per vehicle-kilometre. In a similar fashion, the value of time saving for passenger cars on sections D4250/D4190 and D4050/D1583 was estimated as R0.0656 and R0.0437 per vehicle-kilometre, respectively.

For tourist trips on D4050/D1583, the estimated time saving per vehicle-kilometre was R0.0455. This was derived from the time saving for the average of 1.5 tourists and 0.5 guides in a typical vehicle.[119] No substantial volume of normal tourist traffic was expected on other sections of the upgraded road.

The same method was applied to measure the value of time saving for minibuses. For section D4100, the resulting estimate was R0.3102 per vehicle-kilometre.[120] The value of time saving for minibus traffic on sections

---

[118]The study by ARCUS GIBB in 2004 placed values of R6.71 and R17.14 on unskilled and skilled hourly wages, respectively. An inflation adjustment of 6.5 percent was applied to obtain the 2005 wage rates, resulting in R7.15 and R18.25.

[119]The value of time saving for tourists was R0.0273 per vehicle-kilometre (= [(R9.13 / 60.7) − (R9.13 / 69.1)] × 1.5 occupants). For skilled occupants of a tourist vehicle, the estimated time saving amounted to R0.0182 per vehicle-kilometre (= [(R18.25 / 60.7) − (R18.25 / 69.1)] × 0.5 occupants). The summation of the value of time for both kinds of occupants gave a figure of R0.0455 per vehicle-kilometre on section D4050/D1583.

[120]Estimated as ([R7.15 / 60.4] − [R7.15 / 81.9]) × 10.0 occupants = R0.3102 per vehicle-kilometre on section D4100.

D4250/D4190 and D4050/D1583 was estimated as R0.3102 and R0.2133 per vehicle-kilometre, respectively.

In the case of freight for LGVs and agricultural traffic, a different approach was needed for estimating the value of time saving. The improved road would enable LGVs and agricultural transport to move at a higher speed, allowing a faster turnover of the vehicle fleet and more productive use of the vehicles. In the long run, the owners of vehicle fleets would need fewer vehicles, thus resulting in savings of capital costs. Suppose a new truck costs R1.30 million, its average utilization factor is 70 percent, and the real rates of depreciation and financial return on investment are 15.4 percent and 10.0 percent per annum, respectively.[121] On section D4100 alone, the value of time for LGVs/agricultural traffic per vehicle-hour would be R53.95.[122] If the time saving per 34-km trip resulting from an increase in speed was 0.181 hour, the value of capital savings can be estimated at R9.760 per vehicle trip on this section.[123]

In addition to capital savings, there would also be savings on drivers' wages, which would add up to R1.294 per 34-km vehicle trip.[124] Thus, the combined value of time saving for heavy traffic was R11.054 per vehicle trip on section D4100. Using the same approach, the value of time saving was estimated for sections D4250/D4190 and D4050/D1583 as R15.281 per 47-km vehicle trip, and R16.459 per 75-km vehicle trip, on the corresponding section.

17.8 Economic Appraisal

The economic appraisal of a project is concerned with the effect that the project has on the entire society; it examines whether the project increases the economic welfare of society as a whole. It looks at the present value (PV) of all the incremental annual economic benefits and costs generated throughout the project life; in the case of a road improvement project, this includes savings in VOC, time-costs of travellers, maintenance costs, and other costs such as accidents and other externalities. The PV of annual benefits minus costs over a project's lifetime is then compared with the capital expenditures incurred on upgrading a road.

The annual savings in maintenance, VOC, and time-costs in the current analysis will be quantified in the next section. The impacts of an improved road

---

[121]The average annual cost structure of truck transportation was obtained from the Vehicle Cost Schedule, published by the Road and Freight Association (October 2001).

[122]The value of time per LGV was estimated as R1,300,000 × (15.4 percent + 10.0 percent) / (365 × 24 × 70 percent) = R53.95 per vehicle-hour. Alternatively, it is possible to use annual rental charges for LGVs divided by the number of hours the vehicle is actually transporting merchandise.

[123]The amount of time saved per trip was 0.181 hour per vehicle trip (= 34 km / 53.9 km/hr − 34 km / 75.5 km/hr. The value of capital savings can then be estimated as R9.760 per vehicle trip (= R53.95/hour × 0.181 hour/vehicle trip) on section D4100.

[124]The value of drivers' wage savings was estimated as R7.15 hour × 0.181 hour/vehicle trip = R1.294 per 34-km vehicle trip.

project on accidents could be important in terms of changes in the number of accidents and the monetary value of damage to property and human bodies. In general, such impacts should be properly assessed for "with" and "without" project scenarios. However, this component may not have been significant in this project as a result of the low volume of traffic, and was therefore not included in this study.

Other externalities, such as various taxes and subsidies involved in key project inputs, were captured in commodity-specific conversion factors (CSCFs). Three key CSCFs were identified in this project: infrastructure construction and maintenance costs, truck transportation, and passenger care transportation; their corresponding CSCFs were estimated at 0.876, 0.850, and 0.922, respectively, based on the methodology outlined in Chapter Eleven and the empirical estimation carried out elsewhere.[125] These CSCFs allowed all financial costs of the project inputs to be converted into the corresponding economic costs in order to construct the economic resource flow statement of the project.

17.8.1 Annual Savings in Maintenance Costs, VOC, and Time-Costs

This section summarizes the total savings in maintenance costs, VOC, and time-costs generated by upgrading a gravel road to a tarred road.

a) Maintenance Costs

Annual savings in financial maintenance costs were estimated (costs of the project minus what they would have been in its absence), and these are presented in Table 17.3 by road section. These costs were multiplied by the conversion factor for maintenance costs at 0.876 to generate annual savings of economic resource costs. Details for each year over the life of the project are shown in Table 17.9 by road section and by frequency of maintenance.

A positive result means that some cost savings will be generated, while negatives imply a net increase in resource costs. In this case, each type of maintenance activity would generate savings in economic resource costs. The estimated PV of these savings (using the economic cost of capital for South Africa at 11.0 percent as the discount rate) (Kuo et al., 2003) as a result of road improvement amounted to R137.8 million in 2005 prices. About 57.1 percent of the total savings stemmed from reduced costs of intermediate maintenance. Savings in periodic maintenance accounted for 35.7 percent of the total, and savings on routine maintenance accounted for the remaining 7.2 percent.

---

[125]Taken from Cambridge Resources International (2004).

b) Vehicle Operating Costs

Using the estimates of savings in VOC and time-cost per vehicle-kilometre by vehicle type presented in sections 17.6 and 17.7, and the projected corresponding annual normal, diverted, and generated traffic on each road section shown in Section 17.5, the annual saving in VOC and time-costs for each road section could be estimated and then aggregated to total annual savings. These incremental financial cost savings were translated into incremental economic resource savings by applying economic conversion factors for each type of outlay.

VOC constitutes a major expense for road users. Using gravel roads substantially increases VOC for all vehicle types. These costs would decline as a consequence of the upgrading of the road. The cost savings, or the economic benefits to the existing or normal traffic, are the summation of savings in VOC per kilometre multiplied by the AADT on the road section, the length of the road, and 365 days a year over all types of vehicle. The resulting values were multiplied by the relevant conversion factor at 0.850 for LGVs, HGVs, and agricultural transport, and 0.922 for cars, tourist vehicles, and minibuses.

Table 17.9: Savings in Economic Maintenance Costs (R million, in 2005 prices)

Year	Routine					Intermediate					Periodic					Total
	D4100	D4250	D4190	D4050/D1583	Sub-total	D4100	D4250	D4190	D4050/D1583	Sub-total	D4100	D4250	D4190	D4050/D1583	Sub-total	
2005	1.11	0.65	0.00	0.00	1.76	0.00	0.00	0.00	0.00	0.00	0.00	0.00	0.00	0.00	0.00	1.76
2006	0.16	0.32	0.65	0.82	1.95	6.34	5.04	3.73	13.99	29.11	0.00	0.00	0.00	0.00	0.00	31.06
2007	0.16	0.13	0.09	1.75	2.13	0.00	0.00	0.00	0.00	0.00	0.00	0.00	0.00	0.00	0.00	2.13
2008	0.16	0.13	0.09	0.35	0.73	1.59	2.24	3.73	13.99	21.55	0.00	0.00	0.00	0.00	0.00	22.28
2009	0.16	0.13	0.09	0.35	0.73	0.00	−0.98	−2.80	−3.50	−7.28	11.10	8.82	6.53	24.49	50.94	44.39
2010	0.16	0.13	0.09	0.35	0.73	6.34	5.04	3.73	7.00	22.11	0.00	0.00	0.00	0.00	0.00	22.84
2011	0.16	0.13	0.09	0.35	0.73	−4.76	−2.80	0.00	0.00	−7.56	0.00	0.00	0.00	0.00	0.00	−6.83
2012	0.16	0.13	0.09	0.35	0.73	6.34	4.06	0.93	10.50	21.83	0.00	0.00	0.00	0.00	0.00	22.56
2013	0.16	0.13	0.09	0.35	0.73	0.00	0.00	0.00	−7.00	−7.00	0.00	0.00	0.00	0.00	0.00	−6.27
2014	0.16	0.13	0.09	0.35	0.73	1.59	2.24	3.73	13.99	21.55	11.10	8.82	6.53	24.49	50.94	73.22
2015	0.16	0.13	0.09	0.35	0.73	0.00	−0.98	−2.80	−3.50	−7.28	−15.86	−9.33	0.00	0.00	−25.19	−31.74
2016	0.16	0.13	0.09	0.35	0.73	6.34	5.04	3.73	7.00	22.11	0.00	−3.27	−9.33	−11.66	−24.26	−1.42
2017	0.16	0.13	0.09	0.35	0.73	−4.76	−2.80	0.00	0.00	−7.56	0.00	0.00	0.00	−23.32	−23.32	−30.15
2018	0.16	0.13	0.09	0.35	0.73	6.34	4.06	0.93	10.50	21.83	0.00	0.00	0.00	0.00	0.00	22.56
2019	0.16	0.13	0.09	0.35	0.73	0.00	0.00	0.00	−7.00	−7.00	11.10	8.82	6.53	24.49	50.94	44.67
2020	0.16	0.13	0.09	0.35	0.73	1.59	2.24	3.73	13.99	21.55	0.00	0.00	0.00	0.00	0.00	22.28
2021	0.16	0.13	0.09	0.35	0.73	0.00	−0.98	−2.80	−3.50	−7.28	0.00	0.00	0.00	0.00	0.00	−6.55
2022	0.16	0.13	0.09	0.35	0.73	6.34	5.04	3.73	7.00	22.11	0.00	0.00	0.00	0.00	0.00	22.84
2023	0.16	0.13	0.09	0.35	0.73	−4.76	−2.80	0.00	0.00	−7.56	0.00	0.00	0.00	0.00	0.00	−6.83
2024	0.16	0.13	0.09	0.35	0.73	6.34	4.06	0.93	10.50	21.83	11.10	8.82	6.53	24.49	50.94	73.50
2025	0.16	0.13	0.09	0.35	0.73	0.00	0.00	0.00	−7.00	−7.00	0.00	0.00	0.00	0.00	0.00	−6.27
2026	0.16	0.13	0.09	0.35	0.73	1.59	2.24	3.73	13.99	21.55	0.00	0.00	0.00	0.00	0.00	22.28
2027	0.16	0.13	0.09	0.35	0.73	0.00	0.00	0.00	0.00	0.00	0.00	0.00	0.00	0.00	0.00	0.73
PV@11%	2.40	1.90	1.30	4.40	9.90	15.80	12.90	10.20	39.80	78.70	10.20	8.20	6.30	24.40	49.10	137.75

For diverted and generated traffic, the total benefits were taken to be one-half of the per unit reduction in the above VOC per vehicle–kilometre multiplied by the length of travel and total diverted and generated traffic over 365 days a year.

It should be noted that because construction takes three years to complete, an adjustment was made to exclude each section until it had been upgraded, and to treat VOC on these sections as traffic on gravel road. During the construction period of a particular section, no VOC savings would be realized, since traffic typically uses a temporary bypass.

Table 17.10 presents annual savings in VOC for traffic that would be present on the old road if the project were not to be implemented. The PV of economic VOC resource savings was estimated to be R200.8 million in 2005 prices. This result represented a significant addition to savings in maintenance costs. For diverted and generated traffic by various types of vehicle, VOC savings were estimated to be approximately R5.9 million and R3.8 million, respectively.

c) Time Saving

The value of time saving is determined by an increase in vehicle speed, the length of the road section, and the time value of each occupant travelling or the time value of the vehicles used to transport merchandise plus the time value of the cargo. The speed of each type of vehicle travelling on different road sections was estimated for the "with" and "without" project scenarios, leading to consequent estimates of savings in time-cost per vehicle-kilometre. As with the reduced VOC, road users would experience a rise in their average speed on the improved road, thus reducing their total travel time. In the case of diverted and generated traffic, the benefits were taken to be one-half of time saved between travelling on the upgraded tarred road and travelling on the gravel road.

Once the value of time savings per vehicle-kilometre and per vehicle trip had been estimated for all vehicle types and road sections, a combined annual estimate of time savings for the existing traffic and consumer surplus for diverted and generated traffic was estimated. The total annual benefits in time savings for all normal traffic over the life of the project are presented in Table 17.11. Their PV over the life of the project amounted to R33.11 million in 2005 prices. The time savings for diverted and generated traffic were R0.59 million and R0.46 million, respectively.

Table 17.10: VOC Savings for Normal Traffic (R million, in 2005 prices)

Year	D4100					D4250/D4190					D4050/D1583				Total
	Car	Minibus	LGV/Agri	HGV	Sub-total	Car	Minibus	LGV/Agri	HGV	Sub-total	Car	Tourist	Minibus	Sub-total	
2005	0.0	0.0	0.0	0.0	0.0	0.0	0.0	0.0	0.0	0.0	0.0	0.0	0.0	0.0	0.0
2006	1.2	4.4	0.1	0.3	5.9	0.9	3.4	0.1	0.2	4.6	0.0	0.0	0.0	0.0	10.5
2007	1.2	4.5	0.1	0.3	6.2	2.2	8.3	0.2	0.4	11.2	0.3	0.1	0.5	0.8	18.3
2008	1.3	4.7	0.1	0.4	6.5	2.3	8.7	0.2	0.5	11.7	1.0	0.2	1.4	2.6	20.8
2009	1.3	4.9	0.1	0.5	6.8	2.4	9.0	0.2	0.5	12.2	1.0	0.2	1.5	2.7	21.7
2010	1.4	5.1	0.1	0.5	7.1	2.5	9.4	0.3	0.5	12.6	1.1	0.2	1.5	2.8	22.5
2011	1.4	5.3	0.1	0.5	7.4	2.6	9.8	0.3	0.5	13.2	1.1	0.2	1.6	2.9	23.5
2012	1.5	5.5	0.2	0.5	7.7	2.7	10.1	0.3	0.6	13.7	1.2	0.2	1.7	3.1	24.4
2013	1.5	5.7	0.2	0.6	8.0	2.8	10.6	0.3	0.6	14.3	1.2	0.2	1.7	3.2	25.4
2014	1.6	6.0	0.2	0.6	8.3	2.9	11.0	0.3	0.6	14.8	1.3	0.2	1.8	3.3	26.4
2015	1.6	6.2	0.2	0.6	8.6	3.0	11.4	0.3	0.7	15.4	1.3	0.3	1.9	3.4	27.5
2016	1.7	6.4	0.2	0.7	9.0	3.2	11.9	0.3	0.7	16.1	1.4	0.3	1.9	3.6	28.6
2017	1.8	6.7	0.2	0.7	9.4	3.3	12.3	0.4	0.7	16.7	1.4	0.3	2.0	3.7	29.8
2018	1.9	7.0	0.2	0.7	9.8	3.4	12.8	0.4	0.8	17.4	1.5	0.3	2.1	3.9	31.0
2019	1.9	7.2	0.2	0.8	10.1	3.6	13.4	0.4	0.8	18.1	1.5	0.3	2.2	4.0	32.3
2020	2.0	7.5	0.2	0.8	10.6	3.7	13.9	0.4	0.8	18.8	1.6	0.3	2.3	4.2	33.6
2021	2.1	7.8	0.2	0.8	11.0	3.8	14.4	0.4	0.9	19.6	1.7	0.3	2.4	4.4	35.0
2022	2.2	8.2	0.2	0.9	11.4	4.0	15.0	0.5	0.9	20.4	1.7	0.3	2.5	4.5	36.4
2023	2.3	8.5	0.3	0.9	11.9	4.2	15.6	0.5	1.0	21.2	1.8	0.3	2.6	4.7	37.9
2024	2.3	8.8	0.3	1.0	12.4	4.3	16.2	0.5	1.0	22.1	1.9	0.4	2.7	4.9	39.4
2025	2.4	9.2	0.3	1.0	12.9	4.5	16.9	0.5	1.1	23.0	2.0	0.4	2.8	5.1	41.0
2026	2.5	9.5	0.3	1.1	13.4	4.7	17.6	0.6	1.1	23.9	2.0	0.4	2.9	5.3	42.7
2027	2.6	9.9	0.3	1.1	14.0	4.9	18.3	0.6	1.2	24.9	2.1	0.4	3.0	5.5	44.4

Table 17.11: Time Savings for Normal Traffic (R million, in 2005 prices)

Year	D4100					D4250/D4190					D4050/D1583				Total
	Car	Minibus	LGV/Agri	HGV	Sub-total	Car	Minibus	LGV/Agri	HGV	Sub-total	Car	Minibus	LGV/Agri	HGV	
2005	0.0	0.0	0.00	0.0	0.0	0.0	0.0	0.00	0.0	0.0	0.0	0.0	0.00	0.0	2005
2006	0.1	0.9	0.02	0.1	0.1	0.1	0.9	0.02	0.1	0.8	0.1	0.9	0.02	0.1	2006
2007	0.1	0.9	0.02	0.1	1.1	0.1	0.9	0.02	0.1	1.9	0.1	0.9	0.02	0.1	2007
2008	0.1	1.0	0.02	0.1	1.1	0.1	1.0	0.02	0.1	2.0	0.1	1.0	0.02	0.1	2008
2009	0.1	1.0	0.02	0.1	1.2	0.1	1.0	0.02	0.1	2.1	0.1	1.0	0.02	0.1	2009
2010	0.1	1.0	0.02	0.1	1.2	0.1	1.0	0.02	0.1	2.2	0.1	1.0	0.02	0.1	2010
2011	0.1	1.1	0.02	0.1	1.3	0.1	1.1	0.02	0.1	2.3	0.1	1.1	0.02	0.1	2011
2012	0.1	1.1	0.02	0.1	1.3	0.1	1.1	0.02	0.1	2.4	0.1	1.1	0.02	0.1	2012
2013	0.1	1.2	0.02	0.1	1.4	0.1	1.2	0.02	0.1	2.5	0.1	1.2	0.02	0.1	2013
2014	0.1	1.2	0.03	0.1	1.4	0.1	1.2	0.03	0.1	2.6	0.1	1.2	0.03	0.1	2014
2015	0.1	1.3	0.03	0.1	1.5	0.1	1.3	0.03	0.1	2.7	0.1	1.3	0.03	0.1	2015
2016	0.1	1.3	0.03	0.1	1.6	0.1	1.3	0.03	0.1	2.8	0.1	1.3	0.03	0.1	2016
2017	0.1	1.4	0.03	0.1	1.6	0.1	1.4	0.03	0.1	2.9	0.1	1.4	0.03	0.1	2017
2018	0.1	1.4	0.03	0.1	1.7	0.1	1.4	0.03	0.1	3.0	0.1	1.4	0.03	0.1	2018
2019	0.1	1.5	0.03	0.1	1.8	0.1	1.5	0.03	0.1	3.1	0.1	1.5	0.03	0.1	2019
2020	0.1	1.5	0.03	0.1	1.8	0.1	1.5	0.03	0.1	3.3	0.1	1.5	0.03	0.1	2020
2021	0.1	1.6	0.04	0.2	1.9	0.1	1.6	0.04	0.2	3.4	0.1	1.6	0.04	0.2	2021
2022	0.1	1.7	0.04	0.2	2.0	0.1	1.7	0.04	0.2	3.5	0.1	1.7	0.04	0.2	2022
2023	0.1	1.7	0.04	0.2	2.1	0.1	1.7	0.04	0.2	3.7	0.1	1.7	0.04	0.2	2023
2024	0.1	1.8	0.04	0.2	2.1	0.1	1.8	0.04	0.2	3.8	0.1	1.8	0.04	0.2	2024
2025	0.1	1.9	0.04	0.2	2.2	0.1	1.9	0.04	0.2	4.0	0.1	1.9	0.04	0.2	2025
2026	0.2	1.9	0.04	0.2	2.3	0.2	1.9	0.04	0.2	4.1	0.2	1.9	0.04	0.2	2026
2027	0.2	2.0	0.05	0.2	2.4	0.2	2.0	0.05	0.2	4.3	0.2	2.0	0.05	0.2	2027

17.8.2 Economic Viability of the Project

The economic viability of the project is based on the incremental economic benefits and costs generated over the entire life of the project. The main incremental annual economic benefits are savings in maintenance costs, VOC, and time-costs, as presented in the previous section and summarized in columns 3 to 5 of Table 17.12. The savings expressed in PV were R137.8 million, R210.4 million, and R34.4 million, respectively, using the real economic cost of capital for South Africa (11 percent) as the discount rate.

The major cost of this improved road project would be the construction cost incurred by RAL. After conversion into economic cost, its PV was R277.2 million in 2005 prices. This was the economic opportunity cost of resources that would be employed to upgrade the road. RAL would not gain financially from this project because the estimated value of its resource savings from reduced maintenance activities alone (R137.8 million) fell far short of the proposed investment (R277.2 million). However, apart from RAL, other stakeholders were involved, and their net benefits could easily have carried the project to a positive overall NPV.

Once economic costs and benefits had been estimated on an annual basis, an economic resource flow statement was developed. This statement presents the projected incremental economic investment costs along with the value of generated incremental economic benefits in order to obtain the net resource flow generated by the proposed road improvement. The annual economic resource flow statement shown in Table 17.12 summarizes the investment costs, economic maintenance resource cost savings, economic VOC savings, and time savings. The estimated economic NPV of the whole project was R105.4 million in 2005 prices, using an 11 percent discount rate. This positive economic NPV implies that the country as a whole would be better off with the proposed project. The ratio of PV of benefits to the PV of costs was 1.38.

It is important to note that the proposed road was composed of three separate sections that were, in fact, projects on their own since they had different construction costs and provided different levels of benefits. The analysis could be structured in such a way as to evaluate the economic feasibility of each section of the road.

Table 17.12: Economic Resource Flow Statement (R million, in 2005 prices)

Year	Construction Costs	Savings in Maintenance Cost	Savings in VOC	Savings in Time Costs	Annual Net Benefits
2005	−100.5	1.8	0.0	0.0	−98.8
2006	−102.3	31.1	11.2	1.9	−58.2
2007	−104.1	2.1	19.2	3.2	−79.6
2008	0	22.3	21.8	3.6	47.6
2009	0	44.4	22.7	3.7	70.8
2010	0	22.8	23.7	3.9	50.3
2011	0	−6.8	24.6	4.0	21.8
2012	0	22.6	25.6	4.2	52.3
2013	0	−6.3	26.6	4.3	24.7
2014	0	73.2	27.7	4.5	105.4
2015	0	−31.7	28.8	4.7	1.8
2016	0	−1.4	30.0	4.9	33.4
2017	0	−30.2	31.2	5.1	6.1
2018	0	22.6	32.4	5.3	60.3
2019	0	44.7	33.7	5.5	83.9
2020	0	22.3	35.1	5.7	63.1
2021	0	−6.5	36.5	5.9	35.9
2022	0	22.8	37.9	6.2	67.0
2023	0	−6.8	39.5	6.4	39.1
2024	0	73.5	41.1	6.7	121.3
2025	0	−6.3	42.7	7.0	43.4
2026	0	22.3	44.4	7.2	74.0
2027	0	0.7	46.2	7.5	54.5
PV@11%	−277.2	137.8	210.4	34.4	105.4

Following the same approach as outlined previously, the net economic benefits were found to equal R94.5 million for upgrading section D4250/D4190, as a result of substantial VOC savings. Section D4100 also exhibited a positive economic NPV of R45.6 million, while section D4050/D1583 generated a negative economic NPV of R34.8 million. In other words, section D4050/D1583 should be excluded from the upgrade plan. In so doing, the benefits generated from the overall project would rise to R140.2 million from R105.4 million. Details can be found in Table 17.13.

Appraisal of Upgrading a Gravel Road

Table 17.13: Economic Resource Flow Statement by Road Section (R million, in 2005 prices)

Year	D4100					D4250/D4190					D4050/D1583					Total
	Constr uction Costs	Savings in Maintenance Costs	Savings in VOC	Savings in Time-Costs	Sub-total	Constru ction Costs	Savings in Maintenance Costs	Savings in VOC	Savings in Time-Costs	Sub-total	Constru ction Costs	Savings in Maintenance Costs	Savings in VOC	Savings in Time-Costs	Sub-total	Total
2005	-63.3	1.11	0.00	0.00	-62.2	-37.2	0.65	0.00	0.00	-36.6	0.0	0.00	0.00	0.00	0.0	-98.8
2006	0.0	6.50	6.19	1.07	13.8	-50.2	9.74	4.80	0.82	-34.8	-52.1	14.81	0.21	0.02	-37.1	-58.2
2007	0.0	0.16	6.48	1.12	7.8	0.0	0.22	11.65	2.00	13.9	-104.1	1.75	1.06	0.11	-101.2	-79.6
2008	0.0	1.74	6.79	1.17	9.7	0.0	6.19	12.12	2.09	20.4	0.0	14.34	2.91	0.29	17.5	47.6
2009	0.0	11.26	7.11	1.23	19.6	0.0	11.79	12.61	2.17	26.6	0.0	21.34	3.02	0.31	24.7	70.8
2010	0.0	6.50	7.40	1.28	15.2	0.0	8.99	13.11	2.26	24.4	0.0	7.35	3.14	0.32	10.8	50.3
2011	0.0	-4.60	7.70	1.33	4.4	0.0	-2.58	13.64	2.35	13.4	0.0	0.35	3.26	0.33	3.9	21.8
2012	0.0	6.50	8.01	1.38	15.9	0.0	5.21	14.19	2.44	21.8	0.0	10.85	3.39	0.34	14.6	52.3
2013	0.0	0.16	8.34	1.44	9.9	0.0	0.22	14.76	2.54	17.5	0.0	-6.65	3.52	0.36	-2.8	24.7
2014	0.0	12.85	8.67	1.50	23.0	0.0	21.54	15.35	2.64	39.5	0.0	38.83	3.66	0.37	42.9	105.4
2015	0.0	-15.70	9.02	1.56	-5.1	0.0	-12.89	15.97	2.76	5.8	0.0	-3.15	3.80	0.39	1.0	1.8
2016	0.0	6.50	9.39	1.62	17.5	0.0	-3.61	16.62	2.86	15.9	0.0	-4.31	3.95	0.40	0.0	33.4
2017	0.0	-4.60	9.77	1.69	6.9	0.0	-2.58	17.28	2.98	17.7	0.0	-22.97	4.11	0.42	-18.5	6.1
2018	0.0	6.50	10.16	1.75	18.4	0.0	5.21	17.98	3.10	26.3	0.0	10.85	4.27	0.43	15.5	60.3
2019	0.0	11.26	10.58	1.83	23.7	0.0	15.57	18.71	3.22	37.5	0.0	17.84	4.43	0.45	22.7	83.9
2020	0.0	1.74	11.00	1.90	14.6	0.0	6.19	19.46	3.35	29.0	0.0	14.34	4.61	0.47	19.4	63.1
2021	0.0	0.16	11.45	1.98	13.6	0.0	-3.56	20.24	3.49	20.2	0.0	-3.15	4.79	0.49	2.1	35.9
2022	0.0	6.50	11.91	2.06	20.5	0.0	8.99	21.06	3.63	33.7	0.0	7.35	4.97	0.50	12.8	67.0
2023	0.0	-4.60	12.40	2.14	9.9	0.0	-2.58	21.91	3.77	23.1	0.0	0.35	5.17	0.52	6.0	39.1
2024	0.0	17.60	12.90	2.23	32.7	0.0	20.56	22.79	3.93	47.3	0.0	35.34	5.37	0.54	41.2	121.3
2025	0.0	0.16	13.42	2.32	15.9	0.0	0.22	23.71	4.08	28.0	0.0	-6.65	5.58	0.57	-0.5	43.4
2026	0.0	1.74	13.97	2.41	18.1	0.0	6.19	24.67	4.25	35.1	0.0	14.34	5.80	0.59	20.7	74.0
2027	0.0	0.16	14.54	2.51	17.2	0.0	0.22	25.67	4.42	30.3	0.0	0.35	6.03	0.61	7.0	54.5
PV@ 11%	-63.3	28.40	68.70	11.90	45.6	-131.5	40.70	116.30	20.00	94.6		68.60	25.40	2.60	-34.80	105.4

17.9 Impact on Stakeholders

The measurement of project costs and the economic analysis of the project provided the basic data for assessing the impacts of the project on various stakeholders. The analysis looked into the financial expenditures incurred by RAL and the allocation of project externalities among the stakeholders who would be affected by the road improvement.

The stakeholders identified in the analysis were divided into two groups: RAL and various road users. The road users were further divided as follows: existing road users, who continue driving on the road in the absence of upgrading the road; diverted users, who will switch to the upgraded road from another road or alternative transportation modes; and newly generated traffic, which will be induced to use the road when it is upgraded. There were five vehicle classes in each traffic flow: passenger cars, tourist vehicles, minibuses, LGVs and agricultural transport, and HGVs.

Table 17.14 presents a summary of the economic benefits accruing to each stakeholder. RAL would incur the initial capital expenditure of R277.2 million to upgrade the gravel road to a tarred road. Such an investment would bring a substantial amount of savings in maintenance costs for RAL (equal to a PV of R137.8 million). As a result, the net cost to RAL would be R139.4 million.

The PV of total economic net benefits created by the project was R382.5 million, with 36.0 percent of that amount accruing to RAL in the form of lower maintenance costs. The rest was spread across the different vehicle types using the road, namely minibuses (46.3 percent), passenger cars (12.8 percent), HGVs (3.1 percent), tourist vehicles (0.6 percent), and LGVs/agricultural transport (1.2 percent).

Another facet of the distributional analysis considered the allocation of benefits among the existing, diverted, and generated road users. Out of the total benefits of R244.7 million, the existing road users stood to gain R234.0 million, almost 96 percent of the total net economic benefits. The diverted vehicles would benefit marginally by an amount of R6.7 million, and generated traffic would gain R4.3 million.

Table 17.14: Allocation of Costs and Benefits (R million, in 2005 prices)

Stakeholders	Category	Costs	Benefits	Percentage Distribution
RAL	Investment costs	−277.2		
	Savings in			
	Maintenance costs:			
	Routine		9.9	
	Intermediate		78.7	
	Periodic		49.1	
	Sub-total		137.8	36.0%
Car passengers	Existing		45.9	
	Diverted		2.0	
	Generated		1.0	
	Sub-total		48.8	12.8%
Tourists	Existing		1.8	
	Diverted		0.4	
	Generated		0.2	
	Sub-total		2.4	0.6%
Minibuses	Existing		171.1	
	Diverted		3.8	
	Generated		2.2	
	Sub-total		177.1	46.3%
LGV/agriculture	Existing		4.2	
	Diverted		0.0	
	Generated		0.4	
	Sub-total		4.6	1.2%
HGV	Existing		11.0	
	Diverted		0.5	
	Generated		0.5	
	Sub-total		12.0	3.1%
Total		−277.2	382.6	100.0%

17.10 Dealing with Risk

The above analysis employed the most likely single estimates of the key variables used. This resulted in point estimates of the economic outcomes and the impacts of the project on stakeholders. Different values of these key variables would obviously lead to different project outcomes. Reorganizing this, and in order to help decision-makers, we conducted sensitivity and risk analyses of the project.

17.10.1 Sensitivity Analysis

A sensitivity analysis was conducted to assess the impact of several key input variables on the economic outcomes and stakeholders of the project. It was carried out by changing the value of one of these parameters at a time over a plausible range of possible values and examining the impact this had on the project outcomes.

a) Cost Overruns

Capital cost overruns are quite possible and can have a significant negative impact on the outcome of a project. The effect of capital cost overruns on a range from −10 percent to +40 percent is shown in Table 17.15.

Table 17.15: Sensitivity Test of Capital Cost Overruns (R million, in 2005 prices)

Cost Overruns (%)	Economic NPV	Impacts on Stakeholders					
		RAL	Car	Tourists	Minibus	LGV/ Agri	HGV
−10	133.1	−111.8	48.8	2.4	177.1	4.6	12.0
−5	119.3	−125.6	48.8	2.4	177.1	4.6	12.0
0	105.4	−139.5	48.8	2.4	177.1	4.6	12.0
5	91.6	−153.3	48.8	2.4	177.1	4.6	12.0
10	77.7	−167.2	48.8	2.4	177.1	4.6	12.0
15	63.8	−181.1	48.8	2.4	177.1	4.6	12.0
20	50.0	−194.9	48.8	2.4	177.1	4.6	12.0
25	36.1	−208.8	48.8	2.4	177.1	4.6	12.0
30	22.2	−222.6	48.8	2.4	177.1	4.6	12.0
35	8.4	−236.5	48.8	2.4	177.1	4.6	12.0
40	−5.5	−250.4	48.8	2.4	177.1	4.6	12.0

The economic NPV is very sensitive to changes in construction costs. A 10 percent increase in investment costs would result in a more than 26 percent drop in the project's economic NPV. If actual construction costs increased by more than approximately 38 percent, the project's economic NPV would turn negative, and thus the project would not be economically viable.

The impact of cost overruns would fall on RAL alone. There may be some externalities generated by those who work on the construction phase. However, they would be small, and were ignored here.

b) Initial AADT Level

The traffic projection model was based on 2003 traffic counts, which may not be very precise estimates of the current traffic volume. A sensitivity test was performed to check whether the initial AADT counts would affect the project's economic NPV if changed over a range from −50 percent to +50 percent of the base case. A 10 percent decrease in the values of the initial AADT counts led to a 21 percent decline in the economic NPV. If the actual traffic flow was less than the base case assumption by approximately 48 percent, the economic NPV turned negative.

The main impacts of changes in the initial AADT counts on stakeholders were on private car passengers, minibuses, and HGVs. Table 17.16 shows the results of this sensitivity test.

Table 17.16: Sensitivity Test of the Initial AADT Levels (R million, in 2005 prices)

Initial AADT Levels (%)	Economic NPV	Impacts on Stakeholders					
		RAL	Car	Tourists	Minibus	LGV/ Agri	HGV
−50	−5.9	−139.5	25.9	2.4	91.6	4.6	9.2
−40	16.4	−139.5	30.5	2.4	106.7	4.6	9.8
−30	38.6	−139.5	35.1	2.4	125.8	4.6	10.3
−20	60.9	−139.5	39.7	2.4	142.9	4.6	10.9
−10	83.2	−139.5	44.3	2.4	160.0	4.6	11.5
0	105.4	−139.5	48.8	2.4	177.1	4.6	12.0
10	127.7	−139.5	53.4	2.4	194.2	4.6	12.6
20	149.9	−139.5	58.0	2.4	211.3	4.6	13.1
30	172.2	−139.5	62.6	2.4	228.4	4.6	13.7
40	194.4	−139.5	67.2	2.4	245.5	4.6	14.3
50	216.7	−139.5	71.8	2.4	262.6	4.6	14.8

c) Traffic Growth Rate

This test measured the project's performance under alternative rates of growth in the volume of traffic (ranging from −1 percent to +6 percent). The higher the growth rate, the greater the benefits received by road users, especially minibuses and private car passengers. An increase of one percentage point in the growth rate would raise the economic benefits by 26 percent. Table 17.17 shows detailed results of this sensitivity test.

Table 17.17: Sensitivity Test of Traffic Growth Rates (R million, in 2005 prices)

Traffic Growth Rate (%)	Economic NPV	Impacts on Stakeholders					
		RAL	Car	Tourists	Minibus	LGV/Agri	HGV
−1.0	81.3	−139.5	43.9	2.3	159.2	4.2	11.1
−0.5	93.0	−139.5	46.3	2.3	167.9	4.4	11.5
0.0	105.4	−139.5	48.8	2.4	177.1	4.6	12.0
1.0	132.8	−139.5	54.4	2.4	197.4	5.0	13.0
2.0	163.9	−139.5	60.8	2.5	220.5	5.4	14.2
3.0	199.4	−139.5	68.1	2.5	246.9	5.9	15.5
4.0	240.0	−139.5	76.4	2.6	277.1	6.4	17.0
5.0	286.5	−139.5	86.0	2.7	311.7	7.0	18.6
6.0	339.7	−139.5	96.9	2.7	351.3	7.7	20.5

It should be noted that a higher traffic level in this sensitivity analysis would not result in increased frequency or cost of road maintenance. This explains why the PV of net benefits accruing to RAL remained unchanged.

d) Maintenance Cost Savings

A sensitivity factor was applied to all of the maintenance cost savings to measure the impact on the economic NPV with a range from −50 percent to 0 percent. If the overall maintenance cost savings were, for some reason, reduced by 10 percent, the project's economic NPV would decline by 13 percent from the base case. The project would still be viable from the economic point of view, even if the maintenance cost savings declined by as much as 76 percent. Presumably this factor would affect only RAL, not other stakeholders. Table 17.18 shows the results of this test.

Table 17.18: Sensitivity Test of Maintenance Costs (R million, in 2005 prices)

Maintenance Costs (%)	Economic NPV	Impacts on Stakeholders					
		RAL	Car	Tourists	Minibus	LGV/Agri	HGV
−50	36.5	−208.4	48.8	2.4	177.1	4.6	12.0
−40	50.3	−194.6	48.8	2.4	177.1	4.6	12.0
−30	64.1	−180.8	48.8	2.4	177.1	4.6	12.0
−20	77.9	−167.0	48.8	2.4	177.1	4.6	12.0
−10	91.6	−153.3	48.8	2.4	177.1	4.6	12.0
0	105.4	−139.5	48.8	2.4	177.1	4.6	12.0

e) VOC Savings

Table 17.19 reports on the tests of the impact on the economic NPV and stakeholders for changes in VOC savings over a range from −50 percent to 0 percent. In a situation where the overall VOC savings were 10 percent lower than the estimated value, the economic NPV would have declined by 20 percent from the result in the base case. The project would still be economically viable up to a point where the overall value of VOC savings fell by approximately 50 percent.

Any reduction in VOC savings would reduce the benefits received by all road users, as presented in Table 17.19.

Table 17.19: Sensitivity Test of VOC Savings (R million, in 2005 prices)

VOC Savings (%)	Economic NPV	Impacts on Stakeholders					
		RAL	Car	Tourists	Minibus	LGV/Agri	HGV
−50	0.2	−139.5	25.7	1.2	103.2	2.6	6.9
−40	21.2	−139.5	30.3	1.5	118.0	3.0	8.0
−30	42.3	−139.5	35.0	1.7	132.8	3.4	9.0
−20	63.3	−139.5	39.6	1.9	147.5	3.8	10.0
−10	84.4	−139.5	44.2	2.1	162.3	4.2	11.0
0	105.4	−139.5	48.8	2.4	177.1	4.6	12.0

f) Time Savings

A range from −50 percent to 0 percent for time saving was tested, and the results are shown in Table 17.20. This involved a combination of changes in speed, wage rate of vehicle occupants, and capital cost of cargo to transport goods. A 10 percent reduction in the overall value of time saving implied only a 3.3 percent drop in the value of the project's NPV. The project outcome was not very sensitive to this variable.

Table 17.20: Sensitivity Test of Time Savings (R millions, in 2005 prices)

Time Savings (%)	Economic NPV	Impacts on Stakeholders					
		RAL	Car	Tourists	Minibus	LGV/Agri	HGV
−50	88.2	−139.5	47.5	2.3	162.5	4.3	11.1
−40	91.6	−139.5	47.8	2.3	165.4	4.3	11.3
−30	95.1	−139.5	48.1	2.3	168.3	4.4	11.5
−20	98.5	−139.5	48.3	2.3	171.2	4.5	11.6
−10	102.0	−139.5	48.6	2.4	174.2	4.5	11.8
0	105.4	−139.5	48.8	2.4	177.1	4.6	12.0

17.10.2 Risk Analysis

The above sensitivity analysis shows the variables that would have a significant impact on project outcomes. However, the sensitivity analysis only considers changes in one variable at a time and its impact on the project outcome. It does not account for uncertainties and fluctuations of key variables in the real world. In order to overcome this weakness, a risk analysis was carried out for a number of risk variables identified by the sensitivity analysis. The selected risk variables should have significant effects on project outcomes as well as being subject to uncertainty, as expressed in their probability distributions.

Monte Carlo simulations provide a method of risk analysis to approximate the dynamics and uncertainties of the real world. The risk analysis is performed by simulating the economic analysis many times using distributions for the values of the most sensitive and uncertain variables that affect the project. This process generates a probability distribution of project outcomes.

The risk variables selected for this project were construction cost overruns, initial traffic AADT levels, traffic growth rate, and maintenance cost savings. The probability distributions of each of these risk variables and the possible ranges of values are presented in Table 17.21.

Table 17.21: Probability Distribution for Selected Risk Variables

Risk Variable	Probability Distribution Type		Range and Parameter		
			Min	Max	Likelihood
Construction cost overrun	Step distribution	Construction Costs Overrun Factor	−10.0%	−5.0%	2%
			−5.0%	0.0%	5%
			0.0%	5.0%	40%
			5.0%	10.0%	25%
			10.0%	15.0%	15%
			15.0%	20.0%	9%
			20.0%	25.0%	4%
Initial AADT counts	Normal distribution	Initial AADT Counts Factor	Mean: 0.0% Standard Dev.: 6.5%		
Traffic growth rate	Triangular distribution	Additional Traffic Growth Rate	Minimum: −1.0% Mode: 0.0% Maximum: 6.0%		
Maintenance cost savings	Triangular distribution	Maintenance Costs Savings Factor	Minimum: −10.0% Mode: 0.0% Maximum: 5.0%		

The results of the risk analysis were simulated for 10,000 runs. The simulation results shown in Figure 17.1 indicate that the expected value of the project's economic NPV was R136.6 million, which is higher than the deterministic value of R105.4 million. Figure 17.1 presents the range of possible project outcomes that the economic NPV can take and the likelihood of the occurrence of these values. The economic NPV ranged from the minimum gain of R0.7 million to the maximum gain of R382.0 million. There was zero probability that the economic NPV of the project would become negative under all possible circumstances defined earlier in the risk analysis.

Figure 17.1: Results of Risk Analysis on Economic NPV

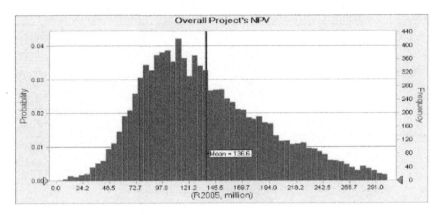

The expected resource cost of this project to RAL was about R160.8 million. This stems from the heavy initial capital cost, partially offset by savings in maintenance costs arising as the various road sections are improved. Figure 17.2 shows that under no circumstances would RAL have had a positive PV of net benefits from this project, since savings in road maintenance costs are far less than the initial investment outlays.

Figure 17.2: Results of Risk Analysis on RAL's NPV

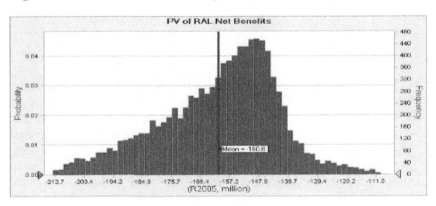

Each of the five classes of road user stood to gain from the improvement of this road. The expected values of their respective benefits were all greater than the values in the deterministic case. At the same time, their respective probability of obtaining negative benefits was virtually non-existent. This simply means that all classes of road users were certain to gain as a result of this project. This is illustrated for private car and minibus passengers in Figures 17.3 and 17.4, respectively.

The risk analysis indicated that the expected benefits received by private car passengers would be R59.6 million, which is larger than the deterministic case of R48.8 million. However, their net benefit was subject to significant variability, with a standard deviation of R11.4 million. The gain ranged from a minimum of R36.9 million to a maximum of R109.0 million. There was zero probability of a negative NPV for this group.

Figure 17.3: Results of Risk Analysis for Car Passengers

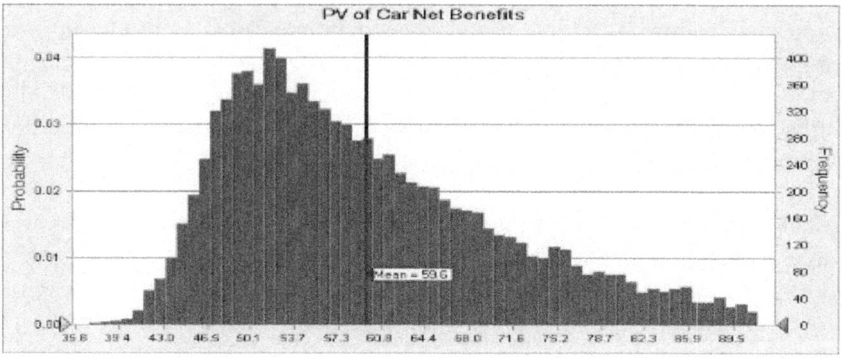

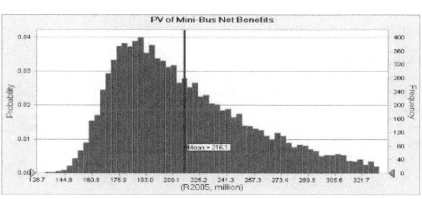

By the same token, the minibus users were expected to gain a mean value of R216.1 million. This resulted mainly from the VOC and time savings of the existing ("without project") road users. This gain was subject to a standard deviation of R41.4 million. Nevertheless, the probability of a negative benefit for this group was nil, as shown in Figure 17.4.

Figure 17.4: Results of Risk Analysis for Minibus Users

It should be noted that the net benefit of upgrading section D4050/D1583 was negative, with a mean value of R38.9 million, under all possible circumstances defined within the risk analysis presented earlier. There was zero probability of a positive benefit resulting from improving this road section as of 2005. On the other hand, the other two sections, D4100 and D4250/D4190, had positive net benefits, with means of R57.3 million and R118.3 million, respectively, and zero probability of a negative benefit.

17.11 Concluding Remarks

This chapter has followed the integrated investment appraisal methodology for evaluating the upgrading from gravel to tarred surface of several road segments in Limpopo province of South Africa. The project was to be carried out by RAL, and no tolls were to be charged. The purpose of this study was to inquire whether the investment costs of each segment would be justified by their economic benefits.

Typically, benefits generated by road improvements included the reduction in resource costs on maintenance by RAL, the reduction in VOC for road users as a result of the improved road surface, time savings for road users because of an increase in average speed of vehicles, and a possible reduction in the costs of accidents. This chapter has described the evaluation of all but the last of these components.

This study shows that for RAL, savings in maintenance costs of R137.8 million would offset a substantial fraction of the initial capital expenditures of R277.2 million required by the improvement. In addition, the improvement of the road would generate a substantial benefit in terms of the savings of time and operating costs accruing to different classes of road user. As a result, the net economic benefit of the project was R136.6 million.

A stakeholder analysis was also carried out for this project. The main beneficiaries of this investment would be the owners and users of minibuses (R216.1 million) and of passenger cars (R59.6 million). Other road users — tourists and owners of light and heavy freight vehicles — would also share the benefits of the improved road, to the value of R2.4 million, R5.3 million, and R14.0 million, respectively.

It is important to point out that the proposed road consisted of three sections for which an individual economic assessment was carried out in this study. It appears that while the overall economic NPV of the project was expected to be approximately R136.6 million, section D4050/D1583 had an expected negative NPV of R38.9 million when evaluated on its own. This section should therefore have been excluded from the investment package, an act that would raise the overall net benefits of the project to R175.5 million.

Appendix 17A: Estimating Vehicle Operating Costs

Estimates of VOC are based on the RED model developed by the World Bank and modified for South African realities by CSIR Transportek in 2003. The costs are essentially dependent upon terrain, roughness of the road, and type of vehicle. For each category, *VOC* is expressed as a function of roughness in the form of cubic polynomials, differing by category of road and type of vehicle. The general form is:

$$VOC = a_0 + a_1 * R + a_2 * R^2 + a_3 * R^3$$

where R stands for the degree of road roughness, which is standardized and expressed in terms of the international roughness index. The results are shown in Table 17A.1. Costs are obviously expected to be higher for travelling on a mountainous road rather than on a level road, and for travelling on a rough road rather than on a smooth one.

Since the original model's output was expressed in 2003 prices, the final results were inflated into the prices for 2005 by using an annual inflation rate of 6.5 percent for each of 2003 and 2004. Table 17A.2 presents the resulting VOC estimates in 2005 prices by type of vehicle, terrain, and road roughness.

Table 17A.1: Estimates of Average VOC by Terrain, Type of Vehicle, and Roughness (R per vehicle-km, in 2003 prices)

Terrain	Vehicle Type	Coefficients of the VOC Function				VOC (R per vehicle-km)		
		a_0	a_1	a_2	a_3	R at 2.0	R at 10.0	R at 20.0
Flat & paved	Car	2.198	-0.028	0.017	-0.00031	2.204	3.261	5.790
	Utility	2.197	-0.016	0.017	-0.00031	2.229	3.388	6.048
	Light bus	2.600	0.027	0.012	0.00010	2.702	4.164	8.722
	Medium bus	3.047	0.027	0.012	0.00011	3.148	4.611	9.227
	Heavy bus	3.788	0.026	0.013	0.00010	3.894	5.463	10.360
	Light truck	2.954	0.162	0.012	-0.00022	3.324	5.554	9.218
	Medium truck	3.397	0.181	0.013	-0.00023	3.809	6.251	10.259
	Heavy truck	4.840	0.223	0.012	-0.00021	5.334	8.083	12.489
	Articulated truck	6.856	0.287	0.023	-0.00047	7.518	11.552	18.021
Mountainous & paved	Car	2.495	-0.028	0.015	-0.00027	2.497	3.458	5.843
	Utility	2.533	-0.015	0.015	-0.00027	2.562	3.631	6.145
	Light bus	2.943	0.025	0.011	0.00014	3.036	4.391	8.811
	Medium bus	3.583	0.038	0.009	0.00018	3.698	5.065	9.462
	Heavy bus	4.534	0.045	0.010	0.00017	4.665	6.154	10.799
	Light truck	3.669	0.161	0.010	-0.00016	4.028	6.092	9.512
	Medium truck	4.260	0.200	0.009	-0.00015	4.696	7.042	10.774
	Heavy truck	6.672	0.244	0.009	-0.00014	7.195	9.835	13.861
	Articulated truck	8.961	0.242	0.018	-0.00029	9.515	12.886	18.637

Table 17A.2: Estimates of Average VOC by Terrain, Type of Vehicle, and Roughness (R per vehicle-km, in 2005 prices)

Terrain	Vehicle Type	VOC (R per vehicle-km)		
		R at 2.0	R at 10.0	R at 20.0
Flat & paved	Car	2.500	3.699	6.567
	Utility	2.528	3.843	6.860
	Light bus	3.065	4.723	9.892
	Medium bus	3.571	5.230	10.465
	Heavy bus	4.416	6.196	11.751
	Light truck	3.770	6.299	10.455
	Medium truck	4.320	7.090	11.636
	Heavy truck	6.050	9.168	14.166
	Articulated truck	8.527	13.103	20.440
Mountainous & paved	Car	2.720	3.837	6.598
	Utility	2.735	3.983	6.906
	Light bus	3.267	4.837	9.913
	Medium bus	3.786	5.366	10.496
	Heavy bus	4.624	6.336	11.786
	Light truck	3.997	6.425	10.487
	Medium truck	4.505	7.210	11.670
	Heavy truck	6.211	9.274	14.200
	Articulated truck	9.459	13.420	20.459

Appendix 17B: Estimation of Average Vehicle Speeds

Estimates of speeds are also based on the RED model developed by the World Bank and modified for South Africa. The average vehicle speed is a function of several factors, and the model was developed to estimate speeds for different types of vehicle under various terrain and road conditions.

For each category, the average vehicle speed S, expressed as the number of kilometres per hour, is calculated as a function of the degree of road roughness:

$$S = b_0 + b_1 * R + b_2 * R^2 + b_3 * R^3$$

The coefficients of the equations were estimated for each type of vehicle by terrain and road roughness and are shown in Table 17B.1. Vehicle speed is faster on smoother roads, for every type of vehicle. Similarly, given the same degree of road roughness, vehicles move, on average, faster on a flat road than on a mountainous road.

Table 17B.1: Estimates of Average Vehicle Speeds by Terrain, Type of Vehicle, and Roughness (kilometre per hour)

Terrain	Vehicle Type	Coefficients of the Speed Function				Speed (Kilometre per Hour)		
		b_0	b_1	b_2	b_3	R at 2.0	R at 10.0	R at 20.0
Flat & paved	Car	87.310930	0.169627	-0.275873	0.007344	86.61	68.76	39.11
	Utility	80.447861	-0.396431	-0.205073	0.005667	78.88	61.64	35.82
	Light bus	84.601774	-0.941928	-0.210988	0.006361	81.92	60.44	32.25
	Medium bus	74.745730	-0.124356	-0.220741	0.006043	73.66	57.47	32.31
	Heavy bus	74.578226	-0.158145	-0.216589	0.005939	73.44	57.28	32.29
	Light truck	79.405651	-1.691452	-0.131311	0.004518	75.53	53.88	29.20
	Medium truck	74.316529	-1.822427	-0.104362	0.003841	70.28	49.50	26.85
	Heavy truck	61.903260	-0.930893	-0.108541	0.003330	59.63	45.07	26.51
	Articulated truck	85.917625	-5.437581	-0.099941	0.000352	75.45	41.89	19.96
Mountainous & paved	Car	67.707011	1.136416	-0.238360	0.005474	69.07	60.71	38.88
	Utility	60.813997	0.637159	-0.178888	0.004143	61.41	53.44	35.15
	Light bus	63.274717	0.715527	-0.222646	0.005474	63.86	53.64	32.32
	Medium bus	53.016936	0.683988	-0.160811	0.003647	53.77	47.42	31.55
	Heavy bus	51.129871	0.615620	-0.145875	0.003264	51.80	45.96	31.21
	Light truck	53.549798	0.218623	-0.144733	0.003569	53.44	44.83	28.58
	Medium truck	49.905646	-0.038640	-0.117567	0.002995	49.38	40.76	26.07
	Heavy truck	36.174877	0.023484	-0.062253	0.001431	35.98	31.62	23.19
	Articulated truck	45.592234	-0.206041	-0.120175	0.003325	44.73	34.84	20.00

References

AFRICON Pietersburg. 2000. "The Long Term Consequences of Various Budget Levels and Flood Damage Assessment on the Northern Province Road Network", Vol. 1, prepared by AFRICON Pietersburg for Roads Agency Limpopo (October).

ARCUS GIBB Ltd. 2004. "Limpopo Integrated Infrastructure Development Plan: Phase II – Benefit Cost Analysis of Selected Projects", Final Report, Appendix I: Flag Boshielo to Mafefe to Sekororo and Ga-Seleka to Mmatladi (March).

Archondo-Callao, R. 2001. *Roads Economic Decision Model (RED) for Economic Evaluation of Low Volume Roads: Software Users Guide*, Version 2.0. Washington, DC: The World Bank.

Cambridge Resources International. 2004. "Integrated Investment Appraisal: Concepts and Practice", Appendix G: "Commodity-Specific Conversion Factors for Non-Tradable Goods and Services in South Africa", 626–635.

Flyvbjerg, B., M. Skamris Holm, and S.L. Buhl. 2002. "Underestimating Costs in Public Works Projects: Error or Lie", *Journal of the American Planning Association* 68(3), 279–295.

Jenkins, G.P. and C.Y. Kuo. 2006. "Evaluation of the Benefits of Transnational Transportation Projects", *Journal of Applied Economics* IX(1), Argentina.

Klevchuk, A. and G.P. Jenkins. 2004. "Capital Appraisal Handbook on Roads", prepared for Roads Agency Limpopo, Limpopo Provincial Government, Polokwane, South Africa (August).

Kuo, C.Y., G.P. Jenkins, and M.B. Mphahlele. 2003. "The Economic Opportunity Cost of Capital in South Africa", *South African Journal of Economics* 71(3), 525–543.

Chapter Eighteen

The ABCs of Electricity Project Analysis

18.1 Background[126]

For the most part, the differences between the analysis of an owner-operated private venture project and that of typical public sector projects are concentrated in the valuation of benefits. Most project costs are indeed cash outlays, just like those of a business venture, but this is not at all generally true on the benefits side. For example, public parks and highways (other than toll roads) rarely yield any cash inflows. The problem, then, is to find ways of estimating the true economic value of their benefits. In other cases (e.g., irrigation projects and toll roads), there is usually some charge for the use of the project's output, but that charge is typically a very poor measure of the project's true benefits. Again, the challenge is to measure the true benefits of the project.

Electricity projects appear to be in a different category, in that one hardly ever sees attempts to measure the actual benefits that users receive from such projects. Yet paradoxically, we still say we are quantifying the value of such benefits. The explanation of this apparent anomaly lies in what is called the "least alternative cost" principle. This principle states that one should not attribute to a project a value of benefits that is greater than the least alternative cost one would have to incur by providing an equivalent benefit stream in a different way.

This principle is fully general, but often seems quite redundant. Thus, irrigation projects provide certain flows of water to a farming area, but with most of them, one cannot even dream of a sensible alternative way to provide the same flows. In those cases, the alternative cost (say, of bringing the water in by truck) is so high as to be irrelevant in the analysis of a project to draw water from a nearby river, so one tries to put an economic value on the river water itself, as it is used for irrigation. However, one does encounter irrigation projects in which pump irrigation (from underground aquifers) is a quite reasonable alternative to drawing water from the river. In these cases, it would be incorrect to attribute to

---

[126]This chapter is mainly taken from "Introduction to Cost-Benefit Analysis prepared for USAID Officers", a training programme prepared by A.C. Harberger for the US Agency for International Aid, as well as "The ABCs of Electricity Project Analysis" (July 2010) and "More on the Cost-Benefit Analysis of Electricity Projects" (July 2010), reports prepared by A.C. Harberger for USAID.

the river-irrigation project a benefit stream that exceeded the alternative cost of getting the same water by way of pump irrigation.

While the least-cost principle can thus sometimes come into play for irrigation projects, one can say that it virtually always is the determining factor in estimating the benefits of electricity projects. The reason is that a next-best alternative of reasonable cost nearly always exists. Indeed, much of the time, this next-best alternative is simply the standard way of doing things. The projects being analysed in such cases then represent attempts to find new or different ways of doing things that are better than the standard alternative. The benefits of the "new or different" way are measured in such cases by the standard costs that would be saved if the "new or different" project were in fact undertaken.

Now let us for the moment think of carrying out a cost–benefit analysis of this project without bringing the standard alternative into the picture in any way. Inevitably, this leads us to think of "this" project as somehow standing alone. At the moment when it is installed, it will presumably be the newest project in an existing system. But over time, the older plants in this system will wear out, so the generating capacity of the system will decline year after year as, one after the other, the older plants are abandoned. The overall generating capacity of the system would thus steadily decline over time. Even without a growing demand for energy, this would mean a market or economic price of electricity that would be steadily rising. In the more likely case of a continuously growing demand, this upward trend of price would be even more exaggerated. It would take a truly terrible project to fail a cost–benefit test when its output was being valued at prices that were increasing exponentially throughout its economic life. One can almost say that cost–benefit analysis carried out under these assumptions would lose virtually all of its power to discriminate between good and bad projects. All would look good in the face of an ever-rising price of energy.

Now let us return to the real world. It obviously makes no sense to assume that our project — call it Plant E — is going to be the last project to be built in our city's electricity network. We simply have to think of the system being operated in a sensible way. In the beginning, Plant E is added to an existing system consisting of Plants A, B, C, and D. Over time, Plant A, the oldest, is likely to be the first to be retired. It will perhaps be "replaced" by Plant F. But by that time, the area's energy demand will likely have grown by enough to justify the addition of yet more capacity, say Plant G. So, maybe five or 10 years down the line, the system is likely to consist of plants B, C, D, E, F, and G. Further on, Plants B and C will presumably also reach retirement age, and maybe Plants H, I, J, and K will be added. The final step (in the analysis of "our" project — Plant E) will come when Plant E itself reaches the point of being retired from the system. At that point, the cost–benefit profile of Plant E will come to an end, perhaps with a blip of extra benefit representing the salvage value of the plant, perhaps with a blip of cost (e.g., for a nuclear plant) for the safe disposal of its remains.

The image we have tried to conjure here is that of a motion picture representing the costs and benefits attributable to Plant E — not standing alone, but embedded in a system that is being managed intelligently, with other plants being retired when their staying in the system would entail more cost than benefits, and with new plants being added in a pattern that reflects the continuing use of cost–benefit principles. All of this lies behind the development of our basic tool of analysis, the "moving picture" of how the system would operate in the presence of our project — i.e., "with" Project E.

But this is not the end. In order to determine the cost–benefit profile of Project E, we have to make a forecast of how the system would operate in the absence of this project. In this scenario, we do not do Project E, but follow some alternative strategy in managing the electricity network. What strategy? There are only two good answers here: a) the best alternative strategy, if we are able to identify such a strategy in specific terms; and b) a "standard" alternative, defined by our best estimates of the typical costs of energy (varying by time of day, season of year, etc.) that we consider would emerge from a proper continuing application of sound cost–benefit analysis.

Answer a) is likely to be feasible, if at all, only in sophisticated modern electricity systems, whose operations are governed by up-to-date computer systems designed to take into account all relevant factors in order to come up with a minimum-cost strategy for the system as a whole. More likely is answer b), which is based on a more general knowledge of the costs of equipment, fuels and other material inputs, labour and other services, etc. This is the line that we will explore, using examples that move progressively from the simplest to the more complex.

18.2 The Simplest Case — A Homogeneous Thermal Alternative

This section is intended to introduce readers to some very basic aspects of electricity economics. It should be thought of as dipping a toe in the water, not as a full-body immersion. In this exercise, we will have one standard alternative — a homogeneous thermal generator. By "homogeneous", we mean that the actual machines used in Plants A, B, C, D, and E would all be physically the same (though of different ages), assuming all of them to be thermal plants (using fuel to generate energy). We will derive costs per kilowatt hour (kWh) based on the use of this standard generating equipment.

Assume we have data telling us that, given the current fuel price, the operating cost of this standard piece of equipment amounts to 4¢/kWh. This mainly covers fuel, but it also takes into account the labour and other inputs involved in the actual operation of the equipment. It definitely does not include any return to invested capital. This will enter our picture at a later stage.

For now, let us simply concentrate on the idea that 4¢/kWh is the appropriate cost of energy, measured at the plant, when that energy is being produced during off-peak hours. Why do we not add a charge for the use of the generating equipment itself? Simply because the addition of some extra kWh of output during off-peak hours does not require any more capital equipment than we already have.

When does the system require additional homogeneous thermal plants? Quite naturally, when demand threatens to push beyond the level of energy that our existing plants can deliver. We measure that capacity in kilowatt (kW) and also use the term "power" to refer to kW. Power in common parlance is something we can have without using it at all, and certainly without using it fully. But, ask economists, when a system has more capacity (power) than it needs to satisfy demand, why charge for the use of that capacity? Nobody loses anything if idle capacity is put to use, while further excess capacity still exists. Thus, economists say, when idle capacity is present, the appropriate charge for energy would cover running costs (variable costs), not capital costs (fixed costs).

This line of thinking naturally leads to the idea of electricity charges that vary through time, being higher during peak-time hours and lower during off-peak hours. Charges linked to capital equipment (generating capacity) should appropriately be concentrated during peak-time hours because if demand increases significantly during these hours, one will actually have to install additional capacity if that demand is to be met. And if one does not install new capacity in such a case, it will take an increase in the price of peak-time energy in order to constrain demand within the limits of the existing capacity.

An example will probably help to clarify how these concepts are actually used. Suppose that new capacity (of the homogeneous thermal variety) costs $800/kW, that the relevant discount rate (r) is 10 percent, and that the relevant depreciation rate (δ) for this equipment is 5 percent per year. Then, in order to justify the addition of a new kW of capacity, the necessary benefit is $(0.15) \times (\$800)$, or $120 per year. If capacity is added that cannot generate such an annual benefit, the investment in that capacity is not justified. Keep in mind, then, that $120 per year is the target revenue that should be expected from new increments of capacity. How can one think of earning this revenue? The answer is from the sale of energy during peak-time hours. Thus, if the system's peak is 3,000 hours per year, the needed peak-time surcharge would be 4¢/kWh. And if the peak were 2,000 hours, the relevant peak-time surcharge would be 6¢ $(= \$120/2,000)$/kWh.

Let us proceed on this latter assumption. Our "standard costs" for energy are 4¢/kWh, off-peak, and 10¢ $(= 4¢$ for operating costs plus 6¢ of peak-time surcharge) during 2,000 peak hours. Our next step is to apply this assumption to different types of hydroelectric projects. (Recall that we have only one type of thermal capacity, reflected in the modifier "homogeneous".) We will consider, in turn, run-of-the-stream (ROS) hydro projects, daily reservoirs, and seasonal hydro storage projects.

18.3 Run-of-the-Stream Hydro Projects

The key characteristic of ROS projects is implicit in the title: energy is generated using river water "as it flows". Typically, an ROS project will be situated on an incline, where water is flowing down a hill or over a waterfall. Such projects typically channel the water through large tubes (penstocks), which carry it from the top to the bottom of the incline and which lead directly into one or more turbines at the bottom of the hill. The running water turns the turbine, generating electric energy.

To evaluate the benefits of such a project, one typically starts on the purely hypothetical assumption that the turbine capacity of the project will be fully used through all of the 8,760 hours of the year. We then divide these hours into 2,000 of peak-time and 6,760 of off-peak use. Employing this information, we obtain for each kW of turbine capacity:

2,000 hours @ 10¢/kWh = $200.00
6,760 hours @ 4¢/kWh = $270.40
Total $470.40/kW

Now, $470.40/kW per year is what the installed capacity would produce if it were fully used all the time. This, of course, is not at all likely to be the case, as streamflow always varies quite significantly, mainly by season of the year, reflecting changes in rainfall and/or snowmelt. Thus, on average, the installed turbines will be used at only a fraction of their full capacity. Simply for our example, we will assume this fraction to be 60 percent. Hence, estimated benefits = 0.6 × $470.40 = $282.24.

We introduce these benefits into our profile of the ROS project, deducting capital costs during the construction phase of the project and maintenance plus (very minor) operating costs during its operating phase. The result is a project profile that we then can evaluate using, of course, the same discount rate (here 10 percent) that we employed in the derivation of the 6¢ peak-time surcharge.

Readers may have noticed that in the above exercise, the analysis was carried out "per kilowatt (kW)" of installed capacity and complemented by an assumption of the fraction (in this case 60 percent) of that capacity that was expected to be utilized in the course of a typical year. But focusing on this feature prompts a question: why 60 and not 40 or 80 percent? It is to this question that we now turn.

First, let us recognize that in any real-world case, the answer will depend on the hydrological characteristics of the stream (and site) in question. There may be rivers whose streamflow is so steady that there is only a 20 or 30 percent difference between the lowest and the highest daily flow during the year. In such a case, there is not much range for choice as to how many kW of turbine capacity to install. But such cases would be hard to find in the real world. Most rivers and streams are subject to very heavy streamflow in the rainy season (or the period of biggest snowmelt). Some even dry up completely in the driest period of the year, and for most, the lowest streamflow is only a modest fraction of the highest one.

Thus, the designers of a typical ROS project are faced with a serious problem of choice. If they build the project so as to make use of nearly all of the streamflow of the year, they will have to install enough turbine capacity to process the huge rainy-season flows. But then, during the rest (which is most) of the year, the much lower streamflow will leave most of the installed turbines idle for many months running. On the other hand, if the designers decide to keep the fraction of capacity use high, they will have to install turbine capacity geared principally to the rate of streamflow in the drier part of the year. They will then end up using their turbines most of the time, but they will be allowing a lot of the stream's annual water flow to go to waste. The dilemma is: either build big, and a lot of that turbine capacity will be idle a lot of the time, or build small, and the problem will not be one of idle turbine capacity but rather one of a lot of water passing by unused (for electricity generation) simply because you do not have the turbines to process it.

This dilemma represents an economic problem — that of weighing benefits against costs. This problem is best tackled at the design stage in order to ensure that whatever choice is made as to how much turbine capacity to install, that capacity is achieved at the lowest economic cost. The key facts needed for solving this problem are obtained from a graph of the expected (likely) streamflow, period by period (perhaps day by day) throughout the year. This graph will most likely have a single peak sometime in the wettest season and a single trough sometime in the driest period. The benefits of adding turbine capacity become smaller and smaller as we contemplate adding successive increments of capacity. The first few kW of capacity will promise 100 percent usage as long as they involve using less than the lowest expected streamflow. On the other hand, the last few kW of capacity that we might add would promise usage only in the few days of absolutely highest streamflows. Hence, it is very likely that benefits will amply exceed cost for the first few kW, while cost will almost certainly exceed benefits for additions to capacity that we can expect to be utilized only a few days per year. Somewhere between these extremes, then, we should be able to find an optimum level for turbine capacity — a point up to which benefits exceed costs for each successive increment to design capacity and beyond which costs exceed benefits for each successive increment. This is the sort of calculation that should be carried out in the process of designing any ROS project. Obviously, it involves repeated applications of the procedure outlined in the first part of this section, with the ultimate choice being for that turbine capacity that yields the greatest expected net present value (i.e., the greatest expected excess of the present value of benefits over the present value of costs).

18.4 Daily Reservoir Hydro Projects

The daily reservoir (DR) can be thought of as a sort of add-on to an ROS project, either at the design stage or later. Here we will assume that we are dealing with an ROS project that is already operating. Moreover, we will assume that this existing project is well designed for its purpose, following the principles presented above.

In our example of an ROS project, the installation was expected to produce peak-time energy during 2,000 hours and off-peak energy during the remaining 6,760 hours of the year. This means that over the course of the year, around 23 percent (= 2,000/8,760) of the water flow would be used to produce electricity that was worth 10¢/kWh, while the remaining 77 percent (= 6,760/8,760) would be used to produce energy worth only 4¢/kWh.

A DR project has two principal objectives: a) to convert to peak-time production much of the water that would normally go to produce off-peak energy in an ROS operation, and b) to utilize some of the water that would otherwise go to waste (again in an ROS case). To accomplish objective a), a small dam is built upstream of the ROS project. It accumulates water during the off-peak hours and then releases that water during peak time. In this way, it produces 10¢/kWh of energy with the same water that would otherwise end up generating energy worth only 4¢/kWh. The substantial net gain of 6¢/kWh is the principal benefit of the DR project.

This benefit comes with a significant cost, however. First and foremost, there is the cost of the dam itself and possibly of a regulating dam downstream of the project, designed to deliver a steady streamflow to downstream users. If the amount of turbine capacity in the project is not increased, the benefit of extra peak-time energy would be limited to the amount by which the turbine capacity of the ROS project exceeded the streamflow-determined ROS output of each day. Thus, a project with 5 MW (= 5,000 kW) of turbine capacity might in one part of the year be processing a streamflow that generated 2,000 kWh during each hour of peak. This could be brought up to 5,000 kWh per peak-time hour, but not further, if one left turbine capacity unchanged. All this benefit would be of type a). Obviously, in periods of the year when the streamflow itself was enough to generate 5,000 kWh/hr, the installed capacity would be fully utilized by the ROS project and the addition of the daily reservoir would have no effect of shifting water (and therefore energy output) from off-peak to peak hours.

Thus, assume:

T_o = initial turbine capacity, in kW
S_i = expected streamflow per hour of day i expressed as the number of kW that the streamflow can generate
H_{p_i} = number of peak-time hours in day i
H_{n_i} = number of off-peak hours in day i (= $24 - H_{p_i}$)

Then we have $H_{p_i}(T_o - S_i) =$ the maximum number of kWh that can be converted from off-peak to peak if T_o remains unchanged. This is a maximum because in periods of very low streamflow, one may not reach an output of $H_{p_i}T$ in peak time, owing to low streamflow throughout the day.

The amount of water available to be shifted from off-peak to peak is simply $H_{n_i}S_i$, the total water flow in off-peak hours. All of this would represent off-peak energy actually produced by the pre-existing ROS project if $T_o > S_i$. In case $S_i > T_o$, the difference $(S_i - T_o)H_{n_i}$ would represent water that passed by without producing any electricity in the original ROS project. So if the increase in generating capacity ΔT is such that $H_{p_i}(T_o + \Delta T) > 24S_i$, that means that, with a capacity increase of ΔT, the full streamflow of the day $(= 24S_i)$ can be processed during peak-time hours. This would include a shift of all the water that had previously gone to produce off-peak energy plus all the water that had "gone to waste" because of limited turbine capacity. The benefit for day i of the DR project would then be the excess of this value over the value of the energy that the original ROS project would have produced.

On days when $(T_o + \Delta T)H_{p_i}$ is smaller than $24S_i$, the augmented project will not utilize the full streamflow of the day at peak time, but may well use it during peak plus off-peak hours. In this case, the gross benefit for day i of the DR project would then be measured by $H_p(T_o + \Delta T)$ multiplied by the peak-time price of energy plus $[24S_i - H_p(T_o + \Delta T)]$ multiplied by the off-peak price of energy. The term in square brackets represents the water that is available $(= 24S_i)$ minus that amount that is used to generate peak-time energy $[=H_p(T_o + \Delta T)]$. From this, as before, we would have to subtract the value of the energy that the original ROS project would have produced.

Just as, for the ROS project, a separate optimization had to be made to determine the optimal level of T, so here a similar process should be used to determine the best level for ΔT, the increment of turbine capacity.

Special note should be taken of the fact that no considerations of electricity demand entered into the above analysis, either of ROS or of DR projects. The reason for this is the way in which such projects fit into the operations of most electricity systems. As we will see in greater detail later, the principle governing the management of electricity systems is that when demand is low, one uses only those sources of energy that have the lowest running cost per kWh. Then, as energy demand increases, additional capacity is turned on, starting first with the second cheapest per kWh, then turning on the third cheapest, and so on up the scale. Only at times of very high (peak) demand does the system resort to its generators with the highest running cost.

The mere contemplation of how an ROS system operates tells us that it has practically zero running costs. All that is needed is for somebody to make sure that the water that is flowing in a given hour is actually channelled through the turbines to generate energy. Because ROS energy is so cheap, it is always, in principle, the first source to be used in cases of low demand. Moreover, it is used every hour of the day, all through the year, being interrupted only for maintenance and repair. Since ROS capacity constitutes only a small fraction of the total capacity of a typical electricity system, it is in fact used all the time and is practically never used only partially for lack of demand for its energy output.

In the case of DRs, once again their running cost is next to zero, but since the great bulk of their output is at peak time, they are then working along with all or nearly all of the other sources of energy in the system, and of these, they (along with ROS installations) have the lowest running cost. Any variation in peak demand will thus be absorbed by other, higher-cost contributors to the supply of peak-time energy. This explains why demand considerations did not enter into the preceding analysis of DR projects.

18.5 Seasonal Hydro Dams

While DRs have the effect of letting managers decide when, within a given day or so, water will be needed to generate energy, seasonal hydro dams aim to allow such water use to be shifted from one part of the year to another. In the typical case for which a seasonal dam will be contemplated, there is one season in which the energy from a given stream will have a high value and another in which that value will be much lower. Some cases could thus arise because streamflow is very heavy in one part of the year and very light in another, while energy demand is pretty steady over the year. Other cases could arise in which the streamflow is pretty steady but demand is highly concentrated, perhaps in winter for lighting and heating, or perhaps in summer for air conditioning.

As in the preceding sections, we will analyse seasonal hydro dams as part of a system in which the "standard" way of generating electricity is using homogeneous thermal capacity. Again, this standard capacity will be assumed to have a running cost of 4¢/kWh, and a capital cost of $800/kW, with a depreciation rate of 5 percent per annum. The relevant discount rate for cost–benefit analysis will, as before, be 10 percent.

The first question to be answered is whether the energy used in a seasonal storage project should be considered as "baseload" or "peaking" capacity. We have already seen how ROS capacity is quite naturally "baseload", while the whole reason for building DR capacity is to augment the system's supply of peak-time energy. In our simplified case of homogeneous thermal capacity, we would have what is called a "stacking pattern", in which ROS capacity sits at the base, homogeneous thermal capacity occupies the middle, and DR capacity occupies the top. This means that when demand is very low, only ROS capacity will be used. When demand exceeds ROS capacity, that capacity will first be fully used, and it will be supplemented as needed by the output of our homogeneous thermal plants. Only in the hours of greatest demand during the day will the water accumulated in DRs be used to "top off" the energy supply coming from ROS and homogeneous thermal sources.

Now we come to the question at hand: what place in this stacking pattern should be occupied by seasonal hydro capacity? Since we already know that ROS capacity belongs in the base and that DR capacity should be used for peaking, we can concentrate on the question of which, to choose between homogeneous thermal and seasonal hydro capacity, should be turned on first. In particular, should seasonal hydro be thought of as part of the base or as an appropriate way to serve peak-time demand?

The best way to focus on this question is to assume that we have one or more seasonal hydro dams already built. They will accumulate water in the wet season and deliver energy in the dry season.[127] To make our analysis quite clear and straightforward, we must bear in mind that the storage capacity of our seasonal dams will not change. The amount of water they can store was determined when they were built. However, the amount of energy they can generate in any given hour is typically subject to change because such dams are designed to leave room for adding turbines (up to some limit).

In a simplified system consisting of seasonal hydro plus homogeneous thermal capacity, we will have a given level of peak demand, say 1,000 megawatts (MW). If our seasonal hydro capacity is used as baseload, its stored water will be spread over 24 hours a day for, say, 9 months of the year. To use the water in this fashion, perhaps only 200 MW of turbine capacity will be needed (because this capacity will be running virtually continuously). If, on the other hand, the seasonal dams are used for peaking, they may be occupied for many fewer days and for varying numbers of hours on these days. The amount of turbine capacity needed in this case will be much larger — say, 600 MW. So we have Case A, where seasonal hydro is used for baseload, in which we would have turbine capacity of 200 MW by hydro, supplemented by 800 MW of homogeneous thermal. Alternatively, for Case B, we would have to install 400 MW of homogeneous thermal capacity plus, as indicated, 600 MW of turbine capacity in our hydro dams.

As we move from Case A to Case B, then, we are subtracting 400 MW of homogeneous thermal capacity and adding 400 MW of turbine capacity in our seasonal hydro dams. Here the cost–benefit analysis is a no-brainer. First, it is much cheaper to add 1 MW of turbine capacity to an existing dam, with a place already prepared for additional turbines, than to add 1 MW of homogeneous thermal capacity, which entails building the whole plant plus its associated turbines. Second, using homogeneous thermal capacity for peaking will involve start-up and shut-down costs, which are practically zero in hydro dams, where turbines can be turned on or off simply by pressing a button or flicking a switch.

How seasonal hydro capacity will be used during the wet season depends mainly on physical conditions such as streamflow and the storage capacity of the hydro dams. Start with the idea of using these dams for peaking all year round, including the wet season. This would mean that excess streamflow — over and

[127]Alternatively, we can think of them as accumulating water in the season of low electricity demand (say, winter) and delivering it in the season of high electricity demand (say, summer).

above that needed to satisfy peak demand — would be stored for later use. But suppose this would lead to the dams being filled before the wet season ends. In such a case, it is much better to use the excess water in off-peak hours rather than allow it to go to waste. This could mean that some thermal plants would be shut down for part or all of the wet season, their place being taken by turbine capacity in the hydro dams.

There is one additional point to be made with respect to the seasonal hydro versus thermal trade-off. In our numerical example, we had 600 MW of seasonal hydro turbine capacity plus 400 MW of thermal capacity as our preferred solution. Under these circumstances, it is clear that for most of the hours of the year when hydro capacity is being used, the system's thermal plants will be operating at full capacity. The resulting number of hours of full-capacity thermal operations can be called the "thermal peak". This can easily be a lot larger than the "system peak" or "demand peak", which we earlier assumed to be 2,000 hours per year.

Now let us backtrack and ask what the logic is behind our earlier derivation of a 6¢/kWh peak-time surcharge, to be applied over a system peak of 2,000 hours per year. That logic was that it was the growth of demand at peak time that called forth the need for more (homogeneous) thermal capacity — hence, the scarcity value of peak-time energy should cover not only the running cost but also the capital cost of thermal capacity. We obtained the 6¢/kWh peak-time surcharge by first calculating the annualized capital cost of thermal capacity of $120/kW (= 0.15 × $800/kW). We then divided this $120 by the 2,000 hours of system peak. That calculation no longer makes sense in the presence of significant amounts of seasonal hydro capacity. Now the thermal peak is going to be significantly longer — say, 4,000 hours per year — because our seasonal dams have enough capacity to deal with more than just the system peak. Hence, if demand grows (at peak as well as off-peak hours), what is going to happen is that our *given* hydro storage capacity will still fill the system peak and more, but the increase in demand will leave a gap that will (under our assumptions) be filled by adding to the number of homogeneous thermal generators in the system. Thus, incremental thermal capacity will operate (again under our assumption of homogeneity) for the 4,000 hours of thermal peak, not just the 2,000 hours of the system or demand peak. Hence, the peak that we should use for the calculation of the peak-time surcharge is 4,000 rather than 2,000 hours, and the resulting surcharge becomes 3¢ rather than 6¢/kWh. The total collected to cover capital cost is exactly the same $120/kW per year as before, only now it is spread over 4,000 rather than 2,000 hours. Why? Because this is the number of hours that newly added homogeneous thermal plants are expected to operate.

Up to this point, we have carried the discussion on the assumption that the price of off-peak energy was equal to its running cost (here 4¢/kWh) and that of peak-time energy was equal to its running cost plus a peak-time surcharge of either 6¢/kWh (without seasonal hydro) or 3¢/kWh (with seasonal hydro). These assumptions make economic sense and can be said to carry out, in our simple example, the lessons of modern electricity economics, a branch of economic analysis set in motion by French technocrats working at or with Electricité de France in the early 1950s. It was their great insight that the true economic marginal cost of electricity would naturally vary by hour of the day, day of the week, and in many cases season of the year, and it was their recommendation that these variations should be reflected in the prices paid by the users of electrical energy. The French started the time-pricing of electricity in the 1950s. They were followed by many (perhaps by now even most) other countries in adopting this innovation. Typically, time-pricing is first applied to large industrial and commercial users, and is then only gradually, and often only partially, extended to domestic customers. However, time-pricing of energy for household use is also now fairly widespread.

But what do we do in cases where time-pricing is not used and where the pricing system therefore does not reflect true economic cost? The answer here is very simple. The fact that the prices paid by users do not reflect the true economic cost of energy does not change that true cost. Even if peak-time energy is given away for free to some users, that does not alter the fact that it costs 10¢/kWh (without seasonal hydro) or 7¢/kWh (with seasonal hydro) in our examples.

Moreover, since our measure of the benefit of hydro projects (whether they are ROS, DR, or seasonal storage) is based on the amount of thermal-generating costs that they end up saving, all the calculations that we have done assuming "prices" equal to 4¢, 10¢, and 7¢ remain valid. But now they should be recognized as measures of system marginal costs of electricity under the relevant assumed conditions. It is by adding up the savings of these costs, which a new project accomplishes, that we obtain a measure of the project's direct benefits.

18.6 Heterogeneous Thermal Capacity — A Vintage Approach

The assumption of homogeneous thermal capacity, which was carried through to this point, has made it easy to describe what we have called the "standard alternative" to each type of hydro project that was analysed. This assumption is now abandoned in favour of a more realistic assumption of heterogeneous thermal capacity. But even here, there are two distinct ways of introducing heterogeneity — one that considers changes taking place over time in the characteristics of the thermal plants that are being added to the system, and another that looks at different design characteristics of thermal plants that have different functional roles within the system.

In this section, we will be concerned with the first kind of heterogeneity. Our thermal system is here assumed to compromise plants dating from different prior years — the oldest are assumed to be the least "thermally efficient" and therefore to have the highest running cost per kWh. The newer the plant, the more efficient it is assumed to be; hence, the lower its running cost per kWh. These assumptions lead to a "stacking pattern" in which the newest thermal plant will be the first one to be turned on (after ROS capacity is fully used). This will be followed by the second newest, then the third, then the fourth newest thermal plant, in ascending order of running cost as older and older plants are turned on. There is nothing that is difficult to understand up to this point. It is simply an application of the idea that whatever the level of demand is, the aim is to use the mix of generating equipment that satisfies demand at the lowest running cost.

But now we have to modify the previous scenario. There, when we added a new plant, its natural function was to fill a "thermal peak" of demand that would otherwise go unmet. Since the equipment being added was fully homogeneous with the already existing thermal plants, it was right to consider this added plant as the last one to be turned on. Now, however, we are assuming that the newest plant is more efficient than the older ones; hence, if we install it, it should be not the last but the first thermal plant to be turned on.

This shift of function gives rise to a new possibility, namely, that it may be worthwhile to add a new thermal plant (say, Plant E) to an existing structure consisting initially of plants A, B, C, and D, even if the system demand for energy remains the same (i.e., is not growing through time). The motive for this addition would in such a case be exclusively the saving of running cost. The "new" system would not produce more energy than the "old" one — the number of kWh would not change, but the saving in running cost might be sufficient to justify the construction of Plant E.

Table 18.1 gives an outline of how a new plant (here Plant E) might turn out to be justified even if the system demand for energy is not increasing. The table is concerned only with the thermal part of the system. There may be ROS capacity serving as baseload, and daily reservoir or seasonal storage capacity serving at peak times, but their contributions are quite naturally assumed to remain the same since system demand is not changing.

Table 18.1: Justifying a New Thermal Plant Even When System Demand Is Constant

Panel 1 — "Old" System			
	Output (MWh)	*Running Cost (¢ per kWh)*	*Total Running Cost ($ million)*
Plant D	300,000	3.0	9.0
Plant C	240,000	3.5	8.4
Plant B	180,000	4.0	7.2
Plant A	120,000	5.0	6.0
Total running cost of thermal plants			30.6
Panel 2 — "New" System			
	Output (MWh)	*Running Cost (¢ per kWh)*	*Total Running Cost ($ million)*
Plant E	300,000	2.5	7.5
Plant D	240,000	3.0	7.2
Plant C	180,000	3.5	6.3
Plant B	120,000	4.0	4.8
Total running cost of thermal plants			25.8
Saving of running cost = $4.8 million/year			
Capital cost of Plant E @ $600/kW × 50 MW = $30 million			

The "old" system (Panel 1) of Table 18.1 is what will occur if Plant E is not built at this time, while the "new" system (Panel 2) represents what will occur if Plant E is in fact constructed. The figures refer to the first year that Plant E will operate if that investment is made.

Panel 1 shows the stacking pattern that will prevail if Plant E is not built. Each plant is assumed to have a capacity of 50 MW, so in Panel 1, Plant D (the newest) is assumed to be operating for 6,000 hours, Plant C for 4,800, Plant B for 3,600, and Plant A for 2,400 hours. Multiply these by 50 MW in order to obtain the MWh shown in the first column of Panel 1. The assumed running costs per kWh are shown in Column 2, and the total running costs for each plant appear in Column 3 (recall that one MWh equals 1,000 kWh).

Panel 2 shows what will happen if Project E is undertaken, in the absence of any increase in system demand. Since all of the plants are assumed to have a 50-MW capacity, and since system demand is unchanged, the net effect of adding Plant E is that Plant A will be retired (or relegated to a standby role). Plant E now becomes the first thermal plant to be turned on, and Plant B becomes the last. As a result, system running costs end up lower than in Panel 1, the total saving being $4.8 million over the year. If the capital cost of building Plant E is $600/KW, for a total of $30 million for a 50-MW plant, the project appears to be worthwhile using the criteria applied in Part I (a 10 percent discount rate plus a 5 percent rate of depreciation for the plant). The required yearly return on capital for Plant E is then $4.5 million, while the estimated actual return is $4.8 million.

It is worth taking time to note the composition of this $4.8 million benefit. Simply looking at the two panels of Table 18.1, one sees that in Panel 2, Plant E occupies the role that Plant D played in Panel 1, Plant D does what Plant C did in Panel 1, Plant C occupies the role previously played by Plant B, and Plant B does what Plant A previously did. This is a perfectly accurate description of the difference between the two panels, but thinking of the new Plant E as taking the place formerly occupied by Plant D is not a helpful way of describing the change. To maximize insight, we have to focus on the fact that it is Plant E that is being introduced into the system. We then have to ask, as Plant E generates its 300,000 MWh, what sources it is in effect replacing. The answer can be found by asking what change takes place in the output of each of the other plants as we move from Panel 1 to Panel 2. The answer is that plants D, C, and B each "lose" 60,000 MWh of output, while Plant A loses all of its 120,000 MWh. These "losses" add up precisely to the 300,000 MWh generated by Plant E in Panel 2.

But this is only the beginning. When Plant E supplants Plant D for 60,000 MWh, the saving of running cost is 0.5¢/kWh, or $5/MWh. When Plant E supplants Plant C, the saving is $10/MWh; when it substitutes for Plant B, $15/MWh is saved. Finally, with regard to Plant A, the saving is 2.5¢/kWh, or $25/MWh. Now, as if by magic, if we take ($5 × 60,000) + ($10 × 60,000) + ($15 × 60,000) + ($25 × 120,000), the result is $300,000 + $600,000 + $900,000 + $3,000,000, equal precisely (and necessarily) to the $4.8 million of saving in total cost that we calculated directly in Table 18.1. Thus, the cost saving for any year t can be represented by $\sum_j H_{jt}(C_j - C_n)$, where C_n is the running cost per kWh of the new plant, C_j is the running cost per kWh of old plant j, and H_{jt} is the number of kWh for which plant j is being displaced by the new plant during year t.

The above analysis works without modification for all cases in which total demand remains the same "with" the new plant as "without" it. However, this is a rather special case. There is a clue as to what the general case looks like when we recall that in our earlier example (Section 18.2), the output of the new plant went 100 percent toward producing energy at the thermal peak and that the peak-time surcharge was actually calculated by asking what that surcharge would have to be in order for investment in a new plant (aimed at covering the increase in demand in the hours of thermal peak) to be justified.

In Table 18.2 and Table 18.3 we examine a situation in which investing in Plant E is not justified if system demand is not increasing, but can be justified if there is a sufficient rate of increase in system demand. Table 18.2 should be self-explanatory as it simply repeats the calculation of Table 18.1, but with lower output for each plant. Now, in Panel 1, Plant D produces 200,000 kWh rather than 300,000. Similarly, each of the other plants has only two-thirds of the output it had in Table 18.1. This simply reflects different demand characteristics in the system. Here Plant D is operating for 4,000 rather than 6,000 hours per year, and Plant A is operating for 1,600 rather than 2,400. In such a system, our cost–benefit analysis would tell us to say no to Plant E if system demand were constant through time. However, suppose demand were growing. If we say no to Plant E, we must do something to contain demand so that it stays within the combined capacity of plants A, B, C, and D. How can we do this? The answer is to use a peak-time surcharge.

Table 18.2: The Case Where Investing in a New Plant Is Not   Justified While System Demand Remains Constant

Panel 1 — "Old" System			
	Output (MWh)	*Running Cost (¢ per kWh)*	*Total Running Cost ($ million)*
Plant D	200,000	3.0	6.0
Plant C	160,000	3.5	5.6
Plant B	120,000	4.0	4.8
Plant A	80,000	5.0	4.0
Total running cost of thermal plants			20.4
Panel 2 — "New" System			
	Output (MWh)	*Running Cost (¢ per kWh)*	*Total Running Cost ($ million)*
Plant E	200,000	2.5	5.0
Plant D	160,000	3.0	4.8
Plant C	120,000	3.5	4.2
Plant B	80,000	4.0	3.2
Total running cost of thermal plants			17.2
Saving of running cost = $3.2 million/year			
Capital cost of Plant E @ $600/kW × 50 MW = $30 million			

For the sake of simplicity, let us assume that the thermal peak is equal to the 1,600 hours that Plant A is running in Panel 1 of Table 18.2. Then we would derive the peak-time surcharge by asking what peak-time surcharge it would take in order for the "next" addition to capacity to be justified. Using our discount rate of 10 percent and our depreciation rate of 5 percent, we would have a "required" return of $4.5 million on the investment ($30 million) in Plant E. We would have cost savings of 0.5¢, 1¢, and 1.5¢ with respect to plants D, C, and B, and these would apply to 40,000 MWh each. The dollar amounts saved would be $200,000, $400,000, and $600,000 respectively, adding up to $1.2 million. Thus, Plant E's energy at peak time (1,600 hours) would have to generate $4.5–$1.2 million of return to capital if the investment in Plant E were to be worthwhile. This would be created over 1,600 hours × 50,000 kW of capacity, or 80 million kWh. The peak-time surcharge (over and above Plant B's running cost) would then have to be $3.3 million ÷ 80 million kWh = 4.125¢/kWh. The peak-time price would be 8.125¢/kWh.

The calculation would be different if the system peak were equal to, say, 1,000 hours (rather than 1,600). Assuming Plant A's turbines to be used at full capacity during this 1,000-hour peak, they would produce 50,000 MWh during this period. Plant E would not be substituting for Plant A during this time, but it would do so (if Plant E were built) for the remaining 30,000 MWh of Plant A's output (as shown in Panel 1). Thus H_{at} would be 30 million kWh, while H_{bt}, H_{ct}, and H_{dt} would each be 40 million kWh. These substitutions would account for a combined saving in running cost of $1.95 million (= $200,000 + $400,000 + $600,000 for plants D, C, and B, as before, plus $750,000 for Plant A, covering the 30,000 MWh that we have calculated for H_{at}). In order to generate the $4.5 million of benefits that are required to justify investing in Plant E, the peak-time surcharge (over Plant A's running cost of 5¢) would have to generate benefits of $2.55 million (= $4.5 million − $1.95 million). Per kWh, this "surcharge" would be 5.1¢/kWh. The peak-time price of energy in this case would be $10.1¢/kWh.[128]

Readers should be aware that the peak-time "prices" that we calculate here do not in any way have to be put into practice (i.e., be actually collected from the power company's customers). They really are measures of the actual economic cost of bringing peak-time energy in line by way of constructing Plant E. Our $4.5 million figure reflects the economic cost of the capital invested in Plant E. If Plant E worked only at peak time, one would have to assign this full $4.5 million of capital cost to the peak period. In our case, the bulk of this cost is being covered by savings of running cost during the off-peak period. The peak-time price we calculated represents the remaining part of this cost, and it thus reflects the true cost of supplying peak-time energy using the investment in Plant E.

Thus, we would use the peak-time prices that we have calculated to measure the benefits of a DR project's adding to the supply of energy at a system peak of 1,000 hours or the benefits of a seasonal hydro project's increasing the supply

---

[128]In this calculation, we assume that the timing of Plant E's introduction into the system would be such that even in Plant E's presence, both Plant A and Plant E would be fully utilized during the 1,000 hours of system peak. This gives rise to the question of how the system is managed during the interval in which system peak demand exceeds 200 MW (the sum of the capacities of plants A, B, C, and D) but falls short of 250 MW (where all five plants would be operating at capacity). The economist's answer to this question is that the peak-time price of energy would move up gradually from 3¢ (= A's running cost) to 8.4¢ (the level that would justify introducing Plant E). The object of such a gradually increasing peak-time price would be to contain peak demand within the 200 MW limit until the point where the introduction of Plant E is optimal. This answer, however, involves too much fine-tuning for the practical world. The practical solution is simply to set the peak-time price at 7.9¢ soon as system peak demand threatens to exceed 200 MW at a price of 3¢, and then introduce Plant E at the point where it can fully substitute for Plant A.

of energy during a system peak of 1,600 hours. The underlying purpose of our calculating peak-time prices based on thermal costs is, therefore, to give us a cost-based way of assigning a value to peak-time energy coming from alternative sources of energy.

18.7 Thermal Capacity That Differs by Type of Plant

In this section we will consider differences in the capital and running costs of thermal plants, based on their physical (engineering) characteristics. For the sake of simplicity, we will confine our examples to three types of facility — big thermal, combined cycle, and gas turbine (GT). There used to be many more relevant variations by type, as there would be significant variations in capital and running costs for coal-fired plants of different sizes. This sort of variation has been greatly reduced as a consequence of the introduction of combined-cycle generating plants. These plants use petroleum or natural gas as fuel, and they use jet engines or similar equipment to generate energy in the first cycle. The second cycle then uses the heat produced in the first cycle to create steam, which then produces additional energy in the second cycle. Once combined-cycle technology came onto the scene, it turned out to be the cheapest way of generating electricity under a very substantial range of demand conditions. Thus, our choice of just three types of generating equipment pretty well reflects the realities of contemporary thermal power industries.

The characteristics of our three types of equipment are:

	Capital Cost (K)	Annualized Capital Cost (= $0.15 \times K$)	Running Cost
Big thermal	$2,000/kW	$300	$200/kW/yr
Combined cycle	$1,200/kW	$180	5¢/kWh
Gas turbine	$600/kW	$90	9¢/kWh

Readers will note that the running costs of big thermal are expressed on an annual basis per kW of capacity rather than on a per kWh basis. The reason for this is that big coal-fired units cannot be turned on and off to meet variations in system demand. As is the case with nuclear capacity, turning them on and off is a costly operation, leading to their characteristic use as baseload capacity, which is turned off only for maintenance and repairs.

Table 18.3 examines the total annual costs of using these three types of capacity in order to meet different durations of energy demand. It is easily seen there that big thermal is the most efficient way to meet an annual energy demand (per kW of installed capacity) lasting 7,500 hours, while combined cycle is best for a demand covering 5,000 hours in the year and also for one covering 3,000 hours. For demands lasting 2,000 and 1,000 hours, however, gas turbines provide the most efficient answer.

If different types of capacity are best for different numbers of hours, critical numbers of hours have to exist marking the "borderline" between two types. These borderlines are found by equating the total costs for two adjacent kinds of capacity. Thus, at 6,400 hours, the total annualized cost of combined-cycle capacity is equal to $180 + (5¢ × 6,400) = $500, exactly the same as the full-year cost ($300 + $200) of a kW of big thermal capacity. Demands with durations longer than 6,400 hours can thus be accommodated most cheaply by big thermal capacity, while new demands lasting somewhat less than 6,400 hours can be more efficiently served by combined-cycle capacity. These answers apply: a) when the new demand stands alone (i.e., when we are building capacity just to satisfy this demand), and b) when the new demand is added to an already optimized system.

In an exactly analogous fashion, we can find that the borderline between combined-cycle and GT capacity is 2,250 hours. For this number of hours, total annual costs of combined-cycle capacity amount to $180 + (2,250 × 5¢), or $292.50, exactly the same as the annual total for GT at capacity, equal to $90 + (2,250 × 9¢) = $90 + $202.50 = $292.50. So again, either for a stand-alone demand or for a new demand within an already optimized system, we would install GT capacity for demands lasting less than 2,250 hours and combined-cycle capacity for demands going up from this point.

Table 18.3: Electricity System Investment Decision as with Three Different Types of Generating Capacity

	Annualized Capital Costs ($/kW)	Running Costs per Year	Total Costs per Year ($/kW)
Use for 7,500 hours/yr.			
Big thermal	300	$200	500
Combined cycle	180	5¢×7,500 = $375	555
Gas turbine	90	9¢×7,500 = $675	765
Use for 5,000 hours/yr.			
Big thermal	300	$200	500
Combined cycle	180	5¢×5,000 = $250	430
Gas turbine	90	9¢×5,000 = $450	540
Use for 3,000 hours/yr.			
Big thermal	300	$200	500
Combined cycle	180	5¢×3,000 = $150	330
Gas turbine	90	9¢×3,000 = $270	360
Use for 2,000 hours/yr.			
Big thermal	300	$200	500
Combined cycle	180	5¢×2,000 = $100	280
Gas turbine	90	9¢×2,000 = $180	270
Use for 1,000 hours/yr.			
Big thermal	300	$200	500
Combined cycle	180	5¢×1,000 = $50	230
Gas turbine	90	9¢×1,000 = $90	180
Borderline between big thermal and combined cycle			
$300 + $200 = $180 + 0.05 N_1			
$320 = $0.05 N_1			
6,400 hours = N_1			
Borderline between combined cycle and gas turbine			
$180 + 0.05 N_2 = $90 + 0.09 N_2			
$90 = (0.09 − 0.05) N_2			
2,250 hours = N_2			

Table 18.4 explores cases in which capacity is being added to an already optimized system. The first step is to identify system marginal costs during hours of quite low system demand. Similarly, system marginal costs equal 5¢/kWh when combined cycle is the most expensive capacity at work (i.e., during periods of intermediate system demand). Then we have system marginal costs equal to 9¢/kWh when GT capacity is marginal. There are times when the system's big thermal and combined-cycle plants are all operating at full capacity and therefore have to be supplemented by gas turbines in order to accommodate the system's

full demand. The system marginal cost of 9¢ occurs when this is the case and when the system's GT capacity is not fully utilized — i.e., when the system is not yet at peak demand.

Now consider the fact that if GT plants were to generate revenues of 9¢/kWh for all of their hours of operation, this would just cover their running costs, but would make no contribution to their capital costs. Thus, just as in the first part of this chapter, where the peak-time surcharge was set at 6¢ in the first example and a thermal peak surcharge in a later example was set at 3¢ in order to cover the annualized capital cost of new homogeneous thermal capacity, we now set a peak-time surcharge of 9¢ in order to cover the annualized $90/kW capital costs of GT capacity over a system peak of 1,000 hours per year.[129]

In Table 18.4 we present three cases, each dealing with how the system should respond to a new set of energy demands: Case 1 considers a new demand with a duration of 7,000 hours per kW per year; Case 2 considers a new demand lasting 4,000 hours; and in Case 3 the new demand has a duration of 1,500 hours. These cases demonstrate how, in an optimized system of the kind with which we are working: a) each new demand can be met by its appropriate type of capacity, and b) when this is done and that new capacity is remunerated at system marginal cost for each hour that it runs, the total remuneration precisely covers the sum of annualized capital costs plus annual running costs for the appropriate type of capacity.

---

[129]When we deal with peak time, we act as if the relevant capacity (here, GT) is absolutely fully utilized over the assumed duration (here, 1,000 hours) for peak demand. In reality, an electricity administration would define peak-time hours in a very sensible way (say, 5–11 p.m. for a lighting peak in winter, 8–11 p.m. in summer), fully recognizing that the GT part of the system would not be operating at absolutely full capacity during these times. The rest of the system (big thermal and combined cycle) would, however, be at full capacity. Setting the peak-time surcharge at precisely 9¢ turns out to be "right" from the standpoint of big thermal and combined-cycle capacity, as is shown in Table 18.4. It is also "right" from the standpoint of GT capacity if it is indeed fully used for the low-hour peak. This is what we assume here. An upward modification of the peak-time surcharge would lead to excess rewards for big thermal and combined cycle.

Table 18.4: Investment Policy in a System with Optimized Capacities and System Peak of 1,000 Hours

---

System Marginal Costs

Big Thermal Capacity — Operates for 6,400 hours or more. System marginal costs when the marginal capacity = zero.

Combined-Cycle Capacity — Operates for more than 2,250 hours and less than 6,400 hours when this is the system's marginal capacity. System marginal costs = 5¢/kWh.

Gas Turbine Capacity — Operates for less than 2,250 hours per year. When this capacity is only partially used (not at system peak), system marginal costs = 9¢/kWh.

Peak-Time Surcharge — Sufficient to cover capital costs of GT capacity during 1,000 hours of system peak. Annualized capital costs of $90 ÷ 1,000 peak-time hours = peak-time surcharge of 9¢/kWh. System marginal cost during 1,000 peak-time hours = 9¢ running cost + 9¢ peak-time surcharge = 18¢/kWh.

Case 1: New demand arises (new factory working three shifts per day), operating for 7,000 hours per year.

    Answer: Build big thermal capacity to meet this demand

"earns" 18¢/kWh during 1,000 peak-time hours	= $180
"earns" 9¢/kWh during 1,250 hours when GT is marginal capacity	= $112.50
"earns" 5¢/kWh during 4,150 (= 6,400 − 2,250) hours when combined cycle is marginal capacity	= $207.50
"earns" zero during 1,000 hours when big thermal is marginal capacity	= 0
Total "earnings"	= $500
Cost of this new capacity = $300 annualized capital cost + $200 running cost	= $500

Big thermal's costs are exactly covered by system marginal costs, including peak-time surcharge.

Case 2: New demand arises (new factory working two shifts per day), operating for 4,000 hours per year.

    Answer: Build combined-cycle capacity to meet this demand

"earns" 18¢/kWh during 1,000 peak-time hours	= $180

"earns" 9¢/kWh during 1,250 hours when GT is marginal
    capacity   = \$112.50
"earns" 5¢/kWh during 1,750 (= 4,000-2,250) hours   = \$87.50

Total "earnings"   = \$380

Cost of this new capacity = 180 annualized capital cost
+ 5¢ × 4,000 hours + \$200 running cost   = \$380

Case 3: New demand arises (population growth leads to new residential demand plus commercial and street lighting), operating for 1,500 hours per year.

    Answer: Build GT capacity to meet this demand
    "earns" 18¢/kWh during 1,000 peak-load hours   = \$180
    "earns" 9¢/kWh during 500 hours when GT is marginal
    capacity   = \$45

    Total "earnings"   = \$225

    Cost of this new capacity = \$90 annualized capital cost
    + 9¢/kWh during 1,500 hours   = \$225

Thus, in Case 1, big thermal is the "right" capacity to meet a new demand of 7,000 hours a year. If it earns system marginal costs, it will earn 18¢/kWh during 1,000 peak-time hours, 9¢/kWh during 1,250 hours, 5¢/kWh during 4,150 hours, and finally 0¢/kWh during the 1,000 hours when big thermal is the system's marginal capacity. As is shown for Case 1, remuneration at these marginal costs will precisely cover big thermal's annualized capital costs of \$300/kW plus its annual running cost of \$200/kW.

Similarly, in Case 2, we have combined-cycle capacity being built to accommodate a new demand lasting 4,000 hours per year. Here remuneration at system marginal cost covers 1,000 hours at 18¢ plus 1,250 hours at 9¢/kWh plus 1,750 hours at 5¢/kWh. The total of these "earnings" is \$380/kW per year, which precisely equals the sum of an annualized capital cost of \$180/kW plus a running cost of 5¢/kWh for 4,000 hours in the year.

Finally, Case 3 explores a new demand lasting 1,500 hours, to be met by adding new GT capacity. Here that capacity "earns" 18¢/kWh for 1,000 hours and 9¢/kWh for 500 hours, for a total of \$225/kW per year. Once again, this amount precisely covers the GT annualized capital cost of \$90/kW plus the GT running cost of 9¢/kWh for 1,500 hours per year.

It almost looks like a "miracle" that a single peak-time surcharge turns out to be the only supplement to system marginal running cost that is needed in order to fully cover both capital and running cost of each type of capacity in a fully optimized system. Perhaps with an excess of zeal we have called this proposition "the fundamental theorem of modern electricity pricing". At any rate, it was a noteworthy discovery in the annals of electricity economics.

As we shall see, a system that follows the rules of marginal cost pricing will tend over time to approach an optimized level. But many of the world's systems fall far short of this point at the present time and probably will still be non-optimized for quite some time into the future. In most of these cases, the non-optimality of the system stems from two sources: a) the presence of older steam and GT plants that will naturally be retired as they live out their economic lives, and b) the fact that combined-cycle technology has not had enough time to reach the levels needed for a fully optimized system. Table 18.5 explores two cases, both dealing with a system that does not have its optimal amount of combined-cycle capacity. These cases deal, respectively, with increases of demand of long (7,000 hours) and short (1,000 hours) duration. These new demands would "normally" (i.e., in a fully optimized system) be met by adding, respectively, big thermal capacity (for the 7,000-hour increment of demand) and GT capacity (for the 1,000-hour increment). However, because of the non-optimality of the system, it turns out that the best response, even to these very long-duration and very short-duration increments of demand, is to add combined-cycle capacity. This strategy is not only the cheapest way of accommodating the new demands; it also moves the system closer to optimality.

Table 18.5: Investment Policy in a Non-Optimized System with "Too Little" Combined-Cycle Capacity

System has "too much" big thermal capacity, which ends up satisfying demands of 4,500 hours or more.

System has "too much" GT capacity, which ends up satisfying all demands of 3,000 hours or less.

System has "too little" combined-cycle capacity, which ends up satisfying demands of between 3,000 and 4,500 hours per year. Recall that combined-cycle capacity has an economic advantage (based on capital and running costs) for demands all the way from 2,250 to 6,400 hours per year. So quite naturally, if a new demand arises within the 2,250–6,400 range, it should be filled by adding combined-cycle capacity. However, owing to the non-optimality of the system, it turns out that the answer to *any* increase in demand is to add combined-cycle capacity, as this brings the system closer to an optimum. The following examples show why this is so.

Case 4: New demand arises of 7,000 hours per year.

> **Answer:** Meet this demand by taking away big thermal from its "margin" at 4,500 hours per year and shifting it to satisfy the new demand of 7,000 hours. No capital cost or marginal running cost is involved since this capacity operates full-time in either case.
>
> Now add combined-cycle capacity to fill the void of 4,500 hours created by shift. This entails $180 of annualized capital cost
> plus $(4,500 \times 5¢) = \$225$ of additional running cost = $405
>
> Total cost of meeting new demand   = $405
>
> Total cost of meeting this new demand by directly building big thermal capacity for this purpose is
> $300 annualized capital cost plus $200 of annual running cost   = $500

Hence, it is cheaper to add combined cycle than to install new big thermal capacity to meet this new demand.

Table 18.5 (continued)

Case 5: New demand arises of just 1,000 hours at peak time (commercial establishments adding to demand for lighting during evening hours).

> **Answer:** Meet this demand by taking GT capacity away from its "margin" of 3,000 hours and shifting it to meet the new peak-time demand of 1,000 hours. There is no capital cost, and there is a saving of running costs of
>
> $(3,000 - 1,000) = 2,000$ hours × 9¢/kWh $= -\$180$
>
> However, we now have the capital cost of combined cycle (= $180) plus running costs of combined cycle $150 (= 3,000 × 5¢) for 3,000 hours.
> Total combined cycle cost $= \$330$
>
> Net cost per kW of building combined cycle to meet the new demand
> $= \$150$
>
> Total cost of meeting the new demand by directly building GT capacity for this purpose is $90 of capital cost + (9¢ × 1,000 hours of running cost)
> $= \$180$

Hence, it is cheaper to add combined cycle than to install new GT capacity to meet the new demand.

In Case 4, the new demand has a duration of 7,000 hours. At first glance it seems natural that this demand should be filled by big thermal, which is the most efficient type of capacity for demands of this length. That is true in an optimized system. But in a non-optimized system, we may already have some big thermal capacity doing what it should not (optimally) do. This is true in our Case 4, where we have some big thermal capacity that is meeting a demand of only 4,500 hours a year. The right answer is to shift this big thermal capacity out of this slot (where it does not belong), to move it to the new 7,000-hour slot (where it does belong), and to replace it in the 4,500-hour slot by combined-cycle capacity, which is optimal for that duration. As Case 4 shows, this set of moves meets the new demand at a total (capital plus running) cost that is lower than the cost of meeting the new demand with new big thermal capacity.

Similarly, we have Case 5, a new demand with a duration of just 1,000 hours. This is taken to be at peak time because if it were away from the peak, this new demand could be met by simply making more intensive use of the system's existing capacity.

Here the casual observer might think that the best way to respond to the new demand would be to add new GT capacity. Again, this would be the right answer if the system were starting from an optimized position. But given the non-optimality of having some GT capacity working as long as 3,000 hours, the best answer is to shift this GT capacity to the new 1,000-hour slot. This saves

9¢ × 2,000 hours of GT running cost per kW of shifted capacity. To replace this shifted GT capacity in the 3,000-hour slot, we introduced new combined-cycle capacity, having an annualized capital cost of $180 and an annual running cost of $150 (= 3,000 × 5¢). The total cost of this combined-cycle operation is $330 per year, but deducting the saving of running cost on the shifted GT capacity, we find a net cost of $330 − $180 = $150. This is obviously lower than the $180 cost of satisfying the new 1,000-hour demand by adding new GT capacity.

Cases 4 and 5 show why it is true that in a non-optimized system that has too little combined-cycle capacity, adding to that particular type of capacity will be the cost-minimizing way of responding to new demands of essentially any duration.

18.8 Some Notes on Solar and Wind Power

The right way to think about solar and wind power is to consider them as the modern counterparts of ROS generation. All of these have the characteristic that the ultimate source of energy experiences natural variations that are beyond our direct control. In the case of ROS projects, we have the possibility of adding DRs, at which point we do control the flow of energy into the system. The counterpart of DRs is to use wind or solar energy to pump water from a lower to a higher level, with the intention of generating electricity through hydro turbines during peak-time hours. This is known as pump storage, and it involves two dams, one above and the other below the incline down which the water flows to the turbines. Pump-storage projects have existed at least since the 1930s, but they have not become very widespread because of the heavy capital costs that they involve. Aside from pump storage, another means of controlling the flow of electricity from wind and solar sources would be through batteries: generate electricity as the wind and sun permit, but use batteries to store that energy so that it can be used at times of high value per kWh. To our knowledge, such use of batteries is still far from being cost-effective.

Thus, our discussion of wind and solar energy will concentrate on the standard case, directly analogous to ROS projects, where the electricity generated by the project is delivered to the system at the time and in the volume determined by the whims of nature.

Solar and wind projects differ from ROS operations in that one does not always encounter diminishing returns to adding turbines or solar panels at a given site. Ten solar panels will catch ten times as much sunlight as one panel, and ten turbines will catch ten times as much wind as one of them (with some exceptions in cases of canyons, etc., which channel the wind in special ways). The generating capacity of solar and wind projects will therefore be determined mainly by the costs of installing more turbines or panels and by the needs of the electricity system.

The standard way of dealing with capacity of these kinds is to assign to their output the relevant system marginal costs. Reverting to our example of Table

18.4, suppose a solar or wind project had a maximum output of 10 MW. To value its expected output for any future year, we would first assign system marginal costs for each hour of operation. Thus, following Table 18.4, we would have 2,360 (= 8,760 − 6,400) hours at zero marginal cost (when big thermal was expected to be the marginal capacity), 4,150 hours at 5¢ (when combined cycle was expected to be at the margin), and 2,250 hours at 9¢, the marginal running cost of GT capacity. These add up to $410/kW per year. However, the solar or wind project would be expected to operate only at a fraction of its capacity, owing to fluctuations in the availability of wind and sunlight. We here assume the relevant fraction to be 30 percent, which reduces the benefit to $123/kW of capacity.

The above calculations assign no part of the peak-time surcharge to the wind or solar project. This is because in both cases, there are likely to be many peak-time hours during which the project will have zero output. In order to meet peak-time demand at such times, some sort of other standby capacity would have to be available. This might consist of older capacity, mainly retired from the system but held for standby purposes for just this kind of contingency. But within the framework of Table 18.4, it would be GT capacity. There may be places where the wind or sun is so reliable that it can be counted on, at a specified intensity, in peak-time hours. If we assume that intensity to be 20 percent of the maximum intensity, then we would add to the above figure of $123 an amount equal to 20 percent of the 9¢ peak-time surcharge multiplied by the 1,000 hours of peak-time use. This would add $18 for a total benefit of $141/kW.

Some discussions of wind and solar power speak of a "necessity" of supplementing these projects with backup peaking capacity (which in our case would be gas turbines). These discussions focus on the unreliability of these sources to provide peak-time power. The backup capacity enters the picture precisely in order to fill this role. We believe that such "packaging" is unnecessary. In coming to this conclusion, we rely on a fundamental principle of project evaluation — namely, the principle of "separable components". This principle says that if we have two projects X and Y, we can define their combined benefit (in present value) as B_{x+y}; their separate, stand-alone benefits as B_x and B_y; and the benefits of each, conditional on the presence of the other, as $B_x|_y$ and $B_y|_x$. It is easy to see that:

$$B_{x+y} = B_x + B_y|_x = B_y + B_x|_y$$

Similarly, for costs:

$$C_{x+y} = C_x + C_y|_x = C_y + C_x|_y$$

Now if the "joint project" $(X+Y)$ is the best option, this means that:

$$(B_{x+y} - C_{x+y}) > (B_x - C_x)$$
$$(B_{x+y} - C_{x+y}) - (B_x - C_x) > 0$$

and therefore:

$$B_y|_x > C_y|_x$$

That is, if the joint project is acceptable, Project Y must pass the test as the marginal project — it must be worthwhile to add Project Y to an initial package consisting only of Project X.

Similarly, it can be shown that if the joint project is best, Project X must pass the test as the marginal project — it must be worthwhile to add Project X to an initial package consisting only of Project Y.

There is no escaping the rigorous mathematical logic of this argument. If a package consisting of a wind project and a backup GT project is the best option, then each of these two components must pass the cost–benefit test as the marginal project, measuring its contribution as what it would add (to benefits and costs, respectively) in the presence of the other. We must therefore evaluate a wind or solar project as being additional to any GT or other standby peaking project with which some would argue it ought to be "packaged".

18.9 Conclusion

The main objective of this chapter is to convey an understanding of the underlying economic principles that characterize the provision of electrical energy. The starting point is that the value of the kWh — the standard "product" that electricity customers buy and consume — will normally exhibit wide variations by hour of the day and season of the year. This occurs in spite of the fact that there is probably no item more physically homogeneous from unit to unit than kWh of 120 volts and 60 cycles. The reason for the variation in value stems from different effective marginal costs of providing energy at different times. When an electricity system is not working at capacity, the effective marginal cost is the highest running cost among the different plants that are operating at the time. As plants are turned on, in ascending order of running cost, the effective marginal cost will be low at times of low demand and high at times of heavy demand on the system's resources. System marginal cost is highest at peak periods because here the true cost must also cover a provision for capital cost recovery of the type of capacity that has to be expanded when peak-time demand increases.

The key to evaluating investments in new generating capacity is to value their expected output at "system marginal cost" at each moment they are expected to operate. Put another way, the benefits that are to be expected from a new plant are the costs that will be saved because of its presence in the system. This is something that seems straightforward and easy to understand, but in fact, it is anything but simple. The subtleties arise because the output of a new plant stretches many years into the future, so the bulk of its cost saving will take place then. The principle guiding the estimation of these future cost savings is that year by year and into the future, the system will continue to follow good cost–benefit principles as it retires old plants and invests in new ones. Any given plant will almost certainly have a trajectory of benefits that starts high and then declines over time. For thermal plants, one can expect that future additions will be more efficient than the current ones, so that today's new plant, which may start as the most efficient one of its class, may end its life as the least efficient of the class, having been bumped from a heavy load factor (high hours of use) at the beginning of its life to lower and lower hours of use as time goes on. Finally, it will be relegated to standby capacity and ultimately to the scrap heap. Hydro storage dams have a similar trajectory of benefits, in this case stemming from their inevitable accumulation of mud and silt. As this occurs, their effective storage capacity inevitably declines. Perhaps ROS projects and daily reservoirs (which can be de-silted quite easily) are the only ones whose benefit streams may escape an inevitable downward drift through time.

The downward trend of benefits of a given project is incorporated into our analysis through an allowance for depreciation. Investment in an asset that does not depreciate can be justified if that asset just yields the required rate of return (opportunity cost of capital). It is the expectation of declining (or ultimately terminating) benefits that leads to first-year benefits covering more than the required rate of return. The use in our exposition of a required rate of return-plus-depreciation in the first year of a project's operating life is intended to capture all of the subtleties referred to in this chapter.

The fact that the future benefits of electricity projects are measured by their expected savings of costs gives rise to another possibility — that the electricity system in question may already have in place a modern and highly sophisticated system of cost control and future investment programming. That is to say, those enterprises or public authorities may already have done a lot of the work needed in order to see how a given new plant will fit into the system and which particular costs it is likely to be saving, hour by hour and year by year, at least for a few years into the future. All we can say here is that, as cost–benefit analysts, we should be grateful when such pieces of luck relieve us of a great deal of work.

Chapter Nineteen

An Integrated Appraisal of Combined-Cycle Versus Single-Cycle Electricity-Generation Technologies

19.1 Introduction

This study describes an integrated financial, economic, and distributive appraisal of an independent power producer (IPP) project for generating electricity. The critical issue is that the private sponsors of the IPP proposed to build a single-cycle electricity-generation plant that was expected to start operating with an 80 percent load factor. A comparative analysis was undertaken of a single-cycle oil-fuel plant and a combined-cycle oil-fuel plant that would produce the same amount of electricity per year. This analysis was made from the point of view of each of the major stakeholders affected — namely the sponsor of the IPP, the public utility that is the off-taker of the electricity, the government, and consumers.

19.2 Background

The energy sector in the country of Adukki has long relied mainly on the generation capacity of hydroelectric power plants.[130] Almost 61 percent of the installed capacity was hydro, and the rest thermal. All of the hydro power plants were owned by the Adukki Electricity Corporation (AEC), the state-owned utility that generates power and handles all of the transmission and distribution of electricity in the country. Heavy reliance on hydroelectric power generation had caused shortages in meeting the demand for power during periods of drought, when the water level in the reservoirs is very low. In addition, the

---

[130]In order to maintain the confidentiality of the information of the original project on which this case was based, the name of the country, the currency, and a number of other elements have been changed. During the period 2006–2008, Adukki achieved an average real GDP growth rate of slightly above 6 percent per year. Estimates indicated that the rate of growth would have been 0.7–0.9 percent higher if electricity shortages had not prevailed in those years. Adukki is aiming to achieve a real GDP growth rate of 7–10 percent annually by 2015 and to position itself as a middle-income country with a per capita income of US$1,000. Furthermore, access to electricity by the population was only slightly over 50 percent. If the government wants to achieve 100 percent national electrification by 2030, the current installed capacity needs to be doubled by 2030 in order to ensure a reliable and sufficient electricity supply.

existing power-generation capacity was not sufficient to sustain higher economic growth prospects, leading to a power deficit. The main challenges faced by the energy sector were the further diversification of the source of electricity generation and the expansion of the total installed capacity.

The potential for power capacity expansion was perceived by the private sector as a profitable opportunity to invest. A proposal was made to the Government of Adukki by Bright Light Electricity Generation Ltd. in which the IPP promised to finance, construct, operate, and maintain a Bright Light Electricity Generation project (BLEG). The planned 126-MW single-cycle gas turbine plant was expected to be operational by 2010 and would be located at a site owned by the government. In addition, the utility would supply the required fuel for the operation of the plant, light crude oil (LCO). The total cost of investment (net of value-added tax, or VAT) was estimated to be almost $134 million. Upon completion, the IPP would add 126 MW of additional capacity to the existing system. The state utility would be the sole buyer of the generated power based on a long-term power purchase agreement (PPA).

In this study, we chose to analyse not only the proposed single-cycle plant, but also a possible combined-cycle alternative. From the utility's perspective the feasibility of the system expansion was evaluated under two alternative scenarios. This analysis served two purposes: to determine which of the two technologies – single- and combined-cycle – is the most efficient from the utility's perspective, and to predict the potential impact of the choice of technology on the electricity tariff.

The financial benefits generated from the utility were measured by the amount of electricity purchased from the IPP and sold to end-users. The generation plants were configured so that the same amount of electricity would be generated no matter which technology was chosen. Comparison between technologies can be determined by the difference between the capital cost and the energy-transformation efficiency of the different technologies employed. The integrated appraisal framework allows analysts to build a model directly on the consolidated financial cash flows statement, which combines the cash flows of the IPP and those of the utility into a single statement.

The economic analysis in this case was an evaluation of the economic value of all the costs saved by using one technology over the other. Either one of the options considered here would supply electricity to these final consumers; hence, the economic benefits must be tied to the relative costs of producing electricity. A key consideration in the choice of technologies would be determining the least-cost method of supplying the needs of the utility given the existing set of generation facilities available and the nature of the growth in electricity demand. It is also interesting to compare the costs of production with the valuation that demanders (on the margin) would place on the incremental electricity generated as a result of the particular electricity pricing structure being used.

19.3 Project Costs and Parameters for the Appraisal of the Single-Cycle Plant

The construction of the proposed 126-MW single-cycle plant would start in 2008. This phase was expected to last for two years. It was anticipated that 56 percent of the cost would be incurred in 2008, while the remaining 44 percent would be spent the following year. The detailed expenditure by component is shown in Table 19.1.

Table 19.1: Single-Cycle Power Plant Investment Costs by Component (million dollars, in 2008 prices)

	2008	2009	Total
Land	0.50	0	0.50
EPC and engineering			
Initial operating tools and mobilization	2.65	2.08	4.73
Gas turbine and related costs	21.88	17.20	39.08
Total EPC contract (excluding VAT)	28.99	22.78	51.77
Other costs	3.96	3.12	7.08
Sub-total	57.49	45.17	102.66
Development costs (excluding VAT)	8.02	6.30	14.32
Financing costs	9.24	7.26	16.50
Total investment cost	**75.25**	**58.73**	**133.98**

EPC: engineering, procurement and construction

19.3.1 Project Parameters and Assumptions

The base case financial model for the single-cycle IPP was developed on the basis of the assumptions and parameters listed below.

a) Investment Costs

- The total investment cost net of VAT was $133.98 million in 2008 prices. Details are shown in Table 19.1.
- Of this investment cost, land was given to the project as a subsidy by the government. At the end of the project's life, the land would be returned to the government.
- The liquidation values of all investment items other than land would belong to the IPP, and were included in the analysis.

b) Technical Parameters

- The rated plant capacity was 126 MW. The maximum plant availability was 91 percent, leading to a maximum installed capacity of 114.66 MW. This was subject to annual deterioration at a rate of 2.5 percent. The average plant availability factor was assumed to be 89 percent.
- It was anticipated that the initial plant load factor in 2010 would be 80 percent, but this was expected to decrease by 3.4 percent per year until it reached 40 percent in 2030.[131] The proposed thermal plant was expected to run during all hours of peak demand, as well as during the off-peak hours when it is required. Taking both peak and off-peak operations into account, the plant was expected to have a final load factor of 40 percent in 2030.
- Five percent of the gross capacity available would be used for auxiliary consumption.

c) Operating and Maintenance Costs

- The plant was expected to commence generating electricity in 2010, with an operating life of 20 years. The operation and maintenance costs that were expected to be incurred during the project's life were both fixed and variable, and are presented below (expressed in 2008 prices).

Fixed Operating and Maintenance Costs
- **Labour:** The wages bill of the project was expected to amount to $2.08 million in 2010. It was projected that 90 percent of the workers hired would be skilled and the remaining 10 percent unskilled. It was assumed that the real wage rate would increase by 3 percent annually.
- **General Administrative Fees and Operating and Maintenance Costs:** The general administrative fees were predicted to be $0.406 million on a yearly basis (excluding VAT), while the operating and maintenance costs would be approximately $0.5 million per annum. These values would increase over time in real terms by 1.5 percent a year.
- **Long-Term Service Agreement (LTSA) and Others:** The LTSA would cover the whole period of time during which the project operates. The annual fee to be paid by the project amounted to approximately $4.97 million. This amount also included the fixed portion of other services.

Variable Operating and Maintenance Costs
- **Fuel:** This was the most important component of the variable operating costs. The quantity of fuel, LCO, required for the single-cycle gas turbine

---

[131]The annual average percentage decrease was calculated as $(PLF_{2030}/PLF_{2010})^{1/(2030-2010)}-1$. This is because as more generating plants are introduced that have lower running costs, this plant would be used for fewer hours each year. In addition, over time, the marginal running costs of this plant would increase as a result of wear and tear.

plant was determined by the energy-transformation efficiency rate, which was estimated to be 32 percent. This means that 32 percent of the energy released from combustion would be converted into electricity. The remaining energy would be dissipated in the form of heat. The amount depends on the fuel density/heat content, which is 47,000 MJ per ton of fuel. The price of LCO was assumed to be $367 per ton, or an equivalent of $49 per barrel.

- **Water, Chemicals, Lubrication Oil, LTSA, and Others:** The water needed for the operation of the plant would be obtained from the local supplier at a cost of $0.000042 per kWh. The cost of lubrication oil for the boiler, together with the cost of chemicals, was estimated at $0.00071 per kWh. Finally, the variable component of the LTSA costs and others was $0.00043 per kWh.

Working Capital
- Accounts payable was expected to be 8 percent of the total operating costs, excluding labour and fuel. The cash balance was projected at 5 percent of total annual operating costs, excluding fuel.
- Accounts receivable of the IPP was estimated to be 8 percent of total PPA revenue.

d) Life of Assets and Residual Values

- All of the investment cost items were expected to have an economic life of 25 years.
- Since the economic life of the assets was longer than the project's operating life, no replacement of the assets would be necessary during the plant's operation.

e) Macroeconomic Variables

- The annual domestic inflation rate was expected to be 8.9 percent; for the United States, it was 3 percent.
- The real exchange rate as of 2008 was 1.21 rupees per US dollar and was assumed to remain unchanged through the project's life, except when a sensitivity analysis was undertaken.
- The VAT rate of 13 percent was assumed.
- The profit earned by private investors would be subject to the corporate income tax rate of 25 percent.

f) Required Rate of Return

- The minimum real rate of return required by private investors was 13 percent.

19.3.2 Power Purchase Agreement (PPA)

The most important aspects of the proposed PPA and related contracts are summarized below.

- The utility would be the only off-taker of the electricity generated by the proposed plant.
- The financial benefits of the project were determined by the PPA with the supplier (IPP) and the sole buyer (the utility). The tariff payment under the PPA consisted of three main components.
  a) The first was a capacity payment based on the available capacity for sale to the buyer.
  b) The second was the availability incentive payment.
  c) The third included the payment made to cover the variable operating and maintenance costs of the IPP, except fuel.
- A *capacity payment component* is a fixed amount designed to cover the capital recovery as well as fixed operating and maintenance costs.
- The capacity payment for the proposed plant was expected to be $295,000/MW/year in 2008 prices (net of VAT). It would be applied to the yearly net available capacity for sale and indexed to the US inflation rate.
- An *availability incentive payment* is provided as a means of motivation so that the average availability factor of the plant within a given period would not fall below 85 percent. If it is above the target, a specific extra payment would be made to the IPP based on each percentage point of excess availability. If it is below the target, a penalty would apply to the IPP.
- The availability incentive payment was set at $150,000 (2008 prices) for each percentage point by which the availability factor exceeded the 85 percent target. The same figure would apply as a penalty to the IPP for each percentage point of shortfall below this target. In both cases, it was indexed to the US rate of inflation.
- A *variable operating and maintenance cost component* is a specific payment per megawatt hour (MWh) of energy generated in a year, net of auxiliary usage.
- The variable operating and maintenance cost component was estimated at $2.91 in 2008 prices (net of VAT) per MWh of metered electricity delivered to the AEC, again indexed to the US price level. The amount of energy sold to the AEC was measured by the net energy generation in the financial model.
- The fuel required for the plant to operate, LCO, would be purchased and supplied by the AEC. This made the AEC a stakeholder whose costs would vary with the price of oil. It was assumed that ultimately the changes in costs paid by the AEC would be passed on to the consumers of electricity through changes in the electricity tariffs.

- The land on which the project would be located was provided by the government as a grant.
- It was expected that the supply contract would be signed by the independent power producer, both its multinational base (in the US) and its local (African) subsidiary. This company would be responsible for designing, engineering, and supplying to the port of Adukki the gas turbine for the power plant. It would also be contracted for field engineering services and performance testing.
- The Engineering, Procurement and Construction (EPC) contract would be signed with the IPP. The contract consisted of delivering the combustion gas turbine from the port to the plant site, commissioning it and testing it. It also included designing, manufacturing, transporting, commissioning, and testing, and the warranty for all other plant equipment.

19.3.3 Project Financing

The IPP approached the Regional Development Bank (RDB) to finance as much as 70 percent of the US-dollar-denominated investment cost of the proposed project. The IPP proposed that the financing of the investments would be 30 percent by equity and 70 percent through a loan from the RDB on a project finance basis. The loan would be disbursed in 2008 and 2009, covering 70 percent of the respective dollar-denominated investment costs incurred in each year.

The loan principal would be repaid in 14 equal instalments after a two-year grace period. Interest would be paid on the balance of the loan remaining from the previous year. During the construction period, interest would be paid, and would be considered depreciated for tax purposes for a period of five years. The annual interest rate to be charged by the bank was set at a real rate of 6 percent.

19.4 Financial Appraisal of the Proposed IPP

One of the important concepts in assessing an investment initiative is to measure the incremental impact that would occur over and above that which would have occurred in the absence of the initiative. The financial appraisal of the proposed single-cycle power plant was carried out on an incremental basis and identified the "with" and "without" project scenarios. In the "without" project scenario, the private investor would not build the single-cycle plant. The AEC may expand its capacity in the future, through either its own generating operations or purchases from other IPPs. In the "with" project scenario, the private project developer would implement the IPP single-cycle plant. Since this plant did not exist in the past, all the new assets were considered to be incremental investment from the perspective of the IPP.

Since the electricity generated would be sold to the public utility, the financial revenue of the IPP would be determined by the power purchase agreement (PPA). The analysis focused on the financial viability of the IPP investment alone. As for the utility, the overall incremental impact would depend on the difference between the additional revenue collected from the sale of the incremental electricity to end-users and any extra cost incurred from purchasing this electricity from the IPP. The project from the perspective of the utility was assessed at a later stage.

The financial appraisal of the project considered two perspectives, namely those of the lender and of the IPP. For the latter, the appraisal examined the ability of the project to generate enough cash to recover the investment costs and also earn a competitive return on equity. From the lender's perspective, the analysis focused on the capability of the project to meet its debt-repayment obligations.

The starting point of the analysis was to develop the financial cash flow statement of the project from the total investment (or the lender's) point of view. It did not consider how the project would be financed. This perspective enable the analyst to assess the capacity of the project to produce an adequate net cash flow to service the cost of the finance, regardless of the source of project financing.

19.4.1 Financial Viability of IPP

Based on the above assumptions and parameters, the financial cash flow statement from the point of view of total investment was developed. This statement was of particular interest to the RDB, which was approached to finance 70 percent of the project's cost. As the principal project lender, the RDB wanted to assess whether the projected net cash flows would be sufficient to cover the debt obligations. To facilitate this evaluation, the project's expected debt service ratios were calculated.

The annual debt service capacity ratio (ADSCR) measures the annual cash flows generated as a multiple of the scheduled annual debt-repayment obligations. The values of this ratio ranged from 1.24 in 2010, gradually improving year by year and reaching 1.99 in the final year of debt service. As Table 19.2 shows, only in the first year was the ADSCR slightly lower than 1.3, the ratio required by the RDB for contracts of this type. During the following years, this ratio improves and is expected to be well above the lender's benchmark. This means that if there were no uncertainties, the project's cash flow during the debt- service period would amply cover its annual debt obligations. However, in an uncertain environment, the base case ratios may not be realized.

The loan life cover ratio (LLCR) is defined as the present value (PV) of the expected net cash flow during the loan-repayment period divided by the PV of the remaining debt service payments, discounted by the interest rate charged on the loan. This ratio allowed examination of the strength of future cash flows beyond any specific years when the ADSCR is not satisfactory. The cash flow projections indicated that the LLCR was 1.51 in the first year of debt service and would reach 1.99 in the final year.

To summarize, based on the debt service ratios computed, the project's annual net financial receipts were projected in the base case analysis to be at least 24 percent higher than the scheduled annual loan repayment. In the first year of operation, the PV of the stream of the future net cash flows over the loan-repayment period was at least 151 percent of the PV of the total scheduled debt repayments.

Private investors in this project would be expected to receive a rate of return on their equity capital that is no less than the target real rate of return of 13 percent. This can be seen from the above annual financial cash flow statement, adjusted for loan disbursements received and interest and principal paid. The resulting financial cash flow statement after financing is presented in Table 19.3 from the owner's perspective. It addresses the question of whether the flow of financial benefits over the lifetime of the proposed project was sufficient not only to cover capital and operating expenditures but also to provide an adequate rate of return on the owner's investment. This was accomplished by taking the financial net present value (FNPV) after financing, using a 13 percent real rate of return on equity as the discount rate. The FNPV was estimated to be 0.37 million rupees in 2008 prices. This implies that private investors would be able not only to recover all the capital and operating costs, but also to earn more than a 13 percent real rate of return on their investment. The relevant internal rate of return (IRR) would be 13.1 percent.

Table 19.2: Financial Cash Flow Statement from Total Investment Perspetive (million rupees, in 2008 prices)

	2008	2009	2010	2011	2012	2013	2014	2015	2016	2017	2018	2019	2020	2021	2022	2023	2028	2030
Inflows																		
Total PPA revenue	0.00	0.00	42.53	41.40	40.30	39.23	38.19	37.18	36.20	35.25	34.33	33.44	32.57	31.72	30.90	30.10	26.44	0.00
Change in accounts receivable	0.00	0.00	−3.40	−0.19	−0.18	−0.18	−0.17	−0.17	−0.16	−0.16	−0.16	−0.15	−0.15	−0.15	−0.14	−0.14	−0.12	1.89
Government fuel reimbursement	0.00	0.00	76.97	72.64	68.57	64.73	61.11	57.69	54.47	51.44	48.57	45.88	43.33	40.93	38.67	36.53	27.55	0.00
Land subsidy	0.61	0.00	0.00	0.00	0.00	0.00	0.00	0.00	0.00	0.00	0.00	0.00	0.00	0.00	0.00	0.00	0.00	0.00
Total residual values																		
Land	0.00	0.00	0.00	0.00	0.00	0.00	0.00	0.00	0.00	0.00	0.00	0.00	0.00	0.00	0.00	0.00	0.00	0.61
Other assets	0.00	0.00	0.00	0.00	0.00	0.00	0.00	0.00	0.00	0.00	0.00	0.00	0.00	0.00	0.00	0.00	0.00	34.38
Total cash inflows	0.61	0.00	116.10	113.85	108.68	103.78	99.12	94.70	90.51	86.53	82.75	79.16	75.75	72.51	69.43	66.50	53.86	36.88
Outflows																		
Investment costs																		
Land	0.61	0.00	0.00	0.00	0.00	0.00	0.00	0.00	0.00	0.00	0.00	0.00	0.00	0.00	0.00	0.00	0.00	0.61
Other investment costs	96.26	75.64	0.00	0.00	0.00	0.00	0.00	0.00	0.00	0.00	0.00	0.00	0.00	0.00	0.00	0.00	0.00	0.00
Operating and maintenance costs																		
Labour	0.00	0.00	2.67	2.75	2.83	2.92	3.01	3.10	3.19	3.28	3.38	3.48	3.59	3.70	3.81	3.92	4.55	0.00
Operating and maintenance	0.00	0.00	8.26	8.24	8.22	8.20	8.19	8.18	8.17	8.16	8.16	8.15	8.15	8.15	8.15	8.15	8.18	0.00
Fuel requirement cost	0.00	0.00	76.97	72.64	68.57	64.73	61.11	57.69	54.47	51.44	48.57	45.88	43.33	40.93	38.67	36.53	27.55	0.00
Change in working capital	0.00	0.00	−0.11	0.00	0.00	0.00	0.00	0.00	0.00	0.00	0.00	0.00	0.00	0.00	0.00	0.00	0.00	0.07
Net VAT liability	−5.82	−4.57	4.83	4.70	4.57	4.45	4.33	4.21	4.10	3.98	3.88	3.77	3.67	3.57	3.48	3.39	2.96	0.00
Corporate income tax	0.00	0.00	0.29	0.48	0.66	0.81	0.95	2.48	2.47	2.46	2.44	2.42	2.47	2.43	2.39	2.34	2.43	0.00
Total cash outflows	91.05	71.06	92.90	88.81	84.84	81.10	77.57	75.65	72.39	69.32	66.43	63.70	61.21	58.78	56.49	54.34	45.66	0.62
Net cash flow before financing	−90.45	−71.06	23.20	25.05	23.84	22.67	21.55	19.05	18.12	17.21	16.32	15.46	14.54	13.73	12.93	12.16	8.20	36.26
Discounted PV of net cash flow			189.47	176.25	160.27	144.62	129.26	114.17	100.83	87.68	74.70	61.88	49.21	36.75	24.41	12.16		
Discounted PV of load repayment			125.47	113.12	101.38	90.22	79.63	69.58	60.05	51.01	42.45	34.34	26.68	19.42	12.57	6.10		
ADSCR			1.24	1.43	1.47	1.50	1.54	1.47	1.52	1.57	1.62	1.68	1.74	1.81	1.90	1.99		
LLCR			1.51	1.56	1.58	1.60	1.62	1.64	1.68	1.72	1.76	1.80	1.84	1.89	1.94	1.99		

Table 19.3: Financial Cash Flow Statement from the Equity Owner's Perspective (million rupees, in 2008 prices)

	2008	2009	2010	2011	2012	2013	2014	2015	2016	2017	2018	2019	2020	2021	2022	2023	2028	2030
Inflows																		
Total PPA revenue	0.00	0.00	42.53	41.40	40.30	39.23	38.19	37.18	36.20	35.25	34.33	33.44	32.57	31.72	30.90	30.10	26.44	0.00
Change in accounts receivable	0.00	0.00	-3.40	-0.19	-0.18	-0.18	-0.17	-0.17	-0.16	-0.16	-0.16	-0.15	-0.15	-0.15	-0.14	-0.14	-0.12	1.89
Government fuel reimbursement	0.00	0.00	76.97	72.64	68.57	64.73	61.11	57.69	54.47	51.44	48.57	45.88	43.33	40.93	38.67	36.53	27.55	0.00
Land subsidy	0.61	0.00	0.00	0.00	0.00	0.00	0.00	0.00	0.00	0.00	0.00	0.00	0.00	0.00	0.00	0.00	0.00	0.00
Total residual values																		
Land	0.00	0.00	0.00	0.00	0.00	0.00	0.00	0.00	0.00	0.00	0.00	0.00	0.00	0.00	0.00	0.00	0.00	0.61
Other assets	0.00	0.00	0.00	0.00	0.00	0.00	0.00	0.00	0.00	0.00	0.00	0.00	0.00	0.00	0.00	0.00	0.00	34.38
Total cash inflows	0.61	0.00	116.10	113.85	108.68	103.78	99.12	94.70	90.51	86.53	82.75	79.16	75.75	72.51	69.43	66.50	53.86	36.88
Outflows																		
Investment costs																		
Land	0.61	0.00	0.00	0.00	0.00	0.00	0.00	0.00	0.00	0.00	0.00	0.00	0.00	0.00	0.00	0.00	0.00	0.61
Other investment costs	96.26	75.64	0.00	0.00	0.00	0.00	0.00	0.00	0.00	0.00	0.00	0.00	0.00	0.00	0.00	0.00	0.00	0.00
Operating and maintenance costs																		
Labour	0.00	0.00	2.67	2.75	2.83	2.92	3.01	3.10	3.19	3.28	3.38	3.48	3.59	3.70	3.81	3.92	4.55	0.00
Operating and maintenance	0.00	0.00	8.26	8.24	8.22	8.20	8.19	8.18	8.17	8.16	8.16	8.15	8.15	8.15	8.15	8.15	8.18	0.00
Fuel requirement cost	0.00	0.00	76.97	72.64	68.57	64.73	61.11	57.69	54.47	51.44	48.57	45.88	43.33	40.93	38.67	36.53	27.55	0.00
Change in working capital	0.00	0.00	-0.11	0.00	0.00	0.00	0.00	0.00	0.00	0.00	0.00	0.00	0.00	0.00	0.00	0.00	0.00	0.07
Net VAT liability	-5.82	-4.57	4.83	4.70	4.57	4.45	4.33	4.21	4.10	3.98	3.88	3.77	3.67	3.57	3.48	3.39	2.96	0.00
Corporate income tax	0.00	0.00	0.29	0.48	0.66	0.81	0.95	2.48	2.47	2.46	2.44	2.42	2.47	2.43	2.39	2.34	2.43	0.00
Total cash outflows	91.05	71.06	92.90	88.81	84.84	81.10	77.57	75.65	72.39	69.32	66.43	63.70	61.21	58.78	56.49	54.34	45.66	0.62
Net cash flow before financing	-90.45	-71.06	23.20	25.05	23.84	22.67	21.55	19.05	18.12	17.21	16.32	15.46	14.54	13.73	12.93	12.16	8.20	36.26
Loan disbursement	67.39	52.95	0.00	0.00	0.00	0.00	0.00	0.00	0.00	0.00	0.00	0.00	0.00	0.00	0.00	0.00	0.00	0.00
Annual loan repayment	0.00	6.01	18.76	17.48	16.26	15.10	13.99	12.93	11.92	10.96	10.05	9.18	8.35	7.56	6.81	6.10	0.00	0.00
Net cash flow after financing	-23.06	-24.12	4.44	7.57	7.58	7.58	7.56	6.12	6.19	6.24	6.27	6.28	6.19	6.16	6.12	6.06	8.20	36.26
FNPV @13%	0.37																	
FIRR (%)	13.1																	

FNPV: financial net present value; FIRR: financial internal rate of return.

Based on the above analyses from both the total investment perspective and the owner's perspective, the participation of private investors in the IPP appeared to be financially viable and bankable.

However, it should be noted that these financial outcomes would occur entirely because of the particular terms of the PPA. As such, their realization would depend on the long-term viability of the PPA from the perspective of the utility and its customers.

19.4.2 Financial Sensitivity Analysis of the IPP

The results of the financial appraisal presented above were largely determined by the values of the parameters and assumptions acquired from the experience of similar power plants, or from the judgment of experts where information was not available. However, some degree of uncertainty and deviation from these values was to be expected, since the revenue and cost items would be incurred in the future. A sensitivity analysis was therefore carried out to identify the critical parameters, those with the strongest effect on the project's outcome, including the FNPV accruing to the equity owners of the project (discounted at a real rate of 13 percent), the annual debt service capacity, and the LLCR.

Investment Costs Overrun: Given that the main items of capital expenditure were negotiated through the supply and EPC contracts, the likelihood of a cost overrun for the IPP would be small. If provision was to be made for the EPC contract price to be adjusted for any changes or additional work approved by both parties, it would be likely that the IPP would require a higher purchase price from the utility in return. If this was the case, the increase in the investment cost would not affect the FNPV of the IPP.

Load Factor: The load factor of the plant is the ratio of the average amount of energy generated relative to its capacity. In other words, it is a measure of the actual electricity generated during a specific time as compared to the maximum amount that could have been produced over the same period of time. In the base case scenario, it was estimated that the initial load factor would be 80 percent, and that it would decline at 3.4 percent per year over the project's life.

The financial outcome for the IPP is insensitive to changes in the load factor, and follows from the design of the PPA. It was in fact designed so that the investor would be virtually unaffected by differences in intensity of plant use.

Capacity Payment: The capacity payment component of the sales tariff, assumed to be $295,000/MW/year under the PPA, had a very significant impact on the project. As Table 19.4 shows, setting this component at $20,000/MW/year less than that which was proposed would cause a considerable reduction of 9.4 million rupees in the value of the FNPV. This would be equivalent to 7 percent of the project's investment costs. The observed sensitivity to this variable was a result of the fact that the capacity payment represented more than 90 percent of the IPP's revenue. In order for private investors to be able to cover their opportunity costs, the capacity payment would have needed to be greater than $294,200/MW/year. The importance of this component was also confirmed by the reported debt service ratios. The lower the amount set by the contract, the more difficult it would become for the net cash flow of the project to cover the scheduled loan repayment.

Table 19.4: Sensitivity Test of Capacity Payment

Capacity Payment (US$)	FNPV (million rupees)	ADSCR 2010	ADSCR 2011	ADSCR 2012	LLCR 2010	LLCR 2011	LLCR 2012
265,000	−14.07	1.08	1.27	1.30	1.33	1.37	1.39
275,000	−9.05	1.14	1.33	1.37	1.39	1.44	1.45
285,000	−4.28	1.20	1.38	1.41	1.45	1.50	1.52
295,000	0.37	1.24	1.43	1.47	1.51	1.56	1.58
305,000	5.02	1.28	1.48	1.52	1.57	1.62	1.65
315,000	9.68	1.32	1.53	1.57	1.63	1.68	1.71
325,000	14.33	1.36	1.58	1.62	1.69	1.74	1.78
335,000	18.98	1.40	1.63	1.67	1.75	1.81	1.84

Variable Operating and Maintenance Cost Component: This is another component of the sales tariff, which covers operating and maintenance costs, except fuel. Its value was expected to be $2.91 per MWh of the metered electricity sold to the utility. The sensitivity analysis revealed that $1 downward deviation from the proposed rate reduced the FNPV by 2.76 million rupees. To ensure a positive FNPV, this component would need to be set above $2.77 per MWh, keeping all other parameters constant. The debt service ratios were also affected by the changes in this parameter. However, the impact on the overall outcome of the project was much lower than that of the capacity payment.

Domestic Inflation: A higher expected rate of inflation in Adukki lowers the reported FNPV of the project. If the inflation rate in the future was 2 percentage points higher than the assumed 8.9 percent annual rate, i.e. an average of 10.9 percent, the FNPV would decline by 0.71 million rupees. This means that the negative effect of domestic inflation on real accounts receivable, real cash balance, and corporate income tax payments would be greater than the positive effect on real accounts payable. A higher rate of domestic inflation would also adversely affect the ADSCR and LLCR ratios, though not significantly.

Real Interest Rate on Foreign Loan: The real interest rate charged on the US-dollar-denominated loan appeared to be a critical variable for the IPP. If the interest rate to be charged by the lender was 1 percent higher than the 6 percent real rate assumed in the base case, the FNPV of the IPP would become −3.19 million rupees. At a rate higher than 6.10 percent per annum, the FNPV would become negative. The importance of this variable is explained by the fact that the share of debt in financing the cost of investment was high, at 70 percent, and the loan had a variable interest rate tied to the London Interbank Offered Rate (LIBOR). Hence, a small increase in the cost of debt would considerably affect the annual debt repayment and consequently the projected net cash flow. A higher real interest rate on the loan would also be reflected in lower debt coverage ratios, making it more difficult for the IPP to service its debt obligations.

19.5 Financial Appraisal of Alternative Electricity-Generation Technologies

The AEC, the sole off-taker of the generated power, is a state-owned, vertically integrated utility company. Since its main task is to generate and provide electricity to meet the nation's demand for the lowest cost, it would have to ensure that the above IPP proposal of a single-cycle plant was the most cost-effective technology to deliver the required electrical energy. The AEC is also responsible for distribution of the electricity throughout the country.

19.5.1 Financial Feasibility of the Single-Cycle Plant from the AEC's Perspective

When the AEC purchased the electricity generated by the proposed IPP plant, the electricity would be sold to its end-users. The average end-user price in Adukki was estimated to be US18.5¢/kWh.[132] This is equivalent to 223.85 rupees/MWh, net of VAT. For the purpose of the analysis, it was assumed that throughout the life of the project, the real tariff rate would remain unchanged, while the nominal tariff rate, denominated in local currency, would be adjusted in line with domestic inflation. However, if the costs of generation from the IPP were higher than the current electricity retail prices (less transmission and distribution costs), one would expect that the electricity tariff charged to the final consumer would be adjusted to produce sufficient additional revenues for the whole electricity system to cover the higher costs.

In order to evaluate the financial feasibility from the perspective of the AEC, the accounts receivable was assumed to be 15 percent of the total revenue generated by the utility. It was also assumed that 8 percent of the electricity purchased from the IPP would be lost during transmission and distribution to the

---

[132]This tariff was estimated as a weighted average of the tariffs charged to different types of consumers.

end-users.[133] The total cost of transmission and distribution was estimated to be 95 rupees/MWh. Since the utility was responsible for providing the amount of fuel required for the IPP's operation, the cost of LCO would become an important element for the AEC. In the base case, the cost of LCO was assumed to be $367 per ton, or an equivalent of $49 per barrel. Moreover, the accounts payable by the AEC to the IPP was predicted to be 8 percent of the total purchases from IPP. The accounts payable owed to others was estimated to be 15 percent of fuel cost, while the cash balance was 10 percent of the total operating cost incurred by the utility. The real rate of return targeted by the utility was 10 percent. The financial analysis from the perspective of the utility was based on the estimation of incremental financial cash inflows and incremental cash outflows of this investment initiative. This assumed that the utility would need the additional electrical energy supply to meet the future demand for electricity. Therefore, the incremental financial benefits (from the utility's perspective) would be measured by the additional revenue obtained from selling to its customers the electricity generated by the additional capacity of the IPP. The incremental financial cost was measured by the extra cost incurred in obtaining electricity from the IPP. Thus, the outflows included the PPA revenue paid to the IPP, fuel purchases delivered to the IPP, transmission and distribution costs, changes in accounts payable, and changes in cash balances. The overall incremental impact on the utility was determined by the difference between the two.

From the perspective of the AEC, the viability of this capacity expansion option would depend on whether the amount of revenue collected from the sale of electricity was large enough to cover the expenses of obtaining this electricity from the IPP. The resulting net cash flow projections for the utility over the life of the project are presented in Table 19.5. As can be seen, the discounted value of net financial cash flows over the life of the project was −257 million rupees, using a 10 percent real discount rate for equity.

Given the assumptions made, it would not be financially attractive for the utility to expand its electricity-generation capacity by making such an arrangement for an IPP to build and operate a single-cycle electricity-generation plant at the current rate of tariffs charged for the additional electricity sold from this generation plant. The AEC would need to raise the electricity rates charged to some or all of its customers to recover the higher than average generation costs of the plant under consideration.

---

[133]Transmission losses accounted for 3 percent. The distribution losses were assumed to account for the remaining 5 percent.

19.5.2 Financial Feasibility of a Combined-Cycle Plant from the AEC's Perspective

A combined-cycle electricity-generation plant would be an alternative option for expanding the electricity-generation capacity of the system. In a combined-cycle power plant there is a gas turbine, which generates electricity in the same way as for the single-cycle plant, and a steam turbine, which uses the heat dissipated from the first cycle to generate additional electricity. This increases the energy-transformation efficiency of the combined-cycle plant to 60 percent,[134] compared with 32 percent in the case of the single-cycle plant. Another important difference between the two technologies is that the capital cost of a combined-cycle plant is on average 40 percent higher than that of a single-cycle power plant with the same generation capacity.[135] In this case, the combined-cycle plant used for comparison purposes was made up of 84 MW of gas turbines plus 42 MW of steam generation. In total, it would have exactly the same generation capacity, 126 MW, as the single-cycle plant.[136]

To facilitate the analysis, the assumptions and parameters of the combined-cycle power plant were assumed to be the same as those of the single-cycle plant described above, except for the following key parameters.

- The investment cost was assumed to be 40 percent higher than the single-cycle alternative. Table 19.6 presents the estimated investment costs of the combined-cycle plant by component.
- The estimated fuel efficiency was 60 percent. As a result, the amount of fuel required for the combined-cycle power plant would be lower.
- Because of higher capital costs, the PPA would imply that the capacity payment component would increase to $377,200/MW/year, net of VAT. The other two components of the payments to the IPP under the PPA were assumed to be the same as for the single-cycle plant option.

The other assumptions and parameters for the utility were as described in the previous section.

---

[134]Information obtained from:
www.gepower.com/prod_serv/products/gas_turbines_cc/en/h_system/index.htm.
[135]Boyce (2001). See also Poullikkas (2004).
[136]While it would reduce average costs to have two gas turbines and one steam generator with a larger total capacity, for the purposes of this analysis, the total capacities of the two alternative-generation configurations were taken to be identical.

Table 19.5: Financial Cash Flow Statement from the Utility's (AEC) Perspective when the IPP Implements a Single-Cycle Plant (million rupees, in 2008 prices)

	2010	2011	2012	2013	2014	2015	2016	2017	2018	2019	2020	2021	2022	2023	2028	2030
Inflows																
Sales of electricity to end-users – peak	79.05	77.08	75.15	73.27	71.44	69.65	67.91	66.21	64.56	62.94	61.37	59.84	58.34	56.88	50.12	0.00
Sales of electricity to end-users – off-peak	79.05	71.82	65.08	58.80	52.94	47.49	42.41	37.69	33.29	29.21	25.42	21.90	18.64	15.62	3.60	0.00
Change in accounts receivable – peak	-11.86	-0.67	-0.66	-0.64	-0.62	-0.61	-0.59	-0.58	-0.56	-0.55	-0.54	-0.52	-0.51	-0.50	-0.44	6.73
Change in accounts receivable – off-peak	-11.86	0.11	0.13	0.14	0.16	0.17	0.18	0.19	0.20	0.20	0.21	0.22	0.22	0.22	0.24	0.24
Total inflows	134.39	148.34	139.71	131.57	123.92	116.70	109.91	103.51	97.49	91.81	86.47	81.43	76.69	72.23	53.51	6.97
Outflows																
PPA revenue paid to the IPP	42.53	41.40	40.30	39.23	38.19	37.18	36.20	35.25	34.33	33.44	32.57	31.72	30.90	30.10	26.44	0.00
Transmission and distribution cost	59.38	55.92	52.67	49.60	46.71	43.99	41.43	39.02	36.75	34.61	32.60	30.70	28.91	27.23	20.17	0.00
Fuel purchases delivered to the IPP	76.97	72.64	68.57	64.73	61.11	57.69	54.47	51.44	48.57	45.88	43.33	40.93	38.67	36.53	27.55	0.00
Change in accounts payable with the IPP	-3.40	-0.19	-0.18	-0.18	-0.17	-0.17	-0.16	-0.16	-0.16	-0.15	-0.15	-0.15	-0.14	-0.14	-0.12	1.89
Change in accounts payable with others	-11.54	-0.30	-0.28	-0.26	-0.25	-0.24	-0.22	-0.21	-0.20	-0.19	-0.18	-0.17	-0.16	-0.15	-0.12	3.59
Change in desired cash balance	17.89	0.57	0.55	0.52	0.50	0.48	0.46	0.44	0.42	0.40	0.39	0.37	0.36	0.34	0.28	-6.50
Net VAT liability	13.30	12.37	11.50	10.68	9.92	9.20	8.53	7.90	7.31	6.76	6.24	5.75	5.30	4.88	3.14	0.00
Total outflows	195.11	182.42	173.11	164.32	156.00	148.14	140.71	133.68	127.03	120.74	114.79	109.16	103.83	98.79	77.34	-1.02
Net cash flow	-60.72	-34.08	-33.40	-32.74	-32.09	-31.44	-30.80	-30.17	-29.54	-28.93	-28.32	-27.73	-27.14	-26.56	-23.82	7.99
FNPV @10%	-257.30															

FNPV: financial net present value.

The financial appraisal of the utility if the IPP implemented a combined-cycle power plant was conducted in the same manner as for the single-cycle power plant. The cash inflows from the sale of the project's electricity were expected to be identical, since the net energy generation delivered to the AEC was calculated to be the same in both cases. This is because the net energy generation is determined by technical factors such as the maximum available capacity, degradation factor, average availability factor, auxiliary consumption, and plant load factor, which were the same for both plants. As specified earlier, the price of electricity charged to the consumers was 223.85 rupees/MWh, net of VAT. However, the cash outflows associated with the alternative technologies were different.

Table 19.6: Combined-Cycle Power Plant Investment Costs by Component (million dollars, in 2008 prices)

	2008	*2009*	*Total*
Land	0.70	0	0.70
EPC and engineering			
Initial operating tools and mobilization	3.71	2.91	6.62
Gas turbine and related costs	30.64	24.07	54.71
Total EPC contract (excluding VAT)	40.59	31.89	72.48
Other costs	5.55	4.36	9.91
Sub-total	80.49	63.24	143.72
Development costs (excluding VAT)	11.23	8.82	20.05
Financing costs	12.94	10.16	23.10
Total investment cost	**105.35**	**82.22**	**187.57**

EPC: engineering, procurement and construction

The FNPV for the utility of using the discount rate of 10 percent real was −123.4 million rupees. This means that the incremental financial benefits realized by the utility during the project's life with constant real electricity tariffs would not be sufficient to cover its incremental costs. The utility, although losing financially, would be better off by 133.9 million rupees over the project's life using the combined-cycle technology, compared to building and operating a single-cycle plant. This estimate was based on same assumptions and parameter values as those used for the analysis of the single-cycle power plant.

19.5.3 Financial Investment in Alternative Technologies from the AEC's Perspective

It is important to identify the main differences in costs between the two technologies that would make it more beneficial for the AEC to purchase electricity from an IPP using a combined-cycle plant instead of the single-cycle plant.

The specific features of these two technologies would affect the AEC's expenditures in two ways. On the one hand, a more expensive combined-cycle plant would require a capacity payment, which must be almost 28 percent higher in order for the IPP to be willing to invest in a combined-cycle plant. On the other hand, the higher energy-transformation efficiency achieved by the combined-cycle plant would reduce the amount of fuel required for this plant to operate. In other words, the projected PPA payment by the AEC in the case of the combined-cycle plant was expected to be higher than for the single-cycle plant, while the projected expense on fuel purchases delivered to the combined-cycle plant was lower.

Table 19.7 presents the difference in the level of expenditures (PPA payment and fuel purchases delivered to the IPP) incurred by the AEC if the IPP was to build a combined-cycle plant, less the expenditures of the AEC if the IPP built a single-cycle plant. The divergence in the amount of PPA payments and fuel purchases throughout the life of the project was estimated at different plant load factors and fuel prices simultaneously. To make these expenditures comparable, their PV was calculated using the 10 percent real rate of return required by the utility as the discount rate.

It appears that the higher the load factor and the price of fuel, the more costly it would become for the AEC to obtain electricity from the single-cycle plant compared to the combined-cycle alternative. When the load factor was high, the amount of fuel required for the plant to operate would be greater. At higher fuel prices, this would translate into higher fuel expenditures incurred by the utility if a single-cycle plant were to be employed. At an average plant load factor of 80 percent and fuel costing $49 per barrel, the AEC would save almost 128 million rupees if the IPP were to use a combined-cycle plant as opposed to the single-cycle plant. This implies that the overall electricity tariff rates charged would need to be higher to pay for the higher fuel costs if the additional electricity obtained by the utility was generated using a single-cycle plant.

It can also be seen from Table 19.7 that if the AEC's cost of capital was 10 percent, then for a price of $49 per barrel of oil, the utility should choose the single-cycle plant only if it were going to use it on average 20 percent of the time, or approximately 1,750 hours per year. If it needed a plant that would operate in the system for more hours per year, it would be much better for it to employ an IPP that was using a combined-cycle generation plant. With oil costing $79 per barrel, the single-cycle plant would be attractive only if it were only going to be used 10 percent of the time, or about 876 hours a year. This is completely unrealistic for any new generation plant that is being introduced into a mature electricity-generation system. At an average price of $79 per barrel and an 80 percent load factor, the selection of the single-cycle plant would cost the public utility an additional amount over the lifetime of the project equal to 250 million rupees (in PV terms using a 10 percent discount rate), or 1.5 times the entire capital cost of the single-cycle plant.

Table 19.7: Expenditure Savings from Choosing a Combined-Cycle Plant Rather Than a Single-Cycle Plant (PV@10%) (million rupees, in 2008 prices)

Initial Plant Load Factor (%)	Light Crude Oil Price (US$/barrel)								
	30	31	45	**49**	55	59	69	79	89
10	−46.04	−45.12	−32.94	−29.57	−24.24	−20.76	−12.06	−3.36	5.34
20	−28.94	−27.41	−7.25	−1.68	7.15	12.91	27.31	41.71	56.11
30	−11.84	−9.70	18.44	26.21	38.54	46.58	66.68	86.78	106.88
40	5.26	8.01	44.13	54.10	69.93	80.25	106.05	131.85	157.65
50	17.09	20.27	61.91	73.41	91.66	103.56	133.30	163.05	192.80
60	28.48	32.06	79.01	91.98	112.55	125.97	159.51	193.05	226.59
70	39.51	43.48	95.59	109.98	132.80	147.69	184.91	222.13	259.34
80	50.26	54.61	111.73	**127.50**	152.53	168.85	209.65	250.45	291.25
90	60.77	65.49	127.52	144.65	171.82	189.54	233.84	278.15	322.45
100	71.07	76.16	143.00	161.46	190.74	209.83	257.57	305.31	353.05

The PVs in Table 19.7 were estimated using a real financial discount rate of 10 percent. This rate is likely to be too high considering that the relevant discount rate should reflect the real weighted cost of capital. For a public utility, a real rate of 6 percent would more closely reflect the AEC's real weighted average cost of capital. Table 19.8 reports the PVs of the cost differences between the combined-cycle versus the single-cycle technology using 6 percent as the discount rate.

The plan was to use this plant at an initial load factor of 80 percent. With this load factor and an average real cost of fuel of $49 per barrel, it was found that the combined-cycle plant had a PV of costs that was 365 million rupees lower than that of the single-cycle plant. At an average price of fuel of $79 per barrel, the cost advantage of the combined-cycle plant had a PV as of 2008 of 572 million rupees, or more than 3.5 times the entire capital cost of the single-cycle generation plant.

In this case, even if the price of oil was as low as $31 per barrel, and even if the plant was to be utilized as little as 10 percent of the time, it would still not be financially worthwhile for AEC to contract for the services of a single-cycle plant.

To summarize, the financial appraisal of the technology under the different scenarios discussed above indicated that it would be more advantageous for the AEC to purchase electricity from an IPP using a combined-cycle plant, since this technology is much more fuel-efficient and hence less costly at high load factors. The fuel consumption at high load factors had a large impact on the AEC's cash flow projections since it was subsidized by the utility. Hence, from the perspective of the public utility, a combined-cycle-technology IPP would be a better private partner from which to purchase electricity. However, under the provision that the utility supplies fuel to the IPP for free, private investors would have preferred to implement the single-cycle plant since it would require less capital, and hence, would be easier to finance.

Table 19.8: Expenditure Savings from Choosing a Combined-Cycle Plant Rather Than a Single-Cycle Plant (PV@6%) (million rupees, in 2008 prices)

Initial Plant Load Factor (%)	Light Crude Oil Price (US$/barrel)								
	30	31	45	**49**	55	59	69	79	89
10	70.74	72.38	93.99	99.96	109.43	115.60	131.03	146.47	161.90
20	101.88	104.61	140.37	150.25	165.92	176.14	201.68	227.23	252.78
30	133.03	136.83	186.75	200.54	222.41	236.68	272.34	308.00	343.65
40	164.17	169.05	233.13	250.83	278.91	297.22	342.99	388.76	434.53
50	183.01	188.54	261.23	281.30	313.14	333.91	385.82	437.74	489.66
60	200.93	207.09	287.97	310.30	345.73	368.84	426.60	484.37	542.13
70	218.16	224.92	313.67	338.18	377.05	402.41	465.80	529.19	592.58
80	234.83	242.17	338.53	**365.15**	407.36	434.89	503.73	572.56	641.39
90	251.03	258.94	362.71	391.37	436.83	466.48	540.60	614.76	688.85
100	266.84	275.30	386.30	416.96	465.59	497.30	576.69	655.88	735.16

19.5.4 Financial Sensitivity Analysis from the AEC's Perspective

A sensitivity analysis was carried out to assess the financial implications for the AEC of changes in key parameters employed in the model. Ultimately, these financial impacts on the electrical utility would be borne by the utility's consumers as it attempts to recover its costs.

Plant Load Factor: The load factor measures the average output compared to the maximum capacity that the plant could theoretically generate during the year. The assumption made in our model was that the load factor was expected to start at 80 percent and then to decline by 3.4 percent per year. The results of the sensitivity analysis for the plant load factor are shown in Table 19.9. A higher plant load factor caused the FNPV of the AEC to become less negative for both the single- and combined-cycle plants. The FNPV of the utility if the single-cycle technology was employed by the IPP is not very sensitive to increases in the plant load factor. However, this is not the case if a combined-cycle plant was to be implemented by the IPP. Increasing the load factor of the combined-cycle plant by 10 percent improved the FNPV of the AEC by almost 18 million rupees (compared to 1 million rupees in the case of the single cycle). This is because the increase in financial revenues from increased sales would be greater than the additional fuel costs; hence, the combined-cycle plant would make a greater contribution to the FNPV if more generation (with a higher load factor) was to take place. The amount of fuel savings resulting from the combined-cycle alternative is shown in the last column of Table 19.9.

Table 19.9: Sensitivity Test of Plant Load Factor (million rupees, in 2008 prices)

Load Factor (%)	FNPV-SC	FNPV-CC	FNPV-CC less FNPV-SC
17	−263.89	−266.39	−2.50
70	−258.13	−141.59	116.53
75	−257.70	−132.43	125.28
80	−257.29	−123.37	133.92
85	−256.87	−114.41	142.46
90	−256.46	−105.55	150.92
95	−256.06	−96.77	159.29
100	−255.66	−88.07	167.59

Fuel Price: The price of fuel plays an important role in the FNPV of the AEC, as shown by the results of the sensitivity test in Table 19.10. An increase in the price of fuel would raise the utility's operating expenditure considerably, resulting in a negative impact on its net cash flow. In particular, the FNPV of the utility was affected more negatively by a change in fuel prices when it used the electricity generated by the single-cycle plant than when it used the combined-cycle technology. If the price of LCO was to increase from $49 per barrel to $52 per barrel, the FNPV would decrease by almost 27 million rupees for the single-cycle plant compared with 14 million rupees for the combined-cycle plant. Thus, keeping everything else the same, the FNPV of the utility was expected to be twice as sensitive to fluctuations in the price of fuel if the private investor built the proposed single-cycle plant. However, in either case fuel price changes would ultimately pass through to final users.

Table 19.10: Sensitivity Test of Fuel Price (million rupees, in 2008 prices)

Crude Oil Price (US$/Barrel)	FNPV-SC	FNPV-CC	FNPV-CC less FNPV-SC
41	−188.50	−86.68	101.82
44	−214.51	−100.56	113.95
46	−231.85	−109.80	122.05
49	−257.29	−123.37	133.92
52	−283.88	−137.55	146.33
54	−301.22	−146.80	154.42
71	−327.23	−160.67	166.56

Real Exchange Rate: The real exchange rate is a crucial parameter for the electrical utility, as shown in Table 19.11. Devaluation of the Adukkian rupee in relation to the US dollar would worsen the FNPV of the utility, no matter which technology was to be chosen. Nevertheless, there would be a difference in the magnitude of the impact of the real exchange rate movement on the utility's FNPV between the two technologies. A change in the real exchange rate from 1.21 rupees to 1.31 rupees per US dollar would cause the FNPV of the AEC to decrease by almost 45 million rupees if the combined-cycle technology was to be employed. The same devaluation would cause a reduction of 56 million rupees in the FNPV if a single-cycle plant was built. The devaluation of the domestic currency would affect the single-cycle plant more since it would require more fuel to operate. Given that the fuel would be imported and priced in US dollars, the impact of the currency devaluation on the FNPV of the utility would be substantial.

Table 19.11: Sensitivity Test of Real Exchange Rate (million rupees, in 2008 prices)

Real Exchange Rate (rupees/dollar)	FNPV-SC	FNPV-CC	FNPV-CC less FNPV-SC
0.90	−85.01	14.60	99.61
1.01	−146.14	−34.36	111.78
1.11	−201.71	−78.86	122.85
1.21	**−257.29**	**−123.37**	133.92
1.31	−312.86	−167.87	144.98
1.41	−368.43	−212.38	156.05
1.51	−424.01	−256.89	167.12
1.61	−479.58	−301.39	178.19

19.5.5 Estimation of the Levellized Financial Costs of the Single-Cycle and Combined-Cycle Plants

Instead of estimating the FNPV from the AEC's point of view for the two different types of plants, it would be possible to measure the financial cost-effectiveness of the two plants by estimating their levellized financial cost of generation. This is carried out by estimating the PV of the full life cycle costs associated with each of the alternative plants and dividing these estimated total financial costs by the PV of the amount of electrical energy generated by the corresponding plant. The results of this analysis are presented in Table 19.12. The difference between the levellized financial costs was 0.034 rupees per kWh, or $0.028 per kWh.

In this case, either of the two technologies would improve the reliability of the electricity supply; however, the single-cycle technology is far more expensive for the public utility.

Table 19.12: Levellized Financial Cost of Energy for the Base Case Scenario

Category	Single-Cycle Plant	Combined-Cycle Plant	Cost: CC less SC
PV of financial cost (million rupees):			
Investment costs	164.46	230.24	65.78
Operating and maintenance costs	76.16	76.16	0
Fuel purchased and delivered to the IPP	377.93	201.56	−176.37
Total	618.55	507.97	−110.58
PV of net energy generated (MWh)	3,297,471	3,297,471	-
Levellized cost of energy:			
Cost expressed in rupees/kWh	0.188	0.154	−0.034
Cost expressed in US$/kWh	0.154	0.127	−0.028

19.6 Economic Appraisal

An economic appraisal evaluates the impacts of the project on the entire society and determines whether the project would contribute to the country's wealth and the economic welfare of its residents. In the context of applying the integrated appraisal framework, the economic evaluation is directly linked to the consolidated financial cash flow statement of the project. The economic analysis is structured so as to be fully consistent with the financial analysis, and is based on the project's financial values and parameters.

These financial values are converted into their respective economic values by making a series of adjustments. The relationship between the financial and economic value of a particular good or service is called a commodity-specific conversion factor (CSCF). This is calculated as the ratio of the economic value to the financial price. Once the conversion factors are computed, they are multiplied by the respective financial values in order to obtain the corresponding economic values.

In this case, the financial analysis from the perspective of the AEC concluded that the choice of technology for this power project was very important. It was estimated that if the plant load factor was higher than 35 percent when the price of fuel exceeded $31 per barrel, the PV of total costs incurred by the utility discounted at 10 percent real for the single-cycle plant would surpass that of the combined-cycle plant. In addition, if the price of fuel was $49 per barrel and if the load factor was above 21 percent, the single-cycle plant would be more expensive than the combined-cycle plant. The first step in the economic appraisal for this project was to identify the technology that would increase the electricity supply at the lowest cost from the economic perspective.

This involved identifying the technology that would result in the lowest resource cost of energy for generating the same amount of power.

19.6.1 Economic Valuation of the Project's Costs

The economic costs of the project were the incremental costs of the country's resources used in the project. Apart from the financial values projected in the consolidated financial statement, a number of economic assumptions and parameters used in the analysis had to be made in order to estimate the economic costs of generating additional electricity by the project.

a) National Parameters

- The economic opportunity cost of capital (EOCK) for Adukki was estimated to be 12 percent real.[137]
- The foreign exchange premium (FEP) on tradable goods was estimated to be 8 percent.
- The shadow price of non-tradable outlays (SPNTO) was estimated to be 1 percent higher than its market price.

b) Economic Value of Tradable Goods and Services

The financial prices of tradable goods are determined in the international markets, and their values may be affected by import duties, VAT, excise taxes, export taxes, and subsidies. The economic values of these items will be free of these distortions, but they must account for the FEP. The tradable inputs of this project, and their related taxes, are described below.

- Imported capital items, including the initial operating tools and mobilization, gas turbine and its related costs, as well as other costs, were not subject to any import duty or VAT.
- The LCO was imported and was subject to a 5 percent import duty levied on the CIF (cost, insurance, and freight) price. It was exempted from VAT.
- Major maintenance materials, both fixed and variable components, were subject to an average tariff of 12 percent. These costs were not subject to VAT.
- Operating and maintenance materials were subject to 20 percent import duty. The 13 percent VAT was not applied on these items.
- Tradable services such as advisory and consulting fees were taxed at 13 percent VAT.

---

[137]The methodology for measuring this parameter is outlined in Chapter 8. See, for example, Kuo et al. (2003).

c) Economic Value of Non-tradable Goods

Non-tradable goods are those not traded internationally. Their economic value is determined by their demand price, their supply price, and the various distortions associated with the market, as well as a series of intermediate inputs required to produce the goods in question. The methodology is outlined in Chapter 11. The non-tradable goods and services used in this project are listed below.

- Infrastructure and civil works were the non-tradable items covered by the EPC contract.
- Non-tradable inputs of the infrastructure and civil works were sourced domestically and were subject to 13 percent VAT when purchased.

d) Labour

- The economic opportunity cost of labour (EOCL) was estimated using the supply price approach discussed in Chapter 12. This approach starts with the market wage paid by the project in the specific region and makes all the necessary adjustments with regard to personal income taxes as well as social security contributions to arrive at the EOCL.
- The labour sourced domestically was composed of 90 percent skilled and 10 percent unskilled workers. The skilled labour was subject to 25 percent personal income tax, whereas the unskilled category was subject to a rate of 15 percent. The corresponding social security contributions were estimated to be 17.5 percent and 10 percent, respectively. It was estimated that in the absence of this project, skilled and unskilled labour would have spent 90 percent and 50 percent of their time, respectively, employed elsewhere.
- Foreign engineers were also employed by the project to work on the activities covered by the EPC contract. The estimation of the EOCL in the case of foreign labour was similar to the approach used for domestic labour, except that it took into account the foreign exchange premium associated with net income repatriated abroad and the amount of VAT collected from the workers' consumption in Adukki. The share of the income repatriated was estimated to be 65 percent. The social security contributions and income tax were assumed to be 15 percent and 25 percent, respectively.

e) Working Capital

- The conversion factor for changes in the desired cash balance was taken as 1.
- The change in the AEC accounts payable with other suppliers had the same conversion factor as fuel.

Using the information presented above, a series of CSCFs for the project outlays was estimated, and is summarized in Table 19.13.

Table 19.13: Summary of CSCFs

Category	CSCF
Investment costs	
Land	1.000
Initial operating tools and mobilization	1.074, same as imported capital items
Gas turbine and related costs	1.074, same as imported capital items
Total EPC contract	0.683 average (infrastructure and civil works, and foreign labour)
Other costs	1.074, same as imported capital items
Development costs	0.937, average tradable and non-tradable services
Financing costs	1.000
Operating and maintenance fixed costs	
General and administration	0.810, same as skilled labour
LTSA and others	0.963, same as major maintenance conversion factor
Operating and maintenance variable costs	
Water	0.918, same as non-tradable good
Chemicals and lubrication oil	1.029, same as fuel conversion factor
Transmission and distribution costs	1.074, same as imported capital items
Fuel purchases delivered to the IPP	1.029
Change in accounts payable for the IPP	0.934, average of CSCFs for major operation and maintenance materials, tradable services (advisory and consulting fees), tradable goods (water) and services (development fees)
Change in accounts payable for the AEC (fuel purchases)	1.029
Change in desired cash balance for the IPP	1.000
Change in desired cash balance for the AEC	1.000

Labour
    Unskilled
    Skilled
    Foreign
	
	0.625
	0.810
	0.604

19.6.2 Economic Evaluation of Selecting an IPP

An economic analysis begins with an economic cost–effectiveness analysis to compare the levellized energy cost of the alternative electricity-generation options when they provide the same amount of electricity. The levellized energy cost methodology is usually used to compare two or more technologies that have different characteristics. In the current case, the two technologies differed in terms of investment costs and fuel usage. The levellized cost was computed as the PV of the total economic costs (including investment cost, operating costs, and fuel expenditure) incurred over the project's life divided by the PV of the net electricity generated by the plant during the same period of time. This represents the costs that ultimately would have to be borne by consumers or financed by the state-owned utility.

Since the net electricity generated by the combined-cycle plant in this case was exactly the same as that of the single-cycle plant over the same period of time, the first step in the economic appraisal of the two alternatives was to compare all the costs expressed in the PV of the resource costs discounted by the real economic cost of capital, which is 12 percent in Adukki. These results are displayed in the upper part of Table 19.14 for the two options. The incremental costs (or cost savings) of the combined-cycle plant compared to those of the single-cycle plant are shown in the lower part of the table. Comparison of these results shows that 120.85 million rupees (in 2008 prices) could be saved by investing in a combined-cycle plant instead of a single-cycle plant, using our assumptions for the base case scenario.

Table 19.14: Economic Resource Costs for Combined-Cycle and Single-Cycle Alternatives (million rupees, in 2008 prices)

	2008	2009	2010	2011	2012	2013	2014	2015	2016	2017	2018	2019	2020	2021	2022	2023	2028	2030
Combined-Cycle Plant																		
Investment costs																		
Land	0.85	0.00	0.00	0.00	0.00	0.00	0.00	0.00	0.00	0.00	0.00	0.00	0.00	0.00	0.00	0.00	0.00	-0.85
Other investment costs	120.31	94.53	0.00	0.00	0.00	0.00	0.00	0.00	0.00	0.00	0.00	0.00	0.00	0.00	0.00	0.00	0.00	-42.97
Operating and maintenance costs																		
Labour	0.00	0.00	2.11	2.18	2.24	2.31	2.38	2.45	2.52	2.60	2.68	2.76	2.84	2.93	3.01	3.10	3.59	0.00
Other fixed operating and maintenance costs	0.00	0.00	6.79	6.80	6.82	6.84	6.85	6.87	6.88	6.90	6.92	6.93	6.95	6.97	6.98	7.00	7.10	0.00
Fuel purchases delivered to the IPP	0.00	0.00	42.22	39.85	37.61	35.51	33.52	31.65	29.88	28.22	26.65	25.17	23.77	22.45	21.21	20.04	15.11	0.00
Other variable operating and maintenance costs	0.00	0.00	1.08	1.04	1.00	0.97	0.94	0.91	0.88	0.85	0.82	0.80	0.78	0.76	0.74	0.72	0.64	0.00
Transmission and distribution cost	0.00	0.00	63.79	60.07	56.58	53.28	50.18	47.26	44.51	41.92	39.48	37.18	35.01	32.98	31.06	29.25	21.67	-4.07
Change in working capital	0.00	0.00	8.98	0.38	0.37	0.35	0.34	0.33	0.32	0.31	0.30	0.29	0.29	0.28	0.27	0.26	0.23	0.22
Total costs	121.16	94.53	124.97	110.32	104.62	99.26	94.21	89.46	85.00	80.79	76.84	73.13	69.64	66.36	63.27	60.37	48.34	-47.88
PV @12%	796.50																	
Single-Cycle Plant																		
Investment costs																		
Land	0.61	0.00	0.00	0.00	0.00	0.00	0.00	0.00	0.00	0.00	0.00	0.00	0.00	0.00	0.00	0.00	0.00	-0.61
Other investment costs	85.94	67.52	0.00	0.00	0.00	0.00	0.00	0.00	0.00	0.00	0.00	0.00	0.00	0.00	0.00	0.00	0.00	-30.69
Operating and maintenance costs																		
Labour	0.00	0.00	2.11	2.18	2.24	2.31	2.38	2.45	2.52	2.60	2.68	2.76	2.84	2.93	3.01	3.10	3.59	0.00
Other fixed operating and maintenance costs	0.00	0.00	6.79	6.80	6.82	6.84	6.85	6.87	6.88	6.89	6.92	6.93	6.95	6.97	6.98	7.00	7.10	0.00
Fuel purchases delivered to the IPP	0.00	0.00	79.16	74.72	70.53	66.58	62.85	59.34	56.03	52.91	49.96	47.19	44.57	42.10	39.77	37.58	28.33	0.00
Other variable operating and maintenance costs	0.00	0.00	1.08	1.04	1.00	0.97	0.94	0.91	0.88	0.85	0.82	0.80	0.78	0.76	0.74	0.72	0.64	0.00
Transmission and distribution cost	0.00	0.00	63.79	60.07	56.58	53.28	50.18	47.26	44.51	41.92	39.48	37.18	35.01	32.98	31.06	29.25	21.67	0.00
Change in working capital	0.00	0.00	5.94	0.27	0.26	0.25	0.24	0.24	0.23	0.22	0.21	0.21	0.21	0.20	0.19	0.19	0.17	-2.84
Total costs	86.54	67.52	158.87	145.08	137.43	130.22	123.44	117.03	110.05	105.39	100.07	95.07	90.36	85.93	81.76	77.84	61.50	-34.14
PV @12%	917.35																	

Table 19.14 (continued)

	2008	2009	2010	2011	2012	2013	2014	2015	2016	2017	2018	2019	2020	2021	2022	2023	2028	2030
Cost savings from choosing a Combined-Cycle rather than a Single-Cycle Plant																		
Investment costs	−34.61	−27.01	0.00	0.00	0.00	0.00	0.00	0.00	0.00	0.00	0.00	0.00	0.00	0.00	0.00	0.00	0.00	12.52
Fuel purchases delivered to the IPP	0.00	0.00	36.94	34.87	32.91	31.07	29.33	27.96	26.15	24.69	23.32	22.02	20.80	19.65	18.56	17.54	13.22	0.00
Change in working capital	0.00	0.00	−3.04	−0.11	−0.11	−0.10	−0.10	−0.10	−0.09	−0.09	−0.09	−0.08	−0.08	−0.08	−0.07	−0.07	−0.06	1.22
Total	−34.61	−27.01	33.90	34.76	32.81	30.97	29.23	27.60	26.05	24.60	23.23	21.94	20.72	19.57	18.49	17.46	13.16	13.74
PV @12%	120.85																	

These results for the base case scenario assumed that both plants would begin with an 80 percent load factor and that the price of fuel was $49 per barrel. Using these parameters, the estimated levellized energy cost as shown in Table 19.15 was 0.146 rupees per kWh for the combined-cycle plant, which was lower than the 0.183 rupees per kWh required for the single-cycle plant. This is equivalent to $0.121 per kWh and $0.152 per kWh, respectively. The difference between the levellized energy costs of the two technologies amounted to 0.037 rupees ($0.031) per kWh. This translates into a 16.5 percent increase in the retail electricity rates that the AEC would have to charge consumers on this quantity of electricity in order to cover the additional costs that would otherwise not be necessary.[138]

Table 19.15: Levellized Economic Cost of Energy for the Base Case Scenario

Category	Combined-Cycle Plant	Single-Cycle Plant	Cost Savings from Choosing a Combined-Cycle versus a Single-Cycle Plant
PV of economic cost* (million rupees):			
Investment costs	205.57	146.83	−58.74
Operating and maintenance costs	68.95	68.95	0
Fuel purchased and delivered to the IPP	207.32	388.72	181.40
Total	481.84	604.51	122.67
PV of net energy generated (MWh)	3,297,471	3,297,471	-
Levellized cost of energy: Cost expressed in rupees/kWh	0.146	0.183	0.037
Cost expressed in US$/kWh	0.121	0.152	0.031

*The economic costs shown in this table differ slightly from those in Table 19.14 because they include the transmission and distribution costs as well as changes in working capital.

As was pointed out in the financial analysis, the higher the load factor and the higher the price of fuel, the more costly it would be for the AEC to obtain the electricity from the single-cycle plant than from the combined-cycle plant. The next step was to make a similar comparison from the economic (as distinct from the financial) point of view.

Table 19.16 shows the PV of the differences in total economic costs (fuel plus capital) over the life of the project if a combined-cycle plant rather than a

---

[138]The AEC would be likely to build these costs into its overall rate structure so that a higher tariff would be charged on the consumption of all customers. Hence, the increase in the average rate would be substantially less than 16.5 percent.

single-cycle plant were to be selected. Table 19.17 presents the results expressed in a different way by measuring the levellized economic cost of energy over the life of the project. They were both simulated for different combinations of plant load factors and fuel prices. For instance, implementing the combined-cycle plant for the base case scenario (fuel cost at $49 per barrel and a load factor of 80 percent) would save 120.85 million rupees in 2008 prices over its lifetime. Equally, it had a levellized cost of generation 0.037 rupees/kWh cheaper than that of the single-cycle plant.

Table 19.16: Resource Cost Savings from Selecting a Combined-Cycle Plant Rather Than a Single-Cycle Plant (million rupees, in 2008 prices)

Initial Plant Load Factor (%)	Light Crude Oil Price (US$/barrel)								
	30	31	45	**49**	55	59	69	79	89
10	−35.85	−35.24	−24.42	−21.02	−16.69	−12.88	−5.25	2.37	10.10
20	−20.80	−19.78	−1.87	3.76	10.92	17.23	29.85	42.47	55.26
30	−5.75	−4.32	20.68	28.54	38.53	47.34	64.96	82.57	100.43
40	9.31	11.14	43.23	53.31	66.14	77.45	100.06	122.67	145.59
50	20.07	22.19	59.35	71.02	85.88	98.97	125.16	151.34	177.88
60	30.45	32.85	74.88	88.10	104.91	119.72	149.35	178.98	209.00
70	40.52	43.19	89.97	104.67	123.39	139.87	172.84	205.81	239.22
80	50.35	53.28	104.69	**120.85**	141.41	159.53	195.76	231.99	268.71
90	59.97	63.17	119.11	136.69	159.06	178.78	218.20	257.62	297.58
100	69.42	72.87	133.26	152.24	176.40	197.68	240.24	282.79	325.93

Note: The resource cost savings from choosing the combined-cycle plant rather than the single-cycle plant for the base case (120.85 million rupees) is slightly different from that presented in Table 19.15 (122.67million rupees) because the former takes into account changes in working capital, where the latter does not.

Table 19.17: Cost Savings per (Levellized) kWh from Selecting a Combined-Cycle Plant Rather Than a Single-Cycle Plant (rupees/kWh, in 2008 prices)

Initial Plant Load Factor (%)	Light Crude Oil Price (US$/barrel)								
	30	31	45	**49**	55	59	69	79	89
10	−0.072	−0.071	−0.049	−0.042	−0.033	−0.025	−0.009	0.006	0.022
20	−0.021	−0.020	−0.001	0.005	0.012	0.018	0.031	0.044	0.058
30	−0.003	−0.003	0.015	0.020	0.027	0.033	0.045	0.057	0.069
40	0.005	0.006	0.023	0.028	0.034	0.040	0.052	0.063	0.075
50	0.009	0.010	0.026	0.031	0.038	0.044	0.055	0.066	0.078
60	0.012	0.013	0.029	0.034	0.040	0.046	0.057	0.068	0.080
70	0.014	0.015	0.031	0.036	0.042	0.048	0.059	0.070	0.081
80	0.016	0.017	0.032	**0.037**	0.043	0.049	0.060	0.071	0.082
90	0.017	0.018	0.033	0.038	0.045	0.050	0.061	0.072	0.083
100	0.018	0.019	0.035	0.039	0.046	0.051	0.062	0.073	0.084

The results were similar to the conclusions reached in the financial analysis when the AEC's expenditures were discounted at 10 percent. That is, if the price of crude oil was higher than $31 per barrel, it would be economically worthwhile to implement the combined-cycle plant so long as the initial load factor was greater than 40 percent. If the price of oil was higher than $45, the combined-cycle plant should be chosen over the single-cycle plant, even if the load factor was as low as 20 percent. These results implied a very substantial negative impact on the prices that would have to be paid by the retail consumers if a single-cycle plant was to be built. Furthermore, as it would involve the waste of fossil fuel, the implementation of a single-cycle generation plant would create more environmental damage than would otherwise be the case.

Because of the lower capital outlays required from private investors in the implementation of a single-cycle generation plant, and because the fuel costs will be borne by the public sector off-taker of the electricity, private investors often prefer to employ single-cycle gas turbine technology. Furthermore, as the capital costs are explicit in the PPA and the fuel costs are not, it might appear to decision-makers that the single-cycle generation plant would be less costly, while in fact it would be much more costly when the full life cycle costs are taken into account.

In the following section it is assumed that these perverse financial incentives have caused decision-makers to select the single-cycle (gas turbine) technology for the IPP, and the stakeholder implications of such a decision are considered.

19.7 Stakeholder Impacts

The purpose of a stakeholder analysis is to identify the impacts that the proposed technology has on different interest groups (stakeholders) in society. Quantification of these impacts is an important part of the analysis, and allows us to determine how much each stakeholder would gain or lose as a result of the project implementation. To be able to undertake this analysis, the projected benefits and costs from the financial and economic appraisal are used.

19.7.1 Identification of Stakeholders and Externalities

The stakeholder analysis of the BLEG project was conducted in order to identify which segments of society in Adukki would benefit and which, if any, would lose from the implementation of the combined-cycle plant instead of the single-cycle plant. This representation emphasizes the fact that the proposed technology would create two types of net benefits: financial net benefits, reaped by the parties that have a financial interest in the project, and externalities, which would accrue to the different segments of Adukkian society affected by the proposed technology.

The stakeholder analysis involved the following steps.

1. The stakeholder impacts of the project were identified item by item by subtracting the financial cash flow statement from the economic statement of benefits and costs.
2. The PV of each line item's flow of externalities was calculated over the life of the project,[139] using the EOCK in Adukki as the discount rate.
3. The PV of the externalities was allocated to the affected groups in the economy.

The reconciliation among the incremental financial flows of the utility, economic resource flows, and distributional impacts of the proposed combined-cycle plant compared to the single-cycle plant is demonstrated in Table 19.18. To ensure that the analysis is performed in a consistent way, the PV of the economic cost savings must equal the PV of financial cost savings plus the PV of the difference in externalities. In other words, the combined-cycle plant would have lower economic costs of 120.85 million rupees; this is composed of financial cost savings of 108.83 million rupees and positive externalities of 12.02 million rupees. This is shown in Table 19.18.

Table 19.18: Present Value of Cost Savings for a Combined-Cycle versus a Single-Cycle Plant (million rupees, in 2008 prices)

	Financial Cost Savings	Externality Savings	Sum of Financial Cost plus Externality Savings	Total Savings of Economic Cost
Investment costs				
Land	−0.24	0.02	−0.22	−0.22
Other Assets	−64.38	6.91	−57.48	−57.48
Operating and maintenance costs				
Fixed costs	0	0	0	0
Variable costs:				
Fuel	176.37	5.04	181.40	181.40
Others	0	0	0	0
Change in taxes and working capital	−2.91	0.05	−2.86	−2.86
Total costs	108.83	12.02	120.85	120.85

---

[139]The value of externalities such as import duties, taxes, consumer surplus, and producer surplus can be measured by the difference between the financial value and the economic value associated with the distortions of the item in question.

19.7.2 Distributive Impacts

In this case, the difference in the PV of financial costs would ultimately be borne by electricity consumers through higher electricity tariffs. The PPA was designed to compensate the private owners of the plant for differences in financial costs they would incur.

The externalities generated by this type of power project are perceived by the government and electricity consumers. In this case, the combined-cycle plant would be supplying the same amount of electricity to consumers as the single-cycle plant over the life of the project, so the additional benefits to consumers would be created by the lower costs of generation rather than increased consumption of electricity. The financial cost savings would be 108.83 million rupees. The externality of 12.02 million rupees represents the additional taxes that would be collected on import duties, corporate income taxes, and VAT, corrected for the additional FEP associated with differences in the volume of tradable inputs used by the two types of plants.

19.8 Conclusion

The evaluation of this project was carried out using the integrated investment appraisal methodology. The proposed project aimed to expand electricity-generation capacity by 126 MW in order to reduce electricity shortages and outages in Adukki. It had been proposed that a single-cycle thermal plant would be built and operated by an IPP. The state utility, the AEC, would be the only off-taker of the additional electricity generated by this plant, and the price paid to the IPP had to be negotiated through a long-term power purchase agreement.

The assessment of the financial feasibility of the private sector involvement in power generation was the first step of this analysis. The financial appraisal of this project was not limited to the evaluation of the IPP's single-cycle plant as a stand-alone project: it was also carried out for alternative combined-cycle technology. This appraisal served the purpose of determining whether the IPP's involvement was justified from the perspective of the AEC, given that the least costly electricity-generation technology must be chosen.

The financial feasibility of the IPP project per se was evaluated from two perspectives, the lender's point of view and the private investor's point of view. With regard to whether the project would be able to service its debt obligations, the projected ADSCR ratios were calculated against the 1.3 benchmark set by the lenders. There would be some risk in the first year, in which the ADSCR is 1.24. However, the LLCR ratios would improve gradually throughout the debt service period, indicating that the project should be able to generate sufficient cash flow to fulfil its debt service obligations.

From the private investor's point of view, the value for the FNPV of the single-cycle IPP would be 0.37 million rupees. This means that the private investor would be able to generate enough cash over the life of the project to cover the investment cost and earn a rate of return no less than the 13 percent real cost of capital.

From the perspective of the AEC, when the IPP is involved in the expansion of the system by building a single-cycle plant, the impact on its financial PV is −257 million rupees using the 10 percent real rate of return required by the utility as the discount rate. This means that the discounted value of the additional revenues from the sale of electricity would not be able to cover all costs under the PPA payment as well as the fuel expenditure incurred by the utility for the operation of the single-cycle IPP. An increase in the electricity tariffs to be paid for by consumers is necessary for the utility to maintain its current financial position; however, the implementation of an alternative combined-cycle plant by the IPP would result in a lower negative financial impact of a PV of −123 million rupees for the AEC. This means that although the combined-cycle plant would be more expensive in terms of capital expenditures (40 percent higher than the single-cycle plant), the fuel savings from its higher energy-transformation efficiency would make the IPP combined-cycle plant a better private partner from which to purchase electricity. The results of the financial analysis indicate that the superiority of the combined-cycle IPP, in terms of cost savings, was more evident at high plant load factors and high fuel prices. It was estimated that as long as the plant load factor is higher than 20 percent and the price of fuel exceeds $49 per barrel, a combined-cycle plant would have a lower PV of total costs incurred for the utility than a single-cycle plant.

Even though the combined-cycle IPP is more beneficial for the AEC, it would provide the wrong incentive to the private investor. If the AEC subsidizes the fuel, the private investor would be more interested in investing in a single-cycle plant since it requires less capital and thus is easier to finance than the combined-cycle technology.

In this chapter, cost–effectiveness analysis was employed to compare single-cycle with combined-cycle technology. The resource cost of the combined-cycle plant as the source of electricity generation would be lower because of its lower fuel requirement compared to the single-cycle option. A full economic appraisal was then carried out to determine the project's contribution to the country's wealth and the economic welfare of its residents. Expansion of the system by employing the most efficient technology, the combined cycle, would be expected to save resource costs equal to 120 million rupees using the 12 percent real EOCK as the discount rate. This is an indication that the implementation of the combined-cycle technology would be justified economically.

To summarize, given the expected load factor of the plant over time, the financial and economic appraisals under the different scenarios discussed above indicate conclusively that it would be more advantageous for the utility and the country if the IPP were to employ a combined-cycle technology rather than a single-cycle thermal technology.

Appraisal of Electricity-Generation Technologies

References

Boyce, P.M. 2001. *Handbook for Cogeneration and Combined Cycle Power Plants.* American Society of Mechanical Engineers.

GE Energy. 2009. "Gas Turbines-Heavy Duty: H System", retrieved in March, 2013 www.gepower.com/prod_serv/products/gas_turbines_cc/en/h_system/ *index.htm.*

Gellings, C.W. and J.H. Chamberlin. 1988. *Demand-Side Management: Concepts and Methods.* Lilburn, Georgia: The Fairmont Press, Inc.

Harberger, A.C. 1972. "Marginal Cost Pricing and Social Investment Criteria for Electricity Undertaking", in A.C. Harberger (ed.), *Project Evaluation.* Collected Papers. London: The MacMillan Press Ltd.

Jenkins, G.P. and H.B.F. Lim. 1997. "Evaluation of the Expansion of Electricity Distribution System in Mexico", Program on Investment Appraisal and Management Case Study Series, Harvard Institute for International Development, Harvard University, Cambridge, MA.

— 1998. "An Integrated Analysis of a Power Purchase Agreement", Program on Investment Appraisal and Management Case Study Series, Harvard Institute for International Development, Harvard University, Cambridge, MA.

Jyoti, R. 1998. "Investment Appraisal of Management Strategies for Addressing Uncertainties in Power Supply in the Context of Nepalese Manufacturing Enterprises", PhD thesis, The Kennedy School of Government, Harvard University (December).

Kuo, C.Y., G.P. Jenkins, and M.B. Mphahlele. 2003. "The Economic Opportunity Cost of Capital in South Africa", *South African Journal of Economics* 71(3), 525–543.

Mun, J. 2004. "Chapter 2: From Risk to Riches", *Applied Risk Analysis: Moving Beyond Uncertainty in Business.* John Wiley & Sons, Inc.

Poullikkas, A. 2004. "Parametric Study for the Penetration of Combined Cycle Technologies into Cyprus Power System", *Applied Thermal Engineering* 24, Issue 11, 1697–1707.

Chapter Twenty

Restructuring the Water and Sewer Utility in Panama

20.1 Introduction

In the 1980s, investments in Panama's water supply and sanitation sector centred on expanding the system capacity to meet the growing demand. However, since the facilities were constructed, maintenance had been neither fully implemented nor properly programmed or maintained. As a consequence, the water supply and sanitation systems were inefficient and functioning under serious constraints.

To remedy these shortcomings, the Panamanian government, with the support of the Inter-American Development Bank (IADB), launched the Public Enterprise Reform Program for the water supply and sewerage sector. The programme's objective was to scale back the public sector's role and to promote the participation of private operators in service delivery. In particular, the programme aimed to strengthen the Instituto de Acueductos y Alcantarillados Nacionales (IDAAN), the public utility responsible for providing water supply and sanitation services, by rationalizing its staff, outsourcing support activities to the private sector, and collecting outstanding accounts.[140]

By 1996, the government had partially achieved the Public Enterprise Reform Program's targets. In response, it launched a more comprehensive reform programme to promote competitive market structures and encourage private sector participation and delivery of services. To this end, the government passed specific legislation, including:

- Law 26 of January 1996, establishing the Public Utilities Regulatory Agency. This agency was created as a financially and operationally independent body. It was responsible for ensuring compliance with the law and its regulations. This provision would protect consumers, promote service under competitive conditions, prevent the IDAAN from abusing its monopolistic position, approve and monitor compliance with tariff regimes,

---

[140]IDAAN had poor performance in collecting water tariffs because of its lack of financial autonomy to set up budgets efficiently and comply with maintenance plans, its inability to apply an adequate tariff structure, outdated technical and customer records, weak administration in effective metering and collection of tariffs, ineffectual coordination in protecting water `resources, and an excessive number of staff.

control the quality of service, and report regularly to the Ministry of Health and other parties.
- Law 29 of February 1996, pertaining to unrestricted competition and consumer affairs.
- Decree-Law 2 of January 1997, establishing a regulatory and institutional framework for the provision of water and sewerage services.

One of the core components of the reform was the restructuring and privatization of IDAAN. There were plans to reduce the workforce, to provide training to the remaining staff and help those made redundant with worker outplacement services, and to bring in a strategic operator from the private sector. IDAAN would be transformed into a corporation, with the private sector controlling at least 51 percent of the share capital. The corporation would be responsible for planning future investments.

After the process of restructuring and privatizing the public utility had started, the water supply systems would be rehabilitated on a priority basis so as to facilitate efficiency improvements. Estimates suggested that between 1997 and 2002, an investment of approximately $200 million would be required to improve the water supply and sewerage systems. IDAAN's financial situation would not permit it to finance investment of this magnitude. An IADB programme was proposed to provide support for the creation of a mixed capital corporation to carry out the rehabilitation of water and sewerage systems. The main purpose of this chapter is to assess whether this water and sewer utility programme would be financially and economically feasible and sustainable.

20.2 Programme Description

The project area, designated as Metropolitan Panama, includes urban zones, suburban areas, and neighbouring rural communities along the strip from Arraijan to Chorrera to the west of the Panama Canal and in the corridor extending from Colon to Panama City, east of the canal. This was a high-priority area because nearly half of the country's population and 70 percent of its urban population were located there.[141]

In 1985, IDAAN's water treatment plants and facilities, together with those of the Panama Canal Authority that served the project area, had an available supply of 206 million gallons a day. For a population of about 1.2 million residents, the gross availability of water was about 166 gallons per person per day. Given these figures, the net daily supply of water available per person should have been more than sufficient if the system were being operated efficiently.

---

[141]Although IDAAN was supposed to serve 100 percent of the urban population and 94.4 percent of the rural population in the project area, its coverage was not as wide because of its inefficiency and poor-quality service.

The key objectives of the programme were: a) to support the restructuring of IDAAN and the private sector entity that would be involved in the management and funding of future investments; b) to habilitate and optimize the water supply systems; and c) to provide technical co-operation. To achieve these objectives, the programme was divided into the three sub-programmes described below.

Sub-programme 1: Restructuring the Public Utility. This sub-programme included downsizing IDAAN and establishing the Sociedad Anonima de Panama Metropolitano (SAPM), which would be fully owned by private investors. The deal that was being discussed with the government was described as follows: the investors would pay nothing up front for their 100 percent stake in the new company, but would obtain the right to all of the net cash flow, beginning in 1998. In return, they would be obliged to obtain financing for implementing the investments of Sub-programme 2.

Sub-programme 2: Rehabilitation Works. This sub-programme consisted of the rehabilitation of the systems supplying water to Arraijan, Chorrera, Colon, and Panama City. On the technical and operational side, it entailed upgrading the distribution networks and developing geographic information systems, technical records, system metering, and operating and control units for the entire Metropolitan Panama area. On the commercial side, it involved upgrading or developing customer records, end-user metering, and flow measurement, as well as detecting and reducing water losses in each of the four targeted systems listed here. The scope of the physical works in each of the systems is as follows:

- *Arraijan system.* This included the purchase and installation of approximately 5,800 customer meters and four stations for macro-metering; the rehabilitation of the Miraflores pumping station, a 1-million-gallon storage tank, 15 kilometres of water mains and pipes, and household connections; and the replacement of 83 control valves.
- *Chorrera system.* This included the purchase and installation of approximately 8,200 households meters and eight stations for macro-metering; the rehabilitation of the El Caimito treatment plant, groundwater pumping plants, an 800,000-gallon storage tank, 33 kilometres of water mains and pipes, and household connections; and the replacement of 90 control valves.
- *Colon system.* This included the purchase and installation of approximately 7,000 meters and four stations for macro-metering; the rehabilitation of a 300,000-gallon storage tank; and the replacement of 99 control valves.
- *Panama City system.* This included the purchase and installation of approximately 34,000 household meters and 36 stations for macro-metering; the rehabilitation of pumping stations, the Chilibre treatment plant, 66-inch and 60-inch transmission pipelines, booster pumping stations, and storage tanks; and the replacement of 946 control valves.

Sub-programme 3: Additional Activities. This sub-programme included improving inter-institutional coordination and the authority responsible for protecting water resources and the water quality of receiving bodies as well as developing feasibility studies and updating the master plan for Panama City's sewerage system.

20.3 Programme Costs and Financing

The estimated total cost of the three sub-programmes was almost $65 million in 1998 prices, of which the cost of Sub-programme 2, the focus of this case study, was estimated at $48.3 million. The projected cost in domestic currency of Sub-programme 2 was B22.7 million, or about 47 percent of the total.[142] The cost estimates were based on contracts with similar characteristics recently awarded in the region, following international bidding. Table 20.1 presents the total capital costs by component of Sub-programme 2.

The IADB would provide financing for 70 percent of the total cost of the programme, which at the government's request, would be drawn on the Single Currency Facility. The proposed terms of the financing were a four-year disbursement period, 19-year amortization period, one-year grace period, and variable interest rates. The remaining financing needed for the programme would come from investor equity contributions.

---

[142]The Panamanian currency unit is the balboa (B). The exchange rate is B1 = US$1.

Table 20.1: Total Costs of Sub-programme 2 by Component (1998 prices)

Category	Foreign Currency (US$ thousands)	Domestic Currency (B thousands)
Engineering and administration	0	3,534
Direct costs:		
Panama		
UFW reduction	3,168	5,393
New physical infrastructure	2,991	1,408
System rehabilitation	7,615	3,373
Colon		
UFW reduction	1,100	1,290
System rehabilitation	67	79
Arraijan		
UFW reduction	744	874
New physical infrastructure	2,835	1,467
System rehabilitation	693	250
Chorrera		
UFW reduction	784	836
New physical infrastructure	3,120	1,468
System rehabilitation	95	51
Concurrent costs	0	630
Contingency 10%	2,321	2,065
Total investment costs	25,533	22,718

UFW: unaccounted-for water.

20.4 Financial Appraisal of the Programme

The financial analysis is the first component of the integrated appraisal of this programme. The principal focus of the analysis was to examine whether the incremental impact of the programme would be financially feasible and sustainable. The incremental impact measures the impacts of the programme that occur over and above what would have occurred in the absence of the programme. This means that there was a need to identify only the effects that were associated with the programme and not include any other effects that would exist whether or not the programme was undertaken.

20.4.1 Programme Parameters and Assumptions

The starting point of the analysis was to develop the incremental financial cash flow statement of the programme from the total investment point of view. It was carried out on an incremental basis for which "with" and "without" programme scenarios had to be identified. In order to do so, the following rationale, hypotheses, and key assumptions were made.

a) Restructuring the Water System

The proposed programme would be expected to substantially improve the water supply and sanitation services as well as enhance the administrative efficiency of IDAAN.

- **Metering and Conservation:** About 45 percent of the residential connections in Metropolitan Panama were not metered at that time. To implement a volumetric tariff system, metering would be necessary. In order to have effective metering of the water, all metered customers would need to receive a 24-hour water service. Under the existing system of fixed monthly charges for water service, unmetered consumers did not face any incremental costs when they consumed additional water. Following implementation of the programme, consumers who switched from a flat fee to a volumetric tariff would have to pay more for higher levels of water consumption and were therefore likely to reduce their consumption. Thus, metering would provide an incentive for water conservation by diverting the relatively low-value uses of water to higher-value uses elsewhere. In addition, economizing on previous water usage would mean that less water would be tapped from the distribution system's sources of bulk supply. Metering would also give SAPM much better operating information, both for efficient management of the system and for better planning of its expansion.
- **Water Leakage:** The existing distribution network in Metropolitan Panama experienced substantial water leakage. The working assumption was that the existing level of physical water losses was approximately 15 percent of all of the water supplied. If the level of water pressure and hours of operation were increased, the water losses would be much greater. The project would include a comprehensive leak detection and repair programme, with the objective of reducing the rate of leakage to 10 percent of water supplied.
- **Unregistered Consumers:** At the time, about 30 percent of potential revenue was lost through unregistered connections as a consequence of inefficient billing and collection. The project included a component to lower this figure to 15 percent.

b) Restructuring the Tariff

- Sub-programme 2 aimed to raise the percentage of residential connections with meters from the existing level of 54 percent of all households to about 91 percent, and these households would receive a 24-hour water supply service. This would represent an increase of 37 percentage points, of which 13 percent of households were previously unmetered but had 24-hour supply, 15 percent were previously receiving an intermittent water supply but coped by using tanks, and 9 percent had only intermittent water supply but did not have tanks. Thus, if the project was fully implemented, only 9 percent of all customers of IDAAN would still not be metered.

- The tariff structure had remained unchanged since 1982. Unmetered residential customers paid, on average, a flat fee of B7.00 per month. Metered residential customers paid a volumetric tariff of B0.80 per 1,000 gallons for consumption up to 10,000 gallons per month, B1.51 per 1,000 gallons for consumption of 10,000 to 30,000 gallons a month, and B1.67 per 1,000 gallons for consumption of more than 30,000 gallons per month. Industrial customers paid B1.51 per 1,000 gallons, and government customers paid B1.36 per 1,000 gallons. According to the IADB loan agreement, when the programme was implemented, the tariff structure would be increased on a one-time basis by 10 percent and adjusted annually thereafter to reflect the rate of domestic inflation.

- It was assumed that unmetered residential customers (both those who received a 24-hour supply of water and those who faced intermittent water supplies) consumed 20 percent more water than residential metered customers. It was estimated that unmetered customers without coping devices consumed 45 gallons per person per day. As the programme entailed an increase in the tariff structure, it was expected that water users would reduce their consumption levels depending on the price elasticity of demand by the different categories of customers. The own-price elasticity of water demand by metered residential customers was assumed to be -0.35, for industrial and commercial customers, -0.60, and for government customers, -0.50.

c) Investment Costs and Residual Values of Assets

- The construction of the programme was to begin in 1998 and last for four years. The total investment cost of the programme would be about $48.3 million in 1998 prices. The detailed expenditures by year and by component are presented in Table 20.2.

- The operation of the programme was assumed to be for a period of 20 years. The fixed assets were expected to have a longer useful life. It was assumed that they would depreciate by 90 percent of their initial cost in real terms by the end of the programme.

- The capital costs during the construction period excluded interest payments.

d) Lowering Operating and Maintenance Costs

- Sub-programme 2 was expected to reduce the cost of personnel and the cost of electricity by 15 percent, and administration costs by 20 percent. It was assumed that these cost savings could take place immediately when the project was implemented in 2002. The costs of operating inputs other than labour were expected to remain unchanged in real terms throughout the life of the programme.

- It was assumed that the SAPM would continue to be exempt from corporate income taxes.

Table 20.2: Capital Costs of Sub-programme 2 by Year and by Component (thousand dollars, in 1998 prices)

Category	1998	1999	2000	2001	Total
Engineering and administration	1,049	1,322	1,049	114	3,534
Direct Costs:					
Panama					
UFW reduction	1,349	2,022	3,842	1,348	8,561
New physical infrastructure	642	1,284	2,152	321	4,399
System rehabilitation	1,604	3,208	5,374	802	10,988
Colon					
UFW reduction	478	717	717	478	2,390
System rehabilitation	29	116	0	1	146
Arraijan					
UFW reduction	324	485	485	324	1,618
New physical infrastructure	860	1,721	1,291	430	4,302
System rehabilitation	189	566	188	0	943
Chorrera					
UFW reduction	341	425	512	342	1,620
New physical infrastructure	918	1,835	1,376	459	4,588
System rehabilitation	29	116	0	1	146
Concurrent costs	180	180	180	90	630
Contingency 10%	799	1,400	1,717	471	4,387
Total investment costs	8,791	15,397	18,883	5,181	48,252

UFW: unaccounted-for water.

e) Working Capital

- The average collection time for the water tariff was 140 days. The programme aimed to reduce it to 70 days.[143]
- About 70 percent of the bills sent to residential water customers were collected. The programme aimed to increase collection efficiency to 80 percent.[144] It was assumed that prior to the project's implementation, 100

---

[143] The programme would strengthen the collection of the water tariff. As a result, the amount of accounts receivable would become smaller and the change in accounts receivable in the first year of operation would be negative in the incremental case scenario compared to the normal stand-alone case.

[144] It was assumed that the efficiency would start from the beginning of the programme.

percent of water bills sent to industrial and government customers were collected.

- It was assumed that accounts payable was equal to two months' worth of operating expenses, excluding labour expenses.
- The desired level of cash balances to be held as working capital was assumed to be one month's worth of all operating expenses, including labour expenses.

f) Foreign Exchange Rates and Required Rate of Return

- The nominal exchange rate with respect to the US dollar is fixed in Panama. The nominal exchange rate was B1 = $1 in the starting year of the analysis. The real exchange rate may vary over time if Panama's inflation rate differs from that of the world price level of tradables.
- The financial opportunity cost of equity capital was 15 percent real.

20.4.2 Financial Feasibility

The cash flow statements of the project entity were estimated for the "with" and "without" scenarios for Sub-programme 2 from the total investment perspective. The difference between them would then measure the incremental contribution of the programme.

The financial analysis of the programme was first conducted in nominal prices to account for the direct and indirect impacts of inflation. The direct impact of inflation on the financial outcome takes place through changes in relative prices of the programme outputs and inputs, plus changes in the value of accounts receivable, accounts payable, and cash balances. The indirect impacts of inflation that alter the tax payments were not relevant in this case because the concessionaire, SAPM, did not pay corporate income tax. The nominal incremental net cash flow was further adjusted for the loan disbursements received, and interest and principal payments made to the IADB, in order to derive the net financial cash flow after debt financing. The nominal incremental cash flows were deflated to arrive at the real incremental cash flow statement, as presented in Table 20.3.

This addressed the question of whether the incremental flow of financial revenues generated by the programme over its life would be large enough to recover the capital and operating expenditures of the programme and also to generate an adequate rate of return on the concessionaire's investment. The financial net present value (FNPV) discounted at a real rate of 15 percent was estimated to be B84.3 million in 1998 prices. This implies that from the investor's perspective, the programme was expected to generate a rate of return on equity capital that was well above its 15 percent real rate of opportunity cost.

In order to determine the bankability of the project, the analysis focused on the ability of the utility to meet its debt-repayment obligations. In the present case, it was important to look at the financial benefits and costs incurred by the entire utility, including the investments made by the programme. The debt coverage ratios were therefore calculated for the utility with the programme.

The resulting financial cash flow statement from the lender's viewpoint, together with the resulting debt service ratios, is presented in Table 20.4. The annual debt service capacity ratio (ADSCR) was calculated as the ratio of the annual net cash flows to the annual debt-repayment obligations, including principal and interest payment. The values of this ratio ranged from 6.34 to 19.31 over the loan-repayment period. They were much greater than 1.4, the minimum rate recommended for this type of project.

The loan life cover ratio (LLCR) was also calculated, where LLCR is defined as the present value (PV) of the net real cash flow during the loan-repayment period divided by the PV of the remaining debt obligation, discounted by the interest rate charged on the loan. The ratios were all greater than 9.60 over the loan period. This indicates that the concessionaire would be able to generate more than sufficient cash flows to cover the loan and interest payments.

The debt service ratios above, along with the estimated FNPV, indicated that the proposed programme would be financially feasible and bankable.

Table 20.3: Incremental Financial Cash Flow Statement from the Equity Perspective (thousand balboas, in 1998 prices)

Category	1998	1999	2000	2001	2002	2003	2004	2005	2006	2007	2008	2009	2010	2019	2020	2021	2022
RECEIPTS																	
Sales revenues																	
Residential unmetered customers					210	311	321	331	331	331	331	331	331	331	331	331	0
Residential metered customers																	
Metered customers without project					1,697	2,716	2,800	2,882	2,882	2,882	2,882	2,882	2,882	2,882	2,882	2,882	0
Unmetered customers with 24-hour supply without project					1,658	1,940	2,005	2,069	2,069	2,069	2,069	2,069	2,069	2,069	2,069	2,069	0
Unmetered customers with intermittent supply without project (coped with tanks)					1,895	2,217	2,292	2,364	2,364	2,364	2,364	2,364	2,364	2,364	2,364	2,364	0
Unmetered customers with intermittent supply without project (did not cope with tanks)					1,184	1,386	1,432	1,478	1,478	1,478	1,478	1,478	1,478	1,478	1,478	1,478	0
Commercial and industrial customers					440	456	471	487	487	487	487	487	487	487	487	487	0
Government					224	228	232	236	236	236	236	236	236	236	236	236	0
Total sales revenues					7,307	9,254	9,554	9,846	9,846	9,846	9,846	9,846	9,846	9,846	9,846	9,846	0
Revenues from recoup of commercial losses					9,490	10,446	10,774	11,095	11,095	11,095	11,095	11,095	11,095	11,095	11,095	11,095	0
Cost savings from reduced bulk water purchase					578	578	578	578	578	578	578	578	578	578	578	578	0
Change in accounts receivable					3,427	-301	150	153	64	64	64	64	64	64	64	64	-3,176
Liquidation value								0	0	0	0	0	0	0	0	0	4,387
Cash inflow					20,802	19,978	21,057	21,672	21,583	21,583	21,583	21,583	21,583	21,583	21,583	21,583	1,210
EXPENDITURES																	
Investment cost																	
Engineering and administration	1,049	1,322	1,049	114	0			0	0	0	0	0	0	0	0	0	0
Direct costs	0	0	0	0	0			0	0	0	0	0	0	0	0	0	0
Panama - UFW reduction	1,349	2,022	3,842	1,348	0			0	0	0	0	0	0	0	0	0	0
- New physical infrastructure	642	1,264	2,152	321	0			0	0	0	0	0	0	0	0	0	0
- System rehabilitation	1,604	3,208	5,374	802	0			0	0	0	0	0	0	0	0	0	0
Comba - UFW reduction	478	717	717	478	0			0	0	0	0	0	0	0	0	0	0
- System rehabilitation	29	116	0	1	0			0	0	0	0	0	0	0	0	0	0
Ayumba - UFW reduction	324	485	485	324	0			0	0	0	0	0	0	0	0	0	0
- New physical infrastructure	860	1,721	1,291	430	0			0	0	0	0	0	0	0	0	0	0
- System rehabilitation	189	566	188	0	0			0	0	0	0	0	0	0	0	0	0
Chumba - UFW reduction	341	425	512	342	0			0	0	0	0	0	0	0	0	0	0
- New physical infrastructure	918	1,835	1,376	459	0			0	0	0	0	0	0	0	0	0	0
- System rehabilitation	29	116	0	1	0			0	0	0	0	0	0	0	0	0	0
Concurrent costs	180	180	180	90	0			0	0	0	0	0	0	0	0	0	0
Contingency	799	1,400	1,717	471	0			0	0	0	0	0	0	0	0	0	0
Total investment cost	8,791	15,397	18,883	5,181	0			0	0	0	0	0	0	0	0	0	0

Table 20.3 (continued)

Category	1998	1999	2000	2001	2002	2003	2004	2005	2006	2007	2008	2009	2010	2019	2020	2021	2022
Operating costs																	
Personnel	0	0	0	0	-2,118	-2,209	-2,302	-2,395	-2,149	-2,444	-2,468	-2,493	-2,518	-2,754	-2,781	-2,809	0
Electricity	0	0	0	0	-1,370	-1,414	-1,459	-1,502	-1,502	-1,502	-1,502	-1,502	-1,502	-1,502	-1,502	-1,502	0
Chemicals	0	0	0	0	-232	-240	-248	-255	-255	-255	-255	-255	-255	-255	-255	-255	0
Materials	0	0	0	0	0	0	0	0	0	0	0	0	0	0	0	0	0
Marketing and administration	0	0	0	0	-1,020	-1,030	-1,040	-1,051	-1,061	-1,072	-1,083	-1,093	-1,104	-1,208	-1,220	-1,232	0
Income tax liability	0	0	0	0	0	0	0	0	0	0	0	0	0	0	0	0	0
Change in accounts payable	0	0	0	0	267	14	14	14	6	6	6	6	6	6	6	6	-287
Change in cash balance	0	0	0	0	-395	-20	-21	-21	-11	-11	-12	-12	-12	-13	-13	-13	474
Cash outflow	8,791	15,397	18,883	5,181	-4,869	-4,900	-5,056	-5,211	-5,244	-5,279	-5,314	-5,350	-5,386	-5,726	-5,765	-5,806	187
NET CASH FLOW	-8,791	-15,397	-18,883	-5,181	25,671	24,877	26,112	26,883	26,827	26,862	26,897	26,933	26,969	27,309	27,349	27,389	1,024
Net cash flow before financing	-8,791	-15,397	-18,883	-5,181	25,671	24,877	26,112	26,883	26,827	26,862	26,987	26,933	26,969	27,309	27,349	27,389	1,024
Debt financing	6,154	10,778	13,218	3,627	0	-4,598	-4,372	-4,154	-3,942	-3,737	-3,539	-3,347	-3,161	-1,739	-1,607	-1,478	0
Net cash flow after debt financing	-2,637	-4,619	-5,665	-1,554	25,671	20,279	21,740	22,729	22,885	23,125	23,358	23,586	23,808	25,570	25,742	25,910	1,024
NPV @ 15.0%	84,336																

UFW: unaccounted-for water.

Table 20.4: Financial Cash Flow Statement of Utility with Project (Lender's Perspective) (thousand balboas, in current prices unless otherwise specified)

Category	1998	1999	2000	2001	2002	2003	2004	2005	2006	2007	2008	2009	2010	2019	2020	2021
RECEIPTS																
Sales revenues																
Residential unmetered customers	5,066	5,327	5,602	5,913	1,498	1,681	1,768	1,856	1,894	1,931	1,970	2,009	2,050	2,449	2,498	2,548
Residential metered customers																
Metered customers without project	10,949	11,493	12,067	12,689	15,214	17,071	17,948	18,840	19,217	19,601	19,993	20,393	20,801	24,859	25,356	25,863
Unmetered customers with 24-hour supply without project					3,534	3,977	4,193	4,412	4,500	4,591	4,682	4,776	4,871	5,822	5,938	6,057
Unmetered customers with intermittent supply without project (coped with tanks)					4,038	4,545	4,792	5,043	5,143	5,246	5,351	5,458	5,567	6,654	6,787	6,922
Unmetered customers with intermittent supply without project (did not cope with tanks)					2,254	2,841	2,995	3,152	3,215	3,279	3,345	3,411	3,480	4,158	4,242	4,326
Commercial and industrial customers	11,309	11,914	12,544	13,262	14,487	15,297	16,143	17,026	17,367	17,714	18,069	18,430	18,799	22,466	22,915	23,374
Government	4,650	4,816	4,992	5,189	5,634	5,847	6,072	6,297	6,423	6,551	6,682	6,816	6,952	8,309	8,475	8,644
Total sales revenues	31,975	33,550	35,206	37,053	46,930	51,258	53,912	56,626	57,759	58,914	60,092	61,294	62,520	74,717	76,212	77,736
Revenues from recoup of commercial losses	0	0	0	0	10,272	11,533	12,133	12,745	13,000	13,260	13,525	13,796	14,071	16,817	17,153	17,496
Cost savings from reduced bulk water purchase	0	0	0	0	626	639	651	664	678	691	705	719	734	877	864	912
Change in accounts receivable	0	−604	−635	−709	2,955	−1,107	−641	−655	−273	−279	−284	−290	−296	−353	−360	−368
Liquidation value																
Cash inflow	31,975	32,946	34,571	36,344	60,783	62,323	66,055	69,381	71,163	72,586	74,038	75,519	77,029	92,057	93,898	95,776
EXPENDITURES																
Investment cost					0	0	0	0	0	0	0	0	0	0	0	0
Engineering and administration	1,049	1,348	1,091	121	0	0	0	0	0	0	0	0	0	0	0	0
Direct costs	0	0	0	0	0	0	0	0	0	0	0	0	0	0	0	0
Panama - UFW reduction	1,349	2,062	3,997	1,431	0	0	0	0	0	0	0	0	0	0	0	0
- New physical infrastructure	642	1,310	2,239	341	0	0	0	0	0	0	0	0	0	0	0	0
- System rehabilitation	1,604	3,272	5,591	851	0	0	0	0	0	0	0	0	0	0	0	0
Colon - UFW reduction	478	731	746	507	0	0	0	0	0	0	0	0	0	0	0	0
- System rehabilitation	29	118	0	1	0	0	0	0	0	0	0	0	0	0	0	0
Arraijan - UFW reduction	324	495	505	344	0	0	0	0	0	0	0	0	0	0	0	0
- New physical infrastructure	860	1,755	1,343	456	0	0	0	0	0	0	0	0	0	0	0	0
- System rehabilitation	189	577	196	0	0	0	0	0	0	0	0	0	0	0	0	0
Chorrera - UFW reduction	341	434	533	363	0	0	0	0	0	0	0	0	0	0	0	0
- New physical infrastructure	918	1,872	1,432	487	0	0	0	0	0	0	0	0	0	0	0	0
- System rehabilitation	29	118	0	1	0	0	0	0	0	0	0	0	0	0	0	0
Concurrent costs	180	184	187	96	0	0	0	0	0	0	0	0	0	0	0	0
Contingency	799	1,428	1,786	500	0	0	0	0	0	0	0	0	0	0	0	0
Total investment cost	8,791	15,705	19,645	5,498	0	0	0	0	0	0	0	0	0	0	0	0

Table 20.4 (continued)

Category	1998	1999	2000	2001	2002	2003	2004	2005	2006	2007	2008	2009	2010	2019	2020	2021
Operating costs																
Personnel	11,979	12,710	13,488	14,351	12,994	13,821	14,693	15,592	16,063	16,548	17,048	17,563	18,094	23,649	24,363	25,099
Electricity	5,210	5,470	5,744	6,049	4,892	5,148	5,416	5,689	5,803	5,919	6,037	6,158	6,281	7,506	7,656	7,810
Chemicals	2,115	2,221	2,332	2,456	2,337	2,459	2,587	2,717	2,772	2,827	2,884	2,941	3,000	3,586	3,657	3,730
Materials	3,208	3,370	3,541	3,730	3,934	4,143	4,360	4,581	4,673	4,767	4,862	4,959	5,058	6,045	6,166	6,289
Marketing and administration	4,900	5,048	5,200	5,357	4,415	4,549	4,686	4,828	4,973	5,124	5,278	5,438	5,602	7,322	7,543	7,771
Income tax liability	0	0	0	0	0	0	0	0	0	0	0	0	0	0	0	0
Change in accounts payable	0	−88	−93	−103	179	−98	−102	−104	−43	−44	−45	−46	−47	−56	−57	−58
Change in cash balance	0	117	124	136	−281	129	135	139	73	75	77	79	81	104	107	109
Cash outflow	36,203	44,553	49,982	37,474	28,469	30,151	31,776	33,443	34,314	35,215	36,141	37,092	38,069	48,156	49,436	50,751
NET CASH FLOW (NOMINAL)	−4,228	−11,607	−15,411	−1,130	32,313	32,172	34,280	35,938	36,849	37,371	37,897	38,427	38,960	43,901	44,463	45,026
NET CASH FLOW (REAL)	−4,238	−11,380	−14,813	−1,064	29,853	29,139	30,439	31,286	31,450	31,270	31,089	30,905	30,720	28,965	28,760	28,553
Debt service coverage ratios																
Net cash flow before financing (real)						29,139	30,439	31,286	31,450	31,270	31,089	30,905	30,720	28,965	27,760	28,553
Debt repayment (real)						4,598	4,372	4,154	3,942	3,737	3,539	3,347	3,161	1,739	1,607	1,478
PV of retaining net cash flow @ 4.90%						386,392	374,766	361,205	346,091	330,064	313,441	296,193	278,292	82,328	55,979	28,553
PV of remaining debt repayment @ 4.90%						40,118	37,262	34,502	31,835	29,260	26,774	24,374	22,058	4,614	3,016	1,478
Annual debt service coverage ratio						6.34	6.96	7.53	7.98	8.37	8.78	9.23	9.72	16.65	17.90	19.31
Loan life cover ratio						9.63	10.06	10.47	10.87	11.28	11.71	12.15	12.62	17.84	18.56	19.31

UFW: unaccounted-for water.

20.4.3 Financial Sensitivity Analysis

The results of the base case financial analysis reported in Table 20.3 for the incremental impact of the project were determined by the single values of the parameters and assumptions made in the model. Those values can differ from reality, and it is important to know how sensitive they are. A sensitivity analysis was conducted to identify the variables that were most likely to affect the programme's financial performance.

Cost Overruns: The programme's financial performance would not be very sensitive to the likelihood of higher than anticipated investment costs. This is on the assumption that any amount of the cost overruns would be financed by additional equity capital. Table 20.5 shows that a cost overrun of 20 percent would reduce the FNPV by only B8 million in 1998 prices. There would be no impact on the debt service coverage ratios.[145] Because of the exemption of the utility from corporate income taxes, the net cash flows during the period of operation would not be altered because of changes in income taxes caused by the cost overruns.

Table 20.5: Sensitivity Test of Capital Cost Overrun (1998 prices)

Cost Overrun (%)	FNPV (thousand balboas)	ADSCR 2003	ADSCR 2004	ADSCR 2005	LLCR 2003	LLCR 2004	LLCR 2005
0	**84,336**	**6.34**	**6.96**	**7.53**	**9.63**	**10.06**	**10.47**
5	82,343	6.34	6.96	7.53	9.63	10.06	10.47
10	80,350	6.34	6.96	7.53	9.63	10.06	10.47
15	78,357	6.34	6.96	7.53	9.63	10.06	10.47
20	76,364	6.34	6.96	7.53	9.63	10.06	10.47
25	74,370	6.34	6.96	7.53	9.63	10.06	10.47
30	72,377	6.34	6.96	7.53	9.63	10.06	10.47
35	70,384	6.34	6.96	7.53	9.63	10.06	10.47

Consumption per Connection: A change in the quantity of water consumed per connection would not seriously threaten the project's financial performance. Table 20.6 shows that, for example, if water users were to consume 20 percent less water than in the base case scenario, the FNPV of the programme would drop by almost B22 million but remain amply positive. As regards debt service ratios, both ADSCR and LLCR would be reduced by a third of their previous

---

[145]If the cost overruns were financed proportionally by the original debt and equity ratio, one would expect the financial NPV to decrease by B4.9 million instead of B8 million when the cost overruns also increased by 20 percent. The ADSCR and LLCR would then be reduced to 5.28 and 8.38, respectively, in the year 2004.

value, but were still very high. The opposite would be the case if water consumption per connection was raised.

Table 20.6: Sensitivity Test of Consumption per Connection (1998 prices)

Consumption per Connection (%)	FNPV (thousand balboas)	ADSCR 2003	ADSCR 2004	ADSCR 2005	LLCR 2003	LLCR 2004	LLCR 2005
−30	52,126	3.28	3.61	3.90	4.84	5.04	5.23
−20	62,806	4.29	4.72	5.10	6.43	6.71	6.97
−10	73,547	5.31	5.84	6.32	8.03	8.38	8.72
0	**84,336**	**6.34**	**6.96**	**7.53**	**9.63**	**10.06**	**10.47**
10	95,162	7.36	8.08	8.75	11.24	11.74	12.22
20	106,015	8.39	9.21	9.97	12.85	13.42	13.98
30	116,888	9.42	10.33	11.19	14.45	15.11	15.74
40	127,778	10.45	11.46	12.41	16.07	16.79	17.50

Water Tariffs: It was assumed that with the programme, water tariffs would be raised by 10 percent from the existing tariff structure. This is a critical variable affecting the financial performance of the programme. Table 20.7 presents the FNPV as well as the debt service ratios over a range of changes in the level of the tariff structure. If the tariff structure remained as it was, the FNPV would fall by more than B14.1 million from the base case scenario, or 29 percent of the programme's investment costs. Table 20.7 also indicates that the projected improvement in efficiency brought about by the proposed programme was such that IDAAN could reduce the tariff structure by almost 40 percent and would be no worse off financially than it had been previously.

Table 20.7: Sensitivity Test of Tariff Structure (1998 prices)

Tariff Structure (%)	FNPV (thousand balboas)	ADSCR 2003	ADSCR 2004	ADSCR 2005	LLCR 2003	LLCR 2004	LLCR 2005
−40	−2,058	1.87	2.07	2.23	2.64	2.74	2.83
−25	27,999	3.42	3.77	4.07	5.07	5.28	5.49
−20	37,229	3.90	4.30	4.64	5.82	6.07	6.30
−15	46,066	4.36	4.80	5.18	6.53	6.81	7.08
−10	54,508	4.79	5.27	5.70	7.22	7.53	7.83
−5	62,556	5.21	5.73	6.20	7.87	8.21	8.54
0	70,210	5.61	6.16	6.66	8.49	8.86	9.22
5	77,470	5.98	6.57	7.11	9.08	9.48	9.86
10	**84,336**	**6.34**	**6.96**	**7.53**	**9.63**	**10.06**	**10.47**

Water Leakage/Commercial Losses: The utility's ability to reduce commercial losses would have a considerable impact on the financial returns of the programme. If the commercial losses after the programme were raised from 15 percent of the water produced, as assumed in the base case, to 21 percent, the FNPV would be reduced by about 20 percent to B67 million (Table 20.8). The debt service ratios would be reduced, though they would still be high. Clearly, this was a critical variable that should not be ignored.

Table 20.8: Sensitivity Test of Commercial Losses (1998 prices)

Commercial Losses (%)	FNPV (thousand balboas)	ADSCR 2003	ADSCR 2004	ADSCR 2005	LLCR 2003	LLCR 2004	LLCR 2005
30	41,305	4.11	4.52	4.89	6.14	6.40	6.65
27	49,911	4.56	5.01	5.41	6.84	7.13	7.42
24	58,518	5.00	5.50	5.94	7.54	7.87	8.18
21	67,124	5.45	5.99	6.47	8.24	8.60	8.94
18	75,730	5.89	6.47	7.00	8.93	9.33	9.71
15	**84,336**	**6.34**	**6.96**	**7.53**	**9.63**	**10.06**	**10.47**
12	92,943	6.78	7.45	8.06	10.33	10.79	11.23
9	101,549	7.23	7.94	8.59	11.03	11.52	12.00

Technical Losses: Table 20.9 shows that a reduction in leakages or technical losses above the targeted 10 percent would not significantly affect the financial viability of the programme. A reduction in the technical losses would lower the operating and maintenance costs and force some water users with illegal connections to become subject to the new volumetric tariff. Because the level of technical losses was rather low to start with, changes in the rate of technical losses would not significantly affect either ADSCR or LLCR.

Table 20.9: Sensitivity Test of Technical Losses (1998 prices)

Technical Losses (%)	FNPV (thousand balboas)	ADSCR 2003	ADSCR 2004	ADSCR 2005	LLCR 2003	LLCR 2004	LLCR 2005
18	81,614	6.20	6.81	7.37	9.42	9.83	10.23
16	82,292	6.23	6.85	7.41	9.47	9.89	10.29
14	82,972	6.27	6.89	7.45	9.52	9.94	10.35
12	83,653	6.30	6.92	7.49	9.58	10.00	10.41
10	**84,336**	**6.34**	**6.96**	**7.53**	**9.63**	**10.06**	**10.47**
8	85,021	6.37	7.00	7.57	9.69	10.11	10.53
6	85,708	6.41	7.04	7.61	9.74	10.17	10.59
4	86,396	6.44	7.08	7.66	9.79	10.23	10.65

Inflation Rate: As Table 20.10 shows, the overall impact of the domestic rate of inflation on the FNPV of the project would be relatively small. A more than threefold increase in inflation from 2 to 6 percent would increase the programme's FNPV by B3.7 million to about B88 million, or 5 percent. This atypical impact of inflation on the FNPV reflects the fact that the programme would significantly reduce the amount of accounts receivable the utility requires. Therefore, an increase in the inflation rate would have a positive impact on the programme's returns because the negative real changes in accounts receivable without the programme were larger in absolute terms than the real changes with the programme.

Since it was assumed that Panama maintains a fixed nominal exchange rate to the US dollar, an increase in the domestic inflation rate with respect to the US inflation rate would bring about an appreciation of the local currency in real terms and would have a positive impact on the financial performance because of the relatively cheaper tradable inputs. Finally, the impact of inflation on the debt service ratios was quite significant, although it had only a small effect on the FNPV.

Table 20.10: Sensitivity Test of Domestic Inflation (1998 prices)

Domestic Inflation (%)	FNPV (thousand balboas)	ADSCR 2003	ADSCR 2004	ADSCR 2005	LLCR 2003	LLCR 2004	LLCR 2005
1	83,107	6.05	6.59	7.06	8.67	8.98	9.28
2	**84,336**	**6.34**	**6.96**	**7.53**	**9.63**	**10.06**	**10.47**
3	85,434	6.63	7.35	8.03	10.67	11.22	11.77
4	86,417	6.93	7.77	8.57	11.77	12.49	13.19
5	87,301	7.25	8.20	9.13	12.96	13.85	14.75
6	88,098	7.58	8.64	9.72	14.22	15.32	16.44
7	88,818	7.91	9.11	10.34	15.57	16.90	18.29
8	89,472	8.26	9.60	11.00	17.00	18.60	20.28

Collection Period: If the average collection period was not reduced from its existing level of 140 days to its target level of 70 days, but instead fell to only 110 days, the programme's FNPV would experience a modest decline of about B4 million, as shown in Table 20.11. Similarly, the impact on the debt service ratios would also be small.

When sensitivity analysis was also carried out for changes in real wage rates and assumed savings in operating and maintenance expenses brought about by the programme, the impacts on the FNPV were also small.

Table 20.11: Sensitivity Test of Collection Period (1998 prices)

Collection Period (days)	FNPV (thousand balboas)	ADSCR 2003	ADSCR 2004	ADSCR 2005	LLCR 2003	LLCR 2004	LLCR 2005
70	84,336	6.34	6.96	7.53	9.63	10.06	10.47
80	83,334	6.31	6.94	7.51	9.62	10.04	10.46
90	82,231	6.28	6.92	7.49	9.60	10.03	10.44
100	81,328	6.24	6.91	7.47	9.58	10.02	10.43
110	80,325	6.21	6.89	7.45	9.57	10.00	10.42
120	79,322	6.18	6.87	7.43	9.55	9.99	10.40
130	78,319	6.15	6.85	7.41	9.54	9.98	10.39
140	77,317	6.12	6.83	7.39	9.52	9.96	10.38

With the financial structure as proposed, this reform would yield a net present value (NPV) of B84.3 million. This is in addition to earning a 15 percent real rate of return on the amount invested in the programme. If this were a competitive industry, this kind of return would almost certainly never occur. However, this is a public utility monopoly. As shown in Table 20.7, if the restructuring of the utility were carried out according to plan, the water tariff rates could be reduced by up to 40 percent from their initial level and still give the private operator a 15 percent real rate of return on the equity investment. Hence, from the financial analysis alone, it would appear that the financial proposal of the institutional restructuring plan was seriously flawed.

20.5 Economic Appraisal

The second component of the integrated investment analysis was the economic appraisal of the programme, which assessed whether the resources used by the programme would generate the greatest net economic benefits to all members of society among the alternative options. The analysis was carried out under the assumption that the current market conditions and the current tax systems, including, among others, personal income tax, corporate income tax, value-added tax, excise duties, import duties, and production subsidies, would remain unchanged over the life of the programme. The measurements of benefits and costs of the programme were based on principles well established in applied welfare economics (see, for example, Harberger, 1971; Dinwiddy and Teal, 1996; Townley, 1998; Mishan and Quah, 2007).

In this integrated investment approach, the measurement of economic benefits and costs was built on the information developed in the financial appraisal, using the domestic currency at the domestic price level as a numeraire. The objective was to measure the incremental economic impacts of the programme, from a base that reflects how the relevant variables would have moved over time in the absence of the programme. The analysis required calculation of the value of key national economic parameters, namely the economic opportunity costs of capital and foreign exchange, the economic value of water, and the conversion factors for all of the inputs used. These factors were then used to convert the outlays of the financial cash flow statement into a statement of economic costs.

20.5.1 National Parameters

The economic opportunity cost of capital for Panama was estimated at approximately 9.26 percent. It was calculated as a weighted average of the rate of time preference for consumption to savers (3.54 percent), the gross-of-tax returns on displaced or postponed investment (9.49 percent), and the marginal economic cost of foreign capital inflows (9.38 percent).[146] The weights were determined by the response of each source to changes in market interest rates. For the purpose of this analysis, 9.3 percent was the rate used for discounting the stream of the economic costs, the economic benefits, and all externalities generated by the programme over its life.

The foreign exchange premium for Panama was estimated at 5.4 percent,[147] and the premium for non-tradable outlays was taken as zero.

20.5.2 The Economic Value of Water

The economic value of water was mainly determined by the demand for water faced by different customers under different conditions before and after implementation of the programme. The supply of water under the existing system served: a) residential metered and unmetered customers; b) industrial and government customers; c) unregistered (non-paying) consumers; and d) physical leaks from the system. Different types of water demanders will place a different value on the water service they receive, depending on the price they are willing to pay for it and the costs of coping with intermittent services.[148] This can be very different from tariffs projected in the financial analysis. In order to meter the customers effectively, the IDAAN would need to maintain an adequate level of water pressure for 24 hours a day. Hence, the programme would involve an improvement in the reliability of the water service, metering, and a reform in the system of pricing the water.

---

[146]Examples can be found in Chapter 8 and Burgess (2010).

[147]The estimate was based on the amount of customs and other import duties, together with the values of imports and exports over the period from 2001 to 2003. See International Monetary Fund (2006).

[148]This is the demand price, which measures the value that demanders place on the goods or services they demand. See, for example, Harberger (1971).

a) Metered Customers under the Existing System

Metered customers included those residential customers with meters in the existing system plus all industrial and government customers that received water 24 hours a day. These customers paid for their water on the basis of a volumetric set of tariffs. As the programme would entail a 10 percent increase in the tariff structure, it is likely that their level of consumption would fall, depending on their price elasticity of demand. Figure 20.1 shows the economic loss incurred with respect to these customers after the implementation of the programme.

Without the programme, the demand for water by those customers with meters was denoted by Q_0. These consumers would lower their consumption by the quantity $(Q_0 - Q_1)$ because of a 10 percent increase in tariffs. The overall savings in the production costs because less water would be prepared for consumption was accounted for when the estimation was made of the incremental change in total cost of production brought about by the project. The loss in consumer surplus by the metered customers is shown by the area P_1ABP_0 in Figure 20.1, of which P_1AEP_0 is a transfer between the vendors and the customers and hence is not a cost for society as a whole. The net loss is the consumer surplus in the triangular ABE. In addition, the reduction in the demand for water would lose the area of EBQ_0Q_1.

Figure 20.1: Demand for Water by Metered Customers

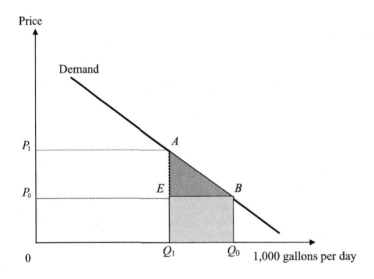

Thus, the total economic loss created by a higher water tariff charged to the demanders would be the economic loss from the reduction in the quantity consumed, $Q_0 - Q_1$, measured by the area ABQ_0Q_1 under the demand curve for water. This category of metered customers, including residents, government and commercial establishments, made up a total of 45 percent of all IDAAN's customers.

b) Unmetered Customers under the Existing System

There were three kinds of unmetered customers under the existing system. Each entailed a different way of measuring the economic benefits for water users.

Demand for Water by Unmetered Customers Who Received a 24-Hour Service without the Project: Figure 20.2 presents the economic analysis for the unmetered consumers, who before the programme received a 24-hour supply of water and paid a fixed charge of B7 per household per month. After implementation of the programme they would have to pay a new volumetric tariff. Suppose these customers obtained a supply of water, Q_0, at the existing flat-fee rate, and there was a zero marginal cost for any additional water consumed. Once they were being metered and facing a tariff schedule with a higher marginal tariff of P_1, then the quantity they consumed would decrease from Q_0 to Q_1. This would result in a loss of economic benefits, measured by the triangular area Q_1AQ_0. Again, a loss of the consumer surplus OP_1AQ_1 resulting from a higher price of water would be a transfer from the customers to the vendors of water, and not an economic cost when viewed for society as a whole.

At the same time, when the programme had been implemented, these customers would save the fixed monthly charge of B7. This can be viewed as a gain in consumer surplus that would be offset by a loss to the vendors created by the volumetric tariff. These people represented approximately 13 percent of the total connected residents who obtained water from IDAAN.

Figure 20.2: Demand for Water by Unmetered Customers who Received a 24-Hour Service without the Programme

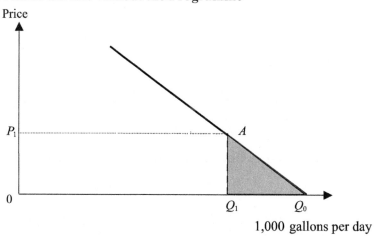

Demand for Water by Unmetered Customers Who Coped with Intermittent Supply Using Overhead Tanks without the Programme: Figure 20.3 shows the situation for those customers who coped with an intermittent water supply by using overhead tanks and who would have to pay a new volumetric tariff with the programme. With the new meters and a 24-hour water supply at an adequate water pressure, these consumers would no longer need the tanks and pumps in order to cope. They would presumably save the marginal running costs of using electricity to fill up the tanks, plus the costs of maintaining and replacing existing tanks. This would be part of the resources saved and considered to be the economic benefits created by metering under the proposed programme. It is shown in Figure 20.3 in the area of OC_0BQ_0.

On the other hand, before the proposed programme these customers paid a flat monthly fee of B7 in 1998 prices, with a zero marginal cost for additional water consumed. Once they were metered and facing a tariff schedule with a higher marginal tariff of P_1, the quantity they consumed would decrease from the current consumption of Q_0 to Q_1. The reduction in consumption would result in a loss of economic benefits, which is measured by the area Q_1ABQ_0. Therefore, with the programme, the total net economic benefits can be measured by the amount by which the saving of resources (represented by the area of OC_0BQ_0) exceeded the economic loss in reduced consumption of Q_1ABQ_0. These people represented approximately 15 percent of the total connected residents who obtained water from IDAAN.

Figure 20.3: Demand for Water by Unmetered Customers Who Coped with Intermittent Supply Using Overhead Tanks without the Programme

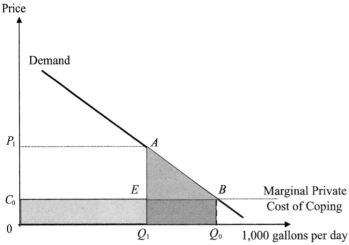

Demand for Water by Unmetered Customers Not Coping with Overhead Tanks without the Programme: The economic analysis for the consumers who were not able to cope with the intermittent water supply by using tanks was influenced by the alternative methods they employed in order to obtain water, along with the associated costs. Figure 20.4 illustrates the programme's economic benefits generated from supplying water to these customers. Although these people had a water connection, the quantity they received was rationed so that they also had to purchase additional water from private vendors for at least part of their consumption.

In Figure 20.4, suppose that the total demand for water of this category is Q_0, of which the volume of water obtained from IDAAN is Q_2 in the absence of the programme. The quantity obtained from vendors or by carrying it to the homes from standpipes is then represented by the volume $Q_0 - Q2$. Of this amount, we can show an amount $Q_3 - Q_2$, which is obtained by households carrying water from standpipes, and an amount $Q_0 - Q_3$, representing the purchase of water from vendors. For this quantity, individuals had to incur heavy coping costs in terms of time and effort in order to bring water to their homes or pay the price of water charged by the private vendors. These coping costs were estimated at B4.4 and B4.5, respectively, per 1,000 gallons of water, and were much higher than the fixed monthly water fees of B7 that IDAAN was charging residential consumers. The coping costs were also higher than the projected water tariff after privatization, including the proposed 10 percent price increase.

Figure 20.4: Demand for Water by Unmetered Customers Not Coping with Overhead Tanks without the Programme

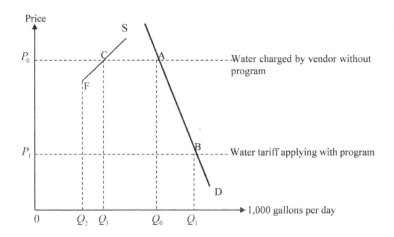

Figure 20.4 illustrates this scenario. The economic benefits from the proposed programme for this category of consumers were measured from three sources. The first is the value placed on the additional consumption $(Q_1 - Q_0)$ resulting from the reduced cost of obtaining water, Q_0ABQ_1. The second is savings resulting from no longer having to carry water by the households,

$Q_2FCQ_3.$[149] The third is the gain from not having to buy water from vendors. On the margin, the value of the coping costs of self-hauling and the price paid to the vendors for the water would be equal. The savings from reduced purchase of water from the vendors is represented by an area of $Q_3CAQ_0.$[150] This group accounted for 9 percent of all connected residential customers.

c) Non-Revenue Water under the Existing System

This category of water is separated into the previous two categories. It consists of pilfered water and water lost to leakage.

A large quantity of water in the existing system was pilfered through illegal connections by non-paying users. The programme was expected to induce these people to pay for the water they used. In response, it was expected that these consumers would reduce the quantity of water they demanded. This reduction in demand for non-paying water would release water that had some economic value to the demanders even though it was stolen. As shown in Figure 20.5, the proposed programme would enhance administration capacity, thereby improving monitoring, policing, and metering of the water system. The consequence, along with the volumetric tariff, would be a decrease in the quantity of water consumed, from Q_0 without the programme to Q_1 with the programme. The resulting economic loss associated with the reduction in the quantity demanded is measured by the triangle Q_0AQ_1. However, the income loss to those who were previously pilfering the water would be much larger. It would be equal to their total loss in consumer surplus as a result of the anti-pilfering programme introduced by the project, OP_1AQ_0.

Unlike pilfered water, which actually has an economic value even though it does not generate revenue for the utility, the water leaking out of the distribution network would not generate any economic benefits. The programme's leak-detection component would retain more water for distribution to consumers and would represent a saving equal to the reduction in the economic costs incurred by the utility to supply the water that leaked from the system.

The water savings from the decrease in consumption brought about by the increase in the tariff structure and the sharp reduction of unmetered connections were estimated to be approximately 15 billion gallons per year. The corresponding reduction in the utility's operating and maintenance costs provided a measure of the economic value of the resources saved. In the appraisal of the programme, this was included in the reduction of operating costs of the utility.

---

[149]It was assumed that vendors set the price of the water they sell at their marginal cost of supply.

[150]In this exercise, the annual value of time spent per household to obtain water in the absence of the programme was assumed to be B35.97, and the water hauled from public taps per household per year was 8,175 gallons.

Figure 20.5: Demand for Pilfered Water

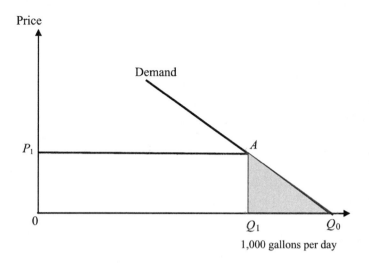

1,000 gallons per day

The programme would also reduce the raw water produced at the Mirshasa plant by 27 million gallons per day and at the Hopaplant by 5 million gallons per day. The economic benefits arising from these savings would be the reduced economic costs of pumping raw water, estimated to be 15 percent of the total operating and maintenance costs.

20.5.3 Conversion Factors of Programme Inputs

The previous section dealt with the incremental benefits of the programme. This section considers the other side of the equation, the incremental costs of the programme. The costs are simply the costs of resources used as a consequence of the implementation of the proposed programme.

Before calculating the economic cost of the programme's inputs, it was necessary to calculate the conversion factors for all of the basic components of its investment and operating costs. These items were first divided into tradable goods (including equipment, machinery, cement, fuel, steel, and chemicals) and non-tradable goods (including freight, handling, and electricity). The economic cost and the conversion factors for each of these items were computed following the methodology developed in Chapters 10 and 11 for tradable and non-tradable goods and services, respectively. The conversion factors for different types of labour — administrative, skilled, unskilled, and foreigners — employed in the programme were also calculated based on the supply price approach outlined in Chapter 12. The conversion factors for the basic tradable and non-tradable goods and services used in this programme are summarized in Table 20.12.

A key economic adjustment that had to be made was for the foreign exchange premium. This variable measures the difference between the market exchange rate and the economic opportunity cost of foreign exchange. This difference arises from the higher taxation of internationally traded goods and services. For Panama, the value of the foreign exchange premium was estimated to be 5.4 percent.

Table 20.12: Conversion Factors of Basic Tradable and Non-tradable Goods and Services

Category	Conversion Factor
Tradable goods and services	
Machinery and equipment	0.915
Steel	0.931
Fuel	0.956
Chemicals	0.947
Cement	0.939
General imported goods	0.915
Non-tradable goods and services	
Freight, handling, and non-tradable materials:	
Handling	0.982
Freight	1.003
Non-tradable materials	0.997
Sand	0.971
Electricity	1.018
Labour:	
Administrative	0.903
Skilled	0.970
Unskilled	1.000
Foreign consultants	0.726

After estimating the basic conversion factors, the conversion factors of the programme inputs or functions were calculated as the weighted average of the economic values of the basic components. The weights are given by the share of the cost of the basic items in the total cost. The aggregate conversion factors of programme inputs or functions are summarized in Table 20.13.

Table 20.13: Conversion Factors of the Programme Inputs or Functions

Category	Conversion Factor
Investment costs	
Supervision and management	0.885
Financial administration	0.903
Execution and coordination	0.814
Direct costs	
UFW reduction	0.921
Reserve tanks	0.950
Reinforcement and secondary network	0.948
Operating and maintenance expenses	
Personnel	0.971
Material	0.927
Marketing and administration	0.903
Cost saving from reduced bulk water purchase	1.017
Liquidation value of investment	0.896
Change in accounts payable	0.949

UFW: unaccounted-for water.

20.5.4 Economic Viability

An economic resource flow statement for the programme was formulated in order to determine whether the proposed programme was justified from the country's perspective. The gross economic benefits (or costs) of the additional (or reduced) consumption of water were estimated based on the methodology outlined in the previous section as a result of the enhanced administrative efficiency and the overall metering system.

Estimates of the economic costs of resources used in the programme were obtained by multiplying each line item in the incremental cash flow statement by the corresponding conversion factors, as displayed in Table 20.13. The resulting economic statement of the programme is presented in Table 20.14. The economic NPV of the programme discounted at the economic opportunity cost of capital for Panama of 9.3 percent was about B10.4 million. This indicates that the proposed programme would have generated a higher economic benefit than the capital would have produced elsewhere in the country.

Up to this point, no consideration has been given to the possibility that if this water concession was to be awarded to a foreign-owned company, it would be likely to result in an increased outflow of profits abroad. When there is an outflow of profits abroad that is greater than the normal opportunity cost of foreign-sourced funds, there would be an additional economic cost in terms of Panama's economic resources. The theoretical framework for the measurement of the economic cost of excess earnings being transferred abroad is discussed in Appendix 13A. In this case, the outflow was far above the economic opportunity cost of the funds used by the programme. The economic NPV of B10.4 million would be the outcome of the programme only if all the "excess" profits were paid to residents of Panama, including all investors in this programme. However, even in this case, one would assume that there would be indifference to a large transfer of income from water consumers to the private owners of the concession. Concern about this issue will be discussed in Section 20.8 when evaluating the impact of foreign financing on the residents of Panama.

20.5.5 Economic Sensitivity Analysis

A sensitivity analysis was conducted to identify the variables that are most likely to affect the outcomes of the programme from the economic perspective. These variables included change in water tariffs, time spent per day in drawing water from public taps, and coping costs per household for those using water tanks.

Table 20.14: Statement of Economic Benefits and Costs of the Programme, Selected Years (thousand balboas, in 1998 prices)

Category	1998	1999	2000	2001	2002	2003	2004	2005	2006	2007	2008	2009	2010	2019	2020	2021	2022
ECONOMIC BENEFITS																	
Sales revenues																	
Residential unmetered customers																	
Residential metered customers																	
Metered customers without project	-	-	-	-	(649)	(669)	(690)	(710)	(710)	(710)	(710)	(710)	(710)	(710)	(710)	(710)	-
Unmetered customers with 24-hour supply without project	-	-	-	-	(530)	(548)	(567)	(585)	(585)	(585)	(585)	(585)	(585)	(585)	(585)	(585)	
Unmetered customers with intermittent supply without project (coped with tanks)	-	-	-	-	2,946	3,047	3,150	3,249	3,249	3,249	3,249	3,249	3,249	3,249	3,249	3,249	
Unmetered customers with intermittent supply without project (did not cope with tanks)	-	-	-	-	5,091	5,266	5,444	5,616	5,616	5,616	5,616	5,616	5,616	5,616	5,616	5,616	
Commercial and industrial customers	-	-	-	-	(815)	(844)	(873)	(903)	(903)	(903)	(903)	(903)	(903)	(903)	(903)	(903)	-
Government	-	-	-	-	(262)	(266)	(271)	(275)	(275)	(275)	(275)	(275)	(275)	(275)	(275)	(275)	-
Total sales revenues	-	-	-	-	5,781	5,986	6,193	6,392	6,392	6,392	6,392	6,392	6,392	6,392	6,392	6,392	-
Non-paying customers	-	-	-	-	(4,429)	(4,570)	(4,714)	(4,854)	(4,854)	(4,854)	(4,854)	(4,854)	(4,854)	(4,854)	(4,854)	(4,854)	-
Cost savings from reduced bulk water purchase	-	-	-	-	588	588	588	588	588	588	588	588	588	588	588	588	
Liquidation value	-	-	-	-	-	-	-	-	-	-	-	-	-	-	-	-	3,930
Total benefits	-	-	-	-	1,941	2,004	2,068	2,127	2,127	2,127	2,127	2,127	2,127	2,127	2,127	2,127	3,930
ECONOMIC COSTS																	
Investment cost																	
Engineering and administration	918	1,161	918	93													
Direct costs	-	-		-													
Panama – UFW reduction	1,243	1,863	3,540	1,242													
- New physical infrastructure	609	1,218	2,041	304													
- System rehabilitation	1,497	2,993	5,015	748													
Colon – UFW reduction	440	661	661	440													
- System rehabilitation	27	107	-	1													
Arraijan – UFW reduction	299	447	447	299													
- New physical infrastructure	812	1,624	1,219	406													
- System rehabilitation	176	528	175	-													
Chorrera – UFW reduction	314	392	472	315													
- New physical infrastructure	870	1,740	1,305	435													
- System rehabilitation	27	108	-	1													
Concurrent costs	162	162	162	81													
Contingency	739	1,300	1,595	437													
Total investment cost	8,133	14,305	17,548	4,802													

Table 20.14 (continued)

Category	1998	1999	2000	2001	2002	2003	2004	2005	2006	2007	2008	2009	2010	2019	2020	2021	2022
Operating costs																	
Personnel	-	-	-	-	(2,057)	(2,145)	(2,236)	(2,236)	(2,350)	(2,373)	(2,397)	(2,421)	(2,445)	(2,674)	(2,701)	(2,728)	-
Electricity	-	-	-	-	(1,395)	(1,440)	(1,485)	(1,530)	(1,530)	(1,530)	(1,530)	(1,530)	(1,530)	(1,530)	(1,530)	(1,530)	-
Chemicals	-	-	-	-	(230)	(227)	(235)	(242)	(242)	(242)	(242)	(242)	(242)	(242)	(242)	(242)	-
Materials	-	-	-	-	-	-	-	-	-	-	-	-	-	-	-	-	-
Marketing and administration	-	-	-	-	(920)	(930)	(939)	(948)	(958)	(967)	(977)	(987)	(997)	(1,090)	(1,101)	(1,112)	-
Excess loss because of foreign financing	-	-	-	-	-	-	-	-	-	-	-	-	-	-	-	-	-
Income tax	-	-	-	-	-	-	-	-	-	-	-	-	-	-	-	-	-
Change in accounts payable	-	-	-	-	253	13	13	13	5	5	5	5	5	5	5	5	(272)
Change in cash balance	-	-	-	-	(395)	(20)	(21)	(21)	(11)	(11)	(12)	(12)	(12)	(13)	(13)	(13)	474
Total costs	8,133	14,305	17,548	4,802	(4,734)	(4,749)	(4,902)	(5,054)	(5,085)	(5,118)	(5,151)	(5,185)	(5,219)	(5,543)	(5,580)	(5,618)	201
Net economic benefits	(8,133)	(14,305)	(17,548)	(4,802)	6,675	6,754	6,970	7,180	7,211	7,344	7,278	7,312	7,346	7,669	7,707	7,745	3,729
NPV @ 9.3 %	**10,406**																

UFW: unaccounted-for water.

Water Tariffs: The programme's economic viability was sensitive to the likelihood of a higher than anticipated change in water tariff. As Table 20.15 shows, an increase in water tariffs of 20 percent would turn the economic NPV negative. This is because of the negative elasticity of demand for water with respect to price, which influences the size of the economic benefits (or losses) received by the consumers. On the other hand, the economic NPV increased if the level of the water tariff was reduced.

Table 20.15: Sensitivity Test of Water Tariffs (thousand balboas, in 1998 prices)

Changes in Water Tariffs (%)	Economic NPV
−15	53,658
−10	45,766
−5	37,495
0	28,845
5	19,815
10	**10,406**
15	618
20	−9,549

Daily Time Spent Fetching Water: The economic outcome of the programme was quite sensitive to the amount of time spent per day on obtaining water from the public taps in the existing situation. Table 20.16 shows that, for example, a 50 percent increase in time spent fetching water from half an hour to three-quarters of an hour per day would raise the economic NPV by more than B5.8 million.

Table 20.16: Sensitivity Test of Time Spent to Fetch Water from Public Standpipes (thousand balboas, in 1998 prices)

Hours Spent per Day Obtaining Water from Public Taps	Economic NPV
0.500	**10,406**
0.625	13,314
0.750	16,222
0.875	19,129
1.000	22,037
1.125	24,944

Savings in Coping Costs for Households with Water Tanks: Table 20.17 shows that the programme's economic outcome would be sensitive to changes in the estimates of households' resource savings from the reduction in coping costs for those who would be using tanks. This was indeed the opportunity cost that they had previously, and that they would then save following implementation of the programme. A divergence of 20 percent would increase the programme's economic NPV by some B5.2 million.

Table 20.17: Sensitivity Test of Savings in Coping Costs for Households with Water Tanks (thousand balboas, in 1998 prices)

Savings in Coping Costs for Households (%)	Economic NPV
−40	85
−30	2,665
−20	5,246
−10	7,826
0	**10,406**
10	12,987
20	15,567
30	18,147

20.6 Stakeholder Analysis

The third component of an integrated investment appraisal is the stakeholder impact analysis. A stakeholder analysis is employed to identify which segments of society reap the benefits of, and which, if any, lose from the implementation of a programme. The stakeholder analysis of a programme builds on the identity that the sum of the financial value of the programme item and all of the externalities associated with the item in the programme equals the economic value of the item. The externalities refer to distortions such as taxes, tariffs, subsidies, and consumer or producer surplus.

On the basis of the identity, the PV of the net economic benefits over the life of a programme discounted by the economic cost of capital should be equal to the PV of the financial net cash flow and the sum of the PVs of all of the externalities generated by the programme, all discounted by the same economic opportunity cost of capital. This means that any programmes will generate two types of net benefits: a) financial net benefits, which accrue directly to those who have a financial interest in the programme; and b) distributive impacts or externalities, which are allocated to different segments of society. In the current case, 9.3 percent was the economic opportunity cost of capital for Panama. To undertake the stakeholder analysis of the programme, the projected incremental benefits and costs from the financial and economic appraisals were used.

20.6.1 Identification of Stakeholders and Externalities

The following steps were undertaken when carrying out the stakeholder analysis:

- Identifying the stakeholder impacts of the programme, item by item, by subtracting the total investment cash flow statement from the economic statement of benefits and costs;
- Calculating the PV of each line item's flow of distributive impacts;
- Allocating the PV of the externalities to the relevant groups in the economy.

The reconciliation among the financial flows, economic resource flows, and distributional impacts of the proposed programme, all discounted by 9.3 percent real, is presented in Table 20.18. To ensure that the analysis was performed in a consistent way, it was confirmed that the economic NPV, as it should be, was equal to the FNPV plus the PV of all externalities (discounted by the same rate). Thus, B10.41 million as shown in Table 20.18 is equal to the sum of the FNPV (B140.18 million) and the PV of all externalities (−B129.77 million) that would be created by the programme.

Table 20.18: Present Value of Financial Cash Flows, Economic Resource Flows, and Externalities for the Programme (thousand balboas, in 1998 prices)

	Financial NPV	PV of Externalities	PV of Fin+Ext	Economic NPV
ECONOMIC BENEFITS				
Sales revenues				
Residential unmetered customers	2,244	−2,244	0	0
Residential metered customers				
Metered customers without project	19,466	−24,260	−4,795	−4,795
Unmetered customers with 24-hour supply without project	14,284	−18,227	−3,944	−3,944
Unmetered customers with intermittent supply without project (coping with tanks)	16,324	5,594	21,919	21,919
Unmetered customers with intermittent supply without project (not coping with tanks)	10,203	27,678	37,881	37,881
Commercial and industrial customers	3,400	−9,486	−6,087	−6,087
Government	1,662	−3,535	−1,873	−1,873
Total sales revenues	67,581	−24,480	43,101	43,101
Non-paying customers	74,479	−107,258	−32,779	−32,779
Cost savings from reduced bulk water purchase	3,973	69	4,042	4,042
Liquidation value	523	−54	469	469
Total benefits	**146,557**	**−131,724**	**14,833**	**14,833**
ECONOMIC COSTS				
Investment cost				
Engineering and administration	3,225	−405	2,820	2,820
Direct costs				
Panama				
- UFW reduction	7,451	−586	6,865	6,865
- New physical infrastructure	3,866	−200	3,666	3,666
- System rehabilitation	9,656	−646	9,011	9,011
Colon				
- UFW reduction	2,101	−165	1,936	1,936
- System rehabilitation	136	−10	126	126
Arraijan				
- UFW reduction	1,423	−112	1,311	1,311
- New physical infrastructure	3,846	−216	3,630	3,630
- System rehabilitation	864	−58	806	806
Chorrera				
- UFW reduction	1,421	−112	1,309	1,309
- New physical infrastructure	4,102	−212	3,889	3,889
- System rehabilitation	136	−9	127	127
Concurrent costs	565	−55	509	509
Contingency	3,879	−279	3,601	3,601
Total investment cost	**42,671**	**−3,065**	**39,606**	**39,606**
OPERATING COSTS				
Personnel	−16,820	486	−16,334	−16,334
Electricity	−10,145	−185	−10,329	−10,329
Chemicals	−1,723	91	−1,632	−1,632
Materials	0	0	0	0
Marketing and administration	−7,498	731	−6,767	−6,767
Excess loss because of foreign financing	0	0	0	0
Income tax liability	0	0	0	0
Change in accounts payable	203	−10	193	193
Change in cash balance	−310	0	−310	−310
Total costs	**6,379**	**−1,952**	**4,426**	**4,426**
Net economic benefits	**140,178**	**−129,772**	**10,406**	**10,406**

20.6.2 Distributive Impacts

The net impact of the proposed programme on all of the affected groups in the country, other than the investors in the programme, was computed by adding up the positive and the negative externalities imposed on each of the groups. It was important to separate the affected stakeholders as well as to quantify the magnitude of the burden imposed (or benefits received) by the proposed programme on each group. The integrated appraisal employed for this programme allowed the realized gains and losses distributed to each particular group of stakeholders to be quantified.

The stakeholders of this programme included the government, commercial and industrial customers, previously metered residential consumers, non-paying consumers without the programme, and paying residential customers who were newly metered as part of the programme. The last category was further broken down into customers with a 24-hour supply of water without the programme, customers with an intermittent water supply without the programme who had coped by means of overhead tanks, and customers with an intermittent water supply who had resorted to public standpipes and water vendors. The distributive impacts of the programme are presented in Table 20.19.

Table 20.19: Distribution of the Programme's Net Benefits among Stakeholders (thousand balboas, in 1998 prices)

Category	Externalities
Government	−1,568
Commercial and industrial customers	−9,486
Residential Customers:	
Metered customers before the programme	−24,260
Unmetered customers with 24-hour supply before the programme	−18,227
Unmetered customers who remained unmetered after the programme	−2,244
Non-paying customers (before the programme)	−107,258
Residential Customers (unmetered with intermittent water before the programme):	
Those who coped using tanks	5,594
Those who coped using public standpipes	27,678
Total	−129,772

The government would realize a net loss of about B1.57 million. On the one hand, the government as a consumer of water would incur a loss of approximately B3.52 million because of the reduction in water consumed as a result of the tariff increase. On the other hand, the government would gain about B3.06 million in import duties on machinery, equipment, and other tradable goods in the construction phase, but would lose B1.11 million in duties because of the lower demand for tradable inputs brought about by the utility's improved operating efficiency.

The residential customers who were metered before the programme and the commercial and industrial consumers would also incur an economic loss related to the reduction in water consumed as a result of the 10 percent increase in tariff. Their losses would be B24.3 million and B9.5 million, respectively. These two groups accounted for a total of 45 percent of all of IDAAN's customers.

It is easy to see the programme's distributive impact on metered customers graphically in Figure 20.1. The economic loss is represented by the area ABQ_0Q_1. This is equal to the sum of the areas of EBQ_0Q_1 and ABE. Consumers' incremental financial outlay is $P_0P_1AE - EBQ_0Q_1$. The programme's distributive impact on metered customers is measured by the net economic impact less the net financial impact. It is equal to the negative of the area $(ABE + P_0P_1AE)$.

Those residential customers who were not metered before the programme but would subsequently receive a 24-hour water supply, and would pay the new water tariff, would realize a loss of about B18.2 million. This group represented 13 percent of IDAAN's customers. Those residential customers who remained unmetered even after the programme would incur a loss of B2.2 million because of the 10 percent increase in the monthly flat fee. These represented 9 percent of IDAAN's customers.

The clear losers from this programme would be those unregistered consumers who as a result of the programme were detected and billed. They would lose about B107.3 million. This can be seen in Figure 20.5. With the implementation of the programme, the economic loss is given by the area Q_1AQ_0. The incremental financial outlay by these water customers is OP_1AQ_1. Therefore, the negative distributive impact on unregistered consumers is $(Q_1AQ_0 + OP_1AQ_1)$ or OP_1AQ_0.

The major beneficiaries of the programme would be those residential consumers who had previously received an intermittent water supply and incurred heavy coping costs in obtaining water. Consumers who were able to cope by using tanks would gain about B5.6 million because their savings in terms of reduced coping costs would exceed the amount of economic losses incurred because of the reduction in their water consumption brought about by the tariff increase. This group made up 15 percent of IDAAN's customers. Furthermore, consumers who had coped by means other than tanks would gain about B27.7 million. This gain reflects the value of coping costs saved because they no longer had to obtain water from the public taps or buy water from private vendors, plus the value of the additional consumption resulting from the reduced cost of water. From this total, we need to subtract the amount they would pay for water with the project. This group represented 9 percent of IDAAN's total customer base.

Table 20.19 also shows that over 82.5 percent of the programme's negative externalities would be incurred by IDAAN's existing illegal and non-paying customers. This group would be hurt by the proposed restructuring and privatization. It is likely that there would be considerable political difficulties in implementing the programme given its potential widespread negative impact, particularly on this group of customers.

20.6.3 Concerns with Current Non-paying Customers

An important contribution made by the stakeholder analysis is that it signals to the analyst some of the areas in which a project may need to be adjusted in order to be sustainable. In this case, a major problem was that most of the people who obtained their water either directly or indirectly from IDAAN would be adversely affected by the changes proposed by this project. In particular, more than 82.5 percent of the programme's negative externalities would be incurred by IDAAN's existing non-paying customers. This group would be likely to pose tremendous political difficulties for the successful implementation of the programme, as some of people had previously been given a free standpipe service because of their low incomes.

It can be seen from the financial analysis that if the programme was unable to collect water tariffs from existing non-paying customers, the programme would still be able to generate a substantial FNPV on the concessionaire's investment of B40.1 million in 1998 prices, discounted at a real rate of 15 percent. The values of the ADSCR, ranging from 4.08 to 11.81 over the loan-repayment period, were also much greater than the minimum rate of 1.4 being recommended for this type of project. In other words, the programme would still be financially feasible and bankable.

Furthermore, the economic NPV of the programme discounted at the economic opportunity cost of capital for Panama of 9.3 percent was expected to increase to approximately B43.19 million from the B10.41 million presented in the previous section. This was because the proposed programme would no longer reduce the consumption of water by existing non-paying customers. The economic NPV (B43.19 million) would then be equal to the sum of the FNPV (B65.70 million) and the PV of all externalities (−B22.51 million) created by the programme, all discounted by 9.3 percent real. The distributed impacts of the programme on various stakeholders are presented in Table 20.20.

From this analysis, it can be seen that if this one change was made to the design of the project, the results of the economic and stakeholder analyses would be greatly improved, while the results of the financial analysis would remain significantly positive.

Table 20.20: Distribution of the Modified Programme's Net Benefits among Stakeholders (thousand balboas, in 1998 prices)

Category	Externalities
Government	−1,568
Commercial and industrial customers	−9,486
Residential customers:	
Metered customers before the programme	−24,260
Unmetered customers with 24-hour supply before the programme	−18,227
Unmetered customers who remained unmetered after the programme	−2,244
Residential customers (unmetered with intermittent water before the programme):	
Those who coped using tanks	5,594
Those who coped using public standpipes	27,678
Total	−22,513

20.7 Risk Analysis

The fourth component of the integrated appraisal considered the nature of the risk associated with the programme. A risk analysis was carried out in which the risk variables had to be uncertain and significant in terms of their impact on the programme outcomes. The variables with the most significant effect were selected from the sensitivity analysis conducted in the previous sections. The range and probability distribution for each of the risk variables were determined, and the appropriate correlations among the variables specified. The output of the analysis was presented as a probability distribution of the important performance variables and their occurrence.

Table 20.21 presents the identified risk variables and their corresponding ranges of values and probability distributions. In terms of relationships among the variables, a negative correlation of 0.80 was modelled between commercial and technical losses. As metering was improved and commercial losses reduced, an increase in the overall water pressure in the system would be required. This would be likely to result in an increased rate of water leakage from the system.

Table 20.21: Probability Distributions and Range Values for Risk Variables

Risk Variable	Base Value	Probability Distribution	Range Values	
			Minimum	Maximum
Commercial losses with programme	15%	Triangular	5%	25%
Technical losses with programme	10%	Triangular	5%	15%
Time per day to draw water from public taps (hours)	0.5	Triangular	0.20	0.80
Divergence from savings in coping costs	0%	Triangular	−30%	30%
			Range	Probability
Investment cost overrun	0%	Step	−15% to −5%	15%
			−5% to 5%	75%
			5% to 25%	10%
Annual consumption per connection of residential metered customers (gallons)	155	Step	125 to 145	30%
			145 to 165	50%
			165 to 205	20%

Based on the underlying uncertainty surrounding each of the variables specified in Table 20.21, a Monte Carlo simulation was carried out over 10,000 trials. The risk analysis presented here was carried out under the assumption that the investors in this programme were all residents of Panama. The rest of the assumptions and parameters used in the analysis referred to the base case scenario outlined in sections 20.4.1, 20.5.2, and 20.5.3.

The results of the risk analysis displayed in Figure 20.6 showed that the expected value of the FNPV discounted at 15 percent was B84.23 million, which was close to the value of the deterministic base case of B84.34 million. The risk analysis also confirmed the programme's robustness from the financial standpoint, with zero probability of the programme outcome having a negative FNPV.

The rest of the statistics of the simulation results are as follows.

Mean value	B84,226 thousand
Median value	B82,278 thousand
Standard deviation	B16,371 thousand
Range: Minimum	B43,731 thousand
Maximum	B144,361 thousand

Figure 20.6: Probability Distribution of the FNPV

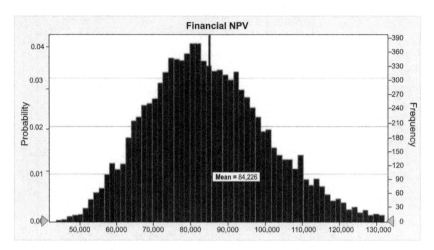

The expected value of the economic NPV was B10.411 million, as shown in Figure 20.7, which is almost the same as the value of the deterministic base case of B10.406 million. The variation in the programme outcomes was also smaller than that for the financial results. The probability of the project having a positive outcome was calculated to be more than 82 percent.

Other economic statistics resulting from the simulations are as follows.

Mean value	B10,411 thousand
Median value	B10,058 thousand
Standard deviation	B10,941 thousand
Range: Minimum	−B23,955 thousand
Maximum	B50,741 thousand

Figure 20.7: Probability Distribution of the Economic NPV

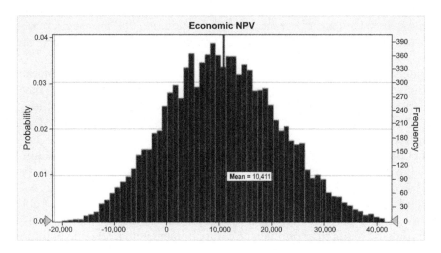

The expected value of all of the externalities was about −B129.58 million, ranging from −B250.74 million to −B45.06 million, as shown in Figure 20.8. This expected value was about the same as in the deterministic case.

Figure 20.8: Probability Distribution of All of the Externalities

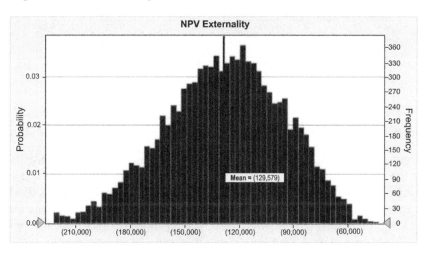

20.8 The Economic Cost of Foreign Financing

The analysis carried out so far was based on the assumption that the programme's investors were Panamanians. However, if the investors were foreigners, the economic outcome of the programme could be quite different.

As water systems have been privatized around the world, the new private operators have frequently been multinational companies. These companies have great expertise in improving the operational efficiency of such public utilities. However, there is a need to make sure that these improvements are obtained at a reasonable cost.

The net financial cash flow after debt financing accruing to the private equity holder of the programme is presented in Table 20.3. It shows that under the proposed arrangements, the FNPV discounted at 15 percent real was B84.336 million. The penultimate row of Table 20.3 is also presented in Table 20.22 below. It is possible to calculate the proportion of the net financial cash flow that would be required to provide the equity holders with a real rate of return of 15 percent (i.e., FNPV = 0): 12.42 percent of the programme's annual net cash flow would be required to provide the private enterprise with an NPV of zero at a 15 percent financial rate of return. This is illustrated in the second row of Table 20.22 for the first few years of the operating phase of the programme.

Table 20.22: Calculation of Excess Return to Foreign Investors (thousand balboas, in 1998 prices)

Category	1998	1999	2000	2001	2002	2003	2004	2005
Net cash flow after debt financing	−2,637	−4,619	−5,665	−1,554	25,671	20,279	21,740	22,729
% share of benefits to make NPV=0	−2,637	−4,619	−5,665	−1,554	3,188	2,519	2,700	2,823
Excess return to foreign investors					22,483	17,761	19,040	19,907
PV of excess return @ 9.3% =142,109								

If the equity holders were domestic residents of Panama, these excess profits (shown in the third row of Table 20.22) would represent a transfer from the water consumers to the private owners of the equity. It would be financially unjustified and, perhaps, politically explosive, but in the aggregate, it would not create an economic loss to Panama. On the other hand, if the private owners were foreign residents, the results would be very different, since the excess profits were estimated in the PV (at the economic discount rate of 9.3 percent) of about B142,109 thousand, which would be an economic cost to the country created by the generous terms of the private concession proposal. Foreigners would then have a claim on this amount of the country's resources.

If the excess profits were properly viewed as non-benefit, then the economic NPV of the programme would turn from a positive value into a negative value. That is:

$$\text{Economic NPV} = \text{FNPV} + \text{PV of all externalities}$$
$$= \text{B}140{,}178 + (-\text{B}129{,}772 - \text{B}142{,}109)\ \text{thousand}$$
$$= -\text{B}131{,}703\ \text{thousand}$$

Moreover, it was unlikely that such an outcome would be the objective of anyone associated with this proposed programme. Table 20.23 shows the distributive impacts of the programme on different stakeholders if the programme was invested by foreigners.

Table 20.23: Distribution of Externalities among Stakeholders of Foreign Equity Holders (thousand balboas, in 1998 prices)

Category	Externalities
Government	−1,568
Commercial and industrial customers	−9,486
Residential customers:	
Metered customers before the programme	−24,260
Unmetered customers with 24-hour supply before the programme	−18,227
Unmetered customers who remained unmetered after the programme	−2,244
Non-paying customers before the programme	−107,258
Residential customers (unmetered with intermittent water before the programme:	
Those who coped with tanks	5,594
Those who coped with public standpipes	27,678
Economic cost of foreign financing	−142,109
Total	−271,880

20.9 Conclusion

The proposed programme showed how the results of the financial and economic appraisals of a programme aimed at improving the overall efficiency of the water utility with no expansion of coverage can differ significantly when viewed from different perspectives.

The programme to support the restructuring of the water and sewer utility would be certain to have a substantial positive impact on the utility's financial performance. For an infusion of B14.5 million of equity capital, it is estimated that the private operator would earn an FNPV of B84.3 million in 1998 prices using 15 percent real as the discount rate. Under the proposal being considered, the plan was to increase tariffs by 10 percent above their current level following the programme implementation.

The programme was also expected to generate significant economic benefits (as much as B10.4 million) for society as a whole if the investment was undertaken by Panamanians. However, the benefits would accrue mainly to the investors. This would almost certainly be damaging to the country because the stakeholders of this programme would pay the price and would be negatively affected by the programme by as much as B130 million. The damage would be much worse if the investment was due to a foreign concessionaire because a substantial amount of the excess profits generated from the proposal would be paid to foreigners. As a result, the simulations yielded a huge negative economic cost to the country. Even though the programme appeared to be financially robust, considerable political risk was present that could bring about a very different financial outcome.

While the rate of return to the concessionaire became clear under the proposal, it was unlikely to be politically sustainable. This is because there were a significant number of negative externalities, of which over 82.5 percent would be incurred by existing customers who were illegal and non-paying consumers, and who would be made worse off by the programme. If the proposed restructuring was able to deliver the cost savings as planned, then a major reduction in the price of water would be possible over time without hampering the financial performance of the utility. It was found that the utility could reduce the water tariff structure for the programme by up to around 40 percent and still remain financially viable. If this were to happen, the majority of customers could be made better off by the programme. In such an event, the economic outcome would also become viable. Alternatively, if the current non-paying customers could not be forced to pay their water tariffs owing to social and political difficulties, the return to the concessionaire's investment would still be well above its 15 percent real rate of opportunity cost, and the financing arrangement would be bankable. As a consequence, the stakeholder impacts would be more balanced, and the economic net benefits to society as a whole would even be enhanced because the consumption of water by this group would not be negatively affected by the proposed programme.

References

Albouy, Y. 1997. "Marginal Cost Analysis and Pricing of Water and Electric Power", Inter-American Development Bank, Washington, DC.

Burgess, D.F. 2010. "Toward a Reconciliation of Alternative Views on the Social Discount Rate", in D. Burgess and G.P. Jenkins (eds.), *Discount Rates for the Evaluation of Public Private Partnerships*. Kingston: John Deutsch Institute for the Study of Economic Policy, McGill-Queen's University Press.

Dinwiddy, C. and F. Teal. 1996. *Principles of Cost-Benefit Analysis for Developing Countries*. Cambridge: Cambridge University Press.

Harberger, A.C. 1971. "Three Basic Postulates for Applied Welfare Economics", *Journal of Economic Literature* IX(3).

Inter-American Development Bank. 1997. "Loan Proposal, Program of Support for Restructuring the National Water and Sewer Utility", Washington, DC.

International Monetary Fund. 2006. "Panama: Selected Issues and Statistical Appendix", IMF Country Report No. 06/3 (January).

Mishan, E.J. and E. Quah. 2007. *Cost-Benefit Analysis*, 5th edition. London and New York: Routledge.

Porter, R.C. 1996. *The Economics of Water and Waste*. Vermont: Ashgate Publishing.

Townley, P.G.C. 1998. *Principles of Cost-Benefit Analysis in a Canadian Context.* Scarborough: Prentice Hall Canada Inc.

Printed in Great Britain
by Amazon

28896157R00334